Management and Leadership in Social Work Practice and Education

D1525710

Management and Leadership in Social Work Practice and Education

Edited by
LEON H. GINSBERG

COUNCIL ON SOCIAL WORK EDUCATION
Alexandria, Virginia

Library of Congress Cataloging-in-Publication Data

Management and leadership in social work practice and
education / edited by Leon H. Ginsberg.
    p. cm.
Includes bibliographical references and index.
  ISBN 978-0-87293-132-9 (alk. paper)
1. Social work administration—United States. 2. Social work
education—United States. I. Ginsberg, Leon H.
  HV95.M264 2008
  361.3068—dc22

                        2008038081

Printed in the United States of America on acid-free paper that
meets the American National Standards Institute Z39-48
Standard.

Council on Social Work Education, Inc.
1725 Duke Street, Suite 500
Alexandria, VA 22314-3457
www.cswe.org

CONTENTS

FOREWORD

Rino J. Patti, Professor Emeritus
School of Social Work
University of Southern California

For several decades Leon Ginsberg has been a leading social work administrator and academic. A former commissioner of a state human services agency, a professor and dean in schools of social work, and, recently, the editor of the journal *Administration in Social Work*, Ginsberg brings to this useful book on social work management a rich background as both practitioner and scholar. Having worked in both agency and academic domains, he is uniquely positioned to understand the demands of management practice and the kinds of information needed by those who work at this craft.

So it is not surprising that Professor Ginsberg has chosen to focus this book on skills and practice guidelines that can be applied easily and directly to the tasks and roles assumed by social work managers, many of whom have not had the benefit of extensive prior educational preparation or experience in management. Nor is it surprising that the authors assembled to produce this book are largely people who are, or have been, administrators. Managers often do not have the time to write for publication, so it is a pleasure to see their extensive contributions to this book. Their insights, based on firsthand experience, give the chapters a currency and authenticity that students and managers will appreciate. The chapters in this book speak in a voice that is easily accessible and specific, without sacrificing the depth that their subjects require.

Social work managers practice in a wide array of human services organizations, at all levels of administration (supervisory, program, and executive), and in variety of line and staff positions. For this reason it is often difficult for managers to apply broad theories and general practice propositions to their particular circumstances. The introductory chapter provides a useful overview of relevant management theories to orient the reader to the latest strategic thinking in the field. But while these theories provide a context, they cannot provide, as Ginsberg is quick to admit, day-to-day guidance on how to address the particular demands that arise in different settings and levels of management. This book seeks to address this challenge by offering chapters on management in specific kinds of organizations and key administrative processes. For example, the reader will find chapters on management in both public and non-profit organizations, in health settings, in schools of social work, in programs for

HIV-AIDS and suicide prevention, and so on.

Cross-cutting these chapters on specific settings are a number of good chapters on specialized management functions, including management of agency research, purchase of service, performance-oriented information systems development, and investment strategies for social agencies. Included here also is an excellent chapter by Joan Levy Zlotnik that provides a wealth of information on how to access social work–relevant research online, on funding sources, strategies for building agency-university collaboration, and trends in evidence-based practice research. These chapters deal with essential skill sets that are increasingly central to the responsibilities of social work administrators.

Two context specific sections in the book, nonprofit agencies and schools of social work, will be especially helpful to managers in these arenas. Six chapters in the section on nonprofits, introduced by Joel Levy, who also contributes to many of these chapters, address in considerable detail such management challenges as leadership, fundraising, financial management, public relations, and human resources administration. The chapters in this section are produced primarily by agency administrators and reflect the latest practices and strategies required in an increasingly complex nonprofit sector.

Another sector-specific part of the book deals with academic administration in social work schools. Aside from occasional monographs, relatively little has been written on this subject in either textbooks or periodicals. Like agency administrators, deans and other academic administrators tend to have little time to devote to writing about their craft, let alone continue with their substantive research interests. This is unfortunate, because new deans and other academic leaders generally have little formal preparation for these jobs, and the transition from teaching and research to management is not easy. Fortunately, this section contains a number of chapters that can serve as something of a primer for new deans as well as an opportunity for seasoned deans to reflect on their practice.

Although this book is mostly about helping managers with context and role-specific skills, it also has a broader purpose: to improve the quality of social work leadership in society. Bruce D. Friedman rightly argues in his chapter, Current Issues in Social Work Management, that social work managers play a key role in policy formulation and advocacy for disenfranchised groups and, to this extent, are key spokespersons for the profession. Yet there is evidence that social workers may be losing out in the competition for top leadership positions in both the public and nonprofit sectors. One of the ways this slide can be stemmed is for social work administrators and social work management scholars and researchers and their respective associations to work on a common agenda concerned with recruitment, education and training, research, mentoring, and the development of practice standards like those promulgated by the Network of Social Work Managers. This book, with its rich blend of contributions from the practice and academic communities, is a promising sign that such collaboration may be in the making.

INTRODUCTION

Leon H. Ginsberg

Leading and managing are among the persistent preoccupations in American life. A review of almost any day's and any town's newspapers will show stories about politics and political figures; presidents, governors, and mayors; school systems and their superintendents; law enforcement managers such as chiefs of police; and, frequently, stories about social agencies and their managers. Clearly, leaders and managers as well as their tasks have high public profiles.

This book is about social work leadership and management, subjects that have been important in the social work literature for much of its 110-year history. Some readers may confuse this book and its contents with "case management," a term that is prominent in the delivery of social services. Barker (2003) defines *case management* as "A procedure to plan, seek, and monitor services from different social agencies and staff on behalf of a client" (p. 58). That process has become common in much of human services work and there are case managers with varying levels of education who perform these services. Sometimes the process is referred to as *case integration* (Barker, 2003) or *case coordination*. However, classic social casework includes such efforts to bring a number of services to bear on a client's needs, and social caseworkers provide referral and coordination services to try to better meet the needs of clients. There are many texts on case management, such as Summers (2008), for those who want to learn more about it.

But this book isn't about case management; it's about the administration and management of human services programs. Both the National Association of Social Workers and the Council on Social Work Education have published books in the past on these subjects. This author's coedited book, *New Management in Human Services*, with Paul R. Keys, who is also a contributor to this volume, was published in two editions, in 1988 and 1995, by NASW Press.

More recently, Rino J. Patti, who edited the journal *Administration in Social Work*, before this editor succeeded him, also edited *The Handbook of Social Welfare Management*, a thorough and detailed text on the subject.

One of the earliest efforts at scholarship about social work leadership and management was the publication nearly 40 years ago of *Social Work Administration: A*

Resource Book, edited by Harry A. Schatz and published by CSWE in 1970. It was large and not nearly as attractive as typical texts today, at a time when social work books from commercial publishers were just beginning. This volume's spiffy cover was far removed from the appearance of Schatz's early efforts. But the social work management literature goes back further. Mary Richmond, whom some consider the founder of modern social work education in the 19th century, was a leader in the development of theories of "scientific philanthropy" when she served in various capacities with Charity Organization Societies and in the first social work education program, at the New York School of Philanthropy (Austin, 2000).

But the literature from the past and more current times on managing and leading social work programs is extensive. Rino Patti (2000) cites *Problems in Administration in Social Work* by P. Atwater, published in 1940 by the University of Minnesota Press. In 1973, Rosemary Sarri wrote *Effective Social Work Intervention in Administration and Planning Roles: Implications for Education* under the auspices of CSWE. Other works include Demone and Harshbarger's *A Handbook of Human Services Organizations*, published in 1974 by Behavioral Publications; R. M. Cyert's *The Management of Nonprofit Organizations*, published in 1975 by D. C. Heath; Harleigh Trecker's *Social Work Administration: Principles and Practices,* published by Association Press in 1977; Mark Miringoff's *Management in Social Welfare*, published in 1980 by Macmillan; Crow and Odewahn's *Management of the Human Services*, published by Prentice-Hall in 1987; and Rino Patti, John Poertner, and Charles Rapp's edited *Managing for Service Effectiveness in Social Welfare*, published by Haworth. Rapp and Poertner also collaborated on *Textbook of Social Administration: The Consumer-Centered Approach* in 1992, published by Longman and, in 2007, by Haworth Publishing. Also in 1988, David Austin published *The Political Economy of Human Service Programs* with JAI Press. The NASW Press published Felice Perlmutter and Wendy G. Crooks's *Changing Hats While Managing Change: From Social Work Practice to Administration* in 2004. Ralph Brody's *Effectively Managing Human Service Organizations*, now in its 3rd edition, was published by Sage in 2004. Barry Dym wrote *Leadership in Nonprofit Organizations: Lessons from the Third Sector*, published by Sage in 2005, and Mark Hughes's *Organizations and Management in Social Work* was also published by Sage, in 2007. *Person-Centered Leadership for Nonprofit Organizations* by Jeanne M. Plas was published by Sage in 2000, and Peter Kettner's *Designing and Managing Programs*, in its third edition, was published by Sage as well. Other important works for students of social work management include Brody's (2005) *Effectively Managing Human Service Organizations;* Dym's (2005) *Leadership in Nonprofit Organizations: Lessons From the Third Sector;* and Hughes's (2007) *Organizations and Management in Social Work.*

That's only part of the literature of social work leadership and management, and more may be published before this book is in print.

In addition to social work's own literature, writers on leadership and management are prolific in world literature. Their tradition is long and ranges from sources in the Bible and the Middle Ages, to the writing of Machiavelli, to modern-day academic and popular writers about leadership and management.

The existing social work leadership and management literature is extensive and cited frequently by the authors of the various chapters here. However, this book differs from much of that literature in several ways. For one, the authors represent both management practice and academic scholarship on management issues. One of the shortcomings in the social work professional literature in our field of professional practice is that few practitioners, compared with teachers and researchers, write about their work. Clearly, practitioners have special insights that professors and other scholars, who often serve as consultants and board members of social agencies, may not have. Several current and former social work managers publish their work in this book, and most of these practitioner-authors are also current social work educators, on a part-time basis. So this book, we hope, transcends the often large gap between the practice of social work and its theoretical bases. Some examples are the chapters authored, or co-authored with his colleagues, by Joel Levy, chief executive officer of the multimillion-dollar Young Adult Institute of New York. Paul R. Keys, a frequent writer on management issues, worked in public social services and as a faculty member before he became a university administrator in Missouri and now in Illinois. This editor is a social worker who moved back and forth between management practice and social work education during his 50-year social work career.

Each author was asked to prepare a practical and accessible treatment of his or her subject. The book is designed for managers and potential managers in both social work agency management and social work education. It is also designed to be a text for social work students, many of whom will become managers within a few years of completing their studies. That is generally the framework of the entire book—practical approaches to leadership and management issues in our field. One goal is to offer direct and rapidly usable information for social agency managers at all levels of responsibility and to directors of social work education programs. Applying theoretical and sometimes abstract concepts to their highly specific and complicated tasks is challenging, and we hope this book will help them in their work. We also hope the book will be used in the classroom by students. BSW and MSW programs are required to educate their students about leadership and management, and many of their graduates quickly become managers and supervisors of social welfare programs. When they assume those roles, we hope they will remember the lessons of this book.

There are some other emphases here that are not often found in the literature. Although deans and directors of social work programs share their insights through groups such as the Bachelor's Program Directors and the National Association of Deans and Directors, their ideas have not been shared often with the larger social work community. In this book, directors such as Michael Daley of the University of South Alabama and Jeannette Takamura of Columbia University offer practical comments on their roles.

In another way, the book is different because it provides some information on management in rural areas, a subject of some importance to those who manage the many nonmetropolitan area agencies.

Historically Black colleges and universities' (HBCUs') social work programs are an important and large segment of social work education. However, they are not often discussed in the professional literature. The chapter by Rufus Sylvester Lynch, Jacquelyn Mitchell, and Eugene Herrington, based in part on a series of meetings of HBCU social work programs, provides special insights into their challenges.

So, with due respect to the existing social work management literature, this book offers itself as a new and different contribution to that literature.

Why so many books on management? Michael J. Austin and Mark Ezell's special issue of *Administration in Social Work* (2004) included articles that noted the relatively small number of management courses in social work schools. The numbers of students who choose the management track in those MSW programs offering them are relatively small, which means sales of related textbooks, which often constitute the bulk of social work publication sales, must also be small.

However, for social work's whole existence, the common belief is that management of services is perhaps the most crucial subject in the lexicon: more important than casework, group work, or community organization; able to achieve massive change with a pen stroke; the basis for the gain or loss of millions of dollars and the employment or unemployment of thousands of social workers. There was never a time when large numbers of social work leaders did not believe that preparing effective managers was at the top of the most critical items on the profession's agenda.

Several reasons form the basis for that belief, including those already mentioned about the essential power of persons in managerial positions. Another is the reality of social workers with a degree of success in line worker and supervisory positions being promoted rather quickly into management. A number succeed and are in demand for other managerial work, but others fail and may drag their programs down with themselves.

Social work may also have a dearth of people interested in and qualified for managerial positions. It is not a subject taught in detail to most students. And many of the students who take such courses don't visualize themselves as potential managers and, consequently, don't take the course content seriously—although managers are what they may become within the first 5 years after they graduate. For many, management isn't what they chose to do when they became social workers, and, therefore, they resist aspiring to or moving into such positions.

There are almost always more social work management jobs than there are those who are qualified to hold them. For educators, the list of vacancies for social work department chairs, deans, or directors tends to exceed the demand for higher-rank professors.

Objectives of the Book

This book is designed to achieve several objectives. The authors, who are distinguished social work leaders, managers, and scholars of management, were oriented with these objectives in mind.

1. Provide practical, easy-to-understand, and up-to-date information about the basics of managing human services programs.
2. Serve as a text for students in courses dealing in part or entirely with the management of social welfare agencies.

3. Provide ideas and suggestions for managers currently employed in human services and social welfare management.

We—the authors and the editor—hope this text meets these objectives.

References

Austin, D. M. (2000). Management overview. In R. L. Edwards and J. G. Hopps (Eds.). *Encyclopedia of social work* (19th ed.; pp. 1642–1658). Washington, DC: NASW Press.

Barker, R. (2003). *The social work dictionary* (5th ed.). Washington, DC: NASW Press.

Brody, R. (2005). *Effectively managing human service organizations* (3rd ed.). Thousand Oaks, CA: Sage.

Dym, B. (2005). *Leadership in nonprofit organizations: Lessons from the third sector.* Thousand Oaks, CA: Sage.

Hughes, M. (2007). *Organizations and management in social work.* Thousand Oaks, CA: Sage.

Summers, N. (2008). *Foundations of case management practice: Skills for the human services.* Pacific Grove, CA: Wadsworth.

1 Basics of Social Work Leadership and Management

Leon H. Ginsberg

The opening chapters of this book trace some basic theories about management and leadership in social work that serve as a backdrop for the rest of the volume.

Chapter 1 is an overview of the current management literature of both social work and general theories of management found in the works of scholars and practitioners in other fields. Tom Peters and Robert Waterman, whose various works on the pursuit of excellence in organizations continue to influence scholarship and practice from the time they were published 30 years ago, have regularly updated their ideas and examples with books, videos, and audio. Other classical theorists, such as W. Edwards Deming, who developed the concept of Total Quality Management, and many predecessors, such as Mary Parker Follett and Luther Gulick, are included as well.

The book also pays some attention, especially in chapter 1, to what some might call "pop" theories of management. The dearth of materials on management, as well as the huge audience for works on the subject, prompts authors to write about the subject from all kinds of perspectives. There are books about Attila the Hun's management theories and even one on the management style of popular television character Tony Soprano, and the management literature pays some serious attention to such classical theorists as Machiavelli. Of course, not all or even most management theories can be covered in a single chapter. One of the goals of the chapter—and the book—is to help readers learn how much literature there is and how much we do not know.

Much of the management literature comes from fields such as business administration and educational leadership, so social workers have usually found it necessary to adapt those disparate foundations to practice in the social work field.

Social work management has a growing literature of its own, some examples of which are included in this first part of the book.

Bruce D. Friedman, president of the National Network for Social Work Managers and chair of the Social Work Department at California State University, Bakersfield, raises some of the current issues faced in the social work management field in chapter 2. The Network, a long-standing forum for those engaged in managing social programs, holds an annual institute. It also is tied to *Administration in Social Work*, the Network's official organ.

Because this book blends issues of leadership and management in social work practice with the management of social work education—as well as teaching students about management concepts—several chapters deal with education for leadership and management. Terri Moore Brown's chapter (3) on preparing students for social agency management focuses entirely on an approach to providing that education.

Part I should serve as a useful introduction for the rest of the book, which focuses on more specialized topics. Please note that some of the chapters in this section will help readers better understand some of the later ones. It is also a good primer on the overall subject of social work leadership and management.

1

Management Theory and Human Services Practice

Leon H. Ginsberg

A majority of licensed social workers are involved, for at least part of their assignments, in managing human services agencies. In the National Association of Social Workers (NASW) study of licensed social workers (Center for Health Workforce Studies, 2006), 69% of the social workers who responded to the survey indicated they were engaged in administration and management. However, most of those carried out administrative and management tasks only part of the time—generally as supervisors or managers of various kinds of client services. Only 20% of those surveyed devoted half or more of their time to administration and management. The study found that almost all licensed social workers (96%) were engaged in some form of direct service to clients. Although the licensed workers who were studied often engaged in consultation (73%) community organizing, (34%) policy development, (30%), and research (19%), these, along with administration and management, were secondary responsibilities to their providing direct services to clients.

Managing Social Welfare Programs

The practices of managing social welfare programs and social workers are explicated in detail in social work's own management literature, which is extensive and growing. However, social work management benefits from the much more extensive general literature on management, which has a long history, as discussed later in this chapter. It comes from such fields of study as business administration, public administration, and specialized fields comparable to social work such as educational and health services administration. To make that literature useful to social work management and other nonprofit fields, however, adaptations must be made, because much of the general management literature focuses on making a profit. Terms such as production and productivity have to be translated into social work terms. Producing automobiles, for example, is not the same as serving clients—although numbers of cases, interventions, and services may serve as proxies for dealing with units of production. Some more commonly used management concepts such as managing by objectives and outcomes, discussed later in this chapter, are more readily translated into the various outcomes social welfare agencies pursue.

Some management literature has an ongoing debate about the qualifications of managers in specialized efforts and organizations. For example, is managing a school significantly different from managing a retail store? Both settings require articulation of objectives, some organizing and structuring, some measurement of efforts, supervision and training of personnel, and other common functions. For some theoreticians, management is management—whether it is management of social services or management of a business. Increasingly, social agencies are turning to the business world for its managers. Even more common, they seek those with educational preparation in public administration. Some universities employ people with successful business management backgrounds instead of educational experience, and, in many cases, they succeed.

In the minds of others, management requires personnel with the specific preparation associated with the endeavor. Social agencies, that approach would say, need social workers as managers. Schools need people specially prepared as educators or school administrators. Businesses require managers with experience in business. The ethical mandates of the professions, including the human services professions, are central to managing organizations effectively that deal with those professions, advocates for managers with subject matter experience believe.

Some of those who hold that only subject matter specialists are equipped to manage programs in specific areas are accused of emphasizing their professions rather than the needs of their organizations. Some lawyers effectively and ethically manage human services agencies. Social workers and business administrators manage some medical practices. So the question of appropriate preparation for quality management is not settled by empirical evidence.

The argument will not be settled by this text, but readers can expect to read about it often in the social work management literature.

The Management Literature

Some of the largest sections of most American bookstores and libraries are those containing academic and popular books on business. And one of the most popular areas of business is management.

Despite management's prominence and focus in American society, managers of all kinds account for only 4.6% of the U.S. workforce, according to *Schott's Miscellany* (2008). The importance placed on management is probably related to the impact managers are seen as having on the rest of the workforce and the economy.

Every professional field, like social work, has its own specialized administration and management literature. Business administration is one of the largest professional fields in higher education, and much of is curriculum is based on studies of and preparation for management positions. Health care fields, especially hospital administration, devote a good bit of their efforts to managing programs and services. Education— elementary, secondary, and higher—has bodies of literature on administration, along with college-level courses, including majors, in the field. Relatively new but growing specialized studies such as hospitality management and sports management also have extensive curricula dealing with management.

Most of the fields draw on the basic concepts of management largely developed in the last century, especially in the works of Frederick W. Taylor, one of the original theorists who created scientific management. (Taylor and his theories are discussed in detail later in this chapter.)

In addition to the specialized, professional literature, management attracts a number of authors and books that may be described as popular or, perhaps, "pop management." Many of these books are quite personal, and most focus on changing behavior in ways that will make one more effective in managing others. Somewhat typical are the books by Randy Gage, whose publicity describes him as a high school dropout, former dishwasher, and now a prosperity expert who is a multimillionaire. One of Gage's suggestions is to start a multilevel or network marketing program—to sell products or services through these devices. Multilevel marketing involves companies—such as Amway or Mary Kay Cosmetics—in which people hire others to become salespersons of their products. Those salespersons hire more salespersons. The people above collect profits and commissions on those below them. If the products are successful, those at the top may earn significant amounts of money. However, as the levels multiply, more and more people are trying to sell products. As a result, many of those engaged in multimarketing endeavors see little profit from them.

Internet marketing is all those messages—usually hundreds—e-mail users receive daily, advertising a wide variety of health, financial, and other kinds of products and services. It is possible that some entrepreneurs earn a great deal by selling to only a tiny fraction of those they contact. Millions of e-mail messages are sent, and even if only a few hundred respond, earnings are possible. Gage markets his books and his ideas and is apparently successful. He also believes in unrestricted commerce:

> If you have a congruent philosophy toward prosperity, you absolutely have to support the right of someone to offer sex for money or to be able to pay for sex, and to support the right of someone to sell crack, crystal meth, or marijuana and use those drugs themselves. (Gage, 2006, p. 180)

But the management literature is much older than these sources and is much more systematic. This chapter traces management literature from very early times to the current era.

Classical Concepts

Several conceptual efforts are used to classify management theorists and theories. Several persisting and well-accepted approaches may be referred to as "classical" ideas about managing. Shafritz , Ott, and Jang (2004) believed that many ancient and later efforts, including works from the 19th and 20th centuries, fall into the classical category. They trace management theory to 1491 B.C.E., with Jethro's urging Moses to delegate authority over hierarchical lines.

As discussed earlier, means for managing the work of organizations and the people who work in them go back to origins such as the writings of Plato and Aristotle. Biblical references about the leaders of ancient peoples, writings about the management functions of a prince by Machiavelli in 1532, which Shafritz, Ott, and Jang (2004) call the first "how to succeed" book, and even theories about the management principles used by Attila the Hun (Roberts, 1990) are found in the management literature. Shafritz and colleagues also cite Adam Smith, the father of economic theory, especially free enterprise, as an early thinker about management. Clearly, those qualify as classic.

In modern management theory, the works of Max Weber and, later, Frederick W. Taylor, are fundamental. The major contribution of Weber (1864–1920) to the literature of management was in his conceptualization of bureaucracy, which continues to have application to larger organizations (Shafritz et al., 2004). Weber showed that large organizations, which are also called bureaucracies, are organized by offices or units into hierarchies—ranked from higher to lower units. The management of organizations is bound by rules that are impersonal, and those who hold positions in such organizations are chosen on the basis of qualifications and suitability for the work. Among many other critics of bureaucracies, Weber knew they become depersonalized and that many people resent and resist them. However, they constitute important structures for organizations, most of which could not function without some formal organizational structure. It is noteworthy that some whose prominence is in literature, such as Franz Kafka and scientists such as Albert Einstein (Isaacson, 2007), were involved in and influenced by large organizations. James G. Marsh and Herbert A. Simon (1958) were prominent more contemporary writers on bureaucracy. (Simon is discussed later as the theoretician who believed many management concepts were proverbs rather than principles.)

Many management authors emphasize the importance of understanding the informal as well as the formal aspects of the organizational structure. Clearly, some things are done well outside the formal system. As a manager, I encounter those realities frequently. While directing a large state agency, a former director explained that the key employees not only worked together daily, many of them also connected socially—at each other's homes, in churches, on fishing trips, and in many other venues. That helped explain positions and decisions that were otherwise hard to understand.

Informal information systems are also found in many organizations. A colleague once had some serious problems with an employee and contacted the human resources department about how to proceed. He noticed that each time human resources was contacted, the employee straightened up and ceased the unacceptable conduct. Someone in human resources was obviously monitoring the situation and tipping off the employee when it appeared that action against the employee was imminent.

One of the most influential of the 20th-century classical theorists of management was Frederick W. Taylor, whose theories achieved such prominence that his work is referred to as an "ism," Taylorism (Goldwag, 2007). Taylor wrote about "scientific management," which focused on strict divisions of labor and treating humans as if they were machines by eliminating sentimentality and emphasizing productivity (Shafritz et al., 2004). Matching humans with their tools and with machines was also a major part of the scientific management movement, which has been a significant approach, especially on management of manufacturing for more than 100 years. Goldwag (2007) says that modern applications of scientific management may be seen in today's fast food restaurants, where people are interchangeable and tasks are carefully defined. Taylor also spoke out against allowing workers to slow or limit their productivity as a means of protecting their jobs and the jobs of others. He believed in relating compensation as closely as possible to work achieved. Weekly, monthly, and annual salaries were less desirable than hourly and daily pay or pay for piecework. Helping the worker understand the rewards of the work performed is central to Taylor's theories. He suggested that workers were hurting themselves and their peers by reducing productivity—that increased productivity increased prosperity for all. That seeming antilabor stance earned Taylor something of a negative reputation, although his ideas were a natural evolution from Weber's concepts of bureaucracy and remain influential.

Another adherent of scientific management, in the manufacture of automobiles, was Henry Ford, who perfected the assembly line approach to vehicle manufacture. Perhaps following Taylor's views, Ford began paying his workers the then-astonishing wage of $5 per day. Such high salaries made it possible not only to keep the workers happy and productive, but also to make it possible for them to purchase their own products (Davis, 2007).

Frank and Lillian Gilbreth were also pioneers in scientific approaches to management for their work on time and motion studies. They are immortalized in the biography, *Cheaper by the Dozen*, written by two of their children (Gilbreth & Carey, 1948) and twice made into movies. The humorous story demonstrated the couple's means for applying scientific management to rearing their 12 children.

POSDCoRB

One of the major organizational theorists of the 1930s was Luther Gulick, whom Shafritz and colleagues (2004) also consider to be a classical writer. He described the need to subdivide work and define the functions of executives, which he did with an acronym, POSDCoRB, perhaps following the tradition of the contemporaneous Franklin D. Roosevelt's New Deal, which founded many services and organizations with acronyms. He was also one of the early management theory list makers. Lists are characteristic of many of the prominent theories of administration and management discussed in this chapter.

POSDCoRB stands for the following management functions: planning, organizing, staffing, directing, coordinating, reporting, and budgeting. The framework continues to be taught and used as a handy way to remember all executive managers must do as part of their work.

Peter F. Drucker

Peter F. Drucker, whom Philipson (2002) calls the father of postwar management, was a highly influential writer and theorist about management for much of the 20th century, especially after he came to England in 1933 and then to the United States in 1937 from Germany. He wrote 33 books on management, which were translated into many languages, on almost every element of administering organizations. One of the concepts he promoted was managing by objectives, a popular 20th-century idea that helped managers formulate goals and carry out their responsibilities with a focus on reaching those objectives.

Drucker believed there were five essential management objectives (Philipson, 2002): setting objectives, organizing, motivating and communicating, measuring, and developing people, including oneself.

Many other classical management theorists in the first half of the 20th century influenced the directions of organizations. Authors such as Chester Bernard, who wrote about the functions of executives (Philipson, 2002); Dale Carnegie, who influenced generations of managers to win friends and influence people (1936); and others helped found the large and pervasive field of management studies.

Management Proverbs

The bubble of formal and carefully defined approaches to managing was burst, to an extent, with the 1946 publication of Herbert A. Simon's *The Proverbs of Administration*. Simon, who later received the Nobel Prize in economics, listed the "principles" of administration found in much of the literature described as classical in this chapter. Four of those principles, he noted, involved how efficiency can be increased (1) by specializing tasks among the work group; (2) by organizing the workers into a hierarchy; (3) by limiting the span of control; and (4) by grouping workers according to purpose, process, clientele, or place. His article, which was something of a landmark in managerial theory, takes a "so what?" attitude toward much of what had been considered to be gospel in organization and management. He demonstrated that they were simply "proverbs," rather than operational principles.

Some still use these "proverbs" in teaching and writing about management. Simon noted that they are generally of no help in organizing and managing. Of course, people are specialized in their work—one person can't do two things at the same time. (Even multitaskers shift between activities, usually within short time spans, so they are not really doing two things at the same time.)

For the second proverb, Simon says hierarchies are often associated with a principle, called "unity of command." Again, he doubts there is a real problem. No person is physically able to respond to two contradictory commands, so the unity of command is obvious and its opposite impossible. Anything else results in confusion and ambiguity, which are greater problems.

In reality, authority is "zoned," Simon (1946) says. Sometimes an employee is called on to respond to a specialist such as the financial manager, although that person is not the employee's line supervisor. The financial manager has a zone of responsibility. That direction may conflict with the tasks assigned by that line supervisor—in which case, the managerial task is to clarify the person to whom the employee must respond if there are contradictory orders. That helps, but the problems persist in most large modern organizations, including universities. Social work professors find they must take orders from registrars, graduate school deans, department chairs, social work or other programmatic deans, financial officers, and many others. To whom is it necessary to respond first or, in the case of conflicts, most definitively?

In state government, I often came into conflict situations with the governor's staff, the attorney general, the state auditor, and many other individuals and offices. One adviser said an official could never go wrong following the written advice of the attorney general— that the attorney general's opinions had the force of law. That was often an effective means of delaying action, which seemed necessary. It worked in the case of state-paid abortions, for example.

Similarly, managers find they must respond to a number of audiences or interest groups, each of which may be critical to the manager's success, but any of which may conflict with another. For example, a manager of a large nonprofit social services agency may find it important to relate carefully to the internal staff, to the contributors who support the agency, to the board of directors that has authority over the agency, to the United Way agencies that may provide financial assistance, to the clients, and to the larger public. In other words, managers have multiple publics. Recognizing and dealing with them is a factor in managerial effectiveness. However, the early management theory "proverbs" do not deal clearly with such phenomena.

Modern Theories of Human Motivation and Management

For much of the 20th century, management theorists gave their attention to and acceptance of a variety of modern approaches, based on empirical studies of organizations and the people who manage them.

Management focus in the classic texts was on productivity in an era when manufacturing was an even greater focus of the American economy than it is today. For social workers, productivity is different in quality from productivity in manufacturing. Of course, social work services can be measured in terms of the activities of the organization. Social services may be quantified by the numbers of clients seen or, as is more customary in modern practices, by the numbers of satisfactory outcomes such as families reunited, patients successfully discharged, or substance abusers whose abuse is suspended or ended. Community organization or macro-oriented social work may be evaluated in terms of organizations successfully created and objectives achieved such as client homelessness overcome, unemployed persons becoming employed, or low-income families overcoming poverty.

The Hawthorne Studies

Perhaps most important in the pre-World War II United States were the Hawthorne Studies, led by the Australian-born Elton Mayo in 1927–1932. In many ways, the Hawthorne findings, which came from a study of the Western Electric telephone company in Chicago, contradicted the scientific management concepts of Taylor and his adherents (Philipson, 2002). The studies pointed to another series of important considerations in managing—the sentiments and reactions of the workers in an industry. For example, rest periods and pay incentives were modified and manipulated during the studies to determine the optimum amount of rest and the most effective means for compensating workers to for improve productivity. Similarly, the lighting in the assembly sites was changed to determine the optimum amount of illumination for effecting productivity increases. What the experimenters found was that lighting, rest periods, and even pay were not significant in increasing worker productivity. During the experiments, productivity continued to increase. Instead of the physical and compensation issues, workers responded to psychological rewards—to being treated as a special work group, to having a say in their work arrangements, and to cooperating with one another in achieving the company's goals. Feelings of worth and job satisfaction were more important than the more tangible issues of rest periods, lighting, and pay patterns.

The Hawthorne experiments changed social sciences and management theories. The human side of management led to theories propounded by later theorists such as Douglas McGregor, whose Theory X and Theory Y continue to influence administration thinkers and scholars (Philipson, 2002). Theory X, the traditional view, following the beliefs of Taylor, suggests that workers dislike their labor and perform as little work as possible. Coercion, control, and appeals to the material needs and desires of workers are viewed as all that make a difference in motivating workers. Theory Y suggests that working is a natural human function, as much as play and leisure. People take pride in their work and appreciate being given opportunities to be imaginative and exercise leadership on the job. Factors such as self-actualization, explicated more fully by Abraham H. Maslow (1970), are often as important to workers as tangible benefits such as salary.

Human relations approaches suggested several developments in management, such as teaching administrators to be sensitive to and react humanely to their employees. Such employee recognition efforts and symbols as service pins, newsletters, years of service awards, and employee-of-the-month and -year designations help increase productivity and improve morale. Some blends of human relations and scientific management, especially those that include additional compensation, are common. For example, those designated as outstanding employees may receive cash bonuses or raises, extra vacation time, and special parking spots.

Another blending of human relations and productivity is found in the works of Blake and Mouton (1964), who developed the managerial grid, which created two axes, concern for people and concern for production. Their concept was that an effective organization had to be deeply concerned with both—measured on scales of 1 to 9. The best organization is one that is highly concerned about its people (workers) and equally concerned about productivity. Cases describing characteristics of organizations are used to illustrate the various points on the grid on which the organization's conduct may place it.

One of the difficulties in using the managerial grid with social work managers is the terminology. Social work programs are concerned about people—that's the business of social work. So trainees have to be helped to understand that services to people are the production of social agencies. Concern for people, the other axis, is about concern for the social work staff, not the clients. By making such clarifications, the grid, which is an unusually helpful educational concept, can be used effectively with social work managers.

Mary Parker Follett

One early philosopher of management, Mary Parker Follett (Graham, 1995), anticipated in some ways the human relations approaches devised from the Hawthorne experiments. Called by some a prophet of management (Graham, 1995), Follett came from a family of some wealth in Massachusetts. She is one of the few women recognized as an innovator in management thinking and one of the only management experts whose work was based on a career in early social work. She finished her education before there were formal social work education programs, and she worked in community-building activities and could probably be called an early large systems or macro social worker. She was one of the first to recognize the potential for schools to be community resources for adult education and community activities after school hours. Vocational placement centers were also among her projects.

As a management theorist, she wrote and spoke extensively about coordination and believed it ought to be achieved through direct contact and communication among the people involved. Coordination, she said, should be considered early in an organization's life and built from the beginning. It should also be continuous because there is no permanent unity, only organizational processes that continually build it, Follett believed.

More current are the writings of Kenneth Blanchard and some of his associates (Blanchard & Johnson, 1983), who authored and coauthored a series of books advising how to be an effective manager in 1 minute in a variety of settings. Lawrence J. Peter (Hull & Peter, 1969) wrote humorously about his Peter Principle, which said most managers were incompetent after being successful at lower levels and then being promoted to their level of incompetence (Hull & Peter, 1969). C. Northcote Parkinson promulgated his Parkinson's Law (Parkinson, 1958), which humorously noted the ways in which organizations expand, whether they need to or not. Murphy's Law makes the point that most organizational efforts eventually go wrong. The concept of Murphy's Law includes a number of statements, such as "Anything that can go wrong will" and "Nothing is as easy as it looks." Murphy's Law—actually a series of humorous and ironic "laws"—has multiple sources in the United States and England from the military and eventually every other kind of organizational endeavor.

Organizational Quality

As some of the foregoing sections suggest, productivity is only one dimension of organizational effectiveness. The quality of production increasingly takes the attention of managers. Over the years, statistical methods became a focus in an effort to eliminate errors and increase quality. Quality is important in all kinds of management, but it became a special focus of manufacturing. Taking steps to ensure quality and meeting specifications is central to production of goods and becomes more important as technical requirements increase. Military equipment, vehicles, aircraft, and tools require careful adherence to quality standards. As the manufacture of goods became more global in the latter half of the 20th century, America found it needed to compete for quality products. The Japanese and German automobile manufacturers and the electronics corporations in several Asian nations produced goods with fewer problems at lower costs, often applying complex quality control procedures. Efforts to hold errors to specific thresholds, often stated in percentages, are characteristic of quality control procedures. Quality control is an industry, itself, often staffed by statisticians and management experts. Applying quality control helped American auto manufacturers meet the standards of quality that were characteristic of German and Japanese vehicles.

Basic quality control is a central part of American life. Opening a new article of clothing usually yields a small piece of paper indicating that it was inspected for quality. Foods of all kinds include Web sites addresses and toll-free telephone numbers asking purchasers to report any quality problems.

Quality control methods are applied not only in manufacturing and other industries but also in government and in social agencies, both governmental and nongovernmental. The goal is to avoid errors in providing client services such as financial assistance and protective services. Quality control units carefully examine a sample of cases and determine the extent to which they were handled properly. In economic assistance programs, for example, the quality control examination of a small, randomly selected sample of cases may find that the agency paid a few dollars too much to that sample. One can then assume that the agency commits similar errors in its whole caseload, perhaps thousands of cases, which may lead to the conclusion that the agency expends millions of dollars in error each year. Historically, quality control measures, especially those applied to large public agencies, have been controversial in the human services industry.

The literature on quality control is extensive, and those who want to pursue the subject further may find it useful to begin by looking at the Wikipedia entries on quality insurance and quality control on the Internet.

Total Quality Management

A seminal set of ideas about quality came from W. Edwards Deming, often called the "Prophet of Quality," who is credited with showing many organizations, especially those in Japan, how to ensure the quality of their products. But in his theories and writing, Deming went beyond inspection for and correction of errors in production and focused as well on relationships with suppliers and customers. He also emphasized quality efforts, from the beginning of the process through every step. Rather than finding and correcting errors at the end, Deming stressed making quality a characteristic of every step in the process up to its ultimate use by consumers. On that basis, he called his approach *total quality management*, sometimes shortened to TQM (Philipson, 2002).

Deming distilled his ideas into 14 points he thought should be followed by managers, and in total, rather than selecting and following only a few. Many of his ideas can also be found in the works of later management theorists, including Peters and Waterman (1982.)

The points, with some interpretation provided in parentheses, come from the Web site, http://www.ValueBasedManagement.Net:

1. Create constancy of purpose for improvement of product and service. (Organizations must allocate resources for long-term planning, research, and education, and for the constant improvement of the design of their products and services.)
2. Adopt the new philosophy. (Government regulations representing obstacles must be removed, and companies need to be transformed.)
3. Cease dependence on mass inspections. (Quality must be designed and built into the processes, preventing defects rather than attempting to detect and fix them after they have occurred.)
4. End the practice of awarding business on the basis of price tags alone. (Organizations should establish long-term relationships with [single] suppliers.)
5. Improve constantly and forever the system of production and service. (Management and employees must search continuously for ways to improve quality and productivity.)
6. Institute training. (Training at all levels is a necessity, not optional.)
7. Adopt and institute leadership. (Managers should lead, not supervise.)
8. Drive out fear. (Make employees feel secure enough to express ideas and ask questions.)
9. Break down barriers between staff areas. (Working in teams will solve many problems and improve quality and productivity.)
10. Eliminate slogans, exhortations, and targets for the work force. (Problems with quality and productivity are caused by the system, not by individuals. Posters and slogans generate frustration and resentment.)
11. Eliminate numerical quotas for the workforce and numerical goals for people in management (To meet quotas, people will produce defective products and reports.)
12. Remove barriers that rob people of pride of workmanship. (Individual performance reviews are a great barrier to pride of achievement.)
13. Encourage education and self-improvement for everyone. (Learning should be continuous for everyone.)
14. Take action to accomplish the transformation. (Commitment on the part of both [top] management and employees is required.) (http://www.ValueBasedManagement.Net).

Stephen R. Covey

Although Stephen R. Covey is not solely a management theorist, one popular and heavily used framework for improving one's performance is his work. His book, *The Seven Habits of Highly Effective People* (2004), is something of a landmark in personal development literature. In recent years, he added an eighth habit. His books and other materials such as calendars and training guides in both printed and electronic form are widely available.

In brief, his habits, several of which are largely self-explanatory, are:

1. Be proactive.
2. Begin with the end in mind.
3. Put first things first.
4. Think win-win.
5. Seek first to understand, then to be understood.
6. Synergize—connect ideas and efforts and help them build on one another. Creative cooperation is a factor in improving organizational life.
7. Sharpen the saw—refine and improve oneself, one's methods, and materials all the time. Dr. Covey suggests that a person's most important resource is him- or herself, so constant improvement efforts are necessary to become one's best.
8. From effectiveness to greatness—keep working to improve one's efforts and one's organization. Dr. Covey believes that most people are not excited or motivated to improve their performances. His eighth habit provides a "road map" for moving toward greatness (Covey, 2006).

Those who are interested in pursuing Dr. Covey's theories should consult his Web site, www.stephencovey.com.

Peters and Waterman

In the 1980s, two management authors became the most prominent and popular of the later years of the 20th century. They followed their landmark book, *In Search of Excellence* (Peters & Waterman, 1982), with several additional books on the same themes, some coauthored with others and some written by the two authors individually. The difference in their works from much of what came before was their effort to distill principles based on observing successful organizations. Much of what they propose builds on the earlier writings mentioned here. The fundamental principles were based on empirical observation.

They based their writing, which Philipson (2002) says became the most popular source of management theories in modern times, on analysis of a large number of excellent organizations, which they whittled down to 62. From these they distilled their principles. Some thought their work was popular because it was simple and readily understood, but Drucker suggested at the time that they made management seem a simple task by avoiding all of the complexity associated with it (Philipson, 2002). Nevertheless, Philipson (2002) argues, *In Search of Excellence* was the impetus for the thousands of popular business and management books that followed.

Among the organizations they chose were large, well-known institutions such as Wal-Mart and IBM, both of which continue to flourish. But they also chose others that were excellent at the time they wrote but had declined or even disappeared within a few years, such as New York Air, one of the first discount airlines. They claimed that the organizations they chose were excellent at the time, not necessarily for all time.

From their observations about the organizations, they distilled 8 principles, which have to do with the ways the organizations operated. In later works, they covered excellent nonprofit organizations from government and the private sector, including some social welfare agencies.

The Eight Principles

An overriding consideration in *In Search of Excellence* was management that was on the scene, that was driven by the organization's values, and that involved direct and personal attention to the organization. Distant, data-studying management has its place, they might say, but being on the scene and being involved in the day-to-day operations were critical management activities.

A Bias for Action was their first principle. Effective, excellent organizations wanted to do something rather than just study and plan. Trying to achieve something, being willing to fail, and simply acting seemed characteristic of excellence. I recall that the bias for action was simply essential to the success of the organizations I have managed. When I came to North Carolina, with a mandate to begin a Master of Social Work (MSW) program, there was resistance and risk. However, we went ahead with announcing the program (a detailed needs assessment had been part of the planning) immediately—and recruited enough students and developed a sufficient curriculum to begin. That seemed to astonish some elements of the Appalachian State University system, which, some told us, had embarked on and then abandoned more than a few graduate programs. Universities are notoriously slow to change and to begin new efforts. Social agencies have similar, cautious approaches to trying new things. In my experience, an orientation to action has tended to pay off—if the actions seemed to have a logical basis and sufficient resources. At Appalachian State, we also developed and offered international study programs for the first time in social work. They were sufficiently subscribed to succeed. Of course, there is not great value in acting on programs that seem doomed to fail. But if there is a plan and a reasonable guarantee of success, it seems wise, according to Peters and Waterman, to go ahead and act.

Close to the Customer, their second principle, changed businesses significantly. Of course, such a principle seems self-evident, although surprisingly large numbers of organizations become mired in satisfying their employees and managers more than in becoming close to the customers whose support sustains them. Wal-Mart's emphasis on low prices and convenient shopping are good examples. IBM's heavy focus on providing consultation and maintenance for the purchases of their products is another. However, it is not as easy to apply this principle to social welfare agencies and educational institutions. Just who is the customer in social work? Few social workers have clearly defined customer bases. Most social workers and those who manage social agencies have to respond to a number of customers or publics, as mentioned earlier. The board of directors; the government, including legislatures and executive agencies; sometimes the press, and clients may constitute customers in the largest sense, for educators, students, university administrators, boards of trustees, parents, and faculty are among the customers who must be satisfied by an educational unit such as a school of social work. The answer for social work managers is to be close to all of these customers, recognizing that their wishes and objectives may conflict from time to time. Sometimes the social work manager must choose among them, but they must be considered in all cases. If there are conflicts, it is useful to explain the reasons for decisions and to maintain the lines of communication. Alienating customers is not a sound resolution of conflicts and is, of course, ideally to be avoided. There often come times when managers have to choose among their customers and publics, but that ought to be a last rather than an early step in resolving conflicts.

The pervasiveness of the concept of being close to customers has extended to some health care practices. Not long ago I, while engaged in a less than pleasant medical procedure, was told by the physician administering it, "I want to do what you want." I don't think I had heard that from a physician before.

Autonomy and Entrepreneurship is a principle involved in dealing with the organization's staff. Sound managers recognize that they can rely on their colleagues to come up with ideas. Excellent organizations encourage staff members to develop new ideas and see them through to fruition. These are the opposite of management, which works as if only the top manager can have ideas and put them into effect. Many of the best ideas come from line staff in social agencies who are in positions to identify needs and potential solutions to them. Agencies have been able to eliminate waiting lists for clients who want services but who are discouraged by how far in advance some agencies must schedule appointments. Excellent and successful corporations such as McDonald's used ideas from local staff to develop such highly profitable innovations as breakfast menus. Clearly, some of the best ideas come from multiple sources within organizations. Encouraging autonomy and entrepreneurship is an important management function.

Productivity through People, similar to the last principle, carries the notions of autonomy and entrepreneurship a bit further by suggesting that the organization's productivity is a product of respecting and working through staff and employees rather than viewing them as simply functionaries who extend the reach of top management. The organization's objectives are reached through the people who staff it, this principle suggests. In professional organizations such as social agencies, the principle is not difficult to see—providing the services of social workers *is* the organization's productivity.

Hands-on, Value-Driven describes the principle discussed earlier of an organization's management maintaining a close, visible tie to all elements of the program. The distant chief executive officer of the social agency is less effective than is the CEO who connects directly and regularly with agency staff as well as with the clients and board of directors. Perhaps most important, the effective manager communicates the values of the organization and ensures they are pursued.

Stick to the Knitting has major applications to business organizations. Peters and Waterman were writing at a time of business mergers, often mergers of a particular kind of effort involving processes that were quite different from what had been the business's primary focus. Some of those businesses ultimately divested themselves of the new acquisitions. In more recent times, acquisitions have made more organizational sense. For example, Sears, with a long history in mail order retailing of clothing, purchased Lands' End, a large mail order clothing company. The marriage was a success, perhaps a greater success than Sears might experience by purchasing financial services organizations. For social agencies, direct practice organizations that attempted to move into community organization and advocacy often had difficulty. Staying with successful operations and avoiding the pitfalls of uncharted territory seemed beneficial to human services agencies. On the other hand, a child protective and foster care organization might reasonably move into adult protective services and foster care, building on its experiences and resources.

Simple Form, Lean Staff is a popular concept from Peters and Waterman. The authors place heavy emphasis on keeping things simple, even when the issues are complicated. Some observers note that relatively complicated organizations manage to govern themselves through only a few layers of structure, while relatively simple organizations govern themselves through large numbers of layers. Generally, the closer top management is to operational personnel, the better off the organization is. If management becomes too far removed from day-to-day operations, as other Peters and Waterman principles suggest, the organization suffers. Of course, oversimplification may also be a source of problems, especially when it is not actually simplifying the effort. Several universities, perhaps following Peters and Waterman, reduced the number of their colleges from 15 or 20 to 4 or 5, which seemed to be functional. However, universities by their nature are specialized—by subject matter, customers, and many other dimensions. What has often occurred is that those universities have hidden their complex nature and become even more difficult to manage. These colleges begat numerous departments and programs within departments, making it difficult for top management, such as provosts and deans, to have a reasonable idea of what was actually going on or what the needs of the organization happened to be.

Simultaneous Loose-Tight Properties are desirable in organizations. Tight auditing and fiscal controls are essential for excellent organizations, for example, to ensure that management knows what is going on and can exercise control. At the other end of the scale, an effective organization also operates loosely, so employees and managers can innovate, change direction, reallocate resources, and respond to changes in the organizational environment. So, effective organizations, including social agencies, have both tight and loose properties.

Social agency managers are influenced by *In Search of Excellence*, even perhaps if they have not read the book or consciously studied the principles it suggests. That is because modern management doctrine generally accepts the principles Peters and Waterman promulgate.

Current Concerns

The more current American management literature focuses on a variety of developments that were not major considerations in earlier writing. For example, much of business has become international in nature. Thomas Friedman's work about the internationalization of almost everything (2007) demonstrates why the preoccupation of all sorts of businesses is no longer national but international. Globalization is en-hanced by modern information technology in which the manufacture of almost everything American is now accomplished in distant parts of the world. Information is also international. Call for help with an American product or service, and the caller is likely to reach an expert at a "call center" in India or another Asian nation. Similarly, people from India are increasingly staffing technology offices of American corporations such as banks and accounting companies. That trend, which is likely to grow, may per-manently change the relationships between the United States and the larger world as well as American employment and management. The other end of the employment spectrum is also becoming increasingly international. Immigrants, both legal and il-legal and often from Latin America, are filling jobs at the lowest compensation levels throughout the United States. Social work is likely to change with the rest of American industry. It is also likely to change the nature of social work, calling on more practice to take place internationally and domestically, with foreign nationals. Social workers who are sensitive to cultural differences and who are multilingual were in great demand in the first decade of the 21st century and are likely to continue being sought by so-cial welfare agencies.

Conclusions and Applications to Social Work

Following the guidance of these myriad theories requires disseminating them widely, not only to the social work managerial staff but also to the totality of agency employees. Having everyone on board with management approaches helps the staff understand the motives and actions of management at all levels. It also helps ensure that the total staff is oriented to results and the pursuit of excellence. Many of the principles in this chapter require actions, not only by top managers but also by every-one who staffs the organization. That is especially true for the principles associated with an orientation toward meeting customers' needs. If everyone shares that kind of orientation, it can happen. If not, staff may seem more interested in their own needs than in those of their clients-customers.

Most of us have seen and been disturbed by store clerks and organizational repre-sentatives, whose job is to be attentive to us and our needs, conducting personal business by telephone. Or we have found that important resources that could have been brought to bear in solving major social problems are diverted, or the need for them is ignored.

In social work, management is crucial to meeting the social objectives to which we are committed. The best-prepared and most skillful social workers cannot resolve human problems in the absence of an effective managerial effort.

Management Basics—Cases

Employee Peer Relationships

William is a new social worker in a rural county community mental health agency. Although he is new to the agency, he comes with a reputation for excellent work in the capital city's comparable agency, where he was employed for 5 years. He relocated after being recruited by the rural agency, which is near his wife's family's home.

For the first year of his employment, William was a valued and productive member of the staff. Clients requested him by name to provide their services. He took on more cases than anyone else in the agency and seemed to be helpful in resolving their problems. Local private practice social workers, as well as local physicians, were pleased with his addition to the staff; he had made it a better agency.

Almost from his first day, William became friendly with the only other male social worker employed by the agency, Charles. They ate lunch together several times each week, their families socialized on weekends, and William became a member of Charles's church, which was similar to the church he had left in the capital city.

Shortly after William began his second year of employment, Charles came to him with a problem. He had received an anonymous insulting letter and a photograph of a man who had dwarfism. Charles showed the letter and photo to William. Charles was short in stature and had a pronounced limp, a result of a childhood case of polio. He was sensitive about his disabilities and was devastated by the letter and photograph. William expressed sympathy and promised to help Charles resolve the problem.

Over the next few weeks, Charles received more letters, photos, and other contacts from the anonymous correspondent. At one point, a florist delivered a funeral bouquet, draped in black, to Charles's house. He also told William about telephone calls he began to receive. Some of these were just calls and hang-ups, but soon the caller began leaving cryptic messages—"Hello, freak," "You should be in a mental institution," and the like. The calls came to Charles both at his home number and in his office. Eventually, the calls began to involve William, too. "Tell your buddy, William, that we're watching him," "Dead child (William had 3 young children, Charles, no children)," and, eventually, came directly to William—calls, sometimes 10 or 15 each night, which ended when William or a family member answered the telephone. These events preceded the widespread use of caller identification, but the telephone company agreed to place a monitoring machine on Charles's home line. The calls, they discovered, came from public telephones.

At one point, after Charles reported telephoned death threats, the local police stationed an officer outside his house for two nights. Charles and William speculated about the source of the harassing telephone calls and mail, assuming, because the behavior was bizarre, that it might be an agency client who was mentally ill.

Both Charles and William reported the situation to the agency director, who listened sympathetically but took no action on his own.

As he became increasingly upset by the threats to his colleague and to himself and his family, William solicited the help of the Federal Bureau of Investigation (FBI) through a friend who was a member of the U.S. Congress. The FBI investigated the situation, spoke to both William and Charles, and reported back to the member of Congress who, in turn, passed the findings along to William.

They noted that at no time was William present when Charles received one of the telephone calls. They also noted that Charles had never been with William when William or a family member received a call. How did William know what calls Charles received? Charles had showed William his letters, but William had no way of knowing who had sent them.

An inescapable conclusion was that Charles initiated and carried out all of the correspondence and telephoning. William confronted Charles with the findings of the FBI investigation, and the telephone calls and mailings subsequently ceased completely. Although Charles continued with the agency, he was passed over for promotions that he sought; William eventually accepted a still better appointment in another state.

Discussion Questions

1. What may have been the genesis of Charles's actions? What were some possible motivations for Charles's behavior?
2. William appears to threaten Charles. What are some of the possible bases for the threat?
3. How might William have prevented the escalation of the problem by behaving differently?
4. What are some steps the agency director may have taken to address the problem after it was brought to his attention?

References

Blanchard, K., & Johnson, S. (1983). *The one minute manager.* New York: Berkeley Publishing Group.

Carnegie, D. (1936). *How to win friends and influence people.* New York: Pocket Books.

Center for Health Workforce Studies. (2006). *Licensed social workers in the United States, 2004.* Albany, NY: School of Public Health, University at Albany.

Covey, S. R. (2004). *The 7 habits of highly effective people.* New York: Free Press.

Covey, S. R. (2006). *8th habit personal workbook: Strategies to take your effectiveness to greatness.* New York: Free Press.

Friedman, T. L. (2007). *The world is flat: A history of the twenty-first century.* New York: Farrar, Straus, and Giroux.

Gage, R. (2006). *Why you're dumb, sick & broke…and how to get smart, healthy & rich.* New York: Wiley.

Gilbreth, F. B., Jr., & Carey, E. G. (1948). *Cheaper by the dozen.* New York: Thomas Y. Crowell.

Ginsberg, L. (2001). *Social work evaluation.* Boston: Allyn and Bacon.

Goldwag, A. (2007). *'Isms and 'ologies: The 453 basic tenets you've only pretended to understand.* New York: Madison Park Press.

Graham, P. (Ed.). (1995). *Mary Parker Follett: Prophet of management—A celebration of writings from the 1920s.* Boston: Harvard Business School Press.

Hull, R., & Peter, R. J. (1969). *The Peter principle.* New York: William Morrow.

Isaacson, W. (2007). *Einstein: His life and universe.* New York: Simon and Schuster.

March, J. G., & Simon, H. A. (1958). *Organizations.* New York: John Wiley & Sons.

Maslow, A. H. (1970). *Motivation and personality* (2nd ed.). New York: Harper and Row.

Parkinson, C. N. (1958). *The pursuit of progress.* London, UK: John Murray.

Peters, T. J., & Waterman, R. H., Jr., (1982). *In search of excellence: Lessons from America's best-run companies.* New York: HarperCollins.

Philipson, N. (Ed.). (2002). *Business: The ultimate resource.* Cambridge, MA: Perseus.

Raymond, F. B., III, & Rank, M. (2003) *Preparing for accreditation in social work education: The self-study and the site visit.* Alexandria, VA: Council on Social Work Education.

Roberts, W. (1990). *Leadership secrets of Attila the Hun.* New York: Warner.

Schott, B. (2008). *Schott's miscellany 2008: An almanac.* New York: Bloomsbury.

Shafritz, J., Ott, J. S., & Jang, Y. S. (2004). *Classics of organization theory.* Florence, KY: Cengage Learning.

Simon, H. A. (1946). The proverbs of administration. *Public Administration Review,* 6, 54–67.

2

Where Have All the
Social Work Managers Gone?

Bruce D. Friedman

As social work is in its second century of existence as a profession, there is the continuing discussion about social work administrators or managers. We continue to look at the field to see social service agencies, whose administrator used to be a social worker, that are now headed by someone with another professional degree. This raises a number of questions, including the title of this chapter, "Where have all the social work managers gone?" This chapter explores those issues and expands on a point-counterpoint discussion that Felice Perlmutter and I had in 2006 in *Administration in Social Work.*

A number of factors relate to the significant change in the role of social workers as administrators of agencies: Some are historical in nature and emerged from the changing nature of the social service delivery environment; some relate to the nature of the profession of social work; and some relate specifically to the higher educational system of which social work education is a part. I explore each of these and make some recommendations for the future.

History of Social Service Agencies in the United States

Social work agencies began to emerge in the mid-1800s in response to the growing immigrant population and the need to assist in their resettlement (Stein, 1958). These agencies were primarily faith-based and had the specific purpose and function of Americanizing those immigrants to prepare them to be contributing members of society. As waves of immigration subsided, the role and function of these agencies changed to adapt to the changing needs of society. In addition, the 1930s and the initiation of the Social Security Act brought the federal government into provision of social services.

The initial directors of these agencies had a normal progression from worker to supervisor and then, eventually, to administrator of the agency (Hoefer, 2003). The values of these agencies were maintained, because the administrators had moved up through the ranks. The changes in needs of agencies as a result of the changing needs of society seemed to change all of that. The Social Security Act and, later, the War on Poverty meant that disenfranchised members of society were being served by government agencies or organizations being subsidized by federal funds. Private agencies changed from providing direct service to disenfranchised members of society to serving a middle-class population; the initial mission changed, and the role of social work became diminished.

The 1960s brought about the War on Poverty and an explosion of social service agencies with federal funding. During this era social service agencies were seen as the solution to communal problems. Federal money was given to agencies because their goal and mission focused on changing the state of the poor and disenfranchised members of society, but there was never enough money to address the problem as it was intended to be addressed. The War on Poverty identified social work as the primary profession to address problems, but the size of the caseload to do the work that needed to be done far exceeded what the profession dictated were optimal case sizes. The optimal caseload was 1 worker to 20 or 25 clients, whereas welfare caseloads began reaching triple digit figures (Schorr, 1986).

Another developmental factor occurred during the late 1800s, with the growth of federated agencies to assist with fundraising efforts of the social service agencies (Brilliant, 1990; Day, 2003; Stein, 1958). Initially, these agencies performed fundraising and community planning functions. Many of the social workers were involved in the community planning and development aspect of these agencies, which led them to administrative positions in these agencies. As the role of these agencies changed in the 1980s and 1990s to primarily fundraising, the role of the social worker in these agencies also diminished.

The Reagan years brought about factors of social accountability for social service agencies. Again, those individuals who held the purse strings did not have a good understanding of the nature of the work of social workers. Thus, agencies were being asked to be more accountable for the expenditure of dollars with an emphasis on "management by objectives," something that was foreign to many social workers, who were providing services to address the overall good of their client systems. Factors of accountability, the nature of the funding streams for services, and the changing nature of societal need were all factors that led to a shift from social workers in administrative roles of agencies to persons with more administrative focus, such as business administration, public administration, or public health.

The Social Work Profession

The social work profession has constantly been struggling between providing services to clients and social advocacy and macrolevel changes. These debates have their origins as far back as the Charitable Organization Society (COS) and the Settlement Houses back in the late 1800s, when there was the question of whether one should effect change in individuals to adapt to society, or societal changes were needed to address the needs of a population group (Day, 2003). Many of these issues relate back to the values of the founding fathers of the United States and the struggle between individual responsibility and community change. As a growing profession, social work initially adopted the work of Mary Richmond's Social Case Work as the driving force for working with individuals. However, one segment of the population also focused on more of the macrolevel changes. As a result, most social workers were trained as direct service practitioners, then they eventually moved up the ranks to administration as a normal progression of their continuing work in the field (Patti, 2000; Skidmore, 1995). This meant that many social work administrators attained their positions without the knowledge and skills to run an agency and had to learn those skills on the job.

As a profession, social work has been slow to recognize the role of the social work administrator as part of its professional workforce. It is as if the natural progression in one's professional career was to advance to administrative positions, but there was no training to get there. In addition, factors of licensure and third-party reimbursement made the clinical realm of practice appear to be lucrative and without the headaches of worrying about agency accountability to funding sources.

On the one hand, there is the notion that social workers, beginning with the bachelor of social work degree, learn to work with systems of all sizes. However, there seems to be an emphasis on the nature of that practice being clinical, and the definition of a client system seems to focus primarily on the individual rather than on mezzo or macro systems.

In the late 1950s, the National Association of Social Workers (NASW) was created to unify all the various groups within social work. Promises were made to maintain some identity for social work managers, but, as Chauncey Alexander (2001) states, social work managers were leaving the association rapidly because their needs were not being met. There was too much emphasis on clinical practice, and the managers were being swallowed up. That led to the creation of the National Network for Social Work Managers in 1985.

Another important factor in the profession has been the role of state licensure. States, as a way to protect their citizens from untrained and unskilled providers, have created clinical social work licenses. Thus, those individuals in administrative roles, with few exceptions, are not subject to the same licensing laws and rules. Many administrators do not feel the need to maintain their licenses, because administrators do not have to be licensed. In addition, the license has meant that those individuals who are licensed are eligible for third-party reimbursement, thus allowing them to bill insurance companies. Supervision needs to be done by someone who is licensed, but it also means those individuals are not able to generate their own billable hours if they are spending a lot of time supervising, thus creating a major dilemma for social work administrators who have been trained in the administrative functioning of the agency but may not be current on day-to-day clinical skills of brief therapeutic treatment techniques that insurance companies usually reimburse.

The profession has witnessed the constant struggle between providing direct clinical services and being involved in leading societal change. Some of this relates to the different skills needed for each. Social casework is a very reactive skill base that mandates that one begins where the client is and then responds by empowering the individual to make those needed changes within the strengths of the individual's ability to do so. On the other hand, macrolevel change is somewhat proactive in that it involves being able to anticipate need, identify the resources or capacity to enable that change, and advocate for change by engaging those power brokers who have the ability to enhance that process. The ability to learn these skills leads to the third area, the educational system.

Social Work Education

A number of authors place a good portion of the blame for the loss of social work managers on the educational system (Austin, 2000; Patti, 2000; Perlmutter, 2006; Wuenschal, 2006). They state that the educational process has not placed enough emphasis on administration as a focus, or that the educational system is market-driven. I explain each of these in detail below. The educational process is only part of the problem, however. As identified above, there are a number of other contributing factors, and the question is whether social work education has been able to respond in a timely manner to those factors. For example, when the War on Poverty was passed as legislation in the 1960s, there was a call for creation of the bachelor of social work (BSW) to address the growing need for social workers. The first programs to grant BSWs were accredited in 1974. However, by that time, social factors had changed, and BSWs were not needed in the public service sector.

From this single scenario, we can see that education does not respond as quickly to societal factors as may be necessary to address those needs. Thus, regarding the loss of social work managers, one should not place blame on the educational process as the sole source of the problem; it is just one source.

Social work education is based on a set of core competencies, the current description of which is in the Educational Policy and Accreditation Standards (EPAS). Each social work program has to demonstrate that it addresses the core competencies as spelled out in the EPAS. Programs can exceed the core competencies and offer more than what is listed, but they are required to address at least the minimum of the 10 core competencies.

These competencies are written in generic terminology to allow each program to describe what it does and how it addresses the competencies to address the local and unique characteristics of the specific region or population the program serves. In addition, each program has to look at its own strengths and identify how those strengths build into the curriculum development of that program to address the competencies. Therefore, there is some flexibility for programs to provide content that may address the administrative needs of the social services community.

However, two other factors contribute to this process: one is the faculty knowledge and skills, and the other is market demand of student enrollment. Let me address the faculty knowledge and skills issue first.

As mentioned previously, many social workers move into administrative positions from direct service positions (Hoefer, 2003; Skidmore, 1995). Social work educators are a subset of the larger arena of social workers. With accrediting bodies requiring that faculty have a PhD, many faculty are completing their post–master's experience as direct service workers, and then moving into doctoral education without allowing for advancement into administrative positions. Thus, there is a loss of faculty with the knowledge and experience in administrative roles to actually teach those roles and functions to students (Patti, 2000). It also means that those faculty members who do have the knowledge and experience are beginning to move closer to retirement age, causing an already small pool to become even smaller. Thus, programs are beginning to look outside social work for people with those skills who can teach in these areas.

The second factor has been student demand. In reflecting back 30 years, to when I received my master of social work (MSW), approximately 80% of the class was interested in direct practice. The rest was spread among groups, families, community organization, and administration. As we look at current trends, a variety of factors has skewed that distribution even more. The child welfare consent decree in the 1980s led to the creation of Title IV-E and students receiving stipends to enter the field of child welfare services. So as not to be undone, community mental health has been pushing to get students to enter into the mental health field. And as we all age, there is a growing need for geriatric social workers. This does not discount the role of social workers in the health field, however. Thus, the growth of the profession and the need for direct care social workers has led people into direct service at entry-level positions. Accompanying the demand for social workers has been growth in social work education programs and the need for faculty to teach practice skills. Thus, faculty are quickly moving from their 2 years of post–master's experience into doctoral education to begin to fill the gap created by the increase in accredited social work education programs.

The focus on clinical positions has had a ripple effect on agencies that used to provide macrolevel services, but can no longer attract students and recent graduates to seek practicum experiences or employment. As mentioned earlier, the role of United Way in the community has changed consistently. In the 1980s, United Way moved more to a focus on fundraising rather than on community planning (Brilliant, 1990). As a result, many people who would have gone to work or done practicum placements at the United Ways no longer had practicum instructors to provide the educational experience. Thus, students were not being exposed to community organizations or administrative practicum experiences as they had been in the past. Given the market factors of social work education programs, there is supply and demand, and with lessening demand, fewer resources are being devoted to that curriculum area.

To address the loss of social work managers and administrators by social service agencies, graduate programs in business, public administration, and public health have created programs in nonprofit management (Gummer, 1987; Keys & Capaiuolo, 1987). Another model has been the development of joint degree programs, where social work partners with business and law to address the administrative needs of nonprofit agencies.

This leads to the question of what this all means, what social work is doing to address the problem, and whether social work needs to do anything, because business, public administration, and public health have taken steps to create graduate education programs to meet the needs of nonprofit management.

Social Work's Response

The social work profession does not have a unified voice, so it is difficult to see many what the profession is doing. The major organizations within the profession, NASW and the Council on Social Work Education (CSWE), have examined the loss of social workers in administrative positions with great concern. CSWE generated a white paper to address these issues, and the Social Work Leadership Institute was created with funding from the John Hartford Foundation to address these factors. Yet, there is another group, a small social work membership organization that has been addressing this concern for more than 20 years and is beginning to gain some recognition for the work it is doing.

The National Network for Social Work Managers (Network) was created in 1985 by Robert Maslyn (2002) and Paul Keys as a way to address the loss of social workers in the upper administrative positions of social service agencies. Initially the Network was created to provide a forum where social work managers could meet and gain support with one another. The Network then created the Institute of the National Network (Institute) as the educational division within the Network to begin to understand and identify factors and develop skills that social workers need to move into upper administrative positions in social service agencies. As a result of the needs identified by managers through the Institute, the Network published *Leadership and Management Practice Standards* (NNSWM, 2004) to begin to address the curricular needs of individuals entering social service administration.

These standards are based on the work of social work administrators in understanding just what it is they need to be able to manage a social service agency successfully. Social service administration is broken down into a number of areas. First are the external factors associated with the organization and how that organization is positioned within the larger more complex societal system. Second are those internal factors that one needs to know to operate the agency properly and maintain its viability.

In a review of various graduate program curricula, a number of studies have compared the curricula in MSW, master of business administration (MBA), master of public health (MPH), and master of public administration (MPA) programs. These analyses found that MSW programs had a strong emphasis on some of the external factors, such as advocacy, public policy, and community organization; whereas, MBA programs stressed internal functioning, such as financial management and human resource management, and MPA programs spanned the boundary between internal and external management, such as strategic planning (Mirabela & Wish, 2000). As a result, no one degree seems to address the total needs of social service agencies. That is why the Network-published *Standards* become so important.

Currently, a number of programs are using the *Standards* to design their curriculum to be in consonance with the needs of social service agencies. Kean University in New Jersey has used the *Standards* to create a post–master's certificate program to provide those individuals who move from direct practice to administration without the appropriate knowledge and skills with a way to gain the knowledge and skills they need to perform their jobs. John Tropman at the University of Michigan, who has a joint appointment in both the School of Social Work and the Business School, uses the *Standards* to design his curriculum in nonprofit management. And this is only the beginning, as programs across the country are looking at the *Standards* as a way to understand the administrative needs of social service agencies, and then to develop curricula to address those needs. They turn to the Network and the Standards as a guide.

The question is also why there needs to be a response from social work. Could business, public administration, or public health not address administration within social service agencies without a social work response? The short answer is no. Social work's role in this area is to focus on the client system. Administrators of social service agencies need to possess skills unique to the social service environment that relate to having to choose between individual needs and agency values (Hasenfeld, 1983; Patti, 2000; Wuenschel, 2006). The changing nature of agency client systems means that the client comes to the agency with "moral and cultural values that determine not only their identity, but also their moral status in the broader social context" (Hasenfeld, 1983, p. 115). Because social work education uses a systems framework to understand the relationship between human need and larger social systems; this creates a values-oriented administrator who can be sensitive to human needs within the larger context of the administrative system and society (Friedman, 2006). Thus, the social work-trained administrator does not look solely at the bottom line but is sensitive to the needs of the clients the agency serves.

To address the need for qualified social work managers, the Network created the certified social work manager (CSWM) certificate; individuals who display these letters have demonstrated competency in at least 10 of the 14 areas of the *Standards*. It signifies that one not only has the academic knowledge, but has also demonstrated the skill through experience to be certified as a social work manager.

The times are changing. Social work managers need to be able to respond to factors and concerns much more quickly than they did before. Whereas the social work agency used to be exempt from public criticism, as a result of unethical business dealings such as Enron's, all organizations are now under public scrutiny. Administrators need to be aware of factors associated with how Sarbanes-Oxley effects their operations. Austin (2000) describes the delicate balance between funders of social services and the needs of the recipients. The ability to have confidence in those administrators to handle this balance is the reason for the *Standards* and the CSWM. Thus, the Network is responding to trends and the loss of social workers in management positions in a positive way that should be adopted by the educational system to begin to provide more confidence in social work administration field.

There is another reason why it is important to rethink the role of administration in social service agencies. In business, the outcome is clear: how to generate a profit. The outcome is different in social service agencies; they seek to generate long-term results (Collins, 2005). These results may take years before there are tangible outcomes, so it is more difficult to see immediate results. This is where social work plays an important role, because the focus is to create systems and mechanisms that may not result in immediate gratification. Social work training prepares the worker for this delayed gratification, for seeing immediate outcomes and being able to look to the future.

Next Steps

More social work administrators are definitely needed in social service agencies, yet social work is unable to produce what is needed to meet that demand. In addition, current social work curricula do not fully address the need, nor do curricula in business administration, public administration, or public health. The values of a social work education help the administrator understand the delicate balance between client needs and accountability to funding sources. The Network has begun to make strides to address these issues, but it is not enough. There needs to be a comprehensive plan to begin to address what has been happening since the profession's beginnings.

First, the *Standards* need to be adopted and integrated into curricula, as they provide the most comprehensive approach to the needs of social work managers. The Network needs to be more involved with education and the profession in helping to promulgate the *Standards*.

Second, the core competencies of social work education need to be more specific in identifying the internal health of an organization. Most social work is done within an agency setting, and, just as there is language that focuses on the bio-psycho-social-spiritual health of an individual client, social service agencies also have a psycho-social-spiritual framework. It is important that the core competencies include language emphasizing that all social work students need to learn how to assess the psycho-social-spiritual needs of the agency where they will work and how to correct any problems that may arise. It is important to help social workers understand the capacity of the agency in relation to its mission and the role it plays in the larger social environment.

Third, the profession of social work needs to recognize that there are specific skills and knowledge are associated with being an agency administrator. Much of the leadership in the field comes from those individuals who are the leaders of these agencies. If we have a loss of administrators, then will there be a loss of leadership? Who will be able to advocate for the needs of the population served by the agency to the larger society if there are no social workers in these leadership positions? Thus, mechanisms need to be made to recognize social work administration, advocate for social workers who may not have the specific current clinical skills to provide administrative supervision to their workforce, and to recognize career paths that move people up to administrative positions. Again, this is where the *Standards* play an important role. To help with the implementation of the *Standards,* the National Network for Social Work Managers developed a tool that quantifies the current level of understanding and skill of each area within the *Standards*. This tool is called the *Self-Assessment Tool* and can be used in conjunction with the *Standards* to help individuals identify their deficiencies. By so doing, the individual will be able to develop a direction for continuing education in social service administration to address those needs.

We cannot change history, but we can acknowledge where we have been, where we are, and where we are going. If we do not change and take some corrective measures now, then we will see fewer and fewer social workers in administrative positions.

Conclusion

A number of factors have interacted to create the problem of a loss of social workers in administrative positions in social service agencies: a combination of historical factors with changes in the nature and mission of social service agencies; factors of the growth of the federal government in providing services to address the needs of those disenfranchised individuals in society; the lack of social workers to meet the growing need of social service agencies; factors within the profession, such as licensure, that cause social workers to focus more on clinical practice rather than macro practice; and the education system that has core competencies that suggest individual practice. Other professions like business, public administration, and public health have responded to the lack of administrators to meet the demand but they do not have the same value orientation as social work. It is not too late to begin to make the change to begin to address this issue. The time is now. The National Network for Social Work Managers has taken steps but they have not received the recognition to make a lasting change. There needs to be a greater embracing of the Network by both the professional and the education community to begin to stem the loss of social workers in administrative positions.

References

Alexander, C. A. (2001). Letter to the National Network of Social Work Managers. Retrieved from http://www.socialworkmanager.org

Austin, D. (2000). Social work and social welfare administration: A historical perspective. In R. J. Patti (Ed.), *The handbook of social welfare management* (pp. 27–54). Thousand Oaks, CA: Sage.

Brilliant, E. L. (1990). *The United Way: Dilemmas of organized charity.* New York: Columbia University.

Collins, J. (2005). *Good to great and the social sector.* Boulder, CO: Jim Collins.

Day, P. J. (2003). *A new history of social welfare* (4th ed.). Boston: Allyn & Bacon.

Faherty, V. (1987). The battle of the Ms: the MBA, MPA, MPH, and MSW. *Administration in Social Work, 11*(2), 33–43.

Friedman, B.D. (2006). Response to Felice Perlmutter: Ensuring social work administration. *Administration in Social Work, 30*(3), 1–4.

Gummer, B. (1987). Are administrators social workers? The politics of interprofessional rivalry. *Administration in Social Work, 11*(2), 19–31.

Hasenfeld, Y. (1983). *Human service organizations.* Englewood Cliffs, NJ: Prentice-Hall, Inc.

Hoefer, R (2003). Administrative skills and degrees: The "best place" debate rages on. *Administration in Social Work, 27*(1), 25–46.

Keys, P. R., & Capaiuolo, A. (1987). Rebuilding the relationship between social work and public administration. *Administration in Social Work, 11*(1), 47–58.

Maslyn, R. T. (2002). Why I founded the National Network for Social Work Managers. Retrieved from http://www.socialworkmanagers.org

Mirabella, R. M., & Wish, N. B. (2000). The "best place" debate: A comparison of graduate education programs for nonprofit managers. *Public Administration Review, 60*(3), 219–229.

National Network for Social Work Managers (NNSWM). (2004). *Leadership and management standards.* Retrieved from http://www.socialworkmanager.org

Patti, R. J. (2000). The landscape of social welfare management in social work. In R. J. Patti (Ed.). *The handbook of social welfare management* (pp. 3–25). Thousand Oaks, CA: Sage.

Perlmutter, F. D. (2006). Ensuring social work administration. *Administration in Social Work, 30*(2), 3–10.

Schorr, A. (1986). *Common decency—Domestic policies after Reagan.* New Haven, CT: Yale University Press.

Skidmore, R. A. (1995). *Social work administration: Dynamic management and human relationships* (3rd ed.). Needham Heights, MA: Allyn & Bacon.

Stein, H. D. (1958). Jewish Social Work in the United States, 1654–1954. In *American Jewish yearbook* (pp. 3 – 97). Philadelphia: The American Jewish Committee and the Jewish Publication Society of America.

Wuenschel, P. C. (2006). The diminishing role of social work administrators in social service agencies: Issues for consideration. *Administration in Social Work, 30*(4), 5–18.

3

PREP for Social Service Agency Leadership:
Directors' Career Paths, Experiences, and Insights

Terri Moore Brown

Over the past decade, budget cutbacks, combined with government and private funding initiatives, are driving social service directors to seek new methods of achieving their agencies' operating, financial, and organizational goals while addressing increasingly complex social problems. As a result, social service directors are turning to collaborative and interorganizational approaches that create synergies among agencies, allowing directors to generate more cost-effective programs that improve community conditions without expending greater resources or duplicating services. To meet the demands of this leaner operating environment, administrators need a different blend of professional competencies. They must understand the multifaceted intricacies of managing interorganizational programs and services (Kaye, 1994; Powell, 1986; Rosenthal & Mizrahi, 1993; Sanfort, 2000); possess diverse knowledge, skills, and cross-disciplinary expertise; and be able to circumvent bureaucratic constraints that hinder efficient and effective social work practice (Barak, Travis, & Bess, 2004; Packard, 2004; Perlmutter, 2006; Wimpfheimer, 2004).

The National Network for Social Work Managers identified two categories of professional competencies that social workers need, external relations and internal relations. Regarding external competencies, administrators must (a) be knowledgeable of current social and public policies and how those policies affect their agencies and consumers; (b) possess advocacy skills; (c) be able to establish relations with the public and community; (d) be able to market their programs and services; and (e) have the skills to govern their agencies (Wimpfheimer, 2004). Among the internal competencies are (a) good planning, program development, and management skills; (b) good budgeting skills; (c) knowledge of how to assess their agency's financial needs; (d) human resource management skills; and (e) knowledge of how to monitor and meet their staff's professional development needs (Wimpfheimer, 2004).

The social work discourse suggests, however, that top administrators in human service agencies may not have the right skills to lead agencies successfully and that social work students are not being trained with the leadership skills they need. In a study of MSW students specializing in administration, Ezell, Chernesky, and Healy (2004) reported that students felt their foundation courses inadequately prepared them for advanced administration courses. Kaye's (1994) study showed that human service executives felt their program marketing efforts for the elderly were weak, insensitive, and ineffective. In another study (Packard, 2000), results from management audits of field practicum agencies conducted by students concentrating in administration revealed that field instructors had limited leadership skills and knew little about management audits or organizational change. Packard concluded that social work graduate education programs need to include more training on leadership and organizational change.

Mulroy's (2004) organization-in-environment framework serves as a guide for persons preparing for careers in social work administration because it emphasizes that administrators need to be committed to social justice and to think about their organizations and communities as tightly intertwined with their social and physical environments. Administrators should think, strategize, and work from the perspective that public policies and social factors continually shape communities and their organizations. This framework supports Livingston's (2003) assertion that career preparation for top-level administrative social service positions is unique in its emphasis on social service agency directors' responsibility to influence policy and environmental change, to work collaboratively with community agencies for client benefit, and to maintain mutually supportive relationships with internal and external interest groups. This framework is important because it represents the core values of the social work profession and the National Association of Social Workers Code of Ethics (National Association of Social Workers [NASW], 1999). Yet, lawyers and those with political and business degrees capture the top-level social service director positions, whereas social workers tend to dominate middle-management agency positions (Perlmutter, 2006). As a result, the number of social workers occupying top-level administration positions in social service agencies seems to be diminishing (Wuenschel, 2006). More research on career patterns, experiences, and insights of social service directors may offer information on how to better prepare social workers with the requisite skills for directing public social service agencies effectively.

Other professions, such as business (DauffenBach, 1980; Kanter, 1993; Mahoney, & Milkovich, 1972), education (Warner, Brazzel, Allen, Bostick, & Marin, 1988), and the military (Daley, 1999; Martin, Rosen, & Sparacino, 2000), have career ladders. Gummer's (1991) study of hierarchical control and collaborative individualism indicates that social work administrators play critical roles in their career outcomes and that their success is based on their ability, first, to tap into resources that provide good ideas and, second, to determine which collaborative relationships can help them turn those ideas into reality. Predicting social service agency directors' career patterns may generate some of those resources and assist social work students and aspiring social service agency directors in preparing for top-level social service positions. Understanding career patterns may also be critical in helping social work educators prepare their students better for social service agency administration.

Literature Review

Few social work students concentrated in administration in the late 1970s and 1980s (Feldman, 1978; Wimpfheimer, 2004), and several decades later, the number has declined further (Bradley, 2005; Council on Social Work Education [CSWE], 2004; D'Aprix, Dunlap, Abel, & Edwards, 2004; NASW, 2004; Thompson, Menefee, & Marley, 1999; Wuenschel, 2006). Toward the end of the 20th century, macro skills, advocacy, social planning, and community organization were de-emphasized in favor of clinical social work and other specializations. In one exploratory study, students specializing in administration reported not only matriculating in an antimanagement climate but also being informed by other students and faculty that administration was not social work (Ezell et al., 2004).

For decades, scholars have debated the role of administration in social work and the need for schools of social work to prepare students for administration. Such debates have led to division and polarization in the literature over the philosophical issues and mission of the social work profession (Ezell et al., 2004; Gambrill, 1997; Gomery, 1997, Stoesz; 1997; Thompson et al., 1999). Some scholars maintain that direct practice is legitimate social work, whereas administration has little to do with social work (Ezell et al., 2004; Perlmutter, 2006). Healy (2004), on the other hand, contends that the social work profession should be committed to practicing leadership and playing a significant role in supervision. Regarding preparation of social work students for administration, some researchers believe administration should have the same prominence in the social work curriculum as do other specializations, such as clinical social work and children and family services (Brilliant, 1986; Healy, Havens, & Pine, 1995), and prepare more students for administration (Brilliant, 1986; Ife, 2001; Neugeboren, 1986; Nixon & Spearmon, 1991; Rees & Rodley, 1995; Videka-Sherman, Allen-Meares, Yegidis, & Yu, 1995). Some in the academy do not believe, however, that administration is significant enough to offer as a specialization option to social work students (Fram, 1982; Friesen & Patti; Hoefer, 2003; Mirabella & Wish, 2000; Wuenschel, 2006). As a result, some faculty members are not interested in teaching administrative courses, and not many social work students are interested in specializing in administration.

Increased accountability, high expectations, scarcity of resources, contracting of services, grant criteria, and program eliminations require social service directors to have multifaceted skills and expertise across disciplines (Barak et al., 2004; Packard, 2004; Perlmutter, 2006; Wimpfheimer, 2004). To maximize leadership roles and competencies, Hart (1988) advocated for social work administrators to borrow from the curricula of MBA programs, learning such skills as cost accounting, marketing, and operation management.

For the present study, two theoretical frameworks stemming from the sociological discourse, internal labor market and external labor market, are used to understand the career choices and patterns of social service agency directors. Labor markets are defined as arenas where employees exchange labor for wages, position titles, and job rewards that are based on a set of organizational policies and procedures. Internal labor markets are viewed as a cluster of jobs with three characteristics: (1) a career ladder comprised of a sequence of positions; (2) entrance into internal labor markets through job entry port positions, which begin at the bottom of career ladder; and (3) advancement of employees as they gain knowledge and skills from entry port position up the career ladder. External labor markets provide workers with key skills organizations need, which enables organizations to identify alternative occupations requiring similar knowledge and skills and, which, in turn, affects hiring patterns. When internal market positions are open to individuals from the external labor market, the advantages of internal labor markets for employees are weakened, making individuals from external markets their competitors (Althauser & Kallenberg, 1981).

Several studies have explored social work career paths (Greenhouse & Haynes, 2004; Le-Doux, 1996; Mondros & Wilson, 1990; Stamp, 1986; Starr, Mizrahi, & Gurzinsky, 1999), preferences (Butler, 1990; Whitley & Wolk, 1999) and influences (Biggerstaff, 2000). A developing body of social work literature addresses training, preparation for advancement, and transition to administration (Calkin, 1982; Cousins, 2004; Hart, 1988). However, few studies in the social work discourse specifically address public social service agency directors' career paths and the preparation required to advance up the career ladder, despite findings that consistently confirm the small numbers of social workers who are graduating with the skills needed for administration (Bradley, 2005; CSWE, 2004; NASW, 2004).

To provide data on agency director career patterns, their preparation for administration, their social and professional backgrounds, and their suggestions for aspiring directors, educators, and mentors, this study sought to answer the following questions: (a) Is there a career pattern leading to the social service agency director position? If yes, what is it? (b) What factors contributed to individuals' decision to serve as an agency director? (c) How did individuals become candidates for agency directorships? (d) How many agency directors had mentors to assist their climb up the career ladder? (e) Are there any relationships among demographic variables, such as education, gender, race, age, marital status, children, and so forth, and having a mentor? (f) What advice would agency directors give to aspirants who desire to move up the career ladder in social service agencies? and (g) What areas of course content and strategies should social work educators use to prepare students for leadership positions in social service agencies?

Methodology

Sampling

The purpose of this exploratory study was to analyze and develop a profile of social service directors' career paths and examine their perceptions of how aspiring directors can prepare to lead social service agencies and how educators can contribute to preparing those aspirants. These data also facilitated development of macro course content for an MSW program in a southeastern university. This descriptive study used quantitative and qualitative data collection methods and purposive sampling procedures. The sample consisted of 430 social service agency directors from 5 southeastern states (Georgia, 159; Virginia, 115; North Carolina, 100; South Carolina, 32; Maryland, 24). These states were selected because a significant number of university graduates from a southeastern university tend to migrate to these states, and the programs and services each state offered were similar. The author noted differences in the organizational structures, job position titles, and social work licensing requirements among the states and kept these differences in mind when analyzing data and drawing conclusions. The list of social service agency directors and mailing addresses was derived from each state's Department of Social Services Web site. Surveys were mailed between June and December 2006, and 185 usable surveys were received, yielding an overall response rate of 50%.

The geographical locations of respondents' social service agencies were 71.9% rural, 11.9% urban, 14.6% suburban, and 1.6% (3) missing responses. The number of persons employed by social service agencies ranged from 7 to 1,200 employees (M=97.7, SD=127.5). North Carolina had the highest number of respondents (34.1%), followed by Georgia and Virginia each with 25.9%, and Maryland and South Carolina each with 7.0%.

Instrument

This researcher attempted to search for an existing survey for the data collection phase of this study, which focused on social work administrators' career paths and their perceptions of how aspiring social worker administrators can prepare for and move into administrative positions. However, the researcher encountered difficulty in finding such an instrument; therefore, this study warranted replication of a survey pertaining to the research questions in this study. As a result, the researcher replicated portions of Touchton, Shavlik, and Davis's (1993) self-report survey. The Touchton and colleagues instrument examined the career patterns and experiences of college presidents. The majority of questions could be used to assess the career paths of persons from other professions, and questions not relevant to this study were eliminated. A 6-page, 47-item survey, with multiple-choice, open-ended, and closed-ended questions, was composed and used to collect data on the career patterns, profiles, and experiences of social service agency directors. The instrument of this study was 6 pages long and included 7 sections: (1) events influencing career paths, (2) work experiences, (3) mentorship, (4) educational background, (5) demographics, (6) agency characteristics, and (7) career advice. Because of the length of the survey, its pages were arranged using a booklet format.

The first section of the survey asked respondents to report on the number of years they served in their positions as social service agency directors; what motivated them to serve in their current positions; how they learned about their agency director positions; and what professional experiences, that is, administrative experience, educational background, financial management, political acuity, and so forth, the search committee felt were important that influenced their decision to hire respondents in their current positions. Respondents were also asked what motivated them to become social workers and to list in sequence their job titles as they climbed up the career ladder. Through multiple-choice questions, respondents identified the type of agency, that is, social services, mental health, hospitals, and so forth, they came from immediately before assuming their current positions.

In the second section of the survey, multiple-choice questions were used to gather information regarding respondents' educational backgrounds and to help respondents identify needed additional professional development training. Examples of such areas included budgeting, conflict management, strategic planning and assessment, grant writing, and so forth. The next section of the survey focused on determining whether respondents had a primary mentor, and if so, how their mentoring relationships formed. Respondents were also asked to describe how their mentors helped them. The fourth section used multiple-choice questions to capture mentors' demographics, that is, position title, gender, and race, followed by asking whether respondents held professional memberships, and if so, which ones. The fifth section of survey included multiple-choice questions focusing on respondents' demographics, followed by a sixth section comprising multiple questions asking respondents to categorize the geographic location of their agencies and report how many personnel their agencies employed. The final section of survey asked respondents what type of advice they would give to aspiring social work directors and to social work education programs preparing students for leadership positions.

Measurement validity and reliability are important considerations when collecting data using self-report surveys. Data collection in this study was highly structured and likely valid because the social service agency directors were asked for factual information about their work experiences and demographic backgrounds. In addition, this researcher was interested in the average response of the total group rather than their individual responses; therefore, a lower item reliability standard was acceptable because the data were analyzed and reported at the group level rather than that of the individual respondents (Gall, Borg, & Gall, 1996).

During the design and after survey development, the survey was tested for clarity and usefulness by having experts, including five social service agency directors, complete the survey and give feedback, and a social work faculty member and a statistician review and give feedback on survey questions and format. Consulting with experts or members of the target population is one method used for content validation (Haynes, Richard & Kubany, 1995; Messick, 1995). As a result of their comments, a few adjustments were made to the survey. It was noted that it took the social service agency directors different lengths of time to complete the survey, and some of them noted it was misleading to say it would take only 10 minutes to complete. As a result, the instructions were changed to say that it would only take a few minutes to complete the survey. Based on the directors' review, the open-ended question regarding what motivated the respondent to become a social worker was changed to a multiple-choice question. All of the experts said it would be interesting to know whether respondents belonged to professional organizations, so a question asking respondents if they were members of professional organizations was added. If respondents reported yes, the respondents were asked to list their organizations.

The social work faculty member and statistician also made suggestions regarding the survey's format, including relocating skip instructions to prevent those instructions from being missed. There was also a suggestion to eliminate placing questions in columns and use one column instead, which prevented respondents from overlooking questions and made the survey easier to read. These changes resulted in converting the survey into a booklet.

After completed surveys were received, respondents' answers were coded individually by assigning numbers to each of their responses and entering them into a data record. Before the data were analyzed, they were checked to identify and correct coding and data entry errors. The researcher independently examined respondents' written responses and interpreted and categorized them into themes. To ensure validity of findings, two social work graduate research assistants also reviewed the directors' written responses and interpreted, categorized, and coded responses into themes. Reviewing data and identifying themes took a good deal of time, and in some instances, there were disagreements about how the data should be categorized. In those situations, the researcher and research assistants discussed why certain data were categorized in one group rather than another until a consensus was reached. There was one occasion where the researcher and reviewers sought feedback from the faculty member who reviewed the survey before dissemination, followed by discussion until a consensus was reached.

SPSS 16 for Windows was used to analyze the data through frequencies, percentages, and means. Chi-square tests of significance and cross-tabulations were used to analyze selected nominal- and ordinal-level variables (e.g., gender, age), and the phenomenological method was used to analyze responses to the open-ended questions. The exploratory nature of this study made it appropriate to rely on open-ended questions, which focused on social service directors' advice to aspiring social service directors and social work educators.

Procedures

A cover letter explaining the study's purpose and requesting the director's participation accompanied the survey mailed to each agency's director, who was told that responses would remain confidential. Persons who did not respond to the survey received a reminder letter and a second copy of the survey 3 weeks after the first mailing. A survey and a self-addressed stamped envelope accompanied each letter. Each survey contained instructions for its completion and return. To preserve each respondent's confidentiality, the principal investigator coded each self-addressed, stamped postcard accompanying each survey. Respondents were instructed to mail the postcard separately from the questionnaire, which notified the principal investigator that the respondents did not need reminders and maintained each respondent's anonymity.

Results

Demographic Characteristics

Respondents' demographic characteristics appear in Table 1. The majority of respondents were female (55.7%). Only a few of the respondents represented persons of color (Blacks=11.9% and other=2.6%). Whites comprised (84.3%) the majority of respondents. The directors ranged in age from 31 to 69 years ($M=63$, $SD=9.8$). The majority was married (78.4%) and had children (86.4%). Nearly 100% of the respondents had an undergraduate degree, slightly more than half (57.3%) had a master's degree, and only 3.8% had a doctoral degree. The undergraduate, graduate, and doctorate major fields of studies were diverse (see Table 1). The total number of

TABLE 1   DEMOGRAPHIC CHARACTERISTICS OF AGENCY DIRECTORS

Variable	(%)	n
Gender		
Female	55.7	103
Male	42.7	79
Age		
31–49 (2 missing)	21.1	39
50–59	57.8	107
60 and over	20.0	37
Race/ethnicity		
White	84.3	156
Black	11.9	22
Other	2.6	5
Marital status		
Married—first marriage	54.6	101
Remarried	22.7	42
Domestic partnership	1.1	2
Divorced/separated	13.0	24
Widowed	1.1	2
Single	6.5	12
Number of children		
0	11.4	21
1	23.2	43
2	41.1	76
3	13.5	25
4	5.9	11
5	1.1	2
6	1.6	3
Education level		
Doctorate	2.7	5
Master's	57.3	106
Bachelor's	97.8	181
No degree	1.6	3
Undergraduate major field of study		
Social work	12.4	23
Sociology	16.2	30
Psychology	11.4	21
Business	10.3	19
Education	8.1	15
History	4.9	9
Other	21.6	40
Missing	15.1	28
Master's major field of study		
Social work	27.0	50
Business	7.6	14
Counseling	5.9	11
Psychology	3.8	7
Political science	2.7	5
Other	5.3	10
N/A	41.1	76
Missing	6.4	12
Doctorate major field of study		
Psychology	0.5	1
Counseling	0.5	1
Human services	0.5	1
Education management	0.10	2
N/A	96.5	177
Missing	0.15	3

Note: N=185; 3 nonresponses for gender; 4 nonresponses for age; 2 nonresponses for race; 2 nonresponses for marital status; 4 nonresponses for children; 1 nonresponse for doctorate; 2 nonresponses for master's; 2 nonresponses for doctorate.

years directors were employed by county department of social services ranged from 1 to 52 years (M=23, SD=10.2) Respondents' salaries ranged from $42,000 to $160,000 ($M$=72,853; SD=19,056.9).

Attraction to and Entry into the Social Work Profession

Directors were asked what attracted them to the social work profession. About 29% reported entering the social work profession because they wanted to make a difference, 18.4% because they enjoyed helping people, and 9.2% because of financial needs and a social work job was available. Only 3.8% reported it was a career goal, and 5.9% responded other. To determine the relationships of agency directors' gender, race, and age to their attraction to the social work profession, a cross-tabulation was performed. A chi-square analysis was performed on the cross-tabulation, which showed no statistically significant relationships between gender, race, and age and directors' attraction to the social work profession.

Pathway to Director

When asked what their entry port was into the social work profession, 42% of directors said social worker, 29.7% said case manager, 17.9% said other, and 10.3% provided no answer. Immediately prior to assuming the directorship, 23.2% of respondents were supervisors, 22.2% were directors, 14.6% were assistant directors, 14.1% were program managers, 6.5% were social workers, and 19.5% held other positions. Further analysis was performed to determine whether there was a relationship between gender, race, and age and directors' entry port into the profession. A chi-square analysis on the cross-tabulations showed no statistically significant relationships.

Immediately before assuming the social work directorship, the majority of directors were working in social service agencies (76.2%). The remainder were in mental health (5.4 %) and other types of agencies (18.3%). The directors were asked how they became candidates for their current director positions. Twenty-four percent read a job advertisement, 24.3% sought out another agency director and discovered the position through that person, 12.4% said they were nominated for the position, and 39% responded other. More than half (52.4%) of the directors were external candidates. When comparing age, older respondents were significantly more likely, χ^2 (77.8%, n=28) 12.92, (p<.001), to be external candidates. Significant differences, χ^2 (62.1%, n=64) 21.089, (p<.001), were found between female and male respondents who were internal candidates, with females significantly more likely than males to report they were internal candidates.

Motivation for advancement varied by years of total experience in the social work profession. The total years of social services experience among respondents ranged from 1 to 52 years (M=23.2, SD=10.2), and tenure in directorships ranged from 1 to 41 years (M=8.74, SD=7.9). Only 17.3% of respondents reported they plan to advance in their careers. More than one-half (55.7%) of respondents said they were motivated to become an agency director as they moved up the career ladder. Nearly 70% of respondents were in their first agency directorship.

Directors were also asked about their interest in becoming a social service director. Twenty percent of respondents said they became an agency director because they enjoyed helping others, 15.1% said it had always been their career goal, and 8.6% said the position was thrust on them. There were no significant associations between pathway to director and gender, race, and age.

To determine respondents' professional development needs, the directors were asked whether, if they had an opportunity for professional development training, what areas they would prefer. Thirty-three percent said they needed additional training in strategic planning and assessment; 14.1% budgeting; 9.2% working with legislators, policymakers and advocacy groups; 8.6% conflict management; 5.9% negotiation skills; 5.4% grant writing; 5.4% working with boards of directors; and the remaining other.

Mentors

Only 27.6% of directors said they had a primary mentor, and 84.3% of all primary mentors were White. Of those primary mentors, the majority was male (60.8%). Chi-square analysis indicated statistically significant differences between female and male respondents who had mentors, χ^2 (35.6%, n=36) 8.92, (p<.001). Female respondents were more likely to have mentors. There were no significant relationships between directors' race, age, marital status, and children and their likelihood of having a mentor.

Agency Directors' Advice to Aspiring Directors

A summary of respondents' statements with shared commonality and high level of agreement were extracted and are presented in Table 2. Respondents urged aspiring directors to gain a solid understanding of social service programs and services and learn good budgeting, financial assessment, planning, program development, human resource, and management skills. For example, one director stated that aspiring directors need to "learn as much as they can about different social service programs; acquire additional training in finance, personnel and other administrative functions that are critical to agency operation." Another director remarked: "The operation of a social service agency is a business. Many individuals with social work backgrounds are not prepared for that reality." "Director is a different skill set," said one director, and you "must expand the way you use and embody social work values, ethics and practice— and long-range mission approach." Another director stated that aspiring directors need to "get involved in state-level committees to get a bigger picture. Work at developing a budget sense, volunteer to manage small grants, and do project development." Another respondent asserted: "Look after your staff! Give them good customer service, and they will, in turn, give back to the community." The overall theme illustrated in these and other comments is that social work director aspirants should gain multi-disciplinary knowledge and diverse skills. Those areas of knowledge and skills include financial management, fiscal controls, performance management, strategic planning and goal setting, mission/vision execution, people management/supervisory skills, results/solution-focused attitudes, change management, mentorship, critical thinking and communication skills (interpersonal and written), leadership, independent thinking, personnel management, conflict resolution, and team building.

These same themes were echoed in the advice social service directors would give to those preparing for administration. The directors emphasized that aspiring social service directors should know current social and public policies and how those policies affect their agencies and consumers. Respondents suggested that individuals pursuing

TABLE 2   AGENCY DIRECTORS' ADVICE TO ASPIRANTS AND SOCIAL WORK EDUCATION PROGRAMS: PREP

Preparation of Self	Relationship Development	Experience	Professional Development
• Know agency mission, goals, and objectives	• Develop and use leadership skills that can motivate employees	• Serve in as many roles as you can and gain a broad knowledge of the entire agency and its services	• Gain strategic planning skills
• Develop and use good writing and oral skills	• Enjoy working with people and making a difference	• Obtain supervisory experience	• Obtain financial management skills
• Develop and exhibit professionalism, commitment, and loyalty	• Join state and local committees	• Don't be afraid to try new positions	• Gain project management skills
• Develop and exhibit critical thinking skills	• Stay in touch with community leaders	• Maximize and demonstrate critical thinking	• Develop skills in program development
• Find a mentor	• Develop exceptional people skills and ethics	• Develop skills in dealing with multiple problems simultaneously	• Develop supervisory skills
• Be flexible and patient	• Develop team-building skills	• Gain experience writing grants	• Gain community development skills
• Have thick skin	• Gain empowerment and motivation skills	• Gain experience in working with the media	• Seek professional leadership training
• Learn to prioritize and budget time	• Develop and use networking skills	• Gain experience in advocacy	• Gain performance management skills
• Develop strong listening skills	• Develop and exhibit good public relations skills	• Gain experience in working with organizational boards	• Know budgets and develop financial management skills
• Develop excellent public speaking skills	• Develop conflict management skills	• Gain experience in public speaking	• Get recruitment personnel management training and experience
• Develop interpersonal skills			• Obtain a master's degree: MSW, MBA, MPA
• Develop time management skills			
• Develop networking skills			
• Learn to be open-minded and flexible			
• Develop and use stress management skills and strive to have a balanced life			

director positions should know how to establish relations with the public and possess advocacy, governing, and marketing skills. For example, one respondent wrote: "The key is aspiring directors should possess skills in community building and have the skills to network with community leaders, and exhibit professional integrity" (see Table 2).

Agency Directors' Advice to Social Work Education Programs

Directors' advice to educators preparing students for leadership and social work administrative positions had strong congruence with that given to aspiring directors. Summary statements by respondents who shared commonality and high levels of agreement were extracted from the survey and are presented in Table 2. Their comments reflected the need for aspiring directors to have multifaceted experience and skills and that faculty can play a critical role in preparing aspirants for top leadership positions in social service agencies. Examples of skills include leadership, strategic planning, organizational development (mission to execution), organizational behavior, people skills, written communication, financial management, conflict resolution, public administration, supervisory and management skills, multidisciplinary experience, strategic/community partnerships, and real-world skills rather than scholarly theories.

Discussion

This study provided a snapshot of social service agency directors' work experience, professional development, educational background, insights, and mentorship about social work administration. From this study, groundbreaking data indicate incongruencies between the real-world skills needed and what the social work literature describes as vital internal and external competencies. With regard to recruiting and selecting directors with the requisite skills to lead public social service agencies, labor market conditions appear to have influenced social service agency director search committees to rely on external rather than internal labor markets. The data suggest that search committees perceive that not all persons with social work degrees have the necessary skills to lead an agency.

These findings show that social workers may lack the critical competencies they need to succeed as top administrators of public social service agencies. Scarcity of resources, competition for services, and so forth make it essential for directors to think more as businesspeople, know how to develop strategic partnerships, and maximize resources without abandoning their deep-rooted commitment to service delivery and executing the mission and purposes of the social work profession. Developing these skills needs greater emphasis in the social work curriculum to better prepare social service director aspirants with high-demand, real-life competencies.

The overall themes uncovered in this study emphasize multidisciplinary knowledge and diverse skills. Table 2 is categorized into themes and summarizes agency directors' advice to social work director aspirants and social work education programs. The model for these themes is called PREP: preparation of self, relationship development, experience, and professional development. One of the most significant survey findings is that several directors urged aspirants to seek master's degrees in business administration or public administration. Those degrees focus on the very skills the directors in this study suggested that aspirants acquire.

Nearly all of the directors had undergraduate degrees, but many were not in social work. The mean age of the directors was 63, so if they sought their degree immediately following high school, few schools offered undergraduate degrees in social work at the time they would have matriculated into college. At that time, the master of social work (MSW) degree was considered the terminal degree, which may account for the high percentage of directors having undergraduate degrees in areas other than social work. Agency directors in this study perceived professional development as a vital component of career development in areas where they and their employees felt they needed additional training. Director comments had a high degree of congruence on the critical competencies and knowledge aspiring directors should possess. Among them were professional leadership, supervisory skills, personnel management, financial management, conflict management, strategic planning, big-picture and solutions-focused thinking, results-focused mindset, change management, mission/vision execution, public speaking, grantsmanship, team building, and collaborative partnerships with legislators, lobbyists, and advocacy groups. Directors felt professional development was essential for themselves and their employees.

The majority of directors held a master's degree; however, it was still surprising that only a little over half of them had graduate degrees. The mean age for directors was 63, and the directors' mean total number of years of employment in social service agencies was 23. This may indicate why more directors did not have master's degrees, because search committees may have considered years of experience in social service agencies to be more important than directors' having a master's degree.

The proportion of directors who had an MSW (27%) was only slightly higher than those with master's degrees in other disciplines (25.3%) and lower than those with no master's degree (41.1%). The finding that not many directors had undergraduate or graduate degrees in social work makes this study very important to the social work profession, because it supports the critical need for schools of social work to reexamine the role administration plays in social work practice and for administrators to redesign the social work curriculum to include additional content.

Study findings indicated that agency directors perceive that their administrative experience, financial management, and personal style and presence were more important to social service search committees than was the type of degree they held. This finding is somewhat consistent with Calkin's (1982) study of female social work administrators' climb up the administrative ladder, which suggests that work experience is an important factor, followed by personality factors and education.

The results show a career pattern among public social service agency directors, with the majority of them following a direct service route leading to mid-level supervision, moving to senior administrative positions, and then assuming social service directorships. This pattern aligns with Bradley's (2005) and Wimpfheimer's (2004) findings that social service administrators tend to follow the direct service route to agency directorships.

The data suggest that search committees hold in high regard directors' work experience in public social service agencies versus work experience from other types of human service agencies, such as mental health, medical, or private human service agencies. The vast majority of agency directors began their careers as social workers, case managers, income maintenance, or eligibility workers and then moved to acquire experience as supervisors, program managers, or assistant directors in social service agencies before serving as agency directors. Many of the directors followed the career path of (a) social worker or case manager, (b) supervisor, (c) program manager and\or assistant director, and (d) social service director.

The choice of whether to have a family does not appear to have prevented directors from climbing the career ladder. The majority of them do have partners and children, and more than half are women. This finding contrasts with those from other studies across disciplines that report children and partners sometimes hindered or prevented aspiring administrators, especially women, from climbing the career ladder (Brown, Ummersen, & Sturnick, 2001; Gardella & Haynes, 2004; Morrison, White, & Van Velsor, 1992).

It is surprising that in this study over half of directors were women, which suggests that more women are breaking the glass ceiling in social service agencies. Not long ago only a few women occupied social work administration positions (Hanlan, 1977; Gardella & Haynes, 2004; Netting, & O'Conner, 2005). Further research is needed in this area to show what factors contributed to the increase of women serving in these positions. Unfortunately, it seems women of color continue to encounter a concrete ceiling as a result of race and gender. Findings from this study continue to support the need for additional persons of color to serve as social service directors. Directors should mirror the diversity of persons served by social service agencies. As cited by Le-Doux (1996), increasing the number of persons of color in the social work profession has been a longtime goal (Chunn, Dunston, & Ross-Sheriff, 1983; CSWE, 1984; Jackson, 1966).

This study also investigated the possible role of mentors in the directors' professional lives. Only a few directors (27.6 %) reported having mentors. Of those with mentors, the majority said those relationships had developed over time. More than twice as many women as men received mentorship, which may suggest that female directors fare better if they have a mentor. Additional research is needed in this area as well. The mean years of experience in social service agencies were 23, which may account for why the majority of the directors in the study did not have mentors. It would have been interesting to know whether they had mentors during their climb up the career ladder and if they were mentoring others.

Implications

The study's findings lend support for revising the social work curriculum to emphasize professional management skills and social work administration. Directors' comments on professional development and advice to educators in schools of social work, and to aspiring agency directors, indicate a need for real-world, practical skills

that enable directors to create and execute on a mission and vision. Directors overwhelmingly express the need for diverse, multidisciplinary knowledge, skills, and
experience, combined with big-picture, strategic-, outcomes-focused thinking. These
findings support the need to emphasize administration in the social work curriculum
alongside other specializations, such as clinical social work and children and family
services (Brilliant, 1986; Healy et al., 1995).

As to why so few persons of color serve as directors, one can speculate that labor
market conditions, such as stereotypes, biases, racism, economic conditions, or education, may prevent persons of color from acquiring top administrative positions in
public social service agencies. Another possible factor is that persons of color may not
see themselves serving as directors. Furthermore, search committees may have difficulty seeing persons of color as directors because they do not represent their perception
of how a director should look or act. It may be difficult for them to visualize persons
of color as independent and competent leaders. These areas call for further study.

It behooves social work education programs to seriously examine whether the social work curriculum prepares students adequately for real-world administration and,
if not, to correct it, because if past hiring practices are precursors of the future, then
few social service agency directors will represent persons of color or have degrees in social work. As a result, policymakers in master of social work programs may consider
exploring the need for multidisciplinary curricula that allows MSW students to interact with business and public administration students or the need to offer a
dual-degree program, MSW and MBA. Findings from this study also support the
need for persons trained in social work administration to fill the gaps created when
older agency directors retire. Study results indicate that respondents will most likely
retire within the next 5 years. Identifying strategies for preparing individuals to assume the directorships of those who will retire and increasing the number of persons
of color to serve in these positions are needed. The social work profession should make
a concerted effort to recruit, train, mentor, and retain in the social service pipeline
more persons of color and others to fill gaps left by retiring directors. Schools of social work should also take more responsibility for filling these gaps by encouraging
students and providing a curriculum that adequately prepares students for future administrative positions in social service agencies. Social work education program
developers should consider creating social work administration certificate programs for
persons who are employed in social services but who need additional training in administration. There is a definite need for schools of social work to identify ways to
attract and prepare social work students for social service administrative positions. In
addition, faculty should remain flexible enough to respond to the changing characteristics of administration in the social work profession and reflect those changes in the
course content they deliver to students.

Social work educators and mentors should encourage persons who show leadership potential to pursue administration and to take advantage of leadership
opportunities and professional development that may benefit them should they decide
to apply for directorships. Even if those aspirants decide in the future that serving as
a director is not for them, they, too, can encourage others who may demonstrate the

potential to lead a social service agency. Director aspirants must also promote their visibility by telling their supervisors and directors within and outside the agency that they are interested in serving as social work administrators.

The services that consumers receive and the policies that drive program development and services are constantly redefined. As a result, the administrative competencies that may be needed to become effective directors are constantly in flux. Based on hiring patterns, people with the right blend of critical competencies that span disciplines appear to be more valued in the workplace of today and the future. Strategic planning, goal setting, leadership, independent thinking, critical thinking, solutions-focused thinking, results, execution, change management, financial management, communication (especially written), and personnel management (specifically performance management and conflict resolution and team building) are the critical competencies that aspirants need to acquire and learn in social work education programs. These competencies were echoed in the advice given by directors.

To fill vacancies once baby boomer directors retire, educators and mentors need to encourage rather than discourage social workers to prepare and seek directorships of public social service agencies. Because many of the respondents in this study do not have degrees in social work but rather in business, sociology, psychology, and so forth, and because of high congruency among the respondents' advice to aspiring directors and social work educators, one can conclude that it is critical for aspirants to think like and have the leadership skills of a business person.

Unless schools of social work address these skill gaps through curricular changes, this trend may accelerate. Administration must be given prominence in the curriculum. Trends in other disciplines, such as business and sports, encourage executive coaching/mentoring to make a positive difference, and this trend may be one that aspiring directors should explore.

References

Althauser, R. P., & Kallenberg, A. L. (1981). Firms, occupations, and the structure of labor markets: A conceptual analysis. In I. Berg (Ed.), *Sociological perspectives on labor markets* (pp. 119–149). New York: Academic Press.

Barak, M., Travis, D., & Bess, G. (2004). Exploring managers' and administrators' retrospective perceptions of their MSW fieldwork experience: A national study. *Administration in Social Work, 28*(1), 21–24.

Biggerstaff, M. A. (2000). Development and validation of the social work career influence questionnaire. *Research on Social Work Practice, 10*(1), 34–54.

Bradley, G. (2005) Education and social service. *Career & Colleges, 25*(3).

Brilliant, E. (1986). Social work leadership: A missing ingredient? *Social Work, 31*(15), 325–331.

Brown, G., Ummersen, C. V., & Sturnick, J. (2001). *From where we sit: Women's perspectives on the presidency.* Washington, DC: American Council on Education.

Butler, A. C. (1990). A revaluation of social work students' career interests, *Journal of Social Work Education 26*, 45–56.

Calkin, C. L. (1982). Women administrators: An exploration of critical factors in women's advancement in social work (Doctoral dissertation, University of Denver, 1982). *Dissertation Abstracts International, 43*, 08A.

Chunn, J. C., Dunston, P. J., & Ross-Sheriff, F. (1983). *Mental health and people of color: Curriculum development and change.* Washington, DC: Howard University Press.

Council on Social Work Education (CSWE). (1984). Task force to recruit students into social work education programs. *Social Work Education Reporter, 32*(1), 14–15.

Council on Social Work Education (CSWE). (2004). *Statistics on social work education in the United States: 2004.* Alexandria, VA: Author.

Cousins, C. (2004). Becoming a social work supervisor: A significant role transition. *Australian Social Work, 57*(2), 175–182.

D'Aprix, A. S., Dunlap, K. M., Abel, E., & Edwards, R. L. (2004). Goodness of fit: Career goals of MSW students and the aims of the social work profession in the United States. *Social Work Education, 23*(3), 265–280.

Daley, J. G. (Ed.). (1999). *Social work practice in the military.* New York: Haworth Press.

DauffenBack, R. C. (1980). *Careers in the labor market: An empirical assessment of the types of careers and their defining characteristics* (ERIC Document Reproduction Service No. ED194828).

Ezell, M., Chernesky, R. H., & Healy, L. M. (2004). The learning climate for administration students. *Administration in Social Work, 28*(1), 57–76.

Feldman, F. L. (1978, January 14). *The social worker as administrator.* University of Southern California, Los Angeles, CA.

Fram, E. H. (1982). Do human service executives need management education? *Administration in Social Work, 6*(4), 69–80.

Friesen, B. J., & Patti, R. J. (1982). A response to Fram. *Administration in Social Work, 6*(4), 81–85.

Gall, M. D., Borg, W. R., & Gall, J. P. (1996). *Educational research: An introduction* (6th ed.). White Plains, NY: Longman.

Gambrill, E. (1997). Social work education: Current concerns and possible futures. In M. Reisch & E. Gambrill (Eds.), *Social work in the 21st century* (pp. 317–327). Thousand Oaks, CA: Pine Forge.

Gardella, L. G., & Haynes, K. S. (2004). *A dream and a plan: A woman's path to leadership in human services.* Washington, DC: NASW Press.

Gomery, J. (1997). Social work and philosophy. In M. Reisch & E. Gambrill (Eds.), *Social work in the 21st century* (pp. 300–310). Thousand Oaks, CA: Pine Forge.

Greenhouse, L., & Haynes, K. S. (2004). *A dream and plan: A woman's path to leadership in human services.* Washington, DC: NASW Press.

Gummer, B. (1991). A new managerial era: From hierarchical control to "collaborative individualism." *Administration in Social Work, 15*(3), 121–137.

Hanlan, M. S. (1977). Women in social work administration: Current strains. *Administration in Social Work, 1*(3), 259–265.

Hart, A. F. (1988). Training social administrators for leadership in the coming decades. *Administration in Social Work, 12*(3), 1–11.

Haynes, S. N., Richard, D. C. S., & Kubany, E. S. (1995). Content validity in psychological assessment: A functional approach to concepts and methods. *Psychological Assessment, 7,* 238–247.

Healy, K. (2004). Social workers in the new human services marketplace: Trends, challenges and responses. *Australian Social Work, 57*(2), 103–114.

Healy, L., Havens, C., & Pine, B. (1995). Women and social work management. In L. Ginsberg & P. Keys (Eds.), *New management in human services* (2nd ed., pp. 128–150). Silver Spring, MD: NASW Press.

Hoefer, R. (2003). Administrative skills and degrees: The "best place" debate rages on. *Administration in Social Work, 27*(1), 25–46.

Ife, J. (2001). *Human rights and social work: Towards rights-based practice.* Cambridge, UK: Cambridge University Press.

Jackson, W. S. (1966). The civil rights of 1964: Implications for social work education. *Social Work Education Reporter, 14*(3), 23–29.

Kanter, R. M. (1993). *Men and women of the corporations.* New York: Basic Books.

Kaye, L. W. (1994). The effectiveness of services marketing: Perceptions of executive directors of gerontological programs. *Administration in Social Work, 18*(2), 69–85.

Le-Doux, C. (1996). Career patterns of African-American and Hispanic social work doctorates and ABDs. *Journal of Social Work Education, 32,* 244–252.

Livingston, V. (2003). Black female career success: The importance of a career plan. *Social Science Journal, 32*(2), 299–305.

Mahoney, T. A., & Milkovich, G. T. (1972). *Internal labor markets: An empirical investigation* (ERIC Document Reproduction Service No. ED072264).

Martin, J., Rosen, L. N., & Sparacino, L. R. (Eds). (2000). *The military family: A practice guide for human service providers.* Westport, CT: Praeger.

Messick, S. (1995). Standards of validity and the validity of standards in performance assessment. *Educational Measurement: Issues and Practice, 14,* 5–8.

Mirabella, R. M., & Wish, N.B. (2000). The "best place" debate: A comparison of graduate education programs for nonprofit managers. *Public Administration Review, 60*(3), 219–229.

Mondros, J., B., & Wilson, S. M. (1990). Staying alive: Career selection and sustenance of community organizers. *Administration in Social Work, 14*(2), 95–109.

Morrison, A. M., White, R. P., & Van Velsor, E. (1992). *Breaking the glass ceiling: Can women reach the top of America's largest corporations?* Reading, MA: Addison-Wesley.

Mulroy, E. A. (2004). Theoretical perspectives on the social environment to guide management and community practice: An organization-in-environment approach. *Administration in Social Work, 28*(1), 77–96.

National Association of Social Workers (NASW). (2004). *CHOICES: Careers in social work.* Washington, DC: Author.

National Association of Social Workers (NASW). (1999). *Code of Ethics of the National Association of Social Workers.* Washington, DC: Author.

Netting, F. E., & O'Connor, M. K. (2005). Lady board of managers: Subjugated legacies of governance and administration. *AFFILIA-Journal of Women and Social Work, 20*(4), 448–464.

Neugeboren, B. (1986). Systemic barriers to education in social work administration. *Administration in Social Work, 10*(2), 1–14.

Nixon, R., & Spearmon, M. (1991). Building a pluralistic workplace. In R. L. Edwards & J. Yankey (Eds.), Skills for effective human services management (pp. 155–170). Silver Spring, MD: NASW Press.

Packard, T. (2000). The management audit as a teaching tool in social work administration. *Social Work in Administration, 36*(1), 39–52.

Packard, T. (2004). Issues in designing and adapting an administration concentration. *Administration in Social Work, 28*(1), 5–20.

Powell, D. M. (1986). Managing organizational problems in alternative service organizations. *Administration in Social Work, 10*(3), 57–69.

Perlmutter, F. D. (2006). Ensuring social work administration. *Administration in Social Work, 30*(2), 3–10.

Rees, S., & Rodley, G. (Eds). (1995). *The human costs of managerialism: Advocating the recovery of humanity.* Sydney, Australia: Pluto Press.

Rosenthal, B., & Mizrahi, T. (1993). Advantages of building coalitions. In M. Austin & J. I. Lowe (Eds.), *Controversial issues in communities and organizations* (pp. 9–22). Needham Heights, MA: Allyn & Bacon.

Sanfort, J. R. (2000). Developing new skills for community practice in an era of policy devolution. *Journal of Social Work Education, 36,* 183–185.

Stamp, G. (1986). Some observations on the career paths of women. *Journal of Applied Behavioral Science, 22*(4), 385–396.

Starr, R., Mizrahi, T., & Gurzinsky, E. (1999). Where have all the organizers gone? The career paths of community organizing social work alumni. *Journal of Community Practice, 6*(3), 23–48.

Stoesz, D. (1997). The end of social work. In M. Reisch & E. Gambrill (Eds.), *Social work in the 21st century* (pp. 368–375). Thousand Oaks, CA: Pine Forge.

Thompson, J., Menefee, D., & Marley, M. (1999). A comparative analysis of social workers' macro practice activities: Identifying functions common to direct practice and administration. *Journal of Social Work Education, 35,* 115–124.

Touchton, J., Shavlik, D., & Davis, L. (1993). *A descriptive study of women in college & university presidencies.* Washington, DC: American Council on Education.

Videka-Sherman, L., Allen-Meares, P. Yegidis, B., & Yu, Y. (1995). Social work deans in the 1990s: Survey findings. In F. Raymond (Ed.), *The administration of social work education programs: The role of deans and directors.* Columbia, SC: National Association of Deans and Directors of Schools of Social Work.

Warner, R. L., Brazzel, J., Allen, R., Bostick, S., & Marin, P. (1988). *Career paths in higher education administration* (ERIC Document Reproduction Service No. ED294506).

Whitley, D. M., & Wolk, J. (1999). Preferred academic and career paths of potential MSW students: What they thinking? *Arete, 23*(1), 53–65.

Wimpfheimer. S. (2004). Leadership and management competencies defined by practicing social work managers: An overview of standards developed by the national network for social work managers. *Administration in Social Work, 28*(1), 45–56.

Wuenschel, P. C. (2006). The diminishing role of social work administrators in social service agencies: Issues for consideration. *Administration in Social Work, 30*(4), 5–18.

II Management and Leadership with Special Groups and in Special Settings

Leon H. Ginsberg

Social work is so large and so specialized that it almost rises to the example of the elephant and the blind men, each of whom describes the animal by the parts he is touching. For some people, social work is synonymous with public assistance. For others, it is essentially child welfare. For still others it is a health or mental health profession. And in the experiences of many, social workers are those who work in and direct community centers and settlement houses. The field is so broad and so diverse that is rare for most of those outside the profession, and many within it, to understand its expansive and comprehensive nature.

The chapters in Part II deal with some of the ways social workers carry out their roles in special settings and with special populations. Except for educators, who need to understand the broad tapestry of the field, social workers are specialized—sometimes highly specialized.

Cynthia Poindexter of Fordham University is a pioneer in working with people who have AIDS and in managing the organizations that serve them. She describes the work of managing AIDS services organizations in chapter 4. Although this editor thinks of her as young (she was my MSW student at the University of South Carolina), Cynthia was one of the early advocates for people with AIDS and helped organize one of the first AIDS service organizations. Many of those with whom she worked—who were also friends of mine—passed on before the life-sustaining protocols that help maintain the lives of many more recent AIDS patients. The nature of AIDS, which continues to be an incurable disease, has modified dramatically since it was first discovered in the 1980s. Of course, Poindexter's insights on managing that kind of specialized organization have applications, as well, to other social work agencies and organizations.

Colleen Galambos, who has a rich and distinguished career in health care settings for social workers, wrote chapter 5. She is editor of the *Journal of Social Work Education* and once edited *Social Work in Health Care*. As is popularly known in the United States, health care is one of our largest industries and one of the "hot button" issues in American politics. Dealing with the cost and availability of health care is raised constantly in most political campaigns, including the current one.

Social work has been involved in health care for decades, originally as the "medical social work" specialty. Now, however, it has broadened to include social work as part of most medical specialties, in discharge planning for those leaving hospitals, for working with families whose members are receiving or need health services, in nursing homes and other extended care facilities, and in working with health planning and health policy. Certainly, health care is one of the more important specialized social work fields. And, again, Galambos's guidance is appropriate for many other fields because health care is, ultimately, part of everything social workers do.

Two preoccupations of American social work have been efforts to help newcomers, especially immigrants, integrate into the American culture and the incidence of suicide among such groups. One of the more interesting intersections of the two is found in Donna Hardina, Jane Yamaguchi, Xong Moua, Molly Yang, and Phoua Moua's findings in chapter 6. Their chapter addresses suicide prevention among the Hmong people, a large population whose members came to the United States after the Vietnam War. Many are well-integrated into American culture, but they do encounter social problems, as first-generation immigrants traditionally have. The study of suicide brings social work full circle—one of the first bases for founding sociology as a social science discipline was the desire to understand why and how suicide occurred as a social problem as well as the means for preventing it.

Of course, social workers are involved in a multitude of social programs of which these are only a small sample. But the principles behind their successes are widely applicable to the work of social workers.

4

Challenges and Skills in
Managing HIV Programs

Cynthia Cannon Poindexter

A manager in an HIV-related program may begin the day by checking the obituaries in the local paper and then handing the newspaper to staff members so that they can do the same. The manager then returns telephone calls from a social work supervisor in a hospital who wants to discuss a problem with a referral, a grants coordinator in a local foundation who wants to know why a report is late, a pharmaceutical representative who would like to stop by, and a legislative aide whose boss is not supportive of state funding of prevention outreach. At the same time she skims a few case records to prepare for several supervisory conversations with case managers that will occur throughout the morning. Between those supervisory conversations she prepares for an important consortium meeting the next day, outlines a plan for staff in-service workshops based on a survey of needs, and sorts through the day's mail as she wanders through the office so that she can listen to the staff and students as they take crisis and informational phone calls. When someone walks in without an appointment to say that he has just tested positive and needs information and medical care, she handles the interview herself because all other staff are busy. That afternoon she meets with the agency's advisory council, works on the foundation report, then eats dinner in the car on the way to drop into a fundraising committee meeting that evening. On the way home in the car she returns a call from the field instructor who wants to arrange meetings with three social work interns.

Managing any social service or social advocacy program can be chaotic. Adding HIV—a life threatening, stigmatizing, and infectious agent—into the mix can take the experience into the realm of trauma. Yet despite intense stress, the work is satisfying, stimulating, and vital. HIV-related programs and organizations are often hybrids, combining social change objectives with social service provision and HIV prevention. As such, these programs espouse a varied value system, being externally and environmentally oriented while focusing on internal challenges (Edwards & Austin, 1991;

I am grateful to Melanie Cohn-Hopwood of the Boston Living Center; James Holmes of Columbia University; Leah Holmes of the Miriam Hospital in Providence; and Jane Edwards of Fordham University School of Social Service for their vital comments on the chapter outline and draft.

Hyde, 1992). Given the nature of HIV disease, the complexity of HIV practice, and the Janus-like orientation of HIV programs, supervisors and managers in the HIV field have concerns that, although perhaps similar to those in other types of human services endeavors, are specifically related to the history and current realities of HIV services in the United States.

This chapter addresses some of the external and internal pressures likely to be faced by community-based macrolevel social work practitioners in the HIV field and suggests some of the skills and approaches that could address them. Dividing organizational challenges into external and internal categories is artificial because the challenges are interactive, dynamic, and mutually influential. This framework may be useful, however, for examining the duality of the vision that managers and directors must maintain: looking outward and inward at all times.

External Pressures

HIV-related social service and advocacy programs, like all human service programs, are susceptible to pressures emanating from the environment. External pressures specific to HIV programs include inappropriately focused public and media attention, marginalization of the issue, debates concerning mainstreaming HIV versus separating it from other social problems, trying to offer multiple interventions with limited resources, a dearth of adequately prepared workers, a disjointed social service system, and a volatile political context.

Lack of Public and Media Salience

When HIV organizations formed a quarter of a century ago in the United States, they were constantly fighting to make people understand that the nation was facing a social, financial, political, and medical emergency. HIV practitioners are still fighting that battle for attention. It seems that the predominant public and media attitude is "AIDS is over." Granted, thanks to pharmaceutical and medical advancements and greatly improved knowledge about prevention and transmission, pediatric infection rates and overall death rates have been reduced, and those success stories have received due attention. However, the bad news is a well-kept secret. Infection rates continue to climb; there is no vaccine, and there is no cure; and treatments, when available and affordable, are onerous, temporary in benefit, and only partially successful. Public perceptions have been aided by large drug companies whose advertising campaigns not only inspire hope, as they should, but also perpetuate false ideas about what it takes to survive the disease and tolerate the drugs. When there is media attention on HIV, it tends to focus on new medical or pharmaceutical advancements, which are presented as revolutionary or miraculous, or, conversely, on a spectacular failure of a vaccine or drug trial. All of these news stories tend to be simultaneously simplified and exaggerated, which furthers the sense that HIV is not a big deal. When the media covers death from HIV, it is almost always focused on countries outside the United States, furthering the myth that the domestic epidemic is no longer of concern. One hardly ever sees good media coverage on the continuing stigma and discrimination or the difficulty with taking the medications or being able to access or afford them.

Managers in HIV programs feel battered by the lack of appropriate and consistent public, media, funder, and political awareness because they must repeatedly fight the same battle for attention and funding for prevention and care. Imagine trying to fight a flood or fire every day when no one seems to know or care that your emergency exists. There is a cyclical effect of this public apathy: Because some outside the HIV field perceive the crisis to be over, the crisis and the numbers of people with HIV continue to grow. HIV is a preventable disease, yet it continues to balloon because of the lack of visible, consistent, and accurate prevention messages. Public complacency and government neglect continue to be frightening, frustrating, and harmful. HIV social service providers and managers sometimes feel as if they will always be swimming against a swift current.

Practitioners in the HIV field have historically been skilled at using public and media events to get attention, and although a collective sigh goes up at the thought, this type of media activity must be continued or revived. HIV advocates paved the way for grabbing attention by using celebrities, politicians, demonstrations, mainstream and alternative television and newspaper coverage, coalitions, confrontation, collaborative experts, and the testimony of persons with HIV. The HIV field became so busy with providing services that activism and public relations understandably fell by the wayside. But it is time for public and political awareness to be moved to the front burner all year long, not just for annual testing day and World AIDS Day. Managers should cultivate ongoing relationships with legislative aides, local journalists, other community-based agency directors, and foundation representatives to make them part of routine information distribution. When a question comes up about HIV, these types of professionals should think immediately of calling the HIV program manager who has been so helpful in the past. Managers should consider information booths at health fairs, informational legislative and journalistic receptions, information packets, free public service announcements, and other inexpensive ways to keep HIV at the forefront of the community's collective awareness. Speakers' bureaus of persons with HIV and caregivers, although not necessarily covered in a social service mission, serve a valuable educational purpose and can raise awareness and donations. This is a short list to jump-start thinking; the key is creative brainstorming about ways to keep both HIV and your agency's name in the public discourse of your local community.

Marginalization and Stigma

Many social action and social service organizations are aligned with vulnerable and denigrated populations. HIV-related programs address the most stigmatized disease in modern history and advocate for the most marginalized individuals. Because HIV is life-threatening, progressive, and incurable; because it is transmissible; because it is associated with drug use and homosexuality; because it disproportionately affects poor people and people of color; and because people are blamed personally for contracting it, the stigma of HIV has been immense. HIV stigma intersects with other intense oppressions to render constituencies on the fringes expendable, invisible, and demonized.

Two and a half decades after the disease was identified, HIV stigma is still an issue, yet some seem to believe that it is not. People with HIV and their caregivers still report that they encounter fear, distancing, distrust, and ignorance when they disclose the presence of HIV in their lives. HIV stigma also continues to challenge workers, supervisors, and managers: The same battles as in the beginning must be fought concerning education, outreach, confidentiality assurances, unwillingness to take HIV tests, and disclosure to family and partners. Discrimination in social service and health care systems must still be monitored and confronted.

HIV-related programs are themselves stigmatized. HIV practitioners carry secondary or associative stigma and must go through their own decisions regarding when, how, and to whom to disclose the nature of their work. HIV managers and policy makers are sometimes, sadly, tempted to distance themselves from their true constituents—the gay community, drug users, sex workers, transgender persons, undocumented immigrants, or mentally ill homeless persons—to placate potential political allies or funding sources.

Managers need support to maintain their courage and resolve to confront the virulent stigma and oppression in which they are steeped each day. It is to be expected that the interwoven oppressions should affect us: We are all part of a racist, homophobic, classist, sexist, xenophobic, HIV-phobic society. As will be discussed later in more depth, affected groups sometimes find themselves pitted against each other for resources and attention rather than organized in solidarity against the common enemies of ignorance and neglect. Social workers, as leaders, educators, and managers, can present an alternative model by actively rejecting and fighting stigma and oppressions, uniting vulnerable communities rather than furthering divisions, and forming organizational cultures that are antioppressive.

Mainstreaming Versus Exceptionalism

HIV is biologically and socially unique. The advent of AIDS demanded and brought forth new approaches in activism and support. When HIV appeared there was no preexisting knowledge or work about the disease, the systems that were already in place did not respond, and those who stepped forward were those who were dying. Social movements do not usually spring forth to be accommodating or mainstream; they are typically radical and reformist in intent. This was certainly the case with the HIV service and activism movement. Immediately there was a backlash: The complaints in public and political discourse, reflected in the media, were that the "AIDS lobby" was taking money and attention from other causes. There were consistent accusations of "AIDS exceptionalism" (Chambre, 2006; Lune, 2007). HIV activists and managers were forced to answer these charges: Why should HIV receive specific funding, for example? It has been exhausting for the managers of HIV programs to have to defend their very need to exist, while at the same time fighting for their financial survival.

HIV advocates and managers realized early on that there were advantages to joining the mainstream. HIV stigma and all the concurrent oppressing factors that were marginalizing people with HIV made it easy for the government, public, funders, and media to continue to neglect the issue. As long as HIV was framed as a problem of deviants, undesirables, and expendable people, it was almost impossible to garner the attention and funding necessary. Strategically it became wise to present HIV as an agent that could infect and affect anyone. A dual stance was necessary: HIV is special, yet it requires the attention of the mainstream (Lune, 2007; Poindexter, 1998). Sometimes this message seemed confusing and dichotomous even to those in the HIV field.

HIV disease has indeed become part of the mainstream. It is no longer unusual; it is part of the fabric of daily life, as are the agencies that came forth from the original emergency. Both the illness and the organizations designed to address that illness are longer-term, less noticed by the public and the media, less fierce, less urgent. It is immaterial whether one believes this situation to be positive or negative; it is simply the new reality.

The question "Why is AIDS special?" continues to come up, so the managers of HIV programs must be prepared with an answer. Managers should balance and espouse both perspectives. Peter Piot, head of the United Nations AIDS Program, says that HIV must be addressed through a balance between mainstreaming and exceptionality (Piot, 2006). Although speaking from a global perspective, his comments are applicable domestically and locally. Clearly, HIV must be dealt with through existing medical, mental health, educational, economic, and public benefits systems. Yet HIV cannot be completely merged into other resources or agendas. Why? HIV is not like anything else. There is no other infectious disease that is this highly stigmatized, with prevention so fraught with moral and political baggage, with no cure or vaccine, this complicated to treat, found in every area of the globe, disproportionately affecting those with the least resources and power, and drawing so little governmental, corporate, and private commitment to provide access to information, testing, treatment, and care. Humanity cannot afford to lose sight of HIV any more than it has already done. We cannot afford greater neglect.

Although there are some benefits to normalizing HIV and emphasizing the common humanity and common needs of persons with HIV, the disease should not be completely folded into mainstream or generic service provision networks. Mainstreaming HIV care completely will lead to poorer care, because it is impossible to stay on top of new developments about this complex illness without focusing on it exclusively. Managers should be clear about these messages, pointing out the uniqueness of HIV and the necessity of addressing it in a unique way, while demanding that mainstream systems continue to do their parts for common human needs and rights.

Providing Multiple Interventions With Limited Resources

At first glance, HIV care seems to imply a specific focused methodology. In reality, advocates, service providers, and managers must work in various ways and programs must have several arms to address the complexity of the HIV pandemic and meet multiple needs.

Goals must include access to voluntary anonymous HIV testing, early diagnosis, accurate education regarding prevention and transmission, decreasing stigma and discrimination, linking prevention and care, connecting persons to community-based organizations, increasing access to expert medical care and medicine, supporting adherence to complicated protocols, and linking HIV care to other services such as mental health, prenatal, and substance use (Janssen et al., 2001). Consequently, contemporary HIV programs and organizations tend to incorporate many domains: health maintenance and prevention of illness (which includes safer sex and drug education to the public, shelters, prisons, parks and streets, and schools, as well as nutrition, yoga, massage, and relaxation classes for those who have HIV); policy analysis and legislative advocacy; case management and crisis intervention (including helping to meet basic survival needs such as food, clothing, and shelter); medical assistance (help to obtain medicine, medical care, and insurance); support to stay on treatment or decide when and how to change treatment; individual, family, couple, and group counseling; education about how to be a better pharmaceutical and medical decision maker; support and education of caregivers; grief counseling for caregivers and survivors; and a continuum of care along a disease trajectory that can include hospice-like care. Managing a range of services this broad in scope can be challenging.

This complexity necessitates multiple skill sets for staff and volunteers, so a manager must be able to envision and provide the training, support, and organizational culture necessary to run a varied network of advocacy and service provision. HIV work has always been "old-fashioned" generalist social work, meaning that quality service provision must occur simultaneously with advocacy and systems work. It is never enough to refer persons with HIV to other organizations, for example, because inevitably roadblocks occur based on stigma—internalized stigma of HIV-infected or HIV-affected persons, institutionalized stigma of the service system, or both. As the HIV-related program staff and managers work to improve access to information, testing, resources, treatment, and medication, and as they seek to address societal and structural inequities, activism and community organizing are just as important as case management, counseling, and crisis intervention.

Not only are HIV practitioners—micro, macro, and generalists—working at multiple levels and domains, they are doing so in organizations that remain understaffed and underfunded. The bulk of HIV care is still done cheaply or free by friends, family members, volunteers, low-paid peers and paraprofessionals, and underpaid trained staff. HIV programs are still struggling financially, still losing the best staff to governmental programs. Managers' advocacy time and skills are drained away from constituency work toward fighting for the survival of the organization; staff and managers find themselves fighting for the continuation of their own jobs. Funding streams have increasingly become biased toward the medical model; as a result, the social, emotional, and spiritual facets of living with HIV—those areas in which HIV-related social service programs have proven so vital—have been shortchanged.

A major strength of the HIV field is that it is an area of practice, policy, and management in which generalist and system orientations thrive and each practitioner must be proficient in multiple methods and think in complex and layered ways. HIV program managers must embrace and be ambassadors for this model: a generalist, multimethods approach combined with specialist knowledge about a unique disease. In addition, managers, as environmental scanners and as those responsible for the continuation of their programs, must continue to advocate for more stable funding for community-based HIV programs.

Shortage of HIV-Trained Workers

Many of the founding pioneers of the HIV service and advocacy field have become disabled or have died of AIDS. These missing laborers, along with an ever-expanding pandemic, have created a huge need for experienced and skilled workers in the HIV field. Yet the social work and human services professions are influenced by the "AIDS is over" trend as well, suffering from a lack of specific HIV training and lack of interest in HIV. People are not coming out of professional and paraprofessional schools educated, recruited, or ready to enter the HIV field. Masters and bachelor-level social workers are no longer entering the HIV field at a high rate. Social workers and other health care and human services professionals do not tend to be adequately prepared to work with persons with HIV or at risk for HIV unless they are HIV specialists. All of these facts have created a crisis for social work and a crisis for the HIV field. This circumstance is also a missed opportunity for trained social workers, because the HIV field offers a chance to use multiple methods; it is a field in which everyone does everything, and in which advanced generalists are born and nurtured.

There are several circumstances leading to HIV care being done by workers who are perhaps not best equipped to do so. Human services workers sometimes find themselves doing HIV practice without any preparation because someone who is HIV-infected or HIV-affected comes forward for services in a social service organization that is not HIV-specific. In community-based HIV-specific programs, which typically offer very low pay, challenging and complicated HIV-related work is being done by people who are not formally trained, and in some cases not necessary highly motivated, to do it. In some governmental programs this situation occurs, ironically, because there are higher pay incentives for those who will agree to do HIV work, so the benefits rather than the desire to work in the HIV field motivates them. All of these situations present challenges to managers, who must scramble to educate, motivate, and monitor workers so that service provision is appropriate, accessible, empathic, empowering, culturally competent, and responsive.

There are implications for the structure and running of HIV programs. Although it is imperative that programs employ HIV-positive peers and members of affected communities, including those without formal education, there is no indication that programs are run best by staff who have no formal training. We need a partnership between community members and professionals; it is not wise to leave HIV programs completely in the hands of underpaid and untrained community members who have not been given support, training, funding, and supervision. There are costs for the persons with HIV, obviously, who deserve the highest possible quality of care. There are also costs for the staff, who are burning out as a result of inadequate support, training, and supervision. Managers are also suffering as staff turnover results, and they are constantly seeking, hiring, and putting new staff on the job.

Managers should advocate for, and become trainers in, postgraduate certificate programs to get social workers ready for HIV practice and to keep them up to date with the knowledge necessary to practice in the field. Managers should offer themselves and their staff, volunteers, and speakers' bureau members as faculty for continuing education workshops and social work classes. As field instructors and supervisors of interns, human services managers and supervisors are consumers of social work schools. In those roles they are positioned to seek assistance in preparing current and future practitioners. Managers can ask the continuing education departments of social work schools to include HIV in their workshops, ask field departments to include HIV in content for field instructors, and ask schools to include HIV content in BSW and MSW classes. NASW chapters can lobby for licensing requirements to include some HIV content every few years.

A Truncated Service System

Instead of being linked through an umbrella organization such as the American Cancer Society, HIV programs and agencies generally are run locally through separate mechanisms. Each HIV program has a unique history and different founder (Chambre, 1999). Collaboration among programs is for the most part voluntary and occurs through goodwill. HIV programs are in competition with each other for funding, service applicants and recipients, individual donors, status, recognition, legitimacy, and expertise. To whatever extent this creates wariness or distrust, there may be holes in the service and referral net, and collaboration can be problematic. Bureaucratic and funding realities may block the needs of the community. The physical, medical, social, personal, and emotional realities of a person with HIV may not match the system's priorities.

Before federal funding was available, innovative, dedicated community-based programs were struggling for survival for many years. After the passage of the Ryan White CARE Act in 1990 and subsequent availability of state and federal programs, HIV services and the funding for them increased. So did competition and bidding for that funding. Some of the pioneering agencies continued to struggle to exist while agencies that had come late to HIV work were well funded (Bielefeld, Scotch, & Thielmann, 2000). It makes sense that large well-established bureaucracies would win competitive bids for state and federal funds, but community-based HIV programs felt further marginalized and unacknowledged. Some of that history still rankles.

In addition, often the loci of HIV care shifts constantly between community-based and institutionally based, because the needs of HIV-infected persons and their families shift rapidly between social/emotional and medical/pharmaceutical support. Often people with HIV and their networks need all these types of services at once. Prevention, support, survival needs, mental health, substance use, and complicated or urgent medical treatments are constantly braided, yet the systems providing these services may be distrustful at best and completely disconnected at worst. Communication between systems can range from nonexistent to dysfunctional. For example, finding common ground may be challenging if one group is advocating self-determination and another is expecting unquestioning compliance (Rier & Indyk, 2006).

Interdisciplinary and interorganizational collaboration is clearly necessary, so HIV program managers must learn to help bridge these differences for the benefit of persons with HIV (Rier & Indyk, 2006). Although it may be difficult for community-based HIV programs to set aside combative histories, different cultural and philosophical orientations, and current funding competition, it is imperative to find ways to collaborate for the good of the constituents. To knit together a safety net that is not unnecessarily unwieldy or duplicative while still offering choice and diversity to persons with HIV, programs must be willing and able to work together. Indeed, several federally funded HIV prevention and service programs require collaboration. Although it can be argued that forced cooperation is an oxymoron, one can appreciate the intention behind these requirements. Each program can work to establish a clear domain or expertise, advocacy, and service delivery and be clear about allies and competition for resources (Cain, 1997).

Despite the historical distrust and incompatibility between the medical and advocacy models, traditional medical institutions and community-based HIV programs can form successful coalitions to expand each other's reach and improve each other's services, bringing greater coherence to care and maximizing resources, if they approach each other's networks with respect and understanding for strengths, history, values, and models (Indyk & Rier, 2006; Rier & Indyk, 2006). HIV program staff and managers must overcome deeply rooted historical resentment at mistreatment and nonresponsiveness of traditional medical systems, and medical personnel must learn to trust advocates and social workers who have made a career of criticizing traditional systems. Such partnerships could benefit vulnerable communities, and if services to persons with HIV are improved, then no effort is too great.

Volatile Political and Economic Context

Human services in the United States have always operated in an unpredictable economic and political climate, and HIV services are certainly at the top of the heap of those struggling to survive in this context. Even though there have been a few brief examples of respite, profound uncertainty and stigma have characterized HIV work regardless of the political party in the White House or Congress.

Funding shifts and shrinkages are common, not necessarily because of anything the agency has or has not done, but because of the vicissitudes of local, state, and federal politics and funding realities. Not only are domestic social service programs suffering everywhere, but funding for HIV prevention, service, and medical programs change based on funding priorities and demographic shifts. One example is the readjustment of Ryan White CARE Act funds in 2006 from urban to rural areas: Agencies that had been accustomed to relatively comfortable funding levels found themselves making decisions about laying off staff and ending programs and/or finding other sources of funding.

Nowhere was the ideological struggle more obvious than in the Bush administration's unrelenting attack on evidence-based HIV prevention and education. Policies censured and restricted federal research applications and reshaped programs through funding restrictions, particularly for the most vulnerable populations (AIDS Alert, 2005). Community-based HIV programs were forced to fill in gaps left by government funding and programmatic restrictions by finding alternative ways to deliver accurate, accessible, relevant, and competent HIV prevention education in the face of political and religious pressure not to do so. Managers are often left with the ethical imperative to provide prevention and care without the funding to do so.

It helps to be experienced, assertive, and well-grounded in the community to establish or continue to provide evidence-based HIV prevention programs, because the current governmental policies and funding procedures are punitive and restrictive (DiFranceisco et al., 1999). Directors and managers must be prepared with alternative successful models, facts and research, professional and community support, foundation and community funding, technical assistance, legislative and advocacy skills, assertiveness, fearlessness, patience, and a high tolerance for intolerance. Managers must train staff and volunteers to implement effective behavior change models even if these are not the models that are being funded (DiFranceisco et al., 1999). And, as is the case with everything HIV program managers do, it helps to have courage, conviction, and a determination to save lives regardless of political, cultural, and religious pressures to the contrary.

Internal Pressures

Internal challenges faced by the managers of HIV programs include the question of identity and loyalty, debates over ownership of the processes, overtaxed resources and staff, ever-changing needs and programs, and threats to organizational functioning.

Identity and Loyalty

HIV programs have changed a great deal since their beginnings, generating debates about their most appropriate roles and responsibilities. When the new emergency arose, it generated an urgent response from community members who knew they were likely to die, and die in an atmosphere of lethal stigma and neglect. The original HIV organizations were founded by people who were not only trying frantically to pull drowning people out of the river, but they also were doing so in a leaky boat while trying to keep from drowning themselves.

A new social movement brought forth a new type of social organization. Although not linked, legislated, governed, or regulated, the early AIDS service organizations had enormous social and political influence, forcing change in health care, federal government response, the pharmaceutical industry, and social service provision. HIV advocates and service providers proposed new ways of being ill and of living life fully. They put forth new ways of being sexual and safe; created ways of reaching the most hidden, confronted bureaucracies; critiqued existing policies; and generated new service models.

The early small grassroots HIV programs were characterized by charismatic effective leadership, committed volunteers, intense involvement with communities at risk, radical activism, mutual support, confrontation of discrimination, collaboration and consensus building, participatory planning and empowerment, innovative programming for prevention and care, and marginal financial status (Arno, 1986; Cain, 1997; Chambre, 1996, 2006; Fleishman, Piette, & Mor, 1990; Hooyman, Fredriksen, & Perlmutter, 1995; Katoff, 1992; Lune, 2007; Maslanka, 1995; Poindexter, 2002, 2003; Rothschild & Whitt, 1986; Wilson, 1995). As organizations with confrontation and activism on one axis and innovative community-driven services on the other, HIV programs stood in direct opposition to the approaches and stances of traditional health care, social services, government agencies, foundations, and corporations, which were often the targets of their activism and sometimes the hostile impediments to their goals.

All social action movements, no matter their focus, tend to become more conservative, corporate, institutionalized, and bureaucratized as their social change goals are replaced with organizational maintenance and survival goals (Zald & Ash, 1965–1966). The natural slide toward conservatism was assisted by the funding crisis in the HIV field: When government funding was offered, HIV programs felt they had to accept it, even when strong and restrictive strings were attached. In addition, government funding tended to heavily influence the services offered, shifting the focus away from volunteer-run self-help services such as buddy programs to more traditional models such as case management and counseling. In recent years HIV programs have been forced by restrictive federal guidelines to move even further away from community-based social work into models that are more individually and medically focused.

Any time activists take to the streets and change the landscape (think Black civil rights movement, gay civil rights movement, antiwar activism) the government wants to accommodate them enough to keep order, but will never trust them completely. The parties may be at the table together but will always eye each other warily. The same was true of the HIV services and advocacy movement. Federal funding (Ryan White CARE Act, Housing Opportunities for Persons With AIDS, Medicaid waivers, etc.), although totally necessary for persons with HIV and their networks, also gave the establishment an opportunity to supplant and control the activists who had invented the method of service delivery and had taken to the streets to demand a federal response (Lune, 2007).

Gradually the members of the radical social movement, positioned in conflict with state and federal officials, became contracting partners with these former enemies. The state and federal influence became more important and in some cases dominant, replacing the influence of community members and persons with HIV. The role of persons with HIV in HIV services became regulated, legislated, and more token rather than central. HIV services, once run by HIV-infected community members, became directed by the state. At one time agency founders and directors, they were now invited to be committee members. As HIV programs grew in staff and funding and more hierarchical in structure, they more closely resembled the organizations they were formed to oppose (Cain, 1997).

Part of the mainstreaming and bureaucratizing of HIV occurred because the disease itself changed from small and urgent to gigantic and chronic. Individual donors and creative fundraisers could no longer carry the load alone. As foundations, state, and federal funding had to support rapidly growing services systems, those services became more uniform and less responsive to individual, community, and cultural concerns. The response cannot be the same as before: The founders and early leaders are disabled or dead, the long-term survivors are exhausted, professionals are in charge, and volunteers are no longer used exclusively (Chambre, 2006). Whatever one's view of the benefits and drawbacks of this situation, it is part of the current reality of HIV service provision and management.

In the HIV field this trend from social movement and alternative organizational network to bureaucratic service provision structure has raised serious questions about whether this is an evolution or a devolution, and whether this process has betrayed the mission to represent the rights and needs of persons with HIV. As painful as it is to have these debates about whether the HIV field has become unethical, sold its soul, or prostituted itself for money, it is even more painful when the debate begins to grow silent because managers are no longer questioning the institutionalizing of the field. Even when this quandary is not articulated or acknowledged, it is still in the shadows, influencing the donor base, the communities at risk, and the possible volunteer corps.

HIV programs stand in balance between communities and bureaucracies, sometimes distrusted by both while they try to satisfy and serve both. HIV programs have always been greatly stressed in the balance of maintaining their commitment and passion while stabilizing funding and organizational functioning (Aggleton, Weeks, & Taylor-Laybourn, 1993). In the current context this tricky negotiation is still the struggle for managers and directors. HIV program staff and managers are aware of the tensions between their histories of responsiveness and empowerment and their current organizational culture of professionalism and bureaucracy (Guenter et al., 2005). Now governmental and community-based leaders need each other, so HIV program managers must continue to maintain the delicate balance between representing the rights and needs of persons with HIV and satisfying the requirements of the funding bureaucracies.

Managers must seek funding where they can, but should be wary about these collaborations considering the ramifications for confidentiality, access to the community, and compromises to organizational values and mission. Although partnerships between community-based AIDS service organizations and governmental organizations can be beneficial for service provision, they can also be challenging because they follow a history of distrust and divergent philosophies and approaches. Government funding can undermine the HIV program's ability to meet community needs, defuse its advocacy agendas, and make it more politically conservative (Cain, 1995). Current challenges or conflicts with communities at risk are often rooted in the past, whether current staff realize it. Understanding the history of HIV programs in the local communities may be worthwhile for HIV program managers, especially if they are new to the organization or community.

HIV programs managers must struggle—in conversation with community members, volunteers, and staff—with questions regarding the true purpose, philosophy, and scope of the organization. If HIV programs are to be just like every other system, except simply focusing on HIV, then the question can be legitimately raised about whether they need to continue as a separate service system. However, if HIV programs can provide professional and ethical services without losing their community-based or advocacy nature, fill in gaps in services while demanding that other systems provide the support they are mandated to provide, deliver prevention programs while working toward the ending of HIV stigma and other oppressions that contribute to the HIV pandemic, and accept governmental funding while working against dysfunctional legislative and governmental policies, then they are honoring their history while shaping the future.

Ownership of the Process and Organization

Similar to the questions of ideology and identity are those that HIV program managers face regarding partnership and empowerment. This issue can manifest itself in conflicts between agency personnel and persons with HIV and between vulnerable community members.

The HIV field is rooted in consumer rights and participation, but over time the distinction between service provider and service consumer has widened. Planning for HIV advocacy, services, and prevention should begin with affected community members, who are obviously the experts on how HIV affects their lives. Yet organizations may mistakenly assume that HIV-infected community members are already fully prepared for participation rather than offering capacity building, technical assistance, research data, and organizational support to make sure that they have the tools they need to be full partners (Dearing, Larson, Randall, & Pope, 1998). Sometimes, rather than working out of a participatory perspective, managers and case managers act as gatekeepers. The financial bottom line, even in the HIV field, seems at times to be more important than grassroots organizing that demands appropriate and accessible care. Rather than working as advocates in solidarity with persons with HIV, some HIV programs seem to have positioned themselves in opposition to persons with HIV, viewing them as takers or users not to be trusted.

Like cancer, HIV can affect anyone and everyone, but unlike cancer, HIV remains highly politicized and stigmatized. In that context sometimes different affected and infected groups position themselves against each other, especially when prevention or service funds are perceived to be scarce. It is disheartening to witness affected communities, more than 25 years into a pandemic, positioning themselves in opposition to each other rather than joining forces to fight the disease or demand sufficient resources for everyone. Yet HIV program managers who are shepherding prevention and care funds often see conflicts over turf and resources. Competing constituencies may feel ownership of the agency, of the problem of HIV, or of the resources, or they may be frightened for their communities or angry at ongoing neglect. As the infection rates grow and funding shrinks, the infighting understandably increases.

HIV program managers have an opportunity to step away from these power struggles and, rather than be participants in them and scrap for influence, understand them as functions of being oppressed and without voice and power in U.S. society. It is to the benefit of the capitalistic systems that people with HIV and other vulnerable communities feel divided against each other in the fight for scarce resources, because if all vulnerable and oppressed people were to organize to demand change, the discriminatory economic forces at work would be in danger of collapse. Managers can help people understand this way of thinking and assist them in rejecting the usual way of doing business. HIV programs are positioned well to keep antistigma, antidiscrimination, and participation on the policy front burner. Programs can strive to be truly community-based, with full participation of people with HIV at every level of planning and implementation, and thus clearly reside in a unique domain. Social justice concerns are not dichotomous with service provision if both are kept at the forefront. A manager can ensure that all groups and processes reflect the diversity of the epidemic, without being guilty of tokenism, and embrace true cultural competence and true partnership.

Stretched to the Limits

With the number of infected persons continuing to climb and no end in sight, and with those persons having increasingly complex social and medical needs, HIV work continues to be difficult, and to be difficult in new ways. More and more persons with HIV are struggling mightily with poverty, powerlessness, access to medical care, and immigration status, so HIV is not the only serious issue in their lives. Increased numbers of service recipients have such limited resources that having HIV is sometimes at the bottom of their concerns. When people with HIV also need addictions services, mental health intervention, and resources for shelter, medications, and/or food, it is more difficult to determine which needs are within the agency's bailiwick and which should be referred to other service systems. In many small community-based HIV programs the workers carry multiple roles at once while managers focus on keeping them all trained, supported, and encouraged.

HIV program staff and managers are susceptible to burnout. In additional to the usual challenges of social work and health care, those in the HIV field may have further stresses related to service provision, such as anxiety about the risk of HIV infection, intense identification and relationships with those who are seriously ill and dying, demands to support the choices of constituents whose choices seem unwise, confusion over complicated legal and ethical dilemmas, high need for cultural competence and social knowledge, accumulation of grief and uncertainty, and uncertainty caused by the trajectory of HIV disease and the complexity of its treatment. They may also be angered or frustrated by insufficient agency and community resources, unstable funding, bureaucratic barriers, stigma and prejudice in the public and in other professionals, and public and political apathy in the face of a growing pandemic (Bennett, Miller, & Ross, 1995; Cushman, Evans, & Namerow, 1995; Demmer, 2002; Liou & Cruise, 1994). Managers are hard-pressed to support employees as they struggle with these stresses, especially if the managers are themselves feeling the same pressures.

In the context of stretched resources and staff, HIV program managers must attend to their own emotional, social, spiritual, and physical needs, but finding the time to do that is so problematic that many managers give up, to the detriment of themselves, their staff, and the agency. Having a peer supervision group or confidential consultant helps. Vacations and leaves of absence may be the answer. Sometimes managers become exhausted or ill but can find no time to take off, no one to substitute for them, and no support in their own supervisors and boards for the need to take a break. Some managers know that they are ineffective but do not admit their exhaustion because they worry about the organization's future. Out of the same concern, some boards and bosses pressure managers to stay on. Managers must advocate for themselves in these situations and educate all levels of the organization about the connection between burnout and quality of supervision and care. Managers must teach self-care to their staffs, model self-care, and support their staffs in caring for themselves. Managers must acknowledge that HIV work, although often highly satisfying and always important, can range from frustrating to heartbreaking.

To avoid, mediate, or address burnout, managers should keep the organization focused on advocacy, collaboration, positive change, problem-solving, interagency cooperation, and empowerment. Perspectives that shift managers and workers toward action are vital. These activities can also change the situations that are causing burnout (Bennett, Miller, & Ross, 1995).

Managers can daily remind themselves what brought them to the work and what keeps them in the work, and help workers, board members, and volunteers do the same. The needs, rights, and strengths of the vulnerable community members, as well as the commitment to social justice, empowerment, and access to resources, outweigh any system barriers or resources gaps. Instead of blaming all frustrations on persons with HIV or thinking that all shortfalls occur only in the HIV field, HIV social workers and managers can be realistic at the same time that they are determined to fight for change. Managers can focus on the concrete positive differences that HIV programs are making in people's lives and help their staff, volunteers, and board members do the same. Managers can continue to hold up the power of respectful nonjudgmental social work relationships, nonstigmatizing organizational spaces, and untiring advocacy to make the world a safer place for persons living with HIV.

Burnout is less likely if the agency's philosophy, supervision, training, and daily work focus on the strength and resilience of the community and on persons with HIV. Instead of viewing persons with HIV as adversaries from whom one must restrict services and benefits, managers and workers are better off seeing persons with HIV as fellow travelers from whom one can learn about health, survival, and culture and with whom one can be partners for change. This has the added benefit of improving advocacy and care because persons with HIV, at risk for HIV, or caring for persons with HIV will realize that they are included and respected. This serves to reduce antagonism and distrust and increase collaboration and cooperation. An improved working relationship eases worker and manager stress and burnout. Taking care of community members does not preclude taking care of ourselves; we are all in the process as partners.

Commitment to the organization, to constituents, and to the cause also increases job satisfaction. Managers and supervisors can help create excitement, motivation, teamwork, pride, and association with the organization and the mission, as well as acknowledge accomplishment, effort, and growth toward the team's objectives. Managers can be leaders and teachers, holding up standards of care and education that keep people excited and engaged. Managers should capitalize on whatever interest and commitment team members present by cross-training them, supporting their sense of dedication, and discovering and using their interests and strengths, regardless of their formal job descriptions.

Changing Needs and Programs

The HIV field tends to stay in flux as infection and illness trends change and as the health and mental health needs of persons with HIV change. Medical and pharmaceutical advances have improved the health of many who have access to them, so the service models developed and implemented from 1981 to 1996, geared to those who were in constant crisis and dying, are no longer universally relevant. HIV programs are still serving those who are in constant multiple crises, critically ill from either HIV or from medication side effects, but they are also now serving people who are in relatively good health or regaining their health. This necessitates redefining the roles of case managers, counselors, and volunteers and ensuring that supportive helpers are available to address the widened range of medical, spiritual, social, and emotional needs of persons with HIV (Chambre, 1997).

Organizations that began with buddy programs, hospital visitors, support groups, and peer counseling now also offer food banks, laundry service, housing assistance, and employment counseling (Cain, 1997). During the first 15 years of HIV services the thought of adding employment counseling would have been unimaginable, but it now makes sense for any HIV-related social service program to provide counseling regarding returning to work, assessing the risk of going off disability benefits, job search and interview skills, workplace disclosure and discrimination, legal rights, and managing insurance costs (Brooks & Klosinski, 1999; Ferrier & Lavis, 2003; Hergenrather, Rhodes, & Clark, 2005).

Managers and directors, in their roles as planners, must stay in advance of these trends. In addition, new treatment protocols and new technological and scientific developments require that practitioners and managers maintain a basic level of knowledge so that public and consumer education, staff development, prevention, and referrals keep pace with evidence. Given the frantic pace of advocacy, service provision, personnel management, and fundraising, managers are frustrated by the lack of time to keep up with the reading necessary to be effective in an ever-changing field. The pace of HIV knowledge proliferation often seems dizzying, and the tracking of demographic trends seems burdensome, but these activities are vital.

HIV program managers and directors have the important task of understanding what the changing infection rates in the local community mean for outreach, programming, staffing, prevention methodology, funding, training, and cultural competence. Again, there often is not enough time for strategic planning, but without an analysis of the trends and how the agency must change to meet them, the organization is constantly behind the community need. Part of the assessment must be how the agency is perceived by various communities and how these communities need the agency to fill in gaps. Managers, already overtaxed with keeping the status quo afloat, are tempted to ignore requests for change. But to be effective they must be open to new methods, approaches, and service technologies.

Challenges to Organizational Functioning

Human services organizations themselves can become marginalized, stressed, under siege, and ailing. Given the financial, political, and interorganizational pressures on HIV programs and the high stress levels of the workers and managers, it is no wonder that HIV programs often suffer conflict within their own walls. Intraorganizational tensions or hostilities can eat up the energy and focus of an agency and keep from focusing completely on the already exhausting needs of its constituency. When the director and board, volunteers and staff, staff and managers, community members and staff, or different types of service constituencies are in conflict or experience distrust, difficult situations begin to seem impossible. Staff morale and turnover can negatively affect advocacy effectiveness, service provision, and rapport with various communities, and poor management and director performance can affect interorganizational relationships, funding, and reputation in the larger community. In both cases agency survival and agency necessity can be threatened.

How are HIV program managers to remain inspirational, effective, and personally and professionally healthy? How does one know how long to stay and when it is time to change jobs? How does a manager assess whether one is doing good in a flawed system? How does one tell if organizational and system problems are negatively affecting one's management style more than one is positively effecting the agency? If a manager is struggling, is it wise to let staff know that, and is it fair not to? If a manager has health challenges, especially if they are HIV-related, disclosure decisions become agonizing. Secrets are corrosive, yet upset and insecure employees are difficult to manage as well. If a manager is also a founder, these questions may be especially poignant; add to those quandaries the fact that successors are not likely to have the same passion, vision, and commitment.

It is important for managers to find ways to get support for themselves within the parameters of confidentiality. Good administrative and clinical supervision are vital. Supportive and confidential peer supervision groups may also be an option.

Managers and directors struggle with whether to acknowledge conflicts rooted in histories of oppression or differences in culture, unsure whether doing so will exacerbate the problems, and are wary of airing the conflicts for fear that funders, media, or the public will get wind of the trouble. In addition, HIV programs are so understaffed, underfunded, and crisis-oriented that managers and directors do not feel they have time to address intraorganizational conflict (Cain, 2002). Yet it is imperative that problems not be allowed to fester. If organizational conflict obstructs staff morale and service provision, managers must take the agency through a process of acknowledging the structural or communication problems, creating the safety necessary to listen to each other respectfully, and building unity, collaboration, conversation, and cohesion.

At times it is painfully necessary to acknowledge the overlapping systems of oppression in which we all work and live and to examine the ways in which oppressive systems affect our own relationships. In that process, time must be spent on focusing on commonalities without divesting people of their diversity. Action plans must replace free-floating anger (Cain, 2002).

Conclusions

HIV program managers face a variety of challenges originating outside the organization and residing inside the organization, leaving them feeling squeezed between competing stakeholders and harsh pressures. It is difficult to maintain balance, health, and perspective when the rest of the world thinks HIV is no longer a problem. Barriers are multiple: Your issue is still highly ostracized, people still accuse your field of an undeserved sense of entitlement, your constituents and their needs are growing while your resources are shrinking, you cannot find enough trained professionals to do the work, the health care and social service systems remain uncoordinated and full of turf fights, and the cultural and political climates are still unfriendly.

Your organization may not be sure of its sense of history, identity, or loyalty; there may be debates about which persons or groups should be making decisions about planning and programming; staff and management alike are frustrated and frightened about the lack of time and resources while they are struggling to provide complicated services to very vulnerable individuals and communities; your field is shifting under your feet all the time; and there are conflicts at every level of your organization. You are dedicated to the cause but more and more wondering whether you are making a difference. You are exhilarated yet exhausted. This is the nature of HIV program management.

This chapter has acknowledged some of the common challenges programs managers face in the HIV field and suggested some starting points for approaches to address these challenges. The intention was to "prime the pump" for the reader's own thinking, collaborative problem-solving, community organizing, and empowering supervision and management strategies in the continuation of the vital work of HIV services and advocacy.

References

AIDS Alert. (2005). Government prevention research "hit list" draws protests from scientists: Recent NIH "hit list" is unprecedented, they say. *AIDS Alert, 19*(1), 1, 3–5.

Aggleton, P., Weeks, J., & Taylor-Laybourn, A. (1993). Voluntary sector responses to HIV and AIDS: A framework for analysis. In P. Aggleton, P. Davies, & G. Hart (Eds.), *AIDS: Facing the second decade* (pp. 131–140). London: Falmer Press.

Arno, P. S. (1986). The nonprofit sector's response to the AIDS epidemic: Community-based services in San Francisco. *American Journal of Public Health*, *76*(11):1325–1330.

Bennett, L., Miller, D., & Ross, M. (1995). Review of the research to date on impact of HIV/AIDS on health workers. In L. Bennett, D. Miller, & M. Ross (Eds.), *Health workers and AIDS: Research, intervention and current issues in burnout and response* (pp. 15–34). Switzerland: Harwood Academic Publishers.

Bielefeld, W., Scotch, R. K., & Thielmann, G. S. (2000). National mandates and local nonprofits: Shaping a local delivery system of HIV/AIDS services. In F. M. Cox, J. L. Erlich, J. Rothman, & J. E. Tropman (Eds.), *Strategies in community organization* (pp. 329–336). Monument, CO: Peacock.

Brooks, R. A., & Klosinski, L. E. (1999). Assisting persons living with HIV/AIDS to return to work: Programmatic steps for AIDS service organizations. *AIDS Education and Prevention, 11*(3), 212–223.

Cain, R. (1995). Community-based AIDS organizations and the state: Dilemmas of dependence. *AIDS and Public Policy Journal, 10*(2), 83–93.

Cain, R. (1997). Environmental change and organizational evolution: Reconsidering the niche of community-based AIDS organizations. *AIDS Care, 9*(3), 331–344.

Cain, R. (2002). Devoting ourselves, devouring each other: Tensions in community-based AIDS work. *Journal of Progressive Human Services, 13*(1), 93–113.

Chambre, S. M. (1996). Uncertainty, diversity, and change: The AIDS community in New York City. *Research in Community Sociology, 6*, 149–190.

Chambre, S. M. (1997, October–December). New tactics: Volunteer programs adapt to meet changing needs of people with AIDS. *Volunteer Leadership*, 17–19.

Chambre, S. M. (1999). Redundancy, third-party government, and consumer choice: HIV/AIDS nonprofit organizations in New York City. *Policy Studies Journal, 27*, 840–854.

Chambre, S. M. (2006). *Fighting for our lives: New York AIDS community and the politics of disease.* Piscataway, NJ: Rutgers University Press.

Cushman, L. F., Evans, P., & Namerow, P. B. (1995). Occupational stress among AIDS social service providers. *Social Work in Health Care, 21*(3), 115–131.

Dearing, J. W., Larson, R. S., Randall, L. M., & Pope, R. S. (1998). Local reinvention of the CDC HIV prevention community planning initiative. *Journal of Community Health, 23*(2), 113–126.

Demmer, C. (2002). Stress and satisfaction among employees in AIDS service organizations in New York. *Evaluation and the Health Professions, 25*(2), 225–238.

DiFranceisco, W., Kelly, J. A., Otto-Salaj, L, McAuliffe, T. L., Somlai, A. M., Hackl, K., et al. (1999). Factors influencing attitudes within AIDS service organizations toward the use of research-based HIV prevention interventions. *AIDS Education and Prevention, 11*(10), 72–86.

Edwards, R. L., & Austin, D. M. (1991). Managing effectively in an environment of competing values. In R. L. Edwards & J. A. Yankey, *Skills for effective human services management* (pp. 5–18). Silver Spring, MD: National Association of Social Workers.

Ferrier, S. E., & Lavis, J. N. (2003). With health comes work? People living with HIV/AIDS consider returning to work. *AIDS Care, 15*, 423–435.

Fleishman, J. A., Piette, J. D., & Mor, V. (1990). Organizational response to AIDS. *Evaluation and Program Planning, 13*(1), 31–38.

Guenter, D., Majumdar, B., Willms, D., Travers, R., Browne, G., & Robinson, G. (2005). Community-based HIV education and prevention workers respond to a changing environment. *Journal of the Association of Nurses in AIDS Care, 16*(1), 29–36.

Hergenrather, K. C., Rhodes, S. D., & Clark, G. (2005). The employment perspectives study: Identifying factors influencing the job-seeking behavior of persons living with HIV/AIDS. *AIDS Education and Prevention, 17*(2), 131–142.

Hooyman, N. R., Fredriksen, K. I., & Perlmutter, B. (1995). Shanti: An alternative response to the AIDS crisis. In F. M. Cox, J. L. Erlich, J. Rothman, & J. E. Tropman (Eds.), *Strategies in community organization* (pp. 417–426). Monument, CO: Peacock.

Hyde, C. (1992). The ideational system of social movement agencies: An examination of feminist health centers. In Y. Hasenfeld (Ed.), *Human services as complex organizations* (pp. 121–144). Newbury Park: Sage.

Indyk, D., & Rier, D. A. (2006). Requisites, benefits, and challenges of sustainable HIV/AIDS system-building: Where theory meets practice. *Social Work in Health Care, 42*(3/4), 93–110.

Janssen, R. S., Holtgrave, D. R., Valdiserri, R. O., Shepherd, M., Gayle, H. D., & De Cock, K. M. (2001). The serostatus approach to fighting the HIV epidemic: Prevention strategies for infected individuals. *American Journal of Public Health, 91*, 1019–1024.

Katoff, L. (1992). Community-based services for people with AIDS. *Primary Care, 19*(1), 231–243.

Liou, K. T., & Cruise, P. L. (1994). Assessing employee attitudes in a community-based AIDS service organization. *Evaluation and the Health Professions, 17*(3), 273–289.

Lune, H. (2007). *Urban action networks: HIV/AIDS and community organizing in New York City*. New York: Rowman & Littlefield.

Maslanka, H. (1995). HIV volunteers. In L. Bennett, D. Miller, & M. Ross (Eds.), *Health workers and AIDS: Research, intervention and current issues in burnout and response* (pp. 151–173). Chur, Switzerland: Harwood Academic Publishers.

Piot, P. (2006). AIDS: From crisis management to sustained strategic response. *Lancet, 368*, 526–530.

Poindexter, C. (1998). Promises in the plague: The Ryan White CARE Act as a case study for legislative action. *Health and Social Work, 24*(1), 35–41.

Poindexter, C. (2002). "Be generous of spirit": Organizational development of an AIDS service organization. *Journal of Community Practice, 10*(2), 53–70.

Poindexter, C. (2003). The South Carolina experience. In B. Willinger & A. Rice (Eds), *A history of AIDS social work in hospitals: A daring response to an epidemic* (pp. 41–50). London: Routledge.

Poindexter, C., & Lane, T. S. (2003). Choices and voices: Participation of people with HIV in Ryan White Title II consumer advisory boards. *Health and Social Work, 28*(3), 196–205.

Rier, D. A., & Indyk, D. (2006). The rationale of interorganizational linkages to connect multiple sites of expertise, knowledge production, and knowledge transfer: An example for HIV/AIDS services for the inner city. *Social Work in Health Care, 42*(3/4), 9–27.

Rothschild, J., & Whitt, J. A. (1986). *The cooperative workplace*. Cambridge, UK: Cambridge University Press.

Wilson, P. A. (1995). AIDS service organizations: Current issues and future challenges. *Journal of Gay and Lesbian Social Services, 2*(3–4), 121–144.

Zald, M. N., & Ash, R. (1965–1966). Social movement organizations: Growth, decay, and change. *Social Forces, 44*, 327–341.

5

Management Skills for Health Care Organizations

Colleen Galambos

In response to market demands, state and federal regulations, and insurance issues, health care organizations are undergoing rapid changes. Working in this type of environment offers the social work manager the opportunity to practice in a fast-paced, interdisciplinary environment in which there is little margin for error. Clients seeking services from these organizations are experiencing crisis or loss and require quick, effective attention. Since managing the immediate presenting crisis, well-being, and safety of the client is of the utmost importance in health care, the social work manager faces certain challenges.

It is an environment that emphasizes continuous quality improvement; knowledge of federal, state, local, and organizational policy; and skill in developing new policies to meet ever-changing demands. Busy crisis situations require strong environmental assessment skills and knowledge about how to use information from the assessment in an administrative plan. Since social workers find themselves in host agencies where social work is one service, but not the primary one, professional advocacy and education are the key to developing a strong social work presence within these organizations. Kirst-Ashman and Hull (2000) refer to these settings as secondary settings and suggest that social work values and perspectives may clash with those of other medical personnel.

The savvy social work manager needs keen interdisciplinary skills to be successful in host health care settings. This chapter discusses the management skills social work administrators need for interdisciplinary collaboration, professional advocacy, professional education, environmental analysis, policy practice, and continuous quality improvement. The importance of developing an evidence-based practice environment is also examined.

Interdisciplinary Collaboration

Health care organizations employ social workers in an environment where a variety of professional staff contribute to the mission of the organization, which generally is a focus on improving health and providing quality medical care. Because of this emphasis, medical personnel with medical backgrounds account for the majority of employees. Social work is classified as an ancillary profession that lends support to the medical mission (Kirst-Ashman & Hull, 2000).

Congruencies in Practice

For proper collaboration to occur, the social work manager must become familiar with the language, common practices, and culture of the facility. It is important to learn who has power and to be respectful of the hierarchy of command. It is common for physicians and nurses to hold key positions within this hierarchy. Social work managers should assess their perspectives and values and determine how social work can contribute to them. Since both medical and ancillary professionals provide quality health care services, the common ground is often quality patient care. However, professional interpretation of good patient care can be different.

A savvy social work manager will determine the congruency between social work values and perspectives and that of other disciplines' values and perspectives. In making this type of careful assessment, the social worker identifies commonalities, which are then used to strengthen interactions and mitigate conflict through a respectful consideration of what is important to other professionals. If managers are aware of what matters to other disciplines, they can use this knowledge to develop strategies to deal with problems.

Communication

Another important skill critical to interdisciplinary collaboration is effective communication. Weiss and Gantt (2004) point out that an effective communicator understands the nature of interacting with others, the importance of altering communication to be more meaningful, and that adjustments in communication are necessary due to different life experiences. They identify two environmental factors that affect interaction. The first is the cultural environment, which is the collective behaviors, attitudes, and values that influence communication messages. The second is the physical environment, which consists of structural and behavioral entities such as practices around formality, privacy, constraints, and distance practices.

In health care settings the purpose of communication is to emphasize interdisciplinary collaboration. Collaboration implies problem solving and solution-focused behavior. The focus is on issues and how to develop outcomes that will benefit everyone. Weis and Gant (2004) identify three skill sets that contribute to cooperative collaborative communications:

- View disagreements from the perspective of the other person.
- Use active listening to identify the meanings and feelings of the other person.
- Use negotiation to solve problems.

The social work manager will use these skills in communications with other disciplines and in performing various functions within the hospital. It is also important that other social workers in the health care facility use this collaborative approach. Social workers can learn this style through training, modeling, and observation. An example of good communication skills is the development of interdisciplinary team meetings attended by the nurse manager, the physician manager, the rehabilitation services manager, and the social work manager to discuss pending patient discharges.

Interdisciplinary and Transdisciplinary Teams

Interdisciplinary health care teams include professionals from a number of backgrounds who share knowledge and disciplinary language; however, new professional collaborations are emerging that are identified as transdisciplinary collaborations (Gehlert & Browne, 2006). Transdisciplinary teams comprise professionals from a variety of backgrounds who develop together a shared language and combine their prospective knowledge and theories to develop new methods and analytical techniques. This new configuration demands that employees have enough medical and biological training to enable them to work effectively on these types of teams. For instance, it is important for social workers to learn basic medical terminology, to be familiar with medications and their side effects, and to understand medical procedures and treatments. This knowledge will help them provide appropriate counseling to patients and their families, ensure that the patient has the best possible environment in which to recuperate, and make relevant resource referrals.

Professional Advocacy and Education

Although it is important to respect other health professionals' points of view, it is equally important to communicate and advocate for the values and standards of the social work profession within secondary settings. The unique contributions of social work are an important addition to both services and the mission of the health care organization. In particular, social workers provide an important environmental and holistic dimension to health care (Gehlert & Browne, 2006).

Systematic Advocacy

Systematic advocacy means bringing the interests of clients to the forefront. In the case of social work managers, advocacy of client issues occurs at the macro level and affects the organization's mission, services, resources, programs, and course of action. Advocacy at this level takes the form of communicating with other decision makers and helping to educate and bring forward the perspective of the client and the client's needs.

Cause Advocacy

Another type of advocacy that is important for a social work manager is cause advocacy, which involves more global issues that affect not only the organization, but society as a whole. This type of advocacy, which involves groups, institutions, and modifications of social conditions (Hardcastle & Powers, 2004), tries to eliminate or lessen the inequalities in health care. For instance, a social work manager may be asked to testify on the impact of Medicaid cuts on health care services for indigent patients. Social workers as political advocates must start by answering this question: What are the structural or environmental factors that create or intensify the problem? (Greene, Cohen, Galambos, & Kropf, 2007).

Health Communication

An important component of advocacy is the ability to communicate messages to a broad audience. The Healthy People 2010 initiative emphasizes the importance of what it terms *health communication* in promoting adequate health care for all citizens (U.S. Department of Health and Human Services, 2000, p. 17; U.S. Office of Disease Prevention and Promotion, 2007). Health communication includes the study and use of communication strategies to inform and influence people, the community, and society. The global impact of good health communication can contribute to (1) better health care outcomes; (2) a reduction in the impact of racial, ethnic, cultural, and socioeconomic differences in care; and (3) improvements in measures targeted at prevention and health promotion (Thomas, 2006).

The Institute of Medicine (2001) indicates that there are disparities in health care between White and minority populations and that some of the differences in health care between the two groups can be attributed to poor communication about the health care needs of specific groups and a lack of cultural competence. Social work managers are in an excellent position to advocate for better health care systems to address these disparities. Advocacy involves confronting others and providing a different perspective. It is important that communication be constructive, informative, and ongoing.

Health Communication Process

Crucial to any advocacy effort is a strong, well-thought-out communication plan. Building on the basic premise of health communication, the social work manager can engage this process to organize advocacy efforts. The health communication process includes four stages—planning, development, implementation, and evaluation (Thomas, 2006).

In the planning stage, which provides the foundation for the advocacy initiative, the problem or issue is identified and stated clearly. Once the problem is identified, then the assumptions that drive the problem are identified. These assumptions can involve demographic information, financial considerations, target population, the impact of the political environment, and so on. These identified assumptions will serve as a force to move the planning process forward.

The next step is to review all available data on the problem. Typical information to collect includes the prevalence of the health problem; the shared characteristics of those affected by the health problem; the consequences of the health problem on a micro, mezzo, and macro level; the possible causes of the problem; and the likely solutions.

Once preliminary information is collected, assess what other information is needed and conduct additional research. Develop objectives for the advocacy project that will help to set priorities for it. Objectives refer to the specific targets to be reached in support of goal attainment and should be impartial and measurable. Strong objectives set clear time guidelines and deadlines for accomplishing tasks. They are realistic, and they can be evaluated. Next, identify the target audience and map out the approach to the advocacy strategy.

The development stage involves creating the materials to deliver the main messages in the advocacy initiative. Resources to develop might include PowerPoint presentations, position statements, letters to the editor, brochures, and so forth. Pay attention to the appropriateness of the materials for the intended audience. Cost factors related to the production of materials should drive decisions about what materials the campaign can use. Plans must also be made to distribute the materials, including deciding who will deliver them and receive them, how they should be delivered, whether to stage an opening event highlighting the problem or solution, and whether efforts will target elected and government officials.

The implementation stage uses the strategy developed in the planning stage to carry out actions; however, this stage highlights the details. Other important tasks are to identify people who will be assigned to specific duties and to develop a communication system that informs everyone involved of the project's progress, successes, and problems. Progress can be tracked using an implementation matrix that identifies tasks and people assigned to complete them. Resource requirements should also be included in the matrix in terms of staff, money, time, and start and end dates. It is important to factor in prerequisites and to establish benchmarks to indicate progress. Some examples of benchmarks are progress, operational, clinical impact, and financial.

The next task in the implementation stage is managing the advocacy effort. The project activities must be monitored through ongoing process evaluations and gauging responses and reactions to the initiative. As problems are identified they should be dealt with through modifying the initial approach and/or eliminating cumbersome steps.

The evaluation stage determines the effectiveness of the approach. Evaluation should include ongoing process monitoring using benchmarks, collected data, and objectives to measure the success of the initiative. Other methods include developing a monitoring and feedback system, surveys, interviews with key stakeholders, and community indicators of success. Problems and successes that emerge from this process may be used to create a more effective approach in the future.

Systematic Approach

A good advocacy effort requires a systematic approach and a certain amount of skill, knowledge, and persuasion. Schneider and Lester (2001) recommend that the following practice principles be used in any advocacy activity:

1. Identify issues and set goals.
2. Get the facts.
3. Plan strategies and tactics.

4. Supply leadership.
5. Get to know decision makers and their staff.
6. Broaden the base of support.
7. Be persistent.
8. Evaluate advocacy effort.

Organizing advocacy efforts into these eight practice steps will ensure an effective approach to resolving inequities and promoting social work values in the health care arena. Social work managers can use this approach to advocate for additional clinical services for patients and families, such as developing a support group for parents of children recently diagnosed with terminal cancer or a support group for patients on a waiting list for heart transplants.

Environmental Analysis

One challenge for social work managers working in health care organizations is to assess and anticipate changes in the environment that will affect the organization. Once these changes are anticipated, the manager must plan a response to them. The types of changes that are likely to occur are policy or political mandates, fiscal or economic factors, population/demographic changes, new and emerging technologies, and alterations in the competitive market place (Swayne, Duncan, & Ginter, 2006). Practice ideologies and rules for different fields of practice may change and influence the types of programs offered (Mattaini, Lowery, & Meyers, 2002). The astute social work manager will keep abreast of these changes and adjust services and organization priorities accordingly. In other words, assessing trends, events, and issues in the environment is an ongoing responsibility of the manager.

Assessment

Assessment tools can be used to determine the best time to conduct an environmental analysis. Mesch (1984) developed one such tool that consists of seven questions managers must ask to determine the need for such an analysis. These questions are:

1. Does the external environment influence capital allocation and decision-making processes?
2. Were previous strategic plans aborted due to unexpected changes in the environment?
3. Has anything unexpected happened in the external environment?
4. Is there competitive growth in health care?
5. Does the organization place an emphasis on marketing?
6. Are external forces driving decisions, and is there more interplay among these decisions?
7. Is the management team unhappy with previous planning efforts?

Answering yes to any of these questions means an environmental analysis may be needed. If there are yes answers to five or more questions, then an environmental analysis is definitely in order.

Environmental Analysis—The Process

Swayne, Duncan, and Ginter (2006) developed a four-step environmental analysis model:

1. *Scan* the environment. Collect and consider external environmental data from other organizations and individuals; organize these data into logical categories of information such as political, regulatory, and economic categories; and identify emerging issues within each category.
2. *Monitor* the identified issues. Scrutinize the sources of the information to confirm or discard trends and to determine the rate of change in the environment.
3. *Forecast* the future direction of the issues. Use information obtained in step 2 to make predictions about future issues and trends.
4. *Assess* the implications of these issues for the organization. The last step involves an evaluation of the forecasted issues and their impact on the organization. A plan is then developed for how the organization will respond to these issues and trends.

Models and tools that assist with the environmental analysis process are designed to bring order to information and connect data together. Moving methodically through each step, the manager identifies the implications of environmental factors on services. With data available, services can be adjusted to meet the demands of a continuously changing environment.

The Institute of Medicine (2001) has identified the need for more focus on the sociocultural factors that may affect medical treatment. An environmental analysis could be used to determine how social work programs in health care settings should respond to this recommendation.

Quality Improvement

Recent reports from the Institute of Medicine describe the inadequacies of the current health care system in the United States. Our system contains many health care disparities, and there is general recognition that the nation must focus on quality improvement. Included in the final report of the Institute of Medicine's Committee on Health Care Quality in America is a call for changes within the health care system and a blueprint for the future. The Institute of Medicine recommends that the American health care system be revised from one that emphasizes treatment of acute episodic care to one capable of handling chronic health conditions and promoting wellness. The report identifies the following six areas for improvement, which are regarded as the six dimensions of quality (Institute of Medicine, 2001; Ransom, Joshi, & Nash, 2005) and include:

1. Care should be safe for patients in health care facilities and at home.
2. Care should be effective and based on the science and evidence behind health care and serve as the standard of care.
3. Care and service should be as efficient and cost effective as possible; waste should be eliminated.
4. Care should be timely, with no waits or delays in receiving care and service.

5. We should strive to achieve patient-centered care in which the health care system revolves around the patient, patient preferences are respected, and the patient is in control.

6. We should strive for equitable treatment. Unequal treatment and disparities in care should be eliminated.

Four Levels of the Health Care System

Ferlie and Shortell (2001) envision the framework for achieving these improvements as occurring within four levels of the health care system. Level A is the patient level and involves everything that happens with the patient. Level B is the microsystem and includes the care delivered by small provider teams. Level C includes the organizational level, the aggregation of the microsystems and supporting functions or the macro system. Level D is the external environment, which includes fiscal mechanisms, policy, regulations, and other external environmental factors. The social work manager has a responsibility to advocate for improvements in health care across all dimensions and at all levels within the framework.

Use of Scorecards

An organizational scorecard can be developed using the six dimensions of quality identified by the Institute of Medicine. A scorecard is a means to organize measures of quality into a framework that includes dimensions of performance and results mandated by the organization. Using this approach, the manager identifies dimensions of performance and realistic outcomes measures and establishes a time frame for when measures are to be taken, such as quarterly reviews. Then, data obtained from this process can be compared or benchmarked against that from other organizations. The six dimensions of quality could be used as a framework for developing the performance measures, and measures could be developed for each quality dimension. As part of the benchmarking process, performance on these measures could be judged against comparable organizations (Ransom, Joshi, & Nash, 2005). For instance, social work managers could use the scorecard method to determine the success of referrals for social work services in the organization.

Processes

Two processes can ensure that social work services are focused on quality care—continuous quality improvement and clinical process innovation. The first process, continuous quality improvement (CQI), is concerned with improving existing practices through the measurement of performance. In this approach, adjustments are made to existing services based on what the data indicate. CQI is designed to measure performance through the use of standards on an ongoing basis.

One approach to CQI that is often used is called the Shewhart Cycle for process improvement, which includes four steps:

1. Plan—problems are recognized and the causes of these problems are identified.
2. Do—a plan or solution is developed to resolve the problem.
3. Check—the plan or solution is systematically tested, results are evaluated, and additional improvements considered.
4. Act—the best solution or plan is implemented (Griffith & White, 2002, pp. 31–32).

After completing step 4, return to the first step (Griffith & White, 2002). The social work manager can use CQI to determine whether the discharge planning process meets the needs of clients, their families, the health care providers, and the health care setting.

The second process is clinical process innovation (CPI) in which the emphasis is on developing and implementing new practices that will lead to improvement. CPI analytically reviews current practices and identifies ways to deliver services (Swayne et al., 2006). A practical example of how CPI could be used in health care settings is in determining the need for and effectiveness of health care ethics committees.

Continuous improvement of the cost and quality of care and services is based in evidence-based practice or the notion that treatment is developed through systematic evaluation of procedures and techniques (Griffith & White, 2002). Managers who are conscientious about quality and improvement must become familiar with evidence-based practice approaches in health care and comfortable with using these methods.

Evidence-Based Practice

There is a strong mandate within the health care environment to use an evidence-based practice (EBP) approach. A simple definition of evidence-based practice is "the conscientious, explicit and judicious use of current best evidence in making decisions about the care of individual patients" (Sackett, Straus, Richardson, Rosenberg, & Haynes, 2000, p. 1). The emphasis on EBP developed in the 1980s to use the best evidence obtained through research to deliver health care more cost effectively (Porter-O'Grady & Malloch, 2007). The American Medical Association further developed this concept in 1992, and it became an important guideline and value in health care (Griffith & White, 2002). EBP uses quantitative and qualitative research outcomes in a selected area of practice and bases practice changes on these findings. In social work, it can assist managers in determining which intervention and clinical approaches are most effective in health care settings.

Evidence-Based Leadership

It is important that managers in health care organizations develop an evidence-based approach to leadership in which available evidence, experience, expertise, and values of the organization influence tasks and projects. DeGroot (2005) defines evidence-based leadership as a "transformational relationship involving organizational stewardship, decision making, and vision translation through reasoned application of empirical evidence from management, leadership, and patient care research." Sources of evidence include systematic literature reviews in which all of the evidence related to a specific issue is summarized; meta-analysis, in which the systematic review is analyzed using statistical methods for combining the results of individual studies; integrative review, which summarizes the findings of research on a particular topic and draws conclusions from it; and exhaustive integrative review, which uses the same rigor and replication as primary research (Porter-O'Grady & Malloch, 2007).

Approaches and Processes

One approach to systematic analysis of scientific literature on outcomes consists of four components that must be in place in organizations:

1. a mechanism that allows for an evidence-based consensus on care;
2. a well-designed process to implement this consensus;
3. a program of outreach that emphasizes disease prevention and health promotion; and
4. developing and using a system that reviews performance and identifies future improvements (Griffith & White, 2002).

In the social work profession, evidence-based practice is receiving increasing attention. Rosen (2003) discussed the reasons why it is important for social workers to adopt an EBP approach, including a commitment to clients' best interest, values-guided practice, goal-directed practice, accountability, and commitment to scientific standards of evidence. Rubin and Parrish (2007) describe a five-step process for evidence-based practice:

1. Formulate an answerable question regarding practice needs.
2. Track down the best evidence available to answer that question.
3. Critically appraise the scientific validity and usefulness of the information.
4. Integrate the appraisal with one's own clinical expertise, client values, and circumstances and then apply it to practice decisions.
5. Evaluate the outcome (using single-case designs if feasible) (p.407).

Creating an Environmental Culture

Social work managers can develop an environment that emphasizes this approach in practice settings. Managers can insure that all members of the social work team receive education and training in EBP and that organizational structures are in place to support such an approach. Franklin and Hobson (2007) advocate for the creation and expansion of university-agency partnerships that support research, supervision, consultation, and technical assistance to facilitate practitioner training and enhance research skills. Social work managers can develop such partnerships through the use of boundary-spanning skills. To be effective, however, training programs must be ongoing. It is contingent on the social work manager to develop and implement cost-effective ongoing training.

The advancement of a constructive culture in which EBP is seen as consistent with organizational values and cultural norms will help facilitate such practices (Miller, 2001). Franklin and Hobson (2007, p. 390) identify the components of such a culture as promoting positive, proactive behavior and interactions; norms of achievement that encourage risk taking, development of one's full potential; and support for one another. This type of culture is associated with a greater willingness to use new and innovative interventions and practices (Glisson & James, 2002; Hemmelgarn, Glisson, & James, 2000; Jaskyte & Dressler, 2005). Organizational leadership is instrumental in developing an environment accepting of innovative practices (Gambrill, 2006). The leader who adopts a decentralized management structure in which employees contribute to the decision-making process is more likely to develop the type of culture that fosters innovation (Franklin & Hobson, 2007).

In addition to creating a positive culture, incentives such as monetary bonuses, increased leave time, adequate time to learn a new skill, and so forth contribute to a practitioner's willingness to adopt new approaches (Corrigan, Streiner, McCracken, Blaser, & Barr, 2001). In addition to these tangible types of support, research indicates that health care practitioners are more likely to use a new intervention when they have sufficient time to learn it and receive support from colleagues when doing so (Hutchinson & Johnston, 2004). Flexibility in implementation, along with clear instructions, also contributes to successful adaptation (Miller, 2001).

Social work needs more focus on high-quality evaluations of programs and intervention studies using designs that can be replicated at multiple sites with multiple populations (Zlotnik & Galambos, 2004). The social work manager is in an excellent position to develop evidence-based services and to foster EBP among supervisees by eliminating or reducing organizational barriers that prevent its adoption. The health care arena has embraced an evidence-based approach to practice. If social work is to remain a health care provider, the profession will need to follow suit.

Conclusion

Societal and marketplace demands will continue to influence health care organizations. As resources become scarcer, the health care environment will demand that services be delivered more efficiently and effectively. In addition, social workers will increasingly be expected to demonstrate that their services make a difference in health care.

Social work managers will be expected to adjust services and professional approaches to comply with regulations, economic conditions, and political realities. The successful manager will be able to practice in interdisciplinary/transdisciplinary teams while advocating for the unique contributions social work brings to health care.

Adjustments in services and approaches must be modified regularly to meet the demands of changing environments. Social work contributions must be evaluated regularly through environmental assessment and continuous quality improvement. To evaluate successful practice, the profession will need to embrace an evidence-based approach to practice. Using the skills and approaches outlined in this chapter will enable social work to continue to be an integral component of the health care team.

References

Corrigan, P. W., Streiner, L., McCracken, S. G., Blaser, B., & Barr, M. (2001). Strategies for disseminating evidence based practices to staff who treat people with serious mental illness. *Psychiatric Services, 52,* 1598–1606.

DeGroot, H. A. (2005). Evidence-based leadership: Nursing's new mandate. *Nurse Leader, 3*(2), 37–41.

Ferlie, E., & Shortell, S. M. (2001). Improving the quality of health care in the United Kingdom and the United States: A framework for change. *Milbank Quarterly, 79*(2), 281–316.

Franklin, C., & Hobson, L. M. (2007). Facilitating the use of evidence-based practice in community organization. *Journal of Social Work Education, 43,* 377–404.

Gambrill, E. (2006). Evidence-based practice and policy: Choices ahead. *Research on Social Work Practice, 16,* 338–357.

Gehlert, S., & Browne, T. (2006). *Handbook of health social work.* Hoboken, NJ: John Wiley & Sons.

Glisson, C., & James, L. R. (2002). The cross level effects of culture and climate in human services teams. *Journal of Organizational Behavior, 23,* 767–794.

Greene, R. R., Cohen, H. L., Galambos, C.M., & Kropf, N. P. (2007). *Foundations of social work practice in the field of aging.* Washington, DC: NASW Press.

Griffith, J. R., & White, K. R. (2002). *The well managed healthcare organization.* Chicago: Health Administration Press.

Hardcastle, D., & Powers, P. (2004). *Community practice: Theories and skills for social workers.* New York: Oxford.

Hemmelgarn, A. L., Glisson, C., & James, L. R. (2000). Organizational culture and climate: Implications for service and interventions research. *Clinical Psychology: Science and Practice, 13*(1), 73–89.

Hutchinson, A. M., & Johnston, L. (2004). Bridging the divide: A survey of nurses' opinions regarding barriers to, and facilitators of research utilization in the practice setting. *Journal of Clinical Nursing, 13,* 304–315.

Institute of Medicine. (2001). *Crossing the quality chasm: A new heath system for the 21st century.* Washington, DC: National Academy Press.

Jaskyte, K., & Dressler, W. W. (2005). Organizational culture and innovation in non-profit human service organizations. *Administration in Social Work, 29*, 23–41.

Kirst-Ashman, K. K., & Hull, G. H. (2000). *The macro skills workbook: A generalist approach*. Chicago: Nelson-Hall.

Mattaini, M. A., Lowery, C. T., & Meyers, C. H. (2002). *Foundations of social work practice: A graduate text*. Washington, DC: National Association of Social Workers.

Mesch, A. H. (1984). Developing an effective environmental assessment function. *Managerial Planning, 32*, 17–22.

Miller, R. L. (2001). Innovations in HIV prevention: Organizational and intervention characteristics affecting program adoption. *American Journal of Community Psychology, 29*, 621–647.

Porter-O'Grady, T., & Malloch, K. (2007). *Managing for success in health care*. St. Louis, MO: Mosby-Elsevier.

Ransom, S. B., Joshi, M. S., & Nash, D. B. (2005). *The healthcare quality book: Vision, strategy, and tools*. Washington, DC: Health Administration Press.

Rosen, A. (2003). Evidence-based social work practice: Challenges and promise. *Social Work Research, 27*, 197–208.

Rubin, A., & Parrish, D. (2007). Challenges to the future of evidence-based practice in social work education. *Journal of Social Work Education, 43*, 405–428.

Sackett, D. L., Straus, S. E., Richardson, W. S., Rosenberg, W., & Haynes, R. B. (2000). *Evidence-based medicine: How to practice and teach EBM*. London: Churchill Livingstone.

Schneider, R. L., & Lester, L. (2001). *Social work advocacy: A new framework for action*. Belmont, CA: Brooks/Cole.

Swayne, L. E., Duncan, W. J., & Ginter, P. M. (2006). *Strategic management of health care organizations*. Malden, MA: Blackwell.

Thomas, R. K. (2006). *Health communication*. New York: Springer.

U.S. Department of Health and Human Services. (2000). *Healthy people 2010: Understanding and improving health*. (2nd ed.). Washington, DC: U.S. Government Printing Office.

U.S. Office of Disease Prevention and Promotion. (2007). Health Communication. *Healthy People 2010* (Vol.1). Retrieved March 15, 2007, from http://healthy-people.gov/Document/HTML/volume1/11HealthCom.htm#.edn4

Weiss, R. M., & Gantt, V. W. (2004). *Knowledge and skill development in nonprofit organizations.* Peosta, IA: Eddie Bowers.

Zlotnik, J. L., & Galambos, C. (2004). Evidence-based practices in health care: Social work possibilities. *Health and Social Work, 29*(4), 257–352.

6

Competition and Cooperation Among Organizations Serving an Ethnic Community
The Case of the Hmong Suicide Prevention Task Force

Donna Hardina, Jane Yamaguchi, Xong Moua, Molly Yang, and Phoua Moua

New organizations often experience difficulties when they try to enter established social service networks. Competition for scarce resources and institutional pressures for new organizations to conform to community values and practices can limit entry for small organizations. This is particularly problematic for ethnic organizations, which often must rely on cooperative agreements with larger organizations or service networks to survive. Such linkages can adversely affect intergroup dynamics within the ethnic community.

In this chapter the authors define the term *ethnic social service organization*, and describe theories that explain the success or failure of social service networks. These theories are then applied to the case of the Hmong Suicide Prevention Task Force. This group was formed by female alumni and faculty of a master's degree program in social work in response to the suicides of eight Hmong teenagers in Fresno, California. The task force attempted to work collaboratively with local organizations to provide preventive counseling services for Hmong adolescents, but encountered resistance from a number of sources: established organizations, ethnic organizations serving the Southeast Asian community, and Hmong community leaders, who often excluded women from traditional decision-making processes.

In addition to the case study, the authors develop a theoretical model that can be used to assess the likelihood that ethnic organizations will enter established social service networks successfully. The implications of this case for administrative practice in social work are also discussed.

Ethnic Social Service Organizations

Ethnic organizations are often formed to provide services that mainstream social service organizations do not offer to members of specific ethnic communities. Often members of ethnic communities face insurmountable language and cultural barriers in applying for services from organizations that represent the dominant culture (Fung & Wong. 2007). In response, ethnic communities develop informal and formal services to serve their members (Hung, 2002). As defined by Iglehart and Becerra (2000), ethnic social service agencies have a majority of board members and staff who are of the same ethnicity as agency clientele and integrate culturally appropriate content into their service delivery process.

Iglehart and Becerra (2000) argue that, to survive in a resource-scarce environment, many ethnic organizations establish contractual relationships for service delivery with mainstream institutions or join existing organizational networks. Little is known about how competing organizations form the service networks necessary to survive or expand service capacity (Provan, Isett, & Milward, 2004). Complicating the competition for resources within ethnic communities may be culturally specific practices and beliefs that specify which members of the ethnic group should be included or excluded from service-related decision making (Yoshihama & Carr, 2002).

Interorganizational Theory and Ethnic Organization Formation

Ethnic organizations often develop explicitly in response to difficulties members of immigrant or historically oppressed ethnic groups experience in obtaining services from traditional nonprofit organizations or public agencies (Iglehart & Becerra, 2000). These traditional or mainstream organizations often integrate values and norms associated with the dominant culture into the service delivery process and, consequently, may deny service to members of socially stigmatized groups or force clients to adapt to the expectations of the organization (Cross & Friesen, 2005). In some instances, ethnic nonprofit organizations are formed to preserve the ethnic group's cultural heritage and to lobby for increased access to services or for greater inclusion in mainstream society (Hung, 2002).

Many ethnic organizations are mutual aid organizations and explicitly incorporate the values and culture of one primary ethnic group into their service delivery procedures (Iglehart & Becerra, 2000). Although fundraising for these organizations often originates within the community served, the monies raised may be insufficient to address the complex needs prevalent in many immigrant or historically oppressed communities. Consequently, many ethnic organizations seek funds from government agencies or foundations to supplement their annual budgets (Graddy & Chen, 2006).

Political economy theory suggests that organizations that serve unique or traditionally oppressed population groups can experience difficulty in obtaining adequate funding streams. According to Alexander (2000), "organizational survival is rooted not only in developing competence but also in the process of creating and maintaining support for their objectives among the public at large and in the broader interorganizational environment" (p. 289). Consequently, to acquire resources needed for organizational formation and maintenance, ethnic organizations often must establish collaborative relationships with local service delivery networks or subcontract with larger organizations to deliver services (Iglehart & Becerra, 2000). Such interorganizational relationships provide a degree of power to the ethnic social service organization by virtue of their ability to reach populations that are often inaccessible to mainstream organizations. Although cooperation with organizations outside the ethnic community can provide the key for economic survival, these ethnic organizations may actually compete for dollars and clients with other organizations serving the same ethnic group. They also may need to compete with organizations from outside the ethnic community with which they may seek to establish joint projects. Large, well-funded organizations have a competitive advantage in obtaining funds and, consequently, may dominate any collaborative arrangement with new organizations seeking to partner with others (Alter, 2000).

This competitive advantage can be best explained using institutional theory: New organizations are most likely to survive if they can establish that their goals and the services they deliver conform to values of community institutions and the larger society (Hasenfeld, 2000; Schmid, 2000). As a result, when an organization joins a community collaborative or contracts with larger organizations, it signals to other organizations that it is ready to comply with accepted rules of conduct. According to Alexander (2000), these organizations have few options for meeting the demands of the larger organizations with which they contract or network.

Resource dependency theory suggests, however, that ethnic organizations do have resources that can be used to reduce the power imbalance between them and the larger organizations with whom they interact. Graddy and Chen (2006) argue that the relationship between government and private contractors is often one of mutual dependence because of the limited availability of some types of specialized services. Ethnic organizations can provide unique services to members of their own communities because of their expertise in meeting the needs of that community. Economies of scale may make it cost prohibitive for larger organizations, especially government agencies, to provide such services.

Consequently, small ethnic organizations may achieve some competitive advantages in relation to providing specialized services to ethnic communities, especially in instances in which there are no service alternatives, demand for these services is great, and inclusion in community service networks is mandated by legislation or prescribed by government or foundation grants and contracts as a precondition of funding (Provan et al., 2004). However, there can be some disadvantages associated with bringing ethnic organizations into established networks of agencies that primarily provide services to the general population. According to Graddy and Chen (2006), due to variations in ethnic-specific management practices and service priorities, when agencies representing diverse ethnic groups attempt to coordinate services with larger networks, "network outputs will be more complex and harder to manage. The counteracting effects may cancel each other out" (p. 537).

Iglehart and Becerra (2000) identify a number of hazards that can have negative effects on relationships between ethnic organizations and large nonprofit or public organizations that typically contract with these smaller groups:

- The ethnic organization does not have access to all of the resources it needs for program operation or survival.
- Informal networks and formal organization arrangements within the ethnic community can perpetuate tensions about gender and social class.
- Efforts to establish interorganizational alliances for service delivery result in contracts for the ethnic agency, whereas mainstream public and nonprofit organizations remain unchanged, delivering services the ethnic community cannot use fully.

◆ Mainstream organizations can simply form alliances to acquire staff and other resources generated by the ethnic organization, leaving that organization unchanged and without sufficient resources to serve the ethnic community.

Given these hazards, the ability of new ethnic organizations to enter into meaningful partnerships with existing organizations can be quite limited. Provan and Milward (2001) argue that service delivery networks can only be judged effective if:

◆ The network provides most essential services.
◆ There are strong relationship ties among organizational members.
◆ New agencies are incorporated into the network as others leave it.

This paper examines the Hmong Suicide Prevention Task Force's efforts to establish an organizational entity with the capacity to provide services and advocate for the appropriate mental health services needed to address a suicide epidemic among Hmong teenagers between 2000 and 2002 in a western city. A task force generally consists of staff members or other representatives of organizations that serve the same community or target population, community leaders, and representatives of constituency groups. Task forces are intended to be time limited and are established to address unmet needs or urgent problems (Speer & Zippay, 2005). Often, task forces start out as informal groups and transition into formal collaborative partnerships (Hardcastle, Wenocur, & Powers, 2004).

Methodology

A case study, using a critical incidence approach, is used to examine the effectiveness of efforts by the Hmong Suicide Prevention Task Force to expand service capacity and establish interorganizational relationships. Critical incidence technique is a qualitative research method that involves exploring the perspectives of participants in community interventions (Hardina, 2002). It is associated with the use of participatory action research methods that involve taking action to promote social change and reflection on the efficacy of those actions by participants (Treleaven, 2001). Critical incidences are defined as events that make a "significant contribution, either positively or negatively to an activity or phenomenon" (Gremier, 2004, p. 66). The critical incident technique requires that participants record observations or be interviewed about their perspectives or experiences in relation to these events (Stitt-Gohdes, Lambrecht, & Redman, 2000). For this case study, data were obtained during a series of interviews with task force members, with those interviewed participating in subsequent analysis and interpretation of the data. Additional data sources include organization documents, meeting minutes, and personal interviews with participants to document their perceptions about events contributing to the development of the task force. Most of the data were collected between 2001 and 2002, during the initial stages of task force development.

The case study includes a brief history of Hmong immigration in the United States and the development of the Hmong Suicide Prevention Task Force to give background and context to the issues examined. This research also focuses on the three criteria for development of successful community networks identified by Provan and Milward

(2001): the capacity of the service delivery network, the strength of relationship ties among members, and the ability of the network to absorb new organizations.

Hmong Immigration and Assimilation in the United States

The Hmong are members of an agrarian culture that formerly lived in the mountains of Laos. Some of the Hmong fought alongside the Central Intelligence Agency (CIA) in the "secret war" in Laos, waged in conjunction with the Vietnam War. After the fall of Saigon, the Office of Refugee Resettlement immediately resettled some of the Hmong in the United States (Fadiman, 1997). Other Hmong families remained in Thai resettlement camps, gradually immigrating to countries outside Southeast Asia (Xiong, 2001).

Large concentrations of Hmong can be found in California, Wisconsin, and Minnesota, but assimilation for this population has been difficult. Seventy-six percent of Hmong are of limited English proficiency; people who lack fluency in English are twice as likely to live in poverty as other Americans. Some of the social problems associated with poverty have had a profound impact on the Hmong: substance abuse, depression, suicide, and domestic violence (Southeast Asian Prevention Intervention Network, 2003). The Hmong also experience high rates of interpersonal discrimination, including negative encounters with individuals, employment discrimination, and police harassment (Hein, 2000).

Although the Hmong experience in the United States is similar to that of other immigrant populations, traditional clan leadership patterns have provided a mechanism for addressing personal and economic crises (Moua, 2001). Hmong clans are rooted in patrilineal kinship and social networks that bind families. Members of each of the 18 clans share a surname, and clan leaders are almost always male and are generally appointed or selected (Moua, 2001). Although clan leaders in Laos were often village, military, or religious leaders, some clan leaders in the United States hold professional degrees and are skilled in facilitating communication between the Hmong community and the dominant culture and garnering resources that community members can use (Yoshihama & Carr, 2002).

The Hmong Suicide Prevention Task Force

In 2001, the Hmong Teen Suicide Prevention Task Force was formed in response to the suicides of eight Hmong teenagers during a 2-year period. This suicide cluster received little attention outside the affected community, and the factors that precipitated the deaths of these children were not always clear (Ellis, 2002a). Yang (2001) interviewed 14 Hmong parents about their perceptions of the causes of teen suicide. The parents viewed the act of suicides as shameful behavior that would disgrace the victim's family. They identified a number of factors as contributing to teen suicide, including poor communication between parents and adolescents, parental adherence to traditional culture and the teenager's need to conform to peer expectations, and parental pressure on the adolescent to succeed in school. Dating was also an area of concern; family status and conflicts among the various clans were additional factors in parental restrictions on adolescent relationships. Family dysfunction and sexual orientation issues appeared to play a role in some of the suicides (Ellis, 2000a).

Few if any of these families had been able to access mental health services from public or nonprofit organizations. Barriers to access included language, unfamiliarity with Western health and mental health practices, and distrust of health care professionals. Rather than seeking help from medical professionals, some families still prefer to obtain medical assistance from shamans, who often treat severe illnesses with herbs and healing rituals (Fadiman, 1997).

To develop a culturally appropriate response to the suicide crisis, four female Southeast Asian master's degree graduates of a social work program formed the task force in 2001. Members also included a Hmong clan leader who worked as a liaison between the county department of social services and the refugee community and a Hmong clinical psychologist. Two of the Hmong members of the task force had family members who had committed suicide. Social work faculty members and representatives of several nonprofit organizations that served the Hmong community were also among the task force's early members. Among the goals established for the task force were

- to increase community awareness about cultural issues in mental health care and suicide in the Southeast Asian community;
- to increase awareness about available services and resources for the Southeast Asian population; and
- to increase culturally appropriate mental health services to the Southeast Asian community.

The task force hoped to accomplish these goals through collaborating with established organizations. Specific objectives for the project included developing culturally appropriate educational materials about teen suicide; establishing a 24-hour crisis hotline; and offering suicide prevention workshops for parents, teens, and social service professionals. They also hoped to place a representative of the Southeast Asian community on the local county's mental health board. The Mental Health Board, a citizens' committee appointed by the Board of Supervisors, plays a major role in advising the county on resource allocation. Task force members reasoned that an appointment to this board would allow for greater advocacy and ultimately result in greater availability of inpatient and outpatient mental health services for the Hmong community.

Initially, the task force seemed well positioned to obtain operating funds. Representatives from a local coalition that advocated for improvements in mental health services for Latinos promised to assist with grant writing and contacts with funders. However, task force members faced many institutional barriers that limited the group's ability to develop organizational capacity and network with local organizations.

Assessing the Effectiveness of the Service Delivery Network

As described by Iglehart and Becerra (2000), ethnic organizations must establish relationships in multiple contexts to survive. To establish itself as a member of the service delivery network, the Hmong Suicide Prevention Task Force needed to form strong interorganizational linkages with local Hmong clan leaders, formal organizations established within the Hmong community, and local agencies and institutions such as county child welfare and mental health services and the local school district. In this section of the paper, the authors use the three criteria identified by Provan and Milward (2001), provision of essential services, strength of relationships among organizational members, and the ability of the system to incorporate new organizations, to examine the degree to which the task force was successful in developing these linkages.

Service Capacity of the Network

According to Iglehart and Becerra (2000), ethnic communities form their own agencies when organizations established to serve the general population fail to address the needs of the ethnic community. During the Hmong suicide epidemic, few of the public or nonprofit agencies were providing inpatient, psychiatric services for children and youth. Low state Medicaid reimbursement rates, shortages of qualified mental health staff, and an increase in demand for services forced long-established service providers to close their inpatient programs for children and youth (Forster & Gateway Psychiatric Services Staff, 2001). All psychiatric beds were licensed for adults only. Although some children and adolescents received outpatient services through juvenile hall, the child welfare system, or the county's mental health department, no in-patient services were available for adolescents.

Although the Hmong community had established four nonprofit organizations that primarily served Hmong clients, only one of the agencies, the family service organization affiliated with a national network, provided mental health services. These services were intended for adults only. In addition, few agencies, either public or private, actually had bilingual or bicultural staff members with professional degrees who were qualified to provide mental health services to Hmong children. Consequently, the service capacity of the existing network with which the task force attempted to link (both outside and within the Hmong community) was very low.

Organizational Ties

The two institutions with the service capacity to address the suicide issue were the county department of social services and the local school district. This school district primarily serves low-income and ethnic children. At the time of the task force was formed, neither of these institutions had Hmong staff qualified to address the suicide issue. Due to lobbying by the Hmong clan leader who served on the task force, the school district applied for and received a large federal grant to provide suicide prevention services to high school students. The grant also allowed the school district to develop training curriculum and provide suicide prevention workshops to local professionals, parents, and students (Ellis, 2002b).

As written, the grant provided funds for five Hmong licensed social workers to provide these services. However, the school district could not locate five licensed Hmong social workers. Subsequently, a Hmong MSW graduate who was one of the founding members of the task force was hired on a full-time basis. Largely due to the intervention of the clan leader who served on the task force, the county department of social services hired a second MSW graduate (also a task force founder) to provide child welfare services. Much of her practice involved suicide prevention services to Hmong adolescents. In addition, the task force placed one of its members on the county mental health board. Among the mental health board's duties was overseeing the provision of public mental health services and ensuring access to care for diverse populations.

The two positions with public agencies that held responsibility for addressing the suicide epidemic and designating a "Hmong" seat on the mental health board represented the formal linkages established with the larger social service network. In these positions, task force members developed successful programs and innovative service delivery methods to serve Hmong adolescents better. However, the task force experienced a number of difficulties in actually joining the larger network.

Integration of the Task Force into the Service Network

Despite these successes, the task force experienced difficulty in working within the Hmong community. Some of these problems related to the internal dynamics of the group. According to one Task Force member there were difficulties:

> identifying core group and leadership. [I] think some of the community folks came to the table with their own agenda and some of the early stages were focused on what the task group would try to do (e.g., provide services, education, research) and who was the service target [in community or mainstream systems].

Establishing a structure that would allow the task force to apply for funds was also problematic. To start applying for grants, task force members concluded they should approach one of the existing Hmong family service agencies about serving as a fiscal agent for the project. Subsequent to this decision, a memo of understanding (MOU) was negotiated with the agency. However, these negotiations proved difficult and ultimately unsuccessful. Representatives of the prospective fiscal agent wanted full control of the services to be provided by the task force, including hiring authority and contacts with potential funders. These lengthy negotiations resulted in depleting task force resources and membership, and discussing the implications of the MOU consumed much of the meeting time. One task force member described the problem:

> It does seem there is some jockeying for control, especially whenever possibility of monies comes up. Also a "passive/feet dragging" response to the group's requests at [the family services agency]. Beyond [the agency] I am led to wonder if there is sometimes some ambivalence in [the male members of the Task Group] work with [Hmong female task force members]—the gender thing. I don't know how much may be gender, how much may be clan and/or not being from the area.

Relationships established with the county department of social services and the local school board were more fruitful initially. Placing two task force members in staff positions enabled them to develop training material, disseminate knowledge to community residents and service and educational professionals, and provide information about the suicide epidemic to the media. One member of the task force was appointed to a seat on the school district advisory board established to monitor the use of the federal grant money received for suicide prevention. Using these institutional resources, the task force was able to hold a workshop on suicide prevention and cultural issues for county mental health and child welfare professionals and conduct a second workshop for Hmong parents and teenagers. Although the task force's efforts to contain the suicide crisis were largely successful, relations with these institutions were somewhat difficult. According to one task force member, these institutions could have allocated more resources to support its prevention efforts:

> The idea of ambivalence and turf come to mind; I was never really clear about those grants that [the school district] got and I doubt they were eager to share/contract out from what has been said. Some of the "natural" support that might come through these organizations would be to allow [the task force members working for the school district and the county department of social services] to represent the organizations or to send a representative [to task force and other collaborative meetings]. That has not been. So it seems that the major systems that would serve/interface with the target group really have not been at the table. Thus we get to the grantwriting issue of interested citizens versus collaboration of agencies—and the latter is more likely to get funding.

Even with these difficulties, the task force was able to obtain a permanent "Hmong seat" on the county mental health board, advocate successfully for an increase in Hmong staff in a county mental health program that served children, obtain local and national media coverage of the suicide issue, develop a culturally appropriate curriculum on the suicide, and provide essential resources and staff support to local institutions so the suicide crisis was alleviated. Although there were numerous suicide attempts among Hmong teens, there were only one or two confirmed suicides in the 4 years following formation of the task force.

However, the task force was unable integrate its services with the other organizations in the network. Despite pressure from some of the clan leaders that it do so, the task force was unable to establish a workable fiscal agent relationship with the Hmong family organization that would have allowed the task force to apply for grants. Although a state agency attempted to broker an agreement among the task force, the family social service agency, and the school district to apply for funds and operate programs collaboratively, the task force withdrew from what it perceived to be an arrangement that was unproductive and had a low probability of success. The task force eventually dissolved, and the Hmong social service agency hired one of its members to provide adolescent health services on a part-time basis.

Discussion: Developing a Theoretical Framework for Network Analysis

Provan and Milward (2001) have identified increased service capacity, the entry of new organizations into existing service networks, and the strength of interorganizational ties as the three primary indicators of the success of interorganizational networks. In the case of the Hmong Suicide Prevention Task Force, establishing strong interorganization ties proved to be elusive. Traditional decision-making patterns in the Hmong community made it difficult for a group of female professionals to enter into a working partnership with community leaders. Competition with the already established Hmong organizations created a situation in which the task force was viewed as a potential competitor, albeit a competitor with resources (steering committee members knowledgeable about suicide prevention and contacts with potential funders) that could be used to benefit other Hmong social service agencies. Organizations outside the Hmong community, such as the school board and the county department of social services, were also eager to acquire the resources of the task force. However, the overall weakness of all three types of interorganizational ties and the task force's inability to acquire funds and full-time staff contributed to its marginalization within both the Hmong and mainstream service delivery networks.

TABLE 1   THE IMPACT OF RELATIONSHIP TIES ON SERVICE CAPACITY AND THE ENTRY OF NEW
           ORGANIZATIONS INTO THE SERVICE SECTOR

Strength of Interorganizational Relationships	High	Low
Strength of intragroup ties	Development of services across gender and class boundaries	Inability to offer services for all community members regardless of gender and class
Strength of the relationship among ethnic organizations	Cooperative working agreements within the community	Competition among ethnic agencies
	Ability to negotiate reciprocal partnership agreements with mainstream institutions	Limited community power to develop service partnerships with larger mainstream institutions that will benefit the ethnic community
	New organizations started within the ethnic community	Limited opportunities to form new organizations
Strength of the relationship between ethnic and mainstream organizations	Creation of strong interorganizational networks that include ethnic and mainstream organizations	Limited collaboration among ethnic organizations and local institutions
	Entry of new organizations into large networks of ethnic and nonethnic organizations	Failure of ethnic organizations to survive
	Partnership agreements with outside organizations that benefit all agency partners	Cooptation of ethnic organizations or acquisition of their resources
	Increased service capacity	Limited capacity to service the ethnic community

Building on the work of both Provan and Milward (2001) and Iglehart and Becerra (2000), we can use the case of the Hmong Suicide Prevention Task Force to create a theoretical framework to explain the success or failure of ethnic organizations in interorganizational networks. Strong relationship ties within ethnic communities can be expected to stimulate the development of services across traditional boundaries of class and gender in such communities. Conversely, weak ties can create a situation in which women and other community members are excluded from decision making. In turn, few services are developed to meet their needs (Yoshihama & Carr, 2002).

Strong relationship ties among ethnic organizations serving the same community are more likely to foster good working relationships, collaborative agreements among these groups that aid service delivery, the ability to acquire critical resources, and the power to bargain with local institutions for reciprocal service agreements that benefit the ethnic community as a whole. Alternatively, weak relationship ties among these organizations result in competition for scarce resources and limit the ability of new organizations to enter the service delivery system within the ethnic community (see Table 1).

Strong ties between ethnic and local institutions foster interorganizational networks that include a mix of ethnic and mainstream organizations, allow the entry of new organizations into the network to replace those organizations that have declined or ended operation, and increase the network's capacity to provide services the ethnic community requires. Weak ties, on the other hand, can result in larger institutions outside the ethnic community coopting and dominating ethnic organizations or mainstream organizations eager to deliver services to the ethnic community acquiring the ethnic groups' resources. The inability of ethnic organizations and these institutions to form strong working relationships limits the ability of the network to provide critical services or allow for the development of culturally competent services by mainstream social service organizations.

Implications for Administrative Practice

Institutional theory suggests that, to survive in a competitive interorganizational environment, new organizations must adapt to the demands of network members and the large institutions that play a large role in sustaining the network (Schmid, 2000). In the case of the task force, its members were required to work cooperatively with two large institutions representing the dominant culture (the school board and the county department of social services) as well as the smaller network of Hmong organizations. The fact that most of the task force members were women and included members who are not Hmong made it difficult for this group to adapt to the expectations of the smaller network, despite the resources it was able to provide. Because the Hmong family service agency had a formal structure and some legitimacy with Hmong clan leaders, it was in a better position to develop a cooperative relationship with institutions outside the Hmong community.

The implications of these findings are that organizations developed to serve the interests of specific ethnic populations are difficult to orchestrate because of competition for scarce resources, weak ties to organizations within and outside the ethnic community, and expectations that the new organization adapt to community norms and traditional decision-making patterns (Iglehart & Becerra, 2000). In contrast, emerging ethnic organizations can establish linkages with larger, established institutions that are eager to exchange resources for access to the ethnic community (Graddy & Chen, 2006). However, such linkages may require ethnic organizations to conform to the expectations and requirements of larger institutions that serve the general population. In some instances, smaller network members may be absorbed by larger organizations or excluded from the network as other members acquire the expertise and capacity to deliver specialized services to ethnic groups.

Conclusions

The case of the Hmong Suicide Prevention Task Force illustrates the difficulties of developing new service organizations in a competitive funding environment. One of the options available to emerging organizations is to exchange service expertise for resources provided by larger, established social service organizations or networks. Although new agencies can be integrated successfully into service networks, and service delivery capacity enhanced, the experience of the task force indicates that these relationships are complex; in some cases the potential hazards of such relationships for small organizations may not outweigh the risks: losing organizational identity or surrendering resources to the larger organizations that dominate the network (Graddy & Chen, 2006; Iglehart & Becerra, 2000). For the large organizations that anchor service networks, their failure to establish working partnership with small ethnic organizations with the expertise to deliver specialized services means that these organizations may never develop the capacity to meet market demand for services to emerging communities. Managers exploring options for joining or creating organizational networks should carefully examine the potential effects of service coordination plans on their organizations.

References

Alexander, J. (2000). Adaptive strategies of nonprofit human service organizations in an era of devolution and new public management. *Nonprofit Leadership and Management, 10*(3), 287–303.

Alter, C. (2000). Interorganizational collaboration in the task environment. In R. Patti (Ed.), *The handbook of social welfare management* (pp. 283-302). Thousand Oaks, CA: Sage.

Cross, T., & Friesen, B. (2005). Community practice in children's mental health: Developing cultural competence and family-centered services in systems of care models. In M. Weil (Ed.), *The handbook of community practice* (pp. 442–459). Thousand Oaks, CA: Sage.

Ellis, A. (2002a, August 11). Lost in America. *Fresno Bee* (Special supplement).

Ellis, A. (2002b, November 18). Funds help Hmong teens. *Fresno Bee*, A1.

Fadiman, A. (1997). *The spirit catches you and you fall down.* New York: Farrar, Straus and Giroux.

Forster, P., & Gateway Psychiatric Services Staff. (2001). *Psychiatric hospital beds in California: Reduced numbers create system slow-down and potential crisis.* Sacramento, CA: California Institute for Mental Health.

Fung, K., & Wong, Y.R. (2007). Factors influencing attitudes toward seeking professional help among east and Southeast Asian immigrant and refugee women [Electronic version]. *International Journal of Social Psychiatry, 53,* 216–231.

Graddy, E., & Chen, B. (2006). Influences on the size and scope of networks for service delivery. *Journal of Public Administration Research and Theory, 16,* 533–552.

Gremier, D. (2004). The critical incident technique in service research. *Journal of Service Research, 7*(1), 65–89.

Hardcastle, D., Wenocur, S., & Powers, P. (2004). *Community practice: Theories and skills for social workers* (2nd ed.). New York: Oxford University Press.

Hardina, D. (2002). *Analytical skills for community organization practice.* New York: Columbia University Press.

Hasenfeld, Y. (2000). Social welfare administration and organizational theory. In R. Patti (Ed.), *The handbook of social welfare management* (pp. 89-112). Thousand Oaks, CA: Sage.

Hein, J. (2000). Interpersonal discrimination against Hmong Americans. *The Sociological Quarterly, 41,* 413–429.

Hung, C. R. (2002). *Asian American participation in civil society in U.S. metropolitan areas.* Paper presented at the 2002 Annual Meeting of the Association for Research on Nonprofit Organizations and Voluntary Action, Montreal, Canada, November 14–16.

Iglehart, A., & Becerra, R. (2000). *Social services and the ethnic community.* Prospect Heights, IL: Waveland Press.

Moua, X. (2001). *Hmong clan leaders' roles and responsibilities.* Unpublished master's thesis. Department of Social Work Education, California State University, Fresno.

Provan, K., Isett, K., & Milward, H. B. (2004). Cooperation and compromise: A network response to conflicting institutional pressures in community mental health. *Nonprofit and Voluntary Sector Quarterly, 33,* 489–515.

Provan, K., & Milward, H. B. (2001). Do networks really work? A framework for evaluating public-sector organizational networks. *Public Administration Review*, *61*(4), 414–423.

Schmid, H. (2000). Agency-environment relations: Understanding task environments. In R. Patti (Ed.), *The handbook of social welfare management* (pp. 133–154). Thousand Oaks, CA: Sage.

Southeast Asian Prevention Intervention Network. (2003). *Is welfare reform a trigger for chemical use/abuse, mental illness, and family violence?* Retrieved March 5, 2002, from http://www.laofamily.org/health/archives/s_spring.htm

Speer, P., & Zippay, A. (2005). Participatory decision-making among community coalitions: An analysis of task group meetings. *Administration in Social Work*, *29*(3), 61–77.

Stitt-Gohdes, W., Lambrecht, J., & Redmann, D. (2000). The critical-incident technique in job behavior research. *Journal of Vocational Education Research*, *25*(1). Retrieved December 26, 2007, from http://scholar.lib.vt.edu/ejournals/JVER/v25n1/stitt.html

Treleaven, L. (2002). The turn to action and the linguistic turn: Towards an integrated methodology. In P. Reason & H. Bradbury (Eds.), *The handbook of action research: Participative inquiry and practice* (pp. 261–272). Thousand Oaks, CA: Sage.

Xiong, C. (2001). *An exploratory study of Hmong perceptions on herbal medicine in treating diabetes.* Unpublished master's project, Department of Social Work Education, California State University, Fresno.

Yang, M. (2001). *Understanding Hmong parents perception of adolescent suicide.* Unpublished master's project, Department of Social Work Education, California State University, Fresno.

Yoshihama, M., & Carr, E. (2002). Community participation reconsidered: Feminist participatory action research with Hmong women. *Journal of Community Practice*, *10*(4), 85–103.

III   Specialized Managerial Processes
Leon H. Ginsberg

Social work managers carry out a number of specialized functions, not all of which are related to the services social workers provide.

One of the premier social work research programs is the Institute for the Advancement of Social Work Research, directed by Joan Levy Zlotnik, the first—and only—director of the organization, who provides her insights in chapter 7. She has a rich background with the two premier social work organizations, the National Association of Social Workers and the Council on Social Work Education. Increasingly, research is a part of the function of every social work agency and institution, and financing of social work programs and social work education is tied, in many instances, to research projects. This book is fortunate to have Dr. Zlotnik as one of its contributors.

A current trend and, in some ways, a priority in social work is evidence-based work, especially evidence-based social work practice. Bowen McBeath and Harold Briggs of Portland State University's School of Social Work are leaders in scholarship about evidence-based work, which they describe in chapter 8. They apply concepts they have developed to evidence-based management, a notion that is new to some and is on the frontiers, in many ways, of social work leadership and management.

Lawrence Martin has studied and written extensively in the social work and management literature on purchasing social services, which he covers in chapter 9. Such purchasing is a central part of nonprofit organization financing in the United States. His insights provide some special guidance to those who are or want to become involved in selling their services to government entities.

A relatively new concern for social work managers is investing their funds. With endowments and diverse funding streams, fiscal management of social work programs becomes more complicated. In chapter 10, Raymond Sanchez Mayers and Fontaine H. Fulghum offer some insights on that subject.

7

Managing Social Work Research

Joan Levy Zlotnik

Today, the role of research in delivery of health and human services programs is growing in importance as managers and administrators focus on enhancing organizational, program, management, supervisory, and staff effectiveness; carry out evaluations addressing both process and outcome variables; and identify culturally relevant, best practices in specific and intersecting fields of social work practice. The current focus on implementing evidence-based practices, sweeping across medicine, nursing and social work, and other disciplines, suggests that managers need to understand research and its applications and to keep abreast of research findings.

The social work profession has a long history of doing research; however, there have been continual tensions between researchers and practitioners. This occurs because the service-delivery community perceives that the research currently underway is not necessarily relevant to its needs, that insufficient attention is paid to translating research into practice, and that researchers perceive that practitioners do not use the findings from empirical research. Therefore, social work managers have critical roles to play as consumers of research, creators of practice-relevant research agendas, and managers of research programs or research centers.

To provide guidance to managers and to those who teach managers, this chapter
* identifies current trends in social work research;
* connects research efforts to evidence-based practice;
* provides examples of information on research resources and funding opportunities;
* suggests ways that agencies and universities can partner to conduct and apply research findings, including community-based research strategies;
* provides information on human participant protections and research ethics; and
* makes recommendations to strengthen the connections between research and practice.

Understanding the Social Work Research Perspective

A 1951 committee of the Social Work Research Group, one of the founding organizations of the National Association of Social Workers (NASW), defined the function of research in a helping profession as providing "a body of verified knowledge directed toward increasing and extending the effectiveness of service to client and community" (Social Work Research Group, 1951, p. 3). Types of research enumerated include

- Determination of need for services
- Evaluation of the adequacy and effectiveness of services
- Investigation of the content of social work processes
- Investigation of the competence required for various operations
- Validation of social work theory and concepts
- Development of methodology and tools for research in social work
- Investigation of the development and sometimes decline of social work services, programs and concepts
- Translation and testing of theory or knowledge drawn from other fields. (Social Work Research Group, 1951, p. 3)

These functions and types are as true today as they were more than a half-century ago.

Definition

Social work research, as defined by the Institute for the Advancement of Social Work Research (IASWR), addresses psychosocial problems; treatment of acute and chronic conditions; and community, organizational, policy, and administrative issues. Covering the life span, social work research benefits consumers, practitioners, policymakers, educators, and the general public by examining prevention and intervention strategies for health and mental health, child welfare, aging, substance abuse, community development, managed care, housing, economic self-sufficiency, and family well-being; studying the strengths, needs, and interrelationships of individuals, families, groups, neighborhoods, and social institutions; and providing evidence for improved service delivery and public policies (IASWR, 2003a). Although examining these issues is not specific to the social work domain, social work's person-in-environment perspective often provides a unique approach to addressing the complex variables and interactions that have implications at the individual practice and policy levels.

Methodology and Study Design

Social work research uses multiple methods, including quantitative and qualitative modalities and ranging from case studies, to surveys, to quasi-experimental designs (with a study and comparison group), to experimental designs where recipients of the intervention to be studied are assigned randomly. Study designs such as community-based participatory research (CBPR) and action research engage consumers and communities more fully in design and implementation and are increasing in popularity.

Social workers engage in program evaluation, frequently evaluating agency-based program innovations. As computer software and statistical data analysis become more sophisticated, it also becomes easier to determine the causal relationships among multiple variables, for example, relationships between length of stay in care and time of entry for foster children, or differential health outcomes related to health disparities.

Analysis of administrative data and of complex surveys, including a range of government surveys (see Box 1 for several sites for such data), can yield important information to guide service delivery, policy, and program planning.

Box 1
EXAMPLES OF DATA SOURCES

Administration on Aging Statistics on the Aging Population:
http://www.aoa.gov/PROF/Statistics/statistics.asp

Bureau of Labor Statistics Occupational Outlook: http://www.bls.gov/oco/home.htm

Census Bureau: http://www.census.gov/

Chapin Hall-Data Systems for Policy Research:
http://www.chapinhall.org/category_editor.aspx?L2=66

Child Welfare Information Gateway, Child Maltreatment Reports:
http://www.childwelfare.gov/pubs/factsheets/canstats.cfm

National Center for Health Statistics: http://www.cdc.gov/nchs/

Office of Applied Statistics, SAMHSA: http://www.oas.samhsa.gov/

Different study designs require different sample sizes, time frames, and funding levels. A manager implementing a research study that includes program evaluation needs to assess carefully which question or questions need to be answered to ascertain what type of study(ies) should be undertaken to best find the answers. Useful information to expand the manager's knowledge of research and research methods and research grant writing can be found at the following Web sites:

- http://www.socialresearchmethods.net/kb/, a Web site put together by William Trochim, a policy professor at Cornell University;
- http://sophia.smith.edu/~jdrisko/qualres.htm, a Web site maintained by James Drisko, a social work professor at Smith College School for Social Work on qualitative research;
- http://www.theresearchassistant.com/index.asp provides a tutorial for behavioral and social science researchers developing research grants, especially to the National Institute on Drug Abuse;
- http://www.biomed.lib.umn.edu/inst/research.pdf provides an overview of designs for clinical research studies; and
- http://www.grants.gov/help/relatedlinks.jsp provides comprehensive information on applying for federal grants and links to numerous other resources about grant writing and research grants.

Current Trends in Social Work Research

As government funding for social and health programs grew over the last century, public funding for social science research, including social work research, also expanded.

Although many foundations support testing innovative and model service delivery strategies, they provide only limited support for full-scale research studies. Funding for innovations, however, usually includes some modest support for program evaluation. The American Cancer Society, Lance Armstrong Foundation, Robert Wood Johnson Foundation, W. T. Grant Foundation, and John A. Hartford Foundation are examples of foundations that support social work research.

The growth of social welfare programs has also seen the creation of local-, state-, and national-level think tanks (e.g., Urban Institute, Brookings Institution, Chapin Hall Center for Children) that undertake social welfare research and program evaluation, often under contract with federal agencies, foundations, and/or service providers, especially large public agencies. Some national associations, for example, the Child Welfare League of America, Council on Social Work Education (CSWE), National Association of State Mental Health Program Directors Research Institute, and American Association of Homes and Services for the Aging have research programs, but frequently they focus more on gathering information and data from and for their own members than on addressing broader issues related to interventions and practice improvements.

National Institutes of Health Support for Social Work Research

National Institute of Mental Health. Since its post–World War II inception, the National Institute of Mental Health (NIMH) has supported the social work profession. It has made major investments training social workers and periodically attempted to examine the research enterprise in the social work profession (Zlotnik, 2008).

In the late 1980s, concerned that there was insufficient attention to knowledge development for social work practice, NIMH funded the Task Force on Social Work Research (TFSWR), which examined the status of research and research training in social work. The task force's work culminated in the publication of the landmark *Building Social Work Knowledge for Effective Services and Policies: A Plan for Research Development* (TFSWR, 1991), and a declaration that there was a crisis in the profession. This resulted in a commitment from social work education and practice organizations—NASW, CSWE, Association of Baccalaureate Social Work Program Directors, Group for the Advancement of Doctoral Education, and National Association of Deans and Directors of Schools of Social Work—to create the Institute for the Advancement of Social Work Research (IASWR).

The TFSWR's reported its recommendations to the NIMH'S National Advisory Mental Health Council, which endorsed the recommendations and directed NIMH to help move the recommendations forward. The developments in social work research since 1993 have been documented (IASWR, 2003a; Zlotnik, Biegel, & Solt, 2002; Zlotnik & Solt, 2006). Both NIMH and the National Institute on Drug Abuse (NIDA) created special social work research infrastructure development programs (Zlotnik, 2008). The success of the social work research center at Washington University led to funding of its Center for Mental Health Services Research (CMHSR; grant # P30 MH068579), which examines the quality of care for persons with mental disorders who are served in nonmental health settings, for example, child welfare and nursing homes, recognizing that service delivery is challenged by "competing demands, co-occurring psychosocial problems, and resource constraints" (CMHSR, 2008).

NIH Plan for Social Work Research. In 2003 Congress requested that the National Institutes of Health (NIH) develop a plan and agenda for social work research (NIH, 2003). Recognizing the value of social work research to NIH's mission to protect and improve the public's health, the plan provided an overview of NIH's investments in social work research and proposed nine recommendations. The trans-NIH social work research working group under the leadership of the NIH Office of Behavioral and Social Sciences Research has worked within NIH and with the social work community to develop and implement these recommendations. Actively involved in developing and implementing the plan are NIMH, NIDA, National Institute of Alcohol Abuse and Alcoholism, National Cancer Institute, National Institute on Aging (NIA), National Institute on Nursing Research, and National Institute on Child Health and Human Development along with the National Heart, Lung, and Blood Institute; the Office of Women's Health Research; and the Office of AIDS Research. Of particular importance were the 3 December 2005 program announcements encouraging *Research on Social Work Practice and Concepts in Health* (http://grants1.nih.gov/grants/guide/pa-files/PA-06-081.html [R01]; PA-06-234 [R03] and PA-06-233 [R31]). Since 2003, NIH has hosted summer research methods institutes on social work research to encourage grant submissions. Topics have included qualitative and mixed methods research, community-based participatory research, and interventions research.

The expanded visibility and activity of social work research at NIH includes funding close to 600 social work research grants since 1993, resulting not only from the output of those 14 schools with NIMH and NIDA funded-research centers, but also from other university- and community-based (e.g., Lighthouse for the Blind) researchers who are making major contributions to our knowledge base. A directory of NIH social work researchers is available on the IASWR Web site. It can be searched by topic to identify the diverse areas, that is, HIV/AIDS; criminal justice; homelessness; cancer survivorship, poverty; and lesbian, gay, bisexual, and transgender (LGBT) issues that the social work research community addresses (IASWR, 2008).

Other Federal Support for Social Work Research

Although NIH is the largest funding source for research, other federal agencies also provide research grants to support studies relevant to social work research and social services delivery. Several of these agencies also have other discretionary grant programs that provide incentives to test new models of service delivery, including the National Institute of Justice; Centers for Disease Control and Prevention (CDC); Bureau of Maternal and Child Health; Administration for Children and Families (ACF) (including the Head Start Bureau, Child Care Bureau, and Children's Bureau); Department of Education; Department of Housing and Urban Development; Department of Homeland Security; Department of Defense; and National Science Foundation. In 2006, CDC developed its first trans-CDC research agenda, *Advancing the Nation's Health: A Guide to Public Health Research Needs, 2006–2015,* (CDC 2006), http://www.cdc.gov/od/science/PHResearch/cdcra/AdvancingTheNationsHealth.pdf, which provides many relevant priorities that social workers might pursue.

Social Work Research Organizations: Roles and Resources

Since the inception of IASWR and the subsequent creation of the Society for Social Work and Research (SSWR) in 1994, both with initial funding support from NIMH, social work research has achieved greater visibility within the profession and in the policy arena, and efforts to strengthen the research/practice connections have expanded.

Institute for the Advancement of Social Work Research. IASWR is a 501(c)3 organization based in Washington, D.C., that strengthens the research capacity of the social work profession; promotes the use of social work research to improve practice, program development, and policy; and enhances the voice of the profession in the national scientific community and in public policy determinations (IASWR, 2003a).

IASWR works at the national level as a facilitator, transmitter, translator, conduit, and advocate connecting the social work profession with federal agencies that fund research, especially NIH, and works with other national organizations that represent other disciplines (e.g., the American Psychological Association), service provider groups (e.g., the American Public Human Services Association), consumers (Anxiety Disorders Association of America), and advocates to highlight the importance of research. IASWR is an active member of the Consortium of Social Science Associations and the Coalition for the Advancement of Health Through Behavioral and Social Sciences Research.

One important role for IASWR is in research agenda development and research synthesis. With support for government agencies and foundations, IASWR has hosted

---

Box 2
RESEARCH AGENDA REPORTS (AVAILABLE FROM HTTP://WWW.IASWRESEARCH.ORG)

• Enhancing the Health and Well-Being of LGBT Individuals, Families, and Communities: Building a Social Work Research Agenda (supported by the Gill Foundation)

• Factors Influencing Retention of Child Welfare Staff: A Systematic Review of Research (supported by the Annie E. Casey Foundation)

• Social Work's Contribution to Research on Cancer Prevention, Detection, Diagnosis, Treatment and Survivorship (supported by the National Cancer Institute)

• Social Work Contributions to Public Health: Bridging Research & Practice in Preventing Violence—Lessons from Child Maltreatment & Domestic Violence (supported by CDC's National Center for Injury Prevention and Control)

• Evaluating Social Work Services in Nursing Homes: Toward Quality Psychosocial Care and Its Measurement (supported by the Agency for Healthcare Research and Quality and the Institute for Geriatric Social Work)

• Partnerships to Integrate Evidence-Based Mental Health Practices into Social Work Education and Research (supported by NIMH)

meetings and prepared reports on the state of social work research related to long-term care, LGBT populations, child welfare workforce, public health, and evidence-based practice (see Box 2). These reports emerged from numerous sources, including meetings of key stakeholders including managers and administrators, direct practitioners and researchers.

Another major role for IASWR is providing technical assistance and training to build the research infrastructure for the profession, especially in social work education programs at the BSW, MSW, and doctoral levels. Summer research methods workshops in Washington, DC, have included university faculty, staff from research centers and think tanks, and service-providing agencies. In 2003, Casey Family Services contracted with IASWR to provide regional training for social work faculty to make them more competitive in responding to requests for applications to carry out research studies. The IASWR Web site provides PowerPoint presentations from conference sessions on how to apply for federal research grant funding as well as links to numerous Web sites related to research funding and research findings (see Box 3).

Box 3
SOURCES FOR RESEARCH OPPORTUNITIES AND RESEARCH FINDINGS

- American Cancer Society
- Center for Retirement Research at Boston College
- Center for the Advancement of Health
- Child Welfare League of America
- Child Trends
- Children's Defense Fund
- Community-Campus Partnerships for Health
- Consortium of Social Science Associations
- Decade of Behavior—FundSource
- HandsNet
- Institute for Women's Policy Research

- Joint Center for Poverty Research
- Justice Research and Statistics Association
- National Association of State Mental Health Program Directors Research Institute
- National Center for Children in Poverty
- National Data Archive on Child Abuse and Neglect
- Society for Women's Health Research
- The Society for the Study of Social Problems
- Urban Institute
- Welfare Information Network
- Welfare Watch

IASWR publishes a weekly e-alert service, *IASWR Listserv Announcements* (see Figure 1), which uses a social work lens to provide information to the field on research funding opportunities, calls for papers for conferences and publications, information on upcoming conferences, new research findings, and important reports.

FIGURE 1   INFORMATION ON THE IASWR LIST SERVER

INSTITUTE FOR THE ADVANCEMENT OF SOCIAL WORK RESEARCH

IASWR

IASWR LISTSERV ANNOUNCEMENTS

*Compiled as a resource to advance social work education, practice,
and policy through social work research.
For more information about IASWR visit www.iaswresearch.org. See information below
on how to subscribe and how to request inclusion of your announcement in future issues.*

IN THIS ISSUE—CLICK BELOW TO GO DIRECTLY TO SECTION

- **CALLS**
- **CALLS FOR NOMINATIONS**
- **CONFERENCES/TRAINING**
- **FUNDING OPPORTUNITIES**
- **NEWS AND NOTICES**
- **ONLINE RESOURCES**
- **PUBLICATIONS**
- **RESEARCH FINDINGS**

To Subscribe to the IASWR Listserv:
Send email to LISTSERV@LISTSERV.SC.EDU
Leave subject line blank and
type in message area:

*Subscribe IASWRLST, then type
your firstname and lastname.*

Another useful resource is on the NASW Web site, http://www.socialworkers.org. IASWR offers a monthly topical review of research related to areas of social work practice. Visit http://www.socialworkers.org/research/naswResearch/0108KeepingUp/default.asp to view topics such as aging, psychosocial care in nursing homes, addictions, veterans, disasters, and posttraumatic stress disorder, among many others.

Launched in 1994, the Society for Social Work and Research (SSWR) (www.sswr.org) is an individual membership organization of close to 1,500 social work researchers with an annual conference that provides a learning and networking venue. The conference focuses on disseminating research findings and teaching research methods. SSWR membership includes a subscription to either *Research on Social Work Practice* or *Social Services Review* as well as a planned e-journal to be launched in the near future.

Evidence-Based Practice

Service providers are increasingly under scrutiny to demonstrate that they are providing evidence-based practices (EBP). To identify evidence-based practices, the social worker should identify the intersection of finding and assessing the best available research evidence, applying his or her ethical practice and critical thinking, and starting where the client is to ensure that the intervention fits with the client's culture, community and wishes. This three-legged definition is important, as EBP is not just about applying research findings to practice. Gibbs' (2003) definition of EBP:

> placing the client's benefits first, evidence-based practitioners adopt a process of lifelong learning that involves continually posing specific questions of direct practical importance to clients, searching objectively and efficiently for the current best evidence relative to each question, and taking appropriate action guided by evidence. (p. 6)

Two different meanings are often used, and confused, with regard to EBP: one defines an approach to answering a question about practice and suggests that the practitioner pursue an evidence-based approach. The second meaning of EBP relates to specific evidence-based practices. Terms such as *empirically supported interventions* and *evidence-informed interventions* may be used as well. Differentiating from the evidence-based practice process described above, Drake and his colleagues define evidence-based practice as a practice that has been established as effective through scientific research according to a set of explicit criteria (Drake et al., 2001). Of particular importance is the idea of "explicit criteria." Different efforts to define EBPs use different criteria that can be ascribed to the level of evidence. For example, during its launch, the California Evidence-Based Clearinghouse for Child Welfare (see http://www.cachildwelfareclearinghouse.org/), needed to determine explicitly and transparently the criteria it be use for different levels of evidence. See Box 4 for an example of defining levels of evidence.

In an effort to strengthen the connections between research and practice, in April 2007, NIMH hosted *Partnerships to Integrate Evidence-Based Mental Health Practices into Social Work Education and Research*, a symposium bringing together representatives from social work education, practice, and research, along with consumers and service providers, to examine the meaning of EBP for the profession and to identify models in use in social work education programs to teach students about evidence-based mental health practices. (The report from the symposium is available at www.iaswresearch.org.) Although it was clear that the research base is insufficient to ensure enough research to inform all areas of social work practice, there are a number of ongoing partnerships between universities and agencies that provide training about EBPs to students and practitioners at, for example, the University of Michigan, University of Southern California, Washington University, Columbia University, and in all of the MSW programs in New York state (IASWR, 2007).

In implementing evidence-based practices, it is unlikely that each individual practitioner has the time or resources to undertake a thorough literature search, review many research journals, and assess the adaptability and adoptability of specific interventions that have been well researched. Thus, Appendix 1 provides Web resources that can be useful to agencies and practitioners in implementing evidence-based practices.

Box 4
THE CALIFORNIA EVIDENCE-BASED CLEARINGHOUSE FOR CHILD WELFARE
(http://www.cachildwelfareclearinghouse.org/)

Specific criteria for each classification system category:

Well-Supported by Research Evidence

♦ There is no clinical or empirical evidence or theoretical basis indicating that the practice constitutes a substantial risk of harm to those receiving it, compared to its likely benefits.

♦ The practice has a book, manual, and/or other available writings that specify components of the service and describes how to administer it.

♦ Multiple Site Replication: At least two rigorous randomized controlled trials (RCTs) in different usual care or practice settings have found the practice to be superior to an appropriate comparison practice. The RCTs have been reported in published, peer-reviewed literature.

♦ In at least one RCT, the practice has shown to have a sustained effect at least one year beyond the end of treatment.

♦ Outcome measures must be reliable and valid, and administered consistently and accurately across all subjects.

♦ If multiple outcome studies have been conducted, the overall weight of the evidence supports the benefit of the practice.

Supported by Research Evidence

♦ There is no clinical or empirical evidence or theoretical basis indicating that the practice constitutes a substantial risk of harm to those receiving it, compared to its likely benefits.

♦ The practice has a book, manual, and/or other available writings that specifies the components of the practice protocol and describes how to administer it.

♦ At least one rigorous randomized controlled trial (RCT) in usual care or a practice setting has found the practice to be superior to an

appropriate comparison practice. The RCT has been reported in published, peer-reviewed literature.

♦ In at least one RCT, the practice has shown to have a sustained effect of at least 6 months beyond the end of treatment.

♦ Outcome measures must be reliable and valid, and administered consistently and accurately across all subjects.

♦ If multiple outcome studies have been conducted, the overall weight of evidence supports the benefit of the practice.

Promising Research Evidence

♦ There is no clinical or empirical evidence or theoretical basis indicating that the practice constitutes a substantial risk of harm to those receiving it, compared to its likely benefits.

♦ The practice has a book, manual, and/or other available writings that specifies the components of the practice protocol and describe how to administer it.

♦ At least one study utilizing some form of control (e.g., untreated group, placebo group, matched wait list) has established the practice's benefit over the placebo, or found it to be comparable to or better than an appropriate comparison practice. The study has been reported in published, peer-reviewed literature.

♦ If multiple outcome studies have been conducted, the overall weight of evidence supports the benefit of the practice.

Lacks Adequate Research Evidence

♦ There is no clinical or empirical evidence or theoretical basis indicating that the practice constitutes a substantial risk of harm to those receiving it, compared to its likely benefits.

♦ The practice has a book, manual, and/or other available writings

that specifies the components of the practice protocol and describes how to administer it.

♦ The practice is generally accepted in clinical practice as appropriate for use with children receiving services from child welfare or related systems and their parents/caregivers.

♦ The practice does not have any published, peer-reviewed study utilizing some form of control (e.g., untreated group, placebo group, matched wait list) that has established the practice's benefit over the placebo, or found it to be comparable to or better than an appropriate comparison practice.

Evidence Fails to Demonstrate Effect

♦ Two or more randomized controlled trials (RCTs) have found the practice has not resulted in improved outcomes, when compared to usual care. The studies have been reported in published, peer-reviewed literature.

♦ If multiple outcome studies have been conducted, the overall weight of evidence does not support the benefit of the practice.

Concerning Practice

♦ If multiple outcome studies have been conducted, the overall weight of evidence suggests the intervention has a negative effect upon clients served;

and/or

♦ There is a reasonable theoretical, clinical, empirical, or legal basis suggesting that the practice constitutes a risk of harm to those receiving it, compared to its likely benefits.

Transporting Research Into Practice

A critical aspect of the EBP process in which managers must be well versed relates to strategies to transport research and evidence-based practices to new settings. To accomplish this, many organizational, staffing, and training issues need to be taken into account. For example, if an aging agency is interested in helping elderly clients decrease their risk of falling, the agency might go through several steps. The first would be to identify what is known about fall prevention research and assess the quality of that information and its applicability to the new setting. The second is to look at what staff training, workload, and service delivery parameters might need to be changed and/or developed to adopt and adapt this new practice. The third relates to evaluation. In adopting and adapting a research-based intervention into practice, it is important to evaluate the intervention carefully so the program manager can understand what worked and did not work and how that information might relate to the intervention itself; to the knowledge and characteristics of the staff that implemented it; or to the characteristics of the client(s), community, and culture where it was implemented.

University/Community Partnerships

Many agencies may not necessarily have the expertise or time to carry out research. University faculty have the expertise, and they need to build a research portfolio and demonstrate their service to both the profession and the community. This sets a context for promoting university/agency research partnerships. Furthermore, because many community agencies serve as field instruction sites for BSW and MSW students, there may also already be a relationship between the agency and the university. Thus, establishing research partnerships between agencies and the university, especially for social work programs, can provide a win-win situation. Research partnerships might focus on evaluation of a project or program, or they might include a needs assessment and information-gathering process. One example would be the University of Maryland School of Social Work's collaboration with the state Department of Human Resources and local Departments of Social Services to examine the factors that effect the recruitment, selection and retention of child welfare workers, (see http://www.family.umaryland.edu/ryc_research_and_evaluation/child_welfare_research_files/cwwrsrs10-07.htm).

To carry out effective research partnerships successfully, the partners should consider a number of issues so the process is as smooth as possible.

- What mechanisms will allow for ongoing and regular communications?
- Who owns the data and who will have access to the data, both in undertaking the specific study and after the study is complete?
- Who owns the study and the subsequent report?
  - Will the academic partner(s) be able to publish results of the study in peer-reviewed publications?
  - Will the agency have the right to halt publication of the study or change reporting of some of the data?

- How will authorship of the study and subsequent reports be determined?
- What if the outcome of the study does not positively support the agency program(s) and/or processes for implementation?
- What are the requirements for Institutional Review Board (IRB) approval?
  - Did the agency assist with the development of the university IRB application?
  - Does the agency have its own IRB or other requirements related to human subjects' participation in research?

CBPR

CBPR is

collaborative approach to research that equitably involves all partners in the research process and recognizes the unique strengths that each brings. CBPR begins with a research topic of importance to the community, has the aim of combining knowledge with action and achieving social change to improve health outcomes and eliminate health disparities. (Community-Campus Partnerships for Health, 2008).

With the growing interest in determining what works best for whom and under what conditions, there is increased interest by numerous research funders, including NIH, CDC, and the Lance Armstrong Foundation, in supporting CBPR models (see Box 5). There is also a lot of interest in CBPR in research related to environmental issues. By its very intent, such research deals with complexity of settings and relationships that need to be built and sustained over time. Although some of the driving forces for model development are in the health care arena, such research models are equally applicable to child welfare, criminal justice, and aging settings.

Box 5
CBPR Principles

- Recognizes community as a unit of identity
- Builds on strengths and resources within the community
- Facilitates collaborative, equitable involvement of all partners in all phases of the research
- Integrates knowledge and intervention for mutual benefit of all partners
- Promotes a colearning and empowering process that addresses social inequalities
- Involves a cyclical and iterative process
- Addresses health from both positive and ecological perspectives
- Disseminates findings and knowledge gained to all partners
- Involves long-term commitment by all partners (Israel, Schulz, Parker, & Becker, 1998)

Community-Campus Partnerships for Health (CCPH) (http://depts.washing-ton.edu/ccph/commbas.html#Principles) maintains an excellent Web site with multiple resources related to CBPR, including reports and presentations, examples of funded proposals, peer-reviewed journal articles, syllabi and course materials, online curricula, electronic discussion groups, principles and policies, memoranda of under-standing, and ethics and institutional review board (IRB) issues. Under electronic discussion groups you can sign up for several resources, including a daily digest of in-formation and resources related to CBPR. This list server was launched in June 2004 through a partnership between Community-Campus Partnerships for Health and the Wellesley Institute to serve the growing network of people involved and interested in CBPR. To subscribe, go to: https://mailman.u.washington.edu/mailman/listinfo/cbpr.

One example in the field of aging that uses a CBPR framework is the Cornell Institute for Translational Research on Aging (CITRA), funded by the NIA in October 2003 as one of the six Edward R. Roybal Centers for Translational Research on Aging (www.citra.org). CITRA has developed a useful model to create researcher/practi-tioner consensus conferences to help address the research/practice gap and to promote implementation of evidence-based practices and practice-informed research.

Research Ethics and Human Participant Protection

When planning a research study, participating in a study, and reporting the findings of a study research ethics issues must be considered. The *Code of Federal Regulations* (CFR) Title 45 Part 46 guides the involvement of human participants in research and the use of IRBs to review and approve research studies and protocols. The IRB or ethics research committee is a federally mandated peer review committee: The 1979 Belmont Report (National Commission for the Protection of Human Subjects of Biomedical and Behavioral Research, 1979) lays out the three principles that under-gird ethical research practices:

1. Respect: Treat each person as a free individual and with dignity.
2. Beneficence: Do good and avoid harm.
3. Justice: Treat people fairly.

Before launching a study, the researchers need to determine whether living individ-uals will be involved: Will these individuals provide data? Will they interact with the researchers? Will they provide identifiable private information? For some studies that include secondary review of data, IRB approval may not be required; however, this should be reviewed carefully. This is especially true in situations of low incidence, for example, in looking at county-level data where the one HIV-positive person in a small rural community might be identified through the analysis. In universities, it is impor-tant for researchers to learn how to complete an IRB proposal and it is useful to serve on an IRB committee. IRBs increasingly include community participants, especially if many community agencies and community settings are involved in the research. When involving community participants in IRBs, it is useful to address time, training, and compensation (see http://www.researchethics.org/Conference_Recommendations.pdf). Due to the concerns about research ethics and research integrity, efforts were undertaken to educate academic and community partners better about research ethics. Useful resources can be found in Box 6. Issues of particular interest to social workers relate to the extent to which certain populations can provide informed consent about research participation. For example, a researcher studying LGBT teens would have to address the issue of informed consent without parental involvement (IASWR, 2005).

Box 6
RESOURCES ON RESPONSIBLE CONDUCT OF RESEARCH AND RESEARCH ETHICS

CSWE National Statement on Research Integrity in Social Work
(http://www.cswe.org/NR/rdonlyres/B69B1FCB-8773-4CAA-8846-
A28F4658090A/0/csweORIbrochure.pdf)

Office of Human Research Protections (http://ohrp.osophs.dhhs.gov)

The Belmont Report
(http://ori.dhhs.gov/education/products/mass_cphs/training_staff/RCReng/RCRBelmo
ntReport.htm)

Ethical Standards and Procedures for Research With Human Beings
(http://www.who.int/ethics/research/en/)

On Being A Scientist: Responsible Conduct in Research
(http://www.nap.edu/html/obas/)

Open Seminar on Research Ethics (http://openseminar.org/ethics/)

Ethics and Research in the Community
(http://ori.dhhs.gov/education/products/mass_cphs/training_staff/RCReng/RCRHome.htm)

Research Next Steps

The NIH and CDC have increased their focus on translational research. Although one level of translation addresses moving research from genes and animals (often referred to as the bench) to real people in clinical settings (often referred to as the bedside), the second level of translation from the bedside to real people in community settings, and with complex needs, is a perfect venue for future social work research efforts. NIH has hosted several meetings on dissemination and implementation science, and Abrams (2007) has articulated the need for systems-level research perspectives and the need to address multiple levels of analysis, from the cell to policy. Addressing how research and policy coincide and/or collide is another area for social work research.

With increased focus on accountability, creating sustainable models for community/university research partnerships also needs more attention. The Children's Bureau has funded several quality improvement center grants (http://www.acf.hhs.gov/programs/cb/programs_fund/discretionary/dis_index.htm) that provide models for system and service improvement through using research and evidence-based practices.

Support to continue such models and to disseminate and create venues to further adapt and evaluate what works also will be critical. Social work education programs and community agencies need to see research partnerships as integral to their functioning, just as field education is integral to social work.

The next decade will see more advances in technology and science, as well as strains on society from the greater disparity in incomes of the rich and the poor; a long war in Iraq and Afghanistan that creates new challenges for those who are serving and those who have experienced trauma and injury; a growing older population that demands the attention of the social work profession; and continued encroachment on the professional roles and identities of social workers. All of these issues provide the stimulus for a robust research program. Thus IASWR, in partnership with its fellow social work organizations and service providers and consumer advocates, will need to secure research funding to support behavioral and social sciences research, to train excellent researchers, and to provide mechanisms to move research to practice and model practices to research.

References

Abrams, D. (2007). Behavior bridges biology and society: Toward systems integration., Keynote address, Consortium of Social Sciences Associations Annual Meeting. Retrieved March 20, 2008, from http://www.cossa.org/annualmtg/COSSA.Abrams.12.07.pdf

Center for Mental Health Services Research (CMHSR). (2008). Description of Center for Mental Health Services Research, Brown School, Washington University. Retrieved March 23, 2008. from http://gwbweb.wustl.edu/cmhsr/cmhsr_overview.html

Centers for Disease Control and Prevention (CDC). (2006). *Advancing the nation's health: A guide to public health research needs, 2006–2015.* Retrieved March 24, 2008 from http://www.cdc.gov/od/science/PHResearch/cdcra/AdvancingTheNationsHealth.pdf

Community Campus Partnerships for Health. (2008). Definition of community-based participatory research. Retrieved August 31, 2008 from http://depts.washington.edu/ccph/commbas.html

Drake, R. E., Goldman, H., Leff, H. S., Lehman, A., Dixon, L. Mueser, K et al. (2001). Implementing evidence-based practices in routine mental health settings. *Psychiatric Services, 52*(2), 179–182.

Gibbs, L. (2003). *Evidence-based practice for the helping professions: A practical guide with integrated multimedia.* Pacific Grove, CA: Brooks/Cole

Institute for the Advancement of Social Work Research (IASWR). (2003a). *Institute for the Advancement of Social Work Research: 1993–2003.* Retrieved March 24, 2008, from http://www.charityadvantage.com/iaswr/IASWR10th%20AnniversaryReport.pdf

Institute for the Advancement of Social Work Research (IASWR). (2003b). *Social work contributions to public health: Bridging research & practice in preventing violence—Lessons from child maltreatment & domestic violence.* Retrieved March 20, 2008, from http://www.iaswresearch.org

Institute for the Advancement of Social Work Research (IASWR). (2003c). *Social work's contribution to research on cancer prevention, detection, diagnosis, treatment and survivorship.* Retrieved March 20, 2008, from http://charityadvantage.com/iaswr/NCIFinalRep91503.pdf

Institute for the Advancement of Social Work Research (IASWR). (2005). *Enhancing the health and well-being of LGBT individuals, families, and communities: Building a social work research agenda.* Retrieved March 24, 2008, from http://charityadvantage.com/iaswr/LGBTFINALREPORT.pdf

Institute for the Advancement of Social Work Research (IASWR). (2007). *Partnerships to integrate evidence-based mental health practices into social work education and research.* Retrieved February 28, 2008, from http://charityadvantage.com/iaswr/EvidenceBasedPracticeFinal.pdf

Institute for the Advancement of Social Work Research (IASWR). (2008, February). *Directory of social work research grants awarded by the National Institutes of Health, 1993–2007.* Retrieved March 20, 2008, from http://www.charityadvantage.com/iaswr/NIHSWRDatabasemarch3008.pdf

Israel, B., Schulz, A., Parker, E., & Becker, A. (1998). Review of community-based research: Assessing partnership approaches to improve public health. *Annual Review of Public Health, 19,* 173–202.

National Commission for the Protection of Human Subjects of Biomedical and Behavioral Research. (1979). *The Belmont report.* Retrieved February 28, 2008, from http://ori.dhhs.gov/education/products/mass_cphs/training_staff/RCReng/RCRBelmontReport.htm

National Institutes of Health (NIH). (2003). *NIH plan for social work research.* Retrieved February 29, 2008, from http://obssr.od.nih.gov/Documents/Publications/SWR_Report.pdf

Social Work Research Group. (1951, May). *The function and practice of research in social work.* A report to the Social Work Research Group. Available from the Social Welfare Archives, University of Minnesota–Twin Cities.

Task Force on Social Work Research. (1991). *Building social work knowledge for effective services and policies: A plan for research development.* Retrieved March 20, 2008, from http://www.iaswresearch.org

Zlotnik, J. L. (2008). Research: History of research. In T. Mizrahi & L. Davis (Eds), *Encyclopedia of social work* (20th ed.), pp. 521–526. Washington, DC: NASW & Oxford Press.

Zlotnik, J. L., Biegel, D. E., & Solt, B. E. (2002). The Institute for the Advancement of Social Work Research: Strengthening social work research in practice and policy. *Research on Social Work Practice*, 12(2), 318–337.

Zlotnik, J. L., & Solt, B .E. (2006). The Institute for the Advancement of Social Work Research: Working to increase our practice and policy evidence base. *Research on Social Work Practice*, 16(5), 534–539.

APPENDIX 1
Useful Resources on Evidence-Based Practice

California Evidence-Based Clearinghouse for Child Welfare. The California Evidence-Based Clearinghouse for Child Welfare provides up-to-date information on evidence-based child welfare practices and facilitates use of evidence-based practices to achieve improved outcomes of safety, permanency, and well-being for children and families involved in the California public child welfare system (http://www.cachildwelfareclearinghouse.org).

Cancer Control PLANET. The Cancer Control PLANET (plan, link, act, network with evidence-based tools) portal provides access to data and resources that can help planners, program staff, and researchers to design, implement, and evaluate evidence-based cancer control programs (http://cancercontrolplanet.cancer.gov/).

Centers for Disease Control and Prevention Community Guides. These guides provide evidence-based recommendations for programs and policies to promote population health and can be useful to professionals addressing a broad array of topics, from alcohol, to cancer, to motor vehicle accident prevention, to sexual health (http://www.communityguides.org).

Cochrane Collaboration. The Cochrane Collaboration is an international, nonprofit organization that produces and disseminates systematic reviews of health care interventions. (www.cochrane.org).

Campbell Collaboration. The Campbell Collaboration is an international, nonprofit organization that reviews the effectiveness of behavioral, social, and psychological interventions in social welfare, criminal justice, and education (www.campbellcollaboration.org).

Evaluation Center at Human Services Research Institute. The Evaluation Center@HSRI is a national technical assistance center dedicated to adult mental health systems change. The Center provides technical assistance in evaluation to states and nonprofit public entities for improving the planning, development, and operation of adult mental health services. The toolkits give users access to some of the most current approaches and instructions on how to implement sound evaluation studies. Toolkits are available in Outcomes Measurement, Evaluation Methodology and Statistics, Managed Care, Performance Measurement & Quality, Internet Evaluation Issues, Multicultural Issues in Evaluation, and Evidence-based Practices (http://www.tecathsri.org).

Evidence-Based Practice and Child Welfare in the Context of Cultural Competency. In June 2007, the University of Minnesota School of Social Work, in collaboration with Casey Family Programs, convened a seminar that brought together judges, legislators, family members, practitioners, administrators, researchers, and educators to address the intersections of EBP and child welfare and cultural competence. The report from the meeting and recommendations for future steps and a video conference are available at http://ssw.cehd.umn.edu/img/assets/27477/Susan%20Wells%20Transcript.pdf.

National Alliance of Multi-Ethnic Behavioral Health Associations. The mission of NAMBHA is to collectively promote the behavioral well-being and full potential of people of color and to eliminate disparities in behavioral health services and treatment. NAMBHA identifies culturally appropriate best practice models (http://www.nambha.org/).

National Association of State Mental Health Program Directors Research Institute (NRI). NRI has useful information about defining evidence-based practices, a directory of several resources that describe criteria for defining which practices are evidence-based, and important information for implementing evidence-based mental health practices. For more information, visit NRI, Inc.'s Center for Mental Health Quality and Accountability at http://www.nri-inc.org/projects/CMHQA/criteria_epb.cfm.

National Implementation Research Network. The National Implementation Research Network (NIRN) seeks to close the gap between science and service by improving the science and practice of implementation in relation to evidence-based programs and practices. NIRN conducts implementation research and creates practical implementation frameworks to guide the transformation of behavioral health systems (http://nirn.fmhi.usf.edu/).

National Resource Center on Evidence-Based Prevention Programs for the Elderly. The center is a nationally recognized source of timely and useful information on evidence-based disability and disease prevention programs for community providers of services to the aging (http://www.ncoa.org/content.cfm?sectionID=11&detail=957).

National Working Group on Evidence-Based Health Care. The National Working Group on Evidence-Based Healthcare represents consumers, caregivers, practitioners, and researchers committed to promoting accurate and appropriate evidence-based policies and practices that improve the quality of health care services in the United States (http://www.evidencebasedhealthcare.org).

Evidence-Based Practice for the Helping Professions. This extensive site is a resource for social workers who want to learn about EBP and how to conduct a search of evidence (http://www.evidence.brookscole.com).

Social Care Institute for Excellence. This is comprehensive resource on developing evidence and using evidence-based practices was created to provide a knowledge base of what works best for people who use social care (http://www.scie.org.uk).

Substance Abuse and Mental Health Services Administration (SAMHSA) National Registry of Evidence-Based Programs and Practices (NREPP). The recently redesigned NREPP supports informed decision making and disseminates timely and reliable information about interventions that prevent and/or treat mental and substance use disorders. A searchable online registry, NREPP allows users to access descriptive information about interventions as well as peer-reviewed ratings of outcome-specific evidence across several dimensions. It also provides information to a range of audiences, including service providers, policymakers, program planners, purchasers, consumers, and researchers (http://www.nrepp.samhsa.gov/).

Substance Abuse and Mental Health Services Administration's (SAMHSA) Center for Mental Health Services' (CMHS) Evidence-Based Practice Implementation Resource Kits. SAMHSA/CMHS has developed six toolkits to guide implementation of mental health evidence-based practices. The toolkits contain information sheets for all stakeholder groups, introductory videos, practice demonstration videos, and a workbook or manual for practitioners. The toolkits cover Illness Management and Recovery, Assertive Community Treatment, Family Psychoeducation, Supported Employment, and Integrated Dual Diagnosis Treatment (http://mentalhealth.samhsa.gov/cmhs/communitysupport/toolkits).

What Works Clearinghouse. Funded by the U.S. Department of Education, this clearinghouse provides educators, policymakers, and the public with a central, independent, and trusted source of scientific evidence of what works in education (http://www.w-w-c.org/).

Blueprints for Violence Prevention. This is Office of Juvenile Justice and Delinquency Prevention (OJJDP) identification of research-based effective programs (http://www.colorado.edu/cspv/blueprints/index.html).

8

Designing Client-Centered, Performance-Based Human Service Programs

Bowen McBeath and Harold Briggs

In response to public calls for greater accountability and budget reductions, policymakers have recently attempted to improve the cost-effectiveness of major social programs serving individuals and families. Federal and state agencies are requiring human service organizations to submit performance reports and identify mechanisms that improve the effectiveness and cost-efficiency of their major programs (Smith, 2003). Policymakers have encouraged service providers to develop innovative, performance-based programs, often by incorporating performance-based and managed care mechanisms into local agencies' purchase-of-service contracts (Courtney, 2000). Thus, in order to receive public funding, agencies have been pressured to develop high-performing human service programs.

Attention to program performance and innovation has elicited varying responses from human service providers. Some agencies have sought to implement *evidence-based programs* to improve client outcomes, particularly in child welfare, medical, mental health, and substance abuse service areas (Chaffin & Friedrich, 2004; Gray, 2001; Norcross, Beutler, & Levant, 2005). In some jurisdictions, service providers are required to use evidence-based programs instead of other service approaches. Because many of these interventions have proved to be efficacious in small-scale, randomized clinical trials, some believe that strict fidelity in implementing them will lead to enhanced program performance over time.

For example, in 2003 the Oregon legislature passed an evidence-based programming requirement law (Senate Bill [SB] 267) that requires specific state agencies to dedicate increasing proportions of their biennial budgets to evidence-based programming. According to the law, an evidence-based program is an efficacious intervention whose components are based on scientific research, including the use of systematic, empirical methods that draw on experiments or observation; rigorous data analysis methods to test formal hypotheses; and measures, research designs, and/or observational methods that allow for reliable and valid data collection. Under the law the state departments of Corrections and Human Services, the Oregon Commission on Children and Families, and the Oregon Youth Authority are required to devote 25%

of their program funding to evidence-based programs in 2005–2007, 50% in 2007–2009, and 75% in 2009–2011.

Other human service providers have attempted to improve program performance and innovation by avoiding the so-called program recipe approach common to evidence-based programs. Instead, some agencies have developed programs that tailor service provision to the specific attributes of individual clients. These *client-centered service approaches* have been influenced by the rise of the consumer advocacy movement in the mental health and developmental disability service sectors (Gowdy, Rapp, & Poertner, 1993; Segal, Silverman, & Temkin, 1993). Client-centered programs generally avoid serving individuals and families in a standardized manner, preferring to adapt services to clients' needs, strengths, and cultural values. It is expected that providing culturally appropriate, tailored services will improve client well-being and, by extension, program outcomes.

The human service managerial role is critical in both approaches, but is substantially different in each. In the evidence-based program framework, the manager must select an appropriate therapeutic intervention and then implement it properly (Fixsen, Naoom, Blasé, Friedman, & Wallace, 2005). The managerial role becomes one of eliminating barriers to program implementation and adhering to an established treatment protocol prescribed by the original program designers and researchers, which is generally in the form of a manual detailing intervention components and forms to use while implementing specified program procedures. Under the client-centered service approach, however, the manager must ensure that frontline staff respond to different client conditions and integrate client preferences with the best available evidence. Human service managers in client-centered programs are instrumental in reducing administrative, supervisory, and frontline barriers to individualized care.

This chapter first introduces evidence-based and client-centered programming approaches and reviews the implications of each for human service managers. Although each approach promotes program performance by seeking to enhance client outcomes, these approaches are not necessarily appropriate for the same organizational and client contexts. This chapter describes the conditions under which each approach should be used. The second half of the chapter provides an integrated framework supporting the development of client-centered, performance-based human service programs. In addition, principles for human service managers and system administrators are introduced using examples from foster care, a field of child welfare practice within the human service sector.

Current Approaches to Improving Human Service Program Performance

Evidence-Based Programming

The terms evidence-based practices, evidence-based treatments, and evidence-supported interventions may be used interchangeably to refer to the evidence-based program approach to human service delivery. To be considered an evidence-based program, a specific therapeutic intervention must be delivered in strict accordance with a program manual and evaluated under randomized clinical trial conditions (Walker, Briggs, Koroloff, & Friesen, 2007). The National Institutes of Health; private accrediting bodies, including the Joint Commission and the Council on Accreditation; and professional membership organizations such as the National Association of Social Workers, National Association of Public Child Welfare Administrators, and American Psychological Association have promoted the evidence-based programming model. As a result, the evidence-based programming approach represents the gold standard of efficacy and scientific credibility in the major human service fields of practice, including child welfare, mental health, and substance abuse (Zlotnick, 2007).

The evidence-based programming approach has been adopted based in part on the purported effectiveness of individual evidence-based programs. Overall, one might argue that individuals enrolled in an evidence-based program will have more positive outcomes than will those receiving standard services. Specific clinically focused interventions have been shown to be more effective in reaching certain client outcomes than usual services (Gibbs & Gambrill, 2002; Gorey, Thyer, & Pawluck, 1998). The evidence-based programming approach offers numerous potential benefits to human service providers: individual evidence-based programs can be adopted wholesale, as their specific intervention components have been developed in advance; such programs have proved to be more effective than some common alternative services. The approach thus appears to promise relief to human service providers struggling to improve client outcomes.

The evidence-based program approach requires that managers attend to the processor of program selection, implementation, and sustainment. Initially, managers must select an evidence-based program. This step requires them to identify a program need related to a specific outcome for a particular client population (e.g., undesirably low parent-child reunification rates among African American families in foster care) (APA Presidential Task Force on Evidence-Based Practice, 2006; Roberts & Yeager, 2004). The manager then uses electronic search engines and databases to identify a list of potential interventions suitable for the specific context and collects evidence from peer-reviewed journal articles and other reports concerning the relative effectiveness of each intervention. Weighing the evidence for or against each intervention allows the manager to select an evidence-based program based on its clinical suitability and evidence of its impact.

Managers are then involved in implementing the intervention. Managers may face personnel and organizational barriers as they implement evidence-based programs in real-world, agency-based environments. Agency staff may need to be trained in delivery of the new program, and agency supervisors may need to ensure that staff adhere to program models (Corrigan, Steiner, McCracken, Blaser, & Barr, 2001; Fixsen et al., 2005). The specific formulation of most EBPs may also limit providers' ability to integrate evidence-based programs with other service delivery techniques they have become accustomed to using (Gold, Glynn, & Mueser, 2006; Kauffman Foundation, 2004). Additionally, because service providers often must bear administrative and programmatic start-up costs, managers seeking to implement evidence-based programs may need to tap agency financial reserves or secure additional funding in advance.

These staff-related and programmatic start-up costs may cause difficulty during program implementation.

Once an evidence-based program has been implemented, its delivery must be sustained over time. Managers must ensure that the intervention continues to be delivered in accordance with its program manual. Given the high turnover rates in the human service sector, managers may need to devote considerable effort to recruiting, training, and supervising new staff in evidence-based programs. Because such programs are rarely appropriate across a wide range of client populations and with large numbers of clients, it is possible for program effectiveness to change if program parameters are altered in response to heavy demand for services and/or client enrollment patterns (Mullen, 2006). Therefore, managers will need to ensure that program eligibility criteria and carrying capacity are not changed over time, particularly if administrators want to improve program performance by increasing the number of clients who use the intervention.

The evidence-based program approach is therefore appropriate for use in only certain practice and agency-based environments. Managers must ensure that any evidence-based program they choose is clinically appropriate for the intended client population and has demonstrable client outcomes. Additionally, the evidence-based program must be able to be implemented faithfully in the particular organizational environment. Appropriate financial and staffing resources must also be available for managers to begin and sustain the delivery of the evidence-based program. If these conditions cannot be met, then the effectiveness of the evidence-based program approach may be reduced.

Client-Centered Service Models

Critiques of evidence-based programming have arisen as the approach has gained support among policymakers and has been incorporated into human service systems. One criticism suggests that few if any evidence-based human service programs have substantial, positive effects on clients; most programs, it is argued, have insubstantial effects (Farabee, 2005). Scholars who have generally dismissed this argument have referred to the Campbell and Cochrane Collaborations' systematic reviews of evidence-based human service programs. Based on these reviews, one cannot make conclusive statements concerning the ineffectiveness of evidence-based human service programming across different client populations (Rubin & Parrish, 2007).

A better-supported criticism concerns evidence-based programs' inability to individualize services in response to different client needs and cultural values. Evidence-based programs may be unable to respond to common client needs and conditions, particularly when used with culturally diverse client populations. Some programs, due to their one-size-fits-all approach—in which all participants receive an identical manualized intervention—may be inappropriate for use with certain cultural groups (Weisz, Jensen-Doss, & Hawley, 2006). Additionally, many evidence-based interventions were developed without the assistance or inclusion of minority clients (Aisenberg, in press; U.S. Department of Health and Human Services, 2001). Researchers' historic exclusion of different minority groups may limit the appropriateness of these programs for individuals from culturally diverse backgrounds. The appropriateness and effectiveness of specific evidence-based programs for different minority populations are therefore uncertain.

This critique has given impetus to the client-centered service perspective. In the human service sector, low-income, minority clients often receive services, and program outcomes for this population are regularly poorer than those for Caucasian individuals and families (Agency for Healthcare Research and Quality, 2003; Hoagwood, Burns, Kiser, Ringeisen, & Schoenwald, 2001). For example, African American children are less likely to leave foster care for permanent placements, such as reunification and adoption, and are more likely to return to care (U.S. General Accountability Office, 2007). Given the disproportionate involvement of racial and ethnic groups in the human service sector (Hill, 2007; Wulczyn & Lery, 2007), it is important for programs to be compatible with the service expectations of culturally dissimilar groups.

Although the evidence-based programming approach cannot easily incorporate client input or different race- and ethnicity-based preferences into service delivery, client-centered service approaches—including the evidence-based process (Gambrill, 2006) and evidence-based management (Kovner & Rundall, 2006) models—specifically incorporate client preferences in service planning. Each model draws from the evidence-based medicine model (Eddy, 2005; Guyatt & Rennie, 2002; Sackett, Straus, Richardson, Rosenberg, & Haynes, 2000) in which service providers integrate the best available evidence, client wishes, available resources, and their clinical expertise before making practice decisions. Evidence is construed broadly and includes standard evidentiary approaches common to the evidence-based programming approach, including data from randomized clinical trials and meta-analyses. The client-centered service approach, however, also refers practitioners to data from direct clinical observation, case studies and qualitative research, and quasi-experimental research (APA Presidential Task Force on Evidence-Based Practice, 2006). These models allow the practitioner to tailor services to culturally distinctive client needs and values (Gibbs, 2007), and thus are more appropriate for diverse client populations than is the evidence-based programming approach. The client-centered approach is thus intended to integrate patient characteristics, culture, and values with empirical approaches to clinical care.

Managerial responsibilities under a client-centered service approach differ considerably from those in an evidence-based programming environment. Under the former, human service managers may view programs as unfinished prototypes and may have to adapt programs to suit the specific attributes and needs of diverse clients. Programmatic changes may be facilitated by trial-and-error experimentation and the use of information systems with real-time program, staff, and client-level data (Pfeffer & Sutton, 2006; Robbins & DeCenzo, 2004). Rather than wait until a manualized intervention has been delivered fully and a program evaluation has been completed before making programmatic changes, managers may make midstream corrections in response to changing agency conditions and new information. Similarly, managers may be able to adopt specific components of evidence-based programs, alter programs during the implementation process, and discontinue clinical programs if field-based evidence suggests they are ineffective or that different services may better suit the client population (Newhouse, 2006; Walshe & Rundall, 2001; Woolston, 2005).

Commitment to organizational change, program improvement, and learning from clients and staff are essential managerial components of client-centered service delivery. Managers must evaluate the appropriateness of services, track changes in client needs and staff activities, and identify whether changes in service delivery improve client outcomes. These tasks are similar to those required of managers in the learning organization (Senge, 1990) and continuous quality improvement (Daft, 2003) management models.

In principle, the client-centered service delivery perspective is appropriate for organizational contexts in which managers are able to develop and shape programs in response to client needs, staff attributes, and empirical knowledge. Agencies are also more likely to engage in client-centered programming if they have integrated information systems that allow regular monitoring of staff activities, service provision, and client outcomes, and if they have experimented previously with different service delivery approaches to improve client outcomes (Johnson & Austin, 2006; Pfeffer & Sutton, 2006).

Designing Client-Centered, Performance-Based Human Service Programs

In principle, human service managers should seek to integrate evidence-based programming and client-centered service approaches, thereby benefiting from the strengths of each perspective. This section provides a number of principles relevant to the design and management of client-centered, performance-based human service programs. These recommendations are anchored by two normative assumptions. First, child welfare agencies must provide socially just services to individuals and families, and one way to do so is to tailor services to client needs and cultural preferences. Second, because human service providers have to demonstrate improvements in client outcomes and program performance, managers must take the issue of governance seriously.

These assumptions are described in more detail, and practice recommendations in different technical areas are presented, below. Given our analytical focus on individuals and families served by human service providers, these recommendations necessarily concern managerial work. Yet, because laws, policies, and markets shape and constrain human service activity (McBeath, 2006; Wells, 2005), higher-order suggestions are presented concerning the administration of human service agencies and multiagency human service systems.

Ensuring Socially Just Service Provision: Principles for Human Service Managers

Human service provision should be aligned with the principle of social justice, which supplies the organizing ethical framework for the social work profession. This chapter draws from a Rawlsian framework in which

> undeserved inequalities call for redress . . . in order to treat all persons equally, to provide genuine equality of opportunity, society must give more attention to those with fewer native assets and to those born into the less favorable social position. The idea is to reduce the bias of contingencies in the direction of equality. (Rawls, 1971, p. 100)

This social justice perspective comports with the medical or therapeutic model of service provision in which the greatest share of public resources is devoted to those with the greatest needs.

Two premises support a socially just human service system. First, services should be tailored in intensity and type to suit clients' needs and cultural values (National Association of Social Workers, 2003). Frontline workers should involve clients in individualized assessments of strengths and needs. Throughout, differences in power and authority between agency staff and clients should be minimized so client preferences can be integrated into the service planning process (Hasenfeld, 1992). Second, service provision should meet clients' biopsychosocial needs and should move them toward positive outcomes. To organize service decisions around clients' sense of time (Goldstein, Freud, & Solnit, 1973), the intensity and type of services provided should be determined by clients' needs and by their ability to adapt to new social environments. It is crucial to ensure that services are provided quickly, yet at a pace that allows individuals and families to adapt to new surroundings and prepare for future transitions. This perspective leads to the following practice principles.

- Identify and meet client needs. Fundamental to a social justice-focused human service system is the capacity to gather accurate and reliable information on client needs over time and to ensure that services are responsive to these needs. These requirements, described below, call for creation of continuous processes that track the needs and service histories of children and families.

- Assess client needs regularly. Client needs are traditionally identified on entry into care but rarely thereafter. For example, usually within the first week of a new foster care placement, foster care caseworkers complete state-required and agency-specific assessments of child and family needs and strengths based on information gathered from biological parents, children, and any available extended family, and then they establish case goals and begin to implement service plans. Because foster care may involve multiple traumatic transitions over time for children and families, however, caseworkers should repeat these assessments of strengths and needs. Biopsychosocial assessments of children and families should be completed at regular intervals and in response to placement changes. More generally, human service providers should identify individual and family needs regularly. When these assessments add valuable information to what was gathered previously, service plans and case goals should be revised accordingly.

- Ensure that services are responsive to different client needs. Ideally, service providers should be able to identify and provide the services needed to move clients toward positive outcomes. Yet, technical uncertainty—the inability to identify which service types and intensities are essential to achieve positive client outcomes—is often difficult to overcome in the human service sector. For example, researchers have had difficulty identifying evidence-based programs that move different types of foster children into appropriate permanent placements in a timely fashion (Hasenfeld, 2005; Thomlinson, 2005). More generally, the relationship between human service technology and client outcomes may be weak or insignificant (Glisson & Hemmelgarn, 1998; Meezan & McBeath, 2008). Thus, service providers may be unable to make services count—that is, to calibrate service provision precisely in response to differing client conditions to move clients toward performance targets.

Human service managers should ensure that the number and type of services provided are appropriate to clients' needs and cultural preferences. At the agency level, it is important for managers to ensure that service intensity is responsive to client needs and that frontline staff are integrating client perspectives into the service planning process. At the system level, managers should examine whether service provision (particularly for critical services) is lower across different racial groups and groups who entered care for different reasons. Where there are such service disparities, managers should survey affected clients to document potential unmet service needs and advocate for more services.

- ◆ Develop utilization review mechanisms. To identify and respond appropriately to clients' changing needs, human service managers should develop utilization management processes similar to those used in health care. Utilization management, which reviews the appropriateness and efficiency of services provided to clients, often occurs in three sequential steps (Wernet, 1999; Wickizer & Lessler, 2002). Before client admission, managers certify that services are needed (preadmission certification). While the case is active, managers examine whether appropriate services are provided at the necessary level of intensity (concurrent review). Finally, upon case closure, agencies retrospectively review which services were received and identify any points at which services were not provided in sufficient number or intensity (retrospective reviews). These steps require detailed, accurate, and reliable information systems that track client diagnostic data and service histories.

- ◆ Ensure that frontline staff individualize service provision. Human service managers should determine whether frontline staff can tailor services to client needs and preferences without additional supports. Given the chronic turnover in human services, caseworkers may be overextended, and supervisors may be juggling administrative and supervisory tasks while also carrying caseloads (U.S. General Accounting Office, 2003). Structural supports should be provided, such as hiring caseworkers or creating job advancement possibilities to retain experienced caseworkers, who are needed to craft appropriate service plans and help individuals and families. Supports should also include more informal processes through which new and existing responsibilities can be managed efficiently.

Human service administrators should be involved in determining whether system-wide resources are adequate for client needs. Although resource needs are likely to arise in the course of regular meetings between system administrators and service providers, administrators should assess for themselves the extent to which human service agencies are struggling with their current resource levels. System administrators should also survey community service providers to determine whether untapped resources exist. If resource levels appear to be inadequate across all agencies, then system administrators and service providers should secure additional funding that will allow for the provision of appropriate services to clients.

Taking Performance Seriously: Principles for Human Service System Administrators

How human service system administrators and managers integrate client-centered considerations within a performance-based context is a question of governance. Governance can be defined as "regimes of laws, rules, judicial decisions, and administrative practices that constrain, prescribe, and enable the provision of publicly supported goods and services" (Lynn, Heinrich, & Hill, 2001, p. 7). In many human service systems, governance and administration may be spread across multiple funders and public and private service providers that are responsible for system maintenance to varying degrees. These agencies may be relatively autonomous and may have few incentives to collaborate with or assist each other.

Various governance models have been proposed to help administrators and managers serve clients and improve performance within multiagency service delivery systems. Two prominent models are the *bureaucratic* and *network* models. The bureaucratic model (Agranoff & McGuire, 2001; Smith & Lipsky, 1993) suggests that human service providers become vassals of the state when they contract with a public funder. Funders may use their financial leverage to require service providers to alter their behaviors, often by reducing agencies' discretion to serve specific client populations or provide services in nonstandard formats. Core tools of bureaucratic management include establishing funding streams (usually by tapping into federal funding sources), drafting requests for proposals that identify the key programmatic and policy requirements that service providers are to follow, and monitoring programs to ensure that service providers are complying with applicable rules, regulations, and standards.

In contrast, the network model acknowledges that public funders and service providers rely on each other strategically: service providers play an essential role in implementing public policies, and funders support the service efforts of service providers (although these agencies often do not depend on any one public contract) (Milward & Provan, 2000). Different implications for management practice emerge from this condition of mutual gain, because public funders have less authority to dictate the terms of service to service providers. Core tools for network administrators thus include clarifying mutual interests, establishing interagency cooperation, and incorporating new service providers into the human service network.

A third model of governance, which might be termed the *client service* model, explicitly incorporates client preferences and needs. This model suggests that service providers provide services to meet the needs of their target communities and constituencies even when doing so may not satisfy organizational goals of stability and longevity (Gutierrez, Glenmaye, & Delois, 1995). From this perspective, human service delivery systems should improve clients' well-being. Client service-focused management involves establishing relationships with client groups and representatives, determining which client needs are most pressing and matching those needs with appropriate service providers, ensuring that service providers have the resources to provide the proper number and type of services, and evaluating whether services have fulfilled client requests.

We argue that system administrators and managers should draw on all three models of governance to organize human service systems around the twin principles of social justice and performance. The strong focus of the client service model on improving client well-being is the basis for human service systems that are dedicated to tailoring services to client needs. This is an image of the human service manager as *advocate*. The network model directs attention to how human service administrators and managers collaborate in the face of diverse funders and service providers that may share few goals or incentives to collaborate. Here, the human service manager is a *facilitator* or *broker*. Finally, the emphasis of the bureaucratic model on resource procurement, program development, and close monitoring of service providers suggests that administrators become *patrons* or *social entrepreneurs* who are able to push service providers to improve performance. These core management roles of advocacy, facilitation, and patronage support the following recommendations.

- Focus the human service system on responding to client needs and improving outcomes. Human service administrators should use bureaucratic tools to ensure that service providers will identify and respond to client needs and improve program performance over time. Essential components of a social justice- and program performance-focused human service system include building client need-focused considerations into requests for proposals and purchase-of-service contracts, selecting service providers based on their expertise in serving clients appropriately and improving client outcomes over time, and redesigning contracts and proposals after the causes of service disparities or suboptimal client outcomes are identified.

- Build client need- and outcome-specific considerations into proposals and contracts. Requests for proposals and purchase-of-service contracts should clearly require human service providers to tailor services to clients and improve client outcomes. These considerations should be built into proposals and contracts through requirements, penalties, and rewards. Contracts that require human service providers to individualize the number and type of services for client needs, and that oblige service providers to use utilization review processes, will send clear signals to agencies and managers. Administrators should prefer human service providers that provide evidence of consistent efforts to individualize services for client needs and cultural values, and that use community resources to supplement their services. Administrators may also provide incentives for agencies to improve client outcomes or to penalize agencies that do not.

- Redesign programs after the causes of service disparities and suboptimal program outcomes are identified. Despite contractual requirements, incentives, and penalties, some service providers nevertheless may provide unsuitable or inappropriate services or ones that do not improve client outcomes. These agencies should not be penalized until it is clear they were capable of tailoring services appropriately or improving client outcomes but chose not to do so. In this situation, human service administrators and agency managers should seek to identify why service disparities exist or how to improve the effectiveness of major programs. Determining why service disparities or suboptimal outcomes exist allows administrators to redesign programs to suit new client needs. If administrators find that service disparities occurred because clients' needs overwhelmed human service providers despite their best efforts, then they should consider providing additional community services.

◆ Provide technical assistance to human service providers. Human service system administrators should ensure that all service providers have the resources and training to conduct thorough assessments, provide appropriate in-agency services, access community resources, and move clients toward positive outcomes. Administrators may find that it is more difficult for some agencies to provide client-centered services and to improve program performance. These providers may be less able to link services to client needs assessments because of inexperienced caseworkers, staff turnover, and/or less technical ability to use utilization review processes; they may have needier clients; or they may not have developed relationships with other service providers. These agencies should receive additional resources and technical assistance. It is also possible to use graduated sanction and incentive systems, which start with easily achievable performance goals and then increase expectations over time and reward service providers for meeting performance milestones. Overall, human service system administrators should avoid setting the bar lower for some agencies, because doing so may create the perception that it is acceptable to shortchange individuals and families.

Discussion and Conclusions

Given the speed with which federal and state policymakers have adopted performance management principles and incorporated performance expectations into human service funding mechanisms (Heinrich, 2007), how managers improve program performance is increasingly relevant. This chapter reviews two managerial approaches for improving client outcomes in human service programs: evidence-based programming, which requires managers to select and implement predesigned interventions, and client-centered service provision, in which managers facilitate the efforts of frontline staff to assess client strengths and needs regularly and tailor services accordingly. Both methods promote use of the best available science in furtherance of human service decision making, although the evidence-based programming perspective relies on a considerably narrower interpretation of what constitutes evidence (i.e., data from randomized clinical trials and systematic reviews).

In part, interest in human service program performance reflects the diffusion of the evidence-based perspective from medicine to human services. Evidence-based medicine involves "the conscientious, explicit, and judicious use of current best evidence in making decisions about the care of individual patients" (Sackett, Rosenberg, Gray, Haynes, & Richardson, 1996, pp. 71–72). Under this model, practitioners are asked to integrate evidence, client values and expectations, available resources, and their clinical expertise before making practice decisions. The current evidence-based programming perspective deviates substantially from this original formulation, as it does not define whether and how client characteristics and preferences and clinicians' prior experience shape service delivery.

It is important for human service managers to demonstrate program effectiveness while supporting the ability of frontline staff to individualize services to clients. Program performance and client-centered service provision are not mutually exclusive constructs, although some evidence-based programs may be unresponsive to differences in clients' cultural expectations and service preferences (Aisenberg, in press). There is significant literature on how managers improve program performance and how human service agencies develop individualized programming. Because these topics traditionally have been examined independently of one another, however, little empirical work exists to inform the development of client-centered and performance-based programs.

This chapter introduces practice principles for managers and system administrators seeking to create these programs. These recommendations focus managerial attention on assessing clients regularly, supporting frontline workers' ability to individualize care, and tracking service use. Human service system administrators are encouraged to reward client-centered practice and high performance, and to provide technical assistance and resources to service providers unable to meet these goals. Overall, these principles suggest that human service providers continuously collect information on clients, staff, services, and program outcomes and retool programs in response to changing client conditions and service availability. Managers have an important role in training frontline staff to listen and respond to client needs. System architects are equally important, as they may reward service providers that take client values and preferences into consideration and penalize those that do not.

These recommendations require managers to engage in data-driven, trial-and-error program improvement processes. Human service providers must be able to propose and test hypotheses, identify program-related uncertainties, and gather evidence to aid decision making. What are optimal strategies for enhancing caseworkers' ability to elicit client preferences, and how can training modules be developed to share this information with new frontline workers? Does individualizing care improve client outcomes, and what sort of information should be collected to test this relationship? Would it be prudent to adopt a particular evidence-based program, given the expected implementation costs? Attention to empiricism, skepticism, and repeated questioning of this sort is necessary for managers to align services with client needs and to identify and remove performance barriers (Senge, 1990).

Such flexibility in service programming is appropriate, given the changing demographics and needs of individuals and families in many human service systems. The disproportionate inclusion of minority clients in the human service sector increases the importance of tailoring programs to client circumstances. A program's guiding philosophy should align (or at least not conflict) with clients' cultural understandings of need and how services should be delivered. Furthermore, clients should view all aspects of the program experience—from each individual program service to the microinteractions between frontline staff and clients—as sensible and empowering. In this manner, disadvantaged, in-need populations will not be subjected to insult or degradation.

In conclusion, it remains unclear what tensions may arise as client-based service approaches are integrated into performance-based environments. Serving clients appropriately and serving them effectively are distinct, yet related, components of service quality and, in broader terms, public accountability. Regardless of whether human service providers adopt evidence-based programming or client-centered service approaches (or neither), managers must demonstrate fluency in collecting and using various types of clinical, staffing, and programmatic information to further decision making. This commitment to subjecting programs to rigorous empirical scrutiny thus constitutes a key aspect of improving the design and delivery of effective, appropriate human service programs.

References

Agency for Healthcare Research and Quality. (2003). *National healthcare disparities report: Summary*. Rockville, MD: Author.

Agranoff, R., & McGuire, M. (2001). American federalism and the search for models of management. *Public Administration Review, 61*, 671–681.

Aisenberg, E. (in press). Evidence-based practice in mental health care to ethnic communities. Has its practice fallen short of its evidence? *Social Work*.

APA Presidential Task Force on Evidence-Based Practice. (2006). Evidence-based practice in psychology. *American Psychologist, 61*, 271–285.

Chaffin, M., & Friedrich, B. (2004). Evidence-based treatments in child abuse and neglect. *Children and Youth Services Review, 26*, 1097–1113.

Corrigan, P. W., Steiner, L., McCracken, S. G., Blaser, B., & Barr, M. (2001). Strategies for disseminating evidence-based practices to staff who treat people with serious mental illness. *Psychiatric Services, 52*, 1598–1606.

Courtney, M. E. (2000). Managed care and child welfare services: What are the issues? *Children and Youth Services Review, 22*, 87–91.

Daft, R. L. (2003). *Management* (6th ed.). New York: Southwestern.

Eddy, D. M. (2005). Evidence-based medicine: A unified approach. *Health Affairs, 24*, 9–17.

Farabee, D. (2005). *Rethinking rehabilitation: Why can't we reform our criminals?* Washington, DC: AEI Press.

Fixsen, D. L., Naoom, S. F., Blase, K. A., Friedman, R. M., & Wallace, F. (2005). *Implementation research: A synthesis of the literature.* Tampa, FL: University of South Florida (FMHI Publication #231).

Gambrill, E. (2006). Evidence-based practice and policy: Choices ahead. *Research on Social Work Practice, 16,* 338–357.

Gibbs, L. E. (2007). Applying research to making life-affecting judgments and decisions. *Research on Social Work Practice, 17,* 143–150.

Gibbs, L. E., & Gambrill, E. (2002). Evidence-based practice: Counterarguments to objections. *Research on Social Work Practice, 12,* 452–476.

Glisson, C., & Hemmelgarn, A. (1998). The effects of organizational climate and interorganizational coordination on the quality and outcomes of children's service systems. *Child Abuse and Neglect, 22,* 401–421.

Gold, P. G., Glynn, S. M., & Mueser, K. T. (2006). Challenges to implementing and sustaining comprehensive mental health service programs. *Evaluation and the Health Professions, 29,* 195–218.

Goldstein, J., Freud, A., & Solnit, A. (1973). *Beyond the best interests of the child.* New York: The Free Press.

Gorey, K. M., Thyer, B. A., & Pawluck, D. E. (1998). Differential effectiveness of prevalent social work practice models: A meta-analysis. *Social Work, 43,* 269–278.

Gowdy, E. A., Rapp, C. A., & Poertner, J. (1993). Management is performance: Strategies for client-centered practice in social service organizations. *Administration in Social Work, 17,* 3–22.

Gray, J. A. M. (2001). *Evidence-based health care: How to make health policy and management decisions* (2nd ed.). New York: Churchill-Livingstone.

Gutierrez, L., Glenmaye, L., & Delois, K. (1995). The organizational context of empowerment practice: Implications for social work administration. *Social Work, 40,* 249–258.

Guyatt, G., & Rennie, D. (2002). *Users' guide to the medical literature: A manual for evidence-based clinical practice.* Chicago: The Evidence-Based Medicine Working Group, JAMA, & Archives of the American Medical Association.

Hasenfeld, Y. (1992). Power in social work practice. In Y. Hasenfeld (Ed.), *Human services as complex organizations* (pp. 257–275). Newbury Park, CA: Sage.

Hasenfeld, Y. (2005). *Worker-client relations: Social policy in practice.* Paper presented at the workshop on New Directions for Research on Social Policy and Organizational Practices, The National Poverty Center at the University of Michigan, Ann Arbor, MI.

Heinrich, C. J. (2007). Evidence-based policy and performance management: Challenges and prospects in two parallel movements. *American Review of Public Administration, 37,* 255–277.

Hill, R. B. (2007). *An analysis of racial/ethnic disproportionality and disparity at the national, state, and county levels.* Washington, DC: Casey-CSSP Alliance for Racial Equity in Child Welfare.

Hoagwood, K., Burns, B., Kiser, L, Ringeisen, H., & Schoenwald, S. K. (2001). Evidence-based practice in child and adolescent mental health services. *Psychiatric Services, 52,* 1179–1189.

Johnson, M., & Austin, M. J. (2006). Evidence-based practice in the social services: Implications for organizational change. *Administration in Social Work, 30,* 75–104.

Kauffman Foundation. (2004). *Closing the quality chasm in child abuse treatment: Identifying and disseminating best practices: The findings of the Kauffman best practices project to help children heal from child abuse.* St. Louis, MO: Author.

Kovner, A. R., & Rundall, T. G. (2006). Evidence-based management reconsidered. *Frontiers of Health Services Management, 22,* 3–22.

Lynn, L. E., Jr., Heinrich, C. J., & Hill, C. J. (2001). *Improving governance: A new logic for empirical research.* Washington, DC: Georgetown University Press.

McBeath, B. (2006). *Shifting principles in a sacred market: Nonprofit service provision to foster children and families in a performance-based, managed care contracting environment.* Unpublished doctoral dissertation, University of Michigan Ann Arbor.

Meezan, W., & McBeath, B. (2008). Market-based disparities in foster care outcomes. *Children and Youth Services Review, 30,* 388–406.

Milward, H. B., & Provan, K. G. (2000). Governing the hollow state. *Journal of Public Administration Research and Theory, 10,* 359–379.

Mullen, E. J. (2006). Choosing outcome measures in systematic reviews: Critical challenges. *Research on Social Work Practice, 16,* 84–90.

National Association of Social Workers. (2003). *Code of ethics* (Rev. ed.). Washington, DC: Author.

Newhouse, R. P. (2006). Examining the support for evidence-based nursing practice. *Journal of Nursing Administration, 36,* 337–340.

Norcross, J. C., Beutler, L. E., & Levant, R. F. (Eds.). (2005). *Evidence-based practices in mental health: Debate and dialogue on fundamental questions.* Washington, DC: American Psychological Association.

Pfeffer, J., & Sutton, R. I. (2006). Evidence-based management. *Harvard Business Review, 84,* 63–74.

Rawls, J. (1971). *A theory of justice.* Cambridge, MA: Harvard University Press.

Robbins, S. P., & DeCenzo, D. A. (2004). *Fundamentals of management: Essential concepts and applications* (4th ed.). Upper Saddle River, NJ: Prentice Hall.

Roberts, A. R., & Yeager, K. R. (2004). *Evidence-based practice manual: Research and outcome measures in health and human services.* New York: Oxford University Press.

Rubin, A., & Parrish, D. (2007). Challenges to the future of evidence-based practice in social work education. *Journal of Social Work Education, 43,* 405–428.

Sackett, D. L., Rosenberg, W. J., Gray, J. A., Haynes, R. B., & Richardson, W. S. (1996). Evidence-based medicine: What it is and what it isn't. *British Medical Journal, 312,* 71–72.

Sackett, D. L., Straus, S. E., Richardson, W. C., Rosenberg, W., & Haynes, R. M. (2000). *Evidence-based medicine: How to practice and teach EBM* (2nd ed.). New York: Churchill Livingstone.

Segal, S., Silverman, C., & Temkin, T. (1993). Empowerment and self-help agency practice for people with mental disabilities. *Social Work, 38,* 705–712.

Senge, P. M. (1990). *The fifth discipline: The art of the learning organization.* New York: Currency Doubleday.

Smith, S. R. (2003). Social services. In L. M. Salamon (Ed.), *The state of nonprofit America* (pp. 151–188). Washington, DC: Brookings Institution Press.

Smith, S. R. & Lipsky, M. (1993). *Nonprofits for hire: The welfare state in an age of contracting.* Cambridge, MA: Harvard University Press.

Thomlinson, B. (2005). Using evidence-based knowledge to improve policies and practices in child welfare: Current thinking and continuing challenges. *Research on Social Work Practice, 15,* 321–322.

U.S. Department of Health and Human Services. (2001). *Mental health: Culture, race, and ethnicity: A supplement to Mental Health: A report of the surgeon general.* Rockville, MD: Author.

U.S. General Accounting Office. (2003). *Child welfare: HHS could play a greater role in helping child welfare agencies recruit and retain staff* (GAO-03-357). Washington, DC: Author.

U.S. General Accountability Office. (2007). *African American children in foster care: Additional HHS assistance needed to help states reduce the proportion in care* (GAO-07-816). Washington, DC: Author.

Walker, J. S., Briggs, H. E., Koroloff, N., & Friesen, B. J. (2007). Implementing and sustaining evidence-based practice in social work. *Journal of Social Work Education, 43,* 361–375.

Walshe, K., & Rundall, T. G. (2001). Evidence-based management: From theory to practice in health care. *Milbank Quarterly, 79,* 429–457.

Weisz, J. R., Jensen-Doss, A., & Hawley, K. M. (2006). Evidence-based youth psychotherapies versus usual clinical care: A meta-analysis of direct comparisons. *American Psychologist, 61,* 671–689.

Wells, R. (2005). Managing child welfare agencies: What do we know about what works? *Children and Youth Services Review, 28,* 1181–1194.

Wernet, S. P. (1999). *Managed care in human services.* Chicago: Lyceum Books.

Wickizer, T. M., & Lessler, D. (2002). Utilization management: Issues, effects, and future prospects. *Annual Review of Public Health, 23,* 233–254.

Woolston, J. L. (2005). Implementing evidence-based treatments in organizations. *American Academy of Child and Adolescent Psychiatry, 44,* 1313–1316.

Wulczyn, F. W., & Lery, B. (2007). *Racial disparity in foster care admissions.* Chicago: Chapin Hall Center for Children.

Zlotnick, J. L. (2007). Evidence-based practice and social work education: A view from Washington. *Research on Social Work Practice, 17,* 625–629.

9
Management & Leadership in Contracting

Lawrence Martin

Several years ago in a large city in southern California, a local chapter of the American Red Cross (ARC) submitted a proposal to its county government to provide specialized transportation services. Unfortunately, the local ARC chapter didn't realize that it was actually submitting a bid in response to an invitation for bids. The ARC chapter was declared the low bidder and awarded the contract. Only then did the ARC chapter director, a social worker, discover that the agency had calculated its costs incorrectly. The director tried to get out of the contract, but the county suspected the director was attempting to lowball the process and threatened legal action. The ARC chapter director decided to honor the contract and provide the service, but at a significant financial loss to the organization.

More recently, in Kansas, a religiously affiliated nonprofit childcare agency entered into a performance-based contract with the state welfare department. The nonprofit agency had little experience as a contract provider and even less experience with performance-based contracting. The nonprofit agency overestimated its performance and underestimated its costs. The result was that the nonprofit agency lost some $2 million on the contract and nearly went bankrupt.

The purpose of these two case examples is not to scare social workers from becoming involved in contracting, but rather to reinforce the notion that a contract represents a business relationship and must be understood in this context. There is a historical predisposition in social work to view the social services and their administration as something separate and apart from other forms of administration, such as business administration (Patti, 2000). Leadership and management in contracting are concerned primarily with understanding the true nature of the business relationship that underpins contracting and ensuring that one's agency and staff are capable of working in this type of environment.

Contracting has been a major mode of government social service delivery since at least the late 1970s (Lohmann & Lohmann, 2002; Martin, 2004) According to some estimates, by the year 2010 as much as 80% of all government-funded social services nationally will involve contracting (Martin 2005). Today, most nonprofit social service agencies receive at least some funding from contracts (Austin, 2003). Most social workers today spend significant portions of their professional careers providing services under contracts.

Despite the obvious importance of contracting, social work has been slow to incorporate contracting into the educational preparation of its practitioners. Consequently, many social workers lack the knowledge and skills necessary to assume leadership and management positions in a contracting environment. One result of this lack of contracting expertise is the increasing number of traditional social work positions being filled by graduates of schools of business and public administration (Perlmutter, 2006). For social workers to compete in a future dominated by contracting, they must be well grounded in this field. To assume leadership and management positions in a contracting environment, social workers must go beyond the basics and learn the myriad policies, procedures, and processes involved in contracting and their attendant risks and rewards.

Risks and Rewards in Contracting for Social Services

This section identifies some of the major leadership and management issues involved in working in a contracting environment and discusses their attendant risks and rewards. The section is organized into five major issue areas: (1) contracts versus grants, (2) mission drift, (3) procurement approaches, (4) compensation mechanisms, and (5) eligibility determinations and referrals.

Contracts Versus Grants

One important leadership and management issue involved in operating in a contracting environment is understanding and appreciating the difference between grants and contracts. Grants are still very much part of the social service funding picture. For example, grant funding from the U.S. Department of Health and Human Services for fiscal year 2006 was estimated at some $257 billion (Domestic Working Group, 2005). But grants are not contracts.

The Federal Grant and Cooperative Agreement Act defines a *grant* as a form of assistance made available to help organizations in discharging their own responsibilities. Although an oversimplification, grants have been called gifts with strings attached; *contracts*, on the other hand, are considered a form of procurement: governments are purchasing goods or services from another party. Contracting connotes a business relationship (a buyer/seller transaction).

One of the major rewards for nonprofit social service agencies involved in contracting is that new funding streams become available. However, there are also risks in becoming involved in contracting that are not attached to grants. Failure to perform under a grant is frequently excused. When a grantee fails to abide by all of the requirements of a grant, the funder frequently excuses the organization, provided the funds were expended for the purposes intended. In contracting, however, failure to abide by the requirements is seldom excused. (Martin, 2001). Even in cases where a government agency might want to waive or excuse the failure, federal, state, or local government laws and regulations generally do not permit such an action.

Leadership and management in a contracting environment involve recognizing the differences between contracts and grants and ensuring that agency policies and procedures reflect the business nature of contract relationships. Leadership and management also involve ensuring that agency staff are educated and trained in contracting issues (Government Accountability Office [GAO], 2006).

Mission Drift

The potential for mission drift is another issue that frequently confronts nonprofit social service agencies operating in a contracting environment. Government contracting priorities can, and frequently do, change. These changes can involve service-delivery methodologies, client mixes, geographical service areas, and other considerations. To continue serving as contractors, nonprofit agencies may have to change their service-delivery approaches. Making minor changes in such approaches to satisfy funding source requirements is a part of everyday life for most nonprofit social service agencies. However, when the changes are so significant that a nonprofit social service agency faces the possibility of changing its basic character, then the issue of mission drift arises. Is the social service agency remaining true to its mission, or is it simply chasing after funding?

Leadership and management in a contracting environment requires being flexible, but also being true to the agency's mission. Flexibility means being able to reconfigure how a nonprofit social service agency does business. Remaining true to agency mission means not trading organizational values for dollars. A common rule of thumb many social work managers use is ensuring that no more than 40 to 45% (at most) of an agency's total operating budget comes from any single source (Martin, 2001). When a single funding source accounts for 50% or more of a nonprofit social service agency's total operating budget, that agency has de facto become a captured entity of the funding source. And with capture invariably comes mission drift.

A social work manager had a large sign in his office that read, "Changed Priorities Ahead." The point of the sign was to remind him to be sufficiently flexible to change priorities, but not values.

Procurement

Procurement is the processes governments use to select contractors and award contracts. All government agencies (federal, state, municipal, and county) have procurement policies and procedures describing when and how they contract. All federal departments and agencies follow the *Code of Federal Regulations* Part 48, Federal Acquisition Regulation (General Services Administration, U.S. Department of Defense, & National Aeronautics and Space Administration, 2005). State and local governments have their own rules and regulations (Martin & Miller, 2006). The good news here is that there is a great deal of commonalty among the various government policies and procedures.

Although learning about procurement may sound far removed from the world of social work, it nevertheless must be mastered if a social service agency is to operate successfully in a contracting environment. In many respects, procurement can be considered a big computer game with lots of rules, some more obvious than others. If you violate any of the rules, GAME OVER! If you master the rules, you advance to the next level where you can win the game (receive a contract).

Governments use two major procurement processes in contracting for social services: the *invitation for bids* process and the *request for proposals* process (Austin, 2002; Martin, 2001; Martin & Miller, 2006).

Invitation for Bids Process

Governments use the invitation for bids (IFB) process when they know a great deal about the social service they want to contract for, including the quantity and quality of the service, the clients to be served, the geographical area to be served, and other important considerations.

With the IFB process, price or cost is usually the determining factor; little, if any, negotiation is involved. A nonprofit social service agency simply completes the IFB package, enters a price to provide the service, and then signs and submits the documents to the government. The contract is usually awarded to the lowest bidder. The crucial point to understand here is that when an IFB package is signed and submitted, it becomes a *legal offer*. All the government has to do is sign its representative's name on the document, and a contract automatically becomes binding. A social worker or a nonprofit social service agency should never agree to something in an IFB that it is not prepared to live with.

Request for Proposals

The request for proposals (RFP) process is used when governments (1) are seeking new and creative ways of providing social services; (2) want to determine jointly with the contractor such issues as the quantity and the quality of the social service, the clients to be served, and the geographical areas to be served; or (3) simply don't want to use the more structured IFB process.

This process usually involves at least some negotiation, and this is the opportunity for a nonprofit social service agency to raise any concerns or make any suggestions about the service-delivery approach, the client group, the service area, and so forth. When negotiations are completed, the conditions are reduced to writing and incorporated into the contract document.

Leadership and management in a contracting environment include knowing the procurement rules and regulations of one's state, county, and municipal governments. The more one knows about the rules of the game, the better positioned his or her social service agency is to compete successfully in a contract environment. Leadership and management also include ensuring that one's staff is knowledgeable about procurement rules and regulations.

Compensation Approaches

From a leadership and management perspective, understanding the risks and rewards of various compensation approaches may be the most important issue when working in a contracting environment. Perhaps no other contracting issue is as important when it comes to risks and rewards.

Contracts can involve a variety of compensation approaches (Ezell, 2007; Martin & Miller, 2006), each of which has its own risks and rewards. Although the number of approaches is restricted only by the creativity of the government contracting agency, there are fortunately fewer general approaches: (1) cost-reimbursement, (2) fixed-price, (3) fixed-fee, (4) performance-based, and (5) capitation.

Cost-Reimbursement Approaches

Under a cost-reimbursement contract, a nonprofit social service agency is compensated only for actual expenses incurred in providing the services. The key word here is *reimbursement*. For a cost to be reimbursable, it must be incurred; this means that, if a nonprofit agency did not actually incur the cost, then it is not reimbursable. To avoid confusion about what is and is not reimbursable, most cost-reimbursement contracts include a budget. If an item of cost is included in the budget and is incurred by a nonprofit social service agency, then it is usually reimbursable. However, the government is the ultimate arbiter of what is and is not reimbursable (Ezell, 2007).

Cash flow is a consideration with cost-reimbursement approaches, as it is with all of the compensation approaches discussed here (Ezell, 2007) Social service agencies must have enough working capital to cover expenses and otherwise survive while waiting for government reimbursement and payment. This lag between the time costs are incurred and revenue is received is an inherent characteristic of contract services. The lag issue is particularly important when it comes to performance-based contracts, where a dozen or more months can separate incurring costs and receiving reimbursement or payment.

One of the rewards to a nonprofit social service agency from a cost-reimbursement contract is that performance is generally not tied to compensation. If an agency encounters problems during contract implementation, it knows that its costs will still be reimbursed. Consequently, there is little financial risk involved when working under such contract. However, cost-reimbursement contracts can still be audited. A government audit team may review a nonprofit agency's financial books and records to ensure that costs reimbursed were actually incurred.

Fixed-Price Approaches

Under fixed-price compensation, a nonprofit social service agency is paid the full contract price on successful completion of the work or provision of services. The operative word here, and for the other compensation approaches discussed later, is *payment*. Unlike cost-reimbursement approaches, there is no relationship in a fixed-price contract between the costs incurred by a nonprofit agency and the compensation paid.

In terms of risk/reward, if a nonprofit social service agency's costs in providing the service exceed the fixed price, then the agency loses money. However, if the agency's costs are less than the fixed price, it gets to keep the difference. Consequently, there is a direct relationship between performance and compensation. An additional reward, or benefit, to a fixed-price contract is that a nonprofit agency does not have much to worry about in terms of financial audits. All the nonprofit social service agency has to do is demonstrate that the service was provided and billed for appropriately.

Fixed-Fee Approaches

In fixed-fee compensation, a nonprofit social service agency receives a predetermined payment each time it provides a unit of some mutually agreed-on service (Ezell, 2007). Fixed-fee compensation approaches are also referred to as *unit-cost* approaches and *fee-for-service*. For example, an agency provides home-delivered meals to elderly and physically disabled individuals. The unit of service here is "one meal," and the fixed-fee compensation might take the form of payment of $6 for each home-delivered meal provided to an eligible client.

In terms of risks and rewards, a nonprofit social service agency incurs significant risk with fixed-fee compensation approaches. Payment is only made for services provided, irrespective of the actual costs incurred. With fixed-fee approaches, as well as the other compensation approaches discussed later, a nonprofit agency *must* have good cost and service utilization data. An agency must know how much it actually costs to provide a service so it does not underprice it. It must also have good service utilization data so it knows how much service it can provide and how many clients it can reasonably be expected to serve.

Performance-Based Approaches

Although all compensation approaches, other than cost reimbursement, have some performance aspects to them, the term *performance-based* refers to a particular class of contracts (McBeath & Meezin, 2006; McEwen & Nelson-Phillips, 2007; Quality Improvement Center on the Privatization of Child Welfare Services, 2006). Government agencies are increasingly turning to performance-based approaches as a means of shifting at least some of the financial risk for performance failure to contractors (Martin, 2002; Romzek & Johnson, 2005). A recent study (McCullough & Associates, 2005) found that more than 90% of state child welfare contracting initiatives can be classified as performance-based.

A performance-based contract can be defined as "one that focuses on the outputs, quality and outcomes of service provision and may tie at least a portion of a contractor's payment as well as any contract extension or renewal to their achievement" (Martin, 2007a).

Performance-based approaches are perhaps best understood by examples. One of the more popular performance-based approaches is called *milestone contracting*. Table 1 is an example of one milestone performance-based approach developed by Oklahoma for providing job training and placement services (Frumkin, 2001; O'Brien & Revel, 2005).

TABLE 1   OKLAHOMA MILESTONE PAYMENT APPROACH

Milestone	Type of Milestone	Payment %
Determination of need	process	10
Vocational preparation	process	10
Job placement	output	10
Job training	process	10
Job retention	quality/outcome	15
Job stabilization	quality/outcome	20
Case closure	outcome	25

Source: Adapted from O'Brien & Revel, 2005; Frumkin, 2001

As Table 1 illustrates, this milestone payment approach ties compensation to accomplishment of specific activities or benchmarks. Sixty percent of the compensation is tied to output, quality, and outcome milestones; the remaining 40% is tied to process milestones. If a nonprofit social service agency fails to achieve any of the performance milestones identified in Table 1, then it loses money on that client.

Table 2 is an example of another milestone approach developed by North Carolina for adoption services (Martin, 2003). In this example, 100% of the compensation is tied to outcome milestones.

TABLE 2   CAROLINA MILESTONE PAYMENT APPROACH

Milestone	Type of Milestone	Payment %
Child placed for adoption	outcome	60
Decree of adoption finalized	outcome	20
Adoption intact for 12 months	outcome	20

Source: Adapted from Martin, 2003

In terms of risk and rewards, milestone compensation approaches place a nonprofit social service agency at considerable risk. There are always factors outside an agency's control that will affect its performance, particularly the accomplishment of outcomes. Nevertheless, no performance, no payment. An additional risk consideration is the length of time allowed for accomplishing some milestones (e.g., see "Adoption intact for 12 months" in Table 2).

An additional risk factor of performance-based approaches is that when compensation is tied to performance, either totally or partially, the performance itself becomes auditable (Martin, 2007b). This so-called dirty little secret of performance-based compensation approaches is seldom discussed. Auditors generally work backward from programmatic reports identifying the outputs, quality, and outcome performance accomplished to the bills submitted to the government and, ultimately, to the compensation paid to a nonprofit social service agency. There must be a clear and documentable audit trail from performance to bills to payments, or the auditors may question costs and perhaps even demand the repayment of some funds (Martin, 2007b).

Capitation Approaches

Capitation approaches, also referred to as *managed-care* and *case-rate* approaches, compensate nonprofit social service agencies at an agreed-on rate to provide services to a client as long as that client remains in service (Ezell, 2007; McCullough & Associates, 2005). Payment can be made up front, when a client enters service, or over the time the client remains in care.

In terms of risks and rewards, the major risk with capitation approaches is that a nonprofit social service agency is making an open-ended commitment to provide services and/or otherwise care for a client, irrespective of cost. Only the most sophisticated nonprofit social service agencies (those that have reliable cost and service utilization data) should become involved in capitation approaches.

From the perspective of leadership and management, social workers need to understand the full implications of the various compensation approaches used in social service contracts. For nonprofit social service agencies, leadership and management also mean developing the capacity to generate reliable cost and service utilization data to support the more currently fashionable and riskier performance-based and capitated compensation approaches.

Eligibility Determinations and Referrals

Another factor that must be included in the risks and rewards of operating in a contracting environment is the issue of who performs eligibility determinations and who makes client referrals.

Governments generally deal with eligibility determinations and client referrals in one of three ways: (1) the functions are included as a component of the contract services to be provided by a nonprofit agency; (2) the government maintains the functions; or (3) the functions are contracted to a third party. The last two situations present significant risks to a nonprofit agency. When operating under any contract payment approach other than cost reimbursement, a nonprofit social service agency that does have control over eligibility determinations and client referrals runs the risk of being unable to provide enough service, or service enough clients, to cover its operating costs. When payments are tied to service levels or number of clients served, relying on someone else for eligibility determinations and referrals is less than optimal.

Summary and Conclusion

Providing services under a contractual arrangement with government can be a worthwhile and rewarding experience for a nonprofit social service agency. Over the last 30 years, government contracting has been responsible for increasing funding to underserved groups (e.g., low income, minorities, and women) and pioneering many social services, from child day care services to adult da care services and many in between (Martin, 2004).

Contemporary approaches to social service contacting have also demonstrated some dramatic successes when governments and nonprofit agencies share resources, talents, and expertise (Martin, 2005).

As discussed here, however, operating in a contracting environment involves understanding and appreciating that one is operating in a business environment, not strictly an assistance environment.

Government contracting represents one of the major sources, if not the major source, of funding for nonprofit social service agencies today. Unfortunately, schools of social work have been slow to include contracting in social workers' educational preparation. Leadership and management in social work today require learning the rules, regulations, policies, and procedures that govern government contracting and procurement as well as the various risk and rewards associated with different compensation approaches, auditing consideration, and other factors.

Recently, the U.S. Department of Health and Human Services funded the School of Social Work at the University of Kentucky (www.uky.edu/SocialWork/qicpcw) to establish a clearinghouse for research on social services contracting with specific emphasis on child welfare services. It is hoped that this clearinghouse will begin providing at least some of the leadership and management in contracting that have been missing from social work education.

References

Austin, D. (2002). *Human services management.* New York: Columbia University Press.

Austin, M. (2003). The changing relationship between nonprofit organizations and public social service agencies in the ear of welfare reform. *Nonprofit and Voluntary Sector Quarterly, 32* (1):97–114.

Domestic Working Group (2005). *Final report issued October 2005.* Retrieved September 22, 2007, from http://www.epa.gov.oig.dwg/reports

Ezell, M. (2007). Managing diverse sources of funding. In J. Aldgate, L. Healy, B. Malcolm, B. Pine, W. Rose, & J. Seden (Eds.), *Enhancing social work management: Theory and best practice from the UK and the USA* (pp. 245–262). London: Jessica Kingsley Publishers.

Frumkin, P. (2001). *Managing for outcomes: Milestone contracting in Oklahoma.* Arlington, VA: PricewaterhouseCoopers Endowment for the Business of Government. General Services Administration, U.S. Department of Defense, & National Aeronautics and Space Administration. (2005). *Federal acquisition regulation.* Retrieved November 28, 2007, from http://www.arnet.gov/far

Government Accountability Office (GAO). (2006). *Grants management: Enhancing accountability provisions could lead to better results.* Washington, DC: Author.

Lohmann, R., & Lohmann, N. (2002). *Social administration.* New York: Columbia University Press.

Martin, L. L. (2001). *Financial management for human service administrators.* Boston: Allyn & Bacon.

Martin, L. L. (2002). *Making performance-based contracting perform: What the federal government can learn from state and local governments.* Washington, DC: IBM Center for the Business of Government. Retrieved from http://www.businessofgovernment.org

Martin, L. L. (2003). *Performance-based contracting (PBC) for human services: A review of the literature.* Orlando, FL: Center for Community Partnerships, University of Central Florida. Retrieved December 10, 2007, from ttp://www.cohpa.ucf.edu/ccp/papers/cfm

Martin, L. L. (2004). The privatization of human services: Myths, social capital and civil society. *Journal of Health & Human Services Administration, 27*(1), 175–193.

Martin, L. L. (2005). Performance-based contracting for human services: Does it work? *Administration in Social Work, 29*(1), 63–77.

Martin, L. L. (2007a). Approaches to performance-based contracting (PBC) for social services. Lexington, KY: Quality Improvement Center on the Privatization of Child Welfare Services, School of Social Work, University of Kentucky Retrieved from http://www.uky.edu/SocialWork/qicpcw

Martin, L. L. (2007b). The evolving state of performance accountability in government contracts and grants. Keynote address, 2007 National Conference on Contracts & Grants, Arlington, VA, December 2–3.

Martin, L, L., & Miller, J. (2006). *Contracting for public sector services.* Herndon, VA: National Institute of Governmental Purchasing.

McBeath, B., & Meezan, W. (2006). Nonprofit adaptation to performance-based managed care contracting in Michigan's foster care system. *Administration in Social Work, 30*(2):39–70.

McCullough & Associates. (2005). *Child welfare privatization: A synthesis of research and framework for decision making.* Chevy Chase, MD: Author.

McEwen, R., & Nelson-Phillips, J. (2007). *The evolution of performance contracting within the Illinois child welfare community.* Chicago: Illinois Department of Children & Family Services.

O'Brien, D., & Revel, G. (2005). The milestone payment system: Results based funding in vocational rehabilitation—2005. *Journal of Vocational Rehabilitation, 23*:101–114.

Patti, R. (2000). *The handbook of social welfare management.* Thousand Oaks, CA: Sage Publications.

Perlmutter, F. (2006). Ensuring social work administration. *Administration in Social Work, 30*(2):3–10.

Quality Improvement Center on the Privatization of Child Welfare Services, School of Social Work, University of Kentucky (2006). *Literature review on performance-based contracting and quality assurance.* Lexington: Author.

Romzek, B., & Johnson, J. (2005). State social services contracting: Exploring the determinants of effective contract accountability. *Public Administration Review, 65*(4):436–449.

10

Investment Strategies for Nonprofit Organizations

Raymond Sanchez Mayers and Fontaine H. Fulghum

In 2006, the Salvation Army reported income from investments of $602 million, a larger amount than the operating revenues of most for-profit or nonprofit organizations (*Nonprofit Times*, 2007). And it was not alone. Of the *Nonprofit Times'* Top 100, an annual review of the 100 largest nonprofits in America, all but 11 had income from investments of more than a million dollars. In total, the Top 100 received investment income of $4.7 billion that fiscal year (Hrywna, 2007). This is an enviable position for an organization, and one that many nonprofits would like to attain. Such attainment flows from a viable investment strategy.

Investing may be defined as the current commitment of funds to receive a future financial gain (Mayers, 2004). Money for investing may come from two main sources: endowment and surplus funds from unrestricted revenue. Many small nonprofits may not have an endowment fund, but most have some surplus monies, even if on a short-term basis. All nonprofits can and should invest a portion of their revenue in ways that produce income for their organizations. Investing is viewed here within the context of a planning process through which the nonprofit develops an investment strategy suitable for the organization within the constraints mandated by governing bylaws, legal statutes, and funder restrictions. The result of this investment process can be an investment mix tailored to the special needs of the organization. This chapter discusses how this can be done and the issues that arise in doing so.

The Context

Nonprofit organizations operate in a stringent regulatory environment at the federal, state, and local levels as well as imposed by private sector standards-setting bodies. Most notable among the private bodies are the American Institute of Certified Public Accountants (AICPA) and the Financial Accounting Standards Board (FASB). In addition, certain accrediting and standards-setting entities have been established specifically aimed at the private nonprofit human services sector. Among these are the Council on Accreditation, the United Way of America and other federated organizations, the BBB

Wise Giving Alliance (a merger of the National Charities Information Bureau and the Council of Better Business Bureaus' Philanthropic Advisory Service), and others (Mayers, 2004). Those most significant here, state governments, the FASB, and the Council on Accreditation, are discussed in following paragraphs.

State Governments

Most state governments have nonprofit corporation acts that govern the operations of nonprofits incorporated in their state. In addition, at least 44 states have passed the Uniform Prudent Investor Act (UPIA) (National Conference of Commissioners on Uniform State Laws [NCCUSL], 1995), which applies to the management of nonprofit trust accounts set up for investment purposes. Even more important is the Uniform Prudent Management of Institutional Funds Act (UPMIFA), passed by 23 states so far and under consideration in others (NCCUSL, 2006). This act specifically applies to the endowments of nonprofit corporations.

Because there are many similarities between UPIA and UPMIFA, they are discussed together. For example, they both adopt the prudence standard for investment decision making. That is, they "direct directors or others responsible for managing and investing the funds of an institution to act as a prudent investor would, using a portfolio approach in making investments and considering the risk and return objectives of the fund" (NCCUSL, 2006, p. 13). We discuss these laws further in the context of decision making on, and management of, investments.

The Financial Accounting Standards Board

Since 1973 the FASB has established standards of financial accounting and reporting for the private, nongovernment sector. In 1995 the organization issued the Statement of Financial Accounting Standards (FAS124): *Accounting for Certain Investments Held by Not-for-Profit Organizations*, which sought to achieve uniformity in recording and reporting nonprofit investments. FAS124 applies to investments in equity securities with readily determinable fair market values (common and preferred stocks) and to all debt securities (corporate and government bonds). It states that these types of investment securities have to be measured at fair value. (FAS124 also mandates disclosure rules for investments in the nonprofit financial statements, but this issue is beyond the scope of this chapter.) However, once an investment policy is developed and implemented, the nonprofit organization and its accountants must adhere to this standard.

The Council on Accreditation

The Council on Accreditation is a standards-setting body with many member organizations, such as the Child Welfare League of America and Family Service of America (now the Alliance for Children and Families). Originally an accrediting body for family and children's agencies, it currently accredits 38 different service areas and more than 60 types of programs. One of its standards, which pertains specifically to investments (see Table 1), says that a nonprofit should have an investment committee, an investment policy, protocols for investment decisions, and established criteria for contracting with an investment adviser. In addition, an organization should periodically review the status of its investments and report such to its governing body (Council on Accreditation, 2008).

TABLE 1 EXCERPT FROM COUNCIL ON ACCREDITATION STANDARDS	FIGURE 1 THE INVESTMENT PLANNING PROCESS

GOV 7: Oversight of Investments

An organization that invests funds has controls to ensure the proper management of investments, including a committee established by the governing body that:

a. follows, and biennially reviews, an investment policy that outlines acceptable levels of risk, criteria for contracting with investment advisors or firms, and protocols for making investment decisions;

b. oversees and reviews both the investment of funds, and the management, purchase, or sale of real estate, securities, and other assets;

c. ensures practices conform to applicable legal and regulatory requirements; and

d. reports the status of investments and investment recommendations to the governing body.

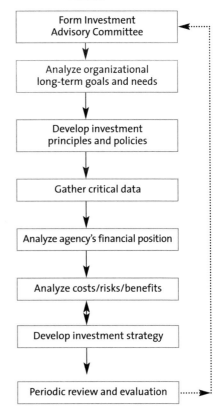

Source: Council on Accreditation (2008); http://www.coanet.org.

Adapted from Mayers, 2004.

The Planning Process

An effective investment plan for the nonprofit organization must reflect critical thought on the part of staff and board members. Such a plan should be the result of a process that includes the following steps: (1) form an investment advisory committee; (2) analyze long-term organizational goals and needs; (3) develop investment principles and policies; (4) gather data from critical agency financial reports and information about suitable investments; (5) analyze the agency's financial condition; (6) analyze the costs/risks/benefits of specific investments; (7) develop an investment strategy which involves an understanding and clarification of investment goals; (8) periodically review and evaluate the agency's investments and investment plan (see Figure 1) (Mayers, 2004). These steps are considered in following paragraphs.

Formation of Investment Advisory Committee

Most nonprofits have a finance committee that operates as a subcommittee of the board of directors. This committee usually works with the executive director/CEO and other staff on budgeting, the audit function, and similar issues. Such a committee may also be involved in investment planning, or the board may want a separate committee made up of other knowledgeable board and staff members to carry out investment planning and implementation.

Analysis of Long-Term Organizational Goals and Needs

The investment committee should view the goals of each investment within the context of the nonprofit organization's needs and any endowment gift restrictions. The organization's board should have a clear idea of its goals before it embarks on an investment program, because its investments should be an integral part of its long-term plan. The primary objective of a nonprofit's investments should be to attain a stable source of funding for operations or other purposes, such as a capital building program.

Organizational goals and needs thus dictate the types of investments an organization might choose. For example, if one key organizational goal is constructing a new homeless shelter, then this type of capital project would require specific investment vehicles suitable for the long term. On the other hand, if an organization wants current operating cash to augment an ongoing program, for example, a teen parenting program, then the investment type selected would be capable of generating current income.

One long-range goal should be the establishment of an endowment fund, along with a marketing plan, to attract donors to it. Although the board may establish specific conditions on gifts and their use, many restrictions come from donors themselves. "A donor restricted endowment fund is created when a donor stipulates that the contributed assets be invested for a specific period of time or in perpetuity" (Larkin & DiTomasso, 2006, p. 121). Donor restrictions may also specify exactly how the interest from the investment is to be spent, for example, on a specific program or program activity. In fact, nonprofits are required to give primary consideration to donor intent as it is expressed in the gift (NCCUSL, 2006). In this case, the agency must view the restriction in light of its organizational goals before accepting the money.

Development of Investment Principles and Policies

A key aspect of this investment planning process is the organization's articulation of the ethical values and financial principles that will shape investment policy. These principles should be codified and made a part of nonprofit organization bylaws to guide an executive director/CEO and/or the investment committee's deliberations.

Policies

Of course, the nonprofit's legal counsel and financial professionals on the board should review investment policies. The organization's investment policy should define

- its investment objectives;
- levels of acceptable risk;
- types of acceptable assets (e.g., stocks, bonds) and their quality ratings;
- levels of responsibility and accountability; and
- establishment of a system for regular review of the policies (BoardSource, 2008; Council on Accreditation, 2008; Fry, 1998).

Values

Along with specific parameters regarding type and allocation of assets, the investment policy may embody some values the organization wishes to reflect, for example, socially responsible investing (SRI). Socially responsible investing "recognizes that corporate responsibility and societal concerns are valid parts of investment decisions . . . . [it] considers both the investor's financial needs and an investment's impact on society" (Social Investment Forum, 2008). According to the Forum's *2007 Report on Socially Responsible Investing Trends in the United States*, approximately 11% of assets under professional management in the United States use the SRI approach. The Forum also identified $2.71 trillion in assets using one or more SRI investing strategies as delineated in following paragraphs (Social Investment Forum, 2007).

Socially responsible investing uses three primary strategies: screening, shareholder advocacy, and community investing (Social Investment Forum, 2008). *Screening* is the evaluation of an investment based on environmental, social, or corporate governance criteria. Screening can use either a positive or negative approach. Positive screening entails purposefully choosing investments, for example, because they are environmentally friendly. So some investors look for investments in corporations that identify themselves as green or eco-friendly. Negative screening seeks to avoid investments whose products or business practices are considered unhealthy for the environment, for human beings in general, or for workers in a particular corporation. In this case, for example, investors may choose to avoid investments in companies that produce cigarettes and other tobacco products or weapons.

Shareholder advocacy can be used when shares of a corporation are purchased. The owner of the stock shares (here, the nonprofit corporation) becomes a part-owner of the corporation, and, as an owner, the shareholder proposes resolutions regarding social and environmental issues to be voted on at shareholder meetings. These resolutions may cover such topics as labor practices, corporate responsibility, or environmental concerns. For example, some shareholder resolutions might involve adding women or minorities to corporate boards of directors; in other instances, resolutions might call on corporations to reduce their greenhouse emissions.

The third approach, *community investing*, "directs capital from investors and lenders to communities that are underserved by traditional financial services institutions" (Social Investment Forum, 2008). Community investing institutions may make or guarantee loans for housing or small businesses, for example, in low-income minority communities that have historically had difficulty securing such funding. One such entity recently invested more than $300 million in projects to create homes for more than 8,000 persons in Massachusetts (Social Investment Forum, 2008).

Gathering Critical Data

The next step in the nonprofit's investment process is gathering data. Having vital internal financial information is crucial to the investment decision-making process. The investment committee should review all information pertinent to the financial status of the organization, which may include past financial statements, along with the audits that accompany them; annual reports; Form 990s (nonprofit tax returns); budget projections; program reports; needs assessments; and reports to external funding sources such as federal, state, and local government entities. Useful external information includes any restrictions on funds by funding sources as well as preliminary information about the types of investments and financial advisers who might be useful in its deliberations. With respect to the last, members of the organization's board of directors might be helpful in this regard.

Analysis of the Organization's Financial Condition

Before beginning an investment program, the nonprofit must make sure it has a sufficiently secure financial base to withstand unexpected events or emergencies, such as the loss of major funding or a disruption of programs because of some natural disaster. Areas that must be reviewed include trend data and projections on revenue and public support, cash flow, and grant support. Also important is to make sure the organization has sufficient liability insurance, as well as an acceptable credit rating, and a surplus as a cushion against emergencies. In the past, funding sources did not approve of nonprofits' having surplus funds. Surplus funds were perceived as wasteful and diverting from program activities, but funders have learned that it is important for organizations to have some extra funds; otherwise, they may return to the funder for every emergency and shortfall. Given the inherent risks associated with any investment, a nonprofit should address any shortcomings in the these areas before implementing an investment program.

Analysis of Costs/Risks/Benefits

The human service organization has to be more cognizant of risk factors associated with investments in light of its charitable function, which recognizes that the money it invests is to be used for the public good. The organization must decide how much risk or uncertainty about the outcome it is willing to assume with respect to loss of principal, fluctuations in the price of securities, and rate of return on investment (Hirt & Block, 1993). Degree of investment risk is related to the type of investment vehicle chosen. Some major categories of risk follow (Huang, 1981):

- Business or financial risk, or that risk concerned with the financial viability of an investment. For example, when shares of a corporation are purchased, the purchaser is taking the risk that the corporation will stay in business and be able to pay dividends on the stock and/or that the stock will appreciate in value as the corporation's profits increase (Gitman & Joehnk, 1990).

- Price-level risk, or that risk concerned with losing money on one's fixed-income investment due to inflation.
- Interest rate risk, which is usually associated with fixed-rate investments and the danger of losing money when interest rates rise higher than the interest on one's fixed-rate investment. For example, if a certificate of deposit (CD) paying 4.2% interest is purchased for 1 year, the buyer is taking the risk that prevailing interest rates may rise, and money would be lost.
- Market risk, or fluctuation in the price of an investment due to events perceived to be related to the earning power of the issuing corporation (Mayers, 2004). For example, when a market analyst forecasts lower earnings for a corporation such as Microsoft, its price per share of stock may decrease.
- Psychological risk, or irrational behavior on the part of an investor related to the vagaries and fluctuations of investment markets.

In addition to risks, there are costs involved as well, for example, brokers' fees, and in the case of mutual funds, sometimes management fees. The UPMIFA requires an organization to minimize its investing costs; however, it states that an organization may prudently incur costs in hiring an investment adviser as long as the costs incurred are appropriate (NCCUSL, 2006, p. 16).

Finally, benefits are to be considered and weighed against the costs and risks. For example, a hedge fund may be riskier than other investments, yet it can also reap greater rewards. The UPMIFA also states that decisions about an individual asset should not be made in isolation but in to the context of the organization's total portfolio and as part of an overall investment strategy (NCCUSL, 2006, p. 12).

Development of Investment Objectives and Strategy

In terms of the organization's investment objectives, nonprofits should keep some factors in mind. Obviously, the nonprofit organization wants maximum return on its investment coupled with minimum risk. To achieve this, the investment committee must consider factors such as (Mayers, 2004):

- Safety of principal: Principal is the amount of money initially invested. Diversification of portfolio can help a nonprofit organization assure the safety of its principal. Indeed, diversification is mandated under UPMIFA: "An institution shall diversify the investments of an institutional fund unless the institution reasonably determines that, because of special circumstances, the purposes of the fund are better served without diversification" (NCCUSL, 2006, p. 13).
- Protection of purchasing power: This goal recognizes that, because of inflation, the price of goods and services increases over time. To protect the value on an investment against inflation, a nonprofit has to try to invest in assets whose value will increase faster than does the rate of inflation. This goal is not always easy to achieve. Because of the uncertainties of world markets and world politics, diversification is an important strategy in furtherance of this goal as well, but within the limitations imposed by legal, moral, donor, funder, and board-imposed restrictions.

- Current income: This occurs when an investment pays a regular amount of interest or dividend to assure a steady cash flow. Investments with a guaranteed stable rate of return include bonds, treasury notes, CDs, and preferred stocks. Although stable, they also usually pay a lower rate of return.
- Capital appreciation: This refers to an increase in the dollar value of an investment. If one pays $50 per share of a stock and sells it for $60, then the capital appreciation on the stock is $10 per share. Of course, an investment may also depreciate in value.
- Liquidity: "Liquidity is the ability to convert an investment into cash quickly at a value similar to the original amount of the principal invested" (Mayers, 2004, p. 194). The importance of this goal depends on the objectives of the investment. That is, if the investment is for a long-term capital program, then liquidity is not important. On the other hand, if the organization is investing quarterly monies from a grant, then it needs to turn around the money quickly so it is available as needed. In this case, the organization needs more liquidity.

Whether investments are meant to meet long- or short-term objectives, no operating monies of a nonprofit, whether revenue or public support, should sit idly in non-interest-bearing accounts. Nonprofits should have, at a minimum, interest-bearing checking accounts and short-term CDs that are readily available. Those with sufficient available cash can set up a bank "sweep account" in which the bank invests monies nightly and redeposits them into the account. Organizations can find out the minimum dollar threshold for this type of account.

- Ease of management and expertise of staff: Managing investments requires financial expertise, skill, and time, characteristics that most nonprofits' staffs do not possess. Although knowledgeable directors may be of assistance, a conflict of interest may arise when board members from the financial sector are responsible for handling investments. Unless an investment is of the simplest type, for example, a CD or an interest-bearing savings or checking account, the wisest course of action for a nonprofit is to seek an investment adviser.
- The investment environment: A number of socioeconomic and political factors influence the investment environment at any given time, for example, general economic conditions; possible effects of inflation or deflation; and expected tax consequences, if any, of an investment (NCCUSL, 2006). Of course, to an investment professional, it is always a good time to invest—what changes is the nature of the investment, which depends on the socioeconomic and political climate.
- Nonprofit organization bylaws or funder restrictions: As mentioned earlier, there may be nonprofit organization bylaws that restrict it to certain types of investments, or a donor to an endowment fund may restrict its use. This makes the matter of investing much easier, if less flexible. Such restrictions are less common now and will be even more so in the future as the UPMIFA states that a nonprofit may invest in any type of investment as part of an overall investment strategy in which risk and return objectives are suited to the organization (NCUSL, 2006). Given these factors, the investment(s) chosen should be diversified and should reflect the values and ethics of the nonprofit organization and its mission.

Periodic Review and Evaluation

As the world of nonprofits and investments is constantly changing, the nonprofit needs to be vigilant about its investments. The circumstances of an organization can change, and so can its investment needs. When periodic strategic plans change for an organization, its investment plan needs to be reviewed and updated as well. With ongoing investments, the committee should expect periodic, monthly, or quarterly reports from its investment manager, whether that person is an in-house staff or board member or an external manager or consultant. The investment committee, along with the executive director/CEO and investment manager, need to review periodically the status of all investments, their rate of return, shares gained or lost, appreciation, and continual congruence of investment goals with organizational needs. Much of this planning and review should take place with consultation from a competent investment adviser.

Choosing an Investment Adviser

Two types of investment advisers may work with the nonprofit and its investment activities. Investment managers may offer services that range from giving advice to actually managing the organization's investment portfolio (Zietlow, 2007). Those who manage portfolios may specialize in one aspect of investments, such as fixed-income securities or specific types of stocks. Investment consultants, on the other hand, do not manage portfolios; instead, they advise the organization when it sets its investment goals and policies and may help secure an investment manager for the organization. Once the organization has decided on an external investment adviser, the nonprofit should contract in writing with the adviser, specifying fees, any additional charges above and beyond the basic fees, and the basis for termination of the contract (Zietlow, 2007).

The investment committee and the executive director/CEO should select an external investment manager based on criteria they developed. Of prime importance is the fit between the organization's values and principles and the investment manager's philosophy. If the investment manager is an employee of a firm specializing in endowment management or nonprofit investments, then the committee will want to know the qualifications of its professionals, the risk management capabilities of the firm, the kinds of internal controls it uses, its fees, the quality and timeliness of its reports, and, most importantly, its reputation in the nonprofit community (Commonfund Institute, n.d.).

Finally, all investment managers of nonprofit funds, whether in-house or contracted, must abide by laws regulating these funds as well as their specific obligations as spelled out under law. For example:

UPMIFA requires a charity and those who manage and invest its funds to
- give primary consideration to donor intent;
- act in good faith, with the care an ordinarily prudent person would exercise;
- incur only reasonable costs; and
- make a reasonable effort to verify relevant facts. (NCCUSL, 2006, p. 2)

In completing this investment planning process, and securing a competent investment adviser where indicated, the nonprofit will be on its way to putting its money to work maximizing resources and increasing operating funds. And it will do this in a way that reflects its mission, purpose, and values. In the future, it may even find its name among those listed in the *Nonprofit Times* Top 100 nonprofits.

References

BoardSource. (2008). *What should our investment policy include?* Retrieved May 9, 2008, from http://www.boardsource.org/Knowledge.asp?ID=3.116

Commonfund Institute. (n.d.). Principles of nonprofit investment management. Wilton, CT: Author. Retrieved April 29, 2008, from http://www.commonfund.org/Templates/Generic/RESOURCE_REQUEST/target.pdf ?RES_GUID=CCAB0290-1E05-40D4-98BA-1AEBF9BF533E

Council on Accreditation. (2008). *Accreditation standards.* New York: Author. Retrieved May 9, 2008, from http://www.coastandards.org/standards.php?navView=private&core_id=807

Financial Accounting Standards Board. (1995). *Statement of Financial Accounting Standard No. 124: Accounting for certain investments held by not-for-profit organizations.* Stamford, CT: Author.

Fry, R. P., Jr. (1998). *Nonprofit investment policies: Practical steps for growing charitable funds.* New York: John Wiley & Sons, Inc.

Gitman, L. J., & Joehnk, M. D. (1990). *Fundamentals of investing.* New York: HarperCollins.

Hirt, G. A., & Block, S. B. (1993). *Fundamentals of investment management* (4th ed.). Homewood, IL: Richard D. Irwin, Inc.

Hrywna, M. (2007). Surging investments pushed large gifts and income. *The Nonprofit Times*, November 1, 2007, pp. 36, 38

Huang, S. S. C. (1981). *Investment analysis and management.* Cambridge, MA: Winthrop Publishers, Inc.

Larkin, R. F., & DiTommaso, M. (2006). *Wiley not-for-profit GAAP 2006: Interpretation and application of generally accepted accounting principles for not-for-profit organizations.* Hoboken, NJ: John Wiley & Sons, Inc.

Mayers, R. S. (2004). *Financial management for nonprofit human service organizations* (2⁻ ed.). Springfield: IL. Charles C. Thomas.

National Conference of Commissioncrs on Uniform State Laws (NCCUSL). (1995). *Uniform Prudent Investor Act.* Retrieved May 10, 2008, from http://www.law.upenn.edu/bll/archives/ulc/umoifa/2006final_act.pdf

National Conference of Commissioners on Uniform State Laws (NCCUSL). (2006). *Uniform Prudent Management of Institutional Funds Act.* Retrieved May 8, 2008, from http://www.law.upenn.edu/bll/archives/ulc/fnact99/1990s/pla94.pdf

Nonprofit Times. (2007, November 1). *The top 100.* Retrieved from http://www.nptimes.com

Social Investment Forum. (2007). *2007 Report on socially responsible investing trends in the United States: Executive summary.* Washington, DC: Author. Retrieved May 9, 2008, from http://www.socialinvest.org/resources/pub/documents/FinalExcSummary_2007_SIF_Trends_wlinks.pdf

Social Investment Forum. (2008). *Socially responsible investing facts.* Retrieved May 9, 2008, from http://www.socialinvest.org/resources/sriguide/srifacts.cfm

Zietlow, J. (2007, June). Step by step: Deciding if you need help with investments. *Exempt.* Retrieved May 8, 2008, from http://www.exemptmagazine.com/full-articles/june07stepbystep.html.

IV   Principles and Issues in Nonprofit Management

Joel M. Levy

There is considerable concurrence in the literature that the job of running and managing large nonprofit organizations has become an increasingly complex, strenuous, and often stressful endeavor. Today's nonprofit leaders have to do much more than create the vision, set the agenda, and articulate the mission of their organizations.

More than ever before, leaders of nonprofit agencies have to be accountable to the mandates of their boards of trustees, their clients, staff, communities, funders, and their many other stakeholders. Today, they have to be even more responsive and sensitive to growing demands from government funders, donors, and service recipients, focusing not only on outputs, but also on outcomes and social impact. They must deal with ever-growing compliance and regulatory issues imposed by all levels of government while adjusting to tightening budgets and demands to demonstrate results, effectiveness, efficiency, and outcomes performance results that address evidence-based management issues with broad, long-term social effects. And they face scrutiny from the media, which all too often focus on the occasional shortcomings of not-for-profit organizations, rather than on their numerous accomplishments. Balancing these demands and competing interests is becoming increasingly difficult.

To be successful in carrying out their organizations' missions in an intensely competitive environment, leaders have to formulate a clear vision of their goals and develop a positive, self-sustaining culture. They have to be articulate communicators, fiscal experts, and effective negotiators. They must be able to forge partnerships with a wide array of external alliances and internal constituencies to maximize their organizations' potential and success.

As a social worker for more than four decades, I have witnessed dramatic changes in the demands made on nonprofit organizations and the people who lead them. Yet what has remained constant is the expectation that nonprofit organizations serve a higher purpose and demonstrate a personal belief in their missions. They must be energized by their intrinsic commitment to meet their clients' needs while creating social change in the broader community and society. Integrating strong, positive, personal social values and building on both principles in the code for social workers and a commitment to social change, social justice, and creating social equity to meet the needs of our vulnerable populations is what drives all of us forward.

Nonprofit organizations are value-driven rather than profit-driven. Our *raison d'être* is to make the world a better place for our most vulnerable citizens. Over the years nonprofit organizations have played a pivotal role in transforming the destinies and changing the lives of millions of individuals. They have done so by engaging in vigorous advocacy, by creating programs and services that address the needs of people with special needs, and by serving as agents for social change and justice.

The chapters that comprise this section take into account the new realities that confront nonprofit agencies and those who lead them. By focusing on the attributes of effective leadership and management and the importance of strategic planning, fiscal management, public relations, fundraising, and resource (personnel) development, we have provided a comprehensive toolbox that will enable leaders of nonprofit agencies to continue their noble tradition of creating social justice and equity for all.

Peggy Pittman-Munke provides in chapter 11 some basic concepts of nonprofit management. My own chapters 12 and 13 deal with fund raising and the management of human resources, which are special issues in the nonprofit management role. Chapter 14 on public relations was written in collaboration with several of my colleagues and covers an increasingly important element of modern nonprofit management. Karen Wegmann and I discuss maximizing financial resources in chapter 15. My collaboration with Philip H. Levy and Joshua Rubin in chapter 17, explaining the necessity of creating a dynamic, outcomes-based strategic plan to achieve organization goals, completes the section.

Many others have noted that today's not-for-profits may be viewed as social entrepreneurs and businesses. Others have noted that businesses should learn from not-for-profits (see Collins, 2005). What is clear today is that great leadership and management skills are required to run a great nonprofit, and nothing less than greatness should be expected from our current not-for-profit leaders.

References

Collins, J. (2005). *Good to great and the social sectors.* New York: HarperCollins.

11

Administration of Social Service Agencies
The Rural/Small Town Challenge

Peggy Pittman-Munke

Both public and private social service agencies in smaller towns and rural areas may fly in the face of community values in many ways. Rural areas and smaller towns often value thrift, self-sufficiency, independence, and strong family values, whereas many social service agencies often are perceived as rewarding people who have violated these values by providing them with services and resources. Social service agencies must deal with community leaders who reflect local values, and these values often influence agency funding and acceptance. Further, even if social service administrators have strong ties to the area, they are often viewed as different by virtue of their education and the values acquired during the course of that education. Professionally educated staff have similar issues in the small community (Buxton, 1976).

Rural culture contains some elements of a frontier ideology, including a belief in hard work and individual initiative (Gilbert, 1982), that are directly opposed to the mandate of most social service agencies, thus complicating both administration and service delivery. There is a time-honored view of rural areas as family farms and closely bonded inhabitants with predictable behaviors, norms, and social values that, although rural areas are diverse, still hold true enough to complicate the work of social service agencies (Stedman & Heberlein, 2001). Today, comparatively few rural Americans make their living from agriculture or live on family farms. In fact, more than 90% of the residents of rural areas have nonfarm jobs (Economic Research Service, 1999, p. 86). However, rural values still prevail. Fluharty (2002) points out that rural local governments have "little or no access to technical assistance, research or grant support" (p. 669); the same conditions complicate local rural social service agency administration.

General Challenges to Administration in Small Areas

Administration is always a challenge and is an even greater challenge when working with small-town and rural social service agencies. For this chapter, *rural* and *small town* are considered synonymous. Some of the biggest challenges come in hiring practices and working with boards as well as in funding. The issues that make rural and small-town areas so desirable as places to live are often the same ones that make administration of social service agencies so difficult. Larger public agencies in rural areas face similar issues but to a lesser degree than do private agencies. Changing the organizational culture can be a major issue.

Other issues affecting both social service delivery and agency administration include geographical barriers and transportation difficulties. Excessive travel time is often an issue when administrators must go to meetings that are generally held in large population centers or when agency staff must make home visits or attend collaborative regional meetings. In some areas of larger states, attending mandated meetings related to funding can take the administrator out of the agency for 2 days because the meeting may be 300 to 500 miles from the agency. Making a home visit in a rural area where two-lane highways and even lesser roads are the norm may take the better part of a day if the client lives in the far reaches of the county. In addition, transporting clients to a state hospital or to other needed services in the more populous part of the state can take a worker out of the office for a full day.

Many rural areas and small towns lack any kind of public transportation, including taxi service, making it difficult for clients to get to appointments. Scarcity of resources is another issue. Needed services often are simply not available. For example, there is no readily available psychiatric hospitalization for adolescents within about 100 miles in the western part of my state. Various medical specialists can only be found across the state line about 150 miles away. The scarcity of foster homes means that children in out-of-home care are often placed 3 or 4 hours away from their home community and social network. Inpatient substance abuse services are virtually unavailable, and waiting lists for outpatient treatment services and children's mental health services are long.

Difficulty in retaining professional staff may also be a problem, but there is an obverse as well: Too few opportunities to move to another position may result in burnout and retention of staff beyond their usefulness to the agency. Collateral issues are professional isolation and lack of opportunity for professional development and growth through continuing education, particularly for small areas that are far from major centers of population (Landsman, 2002). Some states are beginning to help rural and small-town regions some distance from heavily populated areas by offering continuing education online. This is important because continuing education can remove needed workers from their agency for several days if the workers are forced to travel to more populous areas of the state for training, or if providing continuing education is dependent on the local professional community, there is little in the way of real learning or new ideas. I vividly remember one continuing education effort provided by the local branch of a professional society that featured a recent college graduate reporting on an undergraduate research effort that referenced material that was more than 20 years out of date.

Another issue, raised by Ginsberg (1998), is confidentiality. This extends beyond confidentiality related to client issues. Confidentiality in regard to client issues is often violated simply by a community member's seeing a client entering the agency. Often this, combined with reasonable community knowledge of the family's circumstances, can result in community members knowing that help is being sought for a problem. Sometimes, too, there is an effort to gather resources, for example, school clothes for a child who is woefully lacking, and those approached can figure out for which child the clothing is meant. The information is shared with a neighbor, a friend, or fellow church members, often with the best of intentions. However, the result is often shame on the part of the child or family in need.

There is lack of confidentiality regarding board actions, staff issues, and administrator/board relationships and administrator/staff relationships. Although efforts are made to maintain confidentiality in these areas, violations often occur, and these violations become grist for town/community discussion. For example, in one small town, a local agency hired its director's retired father as office manager, and her godmother was the agency's board president. The director also had health issues she would have preferred to keep private. However, her mother shared these issues with her godmother, and her godmother shared them with the rest of the board, whose members shared it with their respective spouses. The agency director was floored to find herself on the prayer list at her church and a number of other local churches. In addition, when several community members called to reach the agency director, her father, who was answering the phones, gave them a full update on his daughter's medical condition because the callers were extended family or friends who were also board members. As a result, a number of board members told the agency director that she should change her doctors, her medication, and her whole physical regime. Several clients also called to express concern, offer suggestions regarding medication, and share, for example, "that my mother had something like this and she did _____ for it." This director lost much of her credibility as a mature and competent adult in the community for a time.

Strengths of rural/small-area practice and agency administration include strong personal and professional relationships within the practice community and the community at large. One result of this connection is often high levels of job satisfaction despite the difficulties associated with rural practice, including social service agency administration. One possible reason for this is that, in a small area, the agency administrator knows the good accomplished by his or her agency. Another possible reason for high levels of satisfaction may be that social service agency staff work in a climate that encourages all that a generalist practice implies, rather than in a bureaucratic setting where roles are clearly differentiated. The amount of variety and the opportunity to use all of one's values and skills probably leads to a much higher level of job satisfaction than do carefully defined roles and tasks, as is the case in larger areas.

Informal communication may be a positive, because many agency directors are able to rely on this method, as well as on traditional publicity methods, to make community members aware of the agency's strengths and offerings (Gumpter, Galtman, & Sauer-Jones, 2000; Sullivan, Hassler, & Otis, 1993). However, informal communication through the town grapevine can also make the community aware very quickly of agency shortcomings. A casual comment made over cards or tailgating about some dissatisfaction with agency process or procedures, or with a staff member, can quickly take on a life of its own. For example, one board member told another in the grocery store that she could never find the agency director in during office hours, but neglected to add that the director had speaking engagements to raise community awareness of the issues and mandatory meetings out of the agency related to clients. The agency director ran into her former high school principal at church, and the principal pointed out to her that she did not seem to be doing her job very well.

Agencies generally reflect the values and culture of the area, because most employees and board members are local residents. Many employees and board members who have education beyond high school did not go far from the area to receive an education or left the area to pursue higher education with a group from the local area. Often the values and norms of even educated citizenry reflect the biases and norms of the regions. Service delivery reflects community norms and values rather than professional norms and values or best practices; this can be a mixed blessing, because input from newcomers to the area is often unwelcome, and when newcomers are hired, they are expected to conform to local norms. However, the agencies generally have no difficulty operating within community norms and values, because agency staff are local people. Sometimes the result is that people in the community who most need services do not apply to the agency for these services because they fear the attitude with which these services will be dispensed. Sometimes too, there is a perception that services are carefully rationed to be dispensed to those deemed as worthy. For example, one agency had a number of services, such as daycare and transportation vouchers, to offer clients but could not offer them to every client because these resources were limited. Clients who were unmarried with children and clients who were seen as less deserving because of substance abuse routinely were not offered these services, nor were most clients of color. Instead, these services went to clients with limited incomes but ties to important community members or to clients the town standards deemed deserving. The availability of these services in the case plan often determined the client's success, thus causing the worker's judgment to be a self-fulfilling prophecy.

Even in child protection, in small areas, substantiation of reported abuse or neglect may vary, depending on the way the investigating worker sees intent or the way the worker views the parenting based on his or her community reputation. In one small community, two toddlers were found wandering around the community clad only in a diaper and shirt in the middle of the night on different occasions. In one instance, the toddler wandered off when the teenage mother, daughter of a family that was well thought of in the community, was asleep, and other members of her family, with whom she lived, did not check on the little one or awaken their daughter before going out for the evening. The worker determined that the charge was unsubstantiated, based on the fact that no one intended to neglect the toddler. In the other instance, the mother of the toddler had worked a double shift and had fallen asleep on the couch in front of the television after she tucked the child into bed. However, this young mother had experienced a comparatively troubled adolescence and was well-known to local agencies. In this case, neglect was substantiated. This mother was referred to parenting classes and was under agency supervision for 6 months. This mother did not plan to neglect her child; she fell asleep, exhausted, after a double shift. Area values affected the decision-making process in both instances.

Organizational Culture

Organizational culture, "the constellation of values, beliefs, expectations, and assumptions that underlie and organize the organization's behavior as a group" (Holland, 1995, p. 1789) is rooted in the local rural culture. Habits of life that prevail in the local community also prevail in the agency. Rarely does organizational culture support innovation and risk taking. Instead, the pressure is on newcomers to the organization and the area to conform to organizational ways of thought.

In some rural areas, for example, computers are treated largely as word-processing entities. In one such area, I was amazed to find that some agencies only allowed the director's computer and, perhaps, the computer of a trusted member of the clerical staff to be hooked up to the Internet. This was permitted primarily so that forms could be downloaded. When I asked about this, I was told that staff would waste time playing games or sending e-mail or would go to shopping or pornography sites on the Web. However, there was no concern about staff members having and using cell phones during working hours. I concluded that in this particular small rural community, cell phones were considered adjuncts to daily life, and computers were still viewed as ways to waste time or worse. Sometime later, when a new director was hired, she attempted to change the organizational culture by initiating staff training where everyone was trained on other uses of the computer, including appropriate Internet use. The staff acted as if there were great interest in the presentation, but 6 weeks later they had not yet found it convenient to allow workmen to come in to wire their offices for computer access. Rather than outright rejection of change, quietly ignoring change is common in rural areas. Soon, the innovation is forgotten, and agency processes and procedures do not change. Agency life continues to be predictable and stable.

However, change is possible in rural agencies. A wise administrator allows plenty of time for the staff to process the potential change, or, if possible, a staff member of long standing who is much respected is encouraged to come up with the idea for the change. If the change comes from outside, such as a funding source, the director may tell several longtime staff members before the change is announced to the agency as a whole, emphasizing the potential loss of the funding source if the agency does not implement the new policy. Then, once the new procedures are announced to the staff as a whole, these longtime staff members are chosen to head the committee that will implement the changes. Slowly, change can happen.

Organizational culture can also subvert stated goals of the organization. Goal displacement takes place when the stated goals of the organization are modified to goals that are similar but are a better fit with the culture of the organization. Sometimes this can be seen in terms of persons offered services and what services are offered. Although policy may state that the agency offers certain services to all who meet the geographical, economic, or other criteria, actually only certain clients, who embody the agency's perspective of good people who are down on their luck, receive services beyond the minimum. Staff may rationalize this displacement by such arguments as "The _____ family would stop going to counseling," or "He has been in treatment before and he never stayed away from the bottle," or "That family doesn't have anyone smart enough to earn a GED." In this way, agencies save critical services for those considered more deserving by local standards rather than wasted on those who are perceived to be unable to profit by the service.

Race frequently plays a role in the quality of services offered. This subversion of original agency goals so that services offered are determined by factors other than the stated criteria often occurs in rural areas. In one relatively small town in the South there were two different public housing units. One rivaled the most expensive apartments in the town in amenities, whereas the other was older and somewhat run-down and had few amenities. The first, newer public housing unit was filled with a number of young couples who had finished college and were saving money for a down payment on a house and a number of older widows who were related to some of the town's leaders. The second housing unit was filled with single-parent Black families with a sprinkling of poor White single parent families in which substance abuse was part of the fabric of daily life. When this disparity was pointed out to one of the workers, she stated, "Those people like to live that way. They wouldn't be comfortable in the new apartments; besides, most of their friends and relatives live in that area."

However, one strength of social service agencies in small town/rural areas is that clients are not merely cases to social service providers, so both providers and clients may feel a stronger connection to each other than is typical of larger areas. In some smaller areas, clients attend the same church or were often grade school or high school classmates, or the children of the clients are in the same school class as the service provider's, or they are connected to the service provider in other ways. Thus, the service provider feels a personal connection, delivering all possible services becomes important to the provider, and many informal resources are accessed as well to provide necessary services and resources unattainable through regular channels. In one small-town agency, a service provider persuaded the local Weight Watchers group leader to provide free service to a severely overweight client, and, as the client began to lose weight, prevailed on a local beautician to provide a new hairstyle and makeup. When asked why she did this for her client, the worker responded that she remembered "what a pretty girl the client was in high school," and "everyone knew that the client's ex-husband was such a jerk to her that no wonder she let herself go and could not get a decent job." The worker had a personal commitment to the client based on their shared high school experience, which caused the worker to see the client as deserving and worthy of all possible effort.

Lines of Authority and Hiring Practices

Formal lines of authority can be found in an organizational chart in *Organization Theory and Design* (Daft, 1998, p. 26). However, there is a difference between formal organizational policy, including the formal organizational chart, and informal organization policy in terms of who actually has the authority to get things done. For the newcomer to rural or small-town agency administration, this often makes understanding the real organization and operation of the agency very difficult.

Resnick and Patti (1980, p. 51) point out that agencies have a number of communication networks by which information is sent and received. *Merriam-Webster's Collegiate Dictionary* (1995) explains that communication is complex and includes nuances of verbal and nonverbal communication such as subtle inflections and tiny gestures. Many times in rural agencies the actual authority is held by a long-term employee or by a person who does not seem to have much connection with the agency, for example, a local politician. The long-term employee may be the director's administrative assistant or a caseworker who is committed to the status quo. A new employee who is not tuned into the informal network may make the mistake of checking with the person at the top of the hierarchy about processes and procedures only to be referred to the person who actually makes decisions or told to do things in a way that offends the informal power structure. Often the informal leader holds expert power (Johns, 1996), that is, the special interconnection of power networks. This informal leader knows "where the bodies are buried" in the agency and the informal power structure in the local area, and is the person who can generally arrange, through connections, to get things done with a minimum of fuss. However, this informal leader often does not have the professional knowledge and expertise needed for agency growth and development and is devoted to maintaining the status quo.

The informal leader can also facilitate the entry of a new worker into the agency system or make it difficult for the newcomer to fit into or to understand agency culture. In one agency, a worker followed the written policy only to find that she had violated many informal norms. The informal leader made it clear to other agency employees that the newcomer, "with her big-city ways," did not fit in with the other workers in the agency. The newcomer quickly found herself on the outside of the group when informal lunch meetings were held or office gossip was circulated. The newcomer decided that working at this agency was not worth her effort and decided to leave. The informal leader assured her that she had made a smart decision. In this case, the loss of this newcomer was a real loss to the agency as well, because she had better computer skills and therapy skills than other agency employees, along with varied experience that could have enriched the services the agency provided. Perhaps it was a coincidence, but about 3 months later, the niece of the informal leader was hired in the same job.

It is important to remember that administration of social service agencies requires skills that are unique and that distinguish these agencies from other enterprises. For this reason, it may be difficult to hire an administrator who is part of the community. Patti (2000) identifies these unique characteristics as the ability to address difficult moral choices; to accommodate community, funder, and client expectations; to advocate for and serve vulnerable populations, and to rely on frontline professionals to provide services. Hasenfeld (1983) reminds us that every service provided by a social service agency has moral consequences for both the lives of clients and, in small areas, the life of the community. The type of services these agencies provide sets them apart from other agencies because the provision of services is "guided by moral considerations" that are a combination of the personal values of the social service worker and "the values underlying organizationally prescribed policies and practices" (p. 116). It is often difficult to help administrators separate their own and their workers' personal values from the values underlying provision of services by the agency: In that case, personal values related to community norms are likely to prevail.

Often private social service agencies have boards that do not understand the relationship of values to service provision or the difference between professional and personal values. Sometimes board members criticize the fact that services are rendered to clients who do not live according to the members' values. In other situations, board members may refer a potential client they know for service alleging that the potential client is a good person when the client does not fit the agency guidelines, and then are angry with agency personnel for declining to serve the referred client.

Another unique aspect of social service agencies that distinguishes them from other community businesses and services is that social service agencies, particularly private nonprofit agencies, rely on a variety of funders, including the local community, local and other foundations, and government bodies to provide funding for operations (Patti, 2000). This variety of funding sources is difficult to manage and requires a seasoned administrator, because each funding source may have different opinions about how services should be delivered, what the agency's goals should be, and how outcomes should be measured to continue funding. Sometimes, too, in small areas, a funder may choose to pull funding if the agency services are provided to clients who do not seem to be deserving, according to community norms. Many times, the number of different fathers of a woman's children may become an issue for some funders in small areas. Funding may be pulled on the basis that the "agency is not serving the deserving people but condoning immorality" on the part of its clients.

Social services agencies are also unique in that, for the most part, they rely on the professional judgment of professional staff to make decisions related to providing services to clients. Hasenfeld (1983) makes this clear: "The core activities in *social service agencies* consist of relations between staff and clients. The relations serve as the vehicle and the tools through which the organization takes jurisdiction over the clients, assesses and determines their needs, works to transform them, and accomplishes some desired results" (p. 10). Patti (2000) points out that, because this is so, agency administrators must help staff develop common goals and must take the lead in expressing values and goals in keeping with social work ethics and values that will serve as inspiration to the professional and nonprofessional staff, volunteers, and supporters, including the board. This often is difficult because social work ethics and values may be the antithesis of the community values as perceived by many volunteers and board members.

So the professional staff must find a way to make social work values and ethics understandable and palatable to all. Often this is easiest in agencies serving children, because everyone involved in the service believes on some level that all children deserve a decent chance at a good life. However, professional agency staff and community members may have very different ideas about what constitutes that decent chance at a good life. Sometimes agencies that deal with young children and their parents, and that are staffed mostly by volunteers, may be more interested in making sure young parents pay for their lapses in judgment rather than in helping young parents to parent while still meeting the developmental tasks of adolescence. One of the services offered by an agency of this type was respite care for young parents. Several of the volunteers did not feel that "these kids" deserved respite care so they could date or go to a school function or hang out with friends, because "these kids had made bad choices and now should live with the consequences and be adult about it." They were willing to provide respite care for approved activities, for example, a church trip. The only problem was that these were teenagers with little family support. The kind of respite and mentoring this agency was established to deliver could make a big difference in whether the teens involved were able to parent successfully and mature to successful adulthood. When volunteers wanted to withhold this help because the young parents had violated community norms, they were violating the values on which the agency's purpose was based.

The informal leader who lacks the appropriate expertise and credentials often is unable to serve as the agency administrator in an increasingly complex world. So the agency is often forced to hire a formal leader who is often an outsider in the community but has the necessary credentials. Sometimes the formal leader is a native of the area *and* understands how things are done in the area. This type of formal leader has an easier time fitting into the organization because he or she understands the local area culture and, therefore, is more likely to understand the agency culture. If the new formal leader is an outsider, staff members generally either ignore the formal leader or organize against him or her. The challenge for new leader is to work with the informal leader to learn the organizational culture and, at least for the first year or two, to go along with the prevailing means of accomplishing agency goals. Change must be introduced incrementally. Process and staff involvement, as well as the acceptance of the informal leader, are very important to the new leader's ultimate success.

Hiring administrators and staff in a rural area is often difficult, primarily because there are too few applicants with the appropriate credentials. This sometimes results in hiring someone who lacks appropriate credentials to serve as an effective administrator, or hiring another agency's problem administrator. In addition, the individuals who are hired may be closely related to other staff or board members. It is often assumed that relatives look out for each other in the job market. Staff members, even if not related by blood or marriage, have several generations of experience with one another in the community, and boundaries between formal agency role and community life are blurred. Community and family connections may become an issue when supervision, promotion, scheduling, and assignment of duties are under consideration. Staff members are often treated differently on the basis of connections outside the agency. The formal leader from outside the area may minimize the importance of these connections and thus may alienate important staff and community members.

Appropriate boundaries between the worker and the client are difficult to maintain. Often, clients who have family or community relationships with the workers or who attend the same church as a worker are treated very differently from those who do not have these connections. Community connection becomes an issue in service delivery when a client expects more than the agency worker can deliver or when a community leader asks for special favors for a client. Formal leaders from outside the community do not always understand the power of community connection. If this factor is ignored, the formal leader's credibility is undermined within both the agency and the larger community. When the sister of a local politician or member of a "first family" calls and asks for consideration for a referral, and the agency administrator from outside the region does not take care of the request in a way that pleases the referring source, the administrator's credibility is often seriously damaged. If an agency staff person who has ties to the power structure in the community is reined in or admonished, the agency administrator may find it difficult to get the business of the agency accomplished in the community and cannot understand what is happening and why, that director will not serve in that job for long. In one small community, a staff member in an agency with a director from "outside" was not working her scheduled hours and was disciplined according to the written personnel policy. The staff member was related to a number of important people in the community, some of whom were on the board. The agency director found herself excluded from a number of important community meetings, and her calls were not returned. She was aware there was an issue and, because she needed to stay in the community, discovered the problem and worked to placate the staff member. She was able to reinstate herself in the professional community and continue to be effective.

The Board of Directors

The board is a major entity in private and nonprofit social service agencies, and its members have great power as well as fiduciary responsibility. Board members are also expected to have exceptional integrity and to guide the organization with skill (Carver, 1997). In rural areas, board seats often are either difficult to fill or seem to be lifetime appointments, often in contradiction to the agency's bylaws. The board's primary responsibilities are to make policy, review the mission statement, secure funding for the organization, review the activities of the agency, and collaborate with the executive director (Carver, 1997). Another major duty of the board is to hire and fire the executive director.

Major issues in rural areas related to the role of the board vis-à-vis that of the administrator of the social service agency have to do with the interconnectedness of small communities. Many times, board members recruit their friends to fill vacancies on the board. On one board in a small town, three of the board members were sorority sisters, two were cousins of the first three, one was an aunt, and one was the former high school principal of the others. Sometimes in small communities, it is so difficult to maintain a full complement of board members that nearly anyone nominated for membership is accepted without regard for qualifications. Most board members are on several boards in the same community, setting up issues of competing loyalties in terms of the agencies they serve. Some board members lack the necessary understanding of their role and attempt to micromanage the agency's daily operations. Some boards take over the hiring process and hire even clerical staff without input from the executive director. Often the hiring process is short-circuited by a recommendation from a friend or relative of a board member, and the members simply express the need to hire the recommended person regardless of qualifications. If the agency director tries to point out a lack of qualifications or other issues, the director, especially if he or she is an outsider, is reminded subtly that, in nonprofit agencies, the director serves at the pleasure of the board.

I remember a board meeting where several board members and the agency director tried to explain to the board chair why the agency should not hire her daughter as long as the board chair remained on the board. Fortunately for all concerned, her daughter did not accept the job. In other instances, the potential new hire is the daughter or son of a friend. Generally the person is hired without any attempt to make sure he or she is a suitable hire.

For many agency boards, their fundraising responsibilities supersede all other duties. Staff time also is often taken up with fundraising, much to the detriment of agency goals. In this case, ethical issues may arise. Board members are not supposed to profit from board membership; however, in some rural areas, members hold printing contracts for agency publicity, cater fundraising events, and are paid fees for legal services they provide to the organization. Sometimes in exchange for small discounts on services, massive public acknowledgement of services is required. It is difficult to help sometimes unsophisticated board members understand that such activities are unethical.

Another issue that may arise in fundraising in small communities is that pressure is put on certain people or groups to donate services or money, whether or not they can afford these services, based on kinship or friendship. One such board member told me he had an aunt who was on seven boards in one small town and expected his small insurance agency to buy tickets for tables at seven fundraisers, be a sponsor for each of these fundraisers, and make a "nice donation" to each of her causes. He finished by saying that the economy in the area was down, and he simply did not have the wherewithal to do this. His aunt did not believe him, and his refusal to support all of her board enterprises resulted in issues within his family. His wife resented the contributions he made to his aunt's causes, and his mother felt he did not do enough to help his aunt.

The egos of some board members can become entangled with fundraising. For example, a local small town agency decided to capitalize on the popularity of a major fundraising attempt by St. Jude's Hospital, an agency with national stature in an adjacent region. St. Jude's Hospital auctions off a house built by local builders in which all the materials and labor are donated. This is a substantial fundraiser; however, when a local agency in a small town attempted this, not only was it unsuccessful at raising substantial funds, the effort took the better part of a year and the agency was lucky to break even. The effort involved major efforts by board members and staff, and detracted substantially from other fundraising efforts such as the annual campaign. Further, as a result of a quarrel among board members about some of the publicity arrangements, another fundraiser that was a comparatively easy source of about $25,000 a year for this agency was given, instead, to another, because one of the local media outlets the board had slighted controlled what local cause would benefit from the fundraiser. At several points, before substantial commitment had been made to the house auction, it was apparent that some board members had overestimated the results of the auction. However, key board members would not back down, and building the house and holding the auction went forward at considerable cost to the agency in financial support, staff time diverted from other work, and community reputation.

Board members may have difficulty collaborating with the agency's executive director if the director is not from the area. Some board members may be related to staff members and may receive reports of agency activities from staff members who do not agree with the picture presented by the executive director. The result may be that the board colludes with the staff to set policy, and the executive director is left out of the loop. Still other local board members look to the executive director as the source of leadership and simply rubber-stamp the director's recommendations. This is more likely to happen when the executive director is a longtime member of the community and a good friend of or related to many board members. Neither of these situations is healthy for the agency.

Conclusion

Location, when it is rural or small town, is an important factor in agency administration and organization. Agency administration in such areas differs qualitatively from agency administration in more urban locales and is influenced both positively and negatively by the small-community setting. Opportunities for community collaboration, creativity, and community understanding are more readily available here than they are in larger areas. Job satisfaction is likely to be higher, and collegial relationships are more likely to be fulfilling in small areas, because these are based only on the work setting as well as community connection and relationships. Relationships with informal community assets such as churches and civic groups often determine the success of the services the agency provides to its clients. Social service agencies are likely to be viewed as important and necessary to community life, and agency administrators may enjoy considerable prestige in the community.

On the other hand, there are also great challenges for the social services agency director in the small-town/rural area. The challenges are balanced by the rewards of living in small communities and being an integral part of community life. To be successful in small-town/rural-area social services agency administration, the administrator needs sharply honed relationship skills; has to understand the community's formal and informal power structures and its issues and problems; and needs to be able to look beyond the organization chart of the agency to determine where actual staff leadership power is located and to work with a board that is interconnected socially and by generations of community relationships. Strong leadership skills, adherence to ethical values, and tact and sensitivity are critical for success, as are patience and understanding of rural, small-town culture, values, and behaviors.

References

Buxton, E. B. (1976). Experiences in rural mental health. In L. Ginsberg (Ed.), *Social work in rural communities: A book of readings* (pp. 29–40). New York: Council on Social Work Education.

Carver, J. (1997). *Boards that make a difference.* San Francisco: Jossey-Bass Publishers.

Daft, R. L. (1998). *Organization theory and design.* St. Paul, MN: West.

Economic Research Service. (1999). U.S. Department of Agriculture. Appendix D.: Two methods of measuring farm linked employment. *Rural Conditions and Trends, 10*(2), 86.

Fluharty, C. W. (2002). Toward a community based national rural policy: The importance of the social services sector. *Child Welfare, 81,* 663–687.

Gilbert, J. (1982). Rural sociology: The grounding of rural sociology. *Rural Sociology, 47,* 609–633.

Ginsberg, L. (1998). Concepts of new management. In L. Ginsberg & P. R. Keys (Eds.), *New management in human services* (2nd ed., pp. 1–37). Washington, DC: NASW Press.

Gumpert, J., Galtman, J. E. , & Sauer-Jones, D. (2002). Toward identifying the unique characteristics of social work practice in rural areas: From the voices of practitioners. *Journal of Baccalaureate Social Work, 6*(1), 24–36.

Hasenfeld, Y. (1983). *Human services organizations.* Englewood Cliffs, NJ: Prentice Hall.

Holland, T. P. (1995). Organizations: Context for social service delivery. In *Encyclopedia of social work* (Vol. 2) (19th ed., pp. 1787–1794). Washington, DC: National Association of Social Workers.

Johns, G. (1996). *Organizational behavior: Understanding and managing life at work.* New York: Harper Collins.

Landsman, M. J. (2002). Rural child welfare practice from an organization-in-environment perspective. *Child Welfare, 81,* 791–819.

Patti, R. J. (2000). The landscape of social welfare management. In R. J. Patti (Ed.), *The handbook of social welfare management* (pp. 3–25). Thousand Oaks, CA: Sage.

Resnick, H., & Patti, R. J. (Eds.) (1980). *Change from within: Humanizing social welfare organizations.* Philadelphia: Temple University Press.

Stedman, R. C., & Heberlein, T. A. (2001). Hunting and rural socialization: Contingent effects of the rural setting on hunting participation. *Rural Sociology, 66,* 599–617.

Sullivan, W. P., Hassler, M. D., & Otis, A. G. (1993). Rural mental health practice: Voices from the field. *Families in Society, 74,* 493–502.

12

Fundraising and the Social Work Manager:
It's All About Relationships

Joel M. Levy and Matt Aubry

Most people join the human services field because they believe in the social work mission of enhancing the lives of vulnerable populations and affording them opportunities for social equality and social justice. This mission is accomplished by building relationships, listening, solving problems, and staying true to the values and principles of your organization and your field.

Few things can make human services managers more uncomfortable than asking for money for their organization. However, fundraising is an essential element of achieving your organization's mission and a critical tool in allowing you to meet the needs of your clients.

Fundraising is not just about asking for money (or, as many think of it, begging for money). Fundraising is the process of creating relationships and alliances with individuals and organizations that give them the opportunity to participate in achieving your mission. Specifically for human services managers, you are providing an opportunity for those who do *not* work in your field to enhance the lives of vulnerable populations and afford them opportunities for social equality and justice.

To be an effective manager and an effective steward of the mission of your organization, you must make the philosophical shift to seeing fundraising as a central and critical element of your work. Fundraising enhances your impact on your organization and fits well with familiar social work functions such as advocacy and developing resources for vulnerable populations.

In this chapter you will learn the basics of fundraising, the tools and knowledge necessary to carry out the task of fundraising. There are many resources for additional training and opportunities to refine your skills, but the process of becoming a fundraiser starts with accepting that fundraising is an honorable and essential element of your job.

Overview and Fundamentals of Fundraising

Human service agencies may be funded in part by government money, which has increased steadily as a funding source over the last 50 years. This funding intensified in the 1980s when, in an attempt to avoid big government, more human services were outsourced to private organizations. This resulted in more community services, with a greater percentage of budgets paid for by government. With this increase in the number of agencies came an increased demand for funds and competition for a limited pool of government money. As agencies' budgets have grown, so has the need to raise funds from the private sector.

In some cases private funds are needed to supplement government funding of basic operational elements. But in most cases additional funds are needed to pay for things that the government can't or won't pay for. This could be start-up services or new programs to address areas of need that the government isn't ready or able to address. AIDS is a powerful example of such a scenario. In the 1980s and early 1990s many social service agencies faced the need to provide services to communities and individuals affected by HIV/AIDS, but the federal government was not yet ready to acknowledge the epidemic or to consider the needs of this population. Agencies were forced to find alternate funding and resources to implement the programs and provide the services they knew were critical to fulfill their missions. Without the willingness of those social workers to raise money to fund HIV/AIDS services, such services would have been a much longer time in coming.

In other cases the government provides some but not all funding for a project. For example, the government may pay for construction of group residences for vulnerable populations, but it won't pay for such things as carpeting, artwork, electronics, or nice quilts and pillows for residents' rooms. The government may deem these things nonessential, but human services managers know that these are critical elements of transforming a residential facility into a home, and they provide the residents with a level of dignity and comfort to which they are entitled. If not for the willingness of agency managers and employees to engage in fundraising, where would these nonessential elements come from?

Creating a Culture of Fundraising in Your Organization

The first element in successful fundraising is to create a culture of fundraising throughout the entire organization. For most organizations this will constitute a significant cultural shift and will require a plan for initiating and following through on that shift. Any culture shift, particularly one directly related to your organization's operations and mission, must begin at the top, with your board. Just as your board of trustees develops the mission, fundraising is one way to gain resources and implement this mission.

Internal communications are an important element in creating a culture of fundraising. It is important to make sure every member of your organization—from staff to volunteers, managers to board members—can articulate your mission, goals, programs, values, accomplishments, and needs. Even if not directly engaged in fundraising, every member of the organization is a de facto ambassador and, by extension, a potential fundraiser. As such, the entire staff should be accurate and respectable representatives.

Overcoming Fears Related to Fundraising

In studies in which people are asked why they gave the last donation they made, about 80% said, "Because someone asked me." Despite this fact, personal solicitation is one of the most difficult strategies to implement. It requires us to engage in an activity—asking for money—that is extremely uncomfortable for most people. For this reason, it is essential to address this fear and provide appropriate education and training to move people past it.

For most people the idea of asking for money is associated with anxiety or dread or some combination of these feelings. One of the strongest methods for overcoming or at least controlling the fear of fundraising is to connect it to your mission. Particularly when it comes to human services, people have chosen to work in this field because of their passion for helping vulnerable populations or to achieve social justice. Human services employees often think nothing of going above and beyond the call of duty, working long hours for low pay, using personal resources, and investing themselves emotionally in an attempt to meet the needs of their clients. When fundraising is considered as just another activity to be undertaken to meet the needs of the organization's clients, the fear will begin to subside and the task will seem more manageable.

Fundraising for social change is about creating healthy attitudes toward money. Generally, nonprofit people are not highly motivated by money, and that attitude carries over into a negative perception of money and all things related to it. By extension, they are often uncomfortable discussing money, admitting to needing money, or, of course, asking for money. Many of these attitudes start in childhood with how we are raised to think about money. With few exceptions, Americans are raised to believe that it is rude to discuss money in public or to ask for money (for many equate fundraising with begging). To be an effective human services manager, it is imperative that you face and address these attitudes. Understanding that fundraising is a tool for doing your job and is really just about building relationships and giving people an opportunity to support your organization's mission is the key to overcoming fears that prevent people from fundraising.

Fears About Asking for Money Fall Into Three Main Categories

The following is a list compiled by Kim Klein (2007) that outlines some of the common fears associated with asking for money and strategies to overcome them.

Things That Will Almost Never Happen

The person will get angry/yell at me. This very rarely occurs but is a common fear, so it must be addressed. Part of the strategy for addressing this fear is to acknowledge that it could happen but would be unjustified. Fundraising is an honorable activity, especially when undertaken by people who believe in the mission and cause; and, assuming the appeals are polite, informed, and appropriate, anything other than a polite, informed, and appropriate response is unnecessary, but should not be interpreted as a personal attack on the fundraiser.

I'll throw up/pass out/die of a heart attack during the solicitation. This could happen if the fundraiser's anxiety reaches a level of extreme physical distress. One strategy for addressing this fear is to role-play the process of asking someone for money. Role-playing helps to confront worst-case scenarios and takes some of the mystery and unknown out of making an appeal, especially for a first-time fundraiser.

Asking a friend for money will have a negative effect on our friendship. If you are approaching someone who is legitimately your friend, then you should be able to predict that person's reaction to your invitation to support your organization. If you predict that person will respond negatively, you don't have to ask him or her.

Things That Can Be Avoided With Training and Preparation

I won't know what to say/I'll say the wrong things/I'll look like an idiot. This fear is best addressed through a strategy of internal communications, training, and providing materials to support funding requests. No one should be sent out to ask for money without complete knowledge of the organization's mission and needs. It is not necessary to memorize every statistic, although it is good to have a few key facts ready.

Things That Definitely Will Happen at Some Point

The person will say no. There are many reasons why people say no to an invitation to donate. They may not be financially able at the time of the request, they may already support another charitable organization, they may not understand or agree with your mission, or they may not have been drawn to any of the particular options for support you offered them. The bottom line is that it's not the end of the world to be told "no." A "no" response can be the beginning of the next potential "yes." If possible or appropriate, consider asking the donor why he or she said "no," and you may be able to get some valuable feedback to help you shape your next appeal. Many times this feedback offers an opportunity to sculpt a new request that *is* geared to the person's interest and that gets a positive response.

Engaging the Board of Directors

Your board of directors is the group that is legally and morally responsible for the actions of your nonprofit organization. New York State Not-for-Profit Corporation Law states that board members must act "in good faith and with a degree of diligence, care, and skill which ordinarily prudent people would exercise under similar circumstances and in like positions," (Charities Bureau, p. 4) and most states have similar language. Board members are legally bound to ensure that the organization earns its money honestly and spends it responsibly, and that it adopts programs and procedures most conducive to carrying out its mission. Therefore, from a purely legal and operational standpoint, it makes sense that any major fundraising initiatives your organization undertakes at least should be approved by, if not created in conjunction with, your board of directors.

Key Elements of Board Operations

In *Securing Your Organization* (2001, p. 51), Michael Seltzer presents some key roles and responsibilities of a successful board. A nonprofit board is comprised of a number of elements, all of which must work together harmoniously for an organization to achieve its mission.

- Members establish and update the organization's vision and mission.
- The chairperson coordinates, motivates, mediates, trains, and encourages board members; leads board evaluation; makes sure the board focuses on governance, not management; acts as chief representative of the organization to its constituencies, and as the principal fundraiser; and works closely with the executive director.
- Other officers work with the executive director and chair to coordinate the board's work and help make things happen.
- Standing committees—development, executive, finance, fundraising, nominating, program—meet regularly.
- Other committees—audit, bylaws, personnel, strategic planning, vision/mission review, and special ad hoc committees such as special events—meet as necessary.
- Meetings address organizational priorities without micromanaging and result in action on committee findings and recommendations.
- Agendas are developed by the chair and executive director to accomplish the board's business.
- Board minutes serve as a brief, readable report of actions taken; items discussed but held over; items postponed; and new business.

The executive director or the chief executive officer (CEO) role exists to support the chairperson in developing and implementing these operations. Demonstrating the CEO's connections to the mission and how this will help the people you serve will attract their assistance in raising the necessary funds to help your organization.

The board must set the example the rest of the organization is expected to follow, and its members often can be the strongest fundraisers in your organization.

Organizations face two common challenges in creating a culture of fundraising within their boards of directors. First, board members often don't understand the importance of taking a leadership role in fundraising and the impact it can have on the culture of the entire organization; second, they are often afraid of asking for money. These two obstacles must be addressed and solved before an agency can fully embrace, and be successful at, fundraising. One strategy involves educating and training the board, first, on the importance of fundraising, and then on the strategies and methods needed. Your board is likely made up of individuals who are passionate about your agency's mission. If you educate them about the critical role fundraising plays in achieving that mission, they will start to accept their role as fundraisers. Having the board understand the general and specific impact fundraising has on the agency and especially on the individuals served is important, especially when they see the connections and they connect emotionally to the needs of your clients and the changes in their lives that can be accomplished by the services fundraising supports. Arranging for board members to visit programs and meet clients to discuss the importance of services is critical and empowering.

Once your board has a philosophical and emotional appreciation for the role of fundraising, set clear expectations and goals for each member to meet and provide training to meet those goals. Many organizations institute give-or-get policies, which means that every board member will either personally contribute (give) a preset amount of money to the organization every year, or that member will raise the money through his or her own efforts (get). In addition to training, be prepared to provide board members with the materials, resources, and support they will need, such as sample letters, press packets, and scripts. Your board members already serve as stewards and models of conduct in governance for your organization; now they must become stewards and models of fundraising for your organization.

The Role of Paid Staff

The role of paid staff in an organization is to oversee the day-to-day functions of the agency and to carry out its mission. The role of staff when it comes to fundraising is to help plan fundraising strategies; set goals related to program and organizational needs; coordinate fundraising activities; keep records; take care of routine fundraising tasks such as renewal appeals and acknowledgements; and assist board members by writing letters for them, forming fundraising plans with them, accompanying them to solicitation meetings, and preparing materials.

Volunteers can augment board committees or support staff in routine tasks as needed. Volunteers are usually willing to work hard for a short time, so they do well at specific projects with measurable outcomes. Many organizations use appointment to their board of directors as a reward for work well done by volunteers.

Ethics of Fundraising

Individual organizations may develop their own codes of ethics when it comes to fundraising, but in general, the Association of Fundraising Professionals (AFP) sets the standards for ethical behavior in fundraising. These standards (AFP, 2007) are based on the principal that "fundraisers are motivated by an inner drive to improve the quality of life through the causes they serve." AFP very clearly outlines the standards and principals it expects fundraisers to adhere to; specifically, AFP members aspire to

+ Practice their profession with integrity, honesty, truthfulness, and adherence to the absolute obligation to safeguard the public trust
+ Act according to the highest standards and visions of their organization, profession, and conscience
+ Put philanthropic mission above personal gain
+ Inspire others through their own sense of dedication and high purpose
+ Improve their professional knowledge and skills so that their performance will better serve others
+ Demonstrate concern for the interests and well-being of individuals affected by their actions
+ Value the privacy, freedom of choice, and interests of all those affected by their actions

- Foster cultural diversity and pluralistic values and treat all people with dignity and respect
- Affirm through personal giving a commitment to philanthropy and its role in society
- Adhere to the spirit as well as the letter of all applicable laws and regulations
- Advocate within their organizations adherence to all applicable laws and regulations
- Avoid even the appearance of any criminal offense or professional misconduct
- Bring credit to the fundraising [profession] by their public demeanor
- Encourage colleagues to embrace and practice these ethical principles and standards of professional practice
- Be aware of the codes of ethics promulgated by other professional organizations that serve philanthropy (AFP, 2007)

Professional Obligations

Members shall not engage in activities that harm the member's organization, clients, or profession.

1. Members shall not engage in activities that conflict with their fiduciary, ethical, and legal obligations to their organizations and their clients.
2. Members shall effectively disclose all potential and actual conflicts of interest; such disclosure does not preclude or imply ethical impropriety.
3. Members shall not exploit any relationship with a donor, prospect, volunteer, or employee for the benefit of the member of the member's organization.
4. Members shall comply with all applicable local, state, provincial, federal, civil, and criminal laws.
5. Members recognize their individual boundaries of competence and are forthcoming and truthful about their professional experience and qualifications. (AFP, 2007)

Presentation of Information

1. Members shall not disclose privileged or confidential information to unauthorized parties.
2. Members shall adhere to the principle that all donor and prospect information created by or on behalf of an organization is the property of that organization and shall not be transferred or utilized except on behalf of that organization.
3. Members shall give donors the opportunity to have their names removed from lists that are sold to, rented to, or exchanged with other organizations.
4. Members shall, when stating fundraising results, use accurate and consistent accounting methods that conform to the appropriate guidelines adopted by the American Institute of Certified Public Accountants (AICPA) for the type of organization involved. (In countries outside the United States, comparable authority should be utilized.) (AFP, 2007)

Compensation

1. Members shall not accept compensation that is based on a percentage of contributions; nor shall they accept finder's fees.
2. Members may accept performance-based compensation, such as bonuses, provided such bonuses are in accord with prevailing practices within the members' own organizations and are not based on a percentage of contributions.
3. Members shall no pay finder's fees or commissions on percentage compensation based on contributions and shall take care to discourage their organizations from making such payments. (AFP, 2007)

Costs of Fundraising

The notion that it costs money to raise money is an accepted precept within the non-profit arena. However, the actual amount that is spent to raise those funds is a matter of concern both within the fundraising world and in the Internal Revenue Service (IRS) and other regulatory bodies. Currently, industry standards expect fundraising costs to equal 25%–35% of the total amount raised. However, the lower that ratio, the better, and industry watchdogs and savvy donors are forcing nonprofits to track their fundraising costs carefully and keep them as low as possible. Fundraising costs can be reduced or contained by using volunteers, planning carefully, and forming strategic partnerships with other organizations or businesses. The ratio of costs to money raised changes depending on the type of fundraising activity. For instance, a golf event or a dinner dance will be a more costly expense than a letter campaign to your donors.

Developing a Fundraising Plan

A strong fundraising plan includes many sources of revenue, because these provide a more stable base for your organization. If an organization focuses solely on foundation support, for example, and that source suddenly runs dry, the organization will collapse. The image of a stool is often used to express the importance and function of multiple streams of revenue: a stool with one or even two legs will not stand well. A stool with three legs is stable, although it requires all three legs to be strong. A stool with four legs is even stronger and can function even if something happens to one of the other legs, thus creating ultimate stability.

Picture the seat of the stool as your organization and each of the legs as a funding source—grants, individual giving, major gifts/planned giving, and earned income/program revenue. When you put them together, you have a very sturdy base to support your organization. So, for example, if your grant program doesn't yield what you were expecting in a year, the organization isn't going to collapse, because the other three legs will support the weight of the organization.

This diversification of funding sources also allows you to reach different donors at different times in their lives and at different giving levels and to develop new donors through various activities in which they would like to participate. Some people would like to participate in golf events, whereas others would like to bring their friends to a dinner, and still others would prefer to give a check. Diversifying your funding sources allows you to build different donors and strengthen your overall fundraising program.

The first step in creating a fundraising plan is to identify exactly what your funding needs are. Make sure that all of your goals are directly linked to your program and organizational needs. Your fundraising goals can include both target dollar amounts and in-kind donations such as computers, office furniture, or similar needs.

Create both short- and long-term goals (see Table 1). Short-term goals are usually those that can be accomplished in 6–12 months; long-term goals are those that can be accomplished in 1–3 years. Make sure your goals are specific, measurable, realistic, and have clear deadlines.

TABLE 1   SAMPLE FUNDRAISING CALENDAR

Month	Fundraising Focus	Board Meeting	Planned Communications
January	Membership sales	Yes	Newsletter: corporate donor story
February	Business & corporate solicitation	No	Spring event invitations
March	Major gift solicitation	Yes	E-mail promotion of online auction
April	Spring fundraising event	No	Newsletter: life income gift story, attend spring event
May	Evaluation and planning	Yes	—
June	Corporate sponsor solicitation for fall event	Yes	Attend fall event, save the date cards
July	Membership sales	No	Newsletter: client story of change
August	Update Web site donation page; prep materials for year-end campaign	Yes	—
September	Fall fundraising event	No	Attend event
October	End-of-year solicitation	No	Direct mail/e-mail
November	Follow up on LYBUNTs*	Yes	Direct mail/e-mail
December	Evaluation and planning	Yes	—

Note: *LYBUNT=Last Year But Unfortunately Not This (fundraising donors)

Separating your fundraising activities allows you to allocate time and energy wisely and make more efficient use of personnel. It also allows time between your events so donors don't become overwhelmed. Remember, not all donors participate in all events.

With realistic expectations based on last year's performance, you can add specific new activities to enhance outcomes and renew external actions at this year's events (see Table 2).

TABLE 2   FUNDRAISING STRATEGY PLANNING WORKSHEET

Sources of Funds	Results Last Year	Goal for This Year	Goal in Next Year	5 Years
Earned income				
Products	_____	_____	_____	_____
Programs/services	_____	_____	_____	_____
Individual gifts/corporate sponsors				
Special events	_____	_____	_____	_____
E-mail solicitations	_____	_____	_____	_____
Direct mail	_____	_____	_____	_____
Phone canvass	_____	_____	_____	_____
Door-to-door canvass	_____	_____	_____	_____
Web site	_____	_____	_____	_____
Workplace solicitations	_____	_____	_____	_____
Membership dues	_____	_____	_____	_____
Annual gifts	_____	_____	_____	_____
Weekly/monthly pledges	_____	_____	_____	_____
Major gifts				
Memorials/honorary gifts	_____	_____	_____	_____
Personal visits	_____	_____	_____	_____
Grants				
Private foundations	_____	_____	_____	_____
Corporate foundations	_____	_____	_____	_____

This chart can be adjusted to your agency and the various interests, strengths, and weaknesses of your donors. Using a SWOT (strengths, weaknesses, opportunities, and threats) analysis for each event, as well as for your overall fundraising plan (see Table 3), can be very effective in planning and enhancing your program.

TABLE 3   SAMPLE WORK PLAN—GOAL $100,000

Source of Funds	Amount	Person Responsible
Annual campaign	$20,000	Tara
Grants	$20,000	Katie
Spring event	$10,000	Kevin
Fall event	$10,000	Julie
Earned income	$2,000	David
Corporate gifts	$10,000	Jaime
Major gifts	$15,000	Sal
Local congregations	$3,000	Jerylen
Membership dues	$10,000	Mike

You may find it useful to use the worksheet in Figure 1 to create an internal audit for your fundraising department and determine whether you have the necessary up-to-date documents. If you are a start-up agency, you will need to obtain these documents before you begin fundraising. Donors, foundations, and other fundraising sources may require much of this information.

FIGURE 1   ORGANIZING WORKSHEET

Name of Your Organization _____

1. Mission Statement:

_____
_____
_____
_____
_____
_____
_____
_____

2. Budgets

   a. The total operating budget for our organization for the upcoming year:
      $_____

   b. The estimated budgets for your projected programs for the year:

Programs	Annual Budget
(1)	$
(2)	$
(3)	$
(4)	$

This worksheet will allow you to focus on the direction you will take, clarify many of the issues you will face, and plan effectively for the future.

Creating a Case Statement

Before you can begin working toward your fundraising goals, you need to create your case statement, or a comprehensive answer to why someone should support your organization. What makes your cause important enough to receive funds? Why is your agency different from all of the other agencies asking for money? You need to define your organization and build a brand that creates an emotional connection with your donor, explain clearly why your clients need their support, and how donors' money will have an impact.

A case statement should include answers to the following questions:

- "Why do you exist?"—the *mission statement*.
- "What do you do?"—your *goals*.
- "How do you accomplish those goals?"—your *objectives*.
  – specific, measurable, and time-limited outcomes that tell how the goals will be met.

- ◆ "How long have you been doing this work? What have you accomplished, or what is your track record?"—your *history*.
- ◆ "Who is involved in this group?"—your *structure*.
- ◆ "How much does it cost for your organization to function, and where do you get your money?"—your *budget* and your *fundraising plan*.

The fundraising plan explains whether the organization has diverse funding sources and understands the fundraising process; what the organization's prospective sources of income are; how income will be raised, or how the organization's financial goals will be reached; and whether the organization's practices are consistent with its mission. Donors want to know that their support will have an impact and that they will be involved in deciding how these monies will be spent. Discussing their ideas up-front helps to gain donors' approval of your plans.

Common Terms and Concepts in Fundraising

As a competent professional, you should to familiarize yourself with industry terms and definitions.

Restricted Funds

Restricted funds are given for a very specific purpose that can be used *only* for that purpose. Government funding is the most common source of restricted funds, but corporations, foundations, and even occasionally individual donors can give restricted funds. These funds are generally used for such things as purchasing new equipment or a facility or refurbishing existing equipment or facilities, or they are in the form of a grant in response to a very specific request. Restricted funds can also come in the form of stocks, bonds, real estate, or other sources of income.

Unrestricted Funds

Unrestricted funds are given for general operating expenses of the agency, which has discretion over how they are spent. The most common source of unrestricted funds is individual giving, although some corporate and foundation support can also come in the form of unrestricted funds. Many donors do not like to fund overhead expenses, preferring instead to give money for specific programs. This is a struggle most non-profits face—finding money to pay the electric bill, rent, salaries, audits, and other necessary operational costs. Unrestricted funds can be used to pay for these expenses, but it's becoming common practice to explain these needs and necessary costs to your donors to encourage them to give unrestricted funds. Many organizations use their annual fund specifically to raise money for overhead costs.

Endowment

This is a specific type of savings account in which an organization invests money, either its own money or unrestricted funds from donors. The principal or core amount that makes up the endowment is not spent but is used to generate interest that is paid out to the organization to augment its annual budget. Your organization will want to invest some of its money and use only the interest from that investment as part of its annual income. The principal that is set aside to be invested is usually referred to as an *endowment*.

Legacy Gifts/Bequests

These gifts, made in honor of someone who has died, can be cash, stocks, real estate, and other physical property. Donors who create these kinds of instruments believe the organization will continue to exist and do important work long after they are dead. Bequests can be made through the transfer of cash, stocks, real estate or other gifts in kind. Bequests account for nearly 10% of all the money given to U.S. nonprofits (Giving USA Foundation, 2007). In most years, money from bequests is equal to the money received from foundations and always surpasses the money from corporations

Planned Giving

Planned giving, arrangements made for an organization to receive contributions from the estate of a donor, generally come from longtime, loyal donors who believe the organization should continue to exist after their own lives are over, and who believe that

FIGURE 2   PLANNED GIVING WORKSHEET

Do I have a will? _____

Which charities do I want to include in my will?

Charity Name   **Amount of bequest**

_____   _____

_____   _____

_____   _____

Whom might I ask to include my organization in his or her will?

_____

_____

Whom do I know who could purchase a large life insurance policy to benefit my organization?

_____

_____

Whom do I know who may want to give my organization a planned gift?

_____

_____

the organization will continue to do a good job for years to come. Donors generally make these commitments during their lifetime to take place after their death. Examples of gifts that may come through a planned giving program include life insurance policies, IRAs, or other retirement plans. Some organizations provide checklists or worksheets for planned giving prospects to help them through the process and to serve as a reminder to include the organization in their estate planning. Figure 2 shows a useful worksheet for potential donors to your organization.

Gifts of Assets

Donors can also give assets to an organization, which generally uses them for capital. The donations are usually so large that donors cannot finance them from their income and must donate cash from savings or other assets (stocks, real estate, art).

Gifts from Estate

Through their wills, trusts, or other estate-planning mechanisms, donors can arrange for nonprofit organizations to receive some or all of their estate. These gifts are used most often for endowments.

Campaigns

These time-limited, intense drives are made to meet specific goals: to raise money, gain new members, or collect specific things (building or playground materials, furniture, etc.). Your organization makes the campaign's goals public; in fact, the purpose of running a specific campaign is to engage the public around a specific and measurable goal. This is in contrast to an annual or holiday fund drive, general appeals for money, or other forms of support. A campaign is an organized, highly publicized event with clear milestones, specific methods of communication, and a measurable goal that can be celebrated at the end of the campaign.

Annual Fund

Individual giving campaigns, which focus specifically on building a base of donors who will give annually, generally seek unrestricted funds to be used for running the organization, such as paying for rent, utilities, groundskeeping, and similar overhead expenses.

Fundraising Pyramid

The standard breakdown of how gifts usually come into organizations is
+ 60% of the income comes from 10% of the donors;
+ 20% of the income comes from 20% of the donors; and
+ 20% of the income comes from 70% of the donors.

The majority of your gifts will be small, but the bulk of your income will come from large donations. A rule of thumb is that 80% of your funds will come from individuals, 11% from corporations, and 9% from grants. Some organizations experience different percentages, but if you have no history of giving from any or all of these sources, basing your prospecting plan around these percentages is a good place to start.

Cultivation of Donors

Cultivating donors is an extension of prospecting, but it involves building relationships with people, companies, and so forth who have been deemed to be good matches for your organization. If they are not already familiar with you or your agency, now is the time to meet them and start building a relationship.

Solicitation

This is the act of asking for donations or support from individuals, corporations, foundations, or other sources. It can take place through various vehicles such as in-person meetings, phone calls, personal letter-writing campaigns, mass direct mailings, e-mails, event invitations, sponsorship opportunities, foundation proposals, workplace giving campaigns, or other opportunities to present a need for support. Solicitations are best when they are timely, compelling, and reference how the solicited resources will be used by the organization or will affect the individuals, community, or group served by the organization. Many corporations and foundations have established specific areas they will support and formats and timelines for any request for funding.

Stewardship

Stewardship, the process by which relationships with supporters are maintained and nurtured, is important because keeping something you already have is easier and less expensive than starting from scratch. Renewing or increasing a gift from a current donor with whom you have maintained a relationship is much easier than soliciting the same size donation from a new donor.

Sources and Types of Fundraising

Individual Giving

Individuals represent approximately 80% of private giving in the United States according to Giving USA Foundation (2007), the yearbook of philanthropy published by Giving USA Foundation and researched and written by the Center on Philanthropy at Indiana University. A broad base of individual donors provides the only reliable funding source for a nonprofit year in and year out, and the growth of individual donations to an organization is critical to its growth and self-sufficiency.

Individual giving campaigns can have several acceptable outcomes, the first of which is obviously a large financial return. Other acceptable outcomes are acquiring new donors or supporters, increased giving, and repeated giving over the years, even if it is at the same level each year. Consistent repeated giving is the cornerstone of any strong individual giving program.

In an individual giving campaign there are generally three goals for each donor: first, to give the biggest gift the donor can afford annually; second, to give gifts to a capital or other special campaign; and third, to remember the organization in the donor's will or to make some kind of arrangement benefiting the organization from the donor's estate.

Getting a donor to give the biggest gift he or she can afford is the result of a powerful and well-crafted appeal that is shaped around the reasons why people give.

Although each person is different, the motivation to make a charitable donation can be attributed to several common motivations: The person cares about the issue, believes in the group, thinks the group's analysis of a problem and vision of a solution are correct, or he or she (or an acquaintance or family) was once in the position of the people the group serves (alcoholics, abused women or children, unemployed, homeless) and is thankful not to be in that position. People may also give because they feel guilty about how much they have or what they have done in their own lives; because the organization expresses their own ideals and enables them to reinforce their image of themselves (for example, a feminist, environmentalist, pacifist, equal rights advocate, good parent, concerned citizen), or because they want to feel more assured of salvation and eternal life. But the most common reason that people give is *because they are asked*, and being asked reminds them what they care about.

Begin by identifying whom you can ask, being sure to include friends, family, neighbors, and business associates. Then evaluate each person on that list based on that person's perceived fit with your organization and his or her giving capacity.

Klein (2007) has an easy-to-use template for prospect lists to organize your fundraising solicitors. Figure 3 shows the most basic information you need for your interactive database.

FIGURE 3   SAMPLE PROSPECT IDENTIFICATION WORKSHEET

Prospector Name: _____

Person I know	Believes in cause?	Gives away money?	Amount to ask for:
_____	❏	❏	$_____
_____	❏	❏	$_____
_____	❏	❏	$_____
_____	❏	❏	$_____

Prospecting

Create a plan based on your fundraising goals (how much you need to raise), the types of funds you need to raise (cash, in-kind, restricted, etc.), and your organization's history of fundraising (who has given, how much, and in response to what motivation or request). An example is shown in Appendix 1.

The charts in the tables, figures, and appendix mentioned previously in this chapter are a good beginning to help you develop a database with information you can use to build a pyramid of successful donor involvement with greater levels of giving. The following paragraphs outline a practical approach to achieving this.

Circles of Support

Circles of support is a fundraising strategy that capitalizes on the fact that people will give when asked personally by a friend or someone they admire, because doing so gives them the opportunity to portray themselves as principled and generous people to someone whose opinion they value.

To create a circle of support campaign, individual members of the organization or board of directors build a "circle" of friends, family members, business associates, or other individuals they can ask to donate. Generally the agency member, or center of the circle, makes a commitment to raise a specific amount of money from that circle. If that amount cannot be raised directly from the within that circle, individual members of the circle create their own circles of support to raise the additional funds.

The second level of a circle of support then becomes the circles that surround individual members of the original circle.

Circles of support provide two benefits to the organization: first, they raise money; and, second, they are used to gain access to new supporters of and advocates for their cause.

Giving Clubs

Giving clubs, or recognition levels, is a strategy to urge annual donors to give more money. Donors buy their way into the club, or achieve a recognition level, by giving a certain dollar amount. For example, in the case of a community orchestra, those giving below $250 are members of the "Audience Guild," whereas those who give $251 or more are in the "Conductor's Circle," and those who give above $1,000 are "Benefactors." People who regularly give $200 can easily be asked to give $300 or more to move up to the Conductor's Circle, and those who consistently give more than $500 can be asked to become Benefactors. The giving levels can be set at any dollar amount, and your organization can offer as many or as few options as it feels are appropriate for your donor base. If 60% of your gifts are for less than $250, you probably don't want to have your first level be $1,000, and you may choose to create two levels below the $250 mark.

Direct Mail

Traditional direct mail refers to a strategy of sending a form letter to hundreds, thousands, or even millions of people via bulk mail asking for donations. The goals of any mail solicitation are to get the recipient (1) to open it, (2) to read it, and (3) to take action. The basic premise of direct mail is volume—sending your letter to up to millions of people, with the goal of approximately 1% return. Direct mail is a long-term proposition for obtaining strong returns. It can take at minimum 3–5 years to cover the costs of starting a direct mail campaign.

For some organizations—primarily large, well-established ones (American Red Cross, Special Olympics, American Cancer Society)—traditional direct mail is a proven and productive method of raising money. These organizations have global name recognition, which increases the likelihood that recipients will open their letters, and they have specific and easily understandable missions to which the majority of people can relate, thereby increasing the likelihood that they will read and take action on the request.

For other organizations, specifically smaller organizations with less universal missions or more complicated goals, traditional direct mail may not be worth the investment of money and time. But an individual giving campaign based on sending appeal letters to your donors and partners is likely to be a productive alternative to a traditional direct mail campaign. The basic direct mail principal of higher returns resulting from larger mailing lists still applies, but instead of using lists, this option achieves growth by mining your board, staff, volunteers, and other supporters for additional names of people from their own networks whom they consider potential prospects for supporting your cause. Engage in public relation/community outreach activities to increase awareness of your organization and cultivate a larger mailing list.

A key element to a successful direct mail or individual giving campaign is soliciting your list several times a year. How many times a year, and in what ways, is a source of debate among fundraising professionals. The answer generally depends on the specific nature and culture of the organization, but in general, "touching" your list 3–6 times a year is good practice.

Recognition is an important part of any campaign, but it is particularly so in individual giving campaigns, because it lays the groundwork for future solicitations and can provide incentives for increased giving. Some examples of types of recognition are
* inclusion in giving societies and councils;
* holiday cards;
* receiving a personal note with the organization's annual report;
* updates on the organization's progress and successes during the year;
* recognizing an individual donor's accomplishments;
* including brief personal notes with all mailings;
* including major donors in some general mailings; and
* including personal e-mails from the executive director or CEO of the organization.

Major Gifts

You should identify a subset of your donors as having the capacity to give larger-than-average gifts and classify them as major gift prospects. As such, you should plan to use a more personalized approach with them. Major gifts can be large cash donations but might also include gifts of property, securities, or bequests of similar assets. Here are the eight steps to the solicitation process.

Eight-Step Solicitation Process for Major Gifts

1. Identification
2. Qualification
3. Development of strategy
4. Cultivation
5. Solicitation and negotiation
6. Acknowledgement
7. Stewardship
8. Renewal (Hodge, 2002)

Before beginning a major gifts program, decide how much money your organization wants to raise in the form of large gifts, the minimum amount that will constitute a major gift, and how many major gifts of varying amounts are needed to reach that goal. You can use the examples in Figure 4 and Table 4 as guides to determine the appropriate distribution of gifts and to establish the correct amounts for major gift solicitations.

Making the Major "Ask"

The standard initial approach is to send a letter describing the organization or the specific need. Include a sentence or two saying that you want to ask the prospect for a gift and requesting a meeting to discuss it further. The letter should be not more than one page and should seek only to raise the prospect's interest enough that he or she is willing to discuss a gift.

Follow the letter with a phone call to schedule a meeting, the ultimate purpose of which is to get the gift. At this meeting it is important to appear poised, enthusiastic, and confident and not to take a rejection personally. The final step, whether or not the prospect agrees to the gift, is follow-up. Send a thank-you letter either for the gift or taking the time to meet with you; document the response in your database; and learn from the experience, positive or negative, to inform your next solicitation.

Capital Funding/Capital Campaign

A capital campaign seeks to raise large sums of money for capital expenditures—typically building, buying, or renovating a facility. Capital campaigns generally have goals in the millions of dollars, so they require extensive planning and research, much more than do general individual campaigns. Capital campaigns usually run for at least 3 years, but can last 10 years or more, depending on the goal. Individual subcampaigns, or drives, may be planned to occur during the period of the capital campaign to support the capital effort or to raise money for other operating or program needs of the organization during the capital campaign. Donors to capital campaigns are usually a few extremely wealthy community members, and their gifts may come in the form of large pledges that are paid in installments over the course of the campaign or in the form of assets, such as savings bonds, inheritances, property, or stocks. Other common major contributors are corporations or banking institutions, particularly if the capital campaign involves mortgages or property leases. A very small percentage of the overall goal comes in the form of individual gifts of $100,000 or less.

FIGURE 4   MAJOR GIFTS: WHAT TO ASK FOR

Possible Gifts	Amount Requested
1. Money:	
Annual gift	_____
Membership	_____
Pledge	_____
Planned gift	_____
Special gift	_____
Challenge/matching gift	_____
Interest-free loan	_____
Other	_____
2. Noncash Assets:	
Art	_____
Real estate	_____
Vehicle	_____
Other	_____
3. Stocks	_____
4. Bonds	_____
5. Life insurance policy, IRA, 401(k)	_____
6. Other	_____

TABLE 4   MAJOR DONOR GIFT RANGE CHART

Major Gifts	Goal: $200,000		
	No. of Gifts	Size of Gifts	Total
	1	$20,000	$10,000
	2	$15,000	$30,000
	2	$10,000	$20,000
	5	$5,000	$15,000
	10	$2,500	$25,000
	15	$1,000	$15,000
	20	$500	$10,000
Total	68 gifts	$500–$20,000	$125,000 (66% of total)
Other Gifts	100	$250	$25,000
	150	$50–$100	$11,000
Total	250 gifts	$50–$250	$35,000 (25% of total)
Remaining Gifts	many	$5–$99	$20,000 (9% of total)

It is generally advisable to undertake a feasibility study before launching a full-scale capital campaign. This study, usually conducted by outside experts, determines whether there is enough support or interest in the community to support your organization in a capital campaign and to identify those individuals and companies most likely to be your major donors.

Typically, 30%–50% of the campaign's total comes from the top three to five donors. Because of the massive nature of a capital campaign, it is imperative that an organization prepare properly, and, in particular, make sure key donors are already committed to participate in the campaign. Ideally, you should be able to announce the contributions of at least one or two of these donors when you officially launch the campaign.

Events

Events can be an integral part of both annual and capital campaigns and are generally a popular method of raising money. Events can also be very effective tools for increasing awareness and growing your mailing list. They are, however, one of the most expensive methods of fundraising, in terms of both hard costs (cash outlays) and soft costs (human resources).

It is important to clarify your goals for an event before you begin the planning process. Possible goals of an event are generating publicity for and increasing awareness of the organization, bringing new people to the organization, and raising money. Raising money does not have to be your primary goal, but at a minimum you should seek to raise enough money from sponsors, ticket sales, or other methods to cover your costs for the event.

Events can provide an opportunity to engage board members and volunteers in specific and measurable ways. Although their participation can offset some of the soft costs, management of these volunteers usually requires time and effort from the fundraising staff to organize meetings, create event materials, coordinate mailings, and serve as a liaison between the volunteers and the organization. However, board members and other volunteers who participate in a well-run, successful event can have a greater sense of ownership, pride, and involvement in the organization and it's mission. Events are also an opportunity to tap into local companies and small businesses by creating sponsorship opportunities that provide advertising and community interaction in exchange for cash or in-kind support for your organization.

Two types of people generally attend events: those who come because of the event and those who come to support your organization. The idea is to attract people to your event who are either already donors whom you want to entice to give more, or people new to your organization whom you want to turn into regular donors. To attract these people, it is critical to link your event to your mission. The temptation might be to focus more on creating a fun and attractive event to get as large an attendance as possible. However, if your event does not do a good job of creating new donors or supporters for your organization, then it becomes a wasted opportunity.

A critical element of successful events is volunteer participation and concrete roles and expectations. The more supporters you put on a committee, the more money you will raise. The more external supporters you develop who invest themselves in the mission, the process, and activities of a successful event, the more access your organization will have to other resources and potential donors. Table 5 shows different models for special events.

TABLE 5   MOST COMMON TYPES OF SPECIAL EVENTS AND THEIR GOALS

Type of Event	Description	Goals/Objectives
Community event	Races, marathons, walk-a-thons, street festivals, galas, cook-offs, fashion shows, home tours, raffles	Raise money through donations, sales of goods, or sponsorships Increase name recognition Recruit new donors/volunteers/clients
Testimonial event	Tribute and award dinners, luncheons, receptions, etc.; recognition event honoring someone	Raise money through tickets to event, donations by honorees and their families, or sponsorships To honor a longtime supporter of or VIP to the organization
Sporting events	Golf , tennis, softball, or bowling tournaments	Raise money through entry fees for teams, sponsorships Increase organization's name recognition Recruit new donors and supporters
Artistic performances	Gallery openings, concerts, theater or studio tours, private performances, opportunities to meet the artists, preview exhibits/performances	Donor recruitment/development Increase connection to organization Recruit new donors
Auctions	Live or silent, can be held as stand-alone events or in combination with other events; can be held live or online	Raise money Provide opportunities to build relationships through donations of auction items

Source: Adapted from Russo, H. (2003). *Achieving excellence in fundraising*. New York: John Wiley & Sons.

A powerful example of an effective mission-oriented event is the YAI/NIPD Central Park Challenge, an annual event to facilitate and celebrate inclusion. It includes a walk-a-thon, a 5K run, and a full day of family activities. The organization's mission centers on the inclusion of people with disabilities in all aspects of their communities. The Central Park Challenge creates an environment in which people of all ability levels join in common activities. The event brings thousands of people together for a fun and inspiring day that transforms YAI's mission into reality. The event itself is a source of revenue and a vehicle for reaching thousands of potential future or long-term donors and ambassadors of the mission. Realization of the organization's mission is the primary goal of the event, with fundraising secondary, which is exactly what makes it a powerful fundraising tool.

House Parties

A house party is a particular type of small event for which someone involved in a nonprofit group invites friends to a party at his or her house. The purpose of the party is to educate the friends about the work of the nonprofit group and to ask them for contributions. In addition to providing an opportunity to discuss an issue, a house party can be the venue for a group of people to meet someone famous or important or who brings interesting information about the issue your group is working on.

Immediately after the house party, it is important to send thank-you notes to everyone who attended and contributed, to make sure to add all attendees to your database, and to send an appeal letter to guests who did not attend.

After an event of any size or type, it is important to do a postevent evaluation, while all of the successes and failures are fresh in everyone's mind. This information will be key to future planning, for either repeating the same event or planning a new one.

Appendix 2 includes an evaluation sheet (Klein, 2007) you can use to identify which elements of your event succeeded and what may need to be revamped.

Tools for Achieving Fundraising Goals

Online Giving

Online giving, the new frontier of fundraising, has had a huge impact on the field in a very short time, while expanding opportunities for fundraising. With a small investment of money and time, an organization can create a basic yet functional Web-based giving portal. In our current Web-oriented culture many people turn to the Internet as their first source of information. If your Web site is a dynamic and inviting platform, it can be a powerful tool in building awareness and raising money.

Tools such as Network for Good, Pay-Pal, and Google Check-Out allow organizations to accept donations through their Web sites without a complicated or expensive e-commerce platform. Organizations that combine online giving with their paper or direct appeals generally report an increase in giving for their overall campaigns, because people find it much easier to go online and make a donation than to remember to write a check and mail it to the organization.

One advantage of using the Internet to raise money is that a Web site can use many forms of media—text, graphics, sound, and animation—to deliver an organization's message much more powerfully and cost-effectively than any other method. In addition, Internet fundraising allows donors to go right to the information that appeals to them, rather than wading through long letters or generic phone scripts. The Internet is also one of the most effective tool for reaching prospective donors from the prime demographic of ages 18–40, a population segment most likely to be strong supporters of causes they believe in, but also one least likely to respond to letters or phone calls.

The Internet also allows for such fundraising activities as online auctions. These auctions can be an attractive alternative to traditional silent/live auction events, which can be time-consuming and expensive to conduct. Sites such as C-Market offer easy-to-use and inexpensive platforms for organizing and executing an online auction; they allow you to solicit and post your own donations or purchase items through their consignment shops. eBay also has a charitable auction site through which sellers can designate their proceeds to benefit different charities.

The popularity of the Internet also creates some disadvantages. For example, the vast number of Web sites competing for users' attention means you must have the resources to monitor any interactive features and keep the site updated and interesting to those who return to it often. Another disadvantage of the Internet is that, despite advances made in access in poor communities and among the elderly, there are still large segments of the population that do not have access to the Internet.

Michael Seltzer (2001) has assembled a few tips, described in following paragraphs, on how to publicize your organization's Web site.

Publicizing Your Web site

After creating an attractive, stimulating site that people will want to return to, you must then do everything you can to drive traffic to your site.

1. Put your e-mail and Web site address on everything that leaves your office, including letterhead, business cards, correspondence, newsletters, annual reports, press releases, advertising copy, and so on.
2. Make sure your Web site address is part of your signature on every e-mail you send.
3. E-mail your Web site address to every Web search engine you can find.
4. Incorporate your Web site address into your voice mail message and announce it at speeches, trainings, meetings, and other opportunities.
5. E-mail the Web masters at organizations similar to yours asking them to link to your site and offer to reciprocate.
6. Update your site frequently.
7. Announce the launch of, or important changes to, your Web site to your constituents and send press releases to local print and electronic media and relevant professional associations.
8. Make your Web site interactive: self-scoring quizzes, bulletin boards, opportunities to sign up for your electronic newsletter, and invitations to join your organization are easy to include.
9. List your Web site on relevant Internet news groups and electronic bulletin boards.

Storytelling

People give emotionally, and the best way to tap into emotions is to tell a story. Stories are a powerful tool because they provide characters and settings to which the listener can relate, and they create images that evoke emotion. People are also more likely to remember stories than they are communications based on facts, figures, or intellectual appeals.

Research into donor motivation has determined that

images or visuals of one person in need engendered more sympathy and funds than statistics about a particular issue or disaster. In several case studies, donors gave more to a charity when they read or heard about one individual as opposed to two or more, or when informed about a particular issue or situation. (Preston, 2007)

Neither *need* nor *tax advantage* makes your organization special. The individual faces and stories of your organization are what make your group special.

Corporate Giving

The key to successful corporate giving is knowing why a corporation gives. Corporations give money primarily because they hope doing so will directly or indirectly help them make more money. In fact, according to the IRS, the average amount companies give away is a mere 1% of pretax profits. Some corporations set up foundations to handle their charitable giving, but their giving priorities support the business and public relations goals of the company. Most companies prefer to give to organizations that are located in the areas where they do business and/or to organizations that can provide national or international exposure. The most common form of corporate giving is employee matching programs, in which companies support and encourage their employees to make charitable donations by matching those donations with either a dollar-for-dollar donation or, in some cases, matching every dollar donated with two dollars from the company. As the use of these programs has grown many corporations have established limits as to the amount each year that can be matched.

When you are considering a corporate giving campaign, the best way to start is to research the large companies operating in your community and see whether they have foundations, matching gift programs, or predefined giving priorities.

Another approach for accessing corporate funds is to create sponsorship opportunities around events and specific naming opportunities. Sponsorships act like advertising for corporations, except that the companies receive tax benefits and unique public relations benefits not associated with traditional advertising. According to a 2004 report, 8 of 10 Americans say that corporate support of causes wins their trust in that company, a 21% increase since 1997, whereas 90% of consumers would consider switching to another company's products or services based on their type and level of community involvement (Cause Marketing Forum, 2004).

In-kind donations are another valuable way that corporations and small businesses can support organizations. In-kind donations can be gifts of products or services the organization would otherwise have to purchase, or contributions of expertise (lending a worker to help a nonprofit with accounting, marketing, or personnel); space (free use of conference or meeting rooms); printing; furniture, or office equipment (computers, fax machines, copy machines); building materials; and so on.

Companies engage in sponsorship and branding relationships with nonprofits for a variety of reasons:

- To create greater public trust in the company
- To enhance the company's image or reputation
- To build "brand awareness"
- To create goodwill now and in the future
- To increase profits for the company
- To attract investors
- To increase employee morale and attract and retain employees
- To provide a competitive advantage (Russo, 2003, p. 185)

Nonprofits, for their part, engage in such partnerships for different reasons:

- To gain more revenue
- To obtain in-kind services or resources
- To diversify income streams
- To facilitate greater capacity to provide a service
- To enhance the organization's reputation
- To increase public recognition and build greater community awareness of the cause
- To attract more volunteers and donors (Russo, 2003, p. 185)

The past few decades have seen many corporations joining with charities in what are called *cause marketing* efforts, in which a corporation donates a certain percentage of its profits from a particular item or a certain amount of each sale to its partner charity. Cause marketing is often a better fit for large regional or national organizations, because the company's usual motivation for the partnership is increased brand visibility and reputation enhancement.

A current national cause marketing example is the partnership between Yoplait Yogurt and the Susan G. Komen Breast Cancer Foundation, in which a portion of the proceeds from each yogurt purchase is donated to the foundation by Yoplait.

With the recent increase in public attention on the theory and practice of corporate social responsibility, more consumer attention is being paid to corporate giving, resulting in an overall increase in corporate philanthropy. A recent study found that 23% of consumers define corporate social responsibility as being actively engaged in the local community. The study also found that

- Americans expect corporations to be engaged in their communities in ways that go beyond just making financial contributions, and
- Americans believe that government should play a role in ensuring the social responsibility of corporations, in some industries more than others.

Online forms of communication continue to change the landscape in which consumers gather and communicate information about how well companies are being socially responsible (Fleishman-Hillard/National Consumers League Study, 2007).

Foundation Funding

Funding from foundations takes the form of grants and can be restricted or unrestricted, depending on the foundation's giving priorities and the nature of your request. Many organizations assume grants are an easy source of funds, but this is not generally the case. Many of the larger foundations report receiving 100 proposals for every 2 they are able to fund. But if you are awarded a grant, it can take 3 months to a year to receive the money, and the process of writing the grant application is generally extremely time-consuming. When considering a grant program, be sure to consider carefully the return you are likely to get on your investment, including the soft costs of staff or volunteer time spent preparing the application.

Types of Foundations

Private charities represent one type of foundation. Private charities have a minimum disbursement requirement based on their charter with the IRS; are assessed excise taxes on their holdings; are required to disclose their financial statements publicly, including revenues received and total disbursement amounts; and are usually funded by a large principal investment, such as a family fortune or corporate dividends.

Public charities represent another type of foundation. Public charities are tax-exempt, receive substantial public support, and are also required to disclose their financial information publicly.

Within these two broad categories, individual foundations have different funding priorities and missions. Some have very broad missions, such as education, and others have very specific missions, such as education in inner cities for elementary school children with learning disabilities. Some foundations support only program costs, some support operating costs, and some support both. It is important to research each foundation's giving priorities and mission carefully before you begin the application process to avoid wasting time on applying to a foundation that won't support either your mission or your funding request.

Table 6 provides an overview of the general characteristics of four common types of foundations.

Basics of a Foundation Proposal

Each foundation, in addition to having its own specific funding focus, may have its own application process. However, all grant proposals share some basic similarities. Table 7 shows some examples of the common elements of a proposal.

It is important to read the giving guidelines of any foundation carefully and follow the requirements. You should also note whether the foundation accepts proposals online, as many now do.

Be aware of reporting requirements when considering the time involved in a grant program, because reporting and tracking requirements can take more time, money, and effort than the award is worth. If you do decide to undertake a grant program, be sure to create a solid stewardship plan to manage the grant's reporting and tracking requirements. This will cut down on the effort it takes to manage the grant and will make applying to extend the grant easier.

TABLE 6 GENERAL CHARACTERISTICS OF FOUR TYPES OF FOUNDATIONS

Foundation Type	Description	Source of Funds	Of Note
Independent foundation	A grant-making organization usually classified by the IRS as a private foundation. May also be known as family foundations; general purpose foundations; special purpose foundations; or private, nonoperating foundations.	Endowment from single source, such as an individual donor or a family or a group of donors.	Most have specific guidelines and give in a few specific fields. About 70% of independent foundations limit their giving to their local area. IRS requires that their 990 tax filings be made public.
Corporate foundation	The philanthropic arm created by a corporation to deal with requests for contributions.	Funds come from a profit-making corporation.	Giving tends to be in fields related to corporate activity or in communities where the company operates. Grants given are generally smaller than those of independent foundations.
Operating foundation	A 501(c)(3) organization classified by the IRS as a private foundation the primary purpose of which is to conduct research, social welfare, or other programs determined by its governing body or establishment charter. It may make some grants, but the sums are generally small relative to the funds used for the foundation's own programs. Very few are also company-sponsored. These foundations commonly operate museums, libraries, or research institutes.	Funds usually come from a single source, but donations from the public are eligible for the maximum deduction.	Grants are generally related directly to the foundation's own programs.
Community foundation	A 501(c)(3) organization that makes grants for charitable purposes in a specific community or region. Funds are usually derived from many donors and held in an independently administered endowment; income earned by the endowment is then used to make grants. Although a few community foundations may be classified by the IRS as private foundations, most are classified as public charities eligible for maximum income tax-deductible contributions from the general public.	Funds are generally received from a variety of donors.	Grants are generally limited to charitable organizations in local communities. 990 tax filings are made public.

TABLE 7   GENERAL GRANT PROPOSAL OUTLINE CHART

Organizational Background	Statement of Need	Goals/ Objectives	Evaluation
This is where you provide your mission statement, the history of your organization, and major organizational accomplishments and goals.	This is your opportunity to explain why your organization exists: what need is it filling in the community (locally or globally). If you are writing the grant for a specific program within your organization, this is also where you describe the purpose of and need for the program.	Clearly state what your organization will accomplish with the funds you are seeking.	Explain the systems or methods you will use to make sure you accomplished the goals and objectives your organization had in mind when requesting the grant.

Social Enterprise Ventures

Efforts that generate funds via a commercial exchange, with revenues benefiting the nonprofit, are a valid fundraising method, though it may seem counterintuitive. However, nonprofit organizations are permitted to earn money, including profits. Nonprofit status simply precludes distribution of any surplus to those with a controlling interest in the organization, such as officers, directors, or staff. Depending on the category of nonprofit organization, the national average for earned income as a percentage of budget ranges from 19% to 56%. Most nonprofit organizations are free to engage in ventures when the proceeds are used to support the organization's mission. If these activities are *related* to the nonprofit's tax-exempt purpose, the organization can generally engage in these ventures without limitation and without incurring tax liabilities.

Examples of common social enterprise ventures include the practice of charging fees for some services, making publications available for sale, or subleasing space to another organization.

Nonprofits can also engage in business activities that are deemed *unrelated* to their organization's mission, but they must pay income taxes on profits derived from those activities. The IRS calls these taxes *unrelated business income taxes* (UBIT). Some nonprofits operate ventures that sell a mixture of related and unrelated products, paying UBIT on the unrelated ones. One example of a nonprofit with a successful unrelated income venture is the Museum Store, operated by Museum of Modern Art in New York City. What began as a small shop in the Museum of Modern Art to generate revenue to support the operations of the museum, has expanded into a business venture not directly related to the museum's mission, but is instead purely income-generating.

Most successful ventures seldom provide more than one third to one half of an organization's annual budget. However, the benefits to enterprise ventures go beyond generating revenue for the organization. They can also strengthen relationships with existing constituencies by providing additional ways to connect with members, funders, clients, volunteers, and other constituents to foster relationships and increase the nonprofit's impact.

Evaluation and Assessment

Periodic evaluation of your fundraising activities, a necessary task for any fundraiser, should be built into your fundraising cycle. It is all too easy to get on the fundraising treadmill and just keep doing the same thing year after year, especially if the activities seem to be raising money. However, some of your activities may be yielding lower results than they have in past years, costs may have increased, the secondary goals of increasing awareness or advancing your mission may have started to slip from focus, or you may be missing new fundraising opportunities. For all of these reasons, it is essential that an evaluation and assessment period be a standard part of your organization's fundraising cycle, as illustrated in Figure 5.

FIGURE 5   THE EVALUATION AND ASSESSMENT CYCLE

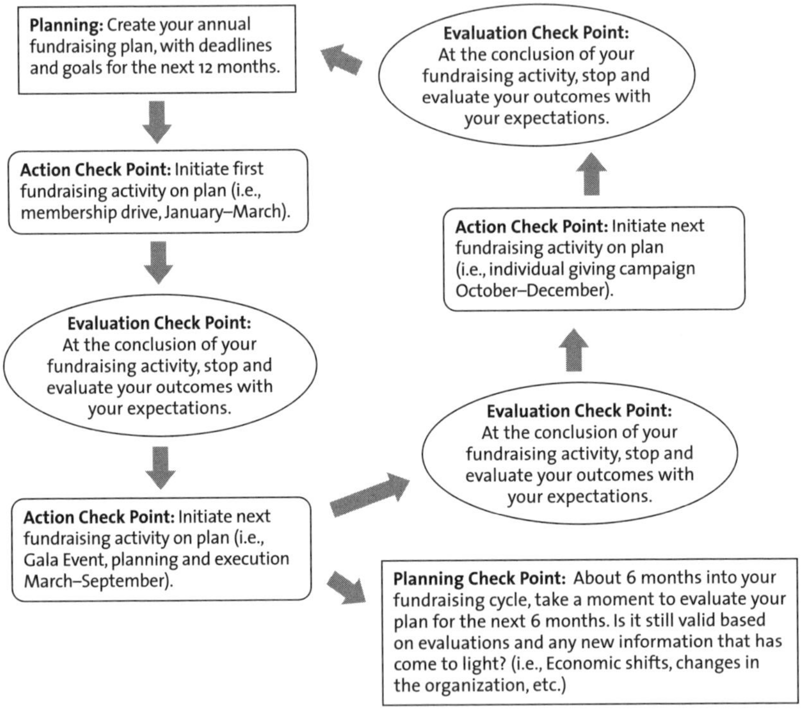

Planning: Create your annual fundraising plan, with deadlines and goals for the next 12 months.

Evaluation Check Point: At the conclusion of your fundraising activity, stop and evaluate your outcomes with your expectations.

Action Check Point: Initiate first fundraising activity on plan (i.e., membership drive, January–March).

Action Check Point: Initiate next fundraising activity on plan (i.e., individual giving campaign October–December).

Evaluation Check Point: At the conclusion of your fundraising activity, stop and evaluate your outcomes with your expectations.

Action Check Point: Initiate next fundraising activity on plan (i.e., Gala Event, planning and execution March–September).

Evaluation Check Point: At the conclusion of your fundraising activity, stop and evaluate your outcomes with your expectations.

Planning Check Point: About 6 months into your fundraising cycle, take a moment to evaluate your plan for the next 6 months. Is it still valid based on evaluations and any new information that has come to light? (i.e., Economic shifts, changes in the organization, etc.)

Conclusion

Building Relationships

Fundraising is about building relationships. As with all relationships, the strongest ones are built on a foundation of mutual interest and respect. The best fundraising relationships result when a donor has been carefully matched to just the right cause and given the opportunity to provide support in the most comfortable way. For example, a prospective donor may show interest in issues related to homelessness but be passionate about working specifically with homeless women and children. This prospect may be enticed to donate to a general program that serves the needs of homeless individuals, but you may form a more productive relationship if you ask this donor specifically to support a women's shelter. If you don't have a program specifically for homeless women, this donor could be a source of seed funding for that type of program, resulting in a much more significant relationship with the donor than if the person had just been asked to write a check for your general program. The more information you are able to gather about your donors' interests, giving capacities, community connections, and so forth, the stronger the relationship and the more significant the donor's participation and support of your organization will be. For example, a highly developed relationship, resulting from a great deal of information gathering, generally results in large gifts that are initiated by the donor. A relationship in the beginning stages, with very little information gathered, generally requires direct solicitation through phone, mail, or e-mail to yield gifts. However, a new relationship does not necessarily mean the gifts will be small, although on average, the gifts are likely to be smaller than with more highly developed relationships. In the middle, you are building relationships and collecting information, but you do not necessarily have a full profile—perhaps you are missing an extensive giving history on which to base predictions. In such scenarios, face-to-face solicitations or invitations to participate in major campaigns will likely yield the best gifts and help to develop the relationship.

Relationships Are Essential to Successful Fundraising

As a social worker you already know how to build and maintain solid relationships; however, it is always important to review the fundamentals. Burnett (2002) presents nine keys to building a relationship:

1. Be honest. If any business area should be honest, it is fundraising. The public expects fundraisers to be honest. Those who don't view fundraisers as inherently honest and trustworthy certainly don't give, so it pays to be seen as honest.

2. Be sincere and let your commitment show. Donors are donors because they care enough to take action and support your cause. Let them see that you care, too, and that is why you're there as well. When this happens, you and the donors are immediately on the same side, sharing a common concern and goal. Your commitment then encourages them to go even further for the cause.

3. Be prompt. Reply quickly and efficiently to any request. Answer letters the next day or sooner if possible. If the issue is important, telephone the donor and explain what action you are going to take. If it will take time to provide a full answer, write or telephone the donor quickly to say that an answer is being prepared and let him or her know when to expect it. Responding promptly shows you take your donor's concerns seriously.

4. Be regular. Regular planned communication keeps donors in touch, informed,

and involved. If you are irregular in your communications, be aware that other fundraisers are not so lax. They also have access to your donors, so they'll be in touch when you are not.

5. Be interesting and memorable. By their very nature, nonprofits have access to compelling material. Use it to the full; present it well. Fundraising is all about telling stories. Make all of your material stand out because of its interesting content, style, and presentation . . . and its unforgettable visuals.

6. Be involving. Don't allow donors to take a passive role. Ask for their opinions, contributions, and even complaints. Encourage feedback in any way you can. Invite them to events, offer visits to projects. Make dialogue be as two-way as you possibly can.

7. Be cheerful and helpful. Advertise your helpfulness. Never let donors feel that asking is a trouble. That's what you are there for—to help them. Teach customer care to all of your colleagues.

8. Be faithful. Always stick to your promises. Let donors see that you are honorable and trustworthy. Stand by your organization's mission and don't compromise what it stands for.

9. Be cost-effective. Donors expect and appreciate good stewardship of their gifts but are generally well aware of the potential for false economies, which they dislike as much as conspicuous waste. Be open and informative, explain your reasons for financial decisions, and show your donors that their money is in good hands (pp. 45–46).

Nonprofit organizations can actually look to some for-profit companies as models of relationship building and relationship management. The Ritz-Carlton Hotel chain is one strong example. Its credo of service is

• The Ritz-Carlton Hotel is a place where the genuine care and comfort of our guests is our highest mission.
• We pledge to provide the finest personal service and facilities for our guests who will always enjoy a warm, relaxed, yet refined ambience.
• The Ritz-Carlton experience enlivens the senses, instills [a sense of] well-being, and fulfills even the unexpressed wishes and needs of our guests.

Replace "guest" with "donor" and "Ritz-Carlton" with your agency's name and you have a powerful and appropriate credo for donor relationship management:

• The Social Work Agency is a place where the genuine care and comfort of our clients and our donors is our highest mission.
• We pledge to provide the finest personal service and recognition for our donors, who will always enjoy a warm and welcome place within our agency.
• The social work agency experience enlivens the senses, instills [a sense of] well-being and fulfills even the unexpressed wishes and needs of our donors.

This may seem a little extreme, or even silly, but the reality is that you cannot nurture the relationships with your donors too much. At worst, they remain stable and reliable donors; at best, they continue to grow their commitment to your organization and become stronger and more significant donors, up to and including making a sizable bequest to your organization that will allow their support to continue after they have passed on.

For social work and human services managers, fundraising can feel like an overwhelming task well outside the scope of their job description and skills. However, with a shift in perspective that allows for understanding the need for fundraising, the recognition that it is simply relationship building, and the willingness to invest in learning the technical aspects of how to raise funds, social work and human services managers can easily make the transition to fundraisers and serve their missions better.

References

Association of Fundraising Professionals. (2007). *Code of ethical principals and standards.* Retrieved June 23, 2008, from http://www.afpnet.org/ka/ka3.cfm?content_item_id=1068&folder_id=897

Burnett, K. (2002). *Relationship fundraising: A donor based approach to the business of raising money.* Hoboken, NJ: Jossey-Bass.

Cause Marketing Forum. (2004). *2004 Cone Corporate Citizenship Study results.* Retrieved September 10, 2008, from http://www.causemarketingforum.com/page.asp?ID=330

Charities Bureau, New York State's Attorney General. (2003). *The regulatory role of the attorney general's charities bureau.* Retrieved September 10, 2008, from http://www.oag.state.ny.us/bureaus/charities/role_1.pdf

Fleishman-Hillard/National Consumers League. (2007). *Rethinking corporate social responsibility.* Washington, DC: National Consumers League.

Giving USA Foundation. (2007). *Giving USA 2007.* Glenview, IL: Author.

Hodge, J. M. (2002). *Gifts of significance.* Retrieved September 10, 2008, from http://www.philanthropy.iupui.edu/TheFundRaisingSchool/PrecourseReadings/pre course_giftsofsignificancehodge.aspx

Klein, K. (2007). *Fundraising for social change.* Hoboken, NJ: Jossey-Bass.

Preston, C. (2007, July 17). New research sheds light on what works in charitable appeals. *The Chronicle of Philanthropy.* Retrieved September 10, 2008, from http://philanthropy.com/news/updates/2700/new-research-sheds-light-on-what-works-in-charitable-appeals

Ritz Carlton Hotel Company. (2008). *Credo.* Retrieved September 10, 2008, from http://corporate.ritzcarlton.com/en/About/GoldStandards.htm

Russo, H. (2003). *Achieving excellence in fundraising.* New York: John Wiley & Sons.

Seltzer, M. (2001). *Securing your organization.* New York: The Foundation Center.

APPENDIX 1
Master Prospect List

Name of Prospect	Contact Info	Solicitor	Amount To Be Solicited	Donor's Area of Interest
_____	_____	_____	_____	_____
_____	_____	_____	_____	_____
_____	_____	_____	_____	_____
_____	_____	_____	_____	_____
_____	_____	_____	_____	_____

Prospect Record

Date:_____

Name: _____

Work address: _____

Work phone: _____ Fax: _____

Cell phone: _____ Home phone: _____

Home address: _____

E-mail: _____

Contact(s):_____

Interest or involvement in nonprofits/philanthropy/community service: _____
_____
_____
_____

Donations to other nonprofits: _____

Other involvement in nonprofits/community service (e.g., volunteering, in-kind donations etc.): _____
_____
_____
_____

Evidence of belief in our organization and/or cause:_____
_____
_____
_____

Occupation:_____

Employer: _____ Matching gift possible? _____

Household composition: _____

Other interests/hobbies:_____

Suggested gift range:

_____

Anything else we should know (e.g., never call home, prefers to communicate via e-mail, makes all decisions with a partner, etc.)_____

_____

_____

_____

Suggested solicitor: _____

Relationship to solicitor: _____

Contact Log

	Date	Method	Outcome	Next Steps
1st contact				
2nd contact				
3rd contact				
4th contact				

_____

Final result:

APPENDIX 2
Special Event Evaluation Form

Approximately how much time did the committee spend on this event? (Be sure to include time spent driving on errands and talking on the phone.) _____

_____

Approximately how much total time did staff spend on this event? _____

_____

Did this event bring in any new donors? _____

How many? _____

Can people who attended this event be asked to become donors?_____

Did this event bring in new money?_____

Does this event have the capacity to grow every year?_____

What would you do the same next time? _____

_____

_____

What would you do differently?_____

_____

_____

List key resources that were part of the success of this year's event, who solicited them, and whether they will be available next year:

_____   _____

_____   _____

_____   _____

_____   _____

What kind of follow-up needs to be done (e.g., thank-you notes, bills to pay, prizes to be sent out, materials to be returned to people who lent them, etc.):

_____   _____

_____   _____

_____   _____

_____   _____

Which committee members did what work?

_____   _____

_____   _____

_____   _____

_____   _____

Which committee members do you think will return next year?

_____   _____
_____   _____
_____   _____
_____   _____

Other comments/notes: _____

_____
_____
_____
_____
_____

13

Human Resources in Social Cause-Based, Entrepreneurial, Not-for-Profit Organizations

Joel M. Levy

There is a wealth of theory available today about the science of managing and motivating complex organizations. This chapter is not meant to be a compilation or a review of this broad base of theory, but rather a reflection of the relevant concepts, guiding principles, and lessons learned over almost 40 years as a practitioner in social entrepreneurial organizations. Although I do review some theoretical perspectives and empirical work, this chapter focuses on relating my experiences at the Young Adult Institute/National Institute for People with Disabilities (YAI/NIPD), from my initial role as a frontline staff member to my current role as the agency's chief executive officer, to three important objectives of human resource management: (1) attracting and hiring talent; (2) motivating, rewarding, and retaining staff; and (3) training and developing staff and manager skills.

One focus of social work is to help vulnerable populations enhance their opportunities for social justice, equality, and supporting human rights issues. To accomplish this, you have to use your scarce resources by building your greatest resource—your staff. To achieve this, you need to engage your staff; build their motivation and their commitment to the agency's mission and enculturate them into your agency's value system; excite them with your vision: to deliver quality services based on a commitment to excellence. You can easily adapt all of the ideas that follow to your agency or practice field.

Brief History of the YAI/NIPD

The YAI/NIPD was founded in 1957 to provide the highest-quality services to people with developmental and learning disabilities to actualize their potential, maximize their independence and inclusion, and facilitate their productivity. Today, the YAI/NIPD is a network comprised of the following seven independent, award-winning, not-for-profit health and human service agencies:

1. YAI/NIPD
2. Premier HealthCare

3. The New York League for Early Learning (NYL)
4. The Rockland County Association for the Learning Disabled (RCALD)
5. The Corporate Source
6. The National Institute for People with Disabilities of New Jersey (NIPD/NJ)
7. The International Institute for People with Disabilities of Puerto Rico (IIPD/PR)

Every day at YAI/NIPD, a staff of 5,500 serves more than 20,000 people, starting at birth and progressing through all of the life cycles. The YAI strives to be a place of hope for infants, children, adults, and seniors with developmental learning disabilities and their families by building brighter futures. First and foremost, the YAI/NIPD is a mission-driven organization, whose mission is best expressed by our model of the *3 Is and a P*. The first I is *individualization*, the second is *independence*, the third is *inclusion*; the P stands for *productivity*. Individualization refers to our belief that each and every person should be treated as an individual, focusing on the person's abilities rather than disabilities. Independence symbolizes our belief that each and every person should be as self-reliant as possible. Inclusion refers to the importance of integrating all members into society and into the decision-making process. P is for productivity, something for which all people strive.

YAI/NIPD's Approach to Human Resources

The YAI/NIPD has used evidence from theoretical and empirical work to help guide, develop, and implement our human resource policies and practices. In this section I briefly outline several lines of research that we have translated into human resources management practice at the YAI/NIPD, a socially based, entrepreneurial organization.

Putting People First

Pfeffer (1998, p. xv) lists seven practices of successful organizations, all of which involve putting people first. Putting people first begins by creating a safe environment, where employees feel secure in their employment. It also includes empowering personnel at all levels of the organization to be involved in decision-making processes and providing them with extensive training. Reducing status distinctions and barriers, such as dress, language, office arrangements, and wage differences across levels, is also consistent with the policy of putting people first.

Our commitment to putting people first is even reflected in our Human Resources Department's mission statement which reads:

> The human resources department recognizes that YAI/NIPD/NIPD's most valuable asset in providing quality services to our consumers is our staff. Therefore, the mission of the human resources department is to ensure the health, safety and active habilitation of our consumers through the recruitment and retention of quality staff.

Effective Management and Organization

In organizations that provide direct services, the way our people work is paramount to the satisfaction of our clients. It is therefore critical to the organization's success that we manage our people effectively as this will lead to worker loyalty and excellent performance.

A number of models for effective management of human service organizations have been developed. To be effective for managing a human service organization, a model must have solid processes for budgeting, planning, monitoring, designing services, supervising, and staffing, as well as a strong leadership core. At the YAI/NIPD, our human resources processes reflect the human service management conceptual model developed by Lewis, Lewis, Packard, and Souflée (2000, p. 11). Our human resources staff are heavily engaged in designing organizational models to offer new services to our consumers in monitoring and evaluating program/service performance; recruiting, motivating, and training our staff; and continuously improving our supervisory processes across our dispersed network in a manner consistent with our mission.

Fostering the right type of leadership throughout the organization is also a key role of our human resource professionals. For the YAI/NIPD, the right type of leadership means aligning our professionals with our mission and our approach to human resource management. At the YAI/NIPD, we strongly believe that optimism is a critical and central component of the right type of leadership. As pointed out by Kouzes and Posner (2003), "Hope is essential to achieving the highest levels of performance. Hope enables people to transcend the difficulties today and envision the potentialities of tomorrow. Hope enables people to bounce back even after being stressed, stretched and depressed. Hope enables people to find the will and the way to unleash greatness" (p. 398). A culture of optimism and hope are integral to the way we recruit, motivate, retain, and train our staff, and, therefore, they are critical to our success.

Our approach to human resource management is closely aligned with the notion of putting people first and of managing staff with positive and effective leadership. We believe the agency's most valuable asset in providing quality services to our consumers is our staff. Recently the YAI/NIPD Network received the American Psychological Association's 2007 National Psychologically Healthy Workplace Award, which, we believe, is a direct result of our management philosophy, treating our staff with respect, and implementing work/life balance programs that are unparalleled in the field of disabilities.

In the following sections I describe some of the YAI/NIPD's human resources policies and programs. I hope you can use the detailed discussion of these programs and polices to help develop and maintain a successful human resource management program at your entrepreneurial social cause agency.

Attracting and Hiring Talent

For an entrepreneurial not-for-profit organization that provides direct services to people with disabilities, the labor market has become an increasingly challenging environment. For example, compensation for providers from government-funded, direct service organizations is limited by a scarcity of funds and lower reimbursement rates for specific services that are set by regulatory agencies. Entrepreneurial not-for-profit organizations can overcome these difficulties through several effective and creative practices.

Word of Mouth

One of the primary ways the YAI/NIPD attracts and recruits its staff is by word of mouth. Current YAI/NIPD staff members are encouraged to voice their opinion regarding who works at the agency, as they receive financial incentives for referring quality candidates who are successful hires. The YAI/NIPD distributes a biweekly Career Opportunities Bulletin to all programs, updating employees on agency vacancies and promoting our word-of-mouth incentives to employees. This bulletin not only strengthens the Word-of-Mouth program, but it also helps to generate interest across the company for open positions in various areas.

Relationships with Universities and Colleges

A second way in which the YAI/NIPD attracts and recruits new staff members is by developing relationships with local universities and colleges through internship programs. Each year, we visit more than 100 high-quality colleges and universities throughout the New York City metropolitan area and the northeastern United States. We also attend dozens of college consortium recruitment events, providing students from over 80 additional colleges and universities with exposure to YAI/NIPD career opportunities. Student internships have always been an important component of our recruitment program. Students provide the YAI/NIPD with the opportunity to reinvest almost 50 years of experience in the field of disabilities in the next generation of professionals. Over the past year, 132 interns received training at YAI/NIPD. In addition, student interns often work at the agency for one or two semesters and, in many cases, are recruited after graduation.

We also use internships at the YAI/NIPD to retrain current staff members for different positions within the agency. As the agency's culture is to encourage employees to pursue or further their education, the YAI/NIPD attempts to find placement options for employees so they do not have to go to another organization to complete their internship requirements. Managers are encouraged to work with the Human Resources Department to identify an appropriate placement for staff members and try to coordinate school schedules and internship hours with the employee's regular responsibilities.

YAI/NIPD's International Exchange Visitor Program, now in its 19th year, is an initiative under the auspices of the U.S. Department of State to provide practical training and enhance international relationships. This program provides an 18-month visa for people who want to work with individuals with developmental disabilities. Over the past year alone, participating countries included England, Spain, Austria, Ireland, Argentina, Australia, and Canada. "YAI/NIPD truly became my home in America," said one staff member. "I made my first friends here, YAI/NIPD helped me complete my master's degree, and I met my husband here. Now I'm preparing to take my citizenship test."

Job Fairs and the Internet

Through the years, we have also experimented with different sources of potential candidates. Two areas where we have had recent success are job fairs and the Internet. Over the past year, commercial organizations or cause-based associations have increasingly sponsored job fairs to provide employment opportunities to their target group(s). We have also experienced increasing success through sponsoring our own YAI/NIPD job fairs, which are coordinated by our Human Resource Department. Program coordinators and supervisors who assist with on-site interviews augment our recruitment staff. We have noted an increasing number of responses to our Internet-based recruiting over the past 6 years from one of our primary target groups, recent college graduates with a bachelor's degree. This is a direct result of our recruitment team's creativity in maximizing the use of employment Web sites. Agencies investing in Web-based personnel systems speed the application process, and, in today's world, e-personnel commerce is a must.

Recruiting, Screening, and Selecting Employees

At the YAI/NIPD, not only do we innovate in our sources of recruits, but we also look to the literature for best practices in the overall recruiting processes. This process begins with assessing the job's requirements, after which we develop job descriptions that contain both task-based descriptions of the role and desirable skills or attributes in a candidate. We then create announcements with key questions to enable our staff to screen résumés appropriately. We develop standard questions to ask during interviews and train the interviewers in both agency-wide interviewing standards (e.g., Equal Employment Opportunity Commission, affirmative action, etc.) and role-specific requirements. Finally, we select the right candidates based on a balance of requirements for the opening, their fit with the company's culture, and their potential for long-term employment.

Motivating, Rewarding, and Retaining Staff

There are some great sources of practical concepts in rewarding and retaining people; one that I have found particularly insightful is *Strategic Tools for Social Entrepreneurs* (Dees, Emerson, & Economy, 2007, pp. 78–89). This book presents results of studies on addressing the roots of employees' intrinsic motivation: appealing to their desire to be a part of an effective organization, to be encouraged to contribute their creativity and energy, to be granted some measure of autonomy and authority, and to be respected by managers and coworkers alike. Applying these concepts builds employee commitment and retention in a cost-effective manner.

A critical challenge in a social entrepreneurial organization is properly motivating, rewarding, and retaining staff in a resource-constrained environment. Therefore, one of the primary issues with which leaders and human resource managers must contend is balancing the need to provide incentives to staff that reward their accomplishments appropriately but do not outstrip a not-for-profit budget. At the YAI/NIPD, we have tried to address this challenge in several different ways.

A Culture of Inclusion

Every organization has its own unique culture, the sum of its values, beliefs, policies, practices, and the knowledge and personality that each employee brings to work each day. According to a survey of 150 U.S. executives by the consulting firm Robert Half International (Dees, 2007, p. 81), potential employees are very interested in the culture of organizations they are considering for employment, and their perception of an organization's culture has a measurable impact on whether they decide to work there. When asked the question, "Other than base salary and bonuses, what do most applicants ask about during job interviews today?" the surveyed executives reported benefits, corporate culture, and job security as the other top three areas of inquiry.

Ownership and Rewards

According to USC business professor Edward Lawler (1996, pp. 32–33) two key traits characterize well-designed, high-involvement organizations—organizations that are by nature high performing. The first is having each employee understand the business. This involves staff members being familiar with your company's vision and strategy and understanding both the competitive landscape and key customer segments. The second trait associated with well-designed, high-involvement organizations is aligning rewards with the overall success of the business. This is a key challenge in social cause organizations, where options and stock warrants are not an available reward. However, by including employees in the mission and vision-definition process and decision-making processes, and by creating a mission-driven culture, an organization can establish a sense of psychic ownership.

Culture for Reinforcing Success

Building an agency culture that treats staff with respect; continually reinforcing opportunities for growth; recognizing their achievements; providing support; enhancing decision making, which empowers them to take the initiative; and setting the bar for excellence creates a very high level of staff productivity. These culture and agency practices allow your greatest assets—your staff—to feel good about their work and themselves.

At the YAI/NIPD, staff inclusion is a critical part of motivating and retaining staff, because it helps to develop a positive workplace environment. For this reason, executive and human resource managers at the YAI/NIPD have put in place policies and programs that formalize staff inclusion.

Participatory management is perhaps the most important policy outlining the agency's position regarding staff inclusion. This policy is used to involve staff at all levels in addressing challenges confronting the agency, department, and program. It also creates a sense of program ownership, enhances staff morale, maintains a direct relationship with the staff, and, ultimately, ensures high-quality services for consumers. Participatory management clearly encourages all levels of our staff to participate proactively in meeting the challenges of the organization, their department, and their individual program through a variety of forums. Therefore, it is important to make your staff members partners in the management and decision-making process by asking them what they think. As a result of employees having a voice and being heard, we have seen them take ownership and become highly motivated, productive, and vested in the organization.

Empowering Your Best and Brightest

We have used participatory management to examine issues that are central to the continued growth and success of the organization. For example, in honor of our 50th anniversary, we have established a strategic planning committee, which allows the best and brightest staff members at all levels to help us chart the future. We know they are the future leaders of the organization, and their perspective is essential in helping to plan for our next 50 years. They see that we respect their expertise and opinions, and they, in turn, become further invested in the organization. One young staff member in her 20s said: "It feels really good to see that YAI/NIPD cares about what I do. I work on the front lines every day, and it's nice to know they take that into account."

Building Trust With Communication and With the Open Door Policy

We have also implemented two other noteworthy polices to nurture staff member involvement. Our communication policy states that staff members are expected to communicate in an open, honest, direct, positive, and constructive manner so that issues can be raised easily, and then addressed and resolved. This policy has been developed so that a clear system encouraging employees to communicate ideas and opinions about improving the agency's programs, systems, and staff member morale to administration is in place.

Our staff members actively use our open door policy. This policy is our way of making sure their voices are heard by providing and reinforcing an organizationally established mechanism for staff members to voice their concerns about any aspect of their employment without fear of retaliation. It is also a way for staff members to communicate their suggestions or recommendations for improving the agency. The director of human resources and human resources managers are always available to respond to staff questions and concerns. How do our staff members feel about the open door? This is what they have to say:

- "Your voice is absolutely heard and respected. You feel empowered to actually change things." Jason, assistant psychologist
- "My ideas are recognized and implemented, I have an impact." Amanda, employment training specialist
- "We feel comfortable talking to administration; they always listen and respond to us." Pat, assistant teacher

- "My voice and opinions are heard loud and clear and respected by all." Diana, assistant supervisor
- "Our ideas are taken into consideration. We always have something positive to contribute to enhance the quality of life of our consumers." Sheila, a coordinator at the International Institute for People with Disabilities of Puerto Rico

Listening to people, and walking the halls to talk to people and get to know them, builds trust over time and earns a great deal of "money in the bank." This is one way to ensure that when you need to make a "withdrawal" at different times, your staff are willing to go the extra distance for your clients and the agency.

The YAI/NIPD also uses staff member feedback surveys to involve employees in setting the agency's direction, evaluating new policies, and providing input about the functioning of individual programs. Employees complete the feedback survey annually, and the findings from the survey are shared with staff members at small town hall-style meetings. Sharing the results with staff members and discussing successes and suggestions for improvement as soon as they are available sends a strong message to staff members that their feedback has been heard.

Staff member inclusion is also promoted via individual program visits. Since the agency has many locations across the greater New York metropolitan area and in New Jersey, executives and senior managers conduct regular visits, scheduled so staff have the opportunity to meet with them individually or in small groups. Every week, the agency's president and I travel throughout the New York area to visit with staff members in our outlying programs. They share their questions and concerns and the successes they have achieved in their programs. We take their suggestions to heart, and they often result in tangible changes. Staff members see that their voices really do make a difference. Recently, we were at a residence in New Jersey, where our staff members set up a game about our agency based on the old game show, *Family Feud*. We were able to have fun, laugh, and get to know each other better. As a result of this program, our staff members also feel more comfortable asking questions and making suggestions. In addition, when the agency wants to examine a particular issue in more detail, having close ties to employees, and having established a culture of inclusion, allows us to build focus groups and teams that can elicit genuine and honest feedback from our employees.

Benefits

Employees have shared with us how important it is that they are working for an agency that makes them feel important, where the culture is supportive and the philosophy is consistent across programs. Developing a nurturing and family-oriented environment is essential. Employees know the agency cares about them personally as well as professionally and is committed to promoting their health and well-being, to reduce stress and improve health outcomes. Our employees say they never have to choose between their jobs and their families. We recognize that an employee's support network is crucial to staff members' ability to have peace of mind while they are at work. We know that if employees are happy in their personal lives, they will be more motivated and effective at work. As an agency, we truly believe that, if we take care of all employees' health and well-being by ensuring they and their families have the best health benefits we can offer, we are providing peace of mind and body. In turn, this allows them to focus their energy on a professional career and on providing the very best services to individuals with disabilities and their families who rely on them every day. Build a gold standard: Treat people as you would like to be treated, and you will build a positive work environment.

Human resources ensure that employees can maximize their benefits so they can focus on their jobs and not worry about personal issues. One health initiative we have put in place is the Take Care New York Program, which assists employees in monitoring their own health via Take Care New York passports that remind staff about their annual physicals, immunizations, and prevention screenings.

Offering an Employee Assistance Program

Another health initiative we implemented is an employee assistance program (EAP), which helps employees in their times of need. If your organization is there for your employees in a time of crisis, they will be there for the agency in a time of need. We have put the EAP in place to provide YAI/NIPD employees with free, confidential assistance to help resolve questions, concerns, or problems by developing coping strategies and solutions. The EAP offers help with life issues such as childcare, child rearing, family and social relationships, emotional problems, legal or financial concerns, trauma, and drug and alcohol abuse problems. This resource adds to our staff's peace of mind and results in better job performance and a higher level of care for the agency's consumers. The EAP provides additional emotional support and resources to assist employees in resolving issues in their personal lives, while keeping their issues confidential and separate from their work.

Use of Intranet

Finally, the Human Resources Department has an intranet site that provides extensive information and support to employees and can be accessed 24 hours a day, at work or in employees' homes. This arrangement makes assistance even more accessible.

Finding Ways to Thank and Reward Staff

As noted previously, one of the major challenges facing not-for-profit executives and human resource managers is balancing the need to provide incentives to staff that reward their accomplishments appropriately but do not outstrip a not-for-profit budget. As the American Express Incentive Services Achieve More survey (1999) shows, the most effective rewards cost little or no money. And since this means that your budget does not have to be an issue when you give employee rewards and recognition, you are limited only by your imagination.

The Achieve More survey offered the best and worst rewards mentioned by respondents. The best rewards list consisted of the following items: a verbal thank you for a job well done, a letter of commendation, a good performance evaluation, and a career-related gift or training. The worst rewards were additional work; being fired or laid off, a T-shirt or other article of clothing, and no recognition or being ignored. Agencies should also refrain from laying people off by using all of the other support and opportunities in the agency to maintain people.

Wondering what to do to reward your employees for little or no money? One practical source of ideas I have found helpful is Bob Nelson's *1001 Ways to Reward Employees* (1994, pp. xv–xvi). He offers such simple ideas as personalize employee business cards with nicknames, give employees an extra hour off for lunch, keep a well-stocked candy jar on your desk and invite employees to partake whenever the urge hits them, write a special memo to recognize a notable team achievement and post it on the department bulletin board and fax it to all locations, have a crazy hat day, post letters of thanks from customers on break room bulletin boards, attach thank-you notes to employee paychecks, throw a barbecue picnic at a nearby park, send flowers home on the first day of work or for an anniversary, or put gold stars on employee computers along with a note of thanks. As a social entrepreneur, you are free to try out innovative new ways to have the most impact on your employees and your organization. The key is to find what resonates with your employees and to do it often.

An annual staff day is one of the major forums we use to acknowledge staff members' achievements and reward our employees. This special day focuses on the agency's nonmanagement employees (i.e., direct support professionals) and shows our appreciation for the important work they do and acknowledges their professional and educational growth. At our annual staff day, we distribute Years of Service Awards, beginning with 5 years, along with our peer recognition awards. Merit Service Awards are presented to part- and full-time direct support professionals who significantly affect the lives of people with developmental disabilities every day. This recognition includes a monetary award. Awardees are recognized by their peers as important role models in the agency. We also present agency-sponsored scholarships to assist direct support professionals in furthering their education in the field. Employees are eligible to apply if they have been employed full time for 1 year, have a very good to excellent evaluation and supervisory approval, and have a received a Merit Service Award. The YAI/NIPD also hosts an annual managers' retreat where managers are recognized for their achievements in similar ways.

Another tool that we routinely use to recognize and reward staff members is an agency-wide fax. The YAI/NIPD's agency-wide fax, called the Friday Fax because it is distributed to all programs every Friday, includes agency-wide recognition for team and individual accomplishments. Announcements of staff member promotions are also included in the Friday Fax. We also now use an alternative personal online system so recognition can go directly to the employee.

Because the YAI/NIPD's work affects local communities, local media are another mechanism to reward and recognize staff members. Articles often appear in local neighborhood papers about the high quality of our employees' work and their impact on a person with disabilities' ability to achieve major milestones.

Training and Developing Skills

The strength of the agency for nearly 50 years has been our ability to develop a farm system by fostering employee growth and development. As a result, the agency promotes primarily from within. This is a tremendous incentive for our employees to stay, as they can see how vested the agency is in them. They experience firsthand the ongoing state-of-the-art training, the depth of support through supervision, mentoring, and job enrichment and growth. Employees also realize how much the agency is investing in them by providing them with so much opportunity, including a menu of educational and career opportunities and scholarships. Our philosophy of promoting from within has resulted in a talented executive and management team with a strong sense of agency philosophy, mission, and organizational history. One hundred percent of our executive management team, including myself, started in a YAI/NIPD program as a direct service professional or program supervisor. A woman who works in one of our residences recently said to me, "I want your job!" I responded by saying, "You *can* have my job! I know, because 30 years ago, I had *your* job." Building opportunities for growth is essential to make people feel important and know they can be part of the growth of the agency.

Developing Future Leaders to Ensure Future Stability of Your Agency

A critical starting point in the process of developing our future leaders is assessing their leadership. To assess leadership potential, we use such practical tools as the Leadership Assessment Summary developed by Larry Bossidy and Ram Charan (2002, p. 151). Once we assess the behavior and performance of our employees, we determine the appropriate way to engage in their development.

We approach training and employee development in a number of different ways. On a daily work level, we use supervision, mentoring, job enrichment, and job growth as our primary tools. On a more formal level, we have established partnerships with local universities and national organizations to provide cost-effective training to key high performers.

Both formal and informal mentorship programs are available to employees who demonstrate potential in leadership or clinical areas and a desire to grow with the agency. This occurs primarily at the program or department level, where a manager (through supervision with employees) identifies an employee who might grow professionally through increased exposure in a particular area.

Job enrichment and job growth are two other ways the YAI/NIPD trains and develops employees. Job growth encourages and supports employees who wish to grow in their current roles or positions by providing increased variety while maximizing the employees' skills and interests. Considered a *horizontal* expansion, job growth has proved to be a great retention tool for employees who do not necessarily have the skills to be promoted to a higher-level position.

Job enrichment, on the other hand, encourages and supports employees to develop additional skills and responsibilities outside of their role while in their current position.

This *vertical* expansion gives employees the opportunity to become eligible for promotions to positions that require better skills and greater responsibilities, for example, management or clinical positions, and facilitates internal promotions.

More formal types of trainings are offered to YAI/NIPD staff members as well. For example, all new managers participate in ongoing managers' training that includes such topics as the agency's philosophy and culture, communication, how to foster a direct relationship with employees, the role of supervision, diversity, sexual harassment, and interviewing. This training also gives new managers direct exposure to senior management. In addition, we have developed partnerships with a number of local colleges and universities for our staff members to receive a discount per credit hour and a 50% agency reimbursement in return for a 2-year-plus postdegree employment commitment.

National surveys about the workplace reveal that when an organization (and, especially, its managers) recognizes employees, good morale, less turnover, and greater retention are the result. As noted previously, building a positive workplace culture fosters a management philosophy that recognizes individual and team accomplishments through supervision and program staff meetings, philosophy that espouses catching employees doing something well and reinforcing it at that moment. This philosophy "puts money in the bank" with employees, so they are more receptive to developmental or constructive feedback when a manager needs to address an issue with the employee. We view supervision, therefore, as supportive rather than disciplinary.

Conclusions

The lessons learned from almost 40 years of managing the employees of the YAI/NIPD are universal and can be applied in any social-entrepreneurial organization. The foundation of our success is recognizing that our people are our most treasured assets. Once leaders recognize this simple tenet, the challenge then become translating this tenet into policies, guidelines, procedures, and actions that resonate with your employees.

Attracting talent is a tremendous challenge to our business. Not only do we wrestle with the typical challenges most enterprises face today, but we also must deal with our inability to control the compensation of our employees. We have met this challenge with a positive culture that makes the YAI/NIPD the most satisfying employer in our industry, with a grassroots or localized approach to recruiting. By establishing strong relationships with local universities, special interest and minority groups, and our employees, we are able to reach a large population of potential recruits cost-effectively.

Employee retention is another area we tackle with an entrepreneurial approach. The foundation of our approach is our participatory management program, a critical pillar of our culture of inclusion. By including our employees in key decisions—for example, the recently chartered Strategic Planning Committee—we "walk the talk" of employee inclusion. Strict adherence to our open door policy is another key reinforcing mechanism of inclusion, and our program visits not only expose our top management executives to the frontline work of direct-care staff, but they also offer a platform for two-way conversation between our most senior and junior staff members.

Rewarding our employees is accomplished without breaking the bank. We encourage our leaders and managers to reward employees throughout the year in innovative ways. We also hold our staff day and managers' retreat, where we celebrate our accomplishments and individual employee excellence. Finally, our human resources managers ensure that our employees get the most of our benefits dollar through benefits management and help create a balanced work-life environment through our EAP.

Our stated preference for promoting from within helps to motivate, reward, and recruit, but it can pose an added training challenge. Through job expansion and enrichment, we expose our best performers to developmental challenges in a controlled manner. Partnerships with local universities and scholarships tied to years of service are also economical ways to retain employees and prepare them for future challenges in areas with higher responsibility.

The challenge of finding policies, procedures, and practices that build a genuine culture of employees are our most valued asset is continuously changing. I hope you find the lessons in this chapter to be useful in managing your organization, as they have been in mine.

You can easily see how proud I am of my agency. Now it's your turn to build on your positive feelings for your agency while engaging all of your staff in being as proud of their agency as you are. Each of the ideas discussed in this chapter can be used in your agency and your practice. Good luck!

References

Hutson, D. (1999, June). New incentives are on the rise. *Compensation & Benefits Review, 32*(5), 40–46.

Bossidy, L., & Charan, R. (2002). *Execution: The discipline of getting things done.* New York: Crown Business.

Dees, G. J., Emerson, J., & Economy, P. (2007). *Strategic tools for social entrepreneurs: Enhancing the performance of your enterprising nonprofit.* New York: John Wiley & Sons.

Kouzes, J. M., & Posner, B. Z. (2003). *The leadership challenge.* San Francisco: Jossey-Bass.

Lawler, Edward. (1996). *From the ground up.* San Francisco: Jossey-Bass.

Lewis, J. A., Lewis, M. D., Packard, T., & Soufflée, F., Jr. (2000). *Management of human service programs* (3rd ed.). Belmont, CA: Wadsworth Publishing.

Nelson, B. (1994). *1001 ways to reward employees.* New York: Workman.

Patti, R. (Ed.). (2000). *The handbook of social welfare management.* Thousand Oaks, CA: Sage Publications.

Pfeffer, J. (1998). *The human equation: Building profits by putting people first.* Cambridge, MA: Harvard Business School Press.

14

Public Relations:

An Essential Tool for Building an Organization's Identity and Promoting the Values, Mission, and Goals of Human Services Agencies

Joel M. Levy, Philip H. Levy, Ben Nivin, and Lynn U. Berman

Social service agencies play a noble role in our society. They often serve our most fragile, vulnerable populations, including children and adults with disabilities, people with life-threatening diseases, the poor, the aged, individuals with substance abuse problems, and families in crisis. Social service agencies also serve as agents of social change. They research and analyze social programs, policies, and regulations, and they serve as advocates for legislative solutions as well as social justice and equity. Throughout their careers, social workers strive to develop positive social acceptance of their service recipients and build support for social change and recognition of their cause.

One might assume that, given these agencies' positive contributions to and significant impact on society, the good works they perform speak for themselves, and that social service agencies do not need to engage in public relations. Yet, to be successful, social service agencies and social workers need to understand the importance of public relations and the role it plays in achieving their objectives.

This chapter focuses on the role of public relations, using the perspective and experience of the YAI/National Institute for People with Disabilities Network (YAI/NIPD, www.yai.org), which, for more than 50 years, has used focused and energetic public relations to promote our organization's mission, vision, and values. Through public relations, YAI/NIPD has communicated effectively to key audiences outside and inside the organization our core values and philosophy: namely, that every person, at every age and level of ability, has the potential for growth and is entitled to the same dignity, respect, and opportunities as all other members of society. By using basic public relations strategies and tools, we have been able to demonstrate how we help the people we serve to achieve their full potential for independence, individuality, productivity, and inclusion in their communities. In short, through public relations, social service and human services organizations can bring their mission to life in a real and tangible way.

What is public relations, and why is it so important for those who work in social service agencies to understand the power of public relations? How can social workers regardless of their organization's size and budget take advantage of public relations tools of to help carry out their agencies' missions and visions? What public relations opportunities are available to social service agencies in the new media era?

To answer these questions, this chapter first defines public relations and why it is essential for social service agencies. Next, we discuss the public relations planning model and specific public relations tools that can and should be part of every agency's outreach toolkit. Because the media offer a powerful method for communicating messages that can enhance support for programs and services, a considerable portion of this chapter focuses on media relations strategies and tactics. We also touch on the role of strategic partnerships and crisis communications strategies. In addition, because new media, such as blogs, podcasts, FaceBook, MySpace, and YouTube, offer important and cost-effective tools for social service agencies, this chapter addresses those opportunities as well. Throughout, we use case studies and examples to illustrate how YAI/NIPD has used public relations tactics to educate our stakeholders and change public perceptions about people with developmental disabilities. This chapter is intended as a practical primer for those in the social work and human services profession who desire to raise the profile of their agencies and achieve organizational goals by using basic public relations strategies and tools.

At the Core of Public Relations: The Relationship

Although there are many definitions of public relations, three are well-suited for the purposes of nonprofit social service agencies. A first definition comes from a textbook commonly used in undergraduate public relations courses: "Public relations is the management of mutually influential relationships within a web of stakeholder and organizational relationships" (Coombs & Holladay, 2007, p. 26). The Public Relations Society of America, the world's largest organization for public relations professionals, with more than 28,000 members, defines *public relations* as the management function that evaluates public attitudes, recognizes the strategies and actions of individuals or organizations with the public interest, and completes procedures to earn public understanding and acceptance. A third definition, from the *Encyclopedia of Social Work* is perhaps the most straightforward: "Public relations is a planned process aimed at bringing an organization's name and message to the public in a systematic and sustained manner" (Brawley, 1983, p. 1675, citing Rossie, 1983, pp. 24–25).

According to Dr. Elizabeth Clark, executive director of the National Association of Social Workers (NASW),

> Public relations is defined by the type of "conversations" (both good and bad) that an organization regularly has with its many publics. It's about being as forthcoming and engaging as one can be about the organization's purpose and mission, as well as the decisions and actions it takes to reach its goals... Public relations relies on an educational versus a sales approach to convey information, and if done well, invites interaction [e-mail interview, March 6, 2008].

The essence of each of these definitions is the *relationship*—and this relationship between an organization and its various publics is the core of any effective public relations effort. Whether the organization desires to create better public awareness about its work, promote its mission and values, raise funds, cope with a crisis, or expand its internal or external constituencies, building relationships with target audiences is the essential element and must be the focus of public relations planning. For example, at many social service and human services agencies, key audiences typically include service recipients, parents, foundations and other funders, the business community, staff, and the media. Through public relations, organizations strive to develop and nurture relationships with each group, recognizing that at the most basic level, each target audience is an "audience of one."

Although the terms *advertising, marketing,* and *publicity* are often used interchangeably with *public relations,* they refer to different but similar activities (see Glossary below). Many people confuse advertising and public relations. Advertising is quite simply publicity that an organization pays for; the organization decides when and where to advertise, and has complete control over the message. On the other hand, as Art Feinglass, founder and president of Access Communications, Inc., has noted, public relations is publicity that you pay for. Although the organization has little control over the media coverage it receives, media "earned" through public relations is often more credible than advertising (Feinglass, 2005, p. 171).

In the *corporate sector,* organizations often use public relations to help achieve marketing and advertising goals; however, public relations is a separate function from marketing and advertising and often encompasses media relations, community relations, crisis management, employee relations, internal communications, investor relations, and public affairs.

Also concerned with helping the organization achieve its goals and objectives, *nonprofit* public relations encompasses media relations, community relations, crisis communications, employee relations, and internal communications. However, unlike the private sector, many nonprofit organizations, especially social service agencies, count social change among their goals.

GLOSSARY

- Advertising: Paid communication of messages targeted for selected audiences, designed to inform and influence them.

- Internal communications: The flow of information between an organization's management and its ranks. Employee communications are a type of internal communications.

- Marketing: The development and distribution of goods and services that meet customer needs.

- Media relations: Outreach to news organizations; a specialized function of public relations.

- Public affairs: Communications focused on the development of public policy.

- Public relations: A planned process that brings an organization's name and message to the public in a systematic and sustained manner.

- Publicity: Media coverage about an organization, including strategic messages, programs and events.

Why Public Relations Is Important

At a time when the complex field of social work is not well understood, and society often ignores, stigmatizes, and discriminates against the people we serve, public relations has the power to make the work of social and human services agencies better known, enabling social and human services agencies to achieve their goals and make people aware of the essential work they do. The tools of public relations enable social workers to communicate about their work, the people they serve, and such issues as social justice and equity.

Public relations can also work to eliminate stereotypes about social workers and service recipients. According to Dr. Richard J. Gelles, dean of the University of Pennsylvania School of Social Policy and Practice,

> The general public and well-educated lay people view social work, social workers and social work agencies through a highly distorted stereotypical lens. This narrow lens assumes that social workers exist to work only with the poor. There are personal and political stereotypes as well, such as that the pay is poor and social workers are all liberals. But the most significant issue is the narrow view that most people have of social work and social service organizations. Using appropriate public relations allow for a more accurate "branding" of the profession and its work and workforce [e-mail interview, March 6, 2008].

As readers will discover in this chapter, media relations is a critical tool for social service organizations, but the public relations toolbox contains a wide range of other ways to expand public awareness and tell the social work story.

Public Relations and Social Work: Promoting Social Change

Public relations, the media, and social work share a long history characterized by a collaboration that has resulted in community action, attitude change, and social reform. At the beginning of the 20th century, alliances of social workers and other reformers with "muckraking journalists" of the Progressive Era educated the public about the social ills of the era, such as child labor, low wages, unsafe factories, and overcrowded housing (Brawley, 2001, p. 1675). As the social work profession developed, social service agencies took on the public awareness and education role, using media outreach to help educate the public about social work and the needs of vulnerable individuals and groups (p. 1675).

More recently, public relations played a major role in transforming the field and lives of people with intellectual and developmental disabilities. Three separate events with public relations elements raised public awareness and changed public attitudes about people with disabilities, contributing to the 1975 consent decree that began the process of closing Willowbrook State School for individuals with developmental disabilities. Illustrating the power of public relations messages, in 1965, Sen. Robert F. Kennedy (D-NY) referred to the Willowbrook State School in Staten Island, New York, as a "situation that borders on a snake pit." Later on, Geraldo Rivera, then a crusading reporter for WABC-TV in New York City, produced a television exposé that featured the deplorable conditions inside Willowbrook. Rivera's graphic reports shocked the public and had a profound impact on changing public perceptions and attitudes pertaining to institutions. Finally, Burton Blatt and Fred Kaplan's *Christmas in Purgatory* (1974), a photo essay of life in five institutions, brought to life social injustice and human rights violations at the institutions and raised questions about the ethical treatment of individuals with developmental disabilities. The publicity generated by these exposures led to the closing of Willowbrook and other institutions and energized the movement toward community living for individuals with developmental disabilities.

In the early 1980s, to broaden awareness about people with disabilities and promote community acceptance, YAI/NIPD worked with the New York State Office of Mental Retardation and Developmental Disabilities to disseminate a public service announcement, "Right at Home, Right in the Neighborhood," which conveyed the message that people with disabilities make good neighbors.

At about the same time, to support families and professionals in ensuring the success of community-based living, YAI/NIPD developed two weekly TV series, *Children with Special Needs* and *On Our Own*. Produced by Joel M. Levy and Philip H. Levy, the programs educated parents, advocates, and service providers on critical issues, ranging from early intervention for infants to the transition from adolescence to adulthood for individuals with developmental disabilities. Between them, the two series garnered numerous media awards, including a local Emmy nomination.

By using public relations, human services organizations can communicate through the media compelling and moving stories of service recipients, raising awareness about an agency's values and work, while eliminating negative public perceptions and stereotypes about the people they serve.

Social workers have a strong commitment to making a positive difference in the lives of service recipients, and to changing society at large. Their work enhances the dialogue on social policies, government funding, program development, and allocation of scarce resources. The NASW Code of Ethics highlights the role social workers play in their ethical responsibility to their clients, their colleagues, their employers, and the social work profession. In each of these areas, effective public relations plays a role, leading to social change and improved lives for the people these agencies serve.

The Challenge of Public Relations Today

Although public relations can clearly play a role in changing public opinion and effecting social change, obtaining media coverage in today's fragmented media market can seem daunting to social service agencies. Social workers typically receive little or no training in public relations tactics, including media relations. Managing large caseloads, limited budgets, and time-consuming administrative responsibilities leaves little time to engage in public relations activities. Adding to these challenges is the intense competition to attract media attention. In addition, with cutbacks in the newspaper and media industries (one in four newspaper jobs has disappeared since 1990; Johnson, 2008), overworked reporters who cover multiple beats have less time to develop stories. To complicate matters still further, the media market is no longer confined to television, radio, and print media; the Internet, blogs, podcasts, and social media channels must be taken into account when planning a public relations program.

As Howard J. Rubenstein, founder and president of Rubenstein Associates, Inc., one of the nation's most prestigious public relations firms, pointed out at YAI/NIPD's 2004 international conference,

> Nonprofits often face greater hurdles in getting their messages heard. Because they usually have fewer resources, nonprofits need to find creative ways to get out their message. If you have a great story and no one hears it, is it a great story? When it comes to pitching stories, it takes persistence, creativity and resourcefulness.

Despite the challenges, public relations does not have to be elaborate, time-consuming, or expensive to achieve successful results. It does, however, necessitate the persistence and creativity that Rubenstein mentions. Above all, it requires a firm, mindful commitment throughout the entire organization to support and engage in the public relations effort. Public relations today is the responsibility of *everyone* in the organization, from the CEO to the clerical support staff. The good news is that, by mastering a few basics and being strategic about how they apply public relations tactics, social service agencies can achieve their public relations goals. In the following section we discuss specific public relations techniques and demonstrate how social service agencies can develop results-getting public relations programs.

Public Relations: Planning is Key

Just as an airplane without a flight plan will lose direction, no organization can be successful in its public relations effort without a solid, systematically developed public relations plan. The plan is a map for public relations activities and provides a way to gauge the success of the effort. According to Art Feinglass, "To get noticed, you need publicity. There are things you can do to get it. Some require time and effort, and others require money. Some don't require much of anything except a plan. Without one, you are unlikely to accomplish much" (Feinglass, 2005, p. 27).

For public relations to be successful, top management must have a clear understanding of what public relations is and must commit resources to the effort. Top management needs to sensitize everyone in the organization to the importance of the public relations program and educate staff to support the public relations plan. Staff at all levels, particularly those at the program level, can provide ideas for human interest stories that will attract media interest and exposure. For most organizations, the public relations plan is an integral part of the organization's overall strategic plan.

Having a public relations strategy is important for all organizations, regardless of size. As was our case when we were a small, struggling agency without the resources for a staff person with public relations responsibility, many small organizations have found creative ways to carry out their public relations campaign. These methods include

- securing a college intern majoring in public relations;
- recruiting volunteers who have experience in public relations;
- consulting board members who may have experience or contacts in public relations; and
- hiring a freelance public relations professional to work on a project basis.

Organizations should work with leadership, board members, and department managers to establish concrete goals, messages, and activities for the public relations effort. Public relations planning and execution should become a shared activity throughout an organization.

There are certain elements to all successful public relations plans, including

- establishment of goals and objectives;
- identification of target audiences (knowing whom the organization wants to reach);
- establishing clear messages;
- choosing appropriate strategies and tactics; and
- evaluating and assessing the public relations effort.

Goals and Objectives

What does the agency want to accomplish in its public relations program? Does it seek to build awareness about its work? Promote its mission, values, and philosophy? Its unique brand? Raise funds? Attract applicants for staff positions? Develop its organizational culture through internal communications? These are among the questions the organization must ask as it seeks to define the goals and objectives for its public relations plan.

For Sheldon Gelman, associate vice president for academic affairs and dean of the Wurzweiler School of Social Work at Yeshiva University, the goal of public relations is effective branding of social service agencies:

> Without good PR, social work organizations cannot effectively portray their services or contributions to clients and funders. The buzz word today is "branding," which helps create a unique identity for the organization. PR is the public face of what is often a poorly understood enterprise [e-mail interview, February 21, 2008].

Public relations goals are closely tied to an organization's mission and vision. They answer questions about who you are, why you exist, whom you serve, and what you value. They inform the organization's goals and communicate its unique brand. YAI/NIPD's Core Mission and Mission of Hope statements work together to articulate our intentions, hopes, and expectations.

YAI/NIPD's public relations goals emphasize the organization's mission, brand, and reputation; its advocacy role in promoting social equity; and its staff relations and culture:

- Bring our mission to life, which includes meeting the needs of the people we serve, creating a society more accepting of the people we serve, and building upon our values.

YAI/NIPD NETWORK'S CORE MISSION

We believe that every person, at every age and level of ability, has the potential for growth and is entitled to the same dignity, respect, and opportunities as all other members of society. We are committed to helping the people we serve to achieve their potential for independence, individuality, productivity, and inclusion in their communities. We dedicate ourselves to the pursuit of excellence in all that we do.

YAINIPD MISSION OF HOPE

Through person-centered planning, self-determination, state-of-the-art programs, and effective advocacy, the YAI/National Institute for People with Disabilities Network builds brighter futures for people with developmental and learning disabilities and their families. Hope is realized each day thanks to the dedication of staff, the courage of consumers and their families, the leadership of members of various Boards, and the generosity and participation of friends and supporters.

- Increase name recognition and reputation as a quality service provider, meeting the needs of service recipients and other stakeholders.
- Increase awareness about issues in the human services field and the people we serve. (This is critical when seeking funds both government and private, generating community support, or advocating on behalf of our clients/consumers.)
- Build social equity and promote social acceptance of our society's most vulnerable citizens.
- Position our organization as an authority and leader on human services issues.
- Boost pride among existing staff and constituents.
- Develop and preserve the cohesiveness of the organization, which reinforces our organization's culture.

Another example of public relations goals comes from the Center for Child Protection and Family Support, a small organization in Washington, DC, that addresses the devastating effects of child abuse through family and children's programming:

- Raise awareness of child abuse/child victimization issues.
- Help the organization gain visibility and become a known and trusted resource for the media and funding sources, and a training and consulting resource for constituents and allied child protection groups.
- Generate attendance and news coverage at a press conference coinciding with the release of new research and at a 1-day, organization-sponsored regional forum on child abuse and victim's rights.
- Lay the foundation for the organization to become the training facilitator of choice for child welfare professionals and help the organization transition from offering free training to fee-based training.
- Assist the organization in developing alliances with organizations that share its mission.

Any social service or human services organization may adapt or modify these goals, depending on its specific mission.

Target Audiences

Audience segmentation, the process of taking an entire market and dividing it into homogeneous groups, is an essential principle in marketing in the corporate sector. Similarly, identifying target audiences is key to successful public relations in the nonprofit sector.

In both marketing and public relations today, no longer can we speak of a mass market. Instead, it is more accurate to think of target audiences as a "public of one." According to a 2007 report from public relations and marketing company Ketchum and the University of Southern California Annenberg Strategic Public Relations Center,

> The theme "public of one" emerged from this year's [study] findings to represent the way communicators should view today's consumer audience. With digital media giving rise to increasing media choice, fragmentation and personal empowerment, the term "mass market" is being outmoded. As a result, it is imperative that communicators view their audience as distinct groupings of individuals. ("Survey Reveals Communicators Are Out of Sync," 2007)

Who does the agency want to reach through its public relations program to accomplish its goals? Social and human service agencies, like most organizations, must direct their public relations efforts at a variety of publics or stakeholders. Each of these audiences constitutes a distinct group of people the organization needs to reach to accomplish its goals. Each group is likely to have its own profile or characteristics, and the messages for each group are often different.

Ralph L. Dogloff, a professor at the University of Maryland School of Social Work, emphasizes the need for social service agencies to define their audiences:

> Public relations educates many groups, including potential service users, of the needs for service and the services available. PR makes the organization visible to multiple audiences. When defining the key people an agency needs to reach, it is important not to overlook the "in-house public," including boards, employees, staff and others who provide services. In many cases, the organization will have multiple communications goals and different PR strategies for each group [e-mail interview, February 29, 2008].

A review of YAI/NIPD's goals in the previous section reveals lists of both *internal audiences* and *external audiences*.

Internal Audiences
- Service recipients
- Families of service recipients
- Staff
- Board members

External Audiences
- Prospective service recipients and their families
- Donors

- Funders, including foundations, corporations, and the government
- Existing and potential partners (individuals and organizations who help an organization carry out its activities and fulfill its mission)
- Social service professionals
- Legislators and other policymakers
- General public
- Media

A note about the last three external audiences: Because social workers advocate for social equity and promote broad-based public acceptance of their service recipients, the general public and policymakers are two important target audiences. In addition, since the media are powerful tools that enable human services agencies to convey their messages to various publics and achieve goals, they should count print, broadcast, and new media among their key target audiences.

Once target audiences are identified, the planning focus must turn to messages and how best to reach each target audience.

Messages

Creating clear, consistent, and well-stated messages about the organization and its mission, values, and culture is fundamental in any successful public relations program. These messages must be fine-tuned so they can be conveyed consistently and succinctly in every communication, including brochures, press releases, newsletters, Web site pages, op-eds, letters to the editor, special events, public service advertisements, blogs, and other public relations outreach.

Organizations should develop several key messages to convey through public relations activities. These messages communicate who you are as an organization and your values. They reflect the organization's culture and mission. They are essentially the organization's "brand." Messages may include the following:

- All service recipients have dignity and worth, and they make valuable contributions to their communities.
- The agency is a cohesive organization, committed to high standards of quality and excellence in all it does.
- The organization is a resource on human services issues.

With the organization's messages articulated and fine-tuned, the plan must focus on strategies and tactics to convey those messages to target audiences.

Public Relations Strategies and Tactics

Media placements in print, radio and television, public service announcements, calendar listings, newsletters (print and electronic), special events, partnerships and sponsorships, press conferences, op-eds, letters to the editor, blogs, FaceBook, YouTube, and other new media: Each is a tool in the public relations toolkit for nonprofit organizations. Social work and human service agencies can use a variety of media outlets to reach key audiences, both internal and external. Because placements in print and broadcast media reach large audiences, agencies can use strategic media relations to tell their story. Any organization, regardless of size, can adopt strategies and tactics.

Media Relations: A Power Tool

On Sunday morning, August 29, 2004, a story appeared in the *New York Times* Job Market column, titled "Off-Court Achievements at the U.S. Open." The article featured Dawn, a person with a developmental disability who received employment training from YAI/NIPD and was hired to maintain the food court at the U.S. Open tennis championship. The article highlighted The Corporate Source, a member of the YAI/NIPD Network that provides job opportunities for people with developmental disabilities, as well as Restaurant Associates, the company that operated the food village at the U.S. Open. The story included quotes from several workers and Mike Sullivan of Restaurant Associates. Similar stories with the consistent message that hiring people with disabilities is a sound business decision appeared on *New York 1 News* (August 25), in *Long Island Business News* (September 10–16), and *Hoy* (August 17). Best of all, this story had legs. Following publication of the *Times* article, a manager at the Yonkers Raceway contacted YAI/NIPD to inquire about hiring 50 of our graduates for the reopening of the raceway, demonstrating that one strategic media placement opens up additional opportunities for an organization.

The messages throughout the U.S. Open articles were clear: (1) people with developmental disabilities make good employees because they are dedicated and capable, and (2) YAI/NIPD is a leader in training people with disabilities. Through a variety of print and broadcast media placements, these messages enabled us to reach our internal and external target audiences. How does this kind of coverage come about? How did our organization manage to get coverage in a major daily newspaper and in other local media?

The answer is quite simply this: with creative media relations and persistence. It took several contacts with the *Times* reporter to interest her in the story, and once she was ready to work on it, we moved quickly to identify for her who would be featured. We also selected appropriate spokespeople for our organization. Our quick response resulted in some outstanding publicity for people with disabilities; our partner, Restaurant Associates; and our agency.

The U.S. Open story is but one example of our media relations successes. At YAI/NIPD, we use a wide array of strategies to convey our messages to target audiences. However, media relations is arguably the most powerful for us, as it can be for other nonprofit organizations. There is no mystery to effective media relations. By understanding how the media work, how best to reach reporters, and what types of stories the media find compelling, social workers and staff in nonprofit organizations will find that being media savvy pays off in increased visibility and credibility.

How the Media Work

Most large media organizations are businesses that seek to make a profit. As a result, they tend to run news stories that are often sensational and involve controversy—the kinds of stories that sell newspapers and advertising. The "good news" stories from many nonprofits often go underreported. According to an October 2007 survey by the Pew Research Center for People and the Press, 1 in 10 Americans said the media do not pay enough attention to the good things that are happening in the country, including positive outcomes and good deeds done by average citizens (see http://people-press.org/reports/display.php3?ReportID=362). Perhaps in response to this sentiment, many news organizations today, especially local ones, are increasingly seeking the kinds of positive stories nonprofits can offer.

What is news and what do media organizations consider to be newsworthy? According to M. Lyle Spencer, former dean of the journalism department at the University of Washington, "News is…any event, idea, or opinion that is timely, that interests or affects a large number of people in a community, and that is capable of being understood by them" (see http://www.socialworkers.org/pressroom/MediaToolkit/default.asp). Note that one criterion used to determine a story's newsworthiness is whether it is "timely." Clearly, social and human service agencies work on some of today's timeliest social issues. They also are concerned with issues affecting the community. This definition suggests that many of the activities and events of social service agencies are indeed newsworthy!

Advocacy is the driving force behind some of the stories YAI/NIPD identifies for media outlets. These stories can be particularly powerful in changing public perceptions and inspiring people and organizations in the social service field to aspire to higher goals. A front page story in the *New York Times* about YAI/NIPD's socialization and relationship programs characterized our organization as "cutting edge" and a "trailblazer" in offering sexuality workshops for people with disabilities (Gross, 2006, p. 1). The story was covered by many newspapers that subscribe to the New York Times News Service, was featured on numerous Web sites, and generated tremendous interest from parents and organizations throughout the United States and abroad who wanted to know more about our program and how to replicate it.

For a story like this to come to life, organizations must be willing to make staff available to ensure the reporter has access to the information he or she needs. In this case, the story began with the reporter's face-to-face meeting with YAI/NIPD President Philip H. Levy and other key staff who provided the background and explained the philosophy behind our organization's programs. We gave the reporter a list of our numerous socialization opportunities for people with developmental disabilities and the locations and times those groups met. We also accompanied the reporter to some of our program sites and arranged for interviews with several couples with disabilities and their parents. Finally, we identified and scheduled phone interviews with other experts in the field outside our organization.

Before approaching a reporter with any story idea, organizations must do their homework to ensure they are approaching the reporters who are most likely to be interested in the story, and, most importantly, that they have all the facts to capture the attention of those reporters.

The media landscape, as noted earlier, is becoming increasingly fragmented, making it more important than ever to know which kinds of stories will appeal to various types of news organizations. Local media, which include community newspapers, radio stations, local cable channels, and local network affiliates, seek stories that appeal to local view-ers, listeners, or readers. National media are those with national audiences, such as the *Wall Street Journal*, *USA Today*; networks ABC, NBC, CBS, and Fox; cable channels such as CNN; and National Public Radio. These news organizations are most likely to be interested in stories on issues of national interest. Trade media, such as *NASW News* and *Social Work Today* are concerned with news about social workers and the social work profession (see http://www.socialworkers.org/pressroom/MediaToolkit/default.asp).

Think Like a Reporter

Successful media relations for social service agencies requires thinking like a jour-nalist and determining what the news hook or human interest element is for each reporter. But how do human service organizations determine which reporters to ap-proach? How can a social service agency determine what kinds of stories will resonate with a given journalist?

A well-developed media list is an essential element in the media relations toolkit. There are a number of ways to assemble a media list that includes basic contact infor-mation, including e-mail addresses, for journalists who cover the types of stories of interest to social service organizations: mental health, at-risk children, and physical health (autism, physical disabilities, etc.). Lists can be purchased from such organizations as Media Contacts Pro (http://www.mediacontactspro.com) or Cision's MediaListsOnline (http://medialistsonline.com), but they can also be assembled using simple searches on Google or Yahoo. Just about every news organization now has a Web site with reporters' contact information. If the information is not available online, it is always appropriate to call the general information number to request contact information for the reporter who covers the particular areas of interest. The increasing number of ethnic media should be included in assembling a comprehensive media list.

Once the media list is compiled, it is time to build and cultivate relationships with the reporters/contacts on the list. After all, the most important part of media relations is the *relationship* one develops with journalists. To help build the relationship, it is im-portant to read the stories these journalists file and watch (or listen to) their broadcast segments. Note the types of issues they cover and watch for linkages with issues rele-vant to the nonprofit or social service agency.

Next, a phone call to introduce the organization is in order. During this conversa-tion, it is important to explain what your organization does, reference a recent story by that journalist, and let the journalist know that your organization's leaders can serve as a resource for future stories on the journalist's reporting beat. This introductory call also should be used to learn more about the reporter and his or her interests. What stories is the reporter working on? When are the reporter's deadlines? How does the reporter prefer to be contacted (by e-mail, phone, or fax)? It is advisable to end the phone call by promising to remain in touch and saying that the organization will help the reporter in the future. The information from this phone conversation should be added to the media list for future reference.

Building an ongoing relationship with reporters takes time but is well worth the ef-fort. Reporters should be on the organization's list to receive newsletters and reports.

Staff at social service agencies should make every effort to attend a "media day" and other conferences that feature reporters and other media professionals. These are excellent opportunities to meet and network with journalists and to pick up valuable tips on working with the media.

Find the Right News Hook

Knowing the preferences of reporters is a good first step in successful media relations. Equally important is finding a news hook for the organization's stories.

Human services agencies are not news-gathering organizations. Regardless of size, most agencies are not quite sure how to identify which stories might capture the media's attention. At YAI/NIPD, a large organization with more than 5,500 employees and 20,000 service recipients across our network, one might assume that finding news stories for the media would be simple. However, our size often makes it difficult to find the good stories within our network of organizations. One strategy we have used with great success is to establish an internal communications system that relies on informal relationships with staff at all levels: coordinators, supervisors, frontline staff, and so forth to gather news for our public relations manager. Program staff provide information about service recipients who might be appropriate for a story as well as news of a staff team that has done exceptional work, or an outstanding fundraising event or program, that can be used in our internal and/or external newsletters and publications. Once a story has been developed well enough to pitch to the media, program staff play an indispensable role in identifying families, parents, and clients who can serve as spokespeople. Developing an internal communications system makes the process much easier.

We like to promote several distinct types of stories to the media, including:

- Stories of hope. For example, people with disabilities who have risen to a new level, such as obtaining a job after years of struggling to do so.
- Trend stories. For example, the national waitlist for an opening in a group home is a major issue and a good tie-in for the opening of a new group residence.
- Once-in-a-lifetime stories. For example, two individuals with developmental disabilities, who met years earlier as residents of the Willowbrook State School and were reunited at YAI/NIPD, got married in 1998, a first for our organization.
- Interesting staff profiles. People with unusual backgrounds, such as a former advertising executive who had a brother with a disability and decided to change careers and join the YAI/NIPD staff.
- Exceptional and inspiring stories, such as a piano player with autism who played in a recital at Carnegie Hall.

Once we have identified a news story, we must do some additional homework. Before contacting a reporter, we need to ensure that each story is newsworthy, has local and human interest, and, if possible, ties into larger trends and current events.

In July 1999 we were able to turn a tragic national news story into an opportunity to share with the public the work we do with people with developmental disabilities. When John F. Kennedy Jr. died in a plane crash, we were able to use the media coverage to highlight Kennedy's work with people with developmental disabilities through the Reaching Up Foundation he founded, which trains people who work in the field. Working with the foundation and City University of New York, we contacted major news organizations about this untold aspect of Kennedy's life. Our ability to respond quickly to requests from CBS and prepare our spokespeople for interviews with Dan Rather earned YAI/NIPD national coverage on a CBS *News Special Report* covering the Kennedy memorial service, as well as CBS *This Morning*, CBS *Sunday Morning*, and CBS *48 Hours*.

As another example, because of the dramatic increase in the number of individuals diagnosed with autism, this topic has received considerable attention in the media. Since the media are always looking for the exceptional and extraordinary story, we were able to attract their attention by pitching the story of a young man with autism, who lives in one of our group residences in New Jersey, who performed Bach's *Prelude in C Major* at Carnegie Hall (Sampson, 2003, p. L1).

Tying stories in with movie releases, holidays, or special events is another media relations strategy. The 2002 release of the movie, *I Am Sam*, provided tremendous opportunities for YAI/NIPD to promote the story of the real Sams (people with special needs who are parents) who are part of our Parents with Special Needs Program, as well as to celebrate the positive portrayal of people with developmental disabilities in the movies. We received favorable publicity in the *Los Angeles Times, New York1 News, Newsday, Active Living Magazine*, and several radio interviews.

The calendar is filled with 12 months of holidays, special months, and commemorations, many of which offer opportunities for nonprofit organizations to find a news hook. A list is available online at http://www.mhprofessional.com/?page=/mhp/categories/chases/content/special_months.html#January.

For example, Valentine's Day was the news hook for media placements about young adults with developmental disabilities who learn dating and socialization skills through one of our programs. An Associated Press reporter interviewed our president, the program's supervisor, and several of the young adults and their parents. Pitching to an Associated Press wire service reporter resulted in the story's appearing on more than 60 major Web sites, including the front page of CNN.com. We knew the story had a major impact based on the numerous e-mails we received applauding us for the program and requesting information for similar programs in other areas.

At a special event, the dedication of a YAI/NIPD group residence in honor of then-New York Mets Manager Bobby Valentine in Queens, New York, our organization promoted the event to the media, along with the principles of community inclusion. The story was picked up by a sportscaster on WNBC-TV, as well as the *Daily News* and several weekly newspapers. Each of these stories highlighted Valentine's commitment to people with disabilities, which served as the news hook for the event. Similarly, the 2005 Special Olympics was the news hook for several articles about two young women, one with Down syndrome and the other on the autism spectrum, both residents of our group residences in New Jersey, who traveled to Japan for the Olympic Games.

Each of these media placements illustrates how to identify a story, and then find a hook to relate the news from your organization to a newsworthy event, whether in your service area, nationally, or even in the international arena, with the Special Olympics.

Be Media Savvy

What does it take to land a front-page news story? Is there a checklist to follow to boost the chances of media coverage? What are some pitfalls to avoid when pitching a story?

To answer these questions, it helps to think like a journalist. Consider that many reporters receive as many as 1,000 e-mail pitches a day, and e-mailed news releases have become a new form of spam, especially if they are not of genuine interest to the reporter. The key to breaking through the clutter is to know what reporters want, and the cardinal rule is to make things easy for them. The following are several tips for successful media relations.

1. *Tailor the pitch.* Whether the organization has purchased a media directory or built a customized list, it is important to know which reporters cover which beats and tailor the pitch accordingly. If the organization has developed a good relationship with the reporter, it is easy to call and say, "I have a story idea I'd like to bounce off you. What do you think of it?"

2. *Know the details.* Before making the pitch, gather all of the details about the story: the key players, correct spellings of names, their ages, and hometowns, and try to anticipate what questions the reporter will ask. Identify the strongest spokespeople for the story, and if the story is for television, make sure to let the reporter know there will be strong visuals to appeal to a TV audience.

3. *Be brief in the pitch.* Increasingly, journalists prefer to receive e-mail pitches for news and feature stories. Many reporters use handheld devices to review their e-mails and don't have time to scroll down through lengthy e-mails or news releases. Because reporters generally do not open attachments because of computer viruses, all text must appear in the e-mail itself or in a hyperlink to the organization's Web site.

4. *Be responsive.* Once you've sent the pitch, be available by phone, including at an after-hours phone number or e-mail, for the reporter's follow-up questions. The organization's ability to respond quickly and obtain additional information often determines whether the reporter writes the story.

5. *Position the organization as a resource for reporters.* In making a follow-up call to the reporter following a news release, a smart approach is to offer to round out the news story with expert interviews, provide additional sources, or send more data or facts. Even when there is no story to pitch, it is a great idea to contact reporters with surveys and other sources of new information that provide perspective on the nonprofit sector and the social work profession.

6. *Consider local papers.* Although everyone strives for a front-page story in the *New York Times,* often the best way to get a media placement is in a local paper. Local newspapers are interested in stories about local people, and they often respond favorably to a story pitch. One strategy is to send the same basic story to different regions, with a different local person featured in each story. Since

publicity often breeds more publicity, getting a story in a local paper can mean that other media will pick it up as well.

7. *Prepare a press kit.* When promoting coverage to media outlets, it is helpful to have a press kit (also called a media kit) prepared that introduces the organization. Two-pocket folders, available at office supply stores, can hold printed copies of news releases, fact sheets about the organization and its activities, backgrounders covering the history and mission of the organization, white papers on an advocacy issue, past media coverage (clips), copies of newsletters, and photographs. If the press kit is sent via mail, it should include a cover letter with reference to previous conversations, if applicable. In a recent survey of 2,000 reporters (TV, radio, print, and online) that asked for preferred ways to receive press kits (print, CD, or online), reporters said the time required to preview and download online kits is an obstacle. For now, they prefer print or CD versions (Don Bates, personal communication, February 27, 2008). Nevertheless, many elements of the press kit should be available on the organization's Web site, preferably in an "Online Newsroom" (described below) or other pages geared to the media.

8. *Don't be discouraged.* Not every good story finds its way to publication or broadcast. Sometimes events outside one's control intervene. In 1998, when two former residents of Willowbrook State School who were reunited at our organization were about to get married, we pitched their story to the media and found great interest from major media outlets, including the *New York Times*, Associated Press, *Good Morning America, Newsday, Daily News*, and a couple of local TV stations. However, just days before the wedding, Special Prosecutor Kenneth Starr released his report on President Clinton, which preempted major coverage of the wedding story despite all our careful preparation and planning. Although we did receive some coverage before and on the day of the wedding, we were proactive, taking photos and submitting a press release about the wedding to several weekly newspapers that were unable to cover the event. We also featured the photos and story in our newsletter.

Writing and Placing News Releases

News organizations are flooded with news releases and e-mail pitches every day. Editors at newspapers and magazines and producers at television and radio stations can pick and choose what releases they read and what stories they cover. Given these odds, what can nonprofit organizations do to compete with large corporations and public relations firms? The way to get your message heard is to present it in the medium and format that reporters want to get it: in a news release that is short, to the point, and well written.

News releases answer the five "W"s and an "H." In no more than about four to six short paragraphs, the release is structured to explain who, what, where, when, why, and how. Beginning with a compelling headline that captures the essence of the story, the news release provides the reporter with a means to determine quickly whether the story is of interest.

A *printed release* is written on the organization's letterhead with a contact name, title, and phone number at the top. The headline (all in capital letters) should be brief and compelling, containing the news hook for the story. A short subhead (in upper- and lowercase) that elaborates on the headline may be included as well. The release time and date appear at the top of the page, usually at the left.

The first paragraph of no more than three or four sentences is arguably the most important because, after the reporter reads it and the headline, he or she should have a good idea about the basic content of the story. This first paragraph should explain the five "W"s and the "H." Succeeding paragraphs flesh out the details and may include a quote from an organization leader. The last paragraph usually contains boilerplate information about the organization: its history, mission, and scope of work. If the news release runs longer than a page, the word "more" appears centered at the bottom of the first page. The end of the release is noted with three pound signs centered in the middle of the page: ###.

An *e-mailed release* uses a similar format, but the subject line assumes greater importance. Without a compelling subject line that includes a news hook, reporters are less likely to open the e-mail and read the rest of the release. The e-mail window can begin with a short, personal message to the reporter, explaining why the story is important and should be covered. In an e-mail release, the contact information, heading, subhead, and complete text may appear as the body of the e-mail text, or this information can be included in a full-text hotlink on the organization's Web site. As noted earlier, avoid attachments; additional information can appear as a hotlink on the organization's Web site. When sending an e-mail release to more than one journalist, it is important to write the recipients' e-mail addresses in the "Bcc" field, so the journalists do not see the addresses of other recipients.

Although some organizations like to send e-mail releases as HTML, the consensus is that HTML releases may look too much like advertisements and could compromise credibility. One excellent tip about e-mail release distribution comes from Don Bates, former director of public relations at the NASW and now academic director, strategic public relations, at The George Washington University: "Don't forget to include your local congressman and state legislators on your news release distribution list. Doing so will help raise awareness about your agency and its activities" (personal communication, February 27, 2008).

At YAI/NIPD, we often use one-page media advisories or media alerts, which we e-mail to reporters, to notify them of special events and stories. The alerts contain essentially the same information as the news releases, but in a shorter form that is easy for reporters to review. A typical media advisory is shown in Figure 1.

With reporters' in-boxes jammed with incoming e-mail pitches, it is important to follow up with a phone call to ensure the reporter saw the e-mail, inquire about whether the story was of interest, and offer additional information. In addition, if a reporter picks up a story, a short thank-you follow-up is also in order. In short, it is the relationship that counts, and follow-up calls can help build relations with the reporter.

FIGURE 1   TYPICAL MEDIA ADVISORY

New York League for Early Learning

MEDIA ADVISORY FOR MONDAY, JUNE 20, 2005

Contact: Lynn U. Berman
XXX-XXX-XXXX (w)
XXX-XXX-XXXX (cell)

A SPECIAL GRADUATION FOR QUEENS TRIPLETS BORN PREMATURELY

WHO: Joseph, Matthew and Leo XXXX, triplets who were born with developmental delays, will be graduating from the New York League for Early Learning's Forest Hills West Preschool. After spending two years at the school, the boys will be attending a regular kindergarten program in the fall.

WHERE: **Forest Hills West Preschool [Address].** The school phone number is **XXX-XXX-XXXX.**

WHEN: **Monday, June 20, 2005; 9:30 A.M.**

WHAT: Edna and Leo XXXX of Middle Village, N.Y., knew their children needed early-intervention services after being born five weeks prematurely. Matthew was born with a hole in his heart; it also took him an hour to drink from his bottle. Leo had sensory issues and extremely rigid movement. Joseph's facial muscles were weak, making eating difficult.

WHY: "Forest Hills West really pushed them," Mrs. XXXX said. "I was always doubtful, thinking in the back of my mind that they will need special education when they get older. All three were a little shy when they came to the school two years ago. Now we can see how happy and proud they are of everything they do."

For children with developmental and learning delays, early-intervention services and preschools like the New York League Early Learning's Forest Hills West offer special education and therapies to infants and children who need the extra help that early intervention provides in motor, intellectual, emotional and social development. Individualized instructional programs and careful attention to each child's needs have helped many students overcome early challenges and achieve their full potential.

The school is a member of the YAI/National Institute for People with Disabilities Network.

For more information about NYL or the YAI/NIPD Network's services, call toll-free 1-866-2-YAI-LINK or visit www.yai.org.
###

Other Media Relations Tools

In addition to outreach to reporters to place stories, other public relations tools are available to nonprofit organizations that enable them to tell their story.

Letters to the editor are an excellent method to gain visibility for the organization and establish credibility. These letters, which should be brief and signed by an organization leader, work well for adding data or new perspectives to an article that ran in earlier in the newspaper or other publication, or for tying national news or trends to a local issue of interest to the community. Some publications demand exclusivity, so it is important to vary the text of the letter if sending it to more than one media outlet.

Op-eds, so called because they appear opposite the editorial page in newspapers, are another outstanding tool to gain visibility for an issue and add to the credibility of the work of social service agencies. Op-eds are opinion pieces on subjects of timely interest. Whether they advocate on an issue, express a point of view, or simply provide information about an issue, the op-ed must convey the organization's message, backed up with facts and other evidence. Most publications have submission guidelines and a word count limit, which can be found online or by calling the editorial department. Many newspapers will only accept op-eds on an exclusive basis. Op-eds usually are submitted under the name of the organization's leadership or a person with specialized expertise in the issue. Another way to promote issues of concern on the editorial pages of newspapers is to set up *meetings with editorial boards*. These meetings give the organization an opportunity to communicate perspectives on critical issues and can result in an editorial about those issues.

Calendar listings are another tool in the public relations toolbox. These listings are ideal for any organization's fundraising events. Most calendar listings have a 2- to 4-week advance notice provision, but it is not difficult to secure these placements. Local newspapers and weeklies gladly accept information on upcoming events.

Letters to the editor, op-eds, and calendar listings can usually be sent to media outlets via e-mail, although some publications' guidelines may specify fax or regular mail submissions.

Special events, such as anniversaries, fundraising galas, and program launches, provide other excellent opportunities for media coverage. Although many of these events raise money for organizations, they also enable agencies to get positive media coverage, build *esprit de corps* among staff, and inform target audiences about programs and activities. Media alerts (discussed earlier) are a great way to inform media outlets about your events and to promote coverage.

Conferences and symposia provide outstanding opportunities to boost awareness of the agency, brand it for quality and expertise, and encourage dialogue on social service issues. By attracting the attention of other organizations, they also help the agency acquire prestige in the profession and set it apart from other groups in its field. Professional associations offer social service organizations excellent opportunities for staff to present at conferences and symposia, and seeking these opportunities should be included in the public relations plan. Whether agency staff serve as speakers or panelists at professional conferences sponsored by other organizations, and whether the agency itself organizes the meetings, the agency should highlight its role on its Web site, in media outreach, and through reciprocal Web links with peer organizations.

Although media outlets generally don't cover conferences, if there are experts on hand discussing current, timely issues, or trends, the media relations effort should use these ties as the news hook. Arranging for experts to be available for interviews before the conference can also generate coverage, while at the same time promoting your conference.

For 29 years YAI/NIPD has organized annual conferences that draw speakers and attendees from throughout the nation and abroad. These conferences serve as major forums for exchanging ideas in our field and presenting the cutting-edge work of our staff. By sponsoring these conferences, we have gained the kind of recognition that has branded YAI/NIPD for quality and expertise and reinforced our national reputation as a leader in the developmental disabilities field. In addition to our conferences, YAI/NIPD produces a wide range of training materials, which we disseminate to organizations around the world that serve people with disabilities. Like our annual conference, these training resources help to set us apart and showcase our expertise.

Using effective spokespeople is a powerful method for communicating what the organization does. Nonprofits in the social and human services field work with people who can often put a face on the work of the organization, enabling it to stand out in a crowded media field. The children, adults, and families an organization serves are often quite willing to be spokespeople. However, whenever service recipients, their photos, or any information identifying them are used, agencies must be mindful of a variety of ethical and legal considerations, including the Health Insurance Portability and Accountability Act (HIPAA) Privacy Rule (http://www.hhs.gov/ocr/privacysummary.pdf). Before releasing photographs, videos, or interviews, the spokespersons or their guardians must sign a release with their express authorization to be identified in newsletters, annual reports, marketing materials, displays, appeals, and media.

In addition, spokespeople must be briefed and trained before having any contact with the reporter. At a minimum, they should be aware of what questions might be asked, and they should rehearse the answers. Many organizations have found value in investing in professional media training for staff spokespeople. Agencies should designate spokespeople who are authorized to respond to media requests for information and implement policies and procedures for staff who answer the phone. These individuals should be trained to find out what the reporter is calling about, collect his or her contact information, and assure the reporter that the appropriate staff will respond in a timely fashion.

The question often arises about the use of *celebrities* to raise the profile of an organization and attract media coverage. Is using a celebrity a smart PR move? Celebrities can provide instant name recognition for the organization, especially if they are people the organization's target audiences admire and trust. Often, a board member may have ties with a local celebrity, or perhaps there is a celebrity who has personal experience with the issues of the organization. For WABC-TV *Eyewitness News* coanchor Bill Ritter, who had a brother with Down syndrome, a partnership with YAI/NIPD was a natural fit. Ritter's involvement, along with that of Dominic Chianese (Uncle Junior from *The Sopranos*), David Eigenberg (Steve Brady from *Sex and the City*), and other celebrities has enabled YAI/NIPD to attract significant media coverage for our Central Park Challenge fundraising and public awareness event over the years.

To highlight Ritter's celebrity support, we crafted an e-mail release event with the headline: "People with Disabilities Hold a Special Place in Bill Ritter's Heart: WABC-TV's Co-Anchor to Support YAI/National Institute for People with Disabilities' Central Park Challenge." In using celebrities, it pays to be cautious. Celebrity endorsements can be harmful to an organization if the celebrity runs into legal problems or attracts negative publicity.

Public service announcements (PSAs) are another option for conveying messages through the media. By definition, PSAs are messages furthering a public interest that a media outlet airs free of charge (Kaiser Family Foundation, 2008, p. 2). Print, radio, and television media outlets all use PSAs from nonprofit organizations. For many nonprofits and social service agencies, PSAs are a central component of public education campaigns designed to raise money, change attitudes, and generate awareness of key social issues, such as substance abuse prevention, AIDS, drunk driving, and the benefits of physical fitness. Today, media outlets are not generally required to run PSAs, although television broadcasters are required to "serve the public interest," and any PSAs they run can count toward that obligation. Cable television stations are under no "public interest" obligation to air PSAs, but, according to a recent report, they donate substantial time anyway (p. 2).

Is it realistic to expect a nonprofit organization to obtain media coverage for its PSAs? Several of the findings from a 2008 report from the Kaiser Family Foundation will be of interest to nonprofit agencies considering whether to use PSAs. First, broadcast and cable TV stations donate on average only 17 seconds an hour to PSAs. This represents .5% of all TV airtime on these channels. However, the time cable donates to PSAs increased from an average of 7 seconds per hour in 2000 to 15 seconds in 2005. On broadcast stations, a greater proportion of donated PSA airtime occurred during the overnight hours (60%), compared to 38% for cable stations and 35% for Spanish-language channels, which varied the times PSAs aired. Nonprofits were the most common sponsors of donated PSAs (71%). As for the types of issues covered through PSAs, more than one of three donated PSAs (38%) concerned a children's issue, and 26% covered a health-related topic such as fitness, cancer, or HIV/AIDS. One of four (26%) donated PSAs featured a celebrity spokesperson of some kind (Kaiser Family Foundation, 2008, p. 2).

These findings might suggest that PSAs are not a realistic option for many social service agencies that do not have the budget or production capabilities to create 30- and 60-second radio or television PSAs. However, organizations can overcome these challenges through partnerships with advertising agencies and video production facilities, which might be willing to donate their creative department's expertise and production facilities. Through these kinds of partnerships, YAI/NIPD has developed a series of PSAs that focuses on key societal issues, such as the value of people with disabilities as hard-working employees and dedicated volunteers. The "evergreen" nature of these PSAs makes them appropriate for cable and television stations to use when they have a time slot to fill.

The organization's *Web site* is a key component in its public relations program, since it is through the Web site that people become familiar with the organization's mission, values, and programs. In his book on public relations for nonprofits, Art Feinglass (2005) identifies a number of elements that should be on every nonprofit's Web site:

- information about the organization's history;
- mission statement;
- names and biographies of board members, officers, and key staff members;
- information on funding sources and current projects;
- policy statements;
- reports on the organization's activities and achievements;
- frequently asked questions, with answers;
- current issue of the organization's newsletter and archived issues of earlier newsletters;
- current annual report;
- online brochure;
- information about how to make a donation; and
- updated calendar of upcoming events (pp. 245–246).

In addition, to assist in media outreach, many nonprofit organizations find it helpful to have an "Online Newsroom" or "Media Center" specifically for journalists. This section of the Web site should contain the following:

- contact information, including cell phone numbers, for key media contacts in the organization;
- biographies of the officers and key staff members;
- news releases, including an archive of past releases;
- organization background, including number of employees, history, and location;
- research data or links to relevant research;
- photos;
- media clips;
- link to list of upcoming events;
- speeches by organization's leaders; and
- downloadable media kit.

Newsletters and publications, both print and electronic, keep external and internal target audiences informed about the organization and its programs. At YAI/NIPD, we have a wide variety of publications, some targeted for a broad audience and others geared to defined groups we want to reach with specific messages. For example, *People in Partnership*, our organization's signature publication, shares inspiring stories of the achievements of the people we serve, and of the impact of our services with government, supporters, media, families, friends, and staff. It shows our many target audiences how we make our mission come alive and connects them personally with our agency. A quarterly e-newsletter, *Working Now*, which profiles businesses and individuals who have gone above and beyond in their support of employment of people with disabilities, is geared for businesses. (We recently transitioned from several print newsletters and publications to e-mailed versions, saving postage and printing costs. *Working Now* replaces the printed *BAC Bulletin*.)

One of our newest online publications is the *Monthly Management Message*, YAI/NIPD's first entirely Web-based, interactive publication for our internal audiences, which provides our managers with current information about organization priorities, initiatives, and events. We also have several other publications for our internal audiences. The *Staff Day Sentinel* captures the excitement and fun of our Annual Staff Awards and Recognition Day and is a useful tool for recruiting new staff and demonstrating our commitment to staff development. The *Friday Fax*, one of the best-known publications among our staff, promotes unity, pride, and cohesiveness throughout our network by keeping staff updated on organization news, benefits, and feature stories, such as tips on exercise, diet, and health issues. Table 1 summarizes how we use a variety of publications and public relations tools to reach our various target audiences.

TABLE 1   YAI/NIPD PUBLIC RELATIONS TOOLS BY AUDIENCE

Public Relations Tool	YAI/NIPD Audience
Board Matters	Board members
Family Matters	Consumers/clients with disabilities, families
Friday Fax	Staff
Monthly Management Message	Managers
People in Partnership	Staff, consumers/clients with disabilities, families, Board members, employers/businesses, Business Advisory Council, donors/funders, legislators, social work and health care professionals, general public, media
Premier HealthCare Connection	Social work and health care professionals
Staff Day Sentinel	Staff
Working Now	Employers/businesses, Business Advisory Council
Annual international conference brochure	Staff, consumers/clients with disabilities, families, legislators, social work and health care professionals, general public/media
Press releases, op-ed pieces, letters to the editor, public service announcements, YouTube, blogs	General public/media
Special events	Staff, consumers/clients with disabilities, families, Board members, donors/funders, legislators, general public/media

Competing for *awards* is another way to boost the organization's visibility and establish credibility. A number of organizations, including professional associations and local governments, invite agencies to apply for awards. Winning an award is an opportunity to write and distribute a news release that also highlights the organization's programs. In 2007, YAI/NIPD received the American Psychological Association's National Psychologically Healthy Workplace Award, which enabled us to garner tremendous recognition and helped set our organization apart from others in the field.

Internally, staff awards are a great way to acknowledge and thank staff for doing a great job. They help build a positive culture, which increases staff retention. Organizations should find many different ways to thank and recognize staff. This is the most cost-efficient communication possible and results in staff feeling respected and valued.

Strategic partnerships involve more people in the work of the organization and allow it to expand its reach and extend limited dollars. At YAI/NIPD, as at many nonprofits, budgets for public relations are limited, so we look for outside help with branding, marketing, and advertising. Our *PR partnerships* with individuals and organizations have been critical in enabling us to expand our capabilities beyond what limited resources would otherwise allow.

To provide counsel and expertise with marketing, public relations, advertising, and Web design, we have established a Corporate Communications Council, comprised of experts in advertising, marketing, and public relations who meet with us periodically and are available for e-mail consultation at other times. This group was instrumental in helping us reexamine and change the way we marketed our annual Central Park Challenge fundraiser by putting a "face" on our posters and advertising and showing the people we serve. In a focus group in which they and other stakeholders evaluated our outreach materials, they reinforced the importance of using coordinated messaging on posters, fliers, advertising, Web site, and banners. A second partnership that has been instrumental in successful media placements has been in-kind sponsorships with media organizations, including local television and cable stations that have provided celebrity spokespersons and/or generous play of our PSAs.

There are several ways organizations can enlist partners. Often, board members have extensive community contacts and can pave the way for partnership connections. In addition, for assistance with public relations activities, public relations and communications organizations, such as the Public Relations Society of America (which has a nonprofit section), can provide contacts and resources on public relations, and sometimes have pro bono programs in partnership with nonprofit organizations.

New Media

Although this chapter has focused thus far on traditional media and public relations strategies, the evolution from "old" media tools to new ones is changing the way public relations practitioners ply their trade. In a 2007 survey of nearly 300 public relations and communications professionals that explored the influence patterns of the new media, 57% reported that social media tools, such as blogs, online videos, and social networks, are becoming more valuable to their activities as more customers and influencers use them ("New Influencer Study Initial Findings Shared," 2007). Should nonprofit organizations have blogs and Facebook, MySpace, or LinkedIn profiles? What about using podcasts and YouTube? Increasingly, the answer appears to be yes—but with certain important caveats.

A *blog* or Web log has a number of public relations advantages. It enables the organization to communicate its key messages through short opinion pieces and commentary, usually from the leadership. It gives voice to the organization on advocacy and other issues of importance to the organization. Comments from blog readers enable the organization to gain important insights about its target audiences and its market. And by using key words used in Web searches and linking to other Web sites with related commentary and also arranging for reciprocal links a blog can optimize the organization's standing among search engines (search engine optimization), bringing more people to the organization's Web site, where the blog is housed. At the same time, a blog can bring unwanted comments from readers, since most blogs are an open, transparent forum over which the blogger has little control.

Don Bates, former public relations director at the NASW and current academic director, strategic public relations, at George Washington University, advises social service organizations considering developing a blog to review other blogs first, preferably in the social work field. Explore how those bloggers write about social work issues. The NASW's blogs (http://www.socialworkblog.org) is a good place to start. Another good resource is Technorati (http://www.technorati.com), which enables visitors to search blogs by subject area. In developing a blog, it is important to consult with people who blog regularly; find out what works and does not work for them. Blog creation software and blog publishing systems are available through online searches on Google or Yahoo. For a blog to be successful, its content must be fresh every few days, requiring a commitment by the organization to devote time and resources to the effort. The blog must also be written in a personal, conversational tone since the objective is to form a relationship with the reader (personal communication, February 27, 2008).

Podcasts, an excellent tool for organizations that wish to make speeches, executive interviews, and presentations available to a large audience, can be made available on the organization's Web site for downloading to MP-3 players.

YouTube (http://www.youtube.com) is another tool enabling broad reach for non-profit organizations. YAI/NIPD has posted several of our PSAs on YouTube (search word: YAI National Institute for People with Disabilities) that reinforce our message about the abilities of people with disabilities, particularly in the workforce.

The growth of such *social media* as Facebook, MySpace, and LinkedIn reflects the power of the Internet to create new communities. Can social service organizations take advantage of social media? According to Don Bates, these new technologies give nonprofit organizations additional opportunities to reach target audiences and create new communities of stakeholders. For example, with a Facebook membership, an organization can reach out to and engage in "conversation" with communities of other Facebook members who have similar concerns. The organization can also create a "Group Page" on Facebook, with its logo, description, Web site URL, and a small ad. At the organization's request, Facebook will distribute the ad to its database of members with an interest in a particular issue (e.g., autism). The organization must pay Facebook a small fee for each responding click on its Facebook page, but the organization can establish a predetermined limit on how much it will pay for this additional exposure (Don Bates, personal communication, February 27, 2008).

Another application of Facebook, one that YAI/NIPD has used, is to encourage runners and walkers at our Central Park Challenge to add information about the fundraiser on their Facebook pages and connect with their Facebook friends.

The new media market is changing rapidly. As Don Bates says, "It's not about blogs, podcasts and Facebook, or the other tools you use. What really counts is the message and the substance of what you have to say. When considering new media, ask yourself: Is this strategic? Will it help the organization?" (personal communication, February 27, 2008).

Crisis Communications

Entire volumes have been written about crisis management. For nonprofit organizations, the danger of a crisis is all too real. Any story that casts the organization in a bad light is a crisis that can damage the organization's reputation, dry up funding sources, destroy staff morale, and disrupt day-to-day programs and activities. Crises can range from a lost client/consumer who fails to return to a group home after a day of work to a serious bus accident with injuries to agency clients and staff. Some agencies have encountered crises related to charges of staff abuse or neglect, and others have had to deal with crises brought on by an external agent or natural disaster. How can a social service agency use public relations tools to manage a crisis effectively?

W. Timothy Coombs, associate professor, Department of Communications Studies at Eastern Illinois University, outlines the components of a crisis communications plan and describes best practices that are relevant for any nonprofit organization (Coombs, 2007):

- Have a crisis management plan and update it at least annually. This plan should list key contact information and reminders of what should be done in a crisis and include forms to document the crisis response. The plan should also establish communications channels for reaching external and internal audiences, including employees and other stakeholders.
- Designate and train a crisis management team, usually comprised of staff from public relations, legal, security, finance, operations, and human resources.
- Each year, conduct an exercise to test the crisis management plan and team.
- Prepare select crisis management messages, including content for "dark" (not posted) Web pages and templates for crisis statements. Have the legal department review and preapprove these messages.

Beyond creating a plan, media training for key spokespeople is essential before any crisis hits. Coombs (2007) suggests several best practices for dealing with the media during a crisis:

- Avoid the phrase, "no comment," which is often interpreted as meaning the organization is guilty and trying to hide something.
- Avoid jargon and technical terms.
- Spokespeople should appear pleasant and avoid nervous mannerisms that might suggest deception.

Once the crisis hits, response must be fast and factually accurate; all messages need to be consistent. Coombs (2007) highlights a number of best practices:

- Be quick and try to respond within the first hour.
- Be accurate. Make sure all facts are checked and rechecked.

- Be consistent. All spokespeople must be informed of the facts and key message points.
- Make public safety the number one concern.
- Use all available communications channels, including the Internet, intranet, and other mass notifications systems.
- Express concern and sympathy for any victims.
- Be ready to provide stress and other counseling for victims and their families, including employees.

In Closing

This chapter has highlighted a number of strategies and tools social service agencies can use to promote social justice and equity. Many of the tools described cost little and are within reach of every social work practitioner. Each day, there are myriad opportunities to highlight the noble work human services professionals do. But public relations requires creativity, persistence, and commitment.

Those of us in the human services field can derive great pride and satisfaction from the work we do. We have a proud tradition of being in the forefront of social reform and social change that improve the lives of the people we serve and free them to achieve their fullest potential. In the truest sense of the word, we are freedom fighters. We work to liberate people from poverty, alienation, discrimination, and the stigma that so many service recipients encounter, and we fight for the civil rights of the most vulnerable individuals in our society. We strive to help them gain public acceptance as valued, contributing members of society. This is why it is incumbent on all of us to use the tools and strategies of public relations to ensure that the voices of the people we serve are heard and heeded.

References

Blatt, B., & Kaplan, F. (1974). *Christmas in purgatory: A photographic essay on mental retardation*. Syracuse, NY: Human Policy Press.

Brawley, E. A. (2001). *Encyclopedia of social work*. Silver Spring, MD: NASW Press.

Coombs, W. T. (2007). *Crisis management and communications*. Institute for Public Relations. Retrieved September 2008 from http://www.instituteforpr.org/research_single/crisis_management_and_communications/

Coombs, W. T., & Holladay, S. J. (2007). *It's not just PR: Publication relations in society*. Boston: Blackwell.

Feinglass, Art. (2005). *The public relations handbook for nonprofits*. San Francisco: Jossey-Bass.

Gross, J. (2006, April 20). Learning to savor of full life, love life included. *The New York Times*, p. 1.

Kaiser Family Foundation. (2008, January). *Shouting to be heard: Public service advertising in a changing television world.* Menlo Park, CA: Author.

Johnson, B. (2008, 18 February). Media workforce sinks to 15-year low. [online] *Advertising Age.*

New influencer study initial findings shared at Society for New Communications research symposium. (2007, December 6). Institute for Public Relations. Retrieved September 2008 from http://www.instituteforpr.org/release_single/new_influencer_study_initial_findings _shared/

Paisley, W. J. (1981). Public communication campaigns: The American experience. In R. E. Rice & W. J. Paisley (Eds.), *Public communication campaigns* (pp. 1). Beverly Hills, CA: Sage.

Rossie, C. (1983). Do it yourself public relations. In *Media resource guide: How to tell your story* (pp. 24–25). Los Angeles, CA: Foundation for American Communication.

Sampson, P. J. (2003, June 25). Keys to expression: Piano virtuosity helps man with autism get his life in tune. *The Record,* p. 1675.

Survey reveals communicators are out of sync with the way consumers use media. (2007). Retrieved from http://www.ketchum.com/2007mediasurvey

15

Maximizing Financial Resources for Quality Programs
Meeting Your Client's Needs

Joel M. Levy and Karen Wegmann

Financial management of a social organization is much like the management of a for-profit organization, in that they both involve clients, employees, and finances. Where a nonprofit differs is in the way funds are raised, managed, and regulated. In this chapter, we discuss the key players in nonprofit finance, how the organization's mission and vision relate to finance, financial reporting, accounting, fundraising, maintaining effective controls, and risk management. This chapter, in essence, focuses on the best way to meet the needs of the clients being served.

Meeting your Client's Needs

Social workers need access to accurate and timely financial information to fulfill their function of managing programs, services, and agencies. Unlike nonprofits, all commercial enterprises have profit maximization as their goal. When seeking a profit, the role of finance is indisputable, and everyone is drawn to it as it manifests the mission of commercial enterprises. The goods or services the commercial enterprise produces are driven by price, competition, and advertising to gain market share, so everything the organization does seeks to maximize sales and profits and get the highest return or earnings for owners or shareholders. By contrast, in the past, nonprofit finance often has been seen as a necessary evil, yet this is far from the truth. Historically, finance was often ignored, and many nonprofits relied on their small size or lack of financial expertise to try and make their finances work. Because of their lack of savvy, administrators appealed to the hearts of government and donors to support the nonprofit's mission.

Social workers worked hard to fulfill their cause using their mission, values, and vision to implement important programs and services to deliver effects that were measured by various outputs and outcomes. These enhanced the lives of vulnerable populations while making society more focused on social justice. Social workers were often excused from having financial knowledge because they were skilled in the services their nonprofit provided, passionate about their mission, and charismatic communicators of the mission and vision of the nonprofit. Times have changed; the Sarbanes-Oxley Act of 2002 permanently changed the playing field of for-profit publicly held corporations, and the law's impact is being felt in the nonprofit sector's use of public funds. Donors increasingly want financial information about the nonprofit before contributing to it, to ensure the nonprofit is stable and well run, and the funds donated are accounted for appropriately. Government is more focused on outcome measures, effectiveness, and efficient use of the funding provided to social service agencies, and foundations are more interested in the social impact their grants achieve. Reviewing the finances of a nonprofit indicates its ability to operate in a sophisticated world.

Accountability, governance, and effective oversight include the financial aspects that are the nonprofit administrators' responsibilities. Nonprofit boards are increasingly holding executives to a higher standard and demanding sound financial structure and operations. In its role of watchdog for the public good, government has mandated that boards of nonprofits have members with sufficient levels of sophistication and expertise to exercise oversight over the financial component of the nonprofit. To perform these responsibilities effectively, the board now requires the social work executive or chief administrator to be financially astute. In fact, all levels within the agency must have some level of financial expertise.

Where it was once hard to find financial information geared to the financial components of nonprofits, this is no longer the case. There is an abundance of financial information geared to nonprofits that provides the tools administrators need to ensure they have the financial knowledge necessary to oversee the organization.

This has manifested itself in the board's evaluation of the nonprofit executive. In fact, without exception, performance evaluations of nonprofit executives must include financial components. The social worker nonprofit executive must demonstrate how financially successful the nonprofit is, not just that the services are of high quality, but that funds are used effectively and efficiently, not just accounted for, but put to the best use possible. Nonprofit executives are expected to excel in the service mission of the nonprofit while simultaneously achieving good financial results. This means that all social worker nonprofit administrators in the organization must understand the role of finance and develop the skills of a good financial manager.

Role of Executives

The role of executives in a profit or nonprofit organization is critical to its success. Because of the regulations surrounding a nonprofit, executives must understand the complicated function of finance. The chief executive must set the tone for the nonprofit by communicating its value, and managers need to share this message and responsibility. By communicating to all within the organization that financial know-how is necessary for services to continue, executives and administrators support those who work in finance. Financial management for social workers is crucial to assure their scarce resources are spent appropriately, to ensure their mission is carried out to meet their special cause, and to build further social value. When the message is successful, program staff rely on financial information to run and maintain new programs and services. In addition, the finance committee is motivated to support program staff by providing accurate and relevant financial information to meet the agency's mission. Establishing a positive agency culture and a fiscal climate that enhances its ability to achieve a greater social impact is paramount.

Mission and Vision

The nonprofit's finance team must have a mission statement that supports the nonprofit's vision and embodies its values. Here is the mission statement for a large human services nonprofit finance team:

> The mission of the Finance Department is to provide the agency with the highest level of leadership and strategic direction in finance, analysis and information technology in meeting the nonprofit's social cause. The Finance Department supports the mission of the Agency with a commitment to excellence, accessibility, customer focus and innovation. They are part of the team that helps build customer satisfaction and excellent services. They achieve their mission with proactive financial management, budgeting, reporting, accounting, cash management and information technology. They strive to provide exemplary service in attaining shared goals and objectives through teamwork, interdepartmental collaboration, maximization of resources and technological advances. Their performance ensures organizational stability and growth through the use of technology in the delivery of strategic financial services. They ensure financial protection by securing and protecting agency funds, regulatory compliance and effective internal control (Wegmann, personal communication, 2003).

A successful finance team will engage staff at all levels, building consensus not only in the importance of financial management but also in sharing the responsibilities, which are both essential to good agency management. Sharing information and training on how to use this information are basic skill requirements of all staff.

Program and finance are joined by a common vision, which is to achieve the mission of the organization. With the consistency of mission and values comes strength, a synergy that empowers individuals at all levels to exceed expectations. As a result, the nonprofit has a greater ability to respond to the demands and requirements of outside entities and stakeholders, thereby strengthening its position in the field. The nonprofit must answer to the demands of funding sources, government regulators, auditors, banks, donors, and clients' family members. Nonprofits are experiencing an increasing demand for both program and financial information, which requires a strong information technology (IT) department. Nonprofits must always be ready to document and justify reimbursement from funding sources to avoid any negative audits that might result in having to return funds.

Financial and Information Reporting

Variance Monthly Reporting

Finance's role is to provide timely, accurate information to program staff so they can run services, communicate operating results, and provide projections to management effectively so management can guide the nonprofit on a sound financial course. This is known as internal reporting, the most common form of which is the variance report. The variance report compares actual amounts to budgeted amounts. A variance report also may compare actual amounts for the current year to the same period during the previous year. This report can be applied to income, expenses, assets, liabilities, and fundraising. Variance reports, which include income and expenses for a given period, are used by program staff to operate programs and by management to evaluate program operations. This report includes line items for all the types of income and expense. Appendix 1 is an example of a variance report package for a human services agency operating residences for individuals with disabilities, known as individual residential alternatives. The reporting period is for the first 7 months of the fiscal year, July 1 though January 31. The first page is a summary Variance Report, or executive overview, with four columns: Budget, Prorated Budget, Actual, and Variance. The annual, or 12-month, budget for income and expense is in the first column; next to it is the 12-month budget prorated for 7 months. The third column is Actual Income and Expense for 7 months, and the last column is the variance or difference between the Prorated Budget and Actual. The actual income amount from funding sources of $20,198,317 and Adjustments to Income resulted in Total Income of $21,340,259. Note that with the Adjustments to Income for items that are expected from government, in the future Actual Income is equal to Budget, so no other income issues exist. The finance department tracks the specific items that make up the adjustments to income category and will follow up with government to ensure they are received. This enables the program managers to concentrate on program operations and expense-related issues. The income adjustments for such items as vacancy, client rent shortfall, etc., present a cash flow shortfall until the government reimburses them.

Notice that the Variance Report package includes a report, "Calculations Used to Determine Income Section of Cover Sheet." This detailed report is quite complex, and the program manager relies on finance staff to perform the calculations and track income adjustments, so the program manager can concentrate on running the program. With proper records, the program manager has immediately available the income information that is critical to determine whether income shortfalls are justifiable, so the manager can expect that the government will reimburse them. Below the Income section is the Expense section, which shows expenses of $21,516,528 and Adjustments to Expense of $3,681, which was the accrual of a reclassification of equipment expense added, resulting in Total Expense of $21,520,209. Total Income less Total Expense gives the excess of expense over income, or a deficit of $179,951. Careful scrutiny is needed for variance reports in each program to identify the troubled areas. The Variance Report for an individual program, Bainbridge IRA, is included in the package. Total income is balanced with Budgeted Income, and

Expenses show an excess of $263,073 over Budget. The Variance Report for the Bainbridge program gives further detail of the types of expenses, also known as functional expenses, of running the program. Each line item of income and expense is compared to budget, and the variance in the right-hand column is the difference between the actual and budget for that particular line item. The variance is expressed as a dollar amount; percentages may be added for ease of review. The program administrator can easily get a sense of how the program is doing financially by reviewing the variance column of the program's income and expenses. Any significant fluctuations appear as large amounts or percentages. These fluctuations may be positive or negative, so the administrator can determine which areas are operating positively and which ones need to be scrutinized by reviewing the variance column. Based on the Bainbridge Variance report, the program manager will investigate the largest negative variance of $156,113 for Personal Service expense. The financial reporting system provides the attachment listing all employees, position titles, and expenses charged to the program. Fringe benefit expense is also over budget by $41,216. Because fringe benefits are directly related to Personal Service expense, identifying overspending in staffing will also explain the Fringe Benefit expense negative variance. The details for Other Than Personal Services (OTPS) expenses are also included for the program manager, who notes that Consumer Food is overspent by $2,931. The program manager understands the workings of the program and knows that several clients living in this residence have behavioral issues that necessitated adding staff to ensure adequate coverage. This was necessary to safeguard client health and safety, thus causing Personal Service expense to go over budget. The organization can appeal this staffing issue to the government through the year-end cost report so it receives adequate reimbursement.

Working collaboratively, finance and program staff identify, analyze, and track variance issues. At the end of the fiscal year, these issues are documented and submitted to the government in an appeal for reimbursement of the items, which may occur only one time or continually. A good financial reporting system is the key to having a Variance Report package the social work manager can use to run the program. Program staff must review variance reports monthly to stay up to date on operations, see emerging trends, and determine action plans. Ways to alleviate a deficit by increasing income might be to increase the number of clients served, negotiate with funding sources to cover base costs, or reduce expenses by renegotiating contracts or reducing nonessential costs.

Program managers, executive management, and finance should review programs that continually run deficits to determine how the deficit can be eliminated through restructuring the program without sacrificing quality. A nonprofit has limited resources to offset a program deficit, which can be difficult, especially if a deficit is continuous or growing.

The key to a good variance report is twofold. First, the accounting systems must capture the transactions related to income and expense. This is completed through good billing, payroll, and accounts payable systems. Second, the budget must be a collaborative effort; the budget is the result of program and finance working together to compile income and expenses at all levels of the agency.

Income Projections

To understand income projections, income itself must be discussed initially. Income is calculated by taking the types of services at the reimbursement amounts for those services multiplied by the total number of services expected to be provided during the budget period, such as a fiscal year. Finance assists the program by compiling the income amounts by funding source and providing guidance with factors such as the number of services that can be provided per staff person or full-time-equivalent (FTE); identifying resource constraints such as availability of staff or space; and noting limitations imposed by funding sources on the maximum number of units or services that may be provided. Program managers ascertain which services and which level of services will be provided, and finance calculates the income budget based on the input of the program manager and the other factors discussed above. This back-and-forth communication process between program and finance continues until the income budget is established. With each round of feedback, income is refined and the income budget is established. The level of income drives the nonprofit, so it is important to be able to determine accurately how much income for services is earned and when that income is to be received. The nonprofit will make spending decisions based upon the amount and timing of income.

Expense Projections

Once the income projections are analyzed, the costs of operating the program must be identified and included in the expense budget. Finance provides a list of all expense types, known as functional expenses. The direct expenses of the program fall into two major categories, Personal Services (PS) and Other Than Personal Services (OTPS). PS expense includes salaries, independent contractors, and fringe benefits, which may be mandated or nonmandated. Law requires mandated fringe benefits, which include Social Security, unemployment and workers' compensation, and disability insurance. Nonmandated fringe benefits include such items as health and dental insurance and pension. Expenses that are not PS are considered OTPS. OTPS expenses include program supplies, client travel and food, medical and therapeutic supplies, rent, utilities, telephone, office supplies, computer services, insurance, audit, legal, etc. The program OTPS list may be quite lengthy, so it is good to balance the number of expense line items that will capture enough detail to enable the program manager and staff to manage the program daily with the ability to review expenses in an efficient manner.

Finance provides the amounts that need to be budgeted for fixed expenses. For example, rent is a fixed expense, and finance calculates the rent expense for the budget year for the program manager, including escalators and add-ons as specified in the lease for the program site. Program managers and financial analysts work as a team to develop the PS and OTPS budget.

Year-to-Year Comparison and Trending Costs

Finance provides historical expense data trends to assist program managers in budgeting accurately for the variable expenses of the program. For example, the expense for program supplies is variable. Finance provides the program supplies expense for the previous year and the number of individuals served or the number of services provided, trending the expense by the average inflationary increase or other information known—such as the vendor from whom supplies are purchased is implementing a 5% price increase for the current year—to provide the budget amount for program supplies. The program manager can review the amount and underlying data to determine whether the expense budget is adequate for the current fiscal year and alert finance if any modifications are necessary. This process is followed for each type of expense necessary to operate the program until a budget amount is established for each expense. The communication between program and finance is the same as described in the Income section.

Balancing

Once the budgeted amounts for income and expenses of the program are determined, they are tallied to reach a total budget for the program. The income and expense budget for the program are then combined to see if they balance. If there is an excess of expense over income, the program will operate at a deficit, and program and finance must identify ways to eliminate the deficit to reach a balanced position. This may be accomplished by finding ways to increase income to the program, reducing expenses, or both. Another approach is to increase income to cover the deficit. One way to increase income is to add additional clients to existing programs, which increases income without materially increasing expenses. Another way is to redesign the program and renegotiate the reimbursement rate. A third way is to increase fundraising, which takes time and generally realizes only incremental growth. If all else fails, redirecting expenses is also required. In many cases, all of the above approaches are required.

The Need to Increase Income—Fund Raising

Available resources are essentially more government funding and using the non-profit's fundraising dollars. Increasing government funding above promulgated trend factors is difficult at best; there may be agreement in concept that the program is valuable, but the amount of increase government is willing to fund is often murky, and an increase may take several years to achieve. If the nonprofit decides to continue operating the program with a deficit, it must use discretionary income from grants, donors, or fundraising. The source of discretionary funds is limited, and, if it is committed to funding a program's deficit, it is not available for other uses, such as to start new services, expand services, or meet lenders' requirements. A program deficit should not be tolerated over the long term because it dilutes the agency's financial strength or its ability to carry on all program operations.

Dependence on fundraising should take place only with the approval of management and the board, and it should achieve strategic objectives, that is, those that further achievement of the organization's mission, such as when a human services nonprofit organization seeks to establish services in an underserved area or provide services for a population in need. In this instance, during the start-up year, the year in which services are established initially, a budget deficit may occur. The budget for the start-up year includes less income than will be available once the program is fully operational because of the greater cost to begin services. The agency is also seeking individuals who need the proposed services. While the services are building, the fixed expenses necessary to run the program—such as hiring a supervisor and paying rent—are at the level they will be once the program reaches capacity. There are not enough services generating income adequate to cover both fixed and variable expenses of the program, so planning for start-up costs before the program begins is essential. Raising funds to implement the program in the phasing-in period is also essential. Negotiating a phase-in budget with your funding source is critical to starting programs.

Control and Monitoring

Control and monitoring are essential for the start-up program, as well as for programs that are fully operational, if it is to succeed and operate balancing income and expense. The budget is used to control and monitor the start-up operations of the program to ensure it is developing in the manner intended. Reviewing the start-up program's variance report provides the key to understanding how long and in what amount the deficit will need to be funded. The variance report allows agencies to monitor and control program operations at all stages of development.

Micromanagement

Along with an executive-level review of the variance report for operations, each program should meet with finance on a monthly basis to review operations and compare the monthly and year-to-date results with the current budget and the previous year. Any variances in income or expense lines must be discussed, and agreement must be reached on whether the particular item will balance out by the end of the fiscal year, and, if not, what actions are needed to attain balanced income and expense. The financial analyst must review the variance report before the micromanagement meeting to ensure that all income or expenses that should be included in the report are shown. Often finance makes accruals for income and expenses that pertain to the service period, but were not recorded until the following month. For example, finance will accrue billing for services provided to clients based upon documentation from the program after the end of the month, as well as expenses for vendor invoices and salary accruals for time sheets submitted after the end of the month. When reviewing the year-end results, it is critical to include billing and expense information received after the end of the year, during the "13th" month. All income and expense for the fiscal year in which services were provided must be included to provide an accurate picture of the results to executive management and the board and to the readers of the audited financial statements.

Budgeting

Before the budget for the fiscal year is finalized, it should be compared to the previous year's actual results to determine whether the budget is attainable and whether its achievement presents an improvement over the past year. Any deviations from prior years' results should be explained. The budget should be developed for the fiscal year and subcategorized by month. The sum of all the individual program budgets produces the overall operating budget for the organization, which is the budget that executive management reviews, along with large categorical budget reports.

Performance-based budgeting incorporates the nonprofit's strategic plan into the organization's performance outcomes and budgeting process. Using this process as a framework to achieve the long-term goals developed by consensus of staff, management, and the board, and documented in the nonprofit's strategic plan, enables the nonprofit to pursue and achieve its social mission. The performance-based budgeting model in *International Handbook of Practice-Based Performance Management* (Julnes, Berry, Aristigueta, & Yang, 2007, p. 379) presents a macro view of the interactions among the nonprofit's strategic plan, budgeting, and performance of programs to achieve the overarching goals tied to social mission. This model does not address managing the specifics of performance, which are done throughout this chapter, but it does provides an executive-level overview and indicator that the nonprofit's micro activities—programs and services to the population in need—are progressing well, that is, they are achieving the goal of meeting the social and human services needs of individuals with disabilities.

Capital Budget

Most budgeting and variance reporting activities appropriately revolve around program operations. It is also important to develop a capital budget and monitor completion of projects from year to year to ensure that an adequate asset base is available to support the current size of program operations and to plan for expansion of assets to support future program growth. The nonprofit's capital budget will use net assets and debt to fund capital projects, but it does not have the ability to raise equity that is available to for-profits. The debt capacity and ability to raise funds are constraints the nonprofit faces when planning for capital projects. Therefore, the capital budget should list projects by level of importance and include costs and time to complete. Net assets or loans used to fund one capital project are not available to fund any other project until the first one is completed. The capital budget may include a new air conditioning system, roof, renovation of program space, new telephone system, or new computers for numerous programs. The executives, program managers, and financial managers must determine the cost of each; the amount of net assets and/or debt that will be used to cover the cost of each project; and when the projects are needed, based on the age of assets being replaced, health and safety issues, and legal requirements. Building in a contingency cost of 10% is wise to cover unexpected costs. The nonprofit manager must prioritize which of the capital projects will take place in the current year and those that will have to wait until the next fiscal year. Large capital projects may need their own capital campaign and may tie up a significant amount of the nonprofit's borrowing capacity for a long time. Completed capital projects should be audited to identify any cost overruns, which should be taken into account in budgeting future projects, and re-imbursement for cost overruns should be appealed to government or foundations wherever possible.

Cash Flow Budget

Adequate cash flow is critical to the smooth operation of the organization; its ability to time reimbursement with payment obligations, namely payroll, is imperative. The cash flow budget is composed of cash receipts or cash inflows and cash disbursements or cash outflows projected on a monthly basis for the fiscal year. As each month occurs, the cash flow budget is updated with actual receipts and disbursements and carefully monitored. Bank lines of credit must be accessed in months when there is a deficit, when cash outflows exceed cash inflows. Chronic deficits in program operations and rapid growth of programs can affect cash flow negatively and must be managed carefully and effectively. *Financial Management for Nonprofit Organizations—Policies and Practices* (Zietlow, Hankin, & Seidner, 2007) explains the five major reasons why cash flow budgets are modified:

1. uncoordinated losses and credit;
2. fluctuations of donations and cash flows (e.g., donations occur seasonally);
3. degree of shortfall or surplus;
4. how long the shortfalls or surplus lasts; and
5. planning for short-term investments or borrowing funds.

Given that the nonprofit normally experiences programs that run deficits, government cost cutting, shifts in donor base, changes in lender policies, and the overarching need to grow and expand programs to fulfill the social and human service mission, strategies to address these obstacles are necessary. Zietlow et al. (2007) also discuss six internal and three external financial strategies nonprofits can use to ameliorate threats to the viability of the nonprofit's cash flow.

Internal Measures

1. A new emphasis on cash forecasting with shorter horizon (month) and interval (weekly). Most nonprofit finance departments need the ability to predict cash is available for daily and long-term liquidity needs.
2. Asset sales. Having a strategic disposition that focuses on the major areas within an organization.
3. Expansion strategy. The ability to obtain land to expand the organization. In addition, using a builder/leaseback enables the builder to take a depreciation (40-year) expense deduction for taxes, whereas the nonprofit would not be able to do this.
4. Asset redeployment. Organize labor and volunteers in major areas.
5. Cost reduction/containment. Having the right amount of resources in place, by downsizing or rightsizing.
6. Treasury strategies. Revise management approach based on benchmarks.

External Measures

1. *Fundraising.* Intensify fundraising efforts.
2. *Bank borrowing.* Detail improvements that will bridge the gap and prove the program's merit for short-term financing.
3. *Merger/acquisition partner or strategic alliance.* Align with a partner who has access to more funding.

External Reporting

A sound financial reporting system is essential to provide the information nonprofit managers need to direct the programs. In addition to internal management needs, outside lenders or banks often provide working capital or loans to cover short- and long-term needs for cash. For instance, a bank loan can provide funds to bridge the time between billing the government for services provided and receiving payment. The financial system must automatically generate the reports necessary to manage the billing and accounts receivable and provide the bank or other lender with the reporting necessary to calculate the loan amounts. Bank loans are generally established based on a percentage of the total accounts receivable up to a certain period. Banks do not want to be completely responsible for the risk; they want the nonprofit to share in it as well. Banks generally lend a portion of accounts receivable, not the total amount. The nonprofit must have an automated system to generate the accounts receivable report from which the loan calculation is made. Appendix 2 shows a bank borrowing base report as of February 29, 2008, and accompanying Accounts Receivable Aging. Notice that the bank loan calculation is based on services billed but not yet paid, known as *accounts receivable.* The bank lends a portion of accounts receivable, not 100%. This nonprofit's bank loan may be for 90% of Medicaid accounts receivable less than 120 days old (borrowing base) plus 85% of other accounts receivable less than 150 days old (borrowing base) up to a maximum of $17 million. Thus, the bank only provides partial financing of accounts receivable. The loan in the amount of $16,608,538 finances 83.9% of the $19,793,649 of Total Eligible Accounts Receivable and 70.6% of the $23,513,125.89 of Total Accounts Receivable. The nonprofit must maintain a fund balance to cover the amount of accounts receivable it has not borrowed against.

Internal managers use the accounts receivable report to follow up on unpaid amounts due from the government. The finance staff relies on program staff to provide accurate information that is used to bill the government for services and to assist with any client information necessary to ascertain client eligibility so the services will be reimbursed.

Financial Statements

Banks and outside stakeholders, such as foundations and contributors, will require standard certified financial statements at least annually and will analyze the statements to determine the financial well-being of the entity. Financial statements must comply with generally accepted accounting principles (GAAP) for which the Financial Accounting Standards Board (FASB) will provide guidance. The standard financial statements for 501(c)(3) organizations required by FASB Statement 117 include the Statement of Activities or Income Statement, Statement of Financial Position or Balance Sheet, and Statement of Cash Flows. The financial reporting system must generate these reports, which are audited by the external audit firm. The audit firm will certify the financial statements and provide an audit opinion. The best audit opinion that may be given is known as an *unqualified* opinion. Banks and other stakeholders will look for audited financial statements with an unqualified opinion as an indication that the nonprofit entity's financial statements are prepared in accordance with GAAP. They also need to represent the financial position of the nonprofit fairly, so banks can rely on them to make decisions regarding loans, and donors can rely on them for making contributions. FASB statements 116 and 117 address financial reporting aspects for the majority of nonprofits. Appendix 3 shows the audited financial statements of a nonprofit human services organization.

Statement of Activities

Nonprofits use the Statement of Activities to define what is known as the Income Statement of for-profits. The Statement of Financial Position shows the Net Asset position of the nonprofit during a certain period, such as 1 year. Net Assets for the period are the difference between income and expenses. Income is government reimbursement for services provided, such as Medicaid and Medicare, contributions, and gains from the sale of assets. Expenses are amounts paid to operate the programs and provide services, such as salaries, fringe benefits, rent, utilities, and supplies. An excess of income over expense results in a surplus, which increases Net Assets; conversely, if expenses exceed income, there is a deficit and a decrease in Net Assets. A nonprofit has an additional challenge that a for-profit does not: It must balance income and expense because the government will take back surpluses, and the nonprofit must raise funds to cover deficits. Wherever possible, the nonprofit must identify programs or areas where the government allows it to keep a surplus, so that, along with capital raised through fund raising, it can use the net assets generated to expand services, grow into the future, and cover funding needs of current program operations. Appendix 3, Statement of Activities, shows an operating loss of $1,703,253. This deficit is more than offset by nonoperating revenues and expenses, or fundraising activities, of $2,466,323, so there is an increase in net assets or a fund balance of $763,070. Note that $112,177 in contributions in the current fiscal year was restricted, and $79,068 of that amount became unrestricted, or available for use to fund computerized health-monitoring systems in residences.

Balance Sheet or Statement of Financial Position

This financial statement is a snapshot of the nonprofit at a particular point. It is analogous to the Balance Sheet of a commercial enterprise and consists of two sections. In Appendix 3, Exhibit A, the $103,064,114 of Total assets and Total liabilities and Net assets are balanced. The first section presents the assets of the organization in order of liquidity, with the most liquid types of assets, such as cash, cash equivalents, money market amounts, and accounts receivable, shown first, followed by investments and fixed assets. Assets of the organization are things the organization owns and uses to carry out its programs and services. The second section of the balance sheet includes Liabilities and Net Assets. Liabilities are amounts the organization owes to creditors that arise in the normal course of running programs and providing services; they are debt the organization incurs to finance some of its assets. The balance of the assets will be financed through Net Assets. Liabilities are shown on the balance sheet by group, with current liabilities, amounts due that are less than 1 year old, followed by long-term liabilities, amounts due that are over 1 year old. Examples of current liabilities are accounts payable, such as amounts due vendors for purchases of medical supplies, and accrued expenses, such as payroll expense earned but not yet paid to staff. Examples of long-term liabilities are notes payable, such as bank lines of credit, mortgages payable (which include loans for property), and capital lease obligations, when the organization decides to finance a piece of equipment rather than purchase it outright. Net assets, the equivalent of equity in a for-profit enterprise, are the other source of financing for assets. Net assets are the accumulation of surpluses from program operations or capital from contributions, such as donations or proceeds from a capital campaign and amounts generated by fundraising events. The fundamental characteristic of the balance sheet is that the total of the two parts of the balance sheet must equal, that is, assets must equal liabilities plus net assets. The balance sheet shows the organization's ability to pay its bills, assets greater than liabilities, and to fund operations, positive amount of net assets.

Statement of Cash Flows

The third required financial statement is the Statement of Cash Flows, Appendix 3, which presents the sources and uses of cash during a given period, such as 1 year. While program managers and finance devote much of their energy to managing income and expenses, through budgeting, variance reporting, and variance analysis, the financial manager of the nonprofit understands that managing cash is a key to the organization's liquidity and viability as an ongoing concern. The Statement of Cash Flows shows the change in cash during the period by inflows and outflows of cash generated by operating, investing, and financing activities. An increase in an asset or a decrease in a liability represents a use of cash, and the converse is true. An increase in a bank loan represents a source of cash, and the converse holds true. The financial manager understands that cash inflows and outflows must be managed carefully so the organization maintains its liquidity, or its ability to pay its bills when due by generating cash receipts through billing for services. Generally, cash management involves matching cash inflows and outflows, for example, accounts receivable and accounts payable, so there is never a shortfall. The social work manager uses the cash flow statement to plan for major program outlays, such as capital expenses and renovations, and to manage cash so nonprofit can always make payroll and pay other expenses on time.

Net Assets or Contributed Capital

Contributions or net assets are classified as permanently restricted, temporarily restricted, or unrestricted. An organization with unrestricted net assets has greater financial flexibility and liquidity than does one that has restricted net assets, because the former can readily use the contributions for any organizational purpose. An organization with restricted or temporarily restricted net assets has less financial freedom than does one whose net assets are primarily unrestricted because it must use the net assets in the future to fund the particular purpose indicated by the donor.

In addition to financial statements, nonprofits generally must file a Form 990 with the Internal Revenue Service (IRS) annually. Potential donors use Form 990, available on the Web, to obtain information about the activities of the nonprofit, including its funding sources, program expenses, and executive compensation. The financial statements accompany Form 990. These external reports must be made available to outsiders, so it is important that the organization take care in preparing them to ensure they supply useful and accurate information. Such information will affect the decisions of current and future donors and foundations, which directly influence the capital contributed to the nonprofit. Form 990 should be a living document that highlights the programs and services a nonprofit offers to fulfill its mission.

Notes to Financial Statements

An important source of information concerning accounting estimates and their effects on the associated accounts is the notes to the financial statements. The notes are the means by which an organization's independent auditors describe some of the underlying detail in the financial statements, disclose important accounting policies, and identify any special or unusual accounting practices the organization has followed in preparing its financial statements. Anthony and Young (1994) state, "In general, conducting an analysis of an organization's financial management requires undertaking ratio analysis, assessing the statement of cash flows, and relying on whatever other information is available" (p. 487).

Ratio Analysis

To increase the usefulness of financial statements, ratios are used to analyze and evaluate the financial well-being of the organization. Ratios generally look at the relationships of financial aspects as presented in the financial statements and are used for internal and external purposes. "The principal purpose of ratio analysis is to allow us to look closely at four categories of financial management: profitability, liquidity, asset management, and long-term solvency" (Anthony & Young, 1994, p. 486).

One technique used to assess an organization's financial management is ratio analysis, which focuses on mathematical comparisons between or among the accounts on a set of financial statements. Ratios allow an analyst to look at the relationships among various parts of a single statement, such as the balance sheet, or to look at the relationships between elements on two different statements, generally the statement of activities and the balance sheet. The current ratio—which examines the relationship between current assets and current liabilities—is an example of the former; the return on assets ratio—whereby the surplus (or an increase in net assets from the statement of activities) is compared with the assets (from the balance sheet)—is an example of the latter.

Indeed, although dozens of ratios can be used to analyze a set of financial statements, most fall into one of these categories. Some of the more important questions that ratios can help answer are discussed here, by category.

Profitability

An organization's profitability—its surplus or change in net assets on its operating statement—can be thought of along two dimensions:

* How large was the overage relative to revenue? Is this amount about right, or is it too small?
* What were the returns on assets and equity? Are these close, given the risks the organization faces in doing business, or are they too low?

Liquidity

Liquidity is the ability to have an asset converted into cash quickly. Questions that could be asked are modified from Anthony and Young (1994), below:

* Is the organization using its cash well? Can it meet its current responsibilities? Is there cash the organization hasn't invested?
* Is the organization managing its accounts receivable? Are the times of collection too long and getting longer?
* Is the organization managing its inventory well? Is there too much inventory on hand? Too little?

Asset Management

To assess an organization's assets properly, one must examine both current and noncurrent portions of the balance sheet. When looking at noncurrent assets, some questions arise:

* What type of fixed assets are there? Are they appropriate for the organization?
* Are the assets being used properly?
* Are the assets aging? Do they need to be replaced? Does the organization have the ability to replace them?

Long-Term Solvency

In determining whether the organization has made sound finance decisions and provided for long-term solvency, one must look to the bottom of the balance sheet as well as the operating statement, and answer these questions:

* Are current liabilities managed well? Can the organization meet obligations when they become due?
* What is the ratio of long-term debt to equity? Does this bode well? Is there too much debt due to risky operations? Can the organization create more debt and still afford to pay old and new debt?

It is a good idea to use industry and historical comparisons to evaluate an organization's ratios. Credit agencies have traditionally published industry ratios that an organization can use for comparison. Ratios should be generated consistently and periodically and examined to see whether emerging trends are in line with the goals of the organization. In addition, the manager needs to exercise judgment, since variations in a ratio over time are not necessarily bad if they are due to actions taken to achieve the organization's mission and social purpose. Reasons why ratios show variations or differences should be evaluated carefully to ensure that the strategic objectives and mission of the nonprofit are being attained.

Developing an Internal Accounting Control System

Identifying areas where abuses or errors are most likely to occur is the initial phase in designing an internal accounting control system. Price Waterhouse's, *Effective Internal Accounting Control for Nonprofit Organizations: A Guide for Directors and Management* offers a checklist for developing an internal accounting control system that includes the following areas:

- Cash receipts: A record and deposit exists of all cash that is meant for the organization. The cash has been reconciled and secured.
- Cash disbursements: Cash can only be disbursed when management has authorized it for valid purposes and all disbursements are properly recorded.
- Petty cash: Petty cash is used only for proper purposes, is safeguarded, and is recorded.
- Payroll: All payroll disbursements are given to authorized individuals, they are recorded, and all legal requirements are in compliance.
- Grants, gifts, and bequests: All grants, gifts, and bequests are in compliance with any restrictions, and they are received and recorded.
- Fixed assets: All fixed assets are safeguarded, recorded, and acquired and disposed of with proper authorization.

Procedures for handling the financial areas must be stated clearly, and there must be a system of checks and balances ensuring that no single individual handles the whole transaction. Known as segregation of duties, this system is imperative for an effective internal control system. Small nonprofits can also divide duties between staff and volunteers, thereby reducing opportunities for error and wrongdoing.

The Board of Trustees and Executive Director

The tone of responsibility and conscientiousness regarding the organization's assets is set and exemplified by the board and executive director. The finance committee helps fulfill that responsibility by making the internal control system work. The board is responsible for issuing checks, requiring certain signatures, setting dollar amounts required for approval, and naming the person who authorizes payments and financial commitments. Its members have responsibility for deposits, such as cash donations. The financial committee and board determine when transfers from the general fund can be made. They also work together to approve plans and commitments before implementation, and they compare financial statements with budgeted amounts, leases, loan agreements, and other major commitments.

The board and executive director must implement personnel policies that determine salary levels, vacation, overtime, and so forth. The board cannot exist without the financial committee, as the two must work in tandem.

The Accounting Procedures Manual

Each organization should have an accounting procedure manual delineating how financial transactions are handled and describing administrative tasks and who is responsible for carrying them out. The manual does not have to be formal, but it should include a simple explanation of how the organization pays bills, deposits cash, and transfers money. By taking time to revise and review the manual, the organization can determine whether the proper controls are in place. In addition, having such a manual facilitates smooth transitions within financial staff, provides a standard for operation, and can be used to create internal audits and train new staff.

Maintaining Effective Controls

The executive director usually oversees daily implementation of policies and procedures. One person within the organization who understands and monitors specific regulations and compliance factors should be responsible for monitoring the process. A management letter, which generally accompanies an audit, asks for responses to each internal control lapse or recommendation. By comparing these letters yearly, the board has a useful tool to monitor its policies and safeguards. Periodically, a nonprofit will need to review the control system that has been established and modify it to fit new circumstances (larger organization, tighter funding, etc.) and regulations. The internal control system's objectives are reliability of financial reporting, operational efficiency and effectiveness, and conformity to laws and regulations (*Developing an Internal Accounting Control System*, 2003).

An example of an internal control policy is preparing financial statements in accordance with generally accepted accounting principles. The internal control system starts with establishing standards, measuring performance, and correcting variations. The control environment should be analyzed from a risk assessment point of view with control activities in different parts of the system, such as cost control, control of cash, and control of physical assets. Cost control is performed through variance reporting and operating budgets that are sufficient in detail and have been approved by management and the board. Fixed-asset control is achieved through capital budgeting and inventory systems. Cost control starts with the chart of accounts, where similar transactions are recorded and classified by function, such as salaries, medical supplies, and so forth, within each program. The internal control system handles allocations of program and personnel costs as well as transactional and physical controls. A good internal control system is inherent in the activities of a nonprofit that has effective program and financial systems, communication channels that share information with staff at all levels of management, and staff inclusion at all levels in decision-making and monitoring processes. Information and communication are essential components, including variance monitoring, income and expense monitoring, and budget monitoring. In addition, internal audits provide more monitoring and are performed to confirm that effective controls are in place. Internal auditing activities must fit the nonprofit's organizational climate and be tailored to the specific programs. The culture of the nonprofit must be ethical and have high expectations for professional conduct and performance. Critical features of the internal control system are that it is economical, objective, and flexible and that the reporting system is meaningful and enforceable. The internal control system must embrace the mission and include the social causes of the nonprofit, which include ethical responsibilities to clients and policies regarding informed consent, conflict of interest, privacy, confidentiality of client information regarding treatment, payment for services, termination of services, referral for services, and other billing and administrative information.

Risk Management

Risk management is a process of evaluating and protecting the organization against possible losses or harm from future events. Risk management for nonprofits includes preventing harm to clients served, in addition to the financial and business risk management found in the for-profit arena. Nonprofits may be affected permanently and unable to recover from disclosures concerning client and staff injury or financial mismanagement. Loss of public or government support due to these occurrences may force the nonprofit to discontinue operations. Risk is any future uncertainty that threatens the nonprofit's ability to accomplish its mission. The board has overall responsibility for risk management in the nonprofit entity. Sarbanes-Oxley, the legislation mentioned earlier, applies to publicly held, for-profit organizations and has affected governance and control of nonprofits. Nonprofits should follow best practices in this area by establishing a code of ethics and corporate compliance program that is known by staff throughout the organization and supported by management and the board. For risk management to be effective, nonprofit managers must believe that promoting safety, protecting clients, and conserving scarce resources free up its staff to focus on the mission-critical functions of serving the social cause.

Summary

Finance has one of the most critical roles in any organization, with nonprofits being no different. Without the aspect of finance, there would be no executives, clients, or employees. This chapter discussed many areas of finance and the many regulations, controls, and responsibilities surrounding this critical portion of an organization. Social organizations have a responsibility to the public, and the finance team has a duty to make sure the organization has the ability to meet the public's demand.

References

Anthony, R., & Young, D. (1994). *The Jossey-Bass handbook of nonprofit leadership & management.* San Francisco: Jossey-Bass

Developing an internal accounting control system—the accounting procedures manual, maintaining effective controls. (2003). Retrieved March 23, 2008, from http://www.labyrinthinc.com/SharedContent/SingleFaq.asp?faqid=55#developing

Price Waterhouse. (1982). *Effective internal accounting control for nonprofit organizations: A guide for directors and management.* Retrieved from http://www.labyrinthinc.com/SharedContent/SingleFaq.asp?faqid=55

Hilton, R., & Joyce, P. (Eds.) (2007). *Handbook of public administration.* Thousand Oaks, CA: Sage.

Julnes, P., Berry, F., Aristigueta, M., & Yang, K. (Eds.). (2007). *International handbook of practice-based performance management.* Thousand Oaks, CA: Sage.

Zietlow, J., Hankin, J., & Seidner, A. (2007). *Financial management for nonprofit organizations—Policies and practices.* New York: John Wiley & Sons.

APPENDIX 1
Individualized Residential Alternatives

VARIANCE REPORT
JULY 1, 2007 THROUGH JANUARY 31, 2008

	BUDGET	PRORATED BUDGET	ACTUAL	VARIANCE
Income	$36,710,630	$21,340,262	$20,198,317	
Adjustments to Income:				
Therapeutic Leave & Vacancy Adjustment				
Hospitalization			177,095	
"Therapeutic Leave"			251,349	
Vacancy			387,150	
Anticipated Additional Income - Res Hab and IRA Supplemental			110,742	
Anticipated Additional Income - Consumer Fees			208,969	
Anticipated Additional Income - Clothing Allowance			6,637	
Total Income		$21,340,262	$21,340,259	($3)
Expense	$36,710,630	$21,340,278	$21,516,528	$1,318,212
Adjustments to Expense:				
Centereach Equipment Reclass from type 650 to 640:			$3,681	
Total Expense		$21,340,278	$21,520,209	($179,931)
SURPLUS/(LOSS)		($16)	($179,951)	($179,935)
Total Adjusted Income		**$21,340,262**	**$21,340,259**	**($3)**
Total Adjusted Expense		**$21,340,278**	**$21,520,209**	**($179,931)**
SURPLUS/(LOSS)		($16)	($179,951)	($179,935)

TABLE 1
INDIVIDUALIZED RESIDENTIAL ALTERNATIVES: CUMULATIVE MONTHLY COMPARISON

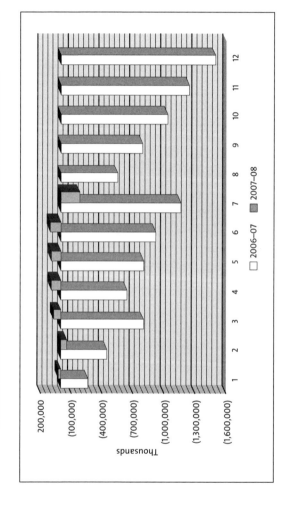

□ 2006–07   ■ 2007–08

CALCULATIONS USED TO DETERMINE INCOME SECTION OF COVER SHEET
JULY 1, 2007 THROUGH JANUARY 31, 2008

Period	Income					$20,198,317
	1. Anticipated Additional Income - Res Hab and IRA Supplemental					
	1a					
July	Supervised Res Hab & IRA Supplemental	8291.62 *	1 months *	280	individuals =	2,321.65
	Land	20.32	1 months	280	individuals =	5,690
	Other	0.06	1 months	280	individuals =	17
Aug-Jan	Supervised Res Hab & IRA Supplemental	8,350.70 *	6 months *	286	individuals =	14,329,805
	Land	26.89	6 months	286	individuals =	46,143
	Other	0.06	6 months	286	individuals =	103
July-Jan	Supportive Res Hab & IRA Supplemental	4,787.55 *	7 months *	69	individuals =	2,312,386
	Land	0	7 months	69	individuals =	0
	Other	0	7 months	69	individuals =	0
						19,015,80
July-Jan	1c Deduction - Accounts Receivable Actual Billed					
	Supervised and Supportive IRA Res Hab					17,555,345
	Supervised and Supportive IRA Supplemental					534,114
						(18,089,459)
July-Jan	1c Deduction - Therapeutic Leave & Vacancy Adjustment					
	Hospitalization					177,095
	"Therapeutic Leave"					251,349
	Vacancy					387,150
						(819,594)
					Total	110,742
	2. Anticipated Additional Income - Therapeutic Leave & Vacancy Adjustment					
					Total	815,594

3. Anticipated Additional Income - Consumer Fees	2,278,202	
3a Prorated Budgeted Income-Consumer Fees		2,069,233
3b Accounts Receivable Actual	Total	208,969
4. Anticipated Additional Income - Clothing Allowance	46,262	
4a Prorated Budgeted Income - Clothing Allowance		39,625
4b Accounts Receivable Actual	Total	6,637
	Total Adjustments	$1,141,942
	Grand Total Adjusted Income	$21,340,259

SUPERVISED IRA
JULY 1, 2007 – JANUARY 31, 2008

	Bainbridge IRA (8 beds) 640-11021			
	Annual Budget	Prorated Budget	Adjusted Actual	Variance
Income:				
Client Fees	88,224	51,464	37,916	(13,548)
Residential Habilitation	812,080	473,713	451,042	(22,671)
Clothing Allowance	1,792	1,045	1,000	(45)
IRA Supplemental	24,173	14,101	14,230	129
Income	926,269	540,323	504,188	(36,135)
VACANCY / REVENUE ADJUSTMENT	0	0	36,135	36,135
Total Income	**926,269**	**540,323**	**540,323**	**0**
Expense:				
Personal Service	495,933	289,294	445,407	(156,113)
Fringe	146,957	85,725	126,941	(41,216)
OTPS	71,229	41,550	51,046	(9,496)
Property and Equipment	96,184	56,107	48,847	7,260
Administration	115,966	67,647	131,156	(63,509)
Total Expense	**926,269**	**540,323**	**803,396**	**(263,073)**
Surplus/(Loss)			**(263,073)**	

Note: OTPS = other than personal services.

BAINBRIDGE IRA
PERSONAL SERVICE 7/07–1/08

Program	Program Name	Dept	Job Title	Employee Name	7/07–1/08
640-11021	Bainbridge IRA	1000	Assistant Psychologist	1	30,625
640-11021	Bainbridge IRA	1000	Assistant Supervisor	2	25,820
640-11021	Bainbridge IRA	1000	Counselor	3	3,617
640-11021	Bainbridge IRA	1000	Counselor	4	4,330
640-11021	Bainbridge IRA	1000	Counselor	5	6,117
640-11021	Bainbridge IRA	1000	Counselor	6	19,570
640-11021	Bainbridge IRA	1000	Counselor	7	21,028
640-11021	Bainbridge IRA	1000	Counselor	8	25,072
640-11021	Bainbridge IRA	1000	Counselor	9	9,592
640-11021	Bainbridge IRA	1000	Counselor	10	6,766
640-11021	Bainbridge IRA	1000	Counselor	11	80
640-11021	Bainbridge IRA	1000	Counselor	12	378
640-11021	Bainbridge IRA	1000	Counselor	13	33,967
640-11021	Bainbridge IRA	1000	Counselor	14	19,138
640-11021	Bainbridge IRA	1000	Counselor	15	21,518
640-11021	Bainbridge IRA	1000	Counselor	16	19,328
640-11021	Bainbridge IRA	1000	Counselor	17	9,086
640-11021	Bainbridge IRA	1000	Counselor	18	6,598
640-11021	Bainbridge IRA	1000	Counselor	19	16,536
640-11021	Bainbridge IRA	1000	Counselor	20	166
640-11021	Bainbridge IRA	1000	Counselor	21	25,856
640-11021	Bainbridge IRA	1000	Counselor	22	4,875
640-11021	Bainbridge IRA	1000	Counselor	23	14,300
640-11021	Bainbridge IRA	1000	Counselor	24	18,828
640-11021	Bainbridge IRA	1000	Counselor	25	16,892
640-11021	Bainbridge IRA	1000	Counselor	26	1,650
640-11021	Bainbridge IRA	1000	Counselor	27	9,578
640-11021	Bainbridge IRA	1000	Housekeeper/Maintenance	28	213
640-11021	Bainbridge IRA	1000	Housekeeper/Maintenance	29	169
640-11021	Bainbridge IRA	1000	Housekeeper/Maintenance	30	210
640-11021	Bainbridge IRA	1000	Housekeeper/Maintenance	31	185
640-11021	Bainbridge IRA	1000	Housekeeper/Maintenance	32	189
640-11021	Bainbridge IRA	1000	Housekeeper/Maintenance	33	2,685
640-11021	Bainbridge IRA	1000	Housekeeper/Maintenance	34	200
640-11021	Bainbridge IRA	1000	Housekeeper/Maintenance	35	205
640-11021	Bainbridge IRA	1000	Housekeeper/Maintenance	36	181
640-11021	Bainbridge IRA	1000	Housekeeper/Maintenance	37	205
640-11021	Bainbridge IRA	1000	Housekeeper/Maintenance	38	179
640-11021	Bainbridge IRA	1000	Housekeeper/Maintenance	39	174
640-11021	Bainbridge IRA	1000	Housekeeper/Maintenance	40	349
640-11021	Bainbridge IRA	1000	Housekeeper/Maintenance	41	178
640-11021	Bainbridge IRA	1000	Housekeeper/Maintenance	42	172
640-11021	Bainbridge IRA	1000	Housekeeper/Maintenance	43	209
640-11021	Bainbridge IRA	1000	Housekeeper/Maintenance	44	236
640-11021	Bainbridge IRA	1000	Housekeeper/Maintenance	45	175

(continued on next page)

BAINBRIDGE IRA
PERSONAL SERVICE 7/07–1/08 *(continued from previous page)*

Program	Program Name	Dept	Job Title	Employee Name	7/07–1/08
640-11021	Bainbridge IRA	1000	Nurse Registered	46	8,276
640-11021	Bainbridge IRA	1000	Psychologist	47	5,130
640-11021	Bainbridge IRA	1000	Psychologist	48	795
640-11021	Bainbridge IRA	1000	Supervisor	49	8,413
640-11021	Bainbridge IRA	1000	Supervisor	50	286
640-11021	Bainbridge IRA	7000	Administrative Assistant	51	26,915
640-11021	Bainbridge IRA	7000	Administrative Assistant	52	251
640-11021	Bainbridge IRA	7000	Administrative Assistant	53	108
640-11021	Bainbridge IRA	7000	Administrative Assistant	54	485
640-11021	Bainbridge IRA	7000	Administrative Assistant	55	321
640-11021	Bainbridge IRA	7000	Administrator	56	211
640-11021	Bainbridge IRA	7000	Assistant Coordinator	57	146
640-11021	Bainbridge IRA	7000	Assistant Coordinator	58	134
640-11021	Bainbridge IRA	7000	Assistant Director	59	888
640-11021	Bainbridge IRA	7000	Assistant Director	60	632
640-11021	Bainbridge IRA	7000	Assistant Director	61	673
640-11021	Bainbridge IRA	7000	Assistant Director	62	637
640-11021	Bainbridge IRA	7000	Assistant Director	63	608
640-11021	Bainbridge IRA	7000	Assistant Director	64	283
640-11021	Bainbridge IRA	7000	Consumer Resource Specialist	65	257
640-11021	Bainbridge IRA	7000	Assistant Director	66	571
640-11021	Bainbridge IRA	7000	Coordinator	67	450
640-11021	Bainbridge IRA	7000	Coordinator	68	27
640-11021	Bainbridge IRA	7000	Coordinator	69	386
640-11021	Bainbridge IRA	7000	Coordinator	70	467
640-11021	Bainbridge IRA	7000	Coordinator	71	552
640-11021	Bainbridge IRA	7000	Coordinator	72	286
640-11021	Bainbridge IRA	7000	Coordinator	73	447
640-11021	Bainbridge IRA	7000	Coordinator	74	610
640-11021	Bainbridge IRA	7000	Coordinator	75	158
640-11021	Bainbridge IRA	7000	Coordinator	76	375
640-11021	Bainbridge IRA	7000	Coordinator	77	530
640-11021	Bainbridge IRA	7000	Coordinator	78	1,254
640-11021	Bainbridge IRA	7000	Coordinator	79	1,223
640-11021	Bainbridge IRA	7000	Coordinator	80	456
640-11021	Bainbridge IRA	7000	Coordinator	81	484
640-11021	Bainbridge IRA	7000	Coordinator	82	587
640-11021	Bainbridge IRA	7000	Coordinator	83	520
640-11021	Bainbridge IRA	7000	Coordinator	84	334
640-11021	Bainbridge IRA	7000	Coordinator	85	536
640-11021	Bainbridge IRA	7000	Director	86	797
640-11021	Bainbridge IRA	7000	Quality Assurance Specialist	87	507
640-11021	Bainbridge IRA	7000	Quality Assurance Specialist	88	357
640-11021	Bainbridge IRA	7000	Quality Assurance Specialist	89	517
640-11021	Bainbridge IRA	7000	Quality Assurance Specialist	90	106

Total Personal Service   445,407

OTPS

BAINBRIDGE AVENUE PROGRAM #640-11021

Acct #	Description	July '07	Aug '07	Sep '07	Oct '07	Nov '07	Dec '07	Jan '08	OTPS Accrual	YTD 07-'08	Budget 12 Months 07-'08	Budget YTD 07-'08	Budget Variance 07-'08
6200-000	Household Supplies	427	454	584	506	101	1,368	616	56	4,112	8,119	4,736	624
6202-002	Office Supplies	444	31	19	37	214	873	351	170	2,140	1,952	1,138	(1,002)
6202-006	Photocopy	129	346	129	446	475	129	131	0	1,784	4,091	2,387	603
6202-008	Postage	32	26	116	24	23	29	21	2	273	254	148	(125)
6202-010	Medical Expense	118	6	270	127	75	542	189	0	1,327	1,307	763	(564)
6210-004	Client Clothing	0	0	933	125	0	163	0	125	1,346	1,450	846	(499)
6210-004	Laundry	0	0	0	0	0	0	79	0	79	0	0	(79)
6212-002	Consumer/Student Food	1,584	3,435	1,687	1,736	146	4,206	1,710	392	14,895	20,509	11,963	(2,931)
6212-004	Refreshment/Training	151	45	48	72	88	128	106	69	708	635	371	(337)
6214-200	Staff Travel	100	318	271	260	159	597	140	72	1,915	1,831	1,068	(847)
6216-000	Program Rec	135	281	383	263	26	1,429	354	530	3,399	2,959	1,726	(1,672)
6224-006	Dues, Subs, & Pubs	0	0	0	0	19	0	15	0	34	72	42	9
6230-002	Building Repairs & Maint.	251	276	1,093	499	349	1,722	0	1,641	5,831	7,864	4,587	(1,243)
6232-000	Utilities	0	1,341	0	619	738	3,207	1,726	115	7,746	12,220	7,128	(618)
6234-000	Telephone/Communications	348	477	174	1,222	257	693	434	88	3,692	3,963	2,312	(1,381)
6238-000	Insurance	0	0	0	0	0	0	0	0	0	1,010	589	589
6260-008	Nyc Ida Service Fee	50	50	500	50	50	500	0	0	1,202	1,792	1,045	(156)
6830-000	Vehicle Expense	403	11	26	5	16	42	60	0	563	1,200	700	137
	Total OTPS	**4,172**	**7,098**	**6,232**	**5,990**	**2,735**	**15,627**	**5,931**	**3,259**	**51,045**	**71,229**	**41,550**	**(9,494)**

PROPERTY & EQUIPMENT

Acct #	Description	July '07	Aug '07	Sep '07	Oct '07	Nov '07	Dec '07	Jan '08	OTPS Accrual	YTD 07-'08	Budget 12 Months 07-'08	Budget YTD 07-'08	Budget Variance 07-'08
6820-100	Vehicle Lease	1,858	1,858	1,861	1,860	1,858	1,865	1,858	0	13,020	23,214	13,542	522
6882-100	Depreciation - Bldg	1,575	1,575	1,575	1,575	1,575	1,575	1,575	0	11,024	19,431	11,335	311
6882-200	Depreciation - Bldg Imp	1,297	1,297	1,297	1,297	1,297	1,297	1,297	0	9,082	16,000	9,333	251
6884-003	Amort of Bond Closing	191	191	191	191	191	191	191	0	1,337	2,312	1,349	12
6250-002	Interest-IDA Capital Lease	3,068	0	0	2,297	3,401	2,724	2,896	0	14,385	25,552	14,905	520
	Total Property & Equipment	**7,989**	**4,922**	**4,924**	**7,219**	**8,323**	**7,658**	**7,818**	**0**	**48,847**	**96,184**	**56,107**	**7,260**
	Total OTPS and P&E	**12,162**	**12,020**	**11,156**	**13,209**	**11,058**	**23,280**	**13,748**	**3,259**	**99,892**	**165,621**	**96,612**	**(3,280)**

APPENDIX 2

Bank Borrowing Base
Dated as of February 29, 2008

Accounts Receivable Aging as of February 29, 2008

Current (0-30)	31 - 60	60 - 90	90 - 120	120 - 150	Total Eligible A/R
$ 11,860,705	$ 6,049,646	$ 572,237	S 1,017,653	$ 293,408	19,793,649

Medicaid Accounts Receivable

Medicaid Receivables < 120 days	15,109,910
Less: Accounts Receivable - Capital Portion	394,142
Eligible Medicaid Accounts Receivable	14,715,769
90% of Eligible Medicaid Accounts Receivable (Borrowing Base)	13,244,192

Other Accounts Receivables

Other Receivables < 150 days	4,588,191
Eligible Other Receivables	4,588,191
85% of Eligible Other Receivables (Borrowing Base)	3,899,962
Total Borrowing Base Maximum = 17,000,000	17,000,000
Current Loan Balance	16,608,538
Excess Availability	391,462

I certify that the above information is true and correct as to the date set forth above.

Signed:

_____
Chief Financial Officer

Accounts Receivables Aging
As of February 29, 2008

	CURRENT	30 DAYS	60 DAYS	90 DAYS	120 DAYS	150 DAYS	180+ DAYS	TOTAL
Medicaid	$9,739,456.85	$4,993,858.14	$264,250.88	$112,344.23	$95,548.66	$61,839.24	$1,275,241.44	$16,542,539.44
Other Insurance	$195,565.40	$144,541.25	$175,467.63	$169,281.06	$132,056.35	$110,788.54	$586,861.15	$1,514,561.38
OMRDD	$1,817,721.00	$855,923.95	$120,588.99	$80,388.52	$36,999.53	$39,424.73	$915,307.09	$3,866,353.81
NYC DMH/ DOE	$0.00	$0.00	$0.00	$628,687.98	$0.00	$0.00	$0.00	$628,687.98
Patient Pay	$107,961.70	$55,322.77	$11,929.60	$26,951.70	$28,803.26	$23,452.17	$706,562.08	$960,983.28
Grand Total	$11,860,704.95	$6,049,646.11	$572,237.10	$1,017,653.49	$293,407.80	$235,504.68	$3,483,971.76	$23,513,125.89

Note: [1] Aging does not include Medicaid Rate Appeal Receivable

APPENDIX 3
Balance Sheet, Statement of Activities, and Statement of Cash Flow

BALANCE SHEET
JUNE 30, 2007

ASSETS

Cash and cash equivalents	$ 4,461,793
Money market-U.S. Government Securities	4,080,799
Accounts Receivable	
Medicaid	30,401,524
New York State	4,039,160
New York City	489,878
Client fees	148,825
Private pay	272,272
Medicare	366,844
Prepaid expenses and other receivables	4,765,042
Bond insurance costs (net of accumulated amoritization	
of $3,073,835)	4,329,371
Fixed assets- at cost(net of accumulated depreciation	
and amoritization of $27,040,043) (Note 3)39,573,930	
Other Assets	10,134,676
Total assets	103,064,114

LIABILITIES AND NET ASSETS

Accounts payable and accrued expenses	$ 20,405,352
Due to New York State (Note 4)	1,896,651
Notes and mortgages payable (Note 5)	37,135,348
Capital lease obligations (Note 6)	27,486,258
Total liabilities	86,923,609
Net assets (Exhibit B)	
Unrestricted	16,107,396
Temporarily restricted (Note 10)	33,109
Total net assets	16,140,505
Total liabilities and net assets	$103,064,114

See independent auditor's report.

The accompanying notes are an integral part of these statements

STATEMENT OF ACTIVITIES
YEAR ENDED JUNE 30, 2007

	Unrestricted	Temporarily Restricted	Total
Operating revenues			
Medicaid	$ 120,016,248		$ 120,016,248
New York State contractual agreements	23,214,854		23,214,854
New York City contractual agreements	1,595,015		1,595,015
Client Fees	4,963,675		4,963,675
Private Pay	677,461		677,461
Medicare	951,154		951,154
Total operating revenues	151,418,407		151,418,407
Operating expenses			
Residential services	69,736,514		69,736,514
Clinical services	55,860,917		55,860,917
Home health care services	8,018,331		8,018,331
Employment initiative services	2,634,267		2,634,267
General support services	16,871,631		16,871,631
Total operating expenses	153,121,660		153,121,660
Change in net assets from operations	(1,703,253)		(1,703,253)
Nonoperating revenues and expenses			
Contributions	734,263	$ 112,177	846,440
Investment income	236,279		236,279
Fund-raising income	(147,390)		(147,390)
Special events	2,255,043		2,255,043
Cost of direct benefits of special events	(725,584)		(725,584)
Other	1,535		1,535
Net assets released from restrictions (Note 10)	79,068	(79,068)	
Total nonoperating revenues and expenses	2,433,214		2,466,323
Change in net assets (Exhibit C)	729,961	33,109	763,070
Net assets – beginning of year	15,377,435		15,377,435
Net assets-end of year (Exhibit A)	$ 16,107,396	$ 33,109	$ 16,140,505

See independent auditor's report

STATEMENT OF CASH FLOWS
Year Ended June 30, 2007

Cash flows from operating activities	$ 763,070
Change in net assets (Exhibit B)	
Adjustments to reconcile change in net assets	
to net cash provided by operating activities	
Depreciation and amortization	4,115,195
Increase in assets	(2,340,044)
Accounts receivable	(1,845,212)
Prepaid expenses and other receivables	(177,927)
Other assets	
Increase (decrease) in liabilities	
Accounts payable and accrued expenses	726,560
Due to New York State	(158,066)
Net cash provided by operating expenses	1,083,576
Cash flows from investing activities	
Fixed asset acquisitions	(6,429,049)
Proceeds from sale of money market-U.S. Government Securities-	
under repurchase agreement	3,009,456
Maturity of certificate of deposit	331,099
Net cash used by investing activities	(3,088,494)
Cash flows from financing activities	
Principal payments on notes and mortgage loans	(10,167,155)
Principal payments on capital leases	(3,126,085)
Proceeds from notes and mortgage loans	17,185,468
Net cash provided by financing activities	3,892,228
Net increase in cash and cash equivalents	1,887,310
Cash and cash equivalents – beginning of year	2,574,483
Cash and cash equivalents – end of year	$ 2,574,483

STATEMENT OF CASH FLOWS
Year Ended June 30, 2007

Supplemental disclosure of cash flow information	$ 3,920,363
Capital lease obligations of $1,710,000 were incurred during the year	
Refinancing of mortgage loans	$ 1,400,378
Debt service reserve fund	109,474
	200,148
	$ 1,710,000

16

Innovative Strategies for Leading and Managing Large Nonprofit Organizations

Joel M. Levy

Leading and managing large nonprofit organizations is a complex and multifaceted endeavor that requires extraordinary skills, persistence, and a clear vision of the organization's mission and goals.

The strategies presented in this chapter are drawn from the findings of some of the most outstanding leadership studies conducted in recent years. Many of these strategies have been tested by and reflect the perspective of the author, whose career as chief executive officer of the YAI/National Institute for People with Disabilities (NIPD) Network spans almost 4 decades. The following is the mission statement for YAI/NIPD:

> Starting at birth and progressing throughout the life cycle, YAI/NIPD strives to build the potential of all people and to be a "place of hope" for infants, children, adults, and seniors. The YAI/NIPD is a large, dispersed, multifaceted human service network of not-for-profit agencies, serving more than 20,000 people in 450 programs through the talent and passion of over 5,600 employees. Starting at birth and progressing through all life cycles, YAI/NIPD strives to be "a place of hope" for infants, children, adults, and seniors with developmental and learning disabilities and their families by building brighter futures.

First and foremost, YAI/NIPD is a mission-driven organization whose mission is best expressed by the model of the "three I's and a P." The first *I* is individualization, the second independence, and the third inclusion; the *P* is productivity. Individualization refers to our belief that each and every person should be treated as an individual, focusing on each person's abilities rather than his or her disabilities. Independence symbolizes our belief that each and every person should be as self-reliant as possible. Inclusion refers to the importance of integrating all members into society as well as into the decision-making process. *P* is for productivity, for which all people strive.

There are three zones of the value chain: administration, results management, and program evaluation (Wei-Skillern, Austin, Leonard, & Stevenson, 2007). The first zone, administration (see Figure 1), focuses on the relationship of inputs, activities, and outputs. This portion of this zone analyzes and examines the effectiveness of internal

FIGURE 1   THE THREE ZONES OF THE VALUE CHAIN

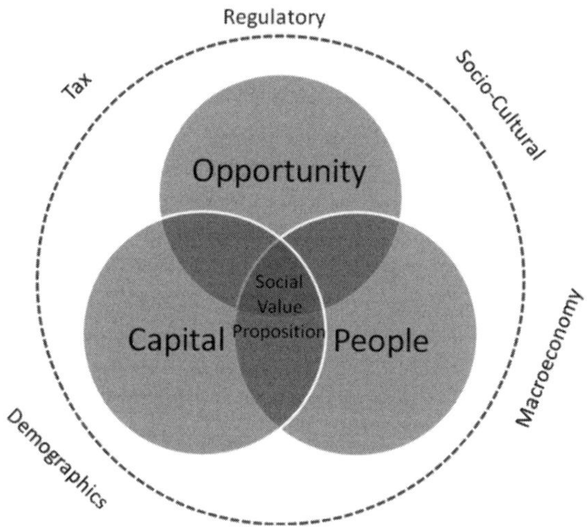

Adapted from Wei-Skillern et al., 2007, p. 23.

operations. By examining the business portion of an organization, we are able to determine what we need to accomplish to perform well.

Each agency operates differently; however, most are guided by their mission, philosophy, and experiences. The right fit must be established on the many decisions leaders are required to make over time because these decisions help them provide long-term social value and impact.

In Figure 1, notice that social value is front and center; however, to be successful, an organization must have good people, capital, and opportunity. The people are necessary, but without the funding, the organization has no chance to be successful. Adequate funding gives good employees the resources to create a great organization.

Results Management

In Figure 2, the sole focus should not be on the immediate outputs but, rather, the more important social aspects. By redirecting the agencies' social value and focusing on long-term projects, the agency is able to guide decisions based on performance outcomes and improve program development.

The second zone, which lies between the organizational boundary and the "normal" data horizon, focuses on results—the external outputs and more visible external outcomes of our actions. "This zone symbolizes the information and analysis necessary to support our management of the results we are producing, and thus guides managerial decision-making and supports learning about how well our actions are being translated

FIGURE 2   AGENCY FOCUS

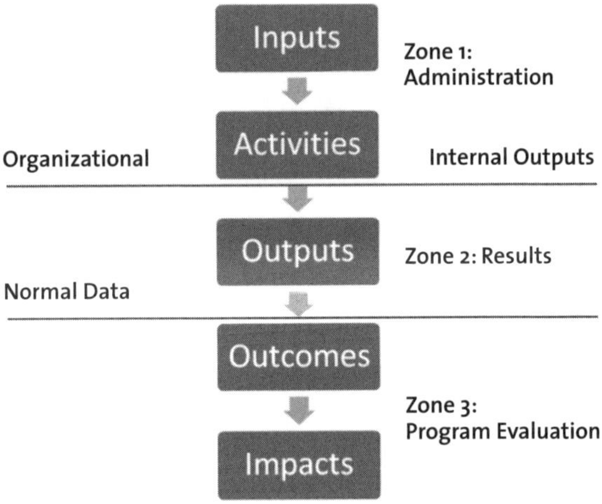

Adapted from Wei-Skillern et al., 2007, p. 332.

into accomplishments" (Wei-Skillern et al., 2007, p. 333). The results management approach to planning exists within the framework of planning and management processes; it is used to underscore better information gathering, decision making, and communication during operational planning. These conclusions can help advance new programs, enhance existing programs, and redefine and improve future programs.

Program Evaluation

The last zone involves program evaluation. According to Wei-Skillern et al. (2007), program evaluation requires collecting and analyzing data, often using quantitative data. By doing research, an organization's leadership is able to examine hypotheses regarding the effectiveness (or lack thereof) of an agency. It makes no difference whether the information comes from quantitative or qualitative research as long as some type of data collection is being done. Adequate time must be spent collecting and measuring data about the outputs and outcomes.

Today more agencies, foundations, and funding sources are using the logical model to demonstrate program development and evaluation. The performance evaluations and management outcomes provide substantiation and thus make research-based decision making more the norm. This can create more cost-effective and efficient services.

The Purpose of Human Services

An organization's purpose is the philosophy of human values partnered with its mission (Taylor & Felten, 1992). Each organization has four interactive and interdependent parts (see Figure 3). To be a *transforming agency*, these parts must produce items of value (Lewis, Lewis, Packard, & Soufflée, 2006). When referring to an agency that involves human services, a transformation occurs from those with problems to those whose problems have been alleviated, at least to some extent. Second, an organization is an *economic agency*, which works for financial gain or not-for-profit agencies and strives to keep the budget balanced or create a surplus. Third, an organization is a *minisociety*, consisting of members who directly influence the agency's effectiveness. Last, an organization is a *collection of individuals*, each of whom is unique in his or her system of values, beliefs, needs, expectations, and skills (Lewis et al., 2006). Agencies need to spend greater resources on their greatest assets, people. Employees can be the agency's greatest resource in meeting the organization's mission and achieving its function. The more the agency reinforces its goal in meeting its social value, the more it reinforces its culture and the important work employees accomplish by meeting their social aim.

FIGURE 3   THE COMPONENTS OF ORGANIZATIONAL PURPOSE

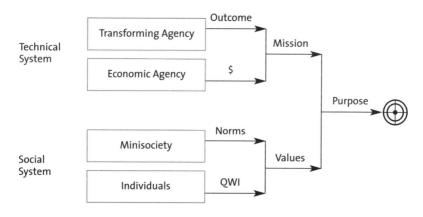

QWL=quality of work life. Adapted from Taylor & Felten, 1992, p. 7

When an organization combines its mission and values, the purpose becomes evident. This in turn, communicates to those within—and outside—the organization why it exists and how it serves the surrounding community. Each is self-reinforcing of the organizational culture and social values, which are in turn like a "fly wheel" that enhances the agency's "greatness" by meeting people's needs. Collins (2001) describes this process as an important part of turning good social agencies into long-lasting, great ones. Continually focusing on long-term agency organizational purpose is critical, while at the same time avoiding mission creep. Agencies need to continue redefining themselves as external factors change; it is possible to do this and still stay true to the mission.

Consumer-Centered

Although client satisfaction seems to be the goal of most social organizations, that is not always be the case (Wei-Skillern et al., 2007). The goal for most service organizations should be to serve their clients effectively. Client satisfaction is important, but it is not the defining factor. The social organization has to focus on serving the masses as opposed to making each person happy. As long as more individuals are served, the organization has met its goal. Although many individuals want their unique interests served, an agency must serve the interests of all individuals—the macro community. Therefore, the purpose at times is not to maximize client satisfaction, but to maintain status quo. At other times, the purpose of the organization may be to create social change. This can lead to conflicts, during which the agency needs to build consensus to resolve whether to serve the most people possible or to serve fewer people with a greater impact. All needs must be balanced: the need to build client satisfaction while also providing the service to meet society's and the broader community's needs.

Building a High-Performance Agency

Agencies that are considered high performing make much better use of their precious resources, including money and employees. They seem to tap into the creativity of each and every person in their building (Dees, Emerson, & Economy, 2002).

According to University of Southern California business professor Edward Lawler, three traits characterize well-designed, high-involvement organizations:

- *Individuals understand the business.* They know its strategy, how it is doing, and whom its customers and competitors are. Successful social enterprises make open communication within and outside the organization a priority, ensuring that employees and stakeholders are well-informed about the organization's workings, its priorities, and its progress toward meeting its goals.
- *Individuals are rewarded according to the success of the business.* They are owners and share in the organization's performance, so that what is good for the business is good for them. Although individuals in most social enterprises cannot own their organizations in a financial sense, they can have psychic ownership of the organization by being involved in developing and implementing its vision and mission, by being involved in the organization's decision-making process, and by feeling they are valued and respected members of the organization
- *Employees are able to influence important organizational decisions.* They decide on work methods, participate in business strategy decisions, and work with each other to coordinate their work. All employees have something to offer their organization; it is often simply just a matter of getting them involved. Once invited to participated, supervisors and managers must follow through by allowing workers to have real decision-making authority, not something less (Lawler, 1986, as cited in Dees, 2002, p. 80).

Most agencies have the ability to perform well; however, some management techniques can be used to help accelerate success. Wei-Skillern et al. (2007) describe a process called reverse planning. This means that planners should start with the end in mind, but not at the expense of exploring other creative directions, consulting stake-holders for new ideas, or involving constituents in the planning process.

The 12 Habits of Highly Effective Organizations

According to Rainey and Steinbauer (1999), the Gallup organization identified 12 characteristics of today's most productive organizations. Curt Coffman, the global practice leader for Gallup, believes these characteristics lead to high performance among workers.

I know the expectations.
I have all I need to complete my work correctly.
My skills are used to my best ability.
I often receive praise for my good work.
My supervisor, or someone at work seems to care about me as a person.
There is someone at work who encourages my development.
At work, others value my opinion.
I believe in the mission and purpose of my organization.
My associates (fellow employees) are committed to doing quality work.
I have a best friend at work.
In the last six months, someone at work has talked to me about my progress.
This last year, I have had opportunities at work to learn and grow. (p. 80)

Furthermore, when Rainey and Steinbauer probed more deeply, they found that employees who feel their organizations give them the opportunity to do what they do best stay longer, which in turn, resulted in lower turnover rates (Dees et al., 2002). Those organizations with happier employees also had a higher customer service satisfaction score. When people feel good about themselves, about their role in meeting the agency's mission, and about bettering the lives of people they are helping, they become more motivated to work hard and engage themselves in meeting the organization's goals. It is important to create agency "treatment plans" for employees as groups and as individuals. Walking the halls, saying hello to employees, and saying thank you is important. Finding ways to interact with staff at all levels is essential.

Socially Entrepreneurial

Social entrepreneurs are different from those in business in terms of their goal. Their objective is to make the world a better place (Sagawa & Segal, 1999). Because of this vision, they receive a different type of feedback from those who are creating value for customers in the form of profits. However, social value does not necessarily lead to monetary rewards for the entrepreneur. This is what makes the social worker and the field of social work so unusual: The social aspect of this career and creating social justice are what make the profession noble.

The best measure of success for social entrepreneurs is not monetary gain, but the extent of social value they create. These individuals act as change agents in the social sector by exhibiting the following behaviors:

* *Adopting a mission to create and sustain social value.* Improving socially is the most important goal, far beyond profits.
* *Recognizing and relentlessly pursuing new opportunities to serve that mission.* Leaders of social organizations must see prospects instead of issues. They are constantly using their vision of their organization to help them achieve goals.
* *Engaging in continuous innovation, adaptation, and learning.* Social leaders are constantly seeking new resources to further their goals.
* *Acting boldly without being limited to resources currently in hand.* Social leaders find ways to get funding and serve their organization. They are not bound by traditional forms of fundraising.
* *Exhibiting a heightened sense of accountability to the constituencies served and for the outcomes created.* Social leaders revisit goals to make sure they are creating value. They want real improvements. (Dees et al., 2002, p. 5)

It is the social return to individuals, communities, and the large population that drives social workers to create social change and equality. Social workers making change on micro, mezzo, and macro levels are one of the aspects of the profession that distinguishes them from other professionals. Fighting for rights, social justice, and social equality should be built into all social agency planning and operations. This in turn is integrated into the agency mission, providing the glue that holds all large agencies together and enabling the organization to attract the best staff to execute its mission.

According to William D. Bygrave, director of Babson College's Center for Entrepreneurial Studies, entrepreneurs exhibit the following characteristics, known as the "10 Ds." Dees et al. (2002) modified them to fit those in the social sector.

* Dreamers—They have a vision of what the future could be like for them, their organizations, and society.
* Decisiveness—They are not procrastinators. They make decisions swiftly, thus helping their success.
* Doers—Once they know their goal, they implement a plan as soon as possible, making adjustments as needed.
* Determination—They execute their projects with total commitment. They seldom admit failure.
* Dedication—They are totally dedicated to their ventures, even if they cost them friendships or family relationships.
* Devotion—They love what they do. This keeps them going when times are tough.
* Details—They are detail-oriented, keeping them abreast of all changes in the industry.
* Destiny—They are in charge of their own destiny rather than dependent on an employer.
* Dollars—Money does not motivate them; however, they realize its importance at keeping their undertaking alive.
* Distribution—They often delegate both duties and recognition. They give others a sense of ownership. (p. 6)

Building a positive work environment, which allows agencies to attract talented staff and take advantage their talents in the most effective manner, is important. Intrinsic rewards, coupled with a work environment that builds on the strengths of each employee, are essential. Affording staff members the opportunity to participate in discussions affecting them is essential to a participatory management approach. When employees have a participatory role, they are far more likely to build their own social and professional commitment.

Current Trends in the Social Sector

Social organizations are alive with change and a new spirit, characterized by trends that have materialized and become stronger:

- Heightened concerns about the effectiveness of traditional governmental and charitable approaches to meeting social needs
- More innovative solutions that lead to improvements
- Adopting some market-based approaches for the social sector
- A growing shift toward privatization of public services, leading to government contracting with both for-profit and nonprofit providers
- A parallel shift toward outcomes-based (rather than needs-based) approaches to funding by both private philanthropies and government agencies
- A more engaged strategic approach to corporate involvement (Dees et al., 2002, p. 13)

Building a social entrepreneur approach allows for a positive environment that permits social change, thereby creating greater opportunities for agencies to distinguish themselves from others. There are many agencies providing services needed; each organization needs to focus on what makes it unique and special. Social organizations should focus on social values and achieve special significance.

These trends are making major strides and changes in the way the social sector operates. At times, the social sector blurs with the business sector, confusing some. Because of this confusion, social entrepreneurs are changing the way they do things, for example, by

reducing the need for charitable assistance rather than simply meeting the need. Motivating people to take responsibility for improving their lives by making them be active in the program (Dees et al., 2001, p. 13).

Social entrepreneurs are also turning away from a reliance of philanthropy on business related methods. Instead, they are exploring commercial methods of generating funds, starting mission-related businesses, and forming mutually beneficial partnerships with corporations (see Figure 4). Because most funding sources now require social returns with measurable outcomes, creative social ventures that serve the needs of vulnerable populations, while maintaining a focus on achieving financial success, are becoming the new social compact.

One of the most important traits to have, according to Allis (2003), is being able to build a solid team. Others include the ability to inspire and provide leadership and

FIGURE 4   ENTREPRENEURIAL STAGES: CHANGING PATTERNS, STRATEGIES, AND ENTREPRENEURIAL ROLES

	Stage I: Entrepreneurial Strategies for the Emerging Venture	Stage II: Entrepreneurial Strategies for the Growing Venture	Stage III: Entrepreneurial Strategies for the Established Venture
Altering patterns of strategic needs of entrepreneurial firms	Strategic framework for forming new ventures. Creativity and opportunity identification (the discovery process). Evaluating & growing opportunities (assessment). Market entry	Financial resource capabilities for nurturing growth by building networks & strategic alliances	Creativity and innovative strategies for breakthrough thinking: reinvention & change to sustain growth. Finding new markets and opportunities: franchising, mergers, & acquisitions.
	The strategic plan: vision and values, the internal & external environment, & organizational strategies for the entrepreneurial team	The strategic plan for the growing venture	Building an entrepreneurial model: learning from failure & serial entrepreneurship
Strategic roles	Creativity, opportunity identification, & evaluation	Opportunity implementation & established growth	Continual innovation & reinvention

Adapted from Gundry & Kickul, 2006, p. 5.

to be persistent. Least important is a college degree. The full results are listed are summarized here:

- Being able to build a solid team
- Leadership and the ability to inspire
- Persistence
- Motivation and ambition
- Integrity
- Ability to communicate effectively
- Confidence
- Being able to execute
- Having a bias toward action
- Having a good idea or plan
- Knowledge for marketing
- Good networking skills
- Having the right advisers
- Knowledge of accounting and finance
- A college degree (p. 77).

It is the personality of the person and how that person fits within the culture of the agency that needs to be considered (Collins, 2001). Organizations have to make sure the right people are in the right positions. A misplaced individual can cause a weak link in an agency and make it less productive. Taking the time to find the right person for the position leads to greater success. Creating the right fit can change an average worker into a successful employee, supervisor, or agency leader. The inverse is also true: A great leader in the wrong agency culture can wreak disastrous results. When hiring and developing staff, look for individuals who are innovative and motivated self-starters and who have the right values, a desire to achieve, and a commitment to serve your population.

Recognizing Stakeholders' Importance

With today's transient workforce, it is surprising to see people stay in one position for a long time. The question many ask themselves is, why do people stay? What makes one person stay in a position when there are many other opportunities out there?

FIGURE 5   COMMUNITIES WORKING COLLABORATIVELY FOR CHANGE

	Networking	Coordination	Cooperation	Collaboration
Definition	Sharing of information for mutual benefit	Sharing information & altering activities for mutual benefit & to achieve a common purpose	Sharing information & altering activities & sharing resources for mutual benefit & to achieve a common purpose	Sharing information & altering activities, sharing resources, & improving the capacity of another for mutual benefit & achieving a common purpose
Characteristics of relationships	Informal; initial level of trust, limited time, & a reluctance to share turf	Formal; dedicated time, higher levels of trust, & some access to each other's area	Formal; substantial amount of time, high levels of trust, & growing access to each other's area	Formal; substantial time commitments, very high levels of trust, &large areas of common turf
Resources	No interagency sharing of resources required	Monitored by the individual organization	Limited sharing of resources (may require written or legal agreement)	Unlimited sharing of resources, risks, rewards, & responsibilities

Adapted from Dees et al., 2002, p. 50.

According to Kouzes and Posner (2007), if we listen to the sensitivity of others, we realize that common values link everyone together:

A chance to be tested, to make it one one's own

A chance to take part in a social experiment

A chance to do something well

A chance to do something good

A chance to change the way things are (p. 151)

It is crucial to thank employees because they accept responsibility and take on challenges that motivate them. Supporting employees with adequate supervision is essential for success.

Stakeholders do not include only employees; other organizations and individuals generally have a stake in social organizations. The government oversees many nonprofits, so it has an interest in the mission. Families of those served, as well as those being served, have a vested concern. Keeping communities abreast of and interested in the social organization's function is also necessary to making it successful. Dees et al. (2002) compiled a chart to delineate a cooperative strategy for all involved that helps build networks inside and outside of the social entity (see Figure 5).

Ownership

Allowing members of an organization to take ownership gives them an interest in its success. Because leaders cannot complete every task themselves, they must be able to delegate. Delegating means more than just giving work to others to complete; it empowers them to be responsible and gives them the authority to do it effectively (Dees et al., 2002). By being given more responsibility, employees can tap into their own skills and creativity to solve problems within their organization and can grow as leaders and help the organization achieve success. When they are responsible, they become more adept at satisfying clients. When employees are more satisfied, they produce pleased customers, and together they make a tremendous organization.

In an entrepreneurial organization delegation allows every employee the chance to become an entrepreneur. The possibilities can be endless if all employees in the organization are energized, creative, and responsive. Delegation is the solution to unleashing the power of ownership within an organization.

Engaging people in the collaborative process and developing intrinsic rewards enhances this process. The agency culture should be developed around a team and collaborative process that can facilitate ongoing self-reinvention. Delegating tasks to people at various levels allows for new, exciting problem-solving potential.

Delegating effectively is not instinctive; it takes a conscious effort on the part of the person doing the delegating—as well as the employee being delegated to—to make sure that the process works. Dees et al. (2002) orchestrated the following six steps for effective delegation:

- *Communicate your expectations.* The work being delegated must be communicated to employees in a way they can understand. Whether it is verbal or written, it should be very detailed. Encourage employees to ask to questions.

- *Furnish context for the work.* Delegation is much more effective when employees understand the big picture—the background information, how it fits into the organization, and how it will meet the agency's goals. This gives employees the power to make informed decisions.
- *Jointly determine standards.* Every project requires milestones, timelines, and goals to provide some way to measure progress. Mutually agreeing on these standards helps both parties have ownership of the task at hand.
- *Grant authority.* Those in charge need the power to accomplish the work. If these individuals have the authority to make decisions without having to seek approval constantly, they can accomplish more.
- *Provide support.* Whether the employees need extra skills or an ear to listen, support should be given.
- *Get commitment.* Whenever you delegate work, be sure you get a positive commitment from the employee that he or she has accepted the work and will complete it according to the agency's standards. (Dees et al., 2002, pp. 76–77)

Delegating keeps all employees involved in the ownership of the success of the organization. They are the owners of the processes—not just those in leadership (Bossidy, Charan, & Burck, 2002). As you delegate you must also provide support and supervision to assure that the staff is following the mission. Blind delegation without this can lead to problems and ruin decision-making processes. Building support and supervision at all levels in the agency affirms continual quality.

Value-Driven/Mission-Driven

Everything within an organization must point to the mission. Notice that, in Figure 6, all entities of the organization lead back to the mission. Therefore, if all items are on board, the mission will be completed.

FIGURE 6   THE ROLE OF THE MISSION IN THE PLANNING CYCLE

Adapted from Dees, Emerson, & Economy, 2001, p. 31.

Strategic Planning

Successful strategic planning is a reality-based activity carried out by and in consultation with those who are responsible for the organization's daily operations. Strategic planning has the greatest chance of successful development and implementation when it involves the staff that will be affected by the plan. Rather than being the exclusive domain of specialized and sophisticated planners, strategic planning is an opportunity for staff at all levels to have a voice in the future of the organization. The development of a strategic plan is more an art than a science; although techniques and guidelines are available, the process depends largely on the abilities and thinking of the persons involved. People who had different values or wondered about strategic planning based their concerns largely on the fact that the process, as it was practiced in the 1970s, did not take into consideration political implications or strategic management considerations (Ansoff, 1979).

As a more sophisticated view of strategic planning has developed, however, experience has proven to be a competent teacher. Strategic planning has been accomplished in recent years with a greater appreciation of its strengths and an understanding of how to avoid its limitations (Bozeman & Schmelzer, 1984).

Strategic planning can be understood as a progression that (1) must be supported by volunteers and leaders; (2) seeks ownership at all levels; (3) requires a commitment of resources; (4) incorporates analysis, thought, judgment, and creativity; and (5) must be tailored to fit an organization's planning culture (Yankey, 1995, p. 2321).

Although strategic planning has many advocates, it also has critics. Some argue that the process is too time-consuming and the world changes too rapidly, often making the plans obsolete (Yankey, 1995). Today strategic planning needs to transition into strategic management, staying more focused as a living process that helps with decision planning and use of resources.

There strategic planning process involves several steps. Yankey (1995) delineated these steps; modified versions of them appear in following paragraphs.

Designing the planning process involves the "planning to plan" concept. Several questions require attention:

- What is the level of commitment to the planning process?
- Who will lead the strategic planning effort?
- Who are the key stakeholders of the organization?
- Which of these key stakeholders will serve on the strategic planning committee?
- How will other stakeholders be involved in the planning process?
- What will be the specific steps and timetable for the planning process?

Leading the strategic planning effort is an important decision in designing the planning process. The organization needs to identify who will head and serve on the committee.

The individual who chairs the committee is significant; he or she must be knowledgeable about the institution and viewed well among members, able to assume an objective role, possess strong planning and group facilitating skills, have influence and be affluent, and should be enthusiastic about the organization (p. 2323).

Selecting the chair and members of the committee is important to building future success. A blending of different skills and people who are open to change based on evidence rather than emotions or unproved proposition is important. However, change will not be embraced fully unless the organization emotionally embraces the new ideas.

Involving Key Stakeholders of the Organization

Those involved in the planning process must be truly engaged in the organization: members of the board of trustees, management officials, staff members, volunteers, clients, and advocacy groups (Yankey, 1995). Involving all of these stakeholders from the beginning allows for a full and open learning environment that builds on participatory involvement and fosters engagement.

Developing Steps and a Timeline for the Planning Process

Once these are clearly defined, the process moves on to a series of analyses, including external, internal, gap, and benchmarking, which provide a context for developing the organization's strategic issues. Strategic programming follows, and the organization develops specific strategies, including strategic goals, action plans, and tactics. Emergent strategies evolve, challenging the intended tactics and altering the realized strategy. Periodically, the organization evaluates its strategies and reviews its strategic plan, considering emergent strategies and evolving changes. It usually takes several years before strategic planning becomes institutionalized and organizations learn to think strategically. Leaders need to incorporate people from all levels of the agency in the strategic planning and management process. A leader cannot understand what is important, what needs to be accomplished, and the effects of the decisions being made without the participation of all levels. Each level of staff provides varied ideas and approaches.

Mission Formulation

When an organization is involved in strategic planning, it must scrutinize its values, beliefs, philosophy, vision, and meaning. Identifying the organization's vision and mission is the first step of any strategic planning process. The vision sets out the reasons for the organization's existence and the "ideal" state the organization seeks to achieve; the mission identifies major goals and performance objectives. Both are defined within the framework of the agency's philosophy and used as a context for developing and evaluating intended and emergent strategies. One cannot overemphasize the importance of a clear vision and mission; none of the subsequent steps will matter if the organization is not certain where it is headed.

Benefits and Obstacles

Illuminating the mission helps an organization retain a shared set of values, define its business, determine the programs it is planning to offer, direct its financial resources, and suggest the kinds of knowledge and skills required to carry out the mission efficiently (Yankey, 1995).

Visioning

A vision is a description of the organization's impending state. A vision must contain deeply held values, experiences, views of the future, intuition, and dreams.

What will the future business of the organization be?

What will the board composition and structure be?

How large will the organization be?

What programs will the organization conduct?

What staff will be required?

What volunteers will be required?

What internal management structures will be required?

What will the funding mix for the organization be?

What facilities will the organization have?

How will success be measured? (Yankey, 1995, p. 2323)

Mission Statement

The mission, the organization's agreed-upon statement of purpose, explains the reason for its existence. It is necessarily broad to encompass the diversity within the organization. The statement is not precise, nor does it need to be, but it does need to be reviewed periodically by the organization to see whether it still encompasses all of the agency's relevant activities. Defining the mission statement could very well be a difficult task because it needs to be in alignment with all of the aspects of the very reason the organization exists.

Goals

Goals need to be both long term and short term: 6 months, 1-year, 3-year, and 10-year goals need to be set so the strategy for reaching these goals can be outlined in the plan. Most organizations recommend setting long-term goals first, and then setting short-term ones: Those goals that can be reached as steps toward attaining the long-term goal.

Objectives

The objectives are the organization's areas of emphasis. Rather than specific statements with a specific goal, objectives state that the organization plans to continue to do quality work in certain areas. These objectives or areas of emphasis should be the product of discussion and review of the organization's current activities as well as activities in which it would like to participate.

Action Plan

The action plan should be designed after the main goals and objectives have been set to attain the mission in a straightforward and measurable way. With an action plan, the goals themselves can be obtained. Without the plan, and the measures it entails, it would be impossible to implement the plan and measure its success.

SWOT Analysis

A SWOT (strengths, weaknesses, opportunities, threats) analysis is an examination of the strengths and weaknesses of the organization in relation to the opportunities and threats presented by its external environment. This step in strategic planning is important in positioning the organization to maximize its strengths and capitalize on its opportunities (Swinton, 2005).

Strategic Issues

A strategic issue can be a policy change affecting mandates, mission, values, product or service, financing, organization, or management (Bryson, 1988). A strategic planning committee must use three approaches to identify strategic issues (Barry, 1986).

- Direct approach—The committee moves from clarifying the mission to determining the issues. This works well when there is no preexisting agreement on goals, no well-defined vision of success, and no higher-ups to impose goals.
- Goals approach—The committee that uses this approach must agree on issues and potential strategies. This helps its members develop strategies for carrying out the mission of the organization (Yankey, 1995). This approach fails when values are diverse, agendas are confusing, and stakeholders are powerful.
- "Vision of success" approach—The vision of success is similar to the visioning activities associated with mission formulation. The organization must create a "best" picture of its future as it fulfills its mission and achieves success. (p. 2325)

An organization needs to focus its decision making on the issues. Once it has done that, then strategic planning can have a positive impact.

Strategy Development Process

Bryson (1988) developed a five-part strategy to help those on the strategic planning committee determine the best strategy by asking these questions:

What practical alternatives might we pursue to address this strategic issue?

What barriers preclude realization of these alternatives?

What major proposals might we pursue to achieve these alternatives?

What major action with existing staff must we undertake to implement these proposals?

What specific action steps must we take to implement the proposals? (p. 46).

According to the literature, there are many ways to develop strategy. However, all of them seem to be variations of one the others. With any development plan, there are obstacles. An appropriate strategy will identify those obstacles and delineate steps to overcome them. Each strategy should contain a timeline and a list of those responsible for finishing the product.

The Strategic Planning Process

Evaluation of the Strategic Plan

After the components from Figure 7 are in place, the plan should be shared throughout the organization. In addition, it may be in the best interest of the organization

FIGURE 7   STRATEGIC PLANNING PROCESS

Adapted from Julnes, Berry, Aristigueta, M., & Yang, 2007, p. 130.

to send it for review in draft form for a final round of feedback (Lewis, Lewis, Packard, & Soufflé, 2002).

Implementation

The keys to successful implementation of the plan are the commitment of all critical internal stakeholders, staff, and board members. In addition, a detailed, clear, and concise action plan is needed. The action plan must communicate clear connections between strategies and operations.

Consistent monitoring and updating of the plan are imperative as well (Bryson, 1988). Organizations must stay focused on the importance of the mission and mandates of the organization when updating the strategic plan.

Optimism/Hope

Constituents want leaders who believe in the capacity of others, who strengthen people's will, who supply the means to achieve, and who express optimism for the future. They also want leaders who are passionate despite obstacles and setbacks. In uncertain times, leaders who are positive and confident in life and business are critical (Kouzes & Pozner, 2007).

Leaders must endeavor to keep hope alive, even when times are difficult. They need to strengthen their employees' belief that a promising future is coming. When leaders keep hope alive, they demonstrate their faith and confidence by accepting responsibility for the quality of their constituents lives. During difficult times, when everything seems to go wrong, they display unwavering commitment to the cause.

Kouzes and Pozner (2007) stress the importance of hope. They say it is essential to achieving the highest levels of performance, as it enables people to transcend the difficulties of today and envision the potential of tomorrow. It also helps those who have been troubled to bounce back and to find the will and the way to unleash greatness.

U.S. Army Major General John Stanford, who survived many tours in Vietnam and was highly decorated, was asked how he develops leaders. He replied,

> The secret to success is to stay in love. Staying in love gives you the fire to ignite other people, to have a greater desire to get things done than other people. A person who is not in love doesn't really feel the kind of excitement that helps them to get ahead and to lead others and to achieve. I don't know any other fire, any other thing in life that is more exhilarating and is more positive a feeling than love is. (Kouzes & Pozner, 2007, p. 389)

The best-kept secret of successful leaders is love; staying in love with leading, with the people who do the work, with what their organizations produce, and with those who honor the organization by using its work. Leadership is not an affair of the head, it is an affair of the heart (Kouzes & Pozner, 2007, p. 399). It is building the positive emotional behavior of staff that helps to overcome resistance and barriers to change. Creating a culture in which people feel good about going to work turns that work into a labor of love. Building positive connections with the mission, staff, supervisors, managers, and other leaders, including the chief executive officer, president, chief operating officers, and divisional administrators, lets everyone in the agency know he or she is connected to the agency's mission. This allows all members to be on the same page within the agency and creates an environment of commitment.

Risk/Risk Taking

In assessing risk, one must understand the factors that may cause the risk to become reality (Dees et al., 2002); in other words, what the likelihood is that an event will occur. Risk factors include the following.

- Quality of management
- Quality of the workforce
- Culture of the organization
- Strength of organizational infrastructure
- Basic enterprise concept
- Level of capitalization
- Prospects of long-term funding
- Changes in the marketplace
- Changes in technology
- Stakeholder backlash
- Competitor reaction (p. 136)

Quality of Management

Managerial risk is one of the most significant risks. Many say that a good manager can succeed with a bad organization, but a bad manager will kill a good one. It is imperative to have the right players, and ensuring that they are an asset and not a risk is central to minimizing managerial risk exposure (Dees et al., 2001).

Alternative Workforces

Although not every social entrepreneur is involved in operating business ventures, social-purpose enterprises that do seek to employ a given target population also represent a unique type of risk. Many social entrepreneurs run businesses with employees who have lost other jobs. In a mainstream business, if workers do not perform well, they are fired. However, in some types of social enterprises, a central element of the mission is to employ individuals who have not been employable. Social organizations usually try to minimize their risk by making sure those individuals have access to support programs (Dees et al., 2001; Greening & Turban, 2000). Developing creative job opportunities for vulnerable populations that offer the opportunity for their integration into the workforce implements a social venture business model.

Culture of the Organization

Having a culture that affirms entrepreneurial approaches to managing the challenges that confront the nonprofit is a crucial factor in the agency's success. Terminating those who are not a good fit for the organization and replacing them with those who value the social mission is key. As a leader, one must also take the initiative to move people into the right positions.

The consulting firm of Robert Half surveyed 150 executives, 34% of whom stated that potential employees are more interested in the culture of an organization than they are in other opportunities. Culture obviously has a huge impact on whether people will work at certain places (Dees et al., 2002). Building the culture in large agencies is an important planning step that requires all aspects of operations to reinforce the culture, values, mission, and vision for the future.

Strength of Organizational Infrastructure

When discussing the strength of an organization, most refer to its ability to manage a particular enterprise. It might also refer to whether the organization can control a market-based venture. Questions to explore in this regard include:
- Are all of your personnel already overextended and unable to cope?
- Does it take you 6 months to get last month's financial statements from accounting?
- Is the organization clear and focused on its mission, or are there competing factions driving conflicting agendas?

In spite of whether the initiative under consideration is a social-purpose enterprise or a new programmatic approach to a social problem, the organization sponsoring the venture brings its own element of risk to the venture's potential for success (Dees et al., 2002). Financial supports are critical for the success of the agency. Training for all people within the agency needs to be available to facilitate ownership and responsibility of a fiscally well-managed agency.

Basic Enterprise Concept

This risk involves those agencies that involve only specific programs or are social enterprises. Questions to ask in this regard include:

* Is the enterprise strategy-tested and reliable?
* Is it new and uncertain?
* Does the enterprise have a degree of risk greater than that of other, similar enterprises?
* What elements/factors make this particular enterprise risky?

According to Gulledge and Sommer (2005), all of these questions must be considered when assessing the risk of a given enterprise; however, the most important risk is that of the concept itself. Whether to take a risk is a vital decision leaders need to face. How the positive outcome can benefit the social cause should not override the negative outcomes, especially if you cannot survive their impact.

Level of Capitalization

The level and structure of capital is the amount of funds an organization has on hand (Dees et al. 2001, p. 139) to start a venture. It could also include basic start-up funds but it should focus on equipment and plant acquisition as well as supplies. Risk in this area is usually focused on the organization's ability to secure the funds needed to start the venture.

Timing of capital infusion is also critical. The practitioner must secure funds at the right time. Although much funding is needed at the beginning, those in charge should be looking for future support as well. Lines of credit are vital to meeting cash flow needs, especially for receivables management to enable the agency to meet its obligations while waiting for payments from its funding sources.

Prospects of Long-Term Funding

Funding risk also includes

* the amount of funds necessary to support the enterprise;
* whether those funds are readily available; and
* the amount of cash flow necessary to support the operation during its start-up and expansion period (Dees et al., 2001, p. 139)

Assessing funding risk should also take into account the cost of accessing needed financial resources. If the organization must travel to numerous meetings, complete reports, and so forth, the process of securing funds might be more onerous than it is truly worth.

Changes in the Marketplace

According to Dees et al. (2001) market risk is inherent in the marketplace. It could include any of the following:

- The presence and actions of competitors
- The impact of capital market resource shifts
- The dynamics of the regional or national markets within with the social enter-
prise operates
- Changes in the tastes or traffic patterns of consumers
- Shifts in the charitable interests of donors (p. 40)

Market risk could include an assessment of shifts in public policies. For example, an educational initiative requiring approval of charter schools will be at risk if the state department of education rules against these efforts.

Stakeholder Backlash

Some believe that charity is charity, and business is business. Those who have op-posing beliefs can create issues. Individuals who have supported the organization in the past may not support it in the future because the organization has changed to a more socially minded institution. Leaders must manage how the idea of social enter-prise is introduced and acted on.

Competitor Reaction

The risk epitomized by competitors is an important aspect of market risk. When engaging in making a profit, competition among players is a given—people discuss it, plan for it, and thrive on it. In the tax-exempt sector, however, we have mixed feelings about competition (Dees et al., 2001). Competition among nonprofits can focus on individual donors, media coverage, and volunteers.

The issue is not whether one competes; it is how one competes that makes the dif-ference. Competitive risk involves a response to competition. Those involved in the not-for-profit sector must adhere to the ideal of fairness and integrity. Becoming part of institution that believes in fairness in advertising and truthful self-promotion is an honor.

Execution Is a Discipline

Execution is about doing things more effectively (Bossidy et al., 2002). People who pinpoint execution as a reason for failure tend to think of it in terms of attention to detail. To understand execution, you have to know that (1) execution is a discipline and integral to strategy; (2) execution is the major job of the business leader; and (3) execution must be a core element of an organization's culture (p. 21). Execution is fundamental to strategy and shapes it (Bossidy et al., 2002). It is worthless to have a strategy if you have no way to make this strategy work.

Execution is a systematic process of investigating what is going to be done and how. It involves questioning, following through, and ensuring accountability. It in-volves making assumptions about the business environment, assessing the organization's capabilities, linking strategy to operations, and having the right people to implement the strategy. The heart of execution lies in three core processes: the peo-ple process, the strategy process, and the operations process.

Innovation

Often an innovation is considered a major invention, such as the light bulb, television, or personal computer (Dees et al., 2002; Lesser, Fontaine, & Slusher, 2000). However, when looking at innovations more closely, we realize they are just new ideas built on old ones. These ideas are simply changed to make something more creative. According to Dees et al. (2002), "innovation involves establishing new and better ways for accomplishing a worthwhile objective" (p. 162). Social entrepreneurs think of them as new and better ways to serve their mission. The following discusses more about each of the key words of this definition.

- *Establishing*... Innovation is about effective action, not simply having an idea. It can be contrasted with invention, which is about generating new ideas.
- *New*... Innovation involves change. To be new in this sense is a matter of degree. Incremental changes count, as opposed to those that are radical.
- *And better*... Innovation must be seen as improvements in the eyes of at least some of the people affected; otherwise, it is a mistake.
- *Ways of*... Innovation can take many forms, including changes in what you are doing, how you are doing it, where you are doing it, or with whom.
- *Accomplishing*... Innovation is about getting results, not just about being different. It is outcomes-oriented.
- *A worthwhile objective*... Innovation is always understood relative to an objective that is deemed worthwhile by those involved. Some may disagree about which objectives are worthwhile. When they do, they also disagree about what counts as a real innovation. (p. 162).

Innovation can occur in all areas of life. In this context, however, the concern is only with innovations for social entrepreneurs. These individuals tend to be involved in creating and delivering products, services, or programs. Schumpeter (1983) used five categories to classify the different ways that businesses can be innovative, modified in the following list for social entrepreneurs.

- *Creating a new or improved product, service, or program*—One with which the users are not yet familiar or one with aspects that are new to consumers.
- *Introducing a new or improved strategy or method of operating*—One that has not been used by the organization adopting it. The new method or strategy can affect one or many of the elements of an enterprise, including how the product is designed.
- *Reaching a new market, serving an unmet need*—Making a product, service, or program available to a group that previously had no access to it.
- *Tapping into a new source of supply or labor*—Finding a labor pool that this organization had not previously used, which lowers costs, improves quality, and/or creates additional benefits for some new group.
- *Establishing a new industrial or organizational structure*—Changing the relationships among existing organizations to improve performance, including mergers, spin-offs, alliances, and other contractual arrangements

- *Framing new terms of engagement*—Changing the terms by which you relate to clients, consumers, suppliers, funders, or employees.
- *Developing new funding structures*—Exploring different options for reducing or covering the costs of producing or delivering your product or service. (p. 163)

When organizations set out on a track of innovation, they must learn to balance the tensions of the innovation process (Burns & Stalker, 1994). To alleviate tension, successful innovators are able to master the following three tensions, as seen in Dees et al., (2001):

- *Using both the beginner's mind and the expert's mind to conceive of viable innovative ideas.* Beginners bring a fresh perspective to situations and can see innovative possibilities better than experts in the field can. A true innovator must maintain a healthy balance between the expert and the beginner. Experts at times miss important issues because of their immersion in the field. By the same token, some beginners are not aware of details the experts know.
- *Being persistent in the face of rejection, but also being open to changing course while persuading others of the merits of your idea.* Innovations change over the course of time. Innovations must adapt to the challenge of making a vision into a reality. An innovator who is set on doing things a certain way will often miss a true innovation.
- *Keeping your ear to the ground while keeping your nose to the grindstone as you implement the idea.* Although innovators feel driven to focus solely on the enterprise and projects, keeping their mind in the game of innovation can keep them abreast of new ideas and services. (p. 166)

If you were to illustrate the different types of people on a bell curve, innovators would account for the fewest individuals. They are the ones who move change along. Early adopters are more careful; they do come around, but they test the waters first. The early majority comprise careful individuals; they finally come along, slowly but faster than most people do. Now, the majority is a skeptical group of people, using an innovation only when everyone else is doing so. Finally, the laggards are the last to accept a change. They enjoy the old ways of doing things and accede to change only when forced (Rogers, 1963).

Building a Brand

At times, McDonald's has been ranked the number one brand in the world. Brands are valuable because they directly influence customers' decisions. By choosing a brand, consumers do not have to make random decisions; they choose a brand they trust.

When an organization is trying to become marketable, it must combine participant benefits with participant costs. Coinciding with that is the mission of the organization and the tactics used to achieve that mission.

Vision

"A powerful way for planners to frame the agency's mission, strategies, goals, and objectives is to develop for the future" (Lewis et al., 2002, p. 44). Senge (1990) introduced the notion of "governing ideas" for an organization. Included in these is the mission, which tells why the organization exists. Core values respond to how the organization wants to present itself. Finally, vision refers to how the organization will evolve.

Senge (1990) describes an organization in this manner:

> A shared vision is not an idea. It is not even an important idea such as freedom. It is, rather, a force in people's hearts, a force of impressive power. It may be inspired by an idea, but once it goes further—if it is compelling enough to acquire the support of more than one person—then it is no longer an abstraction. (p. 209)

According to Senge, shared visions for the future are based on the visions of the members in the organization. Visions cannot be developed and then forced on those involved; it must be a collaborative effort with intensive dialogue.

Yankey (1995) suggests asking the following questions to provide structure to an organization vision.

- What will the future business of the organization be?
- What will the board composition and structure be?
- How large will the organization be?
- What programs will the organization conduct?
- What staff will be required?
- What volunteers will be required?
- What internal management structures will be required?
- What will the funding mix of the organization be?
- What facilities will the organization have?
- How will success be measured? (p. 2323)

A vision statement needs to be inspirational and visionary. These questions focus on the technical components, some of which cannot be answered until much strategic planning has been accomplished (Lewis et al., 2002). The inspirational portions serve as a base or preamble for future planning activities, starting with review of the organization's environment and mission.

Ideas drive funding and agency mission, but vision excites people to achieve beyond their expectations. A leader's job is to create a bridge to meet client's needs through creative programs while meeting funder's needs and policy directions.

Leadership

Leadership can be defined as motivating a group of people to achieve a common goal. Throughout literature, there are many "best practices" in leadership Kouzes and Posner (2002) define five practices of exemplary leadership: (1) model the way; (2) inspire a shared vision; (3) challenge the process; (4) enable others to act; and (5) encourage the heart (p. 13).

These practices can be used by anyone who accepts a leadership challenge. They have stood the test of time, and research confirms they are just as relevant today as they were in the past.

- Model the way—
  - Personalize your own values.
  - Make sure your actions are aligned with your spoken values.
- Inspire a shared vision—
  - Envision the future by verbalizing exciting and noble possibilities.
  - Enlist others in a common vision by appealing to shared desires.
- Challenge the process—
  - Search for opportunities by seeking new ways to improve.
  - Experiment and take risks by constantly producing and learning from mistakes.
- Enable others to act—
  - Collaborate with teammates and build trust.
  - Share power and authority.
- Encourage the heart—
  - Show appreciation for those who excel.

Create a spirit of community to celebrate the successes. (Kouzes & Posner, 2002, p. 22)

Situational Leadership

Situation theorists view leadership effectiveness as a component of the context in which leadership actions or behaviors take place. These theories focus on interaction but add the concept of environmental and social status of the players as variables to consider when defining leadership effectiveness.

Van Seters and Fields (1999) indicated that if the environment was conducive to the leaders' "being in the right place at the right time in the right circumstances, their actions were inconsequential" (p. 34). Those who focused on the social status were concerned with the interactions and characteristics of the situation. In general, situational theorists often attempted to incorporate several components of earlier approaches when defining leadership. The divergence of opinions centered on how such situational factors as social status, power interactions, stress, and external environment could affect the effectiveness of the behaviors, traits, skills, and influence necessary to be effective. One of the best-known approaches to leadership effectiveness using the situational approach is Hersey and Blanchard's (1982) Situational Leadership II (SLII). The SLII model divides leadership effectiveness into four styles (delegating, supporting, coaching, or directing), and includes the development level of the employee (high, moderate, or low) (Blanchard, Zigarmi, & Zigarmi, 1985). The premise is that an employee progresses in and out of various situations, and leaders' effectiveness depends on their ability to assess and diagnose the context of the situation.

Characteristics of Admired Leaders

Kouzes and Posner (2007) were determined to identify the top qualities people admired in leaders. They asked more than 75,000 people an open-ended question: "What seven qualities do you most look for and admire in a leader, someone whose direction you would willingly follow?" (p. 24). Honesty tops the list of characteristics because it is responsible for creating trust among managers and employees at all levels within the agency. The fact that forward-looking is second on the list speaks to the importance of having a vision.

Leadership in large agencies helps to provide vision, providing a clear path for others to follow, and for leaders to follow the ideas of their staff. This helps to create a leader out of each employee.

Evaluation Process

Evaluations are important in any workplace, as they allow employees to gain information regarding their performance. It allows them to understand what items they execute well and what skills need improvement. Assessment within an organization should be an ongoing process, with open lines of communication.

Supervision

The model of supervision in Figure 8 places the leadership role in the middle of all of the responsibilities. This model does not distinguish between the role of a manager or supervisor; it considers the supervisor as a professional involved in managing, mediating, and mentoring. This model always seeks to enhance services to clients (Lewis et al., 2002).

FIGURE 8   A MODEL OF SUPERVISION

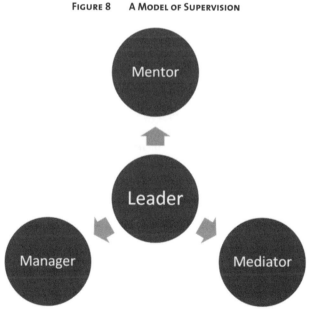

Adapted from Lewis et al., 2002, p. 156.

Characteristics of a leader involve displaying a positive attitude and being cheerfully confident and optimistic. This is a meaningful trait for leaders to project. When leaders demonstrate helping others, they achieve much personal satisfaction while encouraging their benefactor to do the same; the leader sets a moral example.

It is important to offer constructive feedback. Humility and the ability to admit mistakes are powerful qualities in a leader and, perhaps, the most arduous ones for many to demonstrate. The potential to recognize that no leader must emanate perfection is important. When a person makes a mistake, affirm it, learn from it, and carry on.

Leaders must remember to use active listening skills and show followers they care about them. Good listening skills are necessary for winning communications. Studies have shown that people learn 85% of what they know from listening, but forget 75% of what they hear (Olson, 2005). Such statistics are not very encouraging.

When hiring new staff, leaders must help them become a part of the decision-making process. Another important consideration in a personal leadership plan is a commitment to training and development. Leaders must create a learning and growing atmosphere. When followers discuss what causes stress in their work life, they often report that it is a lack of proper and ongoing training (Cordes & Dougherty, 1993). For an organization to be successful, its leader must recognize that the team needs the best tools available. What that equates to is a belief in lifelong learning, and it must be encouraged. Much attention has focused on leadership training, but "followership" training is needed as well (Nelson, 2001). Leadership and followership training are important individually, but it is also important for both leaders and followers to train together as a team.

Conceptual Framework for Human Services Management

Leadership binds and energizes all forces in an organization (Lewis et al., 2002). Leadership involves working with employees to articulate a vision, manage the external environment, oversee the design of organizational process, link elements of the system together, and create a supportive organizational culture (p. 11).

Within human service organizations, there are many different domains of leadership. The managerial domain ranges from executives to first-line managers. It can be divided further into institutional, managerial, and technical levels. Technical skills are those related to accomplishing the agency's core activities: counseling, casework, and other services to clients or community. Conceptual skills address the big picture, and human skills relate to the clients served. Executives need enough knowledge of the program's service delivery technologies to make informed managerial decisions, but conceptual skills are more important in managing all aspects of the organization. People skills are essential and equally important at all levels.

It seems that many organizations that work for a profit, put profits first and their people second. Stanford University professor Jeffrey Pfeffer has determined that there is a direct relationship between a company's financial success and its commitment to treating people as assets.

Even social entrepreneurs are guilty of focusing on performance, measurable outcomes, and the other mechanics of serving clients. Most think people in social organizations inherently put their employees first; however, that is not always the case (Dees et al., 2002).

Pfeffer (1998) lists seven practices of successful organizations—practices that put people first. These include but are not limited to

- employment security;
- selective hiring of new personnel;
- self-managed teams and decentralization of decision making as the basic principles of organizational design;
- comparatively high compensation contingent on organizational performance; and
- fewer status distinctions and barriers, including dress, language, office arrangements, and wage differences across levels (p. 79).

Employees like to be rewarded for a job well done. This does not require a great deal of money; little things can go a long way. Dees et al. (2002 have developed a list of good motivational practices, including pizza parties, birthday cards with a cake and candle, throwing barbecue picnics, reading letters from satisfied customers, holding staff meetings outdoors, and so forth (p. 89). By doing the above positive activities a leader shows that anything is possible when working for those within your organization. The true secret is to make sure the work does not become routine or boring by alternating different motivating activities.

Attracting and keeping employees in a social venture can be challenging. Many assume that people will want to work for a social organization because of the intrinsic reward of helping others. However, it is imperative that social organizations provide extrinsic rewards as well. The pay, benefits, and work environment are often significantly lower in nonprofit organizations than in similar positions in the for-profit arena.

Dees et al. (2001) insist that the intrinsic reward of being involved in an effective organization, to be encouraged to contribute their creativity and energy, to be granted some measure of autonomy and authority, and to be respected by managers and coworkers, is enough to motive them to stay in the organization. By applying these intrinsic rewards in social organizations, potential employees will come to you, and those who are already in place will feel the need to stay (p. 78).

Skill Development

Within many organizations, there are individuals who possess leadership skills. Developing the skills of those potential leaders is significant for any business; doing so maintains employees and reduces costs. Many organizations have employee evaluations that try to determine leadership skills.

An evaluation form should show the positives and negatives of all employees, give their strengths and weaknesses, and show how skills are going to be developed for future growth. No employee is entirely perfect; however, the goal of evaluation and skill development is to nurture the skills employees do have maximum performance.

Dealing with Change

According to Kotter and Cohen (2002), people change what they do because they are shown a truth that influences their feelings rather than being given an analysis that shifts their thinking. This is truer in large-scale organizational change, where new technologies are emerging; mergers and acquisitions are occurring; and restructurings, globalization, and e-business are developing.

Kotter and Cohen have determined that large-scale change occurs in eight stages: push urgency up, put together a guiding team, create the vision and strategies, communicate the vision and strategies effectively, remove barriers to action, accomplish short-term wins, keep pushing for waves of change until the work is done, and, finally, create a new culture to make new behavior permanent (2002, p. 2).

Changing people's behavior is the central challenge. The core problem is behavior: what people do and the need to shift what they do. According to Kotter and Cohen (2002), people need to see a truth to influence the way they feel. Thinking and feeling are essential, and both are found in successful organizations; within change lies the emotions. The flow of see-feel-change creates more power than that of analysis-think-change.

Performance Outcomes Management

Many social enterprises have difficulty maintaining alignment among the resources, activities, and goals of the organization (Wei-Skillern et al., 2007). Social organizations consist of stakeholders, supporters, and clients with differing priorities, purposes, and methods. The managers of these organizations find themselves pulled in many different directions. Many find it a challenge to maintain focus. By using a well-crafted performance management system that is customized to the organization, managers can be successful. Following are three central questions that help articulate a performance framework.

- Which activities are not related to our goals? A well-designed performance system shows which activities are related to the organization's goals, and thus helps to identify and eliminate those activities that do not seem to be very closely related to the organization's main purposes.
- Which goals are not adequately supported by our activities? A good performance system shows which of the organization's purposes do not seem to have enough activities associated with them, thus encouraging development of new ways of trying to achieve the organization's stated purposes.
- What processes need additional improvement? An effective performance system focuses attention on further streamlining and improving the processes that do seem to be working and do seem to be related to the organization's major goals. (p. 341)

As an organization works its way through defining its activities and results, it is building a set of beliefs and hypotheses about important issues. Building a framework can be enormously useful in helping an organization develop a shared understanding of what it is doing and why. The organization is creating a way to remember what it is trying to accomplish; remembering its intentions; and guiding its operational actions, developmental efforts, and investments. With that comes budgeting and allocation of funds.

A performance-based budget (see Figure 9) is an integrated annual performance plan *and* annual budget that shows the relationship between program funding levels and expected results. It indicates that a performance target or a set of targets should be achieved at a given level of spending.

A performance budget formally establishes spending targets (i.e., appropriations) and performance targets, which together form the basis for monitoring all aspects of performance throughout the budget execution cycle. The budget should work in concert with management and the strategic plan. If one part of the system fails, the entire organization will feel the effect.

FIGURE 9   PERFORMANCE BASED BUDGETING

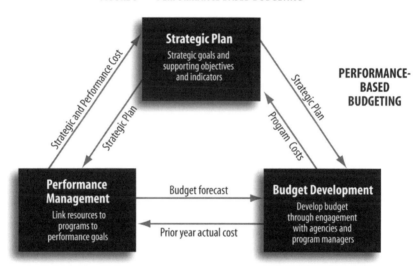

Adapted from SAS, 2006.

The Executive Director and Board Members

The attributes of an executive director are intertwined with the responsibilities of the position. Usually, these individuals have a job description or work list. As these vary from one institution to another, the following are general responsibilities described by Carlson and Donohoe (2002):

As a *visionary*, an executive director is responsible for

- Motivating internal and external stakeholders with a shared picture of the greatness of their nonprofit

- Inspiring passion to achieve what is possible
- Bringing focus to the vision with a strategic plan
- Thinking strategically about the best way to meet community needs
- Evaluating on an ongoing basis the effectiveness of the nonprofit in fulfilling its mission

As a *change agent*, an executive director is responsible for

- Keeping abreast of trends in the nonprofit sector to ensure the organization remains responsive to changing community needs
- Monitoring the nonprofit's internal changes and providing the skills needed to lead, manage, and support the organization at any point in its cycle
- Managing internal change processes by working with stakeholders to set goals and outcomes, create plans, and make change happen
- Persuading and motivating others to accept change as part of the daily routine in the organization, while also acknowledging people's natural resistance to change
- Taking risks by trying new ideas and approaches to achieving the mission

As a *relationship builder*, an executive director is responsible for the following.

- Communicating successfully with internal stakeholders—staff, volunteers, and board
- Managing staff and volunteers in a manner that fosters a healthy culture to ensure that everyone's role on the team is valued and recognized
- Supporting and at times leading the board of directors to ensure its members add value to the organization
- Carrying on the wisdom of the organization's founder while implementing bold new ideas

As a *community creator*, the executive director is responsible for these actions.

- Creating a visible organization with broad stakeholder support
- Communicating with external stakeholders to ensure continuing interest and involvement in the mission
- Building partnerships that further the mission through cooperative efforts and strategic relationships
- Valuing diversity and creating an organizational culture that appreciates and respects differences

As a *resource wizard*, an executive director is in charge of the following.

- Recruiting, mentoring, and recognizing people who raise the funds that allow the organization to thrive
- Communicating and building relationships with funders and donors to gain interest in and support for the mission
- Stewarding and managing funds received so well that the organization's trustworthiness is unquestionable (pp. 5–6)

Little research is conducted on nonprofit executives and boards; however, Herman and Heimovics (1991) investigated the challenges facing chief executive officers (CEOs) and boards of directors of nonprofits. This study centered exclusively on the executive director's or CEO's leadership style and its effect on the survivability of the organization. According to Herman and Heimovics, "Nonprofit chief executives are centrally responsible for the success and failure of their organizations" (p. 128). They acknowledged that this goes against traditional managed-system models that place the authority and responsibility with the board of directors. They countered that effective CEOs will guide the board by using a board-centered leadership style that ensures that board members accept and perform their organization and public fiduciary roles.

Board and Executive Director Partnership

In many nonprofits, boards and executive directors experience tension in their relationship (Herman & Van Til, 1991). In successful enterprises, these individuals tend to work as a team, so the push-pull approach is nonexistent.

Carlson and Donahue (2002) agree, saying that the board should help support community partnerships, while the executive director leads them. The board leads mission-based decisions, while the executive director supports them. It is much easier for boards and executive directors to be successful if their roles are clearly defined. That way, each group knows exactly what is expected of it, instead of one treading on the responsibilities of the other.

Conclusion

The strategies described in this chapter provide a clear road map to leading and managing large nonprofit organizations. The intent of this chapter is to inform as well as to inspire. It is hoped that these strategies will provide leaders—and those who aspire to become leaders—with the tools to define, pursue, and achieve their organizational objectives.

References

Allis, R. P. (2003). *Zero to one million: How to build a company to $1 million in sales.* Durham, NC: Virante, Inc.

Ansoff, H. I. (1979). *Strategic management.* New York: Palgrave McMillan

Barry, B. W. (1986). *Strategic planning workbook for nonprofit organizations.* St. Paul, MN: Amherst H. Wilder Foundation.

Blanchard, K., Zigarmi, P., & Zigarmi, D. (1985). *Leadership and the one minute manager.* New York: William Morrow.

Bossidy, L., Charan, R., & Burck, C. (2002). *Execution: The discipline of getting things done.* New York: Crown Business.

Bozeman, W. & Schmelzer, S. (1984). Strategic planning: Applications in business and education. *Planning and Changing, 15*(1), 35–49.

Bryson, J. M. (1988). *Strategic planning for public and nonprofit organizations: a guide to strengthening and sustaining organizational achievement.* San Francisco: Jossey Bass.

Burns, T., & Stalker, G. M. (1994). *The management of innovation.* New York: Oxford University Press.

Carlson, M. & Donohoe, M. (2002). *The executive director's survival guide: Thriving as a nonprofit leader.* San Francisco: Jossey-Bass.

Collins, J. (2001). *From good to great: Why some companies make the leap and others do not.* New York: HarperBusiness.

Cordes, C. L., & Dougherty, T. W. (1993). A review and integration of research on job burnout. *Academy of Management Review, 18,* 621–656.

Dees, J. G., Emerson, J., & Economy, P. (2001). *Enterprising nonprofits: A toolkit for social entrepreneurs.* New York: John Wiley & Sons.

Dees, J. G., Emerson, J., & Economy, P. (2002). *Strategic tools for social entrepreneurs: Enhancing the performance of your enterprising nonprofit.* New York: John Wiley & Sons.

Greening, D. W., & Turban, D. B., (2002). Corporate social performance as a competitive advantage in attracting a quality workforce. *Business and Society, 39*(3), 254–280.

Gulledge, T. R., & Sommer, R. A., (2005). An introduction to basic enterprise resource planning concepts. *International Journal of Management and Enterprise, 2*(2), 204–218.

Gundry, L. K., & Kickul, J. R. (2006). *Entrepreneurship strategy: Changing patterns in new venture creation, growth, and reinvention.* Thousand Oaks, CA: Sage.

Herman, R., & Heimovics, R. (1991). *Executive leadership in nonprofit organizations: New strategies for shaping executive board dynamics.* San Francisco: Jossey-Bass.

Herman, R., & Van Til, J. (1991) *Do nonprofit boards make a difference?* New Brunswick, NJ: Transaction Books.

Hersey, P. & Blanchard, K. (1982). *Management of organizational behavior: Utilizing human resources.* Upper Saddle River, NJ: Prentice-Hall.

Julnes, P., Berry, F., Aristigueta, M., & Yang, K. (Eds.). (2007). *International handbook of practice-based performance management.* Thousand Oaks, CA: Sage.

Kotter, J. P. (1996). *Leading change.* Cambridge, MA: Harvard Business School Press.

Kotter, J. P., & Cohen, D. S. (2002). *The heart of change: Real-life Stories of how people change their organizations.* Cambridge, MA: Harvard Business School Press.

Kouzes, J. M., & Posner, B. Z. (2007). *The leadership challenge.* San Francisco: Jossey-Bass.

Lawler, E. (1986). *High-involvement management: Participative strategies in improving organizational performance.* San Francisco: Jossey-Bass.

Lesser, E., Fontaine, M., & Slusher, J. (2000). *Knowledge and communities.* Woburn, MA: Butterworth-Heinemann.

Lewis, J. A., Lewis, M. D., Packard, T., & Soufflé, F. (2002). *Management of human service programs.* Florence, KY: Wadsworth.

Nelson, B. (2001). *Please don't just do what I tell you, do what needs to be done: Every employee's guide to making work more rewarding.* New York: Hyperion.

Olson, E. (January, 1995). Organizing for new product development: The moderating role of product innovativeness. *Journal of Marketing, 59*(1), 58.

Pfeffer, J. (1998). *The human equation: Building profits by putting people first.* Cambridge, MA: Harvard Business School Press.

Rainey, H. G., & Steinbauer, P. (1999). Galloping elephants: Developing elements of a theory of effective government organizations. *Journal of Public Administration Research and Theory, 9*(1), 1–32.

Rogers, E. (1964) *Diffusion of innovation* (4th ed.). New York: New York Free Press.

Sagawa, S. & Segal, E. (1999). *Common interest, common good: Creating value through business and social-sector partnerships.* Boston: Harvard Business Press.

SAS. (2006, May). *SAS for performance-based budgeting.* Interactive tour. Retrieved from http://www.sas.com/solutions/pm/

Schumpter, J. A., (1983). *The theory of economic development.* New Brunswick, NJ: Transaction.

Senge, P. (1990). *The fifth discipline: The art & practice of the learning organization.* New York: Doubleday.

Taylor, J. C., & Felten, D. F. (1992). *Performance by design: Sociotechnical systems in North America.* Upper Saddle River, NJ: Prentice Hall.

Van Seters, D. V., & Field, R. H. (1999). The MBA program: Views from a student and a professor. *Journal of Management Education, 13*, 69–71.

Wei-Skillern, J., Austin, J. E., Leonard, H. B., & Stevenson, H. H. (2007). *Entrepreneurship in the social sector*. Thousand Oaks, CA: Sage.

Yankey, J. A. (1995). *Skills for effective nonprofit management*. Hoboken, NJ: Sage.

17

Strategic Planning for Not-for-Profits
A Brief Guide

Philip H. Levy, Joel M. Levy, and Joshua Rubin

Those who look only to the past or present are certain to miss the future.
—John F. Kennedy

Strategic planning can often seem daunting. Careful analysis of an entire organization's portfolio and planning for a point in the distant future can seem overwhelming. The demands of managing a large organization can be a competing force that relegates planning to a backburner. In truth, strategic planning is never an easy thing to do, but it *is* important, and we believe it is critical to a well-functioning, progressive organization and well worth the effort.

Over the past 40 years, policy and program development, devolution, and outsourcing have dramatically changed the not-for-profit community. Strategic planning is an excellent approach to meeting this changing landscape. Using strategic plans as living documents can keep an agency vibrant and evolving to meet dynamic changing needs. In addition, there is a growing need in the United States to justify service funding by demonstrating outcome efficiency and effectiveness. Strategic planning is an excellent way to help achieve this.

To make the process seem less intimidating, we have divided it into six manageable steps. And to make it clearer we have elucidated these generalized steps with specific examples of how we implemented it at YAI/National Institute for People with Disabilities Network (YAI/NIPD), still recognizing that this is but one approach of many that can result in a successful strategic planning process.

YAI/NIPD is an international leader in assisting people with developmental, learning, and other disabilities to achieve their fullest potential through what we term the three *I*s and a *P* (individuality, independence, inclusion, and productivity). YAI/NIPD is a network of seven award-winning not-for-profit health and human services agencies nationally and internationally recognized for excellence and professionalism. We serve more than 20,000 people every day through more than 450 programs and an extraordinary workforce of more than 5,500 talented, dedicated, well-trained professionals.

YAI was founded in 1957 by a small group of concerned parents and a few forward-thinking professionals in the field of human development. They created the Young

Adult Adjustment Center, which grew into the Young Adult Institute and Workshop, Inc. (YAI) when it was incorporated formally in 1964 and eventually became the YAI/NIPD Network. The agency started small, with a single program and several staff, teaching socialization and prevocational skills to seven people and added new programs and services as new needs were identified.

We have always planned how to meet our consumers' needs driven by our mission to serve them by identifying "gaps" in services and creating a plan to match government policy directions with our consumers' needs. This strategic partnership with government, consumers, families, and the community has always been at the nexus of our success.

Why Do It?

Strategic planning requires a great deal of forethought, consensus building, and work. To do it effectively, the busiest (and probably highest salaried) people in an organization must be actively involved, devoting a significant amount of their time (Yankey, 2001) and energy to something that is outside the scope of their day-to-day responsibilities. Difficult, complex, sometimes even painful questions need to be asked and wrestled to consensus. Often diverse input from large groups of stakeholders has to be sought and synthesized. The entire organization needs to be mobilized, and cultures, processes, and people need to be put under a sometimes uncomfortable microscope.

With all the expense of time, money, and emotional energy, why do not-for-profit health and human services providers—often short on both time and money—bother doing strategic planning? Many don't, but many of the most successful have figured out that the cost of not doing it is even higher than the cost of doing it. The absence of a strategic plan often results in the meandering of an organization and a drift away from its mission and primary objectives.

Broadly speaking, there are both internal and external forces providing agencies an incentive to plan strategically. External forces are often the impetus, but once the process is underway, many organizations find that the internal reasons for planning are equally important.

The most obvious reason for organizations to begin a strategic planning process is so that they can meet the agency mission and the changes in the needs of the community they serve (Yankey, 2001). Not-for-profits are set up to meet a particular identified community need, but good administrators will quickly identify related issues that affect their ability to fulfill their mission. Whether incidentally or explicitly, not-for-profit administrators constantly take the pulse of the community they serve and react to the changes they perceive. Sometimes, happily, these changes are the result of organizational successes, when a population served achieves a new level of success that creates a new, higher-level need. Sometimes a particularly intractable problem may force an agency's administration to reconsider the package of services offered in light of the potential to achieve better results through a more efficient strategy.

Another critical external alteration that can prompt a strategic planning process is a change in administration. Many not-for-profits depend primarily on government funding for significant portions of their operating budget. Changes in political administrations can dramatically impact the environment in which a not-for-profit is operating in a number of different ways. Funding levels and priorities may change depending on the organization's congruence with the new administration's ideological outlook, and the regulatory environment in which the organization operates may similarly shift with new leadership in government. As Charles Darwin eloquently put it, "It is not the strongest of the species that survives, nor the most intelligent, but the one most responsive to change." Organizations that wish to survive must pay careful attention to the environmental alterations brought about by policy and leadership changes in government.

And it is not just funding levels and priorities that can change over time. Full-scale changes in funding methodologies can catch an organization flat-footed and unable to meet ongoing obligations despite the appearance that funding levels have remained the same. As foundations and government both look to fund outcomes or levels of productivity, agencies can no longer rest assured that the budget-based rates on which they have come to rely will remain in place. On the other hand, agencies that can anticipate, understand, adjust to, and capitalize on the new funding environment can improve the quality of the services they provide and enhance revenues simultaneously. Every change is an opportunity for reinventing oneself, creativity, and newfound success.

Internal changes can be even more critical causes for strategic reevaluation. Whereas a change in political leadership might have a significant impact on an organization, changes in the organization's leadership will have a huge impact, one which should prompt a rigorous review and an exercise in careful consensus-building.

The biggest change, of course, is an executive leadership change. If that leader was also the founder or builder of the organization, as is often the case in not-for-profits, the need is only heightened, as often people rely on the charisma and vision of the founder for guidance and direction. A new leader will need to create for him- or herself a foundation of legitimacy that is built on group consensus, and a rigorous strategic planning process is a great way to go about building that foundation.

Even in the absence of a new leader, strategic planning can be an important opportunity for an organization to plan for succession and ensure that the next generation of leadership is being identified and groomed. Strategic planning can be an important way by which a leader can create more leaders.

Changes in volunteer leadership likewise are a cause for review and reevaluation. Active, engaged boards of directors are critical components of successful not-for-profit organizations. When the volunteer leadership changes, steps need to be taken to ensure that the board remains a vital and productive component of the equation. A carefully considered plan for addressing the new leadership's priorities can be a valuable mechanism for ensuring collaborative and productive relationships between volunteer leadership and professional staff. The same is true of major supporters. A major new donor likely brings new ideas and priorities to the table along with new funding.

Another important reason to undertake a strategic planning process is to make decisions about priorities and potential areas of growth (Yankey, 2001). Organizations often find themselves torn between different and competing opportunities to serve. Then they must go through the process of determining how best to serve their constituents while ensuring the long-term health of the organization. In these instances a structured planning process is essential to weighing the costs and benefits of different avenues. Choosing between populations to serve, or between services to offer a population, is among the most emotionally difficult things an organization can do for the simple reason that some valid, urgent, and even desperate needs simply will not be met. Every new service an organization provides requires the decision not to provide dozens of others. For all of the stakeholders involved this can create tension, anxiety, and unhappiness. Organizations that make these types of decisions in more haphazard ways, based solely on opportunities that present themselves or snap decisions by a small group of executives, often find that they have drifted from their mission and can no longer offer a coherent vision to their funders, staff, clients, or supporters. That is why a broadly based, stakeholder involved, consensus driven strategic planning process is so critical and is consistent with YAI/NIPD's model of participatory management.

If everything is going well for an organization, its leaders may feel no need to plan. But even in these instances a strategic planning process can be valuable for reenergizing the staff and volunteer leadership. Like a baseball manager calling time-out just to walk to the mound and give the pitcher a pep talk and reconfirm that everyone is on the same page, a strategic planning process can serve as an opportunity to reconfirm a shared mission, values, culture, and vision. More often than not, however, in those instances an organization will learn that they may wish to make a small course correction or take the opportunity to redefine the population they serve or the way in which they serve them.

Another critical reason to undertake a strategic planning process is because of the organizational change it can prompt (Bryson, 1995). In the increasingly competitive environment in which not-for-profit organizations operate, the ability to gather information systematically, track progress rigorously, and make decisions based on data is increasingly critical. The process of creating a strategic plan focuses an organization's leadership on the information they need to run their business efficiently and effectively, creates the mechanisms for data gathering, builds the habits of performance measurement and management, and prepares an organization to make the rapid adjustments that are needed to succeed in a rapidly changing environment (Allison & Kaye, 2005). And it is not just executive staff that needs these critical skills. Distinguished Baruch College professor Frederick Lane emphasizes the important role social workers play in organizational development. "The modern social work professional must be understood as both a service provider and an organizational participant. Understanding and involvement in strategic planning in any organization is essential for both roles" (personal communication, March 12, 2008).

Strategic plans also can be prompted by less momentous factors, such as a milestone anniversary, a year with a round number, a conference someone attended with a session about strategic planning....In the end it doesn't matter what prompts it, the important thing is to engage in it. If you don't, you're leaving your organization's future in the hands of fate. You may succeed nonetheless, but you improve your chances of providing a valuable service to people in need in the most cost-effective, focused, and efficient manner if you invest the time and emotional energy in making the tough decisions and laying the foundation for future success through a rigorous planning process.

The YAI/NIPD Experience

In 2007, our 50th anniversary prompted consideration of a strategic planning process. When we weighed the time and expense against the potential benefit, we realized that many of the previously stated reasons for strategic planning existed for YAI/NIPD.

Changes in Community Need

Two major changes are occurring in the community served by YAI/NIPD. Diagnoses of autism spectrum disorders (ASD) have exploded in the United States. Whereas for many years the prevalence of ASD was estimated at 4 to 5 per 10,000 (Centers for Disease Control and Prevention [CDC], 2007a), the CDC's Autism and Developmental Disabilities Monitoring Network announced in 2007 that 1 in every 150 eight-year-olds in the United States is estimated to have ASD (CDC, 2007b). Even more striking was that the rate in the four counties in New Jersey sampled by the CDC was 1 in every 94 eight-year-olds (CDC, 2007c).

The other major change in the community served by YAI is the lengthening life expectancy of people with intellectual and developmental disabilities. Not long ago there was little cause to consider the needs of older adults with intellectual disabilities (ID); there weren't very many of them. Today, however, as a result of improvements in healthcare and health technology, not only are people with mild ID living longer than ever, but people with severe ID are as well (Horowitz, Kerker, Owens, & Zigler, 2000). The average life expectancy of adults with ID has now reached 66.1 years (Janicki, Dalton, Henderson, & Davidson, 1999). This is still substantially shorter than the 76.5 years that adults in the general population can expect (Horowitz et al., 2000), but children and younger adults with ID can expect to live as long as their peers in the general population, 76.9 years (Fisher & Kettl, 2005).

Change in Administration

After 12 years of Republican George Pataki's administration, 2007 also marked a transition in New York State leadership, as Democrat Eliot Spitzer was sworn in on January 1. One of Governor Spitzer's campaign slogans was "On day one, everything changes," so it was critical that YAI, which relies very heavily on funding from New York State, be prepared for the opportunities and/or threats posed by the new administration.

Changes in Funding Methodologies

YAI began as an agency providing services to people with developmental disabilities through contracts with New York City and State. Today, more than 95% of our revenue still comes from government, but less than 10% comes from contracts with New York State. Some of the growth in other funding sources has come from the creation of new services, such as primary healthcare, which are funded through Medicaid, which now makes up over 60% of our revenue. Much of the growth in Medicaid, however, comes from services that were once under contract with New York State that have been "Medicaided" by the state to increase federal financial participation. This change has occurred gradually over the last decade, but its implications for us are profound. Although the increased federal oversight and audit recoveries have made our funding much less predictable, stepping back to consider our fiscal and political situation nevertheless was very valuable.

Change in Executive Leadership

YAI has been fortunate to have had consistent leadership for nearly 40 years. So a change in executive leadership did not prompt us to develop a strategic plan, but the potential "brain drain" resulting from a significant number of senior leaders approaching retirement age prompted us to make succession planning and accelerated leadership development a key part of our strategic plan. This is consistent with national trends resulting from the aging of professional leadership that came to the field during the deinstitutionalization movement of the mid 1970s.

Competing Priorities and Potential Areas for Growth

We believe that everyone with a disability deserves high-quality services to help them maximize their potential and lead independent, productive, and integrated lives. We serve 20,000 people, but there are many more whom we could help. We could expand our services geographically. We could begin serving people with disabilities outside of the developmental and learning disabilities population we have traditionally served. We could serve people without disabilities whose age presents similar needs and issues and causes them to require assistance. Or, we could stay focused solely on our core constituents. As an organization dedicated to helping, we cannot ignore the fact that more people could benefit from YAI, but we also have to be realistic and realize we cannot serve everyone. Our strategic planning process was invaluable in helping us identify ways to expand our reach while protecting our infrastructure and our core values and services.

Visioning

Dreams are extremely important. You can't do it unless you imagine it.
—George Lucas

The decision to embark on a strategic planning process is a decision to evaluate the direction of an organization. Everything in a strategic plan should flow from the organization's mission and its vision for the future. If you follow Stephen Covey's suggestion and "start with the end in mind," (Wei-Skillern, Austin, Leonard, & Stevenson, 2007, p. 337) you will be sure that everything you do moves you in the best direction possible. As such, the clear articulation of the mission and vision should be a top priority, affected and broadly endorsed by stakeholders, who will be participants in the decision making and implementation process.

People who work in not-for-profit organizations tend to be mission driven. Often their service to their community is a critical component of their identity, and their identification with the organization's consumers is fundamental to their job satisfaction. As a result, conversations about changing (or even just clarifying) the organization's mission, even marginally, are emotionally charged and potentially explosive. The mission is the organization's *why* (Bryson, 1995), so any change to it will need to be broadly endorsed and deeply felt, and the resulting mission statement will need to be clear, explicit, and consistent with the organizational culture.

John Bryson, in his exceptional work, *Strategic Planning for Public and Nonprofit Organizations*, suggests developing a mission statement through reaching consensus answers to six key questions (Bryson, 1995).

1. *Who are you?* This is not the same as what you do, because what you do may change, whereas who you are ought not. If what you do ceased to be necessary, would you fold up shop? No, you would turn your energies to doing something else in service to your community.

2. *What are the problems you exist to address or needs you exist to meet?* Businesses exist to earn money. Not-for-profits exist to meet community needs. Identifying those needs and stating them explicitly is an important piece of the mission drafting process.

3. *What do you do to anticipate the future needs of the people you serve and prepare to meet them?* If you cease to adjust to the changing needs of the people you serve, you will rapidly lose contact with the rationale for your organization's existence. Periodic strategic planning processes are an important opportunity to step back from the day-to-day issues affecting your organization and look proactively at the changing needs they present.

4. *How do you respond to your key stakeholders?* Your organization's health requires that you keep your stakeholders happy. Identifying who they are and how you satisfy them is a critical component of the strategic planning process.

5. *What are your core values?* While these conversations are taking place, organizations should also focus on what they are unwilling to change. What are the core values that make you who you are and that are unalterable without fundamentally undermining yourself? It is important to make those values explicit as a means of establishing parameters for the other conversations, and for aligning your stakeholders with each other and the organization (Allison & Kaye, 2005). This has been called a "values audit," which is a helpful phrase for understanding the nature of the work involved (Pfeiffer, Goodstein, & Nolan, 1986). You might change what you do, but you should try not to change who you are.

6. *What makes you special?* There is no shortage of not-for-profit organizations in the United States. So part of a mission drafting process is identifying the fundamental uniqueness of the group and figuring out how to extend it as far

as possible. If you and your stakeholders are unable to determine what it is about the organization that makes it uniquely valuable to the community you serve, your strategic planning process is likely to fail.

Conversations about the vision for the future also often cut right to the heart of the organization's reason for existing. This is both a potential cause for conflict and a valuable exercise that helps senior management develop the habit of focusing on what is really important. The vision, which is about *where* the organization is going, *what* it should look like, and *how* it should fulfill its mission (Bryson, 1995) should flow directly from your mission. Where you are headed should depend on what it is you're hoping to accomplish. That vision will, in turn, cascade into strategic objectives and initiatives.

Baruch College professor Frederick S. Lane highlights the importance of the visioning exercise.

> Nothing is more important in strategic planning than a consensus on a clear vision for your organization. The questions are fundamental: What should your organization become, say, four years from now? What do your clients need that your organization could provide? (personal communication, March 12, 2008)

University of California professor Michael J. Austin summed up the importance of the vision succinctly. "If you and your organization have no idea of where you are going in the future, how will you ever know if you have arrived?" (personal communication, March 12, 2008)

It is helpful when constructing your vision to ask yourself questions in much the same way you did when you were drafting your mission. John Yankey, in his brilliantly concise and insightful article in the *Encyclopedia of Social Work* suggests a set of 10 questions that can guide a visioning process (Yankey, 2001, p. 2323).

1. What will the organization's future business be?
2. What will the composition and structure of the board be?
3. How large will the organization get?
4. What programs will be run by the organization?
5. What staff will be needed?
6. What volunteers will be needed?
7. What management structure will be necessary?
8. What will the organization's funding mix be?
9. What facilities will the organization have?
10. How will the organization measure success?

It cannot be said often enough that this critical starting point needs to involve as many stakeholders from as broad a cross section as possible (Allison & Kaye, 2005). Implementing the strategic plan will require an enormous amount of hard work and sacrifice from everybody involved. If they do not believe that the boat is headed for a valuable and meaningful shore, they simply won't paddle very hard. That is why it is so essential that every type of stakeholder is involved, from board members to funders to line staff to consumers (Bryson & Alston, 2005). The more people involved in this early stage, the less resistance to change you will experience down the road.

Once you have broad consensus on why you exist and what you want the organization to be, you have a powerful tool. By comparing where you are now with where you hope to be, you can begin to identify the changes that will be necessary to reach your goals (Allison & Kaye, 2005). The clarity that can emerge from the foggy process of negotiating these complicated and emotionally charged statements is remarkable, and can be very compelling to the people who care about your organization and the people it serves.

The YAI/NIPD Experience

When we began our strategic planning process we looked carefully at our mission statement, and we noticed something unsurprising. In the years since it had been written, it had become somewhat dated. Not only had the language we use to speak about the work we do and the people we serve changed substantially, but the parameters of the people we serve had changed somewhat too. Not that we no longer served people with intellectual disabilities, but over the years we had expanded our scope to include people with developmental delays, learning disabilities, physical disabilities, mental illness, and a broad range of other developmental disabilities. We had also expanded our services from the young adults with whom we began to the full life cycle from infants to older adults. To be sure, the vast preponderance of the people we serve continue to be the people for whose benefit the organization was founded, but we had identified many other people who could benefit from our services, and we were assisting them and their families in numerous ways. This was, for the most part, taken for granted, but once we made it explicit through the process of reevaluating our mission, it opened up a wide range of new possibilities.

Remarkably, when we worked through the process to arrive at a vision for our future, our mission was substantially unchanged. Fortunately, we had set very ambitious goals for ourselves, so we have achieved extraordinary things without reaching a plateau. The point on the horizon toward which we had been aiming remained on the horizon and continued to be endorsed by a broad cross section of our stakeholders. Despite the expansion of our mission, the vision of leadership we had for ourselves was consistent.

Similarly, but unremarkably, we found that the values we had established for ourselves decades earlier continued to be values that were broadly shared and deeply held by our leadership, staff, consumers, and other stakeholders. Some of the language seemed out of date, but the timelessness of the concepts and our unflinching adherence to them remained unchanged. In fact, we've literally carved them in stone and placed them in every one of our facilities.

Doing this enabled us to envision the future state and identify the changes we would need to make to our organization to reach that state. With the emotionally challenging work completed, we could turn our attention to gathering and analyzing as much data as possible.

Data Gathering

We can have facts without thinking but we cannot have thinking without facts.

—John Dewey

At this stage of the process, developing a strategic plan becomes a lot like making a fine French sauce. When you're cooking a classically complex sauce you start by adding a wide variety of different ingredients with different flavors that will complement each other. Then you cook it down until your massive pot filled with food has become a small pool of sauce that contains the essence and flavor of everything that went into it.

And so it is with strategic planning. You need to gather an enormous amount of data so that you know as much as possible about what will aid and hinder you as you aim at your future. Every piece of information you can muster about your organization, its finances, its programs, its supporters, and its flaws will help you navigate toward your objective. If you do this analysis carefully and rigorously, you can avoid developing good strategies to solve the wrong problem (Bryson & Alston, 2005). Likewise, everything you can learn about the environment in which you are operating will help you craft a plan that is ambitious yet feasible.

At this stage, two types of analyses are critical: internal and external SWOT (strengths, weaknesses, opportunities, threats) analyses. For both, it is critical to cast as wide a net as possible and to make the difficult decision to be as candid and realistic as you can be (Abraham, 2006).

To conduct an internal SWOT analysis, look at your organization with brutal honesty. How does what you're doing line up with your mission? (Wei-Skillern et al., 2007) What do you do well? What are your core competencies as an organization? What are the key physical resources you have at your disposal? What are your best human resources? Contrarily (and here's where it's really important to be honest), what are you lousy at? What pieces of your organization just don't function very well? Are there departments that are losing money? Are there people who aren't getting the job done? Have your human resource needs changed (Lewis, Lewis, Packard, & Soufflée, 2001)? Are some clients not making the type of progress you want to see them make? Do the opportunities and threats stem from your strengths and weaknesses? Are there prospects for growth built on the foundation of your core strengths? Are there stresses on your organization as a result of the weaknesses you identified? Where is there a strong foundation without a lot built on it? Where are there weak underpinnings with a lot riding on them? Do you have the necessary administrative, financial, and human capacity (Allison & Kaye, 2005)?

Here again it is important to involve a large number of people. None of you is as smart as all of you, so if you're looking for nuance, you're more likely to find it with lots of eyes on the puzzle. And it's critical to create a situation in which all of the people involved feel comfortable telling the hard truths. A sugar-coated SWOT analysis will make everyone feel good, but it won't help you make a successful plan. Whether or not you admit your weaknesses, they're there. And if you don't admit to having them, you surely won't succeed in fixing them.

That same level of brutal frankness should be brought to your external SWOT analysis. Here it is important to consider not just the variables affecting your organization, but also the issues affecting the people your organization serves. Furthermore, it is critical to identify the factors affecting your industry as a whole (Abraham, 2006). Look carefully at your funding environment. Are there structural changes in the economic environment in which you are operating (Abraham, 2006)? How diversified is your funding? Is money drying up? Are there additional sources of revenue that you could access? Are your clients experiencing new types of problems that you're not equipped to deal with? Contrarily, are your clients no longer experiencing an issue that you've focused a lot of resources on? Are there emerging groups of people who could benefit from what you offer? Are there likely donors you haven't contacted? Gather as much information and data as you can so that you know your environment inside and out. Be prepared to admit that some of the things you do well, and that you hoped to do more of, do not make sense in the current operating atmosphere.

Again, these processes have multiple layers of value. Not only are you gathering the information you need to successfully complete your plan, you are introducing to the leadership of your organization a set of habits and frameworks that will improve their long-term ability to stay ahead of emerging trends. As with everything related to the process of strategic planning, you're making a valuable set of tools available to your organization that will pay significant dividends for years to come.

The YAI/NIPD Experience

To conduct our internal SWOT analysis we sent a brief survey to a large portion of our management team. We asked them to tell us what they were experiencing and what they saw coming down the road. We had them prioritize the areas in which they saw opportunity as well as those in which they anticipated trouble. We were able to do this all with an online survey tool, which made it much easier to process and analyze the information as it arrived. Because we had such a large sample size, patterns emerged clearly and avenues to pursue became self-evident.

The external SWOT analysis was similarly robust. By looking at trends in our major funding sources and in the epidemiology of the disabilities we serve, we were able to identify patterns that were too clear to ignore. The rise in ASD diagnoses, the dramatic increases in life expectancy for people with Down syndrome and other intellectual and developmental disabilities, and the ballooning real estate prices in New York City were all external factors that would inevitably impact what we do, how we do it, and for whom. Major ideological shifts in the state agencies that fund us posed significant threats to some of the services we provide, but also provided potential opportunities in some other parts of our agency. Newly passed laws opened doors for us that had not existed before.

In short, taking the time to pull in an enormous amount of information about ourselves, our clients, and our environment enabled us to see things clearly that we otherwise might have missed. Equally importantly, we realized that some things that had seemed really critical were distractions and invested the time and energy that would have gone to them much more efficiently.

Strategizing

Strategy without tactics is the slowest route to victory.
Tactics without strategy is the noise before defeat.
—Sun Tzu

Now that you have all of the ingredients in your pot, you need to cook them down into the exquisitely balanced, multilayered sauce that will move your organization into a brighter future. This is where all the pieces you've constructed come together.

Look at your vision for the desired future state of your organization. Think about what needs to change to get you there. Figure out how you can build on your organizational strengths to make progress while you shore up your weaknesses and navigate the shifting environment. The key here is synthesizing (Abraham, 2006). What are the critical (but possible) things that need to happen to make that vision a reality? Make sure you don't lose sight of the mission. You will never get buy-in if you don't have the needs of the people you serve as a touchstone.

The objective here is to come up with a few key vision elements that flow directly from your mission (Bryson, 1995) through your vision, and that also take into consideration the organization's capacity and the environmental factors that will affect your ability to succeed (Bryson & Alston, 2005; see Figure 1). The more you are able to refine all of this into just a couple overarching themes, the easier it will be for you to develop support from the internal and external stakeholders who will determine your success. It is essential here to agree on the core ways in which you will move toward your vision (Allsion & Kaye, 2005).

FIGURE 1   STRATEGIC PLANNING STRUCTURE

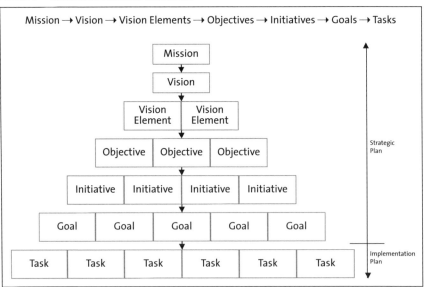

This is no time to think small. You should focus on finding big, audacious goals that are consistent with your vision and clearly related to improving the lives of the people you serve. There should be no doubt in your mind, or anyone else's, that if you accomplish these few things that you will achieve your vision. These will form the core strategies that will drive your organization during the upcoming years (Allison & Kaye, 2005), so they are very important.

During this process many issues will be raised that may not clearly be strategic, but seem critical. Identifying which of them are in fact strategic is essential to ensuring that the process stays on track. Yankey proposes a three-part test for ascertaining whether something is a legitimately strategic issue (Yankey, 2001).

1. Is the issue likely to have an impact on how you carry out your mission?
2. Does the issue require a response from the organization that requires a commitment of human and financial resources?
3. Is there a reasonable expectation that the organization can have an influence on it?

Issues that do not pass the first two tests but pass the third are likely tactical or operational issues that are probably extraneous to the process underway. Although it is critical to ensure that they do not distract you from the strategic issues with which you are struggling, it is equally important not to lose track of them. For many people involved in the process, they will be the things that affect them most on a day-to-day basis, so they will think them critical. If you can address these issues, they will be energized and see additional value in the planning process. You may wish to create a separate team empowered to address these tactical issues so that the strategic planning process can continue unimpeded by the challenges of day-to-day operations (Bryson & Alston, 2005).

Once you have them, the key is to break your goals down into manageable objectives. People need bite-sized pieces or they will be overwhelmed by the size and scope of your plans. Your objectives are likely to seem somewhat vague. They won't be easily measured, but each will be conceptually coherent and have prima facie validity that achieving them will lead to the success of your vision.

This is another place in the process where you will need to reach out broadly to the people needed to implement the plan once it is finalized. If you share responsibility for developing plans with people, they will have ownership of them when it is time for the rubber to hit the road. The more success you have now in working with your colleagues to map out how A leads to B leads to C, the more likely they will be willing to roll up their sleeves and do the meticulous work of implementation planning when the time comes.

Out of these strategic objectives you will need to form initiatives. Break them down still further into the component efforts that must be undertaken to bring them to fruition. These need to be discrete projects assigned to specific people. They should be clearly defined and explicitly stated. Again, the validity of your logic and the comprehensiveness of your plan should be transparent. These initiatives are the building blocks you will use to reach your objectives. It is important to ensure that the initiatives are simple and coherent enough to be implemented within the organizational confines. National Association of Social Workers (NASW) Executive Director Betsy Clark points to a common reason that strategic planning processes fail: "Too often, the strategic plan is grandiose, unmanageable for the staff and available resources" (personal communication, March 17, 2008).

This part of the process is often frustrating. It is not easy. Translating lofty visions into tangible projects can feel like a daunting task. Often people will go around and around, not feeling they are making progress, until there is a sudden "Aha!" moment when the pieces suddenly fall into place. Once you have them, you may find yourself wondering what was so difficult about creating them in the first place. If you do, it's a sign you've done a good job. If they seem obvious to you, they'll seem logically sound to everyone else, and that's what you want. They should be so well-matched that people imagine they are separate pieces of a single whole (Abraham, 2006).

The YAI/NIPD Experience

Our internal SWOT analysis had identified the quality of our services, the commitment of our staff, the excellence of our support departments, and our culture of innovation as the primary strengths of our organization. On the other side of the coin, we identified our heavy reliance on increasingly uncertain and bureaucratically complex government funding, the difficulty of attracting and retaining staff of the caliber our consumers deserve, and the difficulty of implementing new technology solutions as our primary weaknesses and threats.

With those data points in mind we identified three key things we would need to do to achieve our vision of national and international leadership of the field:

1. Maintain and enhance our reputation for excellence, which is built on the quality of our services, staff, technology, materials, and professional activities.
2. Enhance and diversify our funding sources while maintaining the pace of our growth.
3. Remain innovative by identifying new vistas to explore and being one of the foremost providers of new programming.

If we succeed at all three, we will clearly achieve our mission, which is to help people with developmental, learning, and other disabilities and their families improve the quality of their lives through the provision of excellent services, programs, advocacy, and professional education.

From there we crafted nine strategic objectives. Some are focused on continuing to improve on the things we already do well, and others target new services for new clients. In looking at them now, they flow so naturally from the vision elements that they seem inevitable, but that is the result of a lot of hard work and countless discarded drafts.

Those nine strategic objectives flow into 23 strategic initiatives. Each initiative is clear, explicit, and owned by a member of the management team.

Goal Setting

Plans are only good intentions unless they immediately degenerate into hard work.
—Peter Drucker

Up to this point in the process, strategic planning has been lofty, aspirational, and comfortably vague. This is where things change. This is where you come back down to earth. This is where, in the words of NASW Executive Director Betsy Clark, you need to "translate the strategic plan into a business plan" (personal communication, March 17, 2008).

In the absence of measurable goals, neither you nor anyone in your organization will know whether you have achieved your strategic initiatives. If you don't attach meaningful, measurable goals to your initiatives, you will be able to look back in 5 years and declare that you have succeeded regardless of whether any progress has been made. These goals should be expansive enough to capture the broad sweep of the initiatives, but tight enough to leave no room for debate whether they have been reached. And of course, they should be tied to the initiatives closely enough that there is no way to reach the goals without succeeding at the initiatives.

At this point in the process, for the first time, you need not worry about casting a wide net and getting lots of input from people with varied viewpoints. Right now your key constituents are only those people who are responsible for the strategic initiatives. *They* have to set the goals and be held accountable for them (Allison & Kaye, 2005). They will probably need your assistance and your gentle nudging to ensure that the goals are SMART (specific, measurable, achievable, relevant and time-bound). They may be hesitant to commit themselves to such clearly defined structures, because they may be afraid of the consequences of failing to reach them. There is something undeniably comfortable about the haziness of immeasurability. There is something undeniably uncomfortable about being publicly accountable for reaching a number or meeting a clear timeline.

To add to the discomfort, the goals should be outcome measures, rather than process measures, which means that your colleagues will have even less direct control over whether they reach them (Lewis et al., 2001).

And yet, unless you are successful in having your colleagues set these goals and commit to reaching them, the strategic plan will be little more than a set of good intentions, and good intentions don't pave the road to success. If, however, you do succeed, you will have created the structure to do two critical things for your organization. First, the measurable goals will map out the very tangible pathway for reaching your lofty vision and delivering on your mission. Second, and equally as important, they will inculcate in your organizational culture the rigorous performance management practices that ensure ongoing success in an increasingly complex environment. This is the time in the process during which the management of your organization must come to understand that performance measurement is central to their job, not some fashionable trend that will soon disappear (Julnes, Berry, Aristigueta, & Yang, 2008).

Once you have achieved agreement on measurable goals, you will need to ensure that the internal structures are created to measure them. This is a critical step that does not need to be as complicated as it can often seem. Many here will have a tendency to try to create a perfect, and perfectly elegant, automated system for measuring and reporting on all of the goals. That would be nice; but the key is to have the essential data captured and available for analysis. If a simple spreadsheet will do, there is no need to create anything more elaborate and administratively burdensome.

Once your goals have been set and agreed on, all that is left to do is create a document.

When doing so, keep your audiences in mind. Your primary audiences are the managers and staff of the organization who will have to implement the plan and the professional and volunteer leadership who will have to endorse the plan. You want the staff to use and refer to the document frequently. If it sits on a shelf collecting dust, it is unlikely to be implemented successfully. And you want the leaders of the organization to actually read it, so they will know what they've agreed to see the organization do. Both of those things will happen if you do one key thing. **Make it short.** If it is brief, accessible, and user-friendly, the busy people who are your core audiences will find it much more useful than if it is cumbersome and lengthy (Allison & Kaye, 2005).

The YAI/NIPD Experience

YAI is fortunate in that the work we do with our consumers is goal and data driven. For years we have been establishing measurable treatment plans for our consumers and meticulously tracking their progress in achieving their goals. Because most of our senior management grew up in the agency and worked in our programs, they tended to be comfortable with the concept. They may not have been thrilled about committing themselves to public outcome measures, but they were capable of doing so, and with only a moderate amount of nudging, they did.

The bigger challenge, by far, was distilling the document down into something easily readable and simple to understand. We had collected so much information, done so much research, gathered so many ideas, and had so much input that creating a terse, 35-page plan was quite a challenge.

Roll Out

The function of leadership is to produce more leaders, not more followers.
—Ralph Nader

When rolling out your strategic plan there are two critical, and yet seemingly contradictory, things that need to happen. The first is that the leadership of the organization not just endorses, but also actively and enthusiastically promotes the plan. People throughout the organization need to know that the leadership is invested in implementing the plan; otherwise it will be too easy for them to put the plan on a bookshelf in their office and go back to doing whatever it was that they were doing before.

Whether the plan is rolled out at a big meeting or through lower key methods, it is essential to its success that the message is clear: Senior management thinks this is a priority and will be tracking progress and rewarding success.

However, it is just as critical that people throughout the organization feel a sense of ownership of the plan. If it is perceived as being something that is senior management's (or even worse, the author's) responsibility, the plan will be marginalized. This is where the wide net you cast as you began the process is so valuable. The extent to which people see some echoes of their efforts in the plan is the extent to which they will sell it to themselves and save you the trouble. If you have successfully engaged people in the process, they will already be committed to it (Allison & Kaye, 2005).

Ideally, the roll out will generate some "buzz" in the organization. More importantly, it will generate action. If people get excited about it and start trying to craft ways of reaching the goals, you will unleash the creative potential of your colleagues and significantly improve your chances of success.

The YAI/NIPD Experience

We rolled out our strategic plan at our annual management forum. Our president announced its completion to our 400 assembled managers and gave a very brief preview of what it held. Everyone in the room had heard about it before, and most of them had played at least some role in creating it, so nobody was surprised.

We then sent the executive summary out as an attachment to our Monthly Management Message. In this way everybody could review it at their leisure and absorb the nuances.

Most importantly, because each individual initiative has an "owner" from our senior or executive leadership, the plan became a topic of conversation at staff meetings throughout the agency. In this way, it became a part of the fabric of day-to-day life for people at all levels.

Implementation

Vision without implementation is hallucination.

—Benjamin Franklin

Once the plan is written and the rollout is complete, the temptation is to declare success and take a vacation. That would be a tremendous mistake. As eminent University of California professor Michael J. Austin bluntly puts it, "Strategic planning makes no sense unless considerable time is spent implementing the plan which means job functions must change to take into account the new directions (not just implementing the plan on top of 'business as usual')" (personal communication, March 12, 2008). If the plan is going to be turned into action and the goals are to be reached, the discrete tasks that need to be performed must be identified, and progress on them needs to be tracked. Big ideas have to be turned into operational steps, and the focus you achieved during the planning process has to be maintained (Allison & Kaye, 2005). Here is where strategic planning transcends itself and becomes strategic management (Bryson, 1995).

It is up to the leaders of each initiative to determine the tasks and resources needed to reach the goals and to work with their team members to assure success (Abraham, 2006). It is up to the leaders of the organization to track progress toward the goals and hold the leaders of the initiatives accountable for reaching them on a consistent, prearranged basis (Lewis et al., 2001).

This is not to say that the plan drafters' job is done. As soon as the plan is completed, it will likely need to be revised. It needs to be a dynamic, living document. Strategic planning is not something that stops and starts again 3 years later. Strategic planning should flow into strategic management, which in turn leads again to strategic planning (Bryson, 1995). As the organization gains experience and learns new things about itself and its environment, it should constantly correct its course (Abraham, 2006). Like a sailor trimming the sail to stay on course for the point she has selected on the horizon, strategic planners need to be constantly taking in new information that becomes available and using it to keep the organization aimed at its vision for the future. NASW Executive Director Betsy Clark points out that if you adhere too strictly to the plan, "great opportunities may be missed"; but if you are flexible in your implementation, "management can take advantage of emerging trends, market factors, and opportunities" (personal communication, March 17, 2008).

NASW New York City Chapter Executive Director Robert Schachter, in reflecting on his experience with a flexible and carefully crafted strategic planning process said,

> the plan put us onto a more defined and relevant track than we would otherwise have been on, and it sparked ideas that we had not originally considered when the plan was being devised. As a result we can say that the plan was not at all stagnant but changed as we learned from experience. We have a stronger and smarter organization as a result. (personal communication, March 17, 2008)

Strategic planning should cease to be something special or different or momentous. It should be an everyday habit (Bryson & Alston, 2005) as your strategies become part of your everyday operations (Lewis et al., 2001). Gathering information about the environment, obtaining broad stakeholder input, carefully analyzing the strengths and weaknesses of the organization, setting measurable goals and tracking progress toward them, and implementing discrete tasks in pursuit of the organization's mission should all be reflexive acts. When staff at all levels of your organization think strategically about how best to meet the needs of the people you serve as habitually as they come to work in the morning, then you can declare success…and take a well-deserved vacation.

The YAI/NIPD Experience

While the individual initiative leaders were left to break up the tasks and motivate their teams as they saw fit, the leadership of the organization carefully tracked progress toward the goals. The performance measures that were agreed on were reported to the executive leadership routinely and to the board of directors annually. The monthly extended cabinet meetings became a forum at which team leaders could report on their progress and enlist the support of their colleagues.

Conclusion

If one thinks, one must reach conclusions.
—Helen Keller

As you can tell, strategic planning is not primarily about creating a strategic plan. It is about a strategic planning process, strategic management, and creating a strategic organization. If it were just a question of writing a plan, it would be easy. It would also be unimportant, irrelevant, and have little impact. Not-for-profits exist, of course, for the people they serve. Unless your strategic planning process ultimately affects their lives, you need not bother doing it. If, however, you cast a wide enough net to take in the broad range of perspectives and ideas of your stakeholders and then distill it all down into a tight, coherent, ambitious plan with meaningful and measurable outcomes, then you can position your organization to have a positive impact on people's lives for years to come. And that makes all the hard work meaningful and worthwhile.

References

Abraham, S. C. (2006). *Strategic planning: A practical guide for competitive success.* Mason, OH: Thomson South-Western.

Allison, M., & Kaye, J. (2005). *Strategic planning for nonprofit organizations: A practical guide and workbook* (2nd ed.). Hoboken, NJ: John Wiley & Sons.

Bryson, J. M. (1995). *Strategic planning for public and nonprofit organizations: A guide to strengthening and sustaining organizational achievement.* San Francisco: John Wiley & Sons.

Bryson, J. M., & Alston, F. K. (2005). *Creating and implementing your strategic plan: A workbook for public and nonprofit organizations,* (2nd ed.). San Francisco: John Wiley & Sons.

Centers for Disease Control and Prevention (CDC). (2007b). CDC releases new data on autism spectrum disorders (ASDs) from multiple communities in the United States. Retrieved August 31, 2007, from http://www.cdc.gov/od/oc/media/pressrel/2007/r070208.htm

Centers for Disease Control and Prevention (CDC). (2007a). Frequently asked questions—prevalence. Retrieved August 31, 2007, from http://www.cdc.gov/ncbddd/autism/faq_prevalence.htm

Centers for Disease Control and Prevention (CDC). (2007c). *Prevalence of the autism spectrum disorders in multiple areas of the United States, surveillance years 2000 and 2002: A report from the Autism and Developmental Disabilities Monitoring (ADDM) Network.* Retrieved August 31, 2007, from http://www.cdc.gov/od/oc/media/pressrel/2007/f070208.htm

Fisher, K., & Kettl, P. (2005). Aging with mental retardation: Increasing population of older adults with MR require health interventions and prevention strategies. *Geriatrics, 60*(4), 26–29.

Horowitz, S. M., Kerker, B. D., Owens, P. L., & Zigler, E. (2000). *The health status and needs of individuals with mental retardation.* New Haven, CT: Yale University. Retrieved July 27, 2007, from http://www.specialolympics.org/NR/rdonlyres/e5lq5czkjv5vwulp5lx5tmny4mcwhyj 5vq6euizrooqcaekeuvmkg75fd6wnj62nhlsprlb7tg4gwqtu4xffauxzsge/healthstatus_n eeds.pdf

Janicki, M. P., Dalton, A. J., Henderson, C. M., & Davidson, P. W. (1999). Mortality and morbidity among older adults with intellectual disability: Health service considerations. *Disability and Rehabilitation, 21*, 284–294.

Julnes, P. de L., Berry, F. S., Aristigueta, M. P., & Yang, K. (2008). *International handbook of practice-based performance management.* Thousand Oaks, CA: Sage.

Pfeiffer, J. W., Goodstein, L., & Nolan, T. (1986). *Applied strategic planning: A how to do it guide.* San Diego, CA: University Associates.

Wei-Skillern, J., Austin, J. E., Leonard, H., & Stevenson, H. (2007). *Entrepreneurship in the social sector.* Thousand Oaks, CA: Sage.

Yankey, J. A. (2001). Strategic planning. In R. L. Edwards. J. G. Hopps, et al. (Eds.), *Encyclopedia of social work* (19th ed.). Washington, DC: NASW Press.

V   Managing Social Work Education

Leon H. Ginsberg

The concluding part of this book focuses on social work in higher education from a variety of viewpoints. Chapter 18, written by the book's editor, deals with social work education management.

In fact, social work education is one site of a significant amount of social work management and leadership, although little has been published about it. The market for books about social work education management is relatively small, although some doctoral programs offer courses on social work education and its management and include courses from education schools in their curricula.

The Council on Social Work Education, this book's publisher, is the leading developer of materials for social work education, a role it has played throughout its history. Since its early days, it has published and distributed material for social work teachers—case materials, bibliographies, suggested syllabi, and books on specialized subjects. This book follows that tradition and is one of the few that deals with managing social work education programs.

Mark Ezell of the University of Kansas wrote chapter 19 on teaching financial management to social work students, an important subject that is often omitted from educational programs. Ezell is a longtime social work management educator.

Jeanette Takamura's reflections on the role of the graduate social work education program dean—or, as is the case in many programs, director or department chair—comprise chapter 20. It is fitting that her background includes a lengthy career as a public administrator in the U.S. government's Administration on Aging and as the chief executive officer of the profession's first school of social work. Columbia University School of Social Work, originally the New York School of Social Work, began it all in 1898, and she carries forward the tradition in one of the profession's most highly regarded educational institutions.

Bachelor's degree social work, which has existed for almost as long as graduate social work education, became an accredited part of the profession in the 1970s and also has a distinguished history. Michael Daley, director of the BSW program at the University of South Alabama, has a long career in both undergraduate and graduate social work education. He is also one of social work's rural practice theoreticians. He is part of a large cadre of bachelor's program directors throughout the United States. Chapter 21 reflects on that career.

Some of social work's most venerable education institutions are historically Black colleges and universities (HCBUs), a group that has not been extensively described in recent social work literature. Rufus Sylvester Lynch, Jacquelyn Mitchell, and Eugene Herrington, the authors of chapter 22, have extensive experience in those institutions and have involved many of them in thinking about their roles and their distinctive contributions to social work. The profession has a chronic shortage of African American social work practitioners and educators to serve the disproportionately large African American clientele. Many of the most notable African American social workers and leaders of the profession are graduates of HBCUs.

Most of the HBCU schools of social work had their origins before the civil rights movement and before social work schools began heavily recruiting minority faculty and students. In those early days, before the 1960s, many schools of social work were segregated; they could not and did not admit African American students or employ African American faculty.

How HBCUs fit into the new environment is part of the subject matter of the chapter. Part of the impressions the authors communicate come from the efforts of Dr. Lynch, former dean of the Clark Atlanta University School of Social Work and a man with a distinguished career in state government, to mobilize and survey the nation's HBCUs with social work programs, an effort that had not been mounted in recent years and that can make an enormous difference in the profession.

Stanley Blostein's chapter (23) is about research he conducted with associate deans of schools of social work. His work is either a pioneering effort or one whose precedence was long ago. Assistants and associates play difficult and ambiguous roles in social work practice and education. Many of them think their titles convey more authority than they are able to exercise, a source of frustration for them and for those with whom they work. Many are relied on for the basic functions of their schools. Blostein based his chapter on a survey of this large and important group of educators.

The final chapter of Part V, chapter 24, is by Paul R. Keyes, a longtime social work manager and higher education leader whose experiences in the higher levels of university administration are among the few that social workers hold.

18

Some Special Characteristics of Management in Social Work Education

Leon H. Ginsberg

Few materials are written about managing and working within the social work education enterprise, which is actually one of the larger areas of employment for the profession. The 40,000 or more students who study social work each year also constitute a major population within the profession.

Although most graduates of social work doctoral programs take positions in higher education, few formal courses are taught about functioning within those programs. Many learn what they need as kinds of apprentices, studying their major professors and their roles, working as graduate assistants, or teaching courses in the programs in which they are studying.

In addition, social work programs have traditionally used large numbers of part-time or adjunct instructors to teach graduate and undergraduate students. The employment of part-time educators is a growing trend, commensurate with the minimal growth in the cadre of full-time educators in many colleges and universities.

Teaching as a graduate student or part-time instructor is not always realistic preparation for full-time employment as a faculty member. New faculty who have such experiences often say their years of part-time teaching were not relevant preparation for being a faculty member.

In essence, higher education, including social work education, represents a culture that is unknown to most of those who work outside academic settings. Nonacademics who encounter faculty members often say, "Okay, so you're a college teacher." Most faculty members nod in agreement, but they know that teaching is only a part, sometimes a minor part, and the often the least demanding of their responsibilities.

Social work education takes place in institutions of higher education, which are usually named colleges or universities. There are no clear distinctions between colleges and universities. Traditionally, universities were more diverse institutions with a variety of professional schools and colleges as well as traditional units dealing with undergraduate and graduate education in the natural, physical, and social sciences and the humanities. In modern terminology, some small institutions—with fewer than 1,000 students—are named universities. So size and complexity are no longer measures of the distinctions between colleges and universities.

Social work programs in the United States may be termed colleges or, more commonly, schools of social work. Some social work programs are departments within colleges of arts and sciences or in some other kind of unit such as a college of health or health and human services.

In general, social work programs that offer only undergraduate degrees such as bachelor of social work are departments within colleges rather than independent colleges or schools themselves. Some programs that offer master's and doctoral degrees may be their own colleges or schools, although some are departments or divisions within colleges. Higher education is a large industry, and each institution has its own system of administration and structure.

Institutions are also governed differently, depending on their orientation, either public or private (many private institutions are also sectarian and are governed by a religious body) and the state government. In North Carolina and Wisconsin, for example, all state institutions are part of the University of North Carolina or the University of Wisconsin, which have presidents. Chancellors, who report to the presidents, direct the campuses. It is more common for institutions to have their own boards of trustees or directors, who are the ultimate managerial authority for the campuses. Every state has a coordinating or governing board that exercises authority over all of the public institutions and, in some states, must approve even private institutions.

To offer education and degrees, colleges and universities should be accredited by one of the regional accrediting bodies that are recognized by the federal and state governments. Education of all kinds is, in the United States, a function of state governments rather than federal. Some states permit unaccredited institutions or institutions that are accredited by some entity other than one of the regional accrediting bodies. Social work education is accredited by the regional bodies, through their own institutions as well as by the Council on Social Work Education. For a detailed discussion of social work education, see *Social Work Evaluation* (Ginsberg, 2001).

Staff and Supervision

Supervising employees in higher education management differs from those encounters in other kinds of social work management and leadership. Most of these differences are associated with the nature of higher education and the rules and norms under which it operates.

Unknown to most social workers who are not involved in academic life is that, in many ways, professors are guaranteed a high degree of autonomy, which is commensurate with their usual extensive education at doctoral levels and higher education's expectation that professors will write and teach their own beliefs, called academic freedom. Although there are many social work educators whose highest degree is a master's, the increasingly common standard is a PhD or doctor of social work degree.

The requirement for permanent appointment, which is as little as 6 months in social agency personnel policies, is typically 7 years or longer for social work professors.

That is, perhaps, the longest probationary employment of all the occupations and professions, especially those in social welfare.

To achieve permanent appointment, normally called tenure in the specialized language of higher education, which is generally better protected than in other professional work, probationary professors, who usually begin their work as instructors or assistant professors need to accomplish enough to be promoted to the next higher professorial rank, usually associate professor.

Promotion Criteria

Each college or university spells out its criteria for promotion, which are often connected with awarding tenure, for which standards are also spelled out in detail. Depending on the institution, the criteria for promotion and tenure generally include some degree of achievement in teaching, research (often predicated on publication of materials in scholarly sources such as journals and textbooks), and service, which may include service to the community and to the institution. The extent of these expectations varies among institutions. Among the more demanding ones, both public and private, satisfying the research expectations is daunting for many faculty, who are expected to complete significant numbers of scholarly articles in well-regarded publications or scholarly books. Such schools tend to expect faculty to consume as much as half of their workloads doing research and scholarship. Institutions more oriented to teaching have less demanding expectations for research and scholarship but require extensive teaching—perhaps four or five courses per semester compared to two courses in the more research- and scholarship-oriented schools. Quality teaching is almost always expected, but faculty can achieve that. In addition, it is easier for social work educators to attain service credentials than to conduct research and scholarship, which, in many institutions, is the most important and most difficult area to satisfy.

In addition to publishing research, some institutions give credence to obtaining external support in the form of grants and contracts from state and federal organizations and private foundations. Most of such contracts have some elements of research, so they may be given credit as research and scholarship.

Decisions about promotion and tenure are often made by multiple groups—a departmental or school committee (sometimes consisting only of those above the rank to which the faculty member aspires); a university- or college-wide committee, one or more deans and perhaps vice-presidents of the institution; and, ultimately, the president or chancellor and the board of trustees or directors. All of these decision makers, in turn, are influenced by perspectives from faculty colleagues and, increasingly, by evaluations issued by external referees—that is, senior faculty at comparable institutions.

The crucial nature and intensity of these employment issues is so great that the relationship between faculty members and their nominal managers such as social work deans or program directors is looser than one sees in other leadership and management relationships. In some ways, faculty members are independent agents, nearly entrepreneurs, for much of their work life. Although some colleges and universities are unionized, most are not, in part because of the unique relationships between management and employees. Although managers are able to assign teaching and some administrative duties, such as committee service, to faculty, day-to-day supervision is nominal. The institution normally requires faculty to maintain office hours, but those are often limited to perhaps 4 or 5 per week. The rest of the time, faculty members are free to work at home, in libraries, or wherever they choose. Some, usually with permission of those to whom they report and to higher levels of the institution's administration, may engage in paid consultation or private practice with clients.

Opportunities to pursue one's work without significant time or location restraints is typically a boon to self-directed faculty members, who make the most of their opportunities. For those who require external supervision and are less able to maximize their individual achievements, higher education careers often end in disappointing denials of promotion or tenure, usually within the first 6 years of employment.

Other Education Staff

Many social work programs include other categories of staff as well. Some may be considered professional staff, a category between faculty and support staff in status. These positions vary from program to program. Many are researchers or trainers who discharge their responsibilities under grants and contracts for research (sometimes for evaluation of research and demonstration projects carried out by social agencies) or social agency training responsibilities. Some may have nonfaculty educational or administrative responsibilities, such as financial management, searching and applying for grants or contracts, maintaining a social work library, or helping faculty and students with their articles and term papers. Generally, professional staff work regular hours, 35–40 per week, depending on the institution's policies.

Management of Support Staff

In some education programs, there are schisms between some support services workers, such as office assistants and secretaries, and the dean or directors and faculty members. In some ways, conflicts are predictable because of the significant differences between academics and support staff. Usually (not always), faculty and administrators such as deans and directors are paid much more than the support staff, and they are usually subject to very different personnel policies. Faculty may be required to spend only a few hours weekly in their offices and classrooms, whereas support staff members work a specified number of hours per week, close to 8 hours a day.

Support staff roles have also changed. In the times before faculty used computers for much of their work, support staff were needed to duplicate materials and help faculty in other ways to prepare for and teach their classes, prepare correspondence, and otherwise assist them, there is now much less need for such help. Faculty are now more inclined to type and duplicate their own course syllabi and examinations and print their own letters or, more commonly, correspond within and outside the institution by e-mail.

In modern educational institutions, support staff are more likely to be engaged in financial planning and management, preparing personnel-related forms and instruments, preparing class schedules, and providing technical guidance to students to register for courses and meet graduation requirements.

The class differences may lead to conflict-based jealousy and resentments. In many situations, support staff members have more years of service with programs than do faculty or even directors—factors that may lead to support staff's disdain for academic personnel. In many cases, support staff members have less education—perhaps little or no higher education—than do their academic counterparts. Increasingly, with the widespread completion of higher education, many support staff members may hold baccalaureate or even graduate degrees. They also may believe that faculty members are less industrious than they should be, and, on occasion, they are correct.

Social Work Education Chief Executive Officers

Chief executive officer positions in social work education programs are often among the most difficult professions in social work. Although most of the data are anecdotal, there often appear to be an inordinately large number of vacancies for deans and directors of combined master of social work (MSW) and bachelor of social work (BSW) programs, and sometimes for doctoral programs and social work education organizations. Although those positions typically require appointment at the full professor level, vacancies among them are much more common than they are for full professors. Filling those vacancies is often difficult as well. In fact, many are not filled during the first efforts to do so, and the positions are held, often for a year or more, by interim appointments. In some situations, the interim appointees come from college or university units other than social work.

There are a number of reasons for the frequent turnover among social work education chief executive officers. First, the work is difficult. Directors and deans must satisfy a variety of constituents, and sometimes satisfying one group alienates members of others. Constituents include faculty, students, the college or university administration, the accrediting body—the Council on Social Work Education, financial supporters of the program, and the local or state social work community. In some colleges and universities changes in presidents or chancellors may result in substantial replacements of program chief executive officers.

Second, the decisions required of the social work program director may be controversial—recommending or failing to recommend promotion or tenure for faculty members, appointing full- and part-time faculty, suggesting directions for the curriculum, and dealing with student academic and disciplinary issues. Third, because people who occupy these positions often earn more than other members of the faculty, jealousy is often a problem. Others on the faculty may want the job and consider themselves better able to discharge it. Sometimes a lack of stability of the appointment is structured into the position. Some institutions require periodic reappointment of the dean or director, perhaps at 5-year intervals. As the end of the 5-year period nears, opposition to the chief executive officer may become more pronounced. In some unionized institutions, the position is elected. For months before the selection is made, those involved may take sides and selection of the CEO becomes a major preoccupation.

Another issue is the source of the appointment. If the institution's president or chancellor appointed the director or dean and supports that person in the position, support for continued appointment is often provided. When the appointing authority is a higher-level dean (who may be concerned about his or her own survival in the position) support may be a bit more tenuous.

Financing the social work program is also a continuing challenge for social work education CEOs. A number of government and foundation grants and contracts are available to support social work education. In an earlier time, organizations such as the National Institutes of Mental Health funded all graduate social work programs with training grants as did the Children's Bureau and other federal agencies. Most of that grant support has shifted to research projects, which are awarded competitively, typically only to the most research-oriented programs. Foundations such as the Hartford Foundation support education in gerontology for many social work programs. State government programs, funded largely with federal monies, provide training grants for social work students and some faculty who are involved in child welfare programs. There are myriad sources of support, and social work program CEOs must devote considerable amounts of time to securing support for and carrying out projects the support finances.

Most schools of social work, at all levels, find they must focus heavily on independent fundraising from foundations, corporations, alumni, and other individuals.

Maintaining adequate numbers of students is also an issue in many programs. Those that rely heavily on tuition are especially vulnerable to financial problems when student enrollment declines. Some public institutions are financed on the basis of formulas: funding comes to the program via a student enrollment-based formula.

Having enough money to meet the payroll and carry out program obligations is a preoccupation of social work education managers, just as it is for managers in any other kind of work.

Graduate Schools

Graduate schools are also sometimes a source of conflict for MSW programs. Some are highly supportive, whereas others view themselves as supervisors of all graduate programs—monitoring admissions, enforcing procedures that faculty who teach in MSW programs must follow, and otherwise functioning in a rather authoritarian manner. Many top-flight universities do not have graduate schools, leaving operation of programs to the colleges and departments. In many others, particularly those with long histories of undergraduate education and relative recent graduate studies, the graduate school may be a vestige of a time when graduate education was a novelty.

Some universities use standardized tests such as the Graduate Record Examination (GRE) to admit graduate students, including MSW and doctoral students, along with undergraduate grade point averages. MSW programs do not all use the GRE. Some schools find such standardized tests an impediment to effective admissions of MSW students. Although sufficient academic skill is needed to complete the program, some high-priority students, such as members of minority groups, may not fare as well as other applicants on the GRE. Some minority students even avoid applying to programs that use the GRE because of its reputation as being especially difficult for them. This writer, now affiliated with a university that uses the GRE, well remembers attempting to recruit students at a historically African American institution, when he represented a university that did not ordinarily require the GRE. Those institutions that used the GRE were of little interest to potential applicants, whereas the writer found them very interested in his institution.

State Governing or Coordinating Boards

Although most social work programs are so far down the organizational structure that they do not frequently encounter them, every state has some sort of higher education governing or coordinating body such as a board of regents or a commission on higher education. These organizations deal primarily with institution presidents and boards, but when new programs are contemplated or significant departures from existing operations are planned, social work programs may find themselves preparing materials for these state-level bodies. Although such boards typically deal with public institutions, in many states they are also responsible for coordinating and approving the creation of programs in private institutions.

Unionization

Increasingly, social work education programs are part of higher education institutions that have collective bargaining agreements. Higher education systems and individual colleges or universities may be unionized. Several states, including Massachusetts and Pennsylvania, have higher education unions. The unions may be specialized and only applicable to the higher education system, but some are part of larger unions such as the Communication Workers of America or the United Auto Workers. The American Association of University Professors functions as a union for some institutions.

In such situations, methods of selecting leadership such as deans and directors are specified in the union contract, as are working conditions, assignments, and tenure and promotion. Clearly, managing a unionized social work program is different from managing a program that is not part of a collective bargaining agreement.

Higher Education Institutions

Among the complications of managing social work education programs is the nature of higher education institutions, themselves. When most faculty begin their appointments, they have little understanding of colleges and universities apart from their own experience as graduate students. Colleges and universities constitute a special kind of social institution, with their own mores and demands. Increasingly, higher education institutions are compelled to justify themselves and their operations, and financing themselves is a major part of their concerns. Although private institutions historically support themselves with tuition, endowments, and contributions, as well as support from sponsoring bodies, such as religious organizations, public institutions find in the 21st century, that they are only partially supported by state governments. Tuition, fees, foundation grants, and federal government support account for more than half of the support that many institutions—especially some of the best-known public institutions—depend on.

Institutions also compete for reputation within the higher education hierarchy. Organizations such as the American Association of Universities (AAU) identify the top institutions based on criteria such as grants received, faculty publications, and the average scores of entering undergraduate students on the Scholastic Aptitude Test. It is not unusual for an institutional president to campaign to achieve AAU status, which carries with it high potential for federally supported grants and contracts as well as high status within higher education. Such efforts may seem to distort the operations of a college or university, but boards of trustees and state legislatures view such status as important indicators of the value of their investments in the institution.

Keeping Balls in the Air

Most managers in social work find they must keep a number of balls in the air— a metaphor for juggling. This is often a serious issue for social work education managers. Dealing with internal and external constituencies, as discussed earlier, is a major preoccupation of most of those who hold these positions.

Academic politics often take large amounts of time for social work education managers. Although any organization or industry has its political dimensions, those in higher education institutions are sometimes more demanding and contentious than in other kinds of work. A popular and historically old comment, with uncertain attribution, is that academic politics are vicious because the stakes are low. Often the result of sometimes bitter disputes is who gets and does not get the office with the best window or the 9 a.m. rather than the 10 a.m. class. But academic disputes can be bitter and longer-lasting than some of the conflicts in social agencies or in the real politics of state and federal governments. Sometimes the consequences of such disputes threaten professional careers and personal well-being.

The Positives

This discussion focuses primarily on the issues social work deans and directors— of graduate as well as undergraduate programs—face in their day-to-day work. However, there are many positives. There are multiple opportunities to achieve new successes in program development. For some, starting a new BSW or MSW is a particular challenge that can be quite satisfying for a social worker oriented to such creativity. In established programs, a new curriculum, a new grant program, the addition of a branch, attracting new faculty, and improving the quality of the students' education are all positive outcomes for the social work education manager.

Education managers also have some privileges and perks that the rest of the faculty may not have. Invitations to board of governors or trustees social functions, social activities with the president or chancellor, participation in meetings of organizations such as the Association of Baccalaureate Social Work Program Directors or the National Association of Deans and Directors and the Saint Louis Group (an organization of programs with large amounts of external financial support) are all available and attractive to those interested in such activities.

As discussed earlier, education managers are also likely to have larger salaries than most faculty members as well as larger travel budgets. They are also likely to have larger offices. For those who find such perquisites appealing, social work education management is an attractive career.

However, for many social work educators, the attraction to higher education is the opportunity to teach and conduct research as well as publish. The demands of social work education management are often so great they cannot carry out that work. Many directors and deans decide to return to faculty status once they have completed their managerial duties.

Conclusion

This chapter suggests that social work education management is among the most rewarding and challenging careers available to professional social workers. One limitation or challenge is the lack of formal preparation for social work education program directors and other CEOs such as deans. Anecdotally, the failure rate for persons in such positions seems high. Even for those who succeed for a number of years, there is frustration and tensions at several levels—conflicts with faculty, differences with the administration, differences with students, responding to the demands of accrediting bodies, and many others.

Some have suggested a social work education leadership academy, others propose formal mentoring processes. When this writer first became the CEO of a social work education program, his Council on Social Work Education consultant suggested he try to visit two sitting deans, who were successful, to discuss what the job entailed. He did so and learned a great deal from one dean and his associate dean. It was never possible to schedule a meeting with the second dean and, perhaps confirming the point, he was soon replaced in a less-than-pleasant manner.

Informally, most managers of social work education programs consult regularly with one another about ongoing concerns and issues.

The keys to success in social work education management appear to include hard work and frequent and careful communication with constituencies such as students, faculty colleagues, the social work practice community, and the university administration. And perhaps most important to success is a supportive university administration that understands the pressures education CEOs face.

For the long term, the mentoring and leadership academy ideas ought to help develop stronger and more stable social work education management, a goal that has value for the whole profession.

Child Care in the Office

As the new director of an undergraduate social work program that awarded the BSW in a midsize state university, Claude encountered a problem he hadn't seen before in his work at some other universities.

A program secretary cared for her 8-year-old child every afternoon in the office, after the child's father picked the child up from elementary school.

The secretary had worked in the program for the past 20 years, initially as an hourly worker. Before becoming a full-time employee, she had picked up and cared for the child at home. Now she cared for the child 15 hours each week in the office.

Claude's predecessors believed the assistant should be able to operate her office as she saw fit, as long as her work was done. The child used an unoccupied computer to download and play video games. Sometimes she went to classrooms and used the chalkboards. At other times, she sat in offices of faculty members who were away and played video games on their computers. At one time, the child was too ill to attend school, so the secretary brought her to the office for the whole day instead of just the afternoon. On other occasions, when the schools were closed for inclement weather, the child spent the whole day in the office.

The reaction of the faculty was mixed. None were pleased that the child was often present. Some complained about the use of the office for child care. The department chair, who was Claude's immediate supervisor told the secretary that caring for her child in the office was not a right but did not forbid the practice.

Meanwhile, a faculty member who was on maternity leave and gave birth to a son returned to work. She set up her office with stuffed animals and mattresses, signaling a plan to care for that child in the office, too. Again, some faculty complained, but most said nothing.

After 6 months on the job, Claude told the secretary she would have to stop bringing her child to work, that she needed to make other arrangements. She wept and said that Claude didn't care about her and hated children. She complained that the faculty member was bringing her infant child to work as well. Claude explained that policies governing faculty and those governing support staff were different. However, he told the faculty member to cease bringing the child to work. He also consulted with the college dean and the human resources department of the university. Neither gave Claude clear support. Human resources personnel said there were problems with faculty in other departments bringing children to work.

A few months later, Claude saw someone race down a hallway and into a darkened office. Another faculty member told him that the child continued to come to work with her mother when Claude was away. She had hidden in the darkened office, apparently at her mother's instruction, when Claude appeared unexpectedly.

Claude drafted a detailed document of expectations, forbidding the secretary to care for her child in the office, which both the secretary and Claude signed. The secretary complied with Claude's directions. For the next several months, some faculty members said the office atmosphere was tense and hostile. The secretary repeatedly complained to faculty and students about Claude's mistreatment and lack of concern for children. The faculty member with a newborn initiated a campaign to have Claude removed. She met with the college dean to complain about him, and she spoke with faculty members about Claude's denigrating the program's family atmosphere.

Discussion Questions

1. What other steps might Claude have taken to overcome the problem? Were his actions justified? Should he have acted sooner?
2. Why was there so little initial support at higher administrative levels for Claude's actions?
3. Could Claude have suggested other arrangements that would resolve the problem?

False Accusations of Improper Behavior

Sharon was a 35-year-old assistant professor in the English department of a large public university. Two male colleagues made sexual advances toward the recently divorced woman, through invitations and innuendoes, which she rebuffed. Perhaps to defend themselves against charges of sexual harassment, the colleagues charged her with improper behavior with her students, such as socializing and drinking alcohol with them and offering them illegal drugs. She denied the charges. However, she was denigrated in her department as a problem faculty member and required to teach unpopular classes at unpopular times, which would tend to lower her evaluations by her students. She was also told that if she complained or sought legal action, students had been contacted by the male colleagues, and the students would testify that she had engaged in improper acts in any hearing or court case that might ensue. Although she had been awarded tenure a year earlier, she felt she needed to leave for another job because her situation was so uncomfortable.

Discussion Questions

1. Do you think there are elements of the higher education environment that make situations such as this possible? If so, what are they?
2. What possible solutions to the problems would Sharon have? Suggest two or three.
3. How might the department chair or other higher education officials effectively deal with issues such as these?

Student Disagreement with Instructor

A senior social work major visits the director, Suzette, in a BSW program with 100 majors. The student complains that her instructor gave her a grade of C on a paper, but other students earned B with less work. The instructor teaches part-time for the program and practices social work in the community full time. The student wants Suzette to resolve the disagreement. Suzette looks over the paper and tries to explain the instructor's concerns, which the student rejects. Suzette knows she cannot change an instructor's grades and explains that, but she also urges the student to discuss the grade with the instructor again. Suzette also agrees to contact the instructor. The university has a student appeals procedure, and Suzette tells the student how to access it.

Discussion Questions

1. What else might Suzette have been able to do?
2. Suggest the content of Suzette's communication with the instructor.
3. The instructor may believe the issue is one of academic freedom—the right to teach and grade as one chooses. Are there differences in academic freedom for part-time and full-time instructors?

Reference

Ginsberg, L. (2000). *Social work evaluation: Principles and methods.* Boston: Allyn & Bacon.

19

Teaching Financial Management to MSW Students

Mark Ezell

No matter how you perform your non-financial management responsibilities, if "the money is funny" and if the budget is off kilter, you are heading for trouble. (Brody, 2005, p. 225)

Planning for the use of and managing resources are two of the major concerns human services managers face as program managers and executive directors. In their new book, Zietlow, Hankin, and Seidner (2007) assert that financial management functions are increasing and the organization's ability to accomplish its mission depends on effective implementation of these functions. In these times of shrinking resources, Zietlow et al. (2007) point out that skilled financial management can both enhance revenues and reduce costs, allowing a greater proportion of every dollar to be devoted to services.

It is critical to note at the very beginning of this chapter that there are no agencies in our field that identify their mission as breaking even financially. Typically, our mission statements mention resolving the plight or meeting the needs of a particular client group. They usually emphasize individual or social change. Planning, implementing, monitoring, and evaluating the use of resources are tools that we should use to accomplish our missions. Effective financial management should be measured by the amount of positive client change produced. Financial management functions must be kept in that perspective, and organizational leaders need to fight the drift toward the centrality of the budget. Clients are the central concern (Poertner & Rapp, 2007). As Vinter and Kish (1984) say in their classic book on budgeting, "The more the organization knows about where and how it uses resources, the better service job it can do" (p. 2).

For purposes of this chapter, financial management is defined as the tasks and responsibilities associated with three stages of an agency's budget cycle: planning and projecting revenue and expense budgets; implementing and monitoring revenue and expense budgets; and reporting and evaluating the use of financial resources. There is not a lot written in the social work literature about financial management. (And what there is probably is referred to here.) Consensus on this definition is lacking; many include acquisition of funding or fundraising as one of the stages. I do not have a big argument with that. I leave it out of the definition because I can't cover it all in one course. (I discuss this consideration later in the chapter.)

Scandals, Bankruptcies, and Closures

Few people could have missed recent news reports about scandals at several national nonprofit agencies, and they probably know of a local agency or two that closed for financial reasons. The results of egregiously weak financial management knowledge, skills, and practices are clear. The other end of the continuum, agencies achieving their mission and goals; providing high-quality, effective services to clients; and paying staff what they deserve, is also easy to imagine. Even though successful agencies such as this are rarely applauded for strong financial management, it is a big, albeit behind-the-scenes, piece of the puzzle.

Rather than the agencies that fall at either end of the continuum, I'm much more concerned about the thousands of agencies that fall in between these two extremes. Financial management practices aren't so bad that the agency is forced to declare bankruptcy, but they are weak, and agencies plod along functioning well below a satisfactory level of effectiveness or efficiency. They're not totally failing, but clients and staff get less than they deserve. Some might argue that keeping the doors open for a long time is a measure of success in itself. It certainly is not a bad thing, but this is virtually equivalent to the goal of breaking even. To evaluate the results of an agency's financial management practices, we should take a hard look at their service effectiveness, first, followed by such factors as staff turnover, for example. Because the budget is connected to virtually every agency function, fairly small improvements in financial management practices can have multiplier effects.

Numerous studies reveal that social work managers devote a significant amount of time to this activity and rank it as a high priority. Patti's (1977) early study found that although social work managers use less of their time budgeting than they do supervising, for example, they consider it a high priority. Menefee and Thompson (1994) found that "managing resources" ranked toward the lower end of 12 management dimensions in both frequency and importance. This is a little deceptive because other management dimensions, such as "futuring" and "leveraging resources," include aspects of financial management. Menefee's (2000) later description of the tasks of managers as resource administrators explains more fully the long list of and wide-ranging responsibilities necessary to carry out this function effectively.

The National Network of Social Work Managers (2008) is our profession's only national body that credentials social work managers, and it includes financial management among its list of competencies and as part of its certification process.[1]

---

[1] A personal opinion related to state licensing and certification: I find it ironic that many MSWs who work directly with clients are expected and sometimes required to be licensed. The advanced clinical license in Kansas, for example, requires those who sit for the exam to have completed the clinical concentration and a clinical practicum while in school and to have ? years of post-MSW clinical supervision. Agency and program directors, those responsible for supervising dozens of staff, managing millions of dollars, and coordinating services for hundreds of clients, on the other hand, are not expected or required to be licensed as managers. Licensing is a public certification and accountability process meant to establish specific amounts and types of education for certain professionals, continuing education requirements, and public oversight intended to maintain and enforce ethical standards. Although I am skeptical about the benefits of licensing to the public and to clients in general, the tunnel vision described previously is very perplexing.

Figure 1 includes the entire list of competencies from the National Network. All competencies are included so we do not lose sight of the fact that financial management is only one aspect of a social work manager's duties, and that it is difficult, in fact, to disentangle financial management from other duties. There are aspects of governance, for example, that are strongly associated with financial management. Maintaining an organization's nonprofit status by complying with the various provisions of the tax code and filing necessary reports are two such governance activities. I discuss other interdependencies between financial management and other major management functions at the conclusion of the chapter when I suggest that financial management courses might serve as capstone courses in management curricula.

This chapter discusses teaching financial management to master of social work (MSW) students. My experience teaching financial management for over 20 years provides much of the data, as does the literature on the topic, and I include many examples from my class. The class changes every year by about 10% by updating readings and assignments and including new topics as the field continues to mature and laws

FIGURE 1   MANAGEMENT COMPETENCIES OF THE NATIONAL NETWORK OF SOCIAL WORK MANAGERS

These practice standards for social work managers provide a basic framework of knowledge and skills that define effective and sound social work management. The standards are divided into 14 competency areas.

1. Advocacy
2. Communication and Interpersonal Relationships
3. Ethics
4. Evaluation
5. Financial Development
   • Knowledge and understanding of proposal and contract development
   • Ability to identify and access resources from diverse private and public funding sources
6. Financial Management
   • Knowledge and understanding of effective systems and procedures for managing agency resources
   • Ability to develop and use budgets and other financial data and reports to guide agency operations
7. Governance
8. Human Resource Management and Development
9. Information Technology
10. Leadership
11. Planning
12. Program Development and Organizational Management
13. Public/Community Relations and Marketing
14. Public Policy

and regulations change. It would be an error to view this class as the exemplar for all schools; there are good reasons why the course should be different in different places. Competition for curriculum space and the audience—as well as its members' projected futures—are major influencing factors that will cause a course such as this to differ from one place to another, from one time to another. I've been lucky to have the luxury of enough curriculum space to devote the entire course only to financial management. There was either enough room in the curriculum, or, knowing that financial management knowledge and skills are essential to social work managers, we made enough room. Usually a separate course on fund development, grant writing, and fundraising is offered as well. This is not the case everywhere.

Another consideration on the existence and design of the course I mention here is how a school's advanced MSW curriculum is structured. Again, I've been lucky to be at schools whose faculties gave administrative practice in social work a high priority and created concentrations. As such, every year we had a new cohort of MSW students that chose to focus its attention on administrative practice.[2] Concomitant with these students' coursework, they are in administration field placements, usually 3 days a week. Obviously, these two factors, curriculum space and structure, are critical considerations when designing and implementing a course in financial management.

My credentials for teaching and writing about financial management are extensive. I started teaching financial management in 1986 as a new assistant professor at the University of Washington. With the quarter system, classes met for 10 weeks. When we started the course, which included teaching and doing homework with spreadsheet software, the school had two PCs available for student use. This was a long time ago. These PCs had two floppy disk drives, one for the software disk and the other to hold and save data. Actually, we used Microsoft MultiPlan, the precursor to Excel.[3] Associated with teaching the course, helping design the management curriculum, and practicum responsibilities, I've met with dozens of agency representatives over the years to get feedback on the course. As a result of papers written for the course, I've studied budgeting practices indirectly in more than 100 agencies.

In addition to teaching, I've written several chapters on financial management (see Ezell, 2000, 2007, 2008), and I've written several reviews of financial management books. I've done and continue to do research on a variety of issues related to the effectiveness and impact of contracting on social service nonprofits.

The final credential I'll mention is that I've served on approximately 10 boards of directors over the years, and I also helped start and lead a nonprofit agency that continues to operate. Most of the time I've been elected or appointed to be the treasurer, or, at least, to sit on the budget committee. This keeps me in a position to get hands-on experience, stay up to date on budgeting issues, and work with auditors, among other responsibilities.

On our current semester system, the class meets for 15 weeks. In both quarters

---

[2] I use the terms *management* and *administration* interchangeably.

[3] When I left the University of Washington in 1998, it had a beautiful computer lab with approximately 25 computers, set up both for general student use and teaching.

and semesters, students earned 3 credit hours and the class met for between 2½ to 3 hours once a week. Obviously, whether a school is on the quarter or the semester system influences the breadth and depth of the course. With the exception of a sabbatical or two, I've taught the course more than 20 times, as well as workshops here and there, continually updating the content and making revisions as I continue to learn. I estimate that approximately 300 students have taken and finished the course over the years. Almost all of the students were specializing in administrative practice in social work, but a significant handful of clinical/direct service students as well as students from public administration have taken and done well in the course. End-of-term evaluations, measuring a variety of variables, have been consistently positive. Although student satisfaction feedback is important, I think getting feedback from practicing graduates is critical. Alumni survey data and dozens of anecdotal reports have also been very positive. Graduates have found that the knowledge and skills covered in the course are relevant to their practice settings and have contributed to making them better practitioners.[4] Every time I teach the class, I also collect self-report data on financial management knowledge and skills before and during the class. I describe that instrument, as both a teaching and assessment tool, later.

The chapter is divided into four sections. The first discusses the context for designing and teaching the course. Course goals, objectives, and topics are covered in the next section. In the third section, I discuss different teaching techniques I've found to be useful as well as assignments I've used. This section also emphasizes the importance of the link between the class and the field. The final section discusses the advantages of using a financial management course as a capstone course for the management curriculum.

Context for the Class

If a school's curriculum space permits a financial management course, there are several contextual factors that influence the knowledge and skills that should be taught. The more we know about these factors, the more relevant the course will be to both the students and their future agencies of employment. Needs assessments, formal or otherwise, of agencies and delivery systems should be conducted. Also, the more we know about the career progressions of graduates, the more relevant the course can be.

Given public agencies' extensive use of contracting, I emphasize financial management for nonprofits. Although in many states counties deliver human services, all of the states in which I've worked had contracts designed and monitored by state agencies. Nonprofits have to bid on the contracts, and the contents of their bids include many important things such as program designs and staff qualifications. Budgets are a key element in the proposals, even when contracts do not necessarily go to the lowest bidder.[5]

---

[4] Admittedly, graduates who find their financial management preparation to be lacking are unlikely to communicate that directly to me. Alumni surveys should pick this up.

[5] I've worked in Kansas for the last 10 years. Starting in 1996, the state child welfare agency began contracting for all child welfare services except investigations. For-profit agencies are allowed to bid, and some have, but so far contracts have been awarded only to nonprofits.

Often, the bids come down to a quoted price for the service to be provided—X number of dollars per day of residential care or Y number of dollars per month per client, for example.[6] Agencies do not necessarily have to have good financial management practices to prepare their bids and win the contract. Problems arise later when implementing the work at the contracted price when it is below the real cost of service delivery. I cannot emphasize the following enough: *Agencies must have good financial management practices to know how much their services cost for different types of clients, and, therefore, to be able to prepare bids that, if accepted, will permit the delivery of high-quality services.* Occasionally, nonprofits with strong financial management practices do not bid because they know the true costs of their services; and they are aware that the public agency is unlikely to contract at that level. The decision of a nonprofit not to bid is very hard for boards of directors to swallow. Just like most of us, board members accept the American corporate mentality that budget growth is a key indicator of success. Many feel that failure to grow is to die. The more common course of action is for boards and executives to bid on and accept contract terms that are below the real costs, knowing they will have to raise money to make ends meet and not overstress the agency.

Another reason to focus on nonprofit financial management is that public social service agencies usually rely on another public agency (e.g., the Department of Administration) for budget planning, implementation, and evaluation. Public managers in charge of delivering programs and services have very small roles in the budgeting process. As such, public social work managers generally do not have important financial management tools at their disposal.

The career trajectories of graduates, as well as feedback from employing agencies, also influence course and curriculum content. MSW administration graduates frequently become program directors within a year or two of graduation. Some become executive directors of small nonprofits soon after graduation, but this is not the usual pattern. Most management graduates tend to advance to higher-level positions in larger nonprofits. If a significant proportion of graduates is hired by government agencies, however, the emphasis of the course should shift in that direction.

These contextual factors create decision points for those who are planning and teaching courses in financial management. Is there enough curriculum space to have separate courses on financial management and fund development? How much weight should be put on nonprofit budgeting versus public budgeting? Another key decision is whether to emphasize conceptual understanding of financial management versus skill building. Martin (2001) wrote a very good financial management book and is perfectly clear that he emphasizes conceptual understanding. Vinter and Kish (1984), on the other hand, put a lot more emphasis on skills in their book (which is desperately in need of an update). My course uses skill building as the route to conceptual understanding.

---

[6] A common practice is for public agencies to separate the budget part of the bid from the rest of the proposal.

Course Goals, Objectives, and Topics

Two of the most humbling decisions a teacher has to make are, first, what range and depth of content should be included in a course, and second, what to cover during class meeting times. Whether one teaches on a quarter or semester system, the subject of a class—as indicated by the syllabus—includes far more topics and skills than can be covered. What exclusion/inclusion criteria do we use? Even if areas are included in the topical list or readings in the syllabus, what can be included in a lecture, discussion, class exercise, or assignments? There are always some topics on which students have assigned readings, but that's all. We all worry about making the right decisions.

Besides these worries, anyone teaching a financial management course needs to confront the reality that Lohmann and Lohmann (2002) explain:

> Even though social workers willingly acknowledge the importance of financial management, most students and professionals want little to do with it. Probably no topic in the social administration pantheon generates less enthusiasm or greater dread among social work students than the two words *financial management* [emphasis in original]. (p. 2)

The goal of the course is for students to graduate with the knowledge and skills necessary to lead a program or agency through all stages of the budget cycle. A financial management course might cover such concepts and skills as budget planning, resource allocation, problems of fiscal control, fiscal record keeping and reporting, cost analysis, and continuation budgeting. Students should learn how to analyze financial statements and implement sound fiscal controls. Because program and budget planning are inexact sciences, a great deal of emphasis should be placed on techniques to monitor expenses and revenues and on the knowledge to implement corrective action when overspending occurs. Most students think of budgets as expense budgets only. They should leave the course knowing what revenue budgets look like, the importance of the revenue side, and specific skills on forecasting revenues.

An unwritten goal of the course is, at a minimum, to make students comfortable with budget topics. In small agencies, social work managers do just about everything. In larger agencies, they might not have to carry out some of the day-to-day financial management tasks, but they do need to know how to supervise those who do, and what questions to ask.

Topics

A list of potential course topics is included in Figure 2. This list is by no means exhaustive, and, as mentioned previously, instructors have to decide the depth for each topic. Depending on instructors' preferences and teaching styles, all of these topics can be presented to include both knowledge and skills.

By the time students finish the course, they will know how to start a nonprofit organization and will be familiar with relevant tax issues such as unrelated business

FIGURE 2   POSSIBLE CLASS TOPICS

- Stages of the budget cycle
- Activities and tasks in each stage
- Budget planning processes
- Linking budget and program planning
- Types of budgets
- Revenue forecasting and analysis
- Estimating expenses
- Line items/chart of accounts
- Full-time equivalents (FTEs)
- Types of payroll taxes
- Types of employee benefits
- Fiscal years
- Functional budgeting and related concepts
- Indirect costs
- Administrative costs
- Prospective resource allocation
- Budget authority/discretion
- Fiscal controls
- Separation of duties

- Risk management
- Revenue and expense monitoring
- Variance analysis
- Starting a nonprofit corporation
- The IRS and nonprofits
- Boards of directors
- Purchase of service contracts
- Techniques to trim/cut budgets
- Public budgeting
- Advocacy and budgets
- Financial statements
- Basis of accounting
- Identifying and solving ethical dilemmas
- Budget issues related to gender, ethnicity, and sexual orientation
- Cost analysis
- Break-even analysis
- Audits

income. They will be fully versed in all stages of contracting, from requests for proposals (RFPs) and bidding to compliance and reporting. They will gain skills and appreciation of spreadsheet software as tools for financial management. In addition, students will understand the following: commonly used budget planning processes, different budget formats, functional budgeting, break-even analysis, audits, indirect costs, and administrative costs. Throughout the course, ethical issues are raised, and students discuss methods to prevent and resolve them.

Back in the dark ages, when I took my MSW financial management course, we took a course available from the Department of Public Administration. As a result, a great deal of emphasis was placed on public budgeting. Even if the greatest emphasis in a social work financial management course is on nonprofit financial management, time should be devoted to the budget cycles of public agencies, especially at the state level. Because so many social work nonprofits depend on grants and contracts from states, it is wise to know how and when decisions are made. Also, without this knowledge, advocacy by managers, whether for their programs, staff, or clients, has little chance of success.

The financial management class I took also required us to learn basic accounting techniques. Although that process was painful, I appreciate and have used this knowledge a great deal. My perception is that this content is very uncommon in social work courses. Although arguable, I think managers need to understand the underlying accounting practices to fully comprehend an agency's financial statements.

Teaching Techniques and Assignments

The very first thing I do with a new class is to have the students fill out a Sequential Criterion Related Educational Evaluation (SCREE) that I modeled after the work of my late professor, Walter Hudson (1981). Figure 3 shows the layout of the instrument and several sample items. The only instruction I give when I distribute the SCREE on the first day of class is to say that it is not part of the students' grade. Afterward, I briefly discuss its purposes, and because all of them know only a few of the items, I also try to lower their already high anxiety. I remind them that they are

FIGURE 3   LAYOUT AND SAMPLE ITEMS FROM SEQUENTIAL CRITERION REFERENCED EDUCATIONAL EVALUATION (SCREE)

Instructions: Complete every item on this inventory. If you know the correct answer or know how to perform the described task, put an X in the appropriate cell. When you are done, calculate your score and record it in the space provided.

	Test Period		
	1	2	3
1. Do you know the differences among zero-based, performance, line item, and PPBS budgeting?			
2. Do you understand the nature of indirect costs and how they differ from administrative costs?			
3. Do you understand functional budgeting and the role of cost and responsibility centers?			
4. Can you explain the differences between a cash and accrual basis of accounting?			
5. Do you know several ways to forecast revenues?			
6. Do you know how to enter and copy formulas in an Excel worksheet?			
7. Do you understand how certain biases and stereotypes can influence budget decisions and process?			
8. Are you familiar with different types of financial statements?			
9. Do you know what an IRS Form 990 is?			
10. Can you explain unrelated business income and its relevance to nonprofits?			
Total Score (count the number of Xs)	1	2	3

not supposed to do well on the assessment, and if they do, they may not need the class. One of the benefits of such an instrument is that it alerts them from the beginning of the class to the skills and knowledge I think they should have when they finish the course. It focuses their attention when they do their reading, work on their assignments, listen to class lectures and participate in discussions. During the next class session, I report the average and range of scores. I readminister the SCREE at midterm. The only new instruction I give is to tell them to use the same level of truthfulness as they did in the first administration. (It's a joke.) I also tell them it is common, as learning progresses, for students to realize they don't know something they thought they knew during the first administration. They have positive reactions to the second administration of the instrument because they can see they are making progress. I look over the instruments after the students fill them out at midterm and see if their progress is what I think it should be. If there are items that have been covered in readings or in class, but many of them do not indicate mastery, I may need to review them.

I administer the instrument one more time on the last day of class. The scores on the SCREE have been very consistent over the years. For the first administration, students know about 10% of the items on average, and the range of scores is relatively broad. By the end of the term, the average score rises to approximately 90% of the items, and the standard deviation of the scores decreases as the disparities among students' knowledge declines. After the final administration of the instrument, I devote a few minutes to congratulating them for their hard work. I remind them of the first day of class and how little they knew when they started the semester and how they now confidently and comfortably talk about budget issues with new terminology. My experience is that students don't often recognize that their knowledge and skills are increasing. I find it useful to crystallize this as a way to build their confidence.

Teaching Methods

The primary teaching methodology in the course as I teach it is the case study approach. Vinter and Kish's (1984) book describes a small agency from the point when a new program is being planned and budgets negotiated, to the end of the budget cycle, when cost analysis can be conducted. In their book, they include a series of budget exercises to give students the opportunity to apply new knowledge and develop their skills. (The book needs to be updated, but I think the value of doing the exercises, practicing financial management skills, and decision making outweighs the downside.) The late Professor Vinter originally put the exercises into Microsoft Multiplan and made them available at cost. Because software has changed, I converted parts of each assignment to Microsoft Excel for students to work on. As an example of one exercise, the program operates for 6 months, and a budget report shows that unless something changes, it will be $10,000 over budget at the end of the fiscal year. Students are asked to analyze the situation and propose budget cuts so they project a balanced budget at the end of the fiscal year. They come to class prepared to discuss the case, explain their decisions, and defend their choices. The case study method allows them to practice making and defending decisions. They are free to work in groups, and I encourage it. Some students are detail people, others are big picture people. Collaboration is beneficial because most of the exercises require both styles of thinking. It can also be useful to pair less-experienced students with more-experienced ones.

One little trick I use with the Excel worksheets is to include all of the formulas they need in the early assignments, and then include fewer and fewer as the semester advances. They are supposed to be learning how to use formulas, because the formulas and automatic calculations are what make spreadsheet software so useful. More and more students are coming into the class with fairly advanced Excel skills, but this is fairly new to most students. I do emphasize over and over that this is not a computer class, that the software is a budgeting tool only.

I use a grading technique on the case study exercises that places the greatest emphasis on student learning rather than on grades. Almost all students start the class admitting they are very anxious about it, especially the math. In essence, debriefing an exercise in class lets them grade their own work. If there is something they don't understand, and it doesn't come up in discussion, they are to ask about it. In addition to completing all of the steps in the homework, I ask them to write answers to two extra questions: (1) What questions do you still have after completing the assignment? and (2) What did you learn in this assignment? When students tell me what confuses them, I can write explanatory notes to them, and if several students have similar questions, I know I need to address them in class. The second question is an attempt to get them to step back, get away from all the details, and reflect on what they were doing. I hope that by labeling what they just did, they realize how much they have learned.

If students complete these assignments on time and completely, they get the full points. This material is so new to students, and they are so anxious about it, I expect mistakes and misunderstandings, and putting grade pressure on them doesn't seem to help. This approach also seems to contribute to a class atmosphere in which students don't mind explaining their answers and their reasoning, even if they are potentially flawed. I need to understand where and how they got confused .

Besides debriefing the exercises, class time is devoted to short lectures, especially in the first half of the semester. Because students find this material so new and so different, explaining concepts and providing lots of examples is very helpful. In virtually every class meeting, I ask them to describe what they're observing about financial management in their field agencies and to ask questions about it. Obviously, I can't always sort out what different agencies are doing, but students will be able to go back to their placements with new follow-up questions.

Because we offer two sections of the class, one on our Lawrence campus and the other on our Kansas City, KS, campus, an adjunct professor has been teaching one of the sections. We've been lucky to find such an excellent and enthusiastic teacher from the community. Because many students are challenged to understand and work with full-time-equivalents (FTEs), he developed a set of exercises with which students practice (D. Riggin, personal communication, February 22, 2008). An example of a question is: "A program is budgeted for eight full-time staff for an entire fiscal year. If

FIGURE 4   QUESTIONS/ISSUES TO BE ADDRESSED IN THE FINANCIAL MANAGEMENT PAPER

1. What is your agency's fiscal year? Why was this chosen? Describe fiscal policies as they relate to the fiscal year. For example, do all funds have to be expended at the end of the fiscal year, or only obligated? Do you see any dangers in or advantages to having this fiscal year? What are the strengths and weaknesses of end-of-year spending policies?

2. How many FTEs does the agency have overall and in each program? How many of these are "direct service," "support staff," or "managerial?" (The agency may not have definitions of these staff categories, and you may need to create them.) What is the ratio of managerial staff to other staff? What is the ratio of support staff to other staff? Present other ratios relevant to the staffing of your agency/program. Given your knowledge of the issues and your reading for this course, what impresses or concerns you?

3. What the process is used to plan both the expense and revenue budget? What are the roles of the various actors (e.g., board members, managerial staff, other staff, clients) in this process? Does the agency use a budget calendar? Do clients have a role? Does the process include relevant board and staff irrespective of their ethnicity, gender, and/or sexual orientation? How useful is the budget calendar?

4. What are the agency's sources of revenue? How stable have revenues been over the last 3 to 5 years? Describe the "mix" of revenues (e.g., public grants or contracts, donations, fees, etc.). How does the agency forecast revenues? What do you think of the sources and sizes of revenues? Are the forecasting techniques accurate ones?

5. How have budget cuts been handled in the past? Does the agency have a plan for handling new ones? Describe and evaluate how your agency deals with revenue shortfalls. Given your knowledge of the issues and your reading for this course, what impresses or concerns you?

6. While studying your agency's budget practices, did you identify any real or potential ethical dilemmas? Did you observe any instances when budget practices could adversely affect or be more inclusive of ethnic and racial minorities, gay men and lesbians, women, or people with physical or developmental challenges? Explain.

four of the staff are each laid off for 3 months during the year, what is the actual number of FTE staff?"

Another in-class exercise I use to emphasize the importance of monthly revenue and expense monitoring is to distribute an actual monthly report from an agency. The students are to discuss and answer three questions: (1) Do you need all the information presented in this report to monitor revenue and expenses responsibly? (2) What other information do you need? and (3) What are the strengths and weaknesses of the presentation and formatting (e.g., how easy is the report to use)? An example of this exercise is included in Ezell (2008).

Strong Link to the Field

The effectiveness of the class depends heavily on the agencies in which students are placed. The final assignment for the course is a comprehensive paper on budget practices and procedures in their agencies. (Figure 4 includes sample questions from the paper assignment.) The agencies have to be willing to cooperate, but field instructors have not necessarily received training in financial management. When agencies apply to become practicum sites for administration students, we try to make it clear that they have to provide access to budget materials, procedures, and staff. This usually works quite well. If possible, I meet with the field instructors. Occasionally, agencies are nervous about the confidentiality of the information, but we really don't need actual numbers on an expense or revenue budget. We do want to study the format of annual budgets and monthly reports.

Our practicum-learning contract includes several tasks related to financial management, so students are expected to get hands-on experience. Although some of our field instructors are trained in management, they may not have taken a financial management course. Of course, many of the field instructors were trained in direct services and then moved up to administrative positions. Given this situation, I prepared and distributed a list of possible field activities for students to assist agencies. (See Figure 5 for sample items.)

FIGURE 5   SAMPLE TASKS TO BE CARRIED OUT IN THE FIELD

- Describe the process and forms used to monitor revenues and expenditures.
- Develop a plan for a program to absorb a 10% budget cut.
- Analyze and determine the percentage of each agency/program dollar that goes to direct services.
- Analyze the agency's financial statements and prepare observations about its fiscal health.

The final paper students write for the class focuses on their agency's budget planning and implementation process. The purpose of this assignment is to increase their understanding of financial management concepts and budget processes by observing, describing, and analyzing all phases of the budget process in action. I provide a list of questions they must research and answer in their papers. To prepare this paper, they usually have to interview several people. After they describe all of these practices, they analyze them for strengths and weaknesses. The guiding question is: To what degree are agency budget practices, processes, and associated reports useful management tools? Very early in the semester, I consistently ask about their progress on their papers so they don't wait until the last minute, and ask whether they need some coaching on what to tell agency personnel if they are getting any resistance. Several years ago, I started requiring them to submit a draft of answers to about one third of the questions by the 10th week of the semester.

Finally, the last part of the paper requires them to make and defend several recommendations for change. They are also required to make informal presentations in class where the students chose a strength or weakness to discuss. The presentations allow for some cross-pollination from one agency to another. The students usually provide handouts (which are frequently collected after the discussion) so their classmates can see what they're talking about.

Financial Management as a Capstone Course

"We found out very early in our work with tax-exempt organizations that underlying every aspect of nonprofit operations is the budget" (Dropkin, Halpin, & La Touche, 2007, p. xx). Therefore, if financial management is taught at the end of the management curriculum, it can knit together many important management skills. The discussion that follows highlights key management functions that are interdependent with financial management.

Vinter and Kish (1984) repeatedly underscore the importance of strongly linking program planning to budget. All features of a service, from client outreach and staff recruitment and training, to specific interventions have budget implications. When a program is designed, we always ask what qualifications and experience staff should have to deliver services effectively, and how many will be needed. Most social workers realize that if their programs are to have diverse staff members, atypical and, therefore, more expensive recruiting techniques need to be used. To ensure that staff are culturally competent, agencies will need to pay for training and consultants.

As programs are being planned, personnel policies need to be clarified. What benefits will be available to staff and under what conditions (at what cost)? What will be the nature of vacation and sick leave? When staff are sick or on vacation, will the agency need to hire temporary workers? To what degree can and will an agency support social workers' requirements for continuing education?

As managers monitor revenues and expenses, they are monitoring more than the in- and outflow of dollars. When a monitoring report shows overspending, managers need to understand the intricacies of their program to reduce cost overages. They ask questions such as: Is the program being implemented as planned? Are the clients more needy or complicated than projected? Is more supervision of direct service workers needed? Seeing overspending in a monthly budget report is just the red flag to start analyzing program operations. If layoffs are considered as one way to deal with overspending, personnel policies come into play again. Unfortunately, some agencies have to consider cuts in worker benefits. Personnel issues and financial management operate hand-in-hand.

Social work managers represent and advocate for their agencies and programs. If managers are advocating increases in budget, or are fighting decreases, they are likely to be more successful if they have conducted a thorough cost analysis. Many times they address budget planners and appropriations committee members; therefore, the better they can converse in the language of budgets, the greater will be their credibility and chances of success.

Financial management can be an effective capstone course, especially if it is taught using the case method. Using this method requires students to practice solving problems and making decisions in a manner consistent with professional ethics and values. This is exactly what they'll be doing very shortly. The case method simulates actual management practice, but in the low-stakes, safe environment of the classroom. As students make decisions, solve problems, and defend their thinking, they are able to get feedback from classmates and the instructor.

References

Brody, R. (2005). *Effectively managing human service organizations* (3rd ed.). Thousand Oaks, CA: Sage.

Dropkin, M., Halpin, J., & La Touche, B. (2007). *The budget-building book for nonprofits: A step-by step guide for managers and boards* (2nd ed.). San Francisco: John Wiley & Sons.

Ezell, M. (2000). Financial management. In R. J. Patti (Ed.), *Handbook on social welfare management* (pp. 377–93). Thousand Oaks, CA: Sage.

Ezell, M. (2007). Managing diverse sources of funding. In J. Aldgate, L. Healy, B. Malcolm, B. Pine, W. Rose, & A. Bullman (Eds.), *Enhancing human services: Social work management theory and practice in the UK and USA*. London: Jessica Kingsley.

Ezell, M. (2008). Financial management. In R. J. Patti (Ed.), *Handbook on human services management* (2nd ed.). Thousand Oaks, CA: Sage.

Hudson, W. W. (1981). Sequential criterion-referenced educational evaluation: A student/teacher assessment system. *Journal of Education for Social Work, 17*(1), 53–58.

Lohmann, R. A., & Lohmann, N. (2002). *Social administration.* New York: Columbia University Press.

Martin, L. L. (2001). *Financial management for human service administrators.* Boston: Allyn & Bacon.

Menefee, D. T. (2000). What managers do and why they do it. In R. J. Patti (Ed.), *The handbook of social welfare management* (pp. 247–266). Thousand Oaks, CA: Sage.

Menefee, D. T., & Thompson, J. J. (1994). Identifying and comparing competencies for social work management: A practice driven approach. *Administration in Social Work, 18*(3), 1–25.

National Network of Social Work Managers. (2008). Competencies of the National Network of Social Work Managers. Retrieved January 15, 2008, from http://www.socialworkmanager.org/Standards.htm

Patti, R. J. (1977). Patterns of management activity in social welfare agencies. *Administration in Social Work, 1*(1), 5–18.

Poertner, J., & Rapp, C. A. (2007). *Textbook of social administration: The consumer-centered approach.* New York: Haworth Press.

Vinter, R. D., & Kish, R. K. (1984). *Budgeting for not-for-profit organizations.* New York: Free Press.

Zietlow, J., Hankin, J. A., & Seidner, A. G. (2007). *Financial management for nonprofit organizations: Policies and practices.* Hoboken, NJ: John Wiley & Sons.

20

The Graduate Social Work Dean:
Roles and Reflections

Jeanette C. Takamura

This chapter acknowledges the complex nature of social work education and the multiple demands and stresses deans and directors face as leaders and managers of master's programs in social work. A dean of deans, Leon Ginsberg, asked me to write a chapter about the real world of graduate social work education at the master's level and share my personal observations related to educational leadership in our times. I write this from the perspective of a dean, referring to "deans" instead of the lengthier "deans and directors," using feminine pronouns in acknowledgment of the gender distribution within our profession, and relying on "schools" instead of "schools, colleges, departments, or divisions."

With new deans overseeing master's programs in mind, I attempt to identify and attend to several overarching leadership and management issues as well as some of the seemingly mundane, but nonetheless thorny, dilemmas that are inherently part of a dean's everyday work life. These concerns and dilemmas are partly products of the enormous challenges academic institutions face in a world that is changing with considerable speed. They are tied as well to demanding social problems, some of which may be intractable in our current environment or which other professions are often perceived to be addressing more effectively through their policy, practice, and research agendas. Leadership and management issues are also complicated by the state of the profession, which many feel is in crisis. This chapter assumes that governance is shared with faculty around curricular and many other issues and is a topic worthy of its own discussion. The chapter acknowledges, however, that the convergence of very palpable strains in the academy and the profession, along with a host of pressures specific to social work education, make most deanships and the leadership and management of master's-level programs an assignment that, although enormously rewarding, should not be taken up by the faint of heart.

Without any illusions about how germane they will prove to be, I offer several leadership and management pointers for consideration, respectfully recognizing how widely master's programs vary in substantive content and quality. I also attempt to capture a few of the fundamental questions about our profession that arise with regularity and suggest their implications for the education and preparation of social workers. I offer this chapter recognizing the invaluable contributions social workers with master's degrees are making in communities across the nation and, of course, social work education's important role in preparing professionals who dedicate themselves to the betterment of humankind. In so doing, I hope I have come close to honoring Leon's request.

On Becoming a Dean

Discussions of leadership and management within higher education are quick to observe that most presidents of universities have had little or no formal preparation for their positions (Borden, 2005). One can make the same observation about deans of professional schools, including schools of social work. Most deans learn on the job, and their schools lack the resources to afford anything akin to the administrative and management support in private corporations and the federal government.

New deans interested in learning how to lead and manage their schools effectively have a number of formal options. Their own universities may offer executive management workshops and seminars through their human resources departments. For-credit executive management programs and short-term, noncredit programs are also available through business and public administration schools. If these are not feasible, national management associations and professional education companies present short-term seminars for executives and administrators. Online courses are also an option, particularly when time away from the office is impossible to schedule. For deans inclined to focus specifically on social work schools and their concerns, the recently established National Association of Deans and Directors Social Work Leadership Institute may be the most appropriate resource. Finally, the annual meetings of the Council on Social Work Education (CSWE) attend to the full panoply of issues that affect master's programs.

The move into a deanship requires large and small adjustments that can be impossible to fully anticipate and comprehend. The inevitable and necessary redefinition of relationships with colleagues is often sobering for those who transition from the ranks of faculty or from one school to another. It can be jarring for new deans to realize their earlier assumptions and perspectives were faulty. As new layers of information about the university, the different curricular components of the program, its budget, faculty, and students become available to her, a dean may be compelled to seek program and other changes earlier expected. She may find different program areas requiring concentrated attention, or she may be pleasantly surprised to find areas she expected to be problematic were in better shape than originally thought.

A dean is formally approved by university trustees to advance, lead, and manage the school and its master's program as a chief executive officer. She is charged by and reports to her president and provost. A dean is expected to take her school in directions aligned with the vision and the mission of the university. In the process, she must continually educate her superiors and administrative colleagues about the school and its master's program. She must also be responsive to the school's constituencies, which typically include faculty, students, other university administrators, donors, foundations, government agencies, alumni, the health and social service agency community, and the community in which the university is located.

A new dean is often astounded by the interplay of special interests, broad and narrow agendas, individuals, and groups, all of which become much more visible when observed from her new vantage point. A new dean may see for the first time the organizational dynamics that challenge the coherence and potential of a school and its programs. These dynamics and the fluidity of faculty, student, staff, and other interests are viewed widely as part of the nature and culture of the academy. Nonetheless, a dean must assess and juggle the narrow interests of each constituency, among which is sometimes a single dissident faculty member who can consume an extraordinary amount of time and energy if not managed well. With information about the university, the school, and the master's program as a major tool, a new dean must navigate among competing interests to win over constituencies so the school and program are synchronous with or ahead of the rest of the university and trends in the field. This is no small feat, given the inherent tension, for example, between faculty rights and a dean's responsibility for the school and its programs. Deans have the responsibility (and right) to administer their programs within the guidelines provided by the academy, the institution, and the law.

A wise dean navigates through issues fully informed by university and school policies and procedures, federal and state laws, generally accepted accounting principles, and widely embraced ethical standards. When there are competing demands for resources to strengthen one or another of the school's existing programs or to begin new initiatives, a well-thought-through determination criterion is an excellent tool for a dean to use with administrators who manage the school's budget and finances. The determination criterion should reinforce the school's vision, mission, goals, and objectives and make visible expected returns to the master's program from investments of time, energy, and dollars. When they are not available, a dean must determine whether to establish additional administrative policy and procedural guidelines, bearing in mind that their existence can facilitate uniform transactions and, conversely, if overly detailed, can impede progress. In any case, most leadership and management principles recognize the importance of promising only what is deliverable. This applies to large program allocations as well as to requests from individual faculty members.

A new dean comes to appreciate quickly how difficult it can be for faculty who are seeking higher salaries or more resources to compare themselves objectively to others in the larger university, in peer institutions, or across methods and fields of practice within the school. Just as a determination criterion can be helpful in making funding decisions for programs and initiatives, objective faculty performance measures are essential. Yearly measurements should capture the research, publication, funding received from external sources, teaching, and community service achievements by members of the faculty. Although considerable school resources may be dedicated to faculty through research or teaching support and mentoring and other supportive services, these may viewed as a right rather than as a privilege borne out of a conscious investment decision. Even if objective measures are used or a faculty committee has reviewed an individual's full dossier, discussions with members of the faculty about their comparative performance and, accordingly, their salaries can be among the most sensitive of all conversations a dean must have.

isc issues are rarely free from differing perspectives, a dean's objectivity and the ty of formal opportunities for disagreeing individuals or groups to engage in constructive discussions can help to strengthen the school. When a dean finds herself in disagreement with faculty and administrators, as inevitably she often will, she must strive to differ without contributing to or worsening a conflict. Astute deans realize how perilous it is to expect to have socially and emotionally interdependent friendships with faculty, other administrators, alumni, or students about whom they may need to make difficult, objective decisions.

In private corporations and in government, teamwork has become the norm. Rewards are meted out to team members based on their achieving specific outcomes together. In the academy, tenure and material rewards are given to individuals. At the most competitive universities, a positive tenure review has satisfied the decisive factor—that tenured faculty and objective external reviewers have deemed the individual to be the best or among the very best of scholars in a particular area of scholarship. To accomplish this, most tenurable faculty in most schools work for 7 years with a single purpose: to meet or exceed their university's research, publication, funded research, teaching, and service requirements. Tenurable faculty members who have helpful, generous mentors understand that a strong individual portfolio of accomplishments as a scholar and as an educator is an absolute requirement for achieving tenure. This issue has implications for the quality of education offered to master's students, and I return to it later in the chapter.

Borden (2005) concurs that, in the higher education administrator's interactions with all of her constituencies, not just faculty, it's *not* about you. In fact, the most effective leaders check their egos at the door for the duration of their service and remember that constituencies, from overseers to students, relate to the dean's position and to the institution. Because a dean's job is to accomplish as much as possible on behalf of the school and the program, she can better understand its dynamics, needs, and opportunities by listening to its constituencies disproportionately more than she speaks. Periodically she should remind everyone of the need to maintain an institutional focus, to concentrate on substantive issues rather than on personality differences and unproductive agendas, and to keep an eye on the expectable returns on the investment of school time and resources.

A dean who is intent on moving a master's program and a school forward can expect critics and criticism. She knows that relationships change once a deanship begins and when it ends. She knows she must manage information carefully and is mindful of the risk of being quoted and misquoted in and out of context. Anticipating this, a leader keeps her personal life separate from her role as dean and all the deanship entails. And, at the end of her tenure, she leaves behind her executive role and all of the information to which she was privy while in the office of the dean.

The Environment—Understanding the Impact of Relevant Trends

Many of the challenges a social work dean faces are ubiquitous throughout higher education and master's programs in social work. A few, like the yet unresolved definition of social work, are unique to the profession. Taken together, the challenges raise questions for master's programs and social work education that a social work dean cannot ignore. They are challenges around which a dean may be able to galvanize her faculty.

Science and Research

Beginning in the mid-1970s, the landscape of higher education began to shift along with the expansion of the National Institutes of Health research agenda and the Institutes' call for greater rigor in the methodological approaches and analytical tools employed by scientists. Many universities worked feverishly to become Research I institutions,[1] expanding their research infrastructures significantly as they competed for NIH dollars. Frenzied research activity probably reached its highest point when President Bill Clinton and Congress committed to doubling the NIH budget over the 5-year period from 1998 to 2003. With this, the demonstration of the capacity to engage in innovative, state-of-the-art, high-quality scientific scholarship became an imperative for schools of social work embedded in research-intensive, multischool universities where the biomedical sciences, public health, psychology, and other fields and professions with which social workers and social work educators interface were all ramping up their research enterprises. Schools of social work in large research universities could not afford to be left behind, nor could they ignore the enormous incentives offered by the prospect of external funding support from federal agencies and private foundations.

Although all schools are not housed in Research I universities, arguably all master's programs have been affected by the standards and the culture of scholarship within research-oriented institutions. A good number of the contemporary issues before master's programs trace back to the transformation of higher education, triggered by the ascendance of the NIH over 3 decades. In an environment fed by science dollars, quantitative research methods have dominated. Divisions among faculty based on research methods are not uncommon in master's programs, more recently conflated by the profession-wide momentum to adopt evidence-based social work practice as distinct from traditional social work practice.

The Academy Questioned

Members of the academy embrace several core values, of which academic and intellectual freedom are possibly the most important. Among other values is the encouragement of intellectual discourse and behaviors characterized by professionalism and civility. Faculty members expect to be able to conduct research, think, and present their ideas freely. Although this occurs more often than not, some theories and perspectives inevitably are or appear to be accorded greater value in the marketplace of ideas. Dominant perspectives are strengthened by their appearance in top-tier publications, by references to them by influential scholars, by the amount of external

---

[1] Research I universities, as categorized by the Carnegie Foundation for the Advancement of Teaching, give high priority to research, annually award 50 or more doctoral degrees, and receive at least $40 million in federal funding annually (Carnegie Foundation for the Advancement of Teaching, 2007).

funding provided to explore them further, and by the support of colleagues within both a school and the broader intellectual community.

Although the curriculum may be the domain of faculty, a dean is ultimately responsible for administering the school and the master's program. Hence, a dean must be confident that the program's curriculum committee has given careful thought, for example, to how the school upholds the profession's dedication to social justice and protects the freedom of expression of divergent opinions by faculty and students alike. When such confidence is lacking, a dean may need to work with the university's general counsel and faculty to be sure the school's course is unassailable. This is especially important in light of the challenges raised by the National Association of Scholars (NAS, 2007) and by the Foundation for Individual Rights in Education (FIRE), which have taken aim at the most sacred of the social work profession's core values—social justice.

NAS called for the U.S. Department of Education to investigate CSWE (and the accrediting body of schools of education) to determine whether professional social work and education programs deny students their First Amendment right to free speech. NAS has also taken issue with the liberal ideological bent of social work in its complaints to the U.S. Department of Health and Human Services (Harris, 2006). These challenges should stimulate schools to examine and discuss intellectual diversity or intellectual pluralism and their place in master's and other social work programs.

Unprecedented Growth in the Number of Universities and Master's Programs

The explosion in the number and size of universities from the mid-1960s to the current day has presented prospective students with previously unavailable alternatives. There are now approximately 4,000 institutions of higher education, up from 2,329 in 1966, with the majority (908) of new universities and colleges identifying as private, for-profit, followed by public state universities. Not to be overlooked, the private, for-profit University of Phoenix, founded in 1976 to capture the working-adult market, has an enrollment of 116,000 students in 100 degree programs offered at 200 locations in the United States and online throughout the world (Rhodes, 2006).

The growth in the number of higher educational institutions has been followed by a rapid increase in master's programs in social work. Logically, more universities and more colleges will look for more programs to offer and, unless rigorous academic expectations and/or higher application fees are imposed, more social work programs may be expected to emerge, apply for candidacy, and be accredited.

In June 2002 there were 146 accredited master's programs with 26 in candidacy. Over the 5-year period from June 2002 to July 2007, there was about a 27% increase to 184 accredited master's programs with 18 in candidacy (CSWE, 2007). About 20 programs are in candidacy each year for an average period of 18 months. At current rates, about 12 new programs will be added each year, increasing the pool by about 7% per year (S. Schinke, personal communication, January 25, 2008).

There was a steady downward trend in master's program applications between 1994 and 2002, from 46,500 to 27,000. Although application numbers appear to be leveling off at 2002 rates, the 42% decrease in less than a decade, coupled with the increasing pool of master's programs, presents a sobering reality. An informal, rough analysis suggests in gross terms that "each new program accredited since 2002 has reduced the mean number of applicants per program by 5.56% per year through 2006, a trend likely to continue as long as new programs are accredited each year"(S. Schinke, personal communication, January 25, 2008).

During the 2006–2007academic year, there were 24,910 full-time students and 14,656 part-time students. Acceptance rates in 2006, although down by 1% (from 65.8% to 64.8%) from 2005, were still significantly higher than they were for most other professional education programs. However, starting salaries for social workers are significantly lower than for a number of other helping professions, with social workers averaging $42,500 with 2 to 4 years of experience (NASW, 2003) and likely averaging less than $42,000 annually nationwide at the start of their careers. When coupled with the high cost of education, the salaries paid professional social workers and the attractiveness of professions previously closed to women pose enormous disincentives to all but the most socially conscious prospective students.

The downturn and leveling off of applications to schools of social work are not as apparent in other professional education programs. Previously male-dominated professions that women are now entering in significant numbers show dramatically more competitive application and acceptance figures for their professional schools than for schools of social work. Applications to top U.S. business schools have increased as much as 22% and acceptance rates are in the teens (BusinessSchoolAdmissions.com, 2007). Among the 185 accredited law schools, the top 10 schools accepted an average of 13% of their applicants (ranging from 6.8% to 15.6%). The lowest-ranked law school accepted approximately 66% of its applicants. Acceptance rates at the top two U.S. medical schools were even more competitive: 4.7% at first-ranked Harvard and 6.2% at second-ranked Johns Hopkins (*U.S. News and World Report*, 2007). Applications to schools of public health increased by 53% from 1996 to 2006, rising in absolute numbers from 18,470 to 28,233, with an enrollment rate after acceptance (acceptance rates not available) of 26.1% (Association of Schools of Public Health, 2007). Today, there are 40 schools of public health (up from 27 in 1995) offering more than 15 degrees. On average, the 2007 starting salary packages of business school graduates of the top 10 MBA programs was $146,800 (BusinessSchoolAdmissions.com). Law school graduates compare at $62,000 to over $100,000 depending upon their specialization. No information on salaries is available for public health.

Careers in law, medicine, business, architecture and urban planning, and other fields clearly have high appeal for women. Four times the percentage of freshmen women expressed an interest in 2005 in eventually pursuing a law degree in 2005 than in 1966. Over the same time frame, there was a quintupling of interest among freshmen women in medical and dental degrees. Schools must ask how this will affect the quality of applicants to master's programs in social work, and they must ask whether the number of qualified applicants will be high enough to fill all the available spots. If the quality of students entering master's programs is less competitive than is desirable to maintain a strong profession, deans must be certain there is diligent gatekeeping and that their master's programs graduate only those students who have the knowledge, skills, attitudes, values, and character that one would expect of a competent social work professional.

The Rising Cost of Higher Education

Affordability and accessibility—two of the four major issues raised by the Spellings Commission on the Future of Higher Education are continuing dilemmas for universities and colleges (U.S. Department of Education, 2006). The cost of higher education has been on the rise for decades and shows no sign of abating. Only the most determined may be able to shoulder the cost of graduate education on top of the cost of undergraduate education, but not without scholarships, grants, work-study support, and loan forgiveness.

Professions with clearly defined identities and roles held in high public esteem are attracting students who probably would be well suited for social work. Typically these professions promise to their graduates higher salaries and better benefits, the importance of which cannot be overstated. Rhodes (2006) has noted that "being well off financially" was important to 42% of college students surveyed in 1966. Today, 75% of those surveyed regard their financial status as important. This does not bode well for social work education, as debt levels present a significant financial burden among 46% of new social work graduates (Rainey, 2006). Given this situation, it is no surprise that one of the development priorities for most deans is, and will likely to continue to be, student financial aid. However, even securing more financial aid for students is not enough. A 2007 study by the New York chapter of NASW sought information on working conditions from practicing social workers and made unequivocally clear an overriding concern is the need for higher salaries.

A Low Supply of Potential Faculty with Doctoral Degrees

Nearly 300 students were graduated in 2005–2006 by the 69 U.S. doctoral programs that are members of the Group for the Advancement of Doctoral Education in Social Work (GADE). In November 2006, there were 1,637 doctoral students enrolled full time and 917 enrolled part time. If all 184 schools were actively recruiting at once for faculty in 2005, on average each school would have welcomed one new faculty member, assuming a level playing field. Given the high demand for doctoral graduates with sufficient practice experience or who are diverse, most schools will be unable to offer a rich menu of practice courses nor will they be able to diversify their schools without a very heavy reliance on adjuncts. If such is the case, schools will need to work ever more diligently at recruiting and retaining talented adjunct faculty.

Even the availability of capable adjuncts will not satisfy the need for experienced practitioners and teachers for advanced clinical practice courses. The push nationwide towards evidence-based practice is not buoyed by a robust supply of doctoral graduates with rich practice experience who are also trained in this approach. Indeed, this may remain a human resources conundrum for master's programs for many years to come. It has already posed an enormous challenge in efforts to coordinate classroom learning with field education, as most social work professionals in the field are not yet familiar with the theoretical basis, the underlying science, and the interventions and skills associated with evidence-based practice. Strapped for time because of huge workloads and in agencies that are short of resources, many social workers are barely able to provide basic supervision to master's students who feel cheated and demoralized when they are unable to receive assignments or to integrate and apply their coursework in the field. To support field instructors and help them to acquire the knowledge and skills introduced in the classroom, schools must provide these instructors with timely, substantive professional education opportunities.

A Profession in Need of Definition Within an Environment of Complex Social Issues

The nagging, yet unanswered question: "What exactly is social work?" begs for a distinctive, universally embraced definition. The question remains a fundamental source of frustration within highly competitive multidisciplinary contexts. This is because social work roles and functions are increasingly claimed by nursing, public health, law, and other professionals. In health care settings, the roles and functions of other professionals are more widely understood and accepted. Usually social workers must thus fight aggressively for a place at the table.

The knowledge bases of other disciplines and professions such as economics, business, nursing, and medicine are much more clearly associated with defined, widely known skill sets. Thus, they are less likely to be contested. In the world of public policy, for example, economists have secured a strong foothold as experts with powerful analytical tools that can be used to offer new insights into poverty and its alleviation as well as social and economic development. In nonprofit management, business schools are offering programs that can be more attractive to social work managers than the administration and management courses taught in schools of social work. Business schools are also offering specializations in social entrepreneurship, an approach that applies business and finance methods and skills to transform communities and uplift disadvantaged, at-risk populations.

Even if professions have overlapping areas of interest and involvement, it is clear that most social, health, and economic dilemmas are multifaceted, and that one profession alone cannot address these dilemmas satisfactorily. If a viable definition of social work cannot be constructed, social work professionals may simply be compelled to accept further differentiation and specialization mirroring trends in other professions. This will generate more areas of overlap among many professions. What may emerge is a convergence of knowledge and skills suitable for use in highly specialized problem areas by professions that are no longer easily differentiated from each other, except by the excellence and quality of work of its members—i.e., the competent demonstration of leading-edge knowledge and skills, adherence to ethical principles, and the ability to consistently produce significant, measurable results. In the case of social work, the other significant exception should be its commitment to ensuring social justice.

Vision and the School's Mission

Unless a dean plans to be a caretaker, she must be able to articulate a compelling vision of a preferred future for her school and its master's program. Her vision should recognize emerging realities and the directions for her university presented by the president or provost. Her vision should reflect the school's best possible identity and its long-term aspirations. For its successful realization over time, any vision for the school (and program) will require faculty ownership and alignment. Once accepted, this vision serves as a compass and is reinforced by a congruent school mission statement and by relevant program goals and objectives.

The mission statement, as the public declaration of the school's intent, can be a powerful unifying and motivating tool if it succinctly and clearly captures the school's aspirations and identity. Most mission statements are reviewed and revised before reaccreditation. Many are laundry lists of aspirations, others are far too grand. The best mission statements are easily embraced by the school's many audiences. The best statements sometimes emerge organically from the school's vision and thus can help drive collective and individual endeavors and activities.

The vision and the mission for the school and its master's programs should be informed by the larger environment of the university, its other professional schools, and the turf that is shared, claimed, or in play. The neighborhood, city, state, and region within and for which the institution is a resource are factors as well. Schools in national universities that draw students from across the country differ from regional and local schools. Public universities commonly have specific regional or local expectations that must be met. That is, a dean of a public school of social work may need to demonstrate visible leadership on very specific social issues of particular interest to citizens in her community and to her legislators.

The necessary supply of academically trained professional social workers in communities important to the school and the surge in the number of schools of social work must be considered in setting the course of a master's program. Issues already mentioned—that is, the inadequate pipeline of social work doctoral graduates with significant depth of clinical social work practice experience, the small pool of racially and ethnically diverse scholars, and a weak nationwide student applicant pool—have dramatic implications for a school's mission and its master's program goals and objectives.

Financial and human resources are among the most important internal matters to which a dean must attend. As an example, the strengths and interest areas of tenured and tenurable faculty determine to a large measure the courses offered in the second year of a master's program. A heavy ratio of tenured faculty whose work is no longer contemporary will limit a school's curriculum. On the other hand, a school can find itself in a conundrum when courses must be taught, but junior faculty are assigned reduced workloads to support pursuit of their research agendas. Reliance on too many adjuncts in the master's program may run counter to CSWE requirements and to assertions of excellence based on the accomplishments of the school's tenured and tenurable faculty. Unless resources are available to add full-time teaching faculty and staff or additional researchers, a dean must be able to a gauge her school's capacity to juggle its competing teaching and research interests and its realistic timetable for programmatic, curricular, and personnel changes. She must also manage expectations explicitly suggested by the school's mission statement.

On Metrics

Once the school's mission and its goals and objectives are articulated, a system and responsibilities must be in place to capture reliable, timely input, output, and outcome data on the master's program. Some thought should be given to gathering data, beyond that required by CSWE that can be used to tell the school's story effectively to important donors, external sponsors of research, and constituencies in the university and the community. Good information can stimulate midcourse corrections in the curriculum, suggest effective student recruitment and retention strategies, and lead to allocations of financial and personnel resources that are likely to provide the best returns on investment.

Despite its superficiality, the *U.S. News and World Report* (2007) rankings of schools of social work have attracted more attention than they probably merit. Only 10 schools among the 180+ reap the greatest benefit from the survey. Beyond dedicating one's time to striving for program excellence, a dean should consider educating her school's constituencies on the reputational ranking method used and its inadequacies. She should then concentrate on achieving her school's identified objectives and tell her school's story with valid, reliable substantiating data tying the school's accomplishments and its plans to its mission, goals, and objectives.

Co-leadership and Management Teams

In *Good to Great,* Collins (2001) states emphatically that putting the right people in place on an executive team is more important than all the vision and all the strategy in the world. He writes that the greatest leaders "*first* got the right people on the bus, the wrong people off the bus, and the right people in the right seats" (p. 13). Each dean must determine who is right for her administrative team. Given the demands of higher education, basic requirements presumably would include competence; ethics and integrity; good judgment after critical analysis; trustworthiness; an understanding of the larger picture; and the ability to work well with faculty, students, other team members, and administrators from other parts of the university. The ability to connect the dots in an information-rich environment, confront and present hard realities (Collins talks about "brutal facts," pp. 65–89), accountability, stamina, and resilience are important. So are commitments to the institution and to community building, fairness, and civility. If her school has a director of the master's program, a dean will need someone who understands the impact of larger trends as well as the workings of the program and who can lead it with a commitment to excellence. In assembling the right team, a dean must be uncompromisingly honest about what is needed and then persevere in finding the most qualified, most suitable individuals.

The most difficult scenario for a new dean is one in which her administrative team is inherited and change is essential. When this is the case, a new dean needs to secure assurances of unwavering support for her personnel decisions from her superiors. To give administrators notice and time to transition, the intention to institute changes should be made public early in her tenure. As changes are made, a dean should look for competent, productive, positive professionals and consider the multidisciplinary perspectives and contributions of managers with specialized credentials and experience in higher education administration, financial management, curriculum development, and student services. The best administrative team is not necessarily comprised entirely of persons who have social work backgrounds. Individuals with specialized knowledge and skills can accelerate and ease a school's progress towards achieving its mission and its master's program goals and objectives.

Every dean wants to lead and manage her school with a team of trusted colleagues. Based on their observations of large corporations, Heenan and Bennis (1999) have argued that a complex organization is better led and managed by co-leaders who share the same vision and goals for their organization but may have complementary knowledge and skills. When they can disagree in their pursuit of school goals and objectives and deliberately work through differing views with each other within the confines of the team, co-leaders who then proceed as a united front in the best interests of their school are in effect offering their highest and best selves. When co-leadership involves both administrators and faculty, a good school stands its best chance of becoming a great school.

Faculty

More like law firms in which partnerships must be earned and bestowed, universities and schools place enormous pressure on faculty to excel as scholars, teachers, and community leaders. The stresses borne by tenurable faculty, particularly in schools lodged in highly research-intensive universities can be considerable. Although a dean must recruit faculty who have expertise in methods or areas of practice in which there are gaps in the master's program, they must also be sure that newly recruited faculty will enrich the climate and help to sustain a community of scholars. The small pool of doctoral graduates does not ease the task of recruitment, but many deans feel it is far better not to hire than to spend time and resources on individuals who are a poor fit, whose contributions are not likely to exceed the time and energy dedicated to their development by the school, who are extraordinarily self-absorbed or insecure, or whose probability of achieving tenure is no better than a gamble.

Once hired, tenurable faculty can thrive if mentored well by senior faculty invested in their success. They must be encouraged to pursue a clearly defined research agenda. If they did not have opportunities in their doctoral program, they must also be exposed to pedagogical models and instructional strategies that can be used in their classes. Although not all will succeed, both strong, tenurable faculty and those who are not sufficiently competitive or are otherwise inappropriate for academic appointment require careful attention. Deans and their deans for academic affairs would be wise to identify early, through annual reviews, those faculty with inadequate accomplishments to achieve tenure or who are not a good fit. Although discussions about unsatisfactory performance are among the most sensitive in any school, the costs are high for both the school and the faculty member when honest, unambiguous discussions about performance do not occur and remedial plans or career counseling are delayed.

Because of its impact on schools of social work, some mention must be made of the "star system" that emerged as universities pursued Nobel Prize winners, scientists who held important patents, researchers with large NIH and private foundation grants, scholars with exemplary publication records, and public intellectuals. One could argue that a "star" within fields of science in which patents or Nobel Prizes are awarded or high practice incomes can be generated is vastly different from a star in social work. The revenue-generating potential of star faculty in social work is generally less than in the hard sciences. The products of extraordinary research and interventions by scholars in schools of social work are not ordinarily packaged, marketed, and dispensed to millions of consumers. A star's value thus lies in the opportunities to claim authority in specific issue areas or methods, attract external funding, generate new knowledge that can be identified with the school, and enrich students' education. Although these are all significant and positive, the star system may be contributing concomitantly to the erosion of the institutional loyalty that Rhodes (2006) contends was commonplace until recent decades. A dean is most fortunate when she can recruit individuals who have a sense of institutional loyalty and commitment and will strengthen the program through their leadership as scholars. For the sake of the school, a dean must strive to instill and promote a climate in which productive collaboration, collegiality, and consideration for others remain organizational values.

Students

If a master's program accepts students who do not have competitive academic records and do not have critical thinking, strong writing, verbal communication, and other skills associated with professional effectiveness, it must be ensured students know there are nonnegotiable performance standards for professionals. Admitted students should know that admission does not guarantee graduation. Students who lack requisite knowledge and skills must be held responsible for their acquisition through remedial and enrichment opportunities. Some master's programs offer seminars on the social work profession itself and make special writing labs and classes available or have writing centers for students in need of additional assistance. If less-than-competitive students are not held to acceptable academic standards, schools of social work will graduate individuals who will weaken the profession, soil their alma mater's name, and potentially cause harm to their clients.

Student cohorts frequently have distinctive personalities that can affect the climate of a school. Differences in students' confidence and stress levels from the 1st to the 2nd year of the master's program are often palpable, as may be the differences between students in advanced standing programs as compared to traditional 2-year programs. Unfortunately, the confidence levels of less-than-competitive students can be inflated inappropriately when programs compete for them with large financial aid packages.

Administrators who are mature in attitude, sincerely student-oriented, and professional in demeanor can help master's students understand and adjust to the stages of their educational and professional development. Student services administrators can design well-rounded, rich experiences that extend students' educational opportunities well beyond the classroom. In their positions, these administrators may be best able to discern how the school is doing with its most important "customers." A dean should make student feedback and administrators' assessments available to faculty and encourage the examination of available outcome data as the basis for corrections and changes to the master's curriculum. Students who are satisfied with their course and field work and their extracurricular activities, are likely to be the school's best ambassadors over the long term.

Alumni

Alumni can assist the school to achieve its mission, goals, and objectives if they understand the vision and programmatic directions of their alma mater. Like faculty, alumni are sometimes wedded to specific theoretical orientations and methods of practice. They may not understand the differences between a research and a teaching university, the value of evidence-based practice, or the implications of the school's regional, national, or international emphasis. They may not fully appreciate the importance of having a diverse faculty and student body. Their points of reference are likely the curriculum and the composition of the school during their time as master's students. Here is where a dean and staff assigned to work with alumni need to share and discuss emerging trends in master's-level social work education and in social work practice. Alumni with financial resources who understand and support the school's aspirations can help to materialize essential scholarships, professorships, and special programs.

Development

Just as most deans are not schooled in the leadership and management of master's programs, nor are they schooled in development and fundraising. Deans who do not have a development officer in-house should work closely with their university's development office. Although social work was once a profession to which the offspring of wealthy families gravitated, such is not the case today, nor is this likely to be the case in the future. Most students enrolled in schools of social work do not have the resources to pay for their own education unassisted. The majority graduate with sizeable debt burdens and go on to jobs that are not high paying. Fundraising will hence be an even more challenging responsibility in the future and will heighten the importance of students' satisfaction with their educational experiences and of a dean having a compelling story to share with donors about the program and the school.

Idealistic Goals, Realistic Expectations

At some point, every new dean realizes that her honeymoon with school constituencies is over, that thorny issues must be addressed, and that relationships with faculty, administrators, alumni, and students will wax and wane. No dean escapes difficult dilemmas or criticism. Knowing this, a dean should: (1) rely on the university's and the school's policies and procedures as a standard practice; (2) always expect to be held accountable; (3) attempt to communicate decisions as simply and as clearly as possible, and expect that on occasion information that she is privileged to have but not at liberty to disclose will leave her in the uncomfortable position of seeming to be less than forthcoming; (4) expect some misunderstandings by some constituencies or individuals around even the most sound decisions rendered; (5) be as transparent as possible, but not expect that this will satisfy everyone or that universal agreement will result; and (6) always, always strive for excellence because the profession must demonstrate through results that it is second to none in its ability to better the human condition.

Conclusion

The profession and social work education have come a great distance since their early beginnings. Important challenges, large and small, confront deans of schools of social work, among which are a significant shift in the market for social work education, the cost of higher education, the nagging lack of a clear definition of social work and its domain, and overlapping leadership claims by many professions around social issues. These are significant concerns that must be addressed by the profession, national social work organizations, and schools of social work.

A dean of a school with a master's program may be best able to lead and manage if she can maintain and navigate with a strong institutional and program focus as charged by her president and provost. A dean must ensure that her school has a thoughtfully identified and inspiring mission to drive and give coherence to its work. To document and measure the achievement of goals and objectives so the school's story can be told, a dean must be sure there is an institutionalized system for monitoring input, output, and data. She must assemble the strongest possible administrative team composed of members who have the capacity and the temperament to be co-leaders. A dean and her faculty must have a clear sense of the kinds of colleagues who will contribute ably to and build a community of scholars. These faculty, particularly those who are junior and tenurable, must be nurtured and supported to succeed. At the end of the day, their success as scholars, as educators of master's students, and as those who will instill the importance of excellence and competence is what will inspire and prepare competent social workers who can improve the human condition now and in the decades ahead.

References

Association of Schools of Public Health. (2007). [Applications to schools of public health]. Retrieved December 28, 2008, from http://www.naahp.org/PDFs/HealthProfPDFs/ASPH.pdf

Borden, R. H. (2005, July 8). The art of deanship. *The chronicle of higher education*, *51*(44), B9.

BusinessSchoolAdmission.com. (2007). Business school admissions. Retrieved December 28, 2008, from http://www.businessschooladmission.com

Carnegie Foundation for the Advancement of Teaching. (2007). The Carnegie classification of institutions of higher education. Retrieved December 20, 2007, from http://www.carnegiefoundation.org/classifications

Collins, J. (2001). *Good to great.* New York: HarperCollins.

Council on Social Work Education. (CSWE). (2007). *2006 statistics on social work education in the United States: A summary.* Alexandria, VA: Author. Retrieved December 28, 2007, from http://www.cswe.org/CSWE/CMS_Templates/SearchResults.aspx?NRMODE=Published&NRORIGINALURL=%2fCSWE%2fsearchresults%2ehtm%3fquery%3dschools%2520for%2520social%2520worker&NRNODEGUID=%7bD37705C8-3A95-48DB-9C6A-DDDF4C297E4D%7d&NRCACHEHINT=NoModifyGuest&query=Number%20of%20master's%20programs

Harris, S. (2006, October 25). Letter to Admiral John Agwunobi. Retrieved August 30, 2008, from http://www.thefire.org/index.php/article/7428.html

Heenan, D., & Bennis, W. (1999). *Co-leaders: The power of great partnerships.* Somerset, NJ: John Wiley & Sons.

National Association of Scholars. (2007, September 11). The scandal of social work education. Retrieved December 28, 2007, from http://www.nas.org/nasinitiatives/CSWEnitiative/soswe_scandal/scandal_ soc-work-ed_11sep07.pdf

National Association of Social Workers New York Chapter (NASWNYC). (2007, October). Focus group on how working conditions can be improved: A reasonable imperative for social work employers. *Currents, 52*(1), 9–11.

National Association of Social Workers. (2003). *Social work income.* Retrieved December 28, 2007, from https://www.social workers.org/naswprn/surveyTwo/datagram1.pdf

Rainey, A. (2006, April 14). Loan debt could affect career choices. *The Chronicle of Higher Education, 52*(32), A24.

Rhodes, F. T. H. (2006, November 24). After 40 years of growth and change, higher education faces new challenges. *The Chronicle of Higher Education, 53*(14), A18.

U.S. Department of Education. (2006). A test of leadership: Charting the future of U.S. higher education. Washington, DC: Author.

U.S. News and World Report. (2007). America's top medical schools. Received December 28, 2007 from http://gradschools.usnews.rankingsandreviews.com/usnews/edu/grad/rankings/med/brief/mdrrank_brief.php

21

Managing Baccalaureate Social Work Education

Michael R. Daley

Directing a bachelor of social work (BSW) program is a job that often appears very attractive to outside observers. The director position seems to offer a higher salary, has more release time, offers more prestige, and gives the incumbent greater control over what the program does. So what's not to like about all of this for a social work faculty member? From the point of observation of onlookers, the BSW program direction appears deceptively simple.

I had been a BSW director for over 10 years when a good colleague who had been a director summed things up very well. My colleague explained that he was working with a faculty member who had once been a student of his and who was developing quite well. This young faculty member was beginning to reach the point where many of the challenges of the faculty member's role had been conquered, and the person was beginning to look for an upward move. The director's job was beginning to look very attractive. It wasn't long until my colleague moved on to another position, and his protégé became the BSW director. About a year later, my colleague ran into the new program director and asked how things were going. The new director reportedly replied, "Okay, but I need to ask you a question. When I watched you as director, your door was always open, you were always talking to people, and you didn't seem to be working all that hard. But there's a lot of work in this job, and I know you did it. When did you have the time?"

BSW directors play a crucial role in social work education, yet they often enter the position with little or no preparation. Despite the importance of BSW directors for ensuring the business of undergraduate education is carried out, surprisingly little has been written about how to be good in this position. This chapter is a brief practical guide that may prove useful for those who are becoming BSW directors, new directors, and experienced directors. The chapter begins with a general overview of the BSW director position, and then considers the important functional areas of director responsibility. Within these sections, I discuss 16 practical principles for guiding the director.

The BSW Director

Based on the most recent Council on Social Work Education (CSWE) statistics, there are 458 accredited baccalaureate social work programs in the United States (CSWE, 2007b), and each has a full-time person designated as an administrator (CSWE, 2003). The heads of social work programs are appointed under several titles, such as department chair, program coordinator, and program director, depending on the administrative structure and custom of the institution. But the title *program director* is commonly used to refer to them all.

The job of leading a BSW program is difficult because directors are expected to manage in a very complex environment. One key aspect of this complexity is the structure of the programs themselves as they vary considerably in size and auspices. Such complexity makes a one-size-fits-all model of administration or leadership quite difficult. For example, small BSW programs, or those that have 49 or fewer full-time juniors and seniors, constitute 49% of the programs (CSWE, 2007b), although large programs, those with 100 or more full-time juniors and seniors, comprise 18% of the undergraduate programs (CSWE, 2007b). Undergraduate social work programs are also housed in a complex array of university structures, including as stand-alone departments or programs, parts of combined interdisciplinary departments, and combined undergraduate and graduate social work programs. Baccalaureate social work programs are offered at a range of public and private, sectarian and nonsectarian, research, teaching, and urban universities.

This complexity is only the tip of the iceberg. There are issues of personnel management, curriculum design and review, student affairs, fiscal management, interface with the external environment, and accreditation, to name just a few. Given the importance of leadership to effective operation of an academic program, one might expect new directors to receive extensive preparation for their role in directing the BSW program. It would be nice if this were the case.

BSW directors are often figuratively thrown into the pool without anyone asking, or even appearing to care, whether the person knows how to swim! Unfortunately, dumping the director into the pool does not seem to be an uncommon event. In writing of the academic department chairperson, Bennett (1983) says:

> Important? Definitely. Overworked? Probably. Prepared for the job? Rarely. This is the typical academic chairperson. Often almost stumbling into the job, the average chairperson takes quite seriously his or her responsibilities even if how to meet them has to be learned along the way. (p.1)

Bennett (1983) goes on to argue that department chairs are crucial to the success of the university because it is at the department level that the real institutional business is conducted and that the university can better tolerate poor administrators than it can poor chairs. This certainly rings true for BSW directors, who face the same kinds of issues.

Given all of this, where is the BSW director to turn for guidance? Macy, Turner, and Wilson's (2000) *Directing the Baccalaureate Social Work Program* presents a comprehensive resource to new and experienced directors. Another resource is the

Association of Baccalaureate Program Directors, commonly known as BPD, which has provided training at its annual conference for several years (Association of Baccalaureate Program Directors, 1997, 2005, 2006). Generally, directors may not expect much training from the university, and certainly not in the field of social work. These are, indeed, useful resources that address nuts-and-bolts issues likely to confront BSW directors, whether experienced or new. This chapter offers a third option in the form of a practice-oriented, quick guide for BSW directors to help size up principles of practice that add an additional perspective to program direction.

General Approaches to BSW Leadership

Providing effective direction to a BSW program is so challenging because of the type of organizational structure, complex demands of the position, and general lack of preparation for the position. Simply wading through the myriad tasks and responsibilities can be quite daunting absent some guiding principles. The first general principle examines how directors approach learning the job both initially and on an ongoing basis, and two more give a broad overview of the director position.

Principle 1: If You Want to Learn How to Do the Job, You Are on Your Own

Given the importance of the BSW director's position to the success of the program, one might assume that incumbents would be selected carefully for their skill and preparation for the position. But that doesn't seem to be the case, as directors are often chosen for very different reasons (Bennett, 1983). Scholarly or professional accomplishments, being well-liked or politically correct, or being the only one available are common criteria for being selected to direct a BSW program. Even those who have prior administrative experience typically have this experience in a social welfare agency (Macy et al., 2000), and agencies are very different creatures from universities.

Unfortunately, the norm for BSW directors is to be hired into the position without much prior preparation and expect the infamous on-the-job training to work its magic. The way that most new academic directors learn about their duties is by watching how others perform in the position and from colleagues (Lees, 2006). Universities rarely offer much formal training on how to be a director, which certainly has its plusses and minuses.

What's clear is that it is up to program directors to assume responsibility for their professional development in the position. Given that the demands of the program begin from day 1, you should set aside time for reading about heading an academic program, developing a set of contacts with whom to consult about aspects of the job, and engaging in professional development activities related to program administration. Literature on directing a BSW program or being an academic department head can be obtained through the university library, but the key is making the time to read it, because many job-related pressures keep time for reading on the back burner.

Professional contacts on campus can prove useful for consulting about how to handle various kinds of situations or for sharing frustrations, but they can rarely offer advice specific to social work. Additional contacts have to be developed within the social work community among those who are current or former program directors. But you should be aware that, in taking advice from others, they learned the same way and may not have learned the best practices. So outside advice, although valuable, should be evaluated carefully. Professional development activities such the BPD annual conference or the CSWE annual program meeting provide excellent opportunities to get structured training or to engage in networking that can prove valuable to becoming and staying effective BSW directors.

Principle 2: The Director's Position Is a Hybrid Position in a Hybrid Organization

As organizations go, universities are not simple, and the practical significance of this is that many of the traditional theories of management or organizational leadership don't apply at least part of the time. Universities are highly complex organizations (Hage & Aiken, 1970) with intensive technology (Hall, 1982), and these characteristics have implications for the way in which universities operate. The relatively flat administrative structure, coupled with significant freedom and discretion for faculty, is not typical of many organizations. The typical educational program structure used in universities is designed to handle educational and research functions, which are diverse, complex, and very difficult to direct from much distance. Therefore, much decision making is decentralized and pushed to the point where the action occurs, the department or program. This means that program directors and faculty members have a lot of discretion and responsibility. In this type of structure, the program or department head serves as more of a coordinator or manager than administrator.

In a simple world, decentralized program decision making and governance would be the way a university worked, but there is another side to the university that lends itself well to a more traditional hierarchical structure, and that is the business side of the organization. Someone has to pay the bills, keep the records, maintain the grounds, heat and cool buildings, collect money, and do a variety of other more routine jobs. This part of the institution is well-served by a more traditional internal organization with clear lines of reporting, and responsibility for and administration of these jobs or functions are more centralized with less centralized control at the lower levels. Blending the two types of structure—decentralized academic and the centralized business— makes the university organization a hybrid structure.

A BSW director, as the head of the program, must navigate both sides of the organization effectively to satisfy the divergent demands of the university administration. As a result, directors must be flexible and have to be part administrator, part manager, and part coordinator.

As if this were not enough, the position of program director is not purely an administrative one. BSW program directors occupy a hybrid position in which they are an administrator, supervisor, and colleague, all rolled into one. The director's job covers many functions associated with midlevel management such as goal setting, preparing reports, budget administration, planning, and evaluation. However, directors also carry out several job functions typical of supervision. These supervisory functions include assessment of faculty and staff performance and development, motivation, and support of program personnel. Finally, program directors normally maintain line responsibility as a faculty member (Lees, 2006). With this kind of diversity among the functions of the director role, faculty, staff, students, and external constituencies may find it difficult to keep clear in which capacity the director is acting. Sometimes, directors have difficulty figuring this out, too. Any resultant confusion increases the probability of conflict and frustration, and it is important for BSW directors to understand, explain, and manage these varied functions.

A good framework for BSW directors in managing conflicting demands of the job is Kadushin's (2002) work on social work supervision, which identifies the three primary functions of supervisors as administrative, educational, and expressive-supportive supervision. The administrative aspects of the program director position have to do with getting the work done and being accountable to the organization. Educational aspects of the director's job have to do with the professional development of faculty and staff members, and the expressive-supportive functions relate to motivating faculty and staff and giving them a sense of connection to the university.

You should remember that BSW program directors are like the supervisor, a sort of middle person (Kadushin, 2002) with connections to both the administration and the faculty, and are expected to mediate between the two.

Principle 3: The BSW Director Must Be a Generalist

It is a normal process for BSW directors to come from the faculty and, occasionally, from social work practice. In either instance the demands of the previous position and the criteria for success in it are very different from those for BSW directors. Faculty members are prized for their skills in classroom teaching, research, and service or professional achievements, and those from a practice background are recognized for their skill in working with their clients. In any case they are rewarded for developing specialized areas of expertise that can form the basis of their individual activities for the university. In short, these are qualities of individual performance as opposed to group skills. Obviously, to carry out the faculty function that is typically part of the director's role, directors must maintain some of these attributes.

But as a program director, the emphasis shifts from the individual to the collective (Bennett, 1983), and the expectation is to keep the program operating productively. This means addressing the needs of several, often competing, groups at once. In a very real sense, the imperative is for directors to keep the collective going, sometimes at the expense of individual accomplishment. Thus, others determine how directors spend their day, at the expense of the directors' individual time. For example, the administration wants a report...yesterday, a student wants to discuss a grade, there is a meeting with a community group, and a faculty member needs to talk about a grant with a fast-approaching deadline. All of this is likely in a typical day. Rather than focus on individual projects such as classroom assignments, a grant application, service activity, or a research project, program directors must tend to the needs of others first. In so doing they are truly generalists in balancing the demands and needs of different constituencies. This is not the type of position that lends itself to the staunch individualist such as the ivory tower intellectual or lone wolf scholar. Given this overview of the BSW director, the discussion now turns to areas of functional responsibility and provides some suggestions for these areas.

Principles for Functional Areas of BSW Director Duties

In describing the duties of BSW directors, we can identify six areas of functional responsibility: faculty and staff, academics and governance, student affairs, budget and finances, accreditation, and maintenance of self. There are significant challenges for the program director in each of these areas. Principles related to each of these functions are discussed in the following pages.

Faculty and Staff

As Stieglitz (1970) observed many years ago, organizational charts don't tell you much about how an organization works. Formal designations of responsibilities, relationships, and reporting defined by the organizational chart and job descriptions often fall apart when one looks at the way an organization actually works. In fact, the faculty and staff in a BSW program have many interlocking relationships, both in and outside this organizational unit, that don't show up on any organizational chart and that affect what the organization does. These relationships comprise the informal organization that best describes how things really get done (Stieglitz, 1970).

Because the informal organization of a BSW program is not defined anywhere in a university policy manual, and faculty and staff relationships are not always apparent, it is critical for directors to map the informal organization to understand and manage the program. Understanding the informal organization is particularly important because the program is faculty- and staff-intensive in delivering its core services. Effective BSW directors steer the informal organization toward program goals and objectives. Remember that when most BSW program directors discuss their biggest headaches, many of them are about faculty, staff, and personnel issues. Based on this, some important principles for working with faculty and staff are outlined below.

Principle 4: Support the Faculty and Staff and Let Them Do Their Jobs

One of the biggest secrets to being an effective program director is not to overmanage faculty and staff. The way to success lies in getting good people, helping to motivate them, and then not interfering as they do their jobs. This starts with selecting good people who are motivated to achieve program goals and objectives and who can work well with colleagues. Because this is not as easy as it sounds, it pays to collect a lot of information about people before they are hired. A BSW program is a collective effort, and in a very real sense, faculty or staff members who cannot work within the program objectives or be good team players may cause problems. Once the faculty or staff member is on board, directors should meet with this person early and often. Other program demands may often seem more pressing, but directors can be assured that the most disaffected person in the program is there, and actively recruiting the new person into his or her camp and trying to socialize the new person about how things should really be done. Directors should be active in working with the new faculty or staff member to explain expectations, begin the socialization process, and provide support for development that will enable the employee to be successful.

A key function of BSW directors is to help find the resources so faculty and staff can do their jobs well. Educational enhancements such as computers, DVD and video players, sound and visual recording equipment, learning resources for the library, and projectors are important for faculty members to develop state-of-the-art instruction for students, and these all require money. Similarly, scholarly activities and service require resources as well. Funds for travel, mailing, printing, and supplies are essential sources of support for encouraging faculty to engage in these activities. Travel funds to support professional development, participation in service activities, and presentation of research at conferences are another way of encouraging faculty to be productive. The faculty may assist in getting funds for instructional resources, research, or service through grants and other external funding and should be encouraged to do so. But no one is in the position to assess overall needs and to speak for the program like the director. Thus, directors are in the best position to identify program needs and target strategies for meeting them. Chasing external grants just because they are available may seem attractive, but they may end up draining important resources from the program to support them, particularly if they move the program away from its goals and objectives.

The strength of a BSW program is its faculty and staff, and directors probably get too much credit when it succeeds and too much blame when it fails. So it is often difficult to let go of the reins enough to let faculty and staff do their jobs. But the frequently overlooked function of program directors is that of coordinators of activities among colleagues as opposed to traditional administrators in a hierarchical system. Three factors make it difficult for program directors to get into and stay in the coordinator mode. First, directors take the heat when things don't go well. Second, the very nature of university systems is that they tend to reward faculty and staff for individual accomplishments, not contributions to the program. Third, in the traditional models of administration to which many are socialized, directors are expected to be in charge and to tell subordinates what to do. Yet, despite these challenges, effective direction of a BSW program involves a collaborative approach in which faculty are involved in decision making, carry responsibility for important tasks, and work together as a group. For BSW programs, the sum of the parts is greater than the whole. In other words, program faculty and staff who are active and involved are more likely to be productive and committed to the program's success. The important function of directors is to motivate faculty and staff to become involved and active, to build on current strengths, to facilitate communication, and to coordinate activity.

Principle 5: Staff Members Often Represent the Face of the Program

You should not overlook the importance of support staff to the program. Because faculty and staff who serve in a support role carry out most of the key functions of the program, such as education, scholarship, and service, it is easy to overlook the key role staff members play. But make no mistake; when students or outsiders see the program, a staff member is frequently the face they see or the voice they hear. Staff members are often gatekeepers for access to the program, and interaction with them helps to create an image or impression of the program that is transmitted to others. Therefore, staff members should create a good impression for the program.

Good staff members can help the program appear better than it probably is, and weak staff members can make the program look bad. Skilled staff members are hard to find, so it is important to develop and keep them. Secretaries, administrative assistants, budget and grant managers, and contract staff play key roles in program operation and effectiveness, and there are several ways to develop and support them once they are on board. These include permitting time for workshops and classes and travel to professional conferences to support program activities. Staff should also feel supported and valued for what they do; it is crucial that they receive recognition for what they do and that they are treated with respect. Certificates of appreciation, taking them to lunch, and intervening when others are rude or too demanding are examples of this type of support.

But directors who get too busy to tend to this aspect of operations may end up with paperwork that wasn't filed or was lost, incoming calls that were not recorded, inappropriate information being shared with students or those outside the program, and irritated callers who believe they were treated badly. This kind of staff behavior can lead to a bad image for the program and a general perception that the program is poorly run. Poor staff work may also result in work having to be done over and may create unnecessary conflict in and outside the program. In the long run, if good staff support cannot be either developed or maintained, it's time for a change, because staff can do both the program and the director in.

Principle 6: Keep the Conflict In-House

In BSW programs disagreements and conflicts inevitably arise. The disagreements may be about perceived treatment of another faculty or staff member, curriculum, class schedules, pay increases, tenure and promotions, and travel. The specific issue doesn't really matter. As long as a program mechanism for addressing these concerns is used, program disruptions can be minimized.

But in the informal organization, some faculty and staff members feel a need to air their grievances in a broader forum, often outside of the established channels, and this can be disastrous for the program. Unfortunately, once someone starts to sling mud in public, it tends to get on everyone and, as a result, reflects badly on the program. Faculty and staff have external relationships that may make it easy for them to air their issues outside of program channels. These relationships may be with other faculty members, community members, administrators, trustees, or even students. In the end, the person may get what he or she wants, but at a cost to the program, in either resources or reputation. And the end result is that everyone suffers, and not much of this behavior can be tolerated.

Creating a climate of openness and trust is a good way to help minimize program disruption based on grievances (Macy et al., 2000). Working with faculty and staff members in a supportive function to facilitate the resolutions of grievances, however unpleasant they may be, is another important step in resolving the grievances in house. But BSW directors may need to move to a more administrative function when the grievances and/or methods used to present them threaten the program. For example, faculty or staff members who air their program-related grievances with students are acting unprofessionally and can harm the program. This behavior represents a poor role model for students, creates program disruptions, and should be addressed quickly and directly. Chronic grievers may need to be encouraged to find a long-term solution for their grievances in another venue.

Academics and Governance

Universities are not agencies and don't work like them, so don't try to recreate the agency environment from your practice experience. The BSW program is part of a university environment in which decision making is often decentralized, there is a lot of flexibility for operation, and the change process is frustratingly slow. Faculty members have both line and administrative functions, and at times, there seem to be almost no rules.

Principle 7: Faculty Members Should be Involved in Major Program Decisions

In a very real sense, faculty are line workers in the university, as they are the point of contact with the students that produces the educational outcome. But faculty members have curious job descriptions, because they also serve in administrative and supervisory roles in the program. Faculty members evaluate their peers and their program director, and these evaluations affect pay increases and promotion and tenure decisions. Faculty also provides important input into designing the curriculum, specific courses, and academic policies for the program. In other words, although faculty members do the line work of education, they are also management because they help determine what they do and how they do it and who is hired, retained, and promoted, and they evaluate their immediate superior.

So by any definition, faculty members are part of the management team, like it or not. From this standpoint it is wise to keep faculty well-informed and involved. Otherwise, faculty members do not have good information on which to base their decisions. Modern electronic technology makes communicating information relatively easy, but it is not a substitute for regularly scheduled, face-to-face meetings where personal interaction can occur and questions raised. A common view of university administrations is that they hide information, and program directors do not want to get that kind of reputation, which creates distrust. Give faculty more information than they want.

Committees are another way faculty may be kept involved and informed. BSW programs are typically small in that about 86% of them have 10 or fewer faculty members

(CSWE, 2007a). So the possibilities for committees may be limited, especially in smaller programs. You have to have three members just to have a committee, and at this point many programs operate as committees of the whole. But committees with designated responsibilities can serve a valuable function by keeping faculty involved in governance, keeping them informed, and helping directors to provide leadership for the program. The important task for directors with regard to committees is to help determine clear charges, assist committees with focus, and monitor time frames.

Principle 8: Faculty Ownership of the Curriculum Is a Good Thing; Individual Faculty Member Ownership of Courses Is not a Good Thing

At the core of the BSW program is its curriculum, and faculty should have a great deal of involvement in designing and implementing it. The job of program directors is to promote faculty involvement in and coordinate activity related to the ongoing development of academic content. The basic idea here is to get the faculty working together as part of a team, because if the curriculum is to be more than a collection of courses, faculty must collaborate to make it work. Faculty involvement in academic policy and curriculum matters is not only an appropriate application of the concept of faculty governance, but it also promotes commitment to that curriculum. University and external accreditation agencies set some broad limits on academic content of programs, but the program and its faculty generally have broad latitude in this area. As coordinator of activities in academics, program directors maintain responsibility for helping to facilitate faculty cooperation and ensuring that program decisions fall within the parameters set by external constituencies.

Directors should be mindful that the academic program that functions well is one in which faculty are invested in the curriculum, respect each other, and work toward common goals and objectives. Although investment in the curriculum and related policies is a good thing, ownership of specific aspects of it can be harmful. Too much ownership leads to defensiveness about courses and content, lack of trust by other faculty members, and inability to work together. In the extreme, the academic program becomes just a collection of disconnected courses, and valuable instruction time can be wasted. For example, over the years I have discovered more than one faculty member inserting interviewing content into human behavior classes even though this content was offered elsewhere in the curriculum and, in one instance, an introduction to the library in three separate courses. The rationale for both of these was the same—the faculty member wanted to make sure the students had the content. Apparently, there was some level of mistrust of their colleagues or unwillingness to work with them. Faculty members who arrive at ownership of a class are often very resistant to change, even when the curriculum is changing. The director's function is to help everyone remember that the courses and curriculum belong to the program and the university, not to individuals.

Student Affairs

One of the most difficult issues for BSW directors and faculty members is developing an appropriate model for viewing and working with students. Most BSW directors and faculty members come, directly or indirectly, from practice, where their primary work is with clients seeking and using services. Social workers understand the worker-client relationship and its boundaries well, and they often use the framework for this relationship as the basis for viewing faculty-student relationships by new faculty members. Transition to a university creates a new set of relationships with students who are seeking and using services, albeit of a different kind. Yet, the student as client issue is rarely addressed for social work faculty members. Thus, a frequent topic of discussion for social work educators is to what extent the social work faculty-student relationship parallels that of the social-worker client relationship.

Principle 9: Students Are not Clients

Students are not clients, and both perceiving and acting toward students as clients can lead to problems. Useful insight into faculty member-student relationships in social work may be found in the National Association of Social Work's (NASW) Code of Ethics (1999). The NASW Code does have several references to social worker relationships with students, but none of these references is found in the section that addresses social workers' ethical responsibility to clients. Rather, references to social work educators and their students are located in sections two and three of the Code that cover social workers' ethical responsibility to colleagues and in practice settings (NASW, 1999). Based on this students clearly are viewed as colleagues or colleagues-in-training, not as clients.

Principle 10: Avoid the Business Mentality of Students as Customers

One of the current trends in education has been a shift to a business model that identifies students as customers in the institution and purchasers of education. The traditional concept of customer is one of an individual who purchases a tangible good or service. In addition, in thinking about customers, we must also grapple with clichés such as "the customer is always right" and "keep the customer happy," which have been repeated so often they take on the status of axioms. But following this model too obediently can create problems for both the program and the director.

Are students really customers? Well, not in the strict sense of the word. Yes, students do pay for a service, and that service is education. But very few students pay the full cost of this service, as most education is heavily subsidized. Funds from third parties such as state and federal governments, religious organizations, foundations and trusts, and private donors pay part of the cost and make education more affordable for students. If students are customers, then these third parties are their partners, and the interests of both groups have to be taken into account in keeping the customers satisfied, as their interests may not be the same. For example, students may be happy with high grades and a degree, but the third parties expect well-educated, competent graduates. There are also some nonpaying parties, including state higher education agencies, CSWE, and regional accreditation agencies, that have a stake in the process and outcome of this education and have to be satisfied.

Where does all of this leave BSW program directors in terms of satisfying these groups? An answer that meets the needs of all three groups is that the program should provide students with good education, instruction, and advising. These are all important for quality social work education. If program directors lead the program toward these ends, students are likely to feel they got a good education from professionals who care, third parties will feel they are investing in a worthwhile enterprise, and external regulatory agencies will view the program in a positive light.

Good education consists of content and experiences that challenge students to perform in ways that best prepare them for the profession. Educational challenges are not always the experiences that make students happiest, but may be those that have a bigger payoff for students and for the program in terms of employability and program success. Remember, the NASW Code of Ethics requires us to set high standards for the profession, and these standards should begin with students. Good instruction consists of content as well as technique and goes much further than whether students rate the instructor highly.

Achieving good advising can be one of the real challenges for BSW directors. First, faculty have to become invested in advising in actions, not just words. The difficulty is that many universities either don't reward advising or don't appreciate the time-intensive activity required for social work students. Thus, because the institution doesn't reward advising, some faculty members treat it lightly by skipping office hours, neglecting to learn what is required, or not paying attention to what they are doing. But good advising is essential to effective program operation, student retention, and student satisfaction. Students are more satisfied and connected to the program if they believe the faculty know about them and their needs and are accessible. On the other hand, poor advising can generate innumerable problems directors have to fix. Thus, it is important for directors to discuss these kinds of issues with faculty and, one hopes, get them invested in this approach.

Budget and Finances

It is hard to find many social workers who would say they got into the profession to work with money, and unless directors have an administrative background, they are unlikely to have much background in money management. So the learning curve for BSW directors in budget and finances is likely to be fairly steep. Managing budgets and fiscal affairs is complex and takes time to learn, but it is very important to the effectiveness of BSW directors.

Principle 11: Learn How the Money Works and Keep it Clean

A BSW program can do very little without a well-managed budget. Everything a program does requires some kind of resource to make it happen, and the program's budget is the primary source of these resources. Salaries for the director, faculty, and staff; operating funds for phones, travel, and paper; and capital funds for computers, desks, and equipment for instruction are all part of the budget. Good fiscal management helps program operate well; poor management can get the director fired. Because

BSW programs operate with limited funding, effective budget planning and management are critical. A significant aspect of budget management is learning how the funding in the budget works. This means directors must learn something about categorical lines with a budget, timing and management of expenditures, and how money is generated.

Unlike a personal account, program budgets often have money lodged in categories that require dedicated expenditure. For example, lapsed faculty salary money often cannot be used to pay for supplies, and universities often prohibit spending certain kinds for funds for food, drink, or entertainment. Because spending or attempting to spend from unapproved categories will get directors into difficulty, they must learn how the categorical lines in a budget work. Budgets run on an annual cycle, but expenditures do not flow evenly within that cycle. This necessitates attention to expenditures to ensure that the budget is not overrun by year's end. Planning and managing expenditures so there are sufficient funds to cover expenses is essential to keep the program running smoothly. Above all, BSW directors need to learn the areas and limits of flexibility within the program budget and stay within these guidelines. Failure to do so could prove disastrous for the director and the program.

Program budgets often seem to spring into existence each year with relatively few changes from the previous fiscal year's, and directors may have limited ability to effect changes. But planning for new initiatives or additional resources needs to be done well before the budget process gets underway. This means budget planning may need to be done more than a year in advance. In this process directors must understand how the program generates money for the university. In most universities funds are generated as some function of the number of students in the seats, although exactly how this works varies by institution. Remember that social work programs are faculty- and resource-intensive relative to many other programs such as liberal arts with which they compete for budget allocations. Thus, requests for additional funding need well-developed rationales that show tangible rewards for the university.

Accreditation

Of course, there is that thing called *accreditation* that you always thought you knew about until you actually have to deal with it. Accreditation is a fact of life in professional programs and university life. But one can be a faculty member or even a director for some time without ever actually having to respond to an accreditation agency or prepare or direct a self-study. The reason for this is that accreditation does not roll around that often, and most faculty members would like to be far away when it does. Program accreditation involving the CSWE generally occurs every 8 years, and university accreditations by regional associations happen every 10 years. The university and other external audiences generally take external accreditation for the program and university very seriously, and because it is the responsibility of BSW program directors to provide leadership through the accreditation process, it is important to spend time learning about accreditation.

Principle 12: Learn the Rules and Principles of Accreditation

The most important thing to understand about accreditation is that it is an ongoing process and doesn't disappear between cycles. Accreditation standards are really just good educational practices that must be maintained over time. Don't wait until the accreditation cycle moves into full swing before thinking or doing anything about it.

The first task to get up to speed on accreditation is to get a copy of the standards and read them. This may not be the most exciting reading material, but it is important to know what the standards say as opposed to relying on word of mouth. Fortunately, accreditation standards for CSWE and regional accreditation associations tend to be quite compatible, making the job somewhat less onerous. Task number two is understanding what the standards actually mean. The trend in accreditation is for standards to be less proscriptive than in the past. This allows a lot of freedom but also places a lot of responsibility with the program. So in a lot of ways, programs can meet each standard, and it is important to figure out what works for your program and what doesn't. Attending professional conferences where accreditation content is presented and discussing this content with peers can help to clarify how the standards work. Don't be bashful about using consultation either. No rule says you have to know it all, and an experienced consultant can provide an outside viewpoint and suggest ways in which the program can address accreditation standards more effectively.

Principle 13: Involve the Faculty

Because responsibility for directing the self-study that forms the backbone of the accreditation process falls to BSW directors, there is often an implicit assumption that directors will just take care of it. The accreditation process involves a lot of self-examination by faculty and critical review by outside parties that most of us would like to avoid. But accreditation is about the program, not the individuals; in other words, it is about teamwork. An accreditation is much more successful if faculty work together and take ownership of the product. No matter how brilliant an individual faculty member may be, this individual can torpedo an accreditation review by going his or her own way when the rest of the program is headed in another.

The place where teamwork can focus is on the program's goals and objectives. Increasingly, accreditation is less about process and inputs and more about measurable outcomes. Individual programs differ considerably in how they deliver education to BSW students. It is easy to fall into the trap of borrowing a syllabus from another program because the syllabus worked for that program, but beware—it may not fit yours. The goals and objectives of your program provide the key for directing, monitoring, and assessing how well the program is doing. Involving faculty in discussions about the goals and objectives, evaluating how well they are met, and modifying the program to do a better job are really at the core of ongoing accreditation. Therefore, it is critical to involve faculty members in these discussions on a regular basis and allow them access to relevant accreditation standards so they can consider how what the program is doing fits with them.

Maintenance of Self

Last, but certainly not least, is the program director's responsibility to take care of his or her needs over the long haul. Although there are a number of benefits to serving as a BSW program director, such as additional compensation, a reduction in teaching load, greater influence, development of new skills, helping others reach their potential, and greater impact on the program (Lees, 2006), the number of sacrifices can be very draining. In general, the two greatest sacrifices involve the loss of available time for one's own teaching and for scholarship activities (Lees, 2006). For those who were attracted to social work education because of their love of or interest in the classroom or research, the loss of time for these activities can be frustrating. As a colleague once told me, "If you are the best teacher in the department, once you become chair, you won't be anymore." The same thing applies to scholarship because of the loss of available time. Directors may also be affected in terms of university-based rewards over time. Because, in most BSW programs, directors are expected to carry faculty duties, the loss of time for teaching and scholarship may mean a reduction in rewards based on performance in these areas.

Perhaps most frustrating is the changed status of BSW directors with regard to colleagues and students. Certainly relationships with colleagues change once one becomes a program director. Longtime friends and colleagues may suddenly react very differently to the directors, who now assume responsibility in the evaluation, promotion, tenure, and salary determination process. Certainly, there is a tendency for faculty colleagues to be more standoffish if not openly hostile to one of their colleagues who has joined the administration. Or, as one of my colleagues glibly remarked, I had become "a mouse in training to become a rat." Similarly, students tend to view directors in a very different light from other faculty. At some level they all know the director is in a power position with something to give and deny. As students seek to wind their way through their 4+ years of education, they are often looking for shortcuts the director may be able to grant. Directors are thus in the position of saying no to either special favors or requests or exceptions to policy. In addition, directors may be the ones who have to enforce disciplinary procedures. None of these tasks is likely to curry favor with the students. Given these challenges, how is one to survive as a BSW director?

Principle 14: No Good Deed Goes Unpunished

As a program director, you should not expect a lot of thanks. Effective program directors end up making a lot of personal and professional sacrifices to make things work well. But the expectation that faculty, staff, or students will notice or say thanks may be setting up unrealistic expectations. The example cited earlier about the faculty member not noticing all the program director did until she held the position is a good case in point. Perhaps more frustrating is expending extra time, effort, or social or political capital to respond to a request by a faculty member or student only to find that, instead of thanks, extra effort is now expected. So it seems like the good deed is punished rather than rewarded. As a matter of course, to get sources of support and satisfaction, program directors should look in other areas.

Principle 15: Develop Relationships With Peers Who Can Listen and Provide Support

Once one becomes a program director, the notion of who constitutes a peer group has to change. This doesn't mean forsaking one's faculty colleagues, but the relationship with the social work faculty has changed already. The BSW director's peers on campus then tend to be the heads of other academic units. These individuals can listen and share common experiences and responses to them that may be useful for directors. But the heads of other academic departments can rarely offer insight or support specific to social work. As a professional program, social work has many differences that heads of traditional academic programs don't understand and can't offer support for.

It is generally a good practice to develop relationships with other BSW program directors to get the kinds of support needed for social work-related issues. Current and former undergraduate program directors have usually had many similar kinds of experiences and can offer a frame of reference that your issues are to be expected just when you're thinking no one else ever could have had this crazy experience. BSW directors can also offer suggestions about other ways of dealing with particularly frustrating or troubling matters. Professional conferences are a good way to initiate peer relationships and begin networking, and liberal use of the phone or electronic communications is an excellent means of maintaining them.

Principle 16: Make Time for Yourself

Most of the time, there is more for directors to do than there is time available. There are innumerable tasks and requests, from significant ones like budget planning to the mundane such as checking textbook orders. The myriad activities associated with leading the program can consume all available time and energy. Directors are courting burnout if they take things too seriously and unless separate time is made available to recharge their batteries. In some sense time away from director duties is good in and of itself as a means of reenergizing oneself. There is plenty of time to handle most of the minutiae later, and extra energy is vital when the crises come—and they will come. Directors have to plan for the unplanned as rushed deadlines and crises, both major and minor, should be expected at some point in the year.

In addition, some of this time away should be spent on things directors find rewarding. If teaching is one's passion, then work on developing courses, enhancing teaching methods, or integrating new content. The important point is that directors have to give themselves permission to take the time away. Fortunately, the very flow of the job offers some opportunities, as the year and the term have periods of peak and slack activity. Beginnings and ends of academic terms are particularly busy, but summer often moves at a slower pace. It is important to learn this flow and plan for when extra time may be available. This time for self may be the difference between enjoying the job and burning out quickly.

Conclusion

This chapter has provided some practical principles that can be useful for BSW program directors, and although I have attempted to cover several significant aspects of the director's job, the list of principles is not exhaustive. The principles discussed here are general, practical, and broad and are based more on practice wisdom than on scientific reviews of administrative theories. They are not intended as a substitute for continuing education and reading on academic, general, and BSW program administration; fiscal affairs; and accreditation. Rather, they should be viewed as part of a broad-based approach to development as a BSW director. I hope this chapter has added to this development in its own way.

BSW directors hold important positions in social work education. The potential for having a positive influence on the education of many of our future colleagues is exciting and rewarding. But a lot of responsibility goes with the position, because it is complex and challenging and demands that one must learn constantly. This job is never dull and always changing. The BSW program director's job is not for everyone, but those who take it on gain more than they ever imagine.

References

Association of Baccalaureate Program Directors. (1997). *Forging new alliances in social work education.* Presentation at 15th Annual Conference, Philadelphia, PA.

Association of Baccalaureate Program Directors. (2005). *BSW education: Rounding up resources to strengthen and preserve children and families.* Presentation at 23rd Annual Conference of the Association of Baccalaureate Program Directors, Austin, TX.

Association of Baccalaureate Program Directors. (2006). *Building ties— Transforming relationships.* Presentation at 24th Annual Conference Association of Baccalaureate Program Directors, Los Angeles, CA.

Bennett, J. B. (1983). *Managing the academic department.* New York: American Council on Education and Macmillan Publishing.

Council on Social Work Education (CSWE). (2003). *Handbook of accreditation standards and procedures* (5th ed.). Alexandria, VA: Author.

Council on Social Work Education (CSWE). (2007a). *Statistics on social work education in the United States: 2004.* Alexandria, VA: Author.

Council on Social Work Education (CSWE). (2007b). *Statistics on social work education in the United States: 2006.* Alexandria, VA: Author.

Hage, J., & Aiken, M. (1970). *Social change in complex organizations.* New York: Random House.

Hall, R. H. (1982). *Organizations: Structure and process.* Englewood Cliffs, NJ: Prentice Hall.

Kadushin, A. (2002). *Supervision in social work.* New York: Columbia University Press.

Lees, N. D. (2006). *Chairing academic departments.* Boston: Anker.

Macy, H. J., Turner, R., & Wilson, S. (2000). *Directing the baccalaureate social work education program* (2nd ed.). Dubuque, IA: Eddie Bowers.

National Association of Social Workers (NASW). (1999). *Code of ethics of the National Association of Social Workers.* Washington, DC: Author.

Stieglitz, H. (1970). What's not on the organizational chart. In H. A. Schatz (Ed.), *Social work administration: A resource book* (pp. 258–260). New York: Council on Social Work Education.

22

Social Work Education in Historically Black Colleges and Universities
Managing the Legacies and Challenges

Rufus Sylvester Lynch, Jacquelyn Mitchell, and Eugene Herrington

Historically Black colleges and universities (HBCUs) and social work education share similar philosophical and historical backgrounds. Both emerged from mutual-aid traditions significantly colored by religious perspectives, and both experienced notable development in the early 20th century. Religious groups and denominations championed social reform efforts to help poor and immigrant populations, foreshadowing the mission of today's social work educators (Katz, 1983). Individual church leaders and other philanthropists were pioneers in efforts to educate former slaves, creating the foundation for HBCU institutions (Day, 2006; Katz, 1983; Owens, 2001).

HBCUs have developed beyond the efforts of early religious leaders to provide rudimentary learning for the descendants of captives from Africa who were inadvertently brought to America. They are the alma mater of national and international leaders such as E. Franklin Frazier and Martin Luther King Jr., and social work pioneers such as Whitney M. Young Jr. and George Haynes (Greene, 1942; Martin & Martin, 1995). Concurrently, the number of social work education programs has increased to more than 500, well beyond the fewer than 20 schools of social work that formed a loose association in the early 1900s (Council on Social Work Education [CSWE], 2007a; Day, 2006).

However, both HBCU institutions and social work education currently face the reality that things have changed. Perhaps more than in past contexts, continued viability of both relies significantly on obtaining and retaining the leadership and administrative acumen to keep pace with a 21st-century matrix. The challenge must be met by preserving and capitalizing on the legacy of social work education, including the consistent and robust contributions of social work programs in HBCUs that have been acknowledged only obliquely (CSWE, 2007b; Leashore, 2001; Platt & Chandler, 1988).

This chapter is dedicated to the memory of Dr. Bogart R. Leashore, a social work pioneer and graduate of the MSW program at Howard University, a historically Black institution. Dr. Leashore's contributions as a dean, educator, author, and practitioner illustrate the value added to social work education by programs in historically Black colleges and universities. His commitment to HCBUs was evident in the beginning of his professional training and continued until his untimely death.

Context Matters: HBCU institutions and Social Work Program Administration

Dean (2004) uses the terms "post-welfare, globalized, technologized, terrorized, and conservative" to describe the 21st-century context (p. 582). In the academic arena, the contemporary milieu has focused attention on leadership skills and capacity, in both the HBCU and non-HBCU academy, to guide the institutions through the contextually generated challenges (Mactaggart, 2007).

CSWE (2007b) has joined the movement toward a future focus on leadership capacity, engaging an initiative targeted to "identifying viable and successful approaches to developing leaders who are prepared to address the challenges facing both higher education and the profession." Given the initial input that suggests the importance of "multiple aspects of diversity" (p. 10), the initiative might be enhanced by considering the unique HBCU leadership "scholarship for the purpose of service" strategies that foreshadowed today's academic programming such as community service and action research agendas (Adams, 1981, p. 3).

This chapter advances one case for acknowledging, nourishing, and learning from the idiosyncratic, historically generated dynamics that positively and negatively affect HBCU institutions and, therefore, the delivery of social work education within them. An underlying assumption is that HBCU institutions and their social work programs have demonstrated remarkable resilience and have been admirable contributors to their student constituency, their broader constituent community, social work education, and the social work profession. The discussion is also premised on the belief that the institutions' religiously based origins and affiliations have influenced the leadership and management of HBCU institutions and their social work programs.

HBCUs are defined, and the influence of their historically based institutional visions, missions, and goals is explored. HBCU traditions of religious leadership and fiscal sponsorship are addressed as consequential to the emergence and administration of their social work programs. With that backdrop, a discussion of today's HBCUs and master of social work programs within HBCUs follows. The voices of current HBCU social work program administrators who are elicited for their expertise on the special challenges of managing accredited social work programs in HBCU institutions enriches this discussion. In addition, the chapter recommends strategies through which the host institutions, the programs, and CSWE may begin to acknowledge, learn from, and respond to administrative impediments encountered by HBCU social work programs.

Historically Black Colleges and Universities Defined

The Higher Education Act of 1965, as amended, defines an HBCU institution as:

any historically black college or university that was established prior to 1964, whose principle mission was, and is, the education of black Americans, and that is accredited by a nationally recognized accrediting agency or association determined by the Secretary [of Education] to be a reliable authority as to the quality of training offered or is, according to such an agency or association, making reasonable progress toward accreditation.

According to the most recent government data, the more than 100 HBCU institutions enroll 13% of all African American students in higher education, although they account for only 3% of America's 4,084 institutions of higher learning. African Americans accounted for 82% of the fall 2001 enrollment of 289,985 at these institutions. For the 2001–2002 term, a total of 35,648 bachelor, master's, and doctoral degrees were awarded. In 2001, HBCUs had a total economic impact of $10.2 billion and awarded more than 17% of all first professional degrees received by African Americans (Humphreys, 2005; Provasnik & Shafer, 2004).

However, the numbers do not capture the dynamics of the origin, progress, and contemporary complexities of HBCU institutions. Since their birth during the 1800s, one of their distinguishing and defining characteristic has been a legacy of an inspired struggle initiated by African American religious leaders to substitute educational opportunities for the veil of ignorance perpetrated by the institution of slavery. Indeed, the Black church leaders paved pathways for the Black community generally, in addition to providing leadership to educational institutions. As such, they have helped to define the Black academy (Nichols, 2004).

The proscriptions against educating African Americans were especially evident in the southern part of the United States, where educational opportunities were limited, isolated, and often delivered in hostile settings. However, northerners generally shared the strong opposition to education of African Americans held by many southern Whites (HBCU Network, n.d.).

Church leaders first started normal schools and institutes. Higher education curricula followed, initially aimed at preparing for the ministry and training teachers to help educate a struggling Black society. The institutions were developed more fully after the end of the Civil War through continued church sponsorship, philanthropy, and land grant and other public funding (HBCU Network, n.d.).

HBCUs were supported by leaders from a variety of denominations. The vestiges of those early collaborations are reflected today by, for example, inclusion of congregational representation on boards of trustees (Owens, 2001). The sphere of influence of church-based leadership is also evidenced by ownership of the land on which campuses sit, exercise of management authority, leadership positions on boards of trustees, and significant responsibility for financial support. In other instances, the sphere is less profound, limited to employment of denominational staff and faculty and limited, inconsistent support (Wright, 1960).

An infusion of approaches to educational leadership, advanced by two leading African American scholars—W. E. B. DuBois and Booker T. Washington—refined the church-inspired leadership style. Washington urged practical curricula that focused on preparation for agriculture and mechanical trades. DuBois, on the other hand, emphasized liberal arts, in addition to vocational curricula. The Washington model is often associated with land-grant institutions, while DuBois's influence is seen in the privately funded academy (HBCU Network, n.d.).

HBCUs evolved as uniquely distinguishable educational institutions with similar missions, piloted and inspired by religious leaders. The imprimatur of the church-based leadership, notably Christian-based, African American denominations, remains an embedded characteristic of the institutions. Whether the institution's fiscal viability was vested in public or private funding would further refine the developmental path of HBCUs (Evans & Evans, 2002; HBCU Network, n.d.; Sharpe, 2005).

Private Sponsorship

Despite the shared similarities in the missions of all HBCUs, privately funded HBCUs are distinguished by their primary reliance on private funding from churches and philanthropists. Additionally, fiscal support for privately funded institutions has been described as more precarious than that of their public sisters (Wright, 1960).

Private HBCUs initially enjoyed increases in student enrollment and financial support from philanthropists such as John D. Rockefeller and Andrew Carnegie and some public sources (Adams, 1981). However, in the early 20th century, the nation's financial crisis severely restricted philanthropy, resulting in financial desperation for private HBCUs. Consequently, many private institutions joined land-grant HBCUs, already underfunded in comparison to their White counterparts, in experiencing critical financial difficulties during the Great Depression and World War II (United Negro College Fund, n.d.).

In response to this crisis, Dr. Fredrick D. Patterson, president of the Tuskegee Institute, urged private HBCUs to pool their resources and fundraising initiatives. In April 1944, the United Negro College Fund was established to enhance the quality of education, provide financial assistance to deserving students, raise operating funds for member colleges and universities, and increase access to technology for students and faculty at HBCUs. A decade later, the U.S. Supreme Count handed down its opinion in *Brown v. Board of Education*, forcing states to increase funding to HBCUs and to open other colleges and universities to Black students (United Negro College Fund, n.d.; HBCU Network, n.d.).

Public Sponsorship

Public HBCUs were created or, in some instances, re-created by state legislatures between 1870 and 1910, primarily using federal funds dispersed as part of the land-grant movement that originated around the time of the Civil War. The movement was seen as a potential source of funding with which HBCUs could educate the increasing number of recently freed African Americans who wanted to obtain the educational and technical skills offered in colleges and universities (HBCU Network, n.d.; Sharpe, 2005).

The movement can be traced to the 1862 Morrill Land-Grant Act, which provided for the creation of land-grant colleges in each state, with the exception of southern states opposing the Union. Only one Black land-grant institution, Alcorn State University in Mississippi, was created as a result of the legislation, and few of the institutions created were open or inviting to Blacks, particularly in the South. However, several HBCUs were created under the provisions of a second Morrill Act that was passed in 1890 (Alexander, 1987; Brieland, 1987).

Nevertheless, land-grant and other public funding have not been adequate to support operations at HBCUs. Recent efforts to seek funding parity with non-HBCU institutions through the courts have been less than fully successful. For example, in the *Ayers* case, decided in 2000, the U.S. Supreme Court ruled, among other things, that Mississippi HBCUs had been historically underfunded, compared to non-HBUC institutions. However, the ultimate judicial remedy was only minimally responsive to the plaintiffs' demands for relief. The funding increases that were awarded were tied to a formula to provide scholarships to increase the number of students not of color at HBCUs (Mitchell, Osby, Nelums, & Omari, 2004).

The Administration of HBCU Institutions in the 21st Century

The confluence of the Washington and DuBois models and religious leadership continues to color HBCU academic operations. However, the "post-welfare, globalized, technologized, terrorized, and conservative" contemporary milieu has seemingly collided with the historical mission and leadership style that was based largely on Judeo-Christian ethic and proved effective as a vehicle for providing educational opportunities for newly freed slaves and their descendents (Dean, 2004, p. 582; HBCU Network, n.d.).

A lively dialogue is developing regarding the extent to which the traditional mission and leadership style resonates for today's HBCUs. One commentator directly questions whether HBCUs have outlived their usefulness (Williams, 2008). While reaffirming the usefulness and relevance of HBCU institutions, other observers enumerate shortcomings that require attention.

The assessments focus on internal and external issues related to the rather edgy 21st-century intersection of historical mission, leadership, and funding. Specifically noted are uneven graduation rates (Williams, 2008), the recruitment of Black students by non-HBCU institutions, inadequate resources to support high-quality, technologically based academic program challenges, underprepared students, administrative neglect of the dynamics of the external environment, and low endowments and alumni contributions. Institutional ability to increase tuition to cover the increasing costs of operation is restricted by a student population with limited household incomes. Scarce internal and external resources contribute to low faculty salaries and difficulty in competing with non-HBCU institutions for premium African American faculty. Physical plant deterioration further thwarts recruitment of first-rate students and the delivery of state-of-the-art instructional resources (Evans & Evans, 2002; Fields, 2001; Henderson, 2000; Nichols, 2004; Penn & Gabbidon, 2007; Rivers, 2008).

The discourse also touches on legacy-based leadership traditions within which these issues have arisen and through which these issues will be tackled. Clearly, these traditions emerged from adaptive "learning communities" that "made a way" despite the odds, as opposed to formalized protocol (Franklin, 2007, pp. 172–173).

Some observers have questioned whether "romantic notions" of the past are the adaptations for the current context (Minor, 2007, p. 55). In a similar vein, King (2004) calls for attention to faculty involvement in academic decision making at HBCUs as essential to institutional vitality. She further suggests that adopting shared governance might have circumvented the accreditation, operating budget deficits, and loss of academic programs "crises" (p. 1) several HBCUs have experienced. One university president was allegedly ousted based on "a culture of administrative indifference and disregard" for the faculty senate's role, financial problems, problems with academic programming, and deterioration of the equipment and facilities (Kinzie & Alexander, 2007, p. B01). Buck (1999) reports "many top HBCU administrators' salaries are keeping pace with or surpassing those of their counterparts at other institutions," although faculty salaries lag behind their counterparts (p. 1).

Within the religiously inspired adaptive administrative approach, students are viewed as the beneficiaries of the mission, evidenced by flexible admission and accommodation. However, as Rivers (2008) notes, such an approach to 21st-century students might ultimately undermine realization of the mission because students in all institutions have changed over the last 40 years. Therefore, the question arises about the suitability of such traditions to sustain HBCUs as financially viable educational resources that continue to deliver on their historical mission (Thompson, 1933).

On balance, many of the challenges facing HBCUs can be traced to matters related to governance and leadership on fiscal and educational issues. However, such concerns are exacerbated by intersection with a historical mission that, in some respects, competes with current contextual realities. Despite these challenges, HBCUs must compete and comply with the same prerequisites as non-HBCU institutions, some of which face similar difficulties.

To ensure the repositioning of HBCUs to the luster of their former legacy, the institutions must move beyond the comfort of a salvation approach to leadership and management that is more viable in the contemporary environment. As DuBois advised, it is the roots of the tree, the legacy, that are the source of the life of HBCUs. Preservation of the root requires pruning the old ways of operating and, taking into account the context of the current environment, nurturing the growth of a retooled administrative protocol that better responds to the 21st-century matrix (DuBois, 1989).

Therefore, to preserve the institutional legacy within the context of the 21st century requires that HBCUs minimally:

1. Resolve to primarily focus presidential recruitment and retention on endowing the institution with a leader with the vision, skills, and mission affinity that will ensure axiomatic institutional relevance, academic excellence, financial stability, unquestioned ethics, and first-class administrative support to deliver a superior academic product in the 21st-century matrix and beyond.

2. Establish a sound and reliable funding base for existing institutional programs and services.

3. Develop and institute trustee-led strategies to build endowments and/or other external revenue streams essential to continuation of the HBCU legacy of innovation in a technologically advanced environment.

4. Prioritize recruitment and retention of faculty who are at least equal in expertise and dedication to the HBCU mission to that of past scholars who safeguarded an academic environment that produced many of today's leaders, and who are prepared to assume the contemporary roles of contributors to decision making and fundraising.

5. Institute pioneering, strong, and competitive degree offerings that prepare students for careers in the millennium, including hard sciences, technology, and technology-enhanced programs (Evans & Evans, 2002; Fields, 2001; Hawkins, 2004).

There are reports of promising examples of HBCUs that have begun steps to preserve the root of the legacy for the future. These efforts have been attributed to a new cadre of presidents who have introduced leadership and management models different from those traditionally associated with HBCUs. They have essentially replaced the long-standing church-affiliated leadership styles that prioritized inconsistent policies of student accommodation and liberal admission standards. Instead, they have focused on tough decision making, enhanced recruitment, financial management and stability, external fundraising, and accountability (Fields, 2001).

HBCUs are at a crossroad. Movement toward returning these national gems to a posture not only of surviving, but of enjoying sustained prosperity is not only possible but essential. As important, the legacies and future of their social work programs are dependent on the continued growth of the host (Fields, 2001; Turner, 2002).

Social Work Education in HBCUs: The Shared Legacy

Religious responses to poverty provided momentum in the emergence of HBCUs and in the evolution of social work toward professionalization and the institution of accredited social work curricula (Day, 2006). Education directed at professional preparation to meet the needs of marginalized populations is a legacy common to both. Contributions to that common denominator by educators and unique curricula premised on scholarship to support service delivery in work programs in HBCUs are undeniable. Nonetheless, these contributions are not significantly incorporated into the delivery of social work education. Similarly, African American pioneers, early social work education, and social service training programs at HBCUs are not prominently woven into historical accounts of the development of the social work profession (Icad, Spearmon, & Curry-Jackson, 1996; Leashore, 2001).

Whether the origins of social work education are dated to 1885, when Harvard University offered a social reform course, to a later summer course offered by the New York Charity Organization Society, or to the 1-year educational program established as the New York School of Philanthropy (predecessor to Columbia University School of Social Work), social work education developed in response to a recognized need to improve the quality and consistency of services for poor and dependent people through "preparation of competent social work professionals" (Council on Social Work Education, 2007b, p. 4). Concurrently, social work programs in HBCUs were also cultivated. African Americans recognized and pursued the creation of opportunities for training professional social workers, despite the historical lack of recognition by the social work profession of the need for professional assistance to improve the quality of social welfare programs for African American communities. Yet, African American social work pioneers demanded and developed vehicles to educate Black social workers. Consistent with the traditions of HBCUs, the curricula focused on "education for service and racial uplift" (Carlton-LaNey, 1999, p. 313; Platt & Chandler, 1988).

Social Work Education in HBCUs: Institutionalization

Atlanta University School of Social Work (predecessor to the Whitney M. Young Jr. School of Social Work at Clark Atlanta University) is a stellar example of the success of African American social work pioneers in developing the social work profession and professionals. It is recognized as the premier social work program in an institution of color in the world that was established to serve African people and their descendents. The impetus for the school grew out of the recognition of a need for trained personnel to deliver services to a segregated "colored" client population served by organizations such as the National Urban League, the National Association for the Advancement of Colored People, neighborhood centers, and branches of the Young Men's Christian Association and the Young Women's Christian Association (Adams, 1981).

The school opened its doors with 14 students on October 4, 1920, as the Atlanta School of Social Service, the product of the efforts of a collective that was inspired by a speech by Jesse O. Thomas, director of the National Urban League Regional Office in Atlanta, GA. The school was incorporated under the laws of the State of Georgia in 1924 (Adams, 1981).

The school's early curriculum reflected a belief that professional preparation must augment basic social work curriculum content with additional knowledge and skills necessary to serve the specific needs of the African American community. Forrester Blanchard Washington, director of the Atlanta School of Social Work from 1927 to 1947, noted in his writings that "[T]he existence of black people in a predominantly unsympathetic hostile world is sufficient for specialized training for social work in the black community; for this position the writer makes no apologies" (Washington, 1935, p. 84).

The school was granted membership in the American Association of Schools of Social Work in 1928, the first African American school of social work to be accredited in the world. It has continued its accredited status as a charter member, unbroken, under the successor Council on Social Work Education. The school stands today as the oldest accredited social work program in the State of Georgia and was the sole program in the state until 1964 (Whitney M. Young Jr. School of Social Work, 2007–2008).

Social Work Programs in HBCU Institutions: Continuing Contributions and Challenges

Continuing Contributions

Currently, there are 40 accredited social work programs housed in HBCU institutions. According to CSWE (2007a), 12 of these programs offer accredited master's level or a combination of master's and baccalaureate curricula. At least one additional program is in candidacy. Thirty-eight programs offer the BSW degree. Of the 19 HBCUs identified by the National Association of State Universities and Land-Grant Colleges (n.d.), Alabama A&M University, Delaware State University, Florida A&M University, and Southern University at New Orleans house accredited MSW programs. The remainder are among the one-third of accredited programs identified as "private, church-related" (p. 3).

Several HBCUs instituted accredited social work programs that have continued the tradition of education for service. On December 1, 2006, Clark Atlanta University hosted an all-day meeting of the deans of the five HBCU schools of social work with both MSW and PhD programs. In attendance were the deans of Clark Atlanta University, Howard University, Morgan State University, Jackson State University, and Norfolk State University. That meeting eventually resulted in the formation of the HBCU Collaborative Deans and Directors Social Work Group. Operating as Institutional Partners, the Collaborative is designed to support "the mission and needs" of their "respective constituent groups" and other participating HBCU institutions. The Collaborative has resolved to

- identify common issues and concerns unique to the collective mission of HBCU institutions;
- increase student enrollment and retention at all levels in HBCU institutions with accredited social work programs;
- evaluate and design culturally relevant curriculum to meet CSWE standards of practice within various constituent groups;
- facilitate faculty development opportunities;
- increase research productivity and external funding by faculty;
- increase external funding in HBCU social work schools and programs for the purpose of capacity and institutional development; and
- develop and present transparent models for collaborations among HBCU institutions (R. S. Lynch, personal communication, December 15, 2008).

Continuing Challenges

As components within their host institutions, accredited HBCU social work programs share challenges and successes with other social work programs, and experience others that are peculiar to their institutional legacy. However, the special circumstances and triumphs associated with the pioneer leaders and the experiences of the contemporary leaders of those programs have received little, if any attention in the social work literature (Carlton-LaNey, 1999; Leashore, 2001; Martin & Martin, 1995; Platt & Chandler, 1988). The literature that focuses specifically on management and leadership of social work programs in HBCU institutions is notably scarce.

One hopes this discussion will initiate a dialogue on that gap in the literature, augmenting work such as that of Icad and colleagues (1996) on challenges facing baccalaureate social work programs. More specifically, we are adding the voices of current leaders of master of HBCU social work programs to the discourse on the unique challenges encountered in managing an accredited program in an HBCU.

The Drum Majors of HBCU Social Work Programs in HBCUs Speak

The results of a recent survey of the 13 programs offering master's level or a combination of master's and baccalaureate degrees reflect the challenges of their host institutions as well as those that they face as CSWE-accredited programs. The survey instrument was designed to explore the experiences of current deans and directors with selected Council on Social Work Education Accreditation Standards (CSWE, 2001). The instrument contained 7 open-ended questions. Five of the questions elicited challenges experienced in meeting accreditation standards related to curriculum (Standard 2), faculty (Standard 4), student development (Standard 5), nondiscrimination (Standard 6), and program assessment (Standard 8). Two questions asked respondents to identify barriers to meeting accreditation standards related to administrative structure (Standard 3) and program renewal (Standard 7). The results of that survey follow.

Curriculum (Standard 2)

Standard 2 generally requires programs to have "a coherent and integrated" curriculum that is consistent with its goals and objectives and "grounded in the liberal arts," with integrated generalist social work foundation and advanced practice components that are consistent with the Education Policy (CSWE, 2001, pp. 12–13). Respondents were asked to identify major challenges they experienced in meeting Standard 2.

Twelve of 13 respondents report actual or anticipated curriculum challenges. Areas identified include limited resources, maintaining the currency of the curricula, university leadership, incorporating the historical mission and existing curricula, faculty and university leadership investment and comfort with external evaluation, time management, and physical space issues. The remaining institution reports a successful reaffirmation within the last 3 years with adequate faculty and the university support.

Six respondents identify resource impediments to compliance with CSWE Standards as the major challenge. Consistent with the experience of their HBCU host institutions, resource limitations reportedly result in difficulties with meeting Standard 2 requirements because of insufficient faculty to meet course requirement, faculty shortages generally, competitive limitations in recruiting faculty, limited support staff, limited faculty/staff development, the negative impact of low enrollment and faculty shortages on maintaining curriculum, institutional dependence on adjunct faculty, weakened representation on university and program committees because of loss of seasoned tenured faculty, large practice and content course enrollments, faculty facing the combined tasks of new preparations and revision of core courses, inability to abide by university workload policy, minimal release time for scholarly activities, noncompetitive salaries, and the need to explore outside resources to meet faculty and other program needs.

The necessity of blending CSWE curriculum standards with the host institution's lack of consistent leadership is identified by two respondents. Frequent changes in key institutional officers, such as presidents and provosts, are specifically noted. Inadequate instructional technology and concurrently accommodating the host institution's historic education mission (as addressed earlier in this chapter) and CSWE standards are also identified as resource-related impediments to meeting accreditation curriculum requirements.

Faculty (Standard 4)

Standard 4 generally requires programs to have full-time faculty, to use part-time faculty judiciously, to maintain faculty adequate to meet its instructional responsibilities, to assign only master of social work-degreed faculty with practice experience to teach practice classes, and to maintain a faculty workload policy that supports institutional priorities and program goals and objectives (CSWE, 2001, p. 15). Respondents were asked to identify faculty-related challenges they met or anticipated meeting.

Six respondents report having met such challenges. For example, one respondent indicates success with matching expertise with curriculum teaching requirements as a major accomplishment. Two respondents are pleased with having filled faculty vacancies, and others report success with hiring appropriate new faculty adequate to meet faculty/student ratios.

However, respondents also continue to grapple with maintaining required faculty/student ratios; recruitment of faculty for nonurban sites; faculty retention; insufficient senior faculty to teach core courses and to serve as chairs and doctoral committee chairs; overuse of adjunct faculty; inadequate African American male faculty; and noncompetitive faculty salaries.

Student Professional Development (Standard 5)

Standard 5 establishes admissions, course credit, foundation content, advisement, student rights, student performance, and student termination criteria (CSWE, 2001, p 16). The respondents were asked to describe challenges associated with meeting this standard. Responses primarily focus on activities outside the classroom.

Three respondents report no problems with meeting Standard 5. However, 6 respondents have either no dedicated funds or inadequate funds to support student development activities outside the classroom. One respondent tells of plans to initiate a professional development course in fall 2008. Three respondents provide limited developmental opportunities, such as students taking advantage of conference or workshops.

However, a recurring theme in all responses suggests that the noble HBCU mission of inclusion, student accommodation, and liberal admission standards results in a student body that requires more support to be academically and professionally successful. The task is exacerbated by the socioeconomic issues that students are required to juggle, including competing demands from children, family, and full-time employment. Thus, assuming the availability of more professional development opportunities, time that would ideally be devoted to enrichment activities is significantly restricted.

Nondiscrimination and Human Diversity (Standard 6)

Standard 6 essentially requires programs to "provide a learning context" that respects and provides an "understanding of diversity (including age, class, color, disability, ethnicity, family structure, gender, marital status, national origin, race, religion, sex, and values)"; is nondiscriminatory; and operates and delivers the curriculum within that context (CSWE, 2001, pp. 16–17). Respondents were asked to identify the challenges to abiding by the Nondiscrimination and Human Diversity Standard.

Responses tend to reinforce the uniqueness of these programs. The following comments generally encapsulate the multifaceted perceptions of lack of acceptance of the programs' commitment to Standard 6 of the CSWE Accreditation Standards:

> Although they [CSWE] profess that we are able to determine our mission and goals based on the population in our geographic areas, and the mission of our university, [they] often look with disapproval of programs; that focus on the African American or Black experience.

Another respondent notes:

> Our focus on African Americans in urban areas is interpreted [by CSWE] as neglect of other groups despite the fact that we have a required course on diversity. There seems to be an expectation that we cover the numerous areas of diversity equally despite the mission of our university and program to serve disadvantaged African Americans, as well as other groups.

Yet another respondent notes:

> **We do not discriminate** [bold in the original]… CSWE needs educating on this issue…nothing is done around diversity with African American groups or with intergroup African American culture.

Comments from respondents reporting and not reporting challenges are not totally inconsistent. Most respondents identified dynamics associated with integrating and/or infusing nondiscrimination content. However, one respondent who reports no difficulties also comments that HBCUs are by nature and strength nondiscriminatory and accepting of diversity. Dissonance between the missions of HBCUs and non-HBCUs is reported as determining the focus of content in this area. For example, one respondent notes that HBCUs tend to approach this content more from the perspective of race or color than from other diversity categories.

Other challenges noted also seem to resonate around the nature of the institution. For example, in view of the church-based legacy of HBCUs, it is perhaps not surprising that several respondents noted difficulty with content related to gay, lesbian, bisexual, and transgender populations. That student populations are likely predominantly African American and female also complicates the compatibility of realities of programs housed in HBCUs and CSWE accreditation standards. Respondents note voluntary or involuntary efforts to attract male and non-Black students. One respondent notes that a diverse faculty and student population has resulted in the need for "team building and workshop training," although funding for such intervention is not available.

Program Assessment and Continuous Improvement (Standard 8)

Standard 8 essentially requires programs to have an assessment plan and procedures to evaluate the outcome of each program objective and to implement that plan (CSWE, 2001). All respondents indicate efforts to meet this standard, such as instituting processes and procedure; continuous planning, monitoring, and assessment; and pre- and posttests for all classes. Respondents also report current and future challenges that seem to revolve around two general areas, with resource limitations as a recurring theme: administration of tasks and assistance for HBCU institutions that is required to ensure future success.

Many accredited programs may also encounter the challenges to managing the assessment and renewal effort that respondents identify. Included are formulation of clear processes and procedure; ongoing planning, monitoring, and assessment activity; and consistent administration of evaluative instruments to support the assessment effort.

Challenges respondents identify might also be shared with non-HBCU programs. Those include recruitment of faculty with research expertise to replace retiring faculty, consistent collection and analysis of data, distraction of newer faculty from the assessment effort by institutional pressure to engage in scholarship, difficulties of student participation in the effort, and time and resource conflicts of class coverage and assessment activity.

Respondents also specifically identify areas of assistance from which programs housed in HBCUs could benefit. Those areas are

- additional resources to support faculty release time dedicated to implementation of Standard 8;
- equity funding among schools of social work: "Longstanding inequities related to funding when compared to majority White institutions";
- faculty training on assessment: "A consultant is needed to help us put an assessment tool in place that would be useful now and in the future";
- funding for professional staff to assist with assessment and continuous improvement; and
- dedicated space and equipment to expand program curricula, including video labs for student self-evaluation of intervention skills.

As noted, two questions asked respondents to identify key barriers to meeting the requirements of standards 3 and 7. Generally, and as might be anticipated, respondents point to the historically defined culture as a general obstruction to meeting the requirements of these two standards.

Program Governance, Administrative Structure, and Resources (Standard 3)

Standard 3 generally requires "the necessary autonomy and administrative structure to achieve its goals and objectives," including a curriculum that is consistent with both the Educational Policy Standards and institutional policies; administration and faculty participation in formulation and implementation of "recruitment, hiring, retention, promotion, and tenure" policy; a chief program administrator with "demonstrated leadership ability" and other administrators who meet certain criteria; release time for administrators; adequate financial and personnel resources to support program; adequate library resources; and access to assistive technology (CSWE, 2001, pp. 13, 14). Respondents were asked to identify key barriers to maintaining an administrative structure that meets the requirements of the standard and factors that contributed to the barriers.

The barriers to meeting these requirements that respondents identify are consistent with the earlier discussion regarding the leadership issues their host institutions face. Indeed, 11 respondents specifically identify barriers to meeting this standard because of the administrative structure within which they are housed. However, comments from the remaining two respondents also suggest barriers related to the host institution's governance structure.

More specifically, respondents identify several obstacles to compliance with Standard 3, including structural foundation, institutional leaders' minimal understanding of social work, insufficient administrative support for program operations, limited support of scholarship, and restricted ability to attract competitive faculty, including senior faculty.

For example, one respondent notes that institutional leaders' lack of understanding of social work as a professional program resulted in lack of recognition of the need for a director position for each program component and adequate resources to hire experienced directors. Another respondent comments that HBCUs rarely have the resources for personnel and other support for scholarship activities, technological acquisitions, or research infrastructure development. Yet another respondent views restructuring within the host institution and the resulting potential of instability as a barrier.

Three respondents specify contributing factors to maintaining an adequate administrative structure: program position within the host institution, decision-making protocol, restraints on program autonomy as required by the Standards, and variances between CSWE Standards and university priorities and productivity norms.

Program Renewal (Standard 7)

Standard 7 essentially requires "ongoing exchanges with external constituencies," faculty engagement in research and scholarship, and efforts toward innovation and professional and academic leadership (CSWE, 2001, p. 17). The survey asked respondents to identify key barriers to adhering to this standard.

Two themes are reflected in responses indicating barriers to meeting program renewal standards—one related to a historically generated institutional culture that protracts fear of the unknown in the face of the need for change and limited vision for future growth, the other related to time and fiscal resources required for program enhancement. However, 5 of 13 respondents report no barriers, and one notes that "if anything, our faculty tends to be overly involved in community activities that connect us to the practice community."

Lack of resources to support consultants and other expenses is a key barrier identified by 6 of the remaining 8 respondents, as would likely be true for other accredited programs as well. Those respondents also specify the effort and resources associated with the accreditation process, including preparation for the site visit and orientation of the dean, provost, and other administrative officers. These preparations reportedly occur in an environment in which release time is not provided for scholarly activity, classes are large, faculty pay their own professional association dues, merit raises are not awarded, and funds are not available to guide the program through the renewal process.

However, other barriers identified are unique to the HBCU culture, including "traditional oppression of HBCU institutions" by states, absence of administrative vision for future growth, experientially supported fear of the unknown, and historically supported potential for misuse of evaluative data to the detriment of the institution and the program.

The responding deans and directors have provided insight into the realities of leadership issues in accredited social work programs in HBCUs. Because they have the vision to appreciate the value of an effort to initiate a dialogue around the past, present, and future value and challenges of their host institutions and programs, their voices help to provide a baseline from which to continue the dialogue within the social work community.

Their voices affirm the obstacles faced and, perhaps more important, their words reaffirm the continuation of a history of success in delivering social work education. In that respect, we are reminded of inextricably shared legacies of the programs, their hosts, and the social work education community. One hopes the reminder will prompt acceptance of the notion that those challenges and celebrations of success must also be shared by their host institutions and the social work education community. It is in the context of mutuality of legacy and common aspirations for preparing competent social work professionals of the future that the following recommendations are offered. The goal is to encourage attention to the unique leadership challenges of social work programs in HBCU institutions and to underscore the wisdom of the HBCU institution pioneers who nurtured their programs and social work education.

Clarion to CSWE and the Social Work Education Community

Recommendations that are of potential assistance to HBCU social work program administrators have been posited to their institutional hosts. We now turn to our social work colleagues.

Preliminarily, we offer a reminder that social work programs in HBCUs have defied the historical odds that clouded the birth to become "indispensible members of American higher education" (Nichols, 2004, p. 219). They have been and are educating social workers of color, the need for whom has been recognized (Reisch, 2006).

Indeed, in addition to a history of contributions to social work education, the programs figure significantly in the education preparation of today's African American leaders in social work education. They are incubators for the development of leadership and knowledge essential to African American communities. Reportedly, graduates of HBCU baccalaureate and master's degree programs are well-represented among African American deans (House, Fowler, Thornton, & Francis, 2007). Therefore, we urge including programs of social work in HBCUs in the call to embrace "the richness" of the profession and acknowledgment of the "challenges" that it brings (Peebles-Wilkins & Shank, 2003, p. 55).

In that regard and to that extent, we recommend the following initial strategies:

- That CSWE, as the accrediting membership body, assume a leadership role in encouraging the profession's recognition of the challenges faced by its leader colleagues in HBCU Institution social work programs
- That CSWE hear the voices of the deans and directors that have been offered and examine its Educational Policy, Accreditation Standards, and accreditation process to accommodate the unique values and visions of programs in HBCU institutions
- That CSWE purposely and deliberately expand the number of faculty members from HBCU institutions in the cadre of members involved in its accreditation process
- That CSWE engage consideration of strategies that respond to the needs of social work programs in HBCU institutions, to move toward fulfillment of its obligations to preserve and further the viability of its members who have contributed unique scholarship to the profession and educational opportunities to a population of future professionals who would otherwise be lost to the profession
- That CSWE establish a desk or office to assist social work programs in HBCU institutions in navigating the institutional obstacles they face; to provide assistance with meeting standards related to curriculum, student development, and programs assessment; and to develop initiatives such as faculty exchanges
- That CSWE ensure inclusion of HBCU institution faculty and administrators who are not traditional participants in planning and implementing its activities, especially those involving curriculum
- That CSWE provide the leadership and support for the development of strategies to expand research and publication opportunities for HBCU institution faculty
- That the social work education community joins in embracing the contributions and value of HBCU programs to social work education and encourage implementation of these recommendations by CSWE

In essence, the contemporary milieu of economic, social, and political injustice evokes the efficacy of attending to the challenges of managing HBCU social work programs and reconsidering the "education for service" model developed by HBCUs.

Finally, we suggest a fair exchange: the expertise developed by HBCU pioneers who have provided the foundation for preparing future social workers who might otherwise be lost to the profession, for recognition of that knowledge by the social work education community. As Dr. Leashore (2001, p. 1) counseled, "social work would do well to recognize and indeed claim" the pioneers and legacy of social work programs in HBCUs.

References

Adams, F. V. (1981). *The reflections of Florence Victoria Adams.* Atlanta: Shannon Press.

Alexander, C. A. (1987). History of social work and social welfare. In *Encyclopedia of social work* (19th ed.; Vol. 1, pp. 777–788). Washington, DC: National Association of Social Workers.

Ayers v. Fordice, No 4: 75cv009-B-D, 2000 U. S. Dist. LEXIS 9877 (N. D. MS 2000).

Brieland, D. (1987). History and evolution of social work practice. In *Encyclopedia of social work* (19th ed.; Vol. 1, pp. 739–754). Washington, DC: National Association of Social Workers.

Buck, J. (1999). HBCU salaries—The good, bad and ugly. *University Faculty Voice,* 4(1), 4–5.

Carlton-LaNey, I. (1999). African American social work pioneers: Response to need. *Social Work,* 4(4), 311–321.

Council on Social Work Education (CSWE). (2001). *Educational policy and accreditation standards.* Alexandria, VA: Author.

Council on Social Work Education (CSWE). (2007a). *2006 statistics on social work education in the United States: A summary.* Alexandria, VA: Author.

Council on Social Work Education (CSWE). (2007b). *CSWE annual report: 55 years of educating social workers.* Alexandria, VA: Author.

Day, P. J. (2006). *A new history of social welfare* (5th ed.). New York: Allyn & Bacon.

Dean, R. (2004). Looking toward the future in unsettled times [Editorial]. *Smith College Studies in Social Work, 74,* 579–593.

DuBois, W. E. B. (1989). *The souls of Black folks.* New York: Penguin Books. (Original work published 1903.)

Evans, A. L., & Evans, V. (2002). Historically Black colleges and universities (HBCUs). *Education, 123*(1), 3–16, 180.

Fields, C. D. (2001). Parting words. *Black Issues in Higher Education, 18,* 39–41.

Franklin, R. M. (2007). *Crisis in the village: Restoring hope in African American communities*. Minneapolis: Fortress Press.

Greene, L. J. (1942). *The Negro in colonial New England: 1620–1776*. New York: Columbia University Press.

Hawkins, B. D. (2004). Doing more with less. *Black Issues in Higher Education, 21*(9), 44–51.

HBCU Network. (n.d.). The history of HBCU's: DuBois versus Booker T. Retrieved December 15, 2007, from http://www.hbcunetwork.com/The_History_Of_HBCUs.cfm

Henderson, J. (2000, August 3–August 9). Will Historically Black colleges and universities be important in the 21st century? *New Amsterdam News*, 12–13.

Higher Education Act of 1965, 20 USC §§1001, et. seq.

House, L. E., Fowler, D. N., Thornton, P. L., & Francis, E. A. (2007). Minority fellowship program: A survey of African American deans and directors of U.S. schools of social work. *Journal of Social Work Education, 43*, 67–82.

Humphreys, J. (2005). *Economic impact of the nation's historically Black colleges and universities* (NCES 2007-178). U. S. Department of Education, National Center for Education Statistics. Washington, DC: U. S. Government Printing Office.

Icad, L. D., Spearmon, M., & Curry-Jackson, A. (1996). BSW Program in black colleges: Building on the strengths of tradition. *Journal of Social Work Education, 32*, 227–236.

Katz, M. B. (1983). *Poverty & policy in American history*. New York: Academic Press.

King, N. T. (2004). Howard University faculty retreat. *University Faculty Voice*. Retrieved January 10, 2008, from http://www.facultyvoice.com/Opinions/HowardRetreat.html

Kinzie, S., & Alexander, K. L. (2007, March 10). Ouster sought of Howard president: Panel accuses Swygert of "incompetence." *Washington Post*, p. B01.

Leashore, B. R. (2001, February/March). African-American pioneers in social work and social welfare. Retrieved February 4, 2008, from http://naswnyc.org/d18.html

Mactaggart, T. (2007, October). The realities of rescuing colleges in distress. *Chronicle of Higher Education, 54*(7), B11.

Martin, E. P., & Martin, J. M. (1995). *Social work and the Black experience*. Washington, DC: National Association of Social Workers.

Minor, J. T. (2007). Success of HBCUs means looking forward, not backwards. *Issues in Higher Education, 24*(4), 55.

Mitchell, J., Osby, O. S., Nelums, M., & Omari, S. R. (2004, September). *The shadows of Brown/Ayers: A perspective on the failure of human capital development.* Paper presented at the Patterson Research Conference: Still Not Equal: Expanding Opportunity in Global Societies, Washington, DC.

National Association of State Universities and Land-Grant Colleges. (n.d.). About us—membership listing. Retrieved February 4, 2008, from http://www.nasulgc.org/NetCommunity/Page.aspx?pid=249&srcid=236

Nichols, J. C. (2004). Unique characteristics, leadership styles, and management of historically Black colleges and universities. *Innovative Higher Education, 28*(3), 219–229.

Owens, I. (2001). *Stories told but yet unfinished: Challenges facing African American libraries and special collections in historically Black colleges and universities.* New York: Haworth Press.

Peebles-Wilkins, W., & Shank, B. W. (2003). A response to Charles Cowger: Shaping the future of social work as an institutional response to standards. *Journal of Social Work Education, 39*, 49–56.

Penn E. B., & Gabbidon S. L. (2007). Criminal justice education at historically Black colleges and universities: Three decades of progress. *Journal of Criminal Justice Education, 18*(1), 137–162.

Platt, T., & Chandler, S. (1988).Constant struggle: E. Franklin Frazier and Black social work in the 1920s. *Social Work, 38*, 293–297.

Provasnik, S., & Shafer, L. L. (2004). *Historically Black colleges and universities, 1976–2001* (NCES 2004-062). U. S. Department of Education, National Center for Education Statistics. Washington, DC: Government Printing Office.

Reisch, M. (2006). Workforce study all short [editorial]. *Social Work, 51*(4), 291–293.

Rivers, L. E. (2008, January 14). Historically Black colleges: Black universities are still needed [Editorial]. *Atlanta Journal-Constitution.* Retrieved January 26, 2008, from http://www.ajc.com/search/content/opinion/stories/2008/01/14/historice0114.html

Sharpe, R. V. (2005, Winter-Spring). All land grants were not created equal: The benefits of white privilege. *Review of Black Political Economy,* 29–38.

Thompson, C. H. (1933). Introduction: The problem of Negro higher education. *Journal of Negro Education, 2*(3), 257–271.

Turner, B. (2002). HBCUs: An educational system at the crossroads. *Black Issues in Higher Education, 19*(14), 50.

United Negro College Fund. (n.d.). About UNCF. Retrieved December 20, 2007, from http://www.uncf.org.aboutus/faqs.asp

Washington, F. B. (1935). The need and education of Negro social workers. *Journal for Negro Education, 4*(1), 76–93.

Whitney M. Young Jr. School of Social Work. (2007–2008). *Master of social work education* [Brochure]. Atlanta: Author.

Williams, W. (2008, January 14). Historically Black colleges: Is their purpose gone? [Editorial]. *Atlanta Journal-Constitution.* Retrieved January 18, 2008, from http://www.ajc.com/search/content/opinion/stories/2008/01/13/williamsed_0114.html

Wright, Stephen J. (1960). Some critical problems faced by the Negro church-related college. *Journal of Negro Education, 29*(3), 339–344.

23

A National Survey of Associate Deans in U.S. Accredited Graduate Social Work Programs
A Review of Their Roles and Characteristics

Stanley Blostein

Much of the work of colleges and universities is done at the academic department level. Yet, most institutions of higher learning pay little attention to either the preparation of academic department leaders or their succession into the position (Bolton, 1996; Wolverton, Wolverton, & Gmelch, 2005).

One of the most glaring shortcomings in the leadership area is the scarcity of sound research on the training and development of leaders (Conger & Benjamin, 1999, cited in Jackson & Gmelch, 2003). Because many associate deans first received their training in research and teaching, they scarcely anticipate their current leadership positions and thus have had minimal management training. As executives in higher education, academic deans have participated in studies on various aspects of the position (Layman, Bamberg, & Jones, 2002). Less attention has been given to the administrative support staff that enables deans to sustain the mission of the college or school, particularly associate and assistant deans. Considering the importance of these positions to the administration of academic colleges and schools, it is critical to learn more about them (Jackson & Gmelch, 2003).

Introduction

This lack of attention can be ascribed as well to social work education programs, which have committed few if any resources to understand their own institutional structure and processes. This is the enterprise that is responsible for educating social work practitioners as well as future social work educators and leaders (Shera & Bogo, 2001). Yet, these very same programs commit resources (usually in the form of research and publishing) to describing the conditions of the administrative curriculum (see, e.g., Ezell, Chernesky, & Healy, 2004) and to recommending administrative practices in human service organizations (Austin & Ezell, 2004; Hoefer, 2003; Lohmann & Lohmann, 2002; Patti, 2000, 2003). Why this lack of attention by social work faculty who teach and write in the area

I am indebted to Dr. Ashley Fujii and Dr. Tom Gregoire for assistance in the preparation of this study. Appreciation is expressed to those associate deans who took from their responsibilites what is already limited time to participate in this study.

of administration can only be conjectured. Certainly, one reason could be the over-whelming attention by social work faculty and students to clinical practice. In addition, there is the issue of the larger environment in which social work education exists—an in-stitution of higher education, an institution that places great value and gives rewards to those faculty who publish in "appropriate" peer-reviewed, academic journals (Cowger, 2003.) Bennis and O'Toole (2005) describe this last point in their discussion of how busi-ness schools have lost their way by "measure[ing] themselves almost solely by the rigor of their scientific research" (p. 1). There is little value given to writing about academic pro-grams, for which there is little or no financial support, either from the institution itself or from outside funders. But if social work is to meet its stated commitment to the larger so-ciety, it must begin to understand the context in which this commitment is to be met (Reisch & Gorin, 2001). This exploratory study is intended as a step in that direction.

In 1893, at the International Conference of Charities, Anna Dawes (1893, p. 204) called for the establishment of a course of study for "charitable workers [in] some es-tablished institution or in an institution by itself." Four years later, at the National Conference of Charities and Corrections, Mary Richmond (1897, p. 186) called for a training school in applied philanthropy, while cautioning that universities might foster "too exclusive attention to charitable theory." The drive for professional recog-nition, however, was stronger than this caution, and the establishment of programs began. From this beginning, graduate social work education has grown to 170 pro-grams (Council on Social Work Education [CSWE], 2005) in public and private higher education institutions in the United States. At this time, the practice of social work as recognized by the profession is based on the individual's having obtained a pro-fessional degree from a program accredited by CSWE.

Although social work programs are looked to for guidance and analysis of the myriad problems the discipline addresses, there has been little attention to (and consequently, sparse literature about) the structure and operation of social work education, itself. What literature exists focuses on the role of the dean (Munson, 1994), the role of faculty, the teaching-learn-ing process and related technology, and the characteristics and status of students. There is extensive literature on various parts of the curriculum, each with a number of subtopics. These include issues of cultural competence; models and methods of practice; educational techniques and technology; issues related to continuing education, licensure, international social work, and supervision; ethical issues; and myriad other topics (for a discussion, see Mohan, 2002). At the same time, much of the noncurriculum-focused literature that does exist looks at the satisfaction/dissatisfaction of deans; ranking schools by reputation; the publication records of faculty; and recruitment of students and tools for assessing appli-cants. Other disciplines, most notably business, medicine, dentistry, nursing, law, and education, have looked at and begun to assess the structure of their educational programs and their impact on the practice of the respective disciplines (see, for example, Bennis & O'Toole, 2005; Chmar, Weaver, Ranney, Haden, & Valachovic, 2004; Cuffman, 1999; Jackson, 2004; Lee & Hoyle, 2002; Rogers, 1988; Sullivan, 1983; Yrle, Hartmen, Grenier, & Lundberg, 2001). Social work lags far behind in this endeavor.

The decision to focus this study on the associate dean position in accredited grad-uate programs (the term *program* includes colleges, schools, divisions, and departments) is based on the need to describe senior management roles initially to understand better how social work programs function as organizational entities. This process has begun for the role of deans (see, for example, Munson, 1994; Rank, 2000), but not for others in senior management positions. The decision to look only at individuals who carry the title *associate dean* and to review only programs that are accredited at the graduate level, is based on the attempt to maintain as much consistency, clarity, and comparability in the data collected as possible.

At the same time, it is recognized that the use of organizational titles is not consistent from one program to another in higher education institutions. It is assumed, however, that the levels of dean and associate dean are in a relatively consistent position in most of higher education; that is, the dean level is usually responsible to a provost, senior vice president, vice president for academic affairs, or a similar hierarchical position in the institution of which the social work program is a part. Based on this assumption, the study did not look at programs that were headed by those with the title of director/assistant director or chair/vice chair, although there are almost certainly individuals in such positions who are comparable with deans/associate deans. With the limited information available on social work program organizational structure, it is simply not possible to assess what exists in higher education. These limitations do provide some direction for further research, and this is addressed more fully later.

I begin by discussing the methodology used to identify potential respondents and describing the data collection process. The limitations and findings of the study are discussed and organized in three major areas: organizational characteristics, social work program characteristics, and individual functions and characteristics of associate deans.

Methodology

CSWE does not maintain lists of individuals in the role of associate deans (Todd Lennon, personal communication, July 6, 2004), which does not mean that individuals do not maintain informal lists. CSWE maintains lists of deans (and directors) of programs, as well as directors of MSW programs, but the latter are not necessarily in associate dean positions. I compiled a list of associate deans using the CSWE list of all accredited programs by state (CSWE, 2005) and reviewing the individual program Web sites. In the summer of 2005, when this study was initiated, 170 graduate accredited programs were listed. In some instances, administrative staff were identified separately on the program Web site; in other instances, I had to review lists of faculty to identify those with the title of associate dean. This process may have missed some associate deans. Individuals with titles such as *associate director* or *associate chair* were omitted, as it would not be possible to determine comparability with associate dean positions. Forty-seven programs were identified with associate deans, comprising a total of 62 individuals. Messages were sent by e-mail to all 62 individuals to explain the purpose and voluntary nature of the study and to ask for their participation. Questionnaires were offered to all individuals identified, although a small number of schools had more than one associate dean position. In response to the initial informational e-mail message sent to these 62 individuals, 2 were out of the country, 1 declined to participate, and 4 were either no longer in an associate dean position or were associated with university administration rather than social work program administration. This produced a total of 55 in the pool of potential respondents. Those who volunteered to participate were directed to a link in the message that took them to the site of the questionnaire. They were informed that going to the linked site would be considered as their voluntary agreement to participate in the study. However, they could terminate at any point before or while responding to the questionnaire.

I designed the instrument used to collect data based on the literature that describes (1) general theories of management and organization (Anthony & Young, 2003; Bennis, 1993; Ginsberg & Keys, 1995; Lohmann & Lohmann, 2002); (2) literature that describes administration in higher education (Cronin & Crawford, 1999; Eberlein, 1992; Edwards, 1992; Gmelch, Wolverton, Wolverton, & Sarros, 1999; Honan & Teferra, 2001; Jones & Holdaway, 1996; Koerner & Mindes, 1997; Rosser, Johnsrud, & Heck, 2003; Wolverton et al., 1999); and (3) literature that addresses leadership in specific disciplines (see previous discipline-related citations in Introduction section).

The questionnaire contained three major areas: (1) organizational characteristics, (2) social work program characteristics, and (3) individual functions and characteristics. The first area sought information on the social work program's host institution, including name, location, size, and auspices. The second area focused on the social work program, including number of students, number of faculty (tenure- and non-tenure-track), and budget. These first two areas sought to identify the organizational environment in which the associate deans functioned. Area three was intended to obtain information on the individual functions and characteristics, including gender, age, race/ethnicity, academic rank, tenure status, and length of time in the associate dean position. In addition, there was a series of questions seeking to identify areas of academic expertise and to explore the individual's perception of the role of associate dean. Finally, this area identified a series of functional areas, both administrative and faculty-related, that the respondent was asked to rank in importance. These areas are discussed in more depth in the section on findings. Several individuals who were serving as associate deans in social work programs at that time reviewed this instrument, and a number of their suggestions were incorporated into the final instrument.

The instrument was formatted at a commercial Web site (www.surveymonkey.com), which permitted constructing each question to allow for maximum flexibility in responses, including skip logic, required answers, open-ended answers, and randomized multiple-choice answers. Safeguards were ensured at the Web site, and all usual protocols involving human subjects were followed, including no attempt to identify individual respondents, attention to sensitivity of information sought, ability of respondent to discontinue questionnaire at any point, full and complete disclosure of the purpose of the study, and voluntary nature of participation. I clarified in my original message to potential respondents that I was conducting the study as an independent researcher, and the study was not under the auspices of The Ohio State University. (This was due to the research policy of the university, which did not allow for individual research by emeritus faculty without involvement of a regular faculty member.)

The original e-mail message sent to the individuals identified as associate deans explained that the purpose of the study was to describe the functions and characteristics of associate deans. The Web address of the questionnaire was provided, and the message specified that completing the questionnaire constituted the respondent's agreeing to participate. The e-mail address and telephone number of the writer were provided as well, and the recipients of the message were encouraged to contact me with any questions. Recipients were asked to complete the questionnaire within 2 weeks. A week after the initial message, a follow-up message was sent to all on the list thanking those who had completed the questionnaire, encouraging others to do so, and again providing the Web address.

A total of 32 responses were received from the 55 individuals contacted, representing a response rate of 58%. Of the 47 programs identified as having associate deans, responses were received from 29 different programs, or 62%. (Individuals in 3 programs with more than 1 associate dean responded.) A review of the characteristics of these 29 programs indicates they appear to be representative of the 47 programs with associate deans in terms of numbers of students, number of faculty, size of budget, and geographic distribution. (See Findings, Organizational Characteristics for details.)

Limitations of the Study

The primary limitation of this study is imposed by the relatively small number of individuals identified as associate deans (55) and the subsequent number of responses (32), although this represents a response rate of 58%, which is generally considered more than adequate for a study of this size and type (Royce, 2004). The findings represent situational accuracy to the extent of the ability to identify associate deans. The fact that the study is exploratory, and there is no attempt to generalize beyond those who responded, tends to mitigate this limitation. A second limitation is imposed by the lack of literature in the area under study, that is, the administrative structure of social work education programs. This required translating from other professions and disciplines of, for example, the functional areas in which individuals are engaged. At this stage, it is not possible to determine whether these translations are accurate. A third limitation is imposed by the methodology of data collection itself, as well as the means by which the initial list of associate deans was compiled, that is, by using Web sites to identify individuals, e-mail messages for initial contacts, and the Internet for distribution and response to the data collection instrument. Although there have been some initial efforts to evaluate this approach (see, for example, Lamb, 2004), without further research, it is too early to determine its efficacy.

Findings

Organizational Characteristics

Of the 29 programs, 26 (90%) were designated as schools and 3 (10%) as colleges. Auspices of the programs were 59% public and 41% private. To have some gauge of the size of the host institution in which the social work program was located, respondents were asked for the total number of students in the institution (see Table 1). (Note: Each table indicates the number of responses to that specific question.) The geographic distribution of respondent programs was 9 from the Northeast/Mid-Atlantic region; 3 from the Southeast; 8 from the Midwest, and 9 from the West.

TABLE 1   TOTAL NUMBER OF STUDENTS IN HOST
           INSTITUTION BY NUMBER OF RESPONDENTS
           (N = 32)

Number of Students	Number of Respondents
Fewer than 5,000	1
5,001–10,000	3
10,001–15,000	6
15,001–20,000	2
20,001–25,000	4
25,001–30,000	6
30,001–35,000	4
35,001–40,000	2
More than 40,000	4

Note: N reported in tables varies depending on number of
      responses to question.

In consideration of the apparent practice of selecting experienced faculty members to move into an associate dean (as well as a dean) position, and in light of the wide range of administrative functions expected of associate deans, the respondents were asked whether their host institution provided any orientation or training for individuals recently appointed to an associate dean position. This kind of orientation or training is relatively common for recently appointed deans and chairs of departments. Respondents indicated that slightly less than 1 in 5 (18.8%) institutions provided such assistance, whereas 4 of 5 (81.2%) did not. This might be due to an assumption that an experienced faculty member, regardless of experience or education as an administrator, is ready to move into an administrative position. This can be seen by reviewing the qualifications called for in searches for deans (and the rare searches for associate deans), which are essentially the same qualifications stated in searches for full professors.

Again, in an attempt to describe the institutions in which associate deans function, respondents were asked for the total budget of the social work program. Although the intent was to determine the operating budget of the program, there was some confusion about whether to include various forms of grant monies. Nevertheless, the responses, although there were only 22 of them, provide one more interesting piece of the overall description of the host institutions. The fact that 5 respondents did not know the size of the budget was of some surprise. Table 2 shows the total budget of the social work programs of the respondents.

TABLE 2   TOTAL BUDGET OF SOCIAL WORK PROGRAM BY NUMBER OF PROGRAMS (N = 22)

Total Budget of Social Work Program	Number of Programs
Less than $1 million	1
$1–2 million	3
$3–4 million	6
$5–6 million	3
$7–8 million	2
$9–10 million	1
Over $20 million	1
Unknown	5

In response to the question about the number of tenure-track faculty in the program, 27 of the respondents provided the following in a range of 14–45 faculty (see Table 3).

TABLE 3   NUMBER OF TENURE-TRACK FACULTY BY NUMBER OF PROGRAMS (N = 27)

Number of Tenure-Track Faculty	Number of Programs
10–15	1
16–20	9
21–25	5
26–30	8
31–35	0
36–40	2
41–45	2

TABLE 4   NUMBER OF NON-TENURE-TRACK FACULTY BY NUMBER OF PROGRAMS (N = 27)

Number of Non-Tenure-Track Faculty	Number of Programs
1–10	6
11–20	7
21–30	6
31–40	5
41–50	1
51–60	0
61–70	2

Respondents were also asked to provide the number of non-tenure-track faculty who teach in an academic year. Again, as there is no agreed definition of *non-tenure track* (the term includes half-time, part-time, adjunct, clinical, faculty who are not tenure track, and other designations), the comparisons of one program to another are extremely limited. At the same time, these numbers provide an additional element of the organizational characteristics in which associate deans function. The information in Table 4 came from 27 of the respondents, indicating a range of 3–70, with a mean of 27. The fact that there are, on average, an equal number of non-tenure-track faculty as there are tenure-track certainly warrants further exploration, from the perspective of both this study and the perspective of the impact on the curriculum.

Individual Characteristics

Questions were asked in this section of the survey instrument to determine the characteristics, both as faculty members and as administrators, of the associate deans who responded. Slightly more women than men responded, with 42.3% men and 57.7% women; 11.5% were 36–45 years of age; 38.5% were 46–55 years of age, and 50% were 56–65 years of age. None of the respondents was younger than 35 or older than 65. The race/ethnicity of the respondents was more than 92% Caucasian.

A variety of titles are used for associate deans, with the title of associate dean for academic affairs being the most frequent, used by 11 of the 26 respondents. Other titles reported were associate dean (6); associate dean and director of the MSW program (5); associate dean for research (3); and associate dean for student affairs (1). Considering the small number of respondents, there was no attempt to associate titles with functions.

In response to a question about holding academic rank, 84.6% reported they did have academic rank. The academic ranks held by the 24 respondents were 9 professors, 14 associate professors or associate professor emeritus, and 1 senior lecturer.

Of the 26 respondents to a question about their responsibilities before moving into an associate dean position, 19 (73.1%) said they had moved into the associate dean position from a faculty position in the same program, whereas 7 (26.9%) had not. Of these seven, 4 had come from another program, and 3 did not specify the circumstances. Of some surprise was that only a little more than a third of the associate deans (38.5%) reported having served as the director of the master of social work program, whereas 61.5% did not. (The requirement to have an individual designated as the director of the MSW program is related to accreditation requirements.) In response to a question about the length of time for appointment as associate dean, only 8 individuals responded, and there is insufficient information to report. (Of interest, however, was the response of one individual who said that the length "seems like a life sentence some days.") A question about the amount of time in paid teaching positions in higher education, before accepting their current associate dean position, elicited responses ranging from "less than a year" to 36–40 years (see Table 5). The responses to these two questions suggest the need for further study of the career paths of administrators in social work education.

When asked to indicate all their areas of teaching, for example, courses they currently teach and previously taught, respondents reported the following curriculum areas in rank order by number of respondents choosing each area (see Table 6).

As doctoral courses were ranked first in areas of the curriculum respondents taught, it is assumed that advising doctoral students and chairing or serving on doctoral committees is a part of the responsibilities for those teaching doctoral courses. These activities can occupy a significant amount of time, and respondents were asked the number of such students they currently advised. The range of the 19 respondents to this question was from none to 10 students, with the mean being 3.95 students and the median and mode being 3. It is also of some interest to note that, in response to a question about how they perceived themselves as administrators and faculty, respondents (N=26) overwhelmingly (77%) described themselves as administrators or primarily administrators with some faculty responsibilities. The remainder described

TABLE 5   LENGTH OF YEARS IN TEACHING PRIOR TO
ASSOCIATE DEAN POSITION BY NUMBER OF
RESPONDENTS (N = 23)

Years in Teaching	Number of Respondents
Less than 1	3
1–5	7
6–10	4
11–15	3
16–20	1
21–25	4
26–30	0
31–35	0
36–40	1

TABLE 6   AREAS OF THE CURRICULUM TAUGHT BY RANK
ORDER CHOICE OF RESPONDENTS (N = 33)

Teaching Area	Rank
Doctoral courses	1
Research (graduate)	2
Clinical practice (graduate)	3
General foundation practice (graduate)	4
Human behavior (graduate)	5
Undergraduate courses	6
Field	7
Policy (graduate)	8T
Administration (graduate)	8T
Diversity (graduate)	10
Community organization/ development	11

themselves as administrators and faculty equally. Yet, as can be seen in Table 6, administration was tied for 8th place in the ranking of 11 curriculum areas.

In response to the question of how many courses are taught in an academic year, in addition to their responsibilities as associate deans (noting that an academic year might be either two semesters or three quarters), there were 25 responses, with a range of 0–3 courses. The mean was 1.36 courses, with the median and mode being 2 courses.

Respondents were asked to list the professional organizations to which they belonged as part of the effort to identify their individual characteristics. Thirty-two responded to this question; all belong to the Council on Social Work Education; 27 belong to the

National Association of Social Workers, and 21 belong to the Society for Social Work Research. Of little surprise was the wide range of other organizations mentioned, reflecting the respondents' individual interests. Among these were the American Psychological Association, the Academy of Management, the Association for Community Organization and Social Administration, the National Association of Black Social Workers, the Child Welfare League of America, various state associations of deans and directors, and others. (It should be noted that, among these others, one respondent listed the Harley Owners Group, which suggests that the burdens of the position have not overwhelmed a sense of humor, probably a useful attribute.)

Central to one purpose of this study was the attempt to begin to determine (1) how associate deans perceive their administrative position vis-à-vis their role as faculty member (discussed previously); (2) their career goals; and (3) based on their stated career goals, whether they believe the position of associate dean helps or hinders career advancement. Of the 26 respondents to a question about career goals, 6 indicated they would like to move into a position as dean; 6 would like to remain an associate dean; 6 would like to return to a full-time faculty position, and 6 were not sure of their goals. One indicated that his or her career goal was to move into program development, and one had retired.

In response to a question about whether the position of associate dean helps or hinders career advancement, there were 26 responses. One respondent felt it greatly hinders career advancement; 8 felt it hinders advancement; 5 said it neither helps nor hinders advancement; 10 felt it helps career advancement, and 2 said it greatly helps advancement. Of most note for these responses was the divergence of opinions.

Reflective of these responses, the respondents indicated a range of 50%–100% of their total work time committed to administrative responsibilities, with a mean of 80%, and a range of 10%–40% of their time committed to faculty responsibilities, with a mean of 20%.

Of some interest, although again we are dealing with small numbers, of the respondents who said they would like to move into a dean position, 4 were men and 2 were women. Those wishing to remain an associate dean were 4 women and 2 men. Of those who indicated they would like to move into a dean position, 4 said that being associate dean would help or greatly help their goal, whereas 2 said it would hinder their goal. Of the 6 who professed a goal of wishing to return to a faculty position, 4 felt being associate dean hindered this goal, 1 felt it neither helped nor hindered, and 1 felt it helped.

Respondents were asked to review a list of 20 administrative functional areas and a list of 14 faculty functional areas and indicate their perception of the importance of each area, using a 5-point scale:

1. Highest priority/critical
2. High priority/very important
3. Moderate priority/important
4. Limited priority/routine
5. Lowest priority/if time permits.

These 5 responses were combined into 3 categories: the first category combined 1 and 2 in the scale (column C in Tables 7 and 9); the second category reflected 3 in the

TABLE 7   ADMINISTRATIVE FUNCTIONAL AREAS BY PERCENTAGE OF RESPONDENTS RANKING
HIGHEST PRIORITY AND HIGH PRIORITY

A Functional Area	B Number Ranking Functional Area	C Combined Highest Priority/Critical & High Priority/ Very Important (%)	D Moderate Priority/ Important (%)	E Combined Limited Priority/Routine & Lowest Priority/ If Time Permits (%)
Budget/financial matters	22	45	23	32
Supervising staff (nonfaculty)	25	44	36	20
Faculty workloads	22	91	0	09
Faculty evaluations	16	69	06	25
Mentoring faculty	23	74	17	09
Admissions	17	47	06	47
Relationships with units within institution	25	44	52	04
Individual student issues	24	71	12	17
Faculty–student conflicts	23	78	09	13
Faculty–faculty conflicts	19	79	16	05
Relationships with field organizations	15	33	20	47
Relationships with other than field organizations in community	22	23	45	32
Relationships with donors/alumni(ae)	19	32	32	37
Curriculum development	23	83	09	09
Class scheduling	20	85	0	15
Continuing education	16	19	19	63
Accreditation of program	24	96	0	04
Market of program	17	65	16	18
Obtaining funded research	18	56	17	28
Advanced training for self as associate dean	16	25	25	50

scale (column D); and the third combined 4 and 5 in the scale (column E). This was done partially to accommodate the relatively small number of respondents, and partially to reflect the pattern of responses. This information, along with the number of respondents to each functional area, is reported in Tables 7 and 9. In addition, 2 tables (8 and 10) show the ranking of each of the functional areas (administrative and faculty) based on the number of respondents who ranked the functional area as highest priority and high priority.

There appears to be a high level of agreement among the respondents on the importance of the 5 top-ranked administrative functional areas, that is, program accreditation, faculty workloads, class scheduling, curriculum development, and faculty-faculty conflicts (see Table 8). This agreement is not as evident in looking at the faculty functional areas, possibly because most respondents spend only about 20% of their time on faculty functions (see Table 10). However, it is of interest that, in the faculty functional areas, there was some discrepancy about a number of functions, particularly those ranked as the bottom 5 of the 14, that is, service on institutional committees, service as a consultant, relationships with alumni and donors, community

TABLE 8   RANK OF ADMINISTRATIVE FUNCTIONAL AREAS BASED ON RANKING AS HIGHEST PRIORITY AND HIGH PRIORITY COMBINED

Functional Area	Combined Rank
Budget/financial matters	13
Supervising staff (nonfaculty)	14T
Faculty workloads	2
Faculty evaluations	9
Mentoring faculty	7
Admissions	12
Relationships with units within institution	14T
Individual student issues	8
Faculty–student conflicts	6
Faculty–faculty conflicts	5
Relationships with field organizations	16
Relationships with other than field organizations in community	19
Relationships with alumni/donors	17
Curriculum development	4
Class scheduling	3
Continuing education	20
Accreditation of program	1
Marketing of program	10
Obtaining funded research	11
Advanced training for self as associate dean	18

TABLE 9   FACULTY FUNCTIONAL AREAS BY PERCENTAGE OF RESPONDENTS RANKING AS HIGHEST PRIORITY AND HIGH PRIORITY

A Functional Area	B Number Ranking Functional Area	C Combined Highest Priority/Critical & High Priority/ Very Important (%)	D Moderate Priority/ Important (%)	E Combined Limited Priority/Routine & Lowest Priority/ If Time Permits (%)
Preparation for classes taught	20	65	35	0
Student conferences	19	53	32	16
Grading & reviewing course material	20	65	30	05
Field/practicum activities	9	33	33	33
Curriculum development	20	75	15	10
Research related to courses taught	14	79	14	07
Research other than course-related	20	80	05	15
Obtaining funded research	17	59	29	12
Service on social work program committees	20	75	20	05
Service on institutional committees	21	52	29	19
Relations. with alumni/donors	16	38	25	38

Note: Percentages do not always total 100% as a result of rounding.

service, and service on institutional committees. There were widely diverging views about the importance of individual areas. This was not a focus of this study, so it was not explored further, but it certainly merits further study.

Discussion

In the context of this study, and as an initial step in describing and analyzing the organizational structure of graduate social work programs, the section on organizational characteristics presents a number of characteristics of this group that call for further exploration. Although there is no attempt to extrapolate these data beyond the group of respondents, an initial step for further research would be to describe the organizational and administrative structure and processes of all accredited graduate programs, beyond that required for accreditation. The finding that the host institutions

TABLE 10   RANK OF FACULTY FUNCTIONAL AREAS BASED ON RANKING AS HIGHEST PRIORITY
           AND HIGH PRIORITY COMBINED

Functional Area	Combined Rank
Preparation for classes taught	5T
Student conferences	9
Grading & reviewing course material	5T
Field/practicum activities	14
Curriculum development	3T
Research related to courses taught	2
Research other than course-related	1
Obtaining funded research	8
Service on social work program committees	3T
Service on institutional committees	10
Student advising	7
Community service	11
Service as consultant	13
Relationships with alumni/donors	12

for this group encompassed a total number of students from fewer than 5,000 to more than 40,000, with a median of 20,001–25,000, strongly suggests that the structure of the host institution plays a significant role in the structure (and thus the operation and nature of the outcomes) of the social work program. The budgets of the social work programs suggest a similar type of interplay, with annual budgets from less than $1 million to more than $20 million. Another finding related to organizational characteristics that seeks further exploration is the median numbers of tenure-track and non-tenure-track faculty, 21–25 and 21–30, respectively. The ratio between the two groups, and the ratio to students, program budget, and focus of the program, would be useful in assessing program outcomes. Of interest would be a description of how social work programs differ from or are similar to other professional programs, for example, law, medicine, nursing, education, or architecture.

The data on individual characteristics of associate deans show some of the most interesting findings. One cannot tell from the small group of respondents whether they are representative of all programs, but this issue clearly deserves further study. The finding that more than 92% of the respondents are Caucasian certainly raises questions, particularly in a profession that places so much emphasis on diversity in its stated purposes and its curriculum. The limited respondent interest in moving into a dean position suggests a need for further study as well. On the surface, an individual who has served as an associate dean would appear to be a viable candidate for dean.

The most common title respondents used is associate dean for academic affairs, which appears consonant with the functions (which are discussed later in this section). Of some surprise was the small number (5) of respondents who also had the title of director of the MSW program, which had been assumed to be one of the primary responsibilities of associate deans. This may just be a function of the idiosyncratic way of assigning titles in higher education, because the data on functional areas strongly suggest these respondents have major responsibilities in most aspects of the graduate program. What is not known at all is how much these individuals are involved in doctoral education, which is not accredited by CSWE, is usually organizationally reflective of the host institution, and appears to be more and more significant to a program's perceived success. That many respondents said they taught doctoral courses, consider doctoral education as one of their areas of expertise, and usually serve on doctoral committees, suggests a major commitment in this area.

Of no surprise was the finding that almost all of the respondents were tenured and held the rank of either professor or associate professor. Further study might focus on the career paths of administrators, including deans and associate deans, in social work programs. The respondents to this study reported that most are experienced faculty members, raising the question of the efficacy of moving faculty members, whose careers center on their role as faculty, into administrative positions. Although this debate has gone on in social work, as well as in other disciplines, for a number of years, the question remains and is still valid: Does one who has performed at a high level as a faculty member (or practitioner) necessarily have the skills and knowledge to function at a high level as an academic (or nonprofit organization) administrator? If the announcements for dean and associate dean positions are any indicator, most feel the answer is yes, because the position descriptions are almost identical to descriptions for senior faculty positions; that is, "established research agenda; national or international reputation; record of successful grant writing," and often giving a nod to "administrative experience." Little if anything is mentioned about basic administrative skills. This is partially reflected in the responses to areas of the curriculum in which the respondents taught. Administration tied for 8th place out of 11; ranked 1st and 2nd were doctoral courses and research.

The respondents clearly perceive themselves as either administrators or primarily administrators with some faculty responsibilities, with 20 of the 26 responses in these two categories. Yet, at the same time, only 6 said they would like to move into a dean position, and 6 others indicated they would like to remain an associate dean. Although it seems logical that experienced associate deans would be likely candidates for dean positions, this does not appear to be a popular career path. The respondents were about evenly split between those who felt being an associate dean helped and those who felt it hindered their career advancement. This is obviously tied to whether the individual wished to return to a faculty position or remain in administration, either as an associate dean or dean. The area of administrative career choices and advancement in social work programs remains unclear, but this study appears to have identified a number of the components of the issue that deserve further examination. The answer to the question of who makes a successful dean, associate dean, or other administrator would be of immense value to a number of practice-based professions.

Central to the purpose of this study were the data obtained on administrative functional areas, which numbered 20, and faculty functional areas, which numbered 14, in which the respondents are involved. It appears that the respondents, as associate deans in relation to deans, function in a similar way as senior administrators do in other types of organizations, that is, deans function as chief executive officers, and associate deans function as chief operating officers. The dean frequently assumes responsibility for organizational liaison with units higher in the host institution, for example, provosts and president, with alumni and donor groups, and with organizations and individuals in the larger community, other than field agency sites. Associate deans assume responsibility for primarily internal functions, for example, accreditation of the program, faculty workloads, class scheduling, curriculum development, and resolution of faculty–faculty conflicts. This workload is combined with faculty functions, for example, research, both course and noncourse-related; activities related to courses taught; and service on social work program committees. An important question is how time is allocated among these functions; the answers to this question are crucial to assessing the overall functioning of the social work program.

Conclusions

The basic thesis behind this study is that researchers in social work education need to expand the attention given to the enterprise of which they are a part. The structure, roles, and functions of social work programs within higher education are critical components in the quality and outcomes of those programs. It is all well and good that programs in higher education, including social work, strive to move up in the various rankings (a number of which are currently under a great deal of criticism), but these dubious rankings do little to uncover how well students are learning what the faculty say they are supposed to learn. There is a legitimate argument to be made that rankings based on reputational surveys are heavily biased toward programs with faculty who publish a great deal, and have little to do with the quality or effectiveness of the program. This can be determined partially through the kinds of research on students and curriculum that is currently conducted, but such research needs to begin looking at the social work education enterprise as well. It is not enough simply to structure the administration of a social work program based on what it has always been or the idiosyncrasies of individual deans. The study findings suggest, as have other studies (Edwards, 1992), that the influence of the host institution has an impact on the practices of program administrators, including, of course, associate deans. Because social work programs are located in such a wide variety of institutions, it would be helpful to assess this impact.

The transition from full-time faculty member to associate dean deserves a closer look, particularly in the context of what knowledge and skills are needed. Related to this as well is the need for training when individuals move into an associate dean position. The model used to look at associate dean positions in schools of education (Jackson & Gmelch, 2003) would be a useful tool for an expanded review of the roles and characteristics of associate deans of social work programs. Previous research has demonstrated that, in the case of deans (for example, Feldman, Ottoman, & Ottman, 1999; Munson, 1994; Rosser et al., 2003), the role of the associate dean is to supplement the role of the dean in specific functional areas. These two distinct but comple-mentary areas of responsibility, that is, external functions and internal functions, need to be specified to establish the roles and functions of associate deans appropriately. Gmelch et al. (1999), cited in Rosser et al., (2003) stress this point:

> The former vision of the dean as a scholarly leader has been replaced by an ex-ecutive image of the dean as politically astute and economically savvy...The pressure to get more involved in development has shifted the traditional role of the dean as chiefly an academic-policy setter and the liaison between professors and the administration to entrepreneur and politician. (p. 2)

These shifts in the role of deans must also be reflected in shifts in the role of asso-ciate deans. Social work programs would do well to heed the observations and advice of Bennis and O'Toole (2005) to business schools:

> During the past several decades, many leading business schools have quietly adopted an inappropriate—and ultimately self-defeating—model of academic excellence. Instead of measuring themselves in terms of the competence of their graduates, or by how well their faculties understand important drivers (of per-formance), they measure themselves almost solely by the rigor of their scientific research. (p. 1)

Whether this applies as well to social work education can be determined only if the profession as a whole, and particularly social work educators, begins to look closely at the organization and structure of educational programs. Some 36 years ago, Harry Specht (1972) forecast massive changes in social work, including a separation of so-cial work practice from social work education. A question that must be addressed is whether the practice of social work and social work education have gone their sepa-rate ways. To do this, we need to begin looking more closely at the administrative and procedural processes of social work education.

References

Anthony, R., & Young, D. (2003). *Management control in nonprofit organizations.* Boston: McGraw-Hill/Irwin.

Austin, M., & Ezell, M. (2004). Educating future social work administrators. *Administration in Social Work, 28*(1), 1–3

Bennis, W. G. (1993). *Beyond Bureaucracy: Essays on the Development and Evolution of Human Organizations.* San Francisco: Jossey-Bass.

Bennis, W. G., & O'Toole, J. (2005, May). How business schools lost their way. *Harvard Business Review,* 1–9

Bolton, A. (1996). The leadership challenge in universities: The case of business schools. *Higher Education, 31*(4), 491–506.

Chmar, J. E., Weaver, R. W., Ranney, R. R., Haden, N. K., & Valachovic, R. W. (2004). A profile of dental school deans, 2002. *Journal of Dental Education, 68*(4), 475–487.

Conger, J., & Benjamin, B. (1999). *Building leaders: How successful companies develop the next generation.* San Francisco: Jossey-Bass

Council on Social Work Education (CSWE). (2005). Accredited programs. Retrieved from http://www.cswe.org

Cowger, C. (2003). The values of the research university should be maximized to strengthen social work education. *Journal of Social Work Education, 39*(1). Retrieved from http://www.cswe.org/publications/jswe/03-1cowger.htm

Cronin, B., & Crawford, H. (1999). Do deans publish what they preach? *Journal of the American Society for Information Science, 50*(5), 471–474.

Cuffman, D. (1999). *A study of the roles of assistant and associate deans in institutions accredited by the Commission on Colleges of the Southern Association of Colleges and Schools.* Unpublished doctoral dissertation, East Tennessee State University, Johnson City.

Dawes, A. (1893). The need of training schools for a new profession. *Proceedings of the International Congress of Charities,* Chicago, IL.

Eberlein, S., (1992). *Perception of gender differences in leadership styles of higher education administrators.* Unpublished doctoral dissertation, University of Wisconsin-Madison.

Edwards, M. (1992). *Assessing the leadership profile of appointed second-line administrators in the American community college: A case study.* Unpublished doctoral dissertation, Florida International University, Miami.

Ezell, M., Chernesky, R., & Healy, L. (2004). The learning climate for administration students. *Administration in Social Work, 28*(1) 57–76.

Feldman, R., Ottoman, D., & Ottman, R. H. (1999). The human resource crisis in social work education. *Journal of Social Work Education, 35*(2), 178–182.

Ginsberg, L., & Keys, P. R. (Eds.) (1995). *New management in human services* (2nd ed.). Silver Spring, MD: NASW Press.

Gmelch, W., Wolverton, M., Wolverton, M. L., & Sarros, J. (1999). The academic dean: An imperiled species searching for balance. *Research in Higher Education, 40*(6), 717–740.

Hoefer, R. (2003). Administrative skills and degrees: The "best place" debate rages on. *Administration in Social Work, 27*(1), 25–46.

Honan, J., & Teferra, D. (2001). The US academic profession: Key policy challenges. *Higher Education, 41,* 183–203.

Jackson, J (2004). Toward a business model of executive behavior: An exploration of the workdays of four college of education deans at large research universities. *The Review of Higher Education, 27*(3) 409–427.

Jackson, J., & Gmelch, W. (2003). How associate deans' positions are designed within the context of the top 50 colleges and schools of education. *Peabody Journal of Education, 78*(2), 88–110.

Jones, D., & Holdaway, E. (1996). Post-secondary department heads: Expectations for academic leadership and authority. *International Journal of Educational Management, 10*(3), 10–20.

Koerner, M., & Mindes, G. (1997). *Leading from the middle: Critical mentoring from the vantage of the associate dean. Feminist research and collaborative conversations.* Paper presented at the annual meeting of the American Association of Colleges for Teacher Education, Phoenix, AZ, February 28-March 1

Lamb, J. (2004). Online resources for social survey researchers. *Social Research Update, 41.* Retrieved from http://www.soc.surrey.ac.UK/sru/SRU41.html

Layman, E. J., Bamberg, R., & Jones, H. P. (2002). Filling the position of lead administrator in schools of allied health: The experience of search committees. *Journal of Allied Health, 31*(4), 197–203.

Lee, A., & Hoyle, E. (2002). Who would become a successful dean of faculty of medicine: Academic, or clinician or administrator? *Medical Teacher, 24*(6), 637–641.

Lohmann, R., & Lohmann, N. (2002). *Social administration.* New York: Columbia University Press.

Mohan, B. (2002). The future of social work education: Curricular conundrums in an age of uncertainty. *Electronic Journal of Social Work, 1*(1), 1–10.

Montez, J., Wolverton, M., & Gmelch, W. (2002). The roles and challenges of deans. *The Review of Higher Education, 26*(2), 241–266.

Munson, C. (1994). A survey of deans of schools of social work. *Journal of Social Work Education, 30*(2), 153–163.

Patti, R. 2000). *The handbook of social welfare management.* Thousand Oaks, CA: Sage Publications.

Patti, R. (2003). Reflections on the state of management in social work. *Administration in Social Work, 27*(2), 1–11.

Rank, M., & Hutchison, W. (2000). An analysis of leadership within the social work profession. *Journal of Social Work Education, 36*(3), 487–503.

Reisch, M., & Gorin, S. (2001). Nature of work and future of the social work profession. *Social Work, 46*(1), 9–19.

Richmond, M. (1897). The need of a training school in applied philanthropy. *Proceedings of the National Conference of Charities and Corrections.* Boston: National Conference of Charities and Corrections.

Rogers, M. A. (1988). *Dimensions of leadership of assistant and associate deans in collegiate schools of nursing.* Unpublished doctoral dissertation, University of South Carolina, Columbia.

Rosser, V., Johnsrud, L., & Heck, R. (2003). Academic deans and directors: Assessing their effectiveness from individual and institutional perspectives. *The Journal of Higher Education, 74*(1), 125.

Royce, D. (2004). *Research methods in social work* (4th ed.). Pacific Grove, CA: Brooks/Cole.

Shera, W., & Bogo, M. (2001). Social work education and practice: Planning for the future. *International Social Work, 44*(2), 197–210.

Specht, H. (1972, March). The deprofessionalization of social work. *Social Work,* 3–15.

Sullivan, S. (1983). *Job satisfaction of associate and assistant deans in accredited United States law schools.* Unpublished doctoral dissertation, University of Missouri-Columbia.

Wolverton, M., Wolverton, M. L., & Gmelch, G. (1999). The impact of role conflict and ambiguity on academic deans. *The Journal of Higher Education, 20*(1), 80–106.

Yrle, A., Hartmen, S., Grenier C., & Lundberg, O., Jr. (2001). Business college administrators: Organizational networking activities. *Team Performance Management: An International Journal, 7*(5/6), 69–76.

24

The Social Work Educator Potential in Higher Education Administration

Paul R. Keys

Higher education administration is an overlooked field of practice for social work management practitioners. This highly specialized branch of management presents a major future opportunity for the advancement of social work knowledge, skills, abilities, and values (KSAVs), but only if social work educators, professional associations, and social work management practitioners capitalize on the opportunities. There are striking if not nearly identical matches between social work manager standards and the requirements of higher education management. Bridging this gap, however, will not be easy and will take a concerted effort if it is to move forward.

In this chapter the terms *management* and *administration* are used interchangeably, though the distinction between them has been explored and documented by the National Network for Social Work Managers (NNSWM), Bob Maslyn (2002), one of the Network's founders, put it this way:

> What we wanted was Social Work Management, embracing all the leadership ideas that "manager" and "executive" connoted, much more than the limited vision of "administrivia" and paper-clip counting that "administration" seemed to infer, and competitive to MBAs and other disciplines who acted like they owned the word "management." Yet we also found that the American Society for Public Administration (ASPA) and other such associations, while embracing "management" more than NASW did, were disinterested in the "social work" aspect.

Higher Education Administration Is Organizational Management

Historically, Western colleges and universities and their academic organizational structure, unique culture, and traditions evolved from the Middle Ages.

The terms college and university originally had very similar meanings. Only with the passing of centuries did "university" come to signify an educational institution composed of more than one college. The word college means literally "union formed by law," or a group of people associated in some common function. The ancient Roman craft guilds were called collegia. (*Encyclopaedia Britannica Online*, 2007)

Hence the philosophy of management of universities evolved as one of coequal "partners," and that structure generally still exists as today's modern university management system. Today's college and university governance structures are considered to be collegial, and university governance as written into most bylaws is commonly referred to as having a culture of collegiality. Today's academic managers, as well as governing boards and faculty and staff, accept and abide by this form of management.

Founded by Andrew Carnegie in 1905 and chartered in 1906 by an act of Congress, the Carnegie Foundation for the Advancement of Teaching is an independent policy and research center with a primary mission "to do and perform all things necessary to encourage, uphold, and dignify the profession of the teacher and the cause of higher education."

The foundation maintains a standardized set of generally accepted categories of higher education institutions. In general these are Associate's Colleges (generally 2-year), Doctorate-Granting Universities, Master's Colleges and Universities, and Baccalaureate Colleges. There are also classifications of Special Focus Institutions and Tribal Colleges (Carnegie Foundation for the Advancement of Teaching, 2007). This chapter generally uses the term *institution* to refer to all categories.

Academic administration suffers in major ways from management in the corporate, public, and nonprofit sectors and from what a manager might term *general administration*. Colleges and universities as noted previously evolved historically from equal partnerships, which underlies their current management structure and styles.

Although collegial, the modern university does have some separate, distinct, and to some degree hierarchical organizational structures as well for some functions. There is a distinct difference in structure and style between the academic side (academic affairs) and the administrative side of a university. The administrative structure more typically resembles hierarchical corporate, government, and nonprofit management structures, with departments, divisions, and a vice president.

The academic side, however, typically has faculty and staff, a program head or director over specific academic programs, a department chairperson, dean, a provost and/or vice president for academic affairs, and a chief executive officer (CEO), called president or chancellor. A major difference in academic administration is that supervisees, that is, the faculty—according to university policies and traditions—not only have major say about governance and about hiring academic managers and CEOs, but also, by policy, they formally and continually rate managers and the CEO after these individuals are hired. Given these differences, some faculty may even believe, probably based on the collegial academic tradition and the freedom of faculty to choose their own work hours, that they basically do not have supervisors (Dowdall & Dowdall, 2005).

Faculty have great latitude over work hours and duties. Indeed, faculty members typically do not report day-to-day to anyone, though they have set office hours, major curriculum development, committee responsibilities, and meeting times. This is especially true of senior faculty who have achieved the rank of full professor with tenure. Historically, though, this has changed in recent years with the notion of posttenure review; formerly, full professors were not formally evaluated by anyone.

Most often removal of a tenured faculty member can take place only because of misfeasance, malfeasance, or nonfeasance, though in practice it only takes place in a formal reduction in force or retrenchment due to fiscal reasons, and, normally, a governing board must declare a state of emergency for this to take place. Academic freedom is the purpose of the tenure system, to assure that faculty are free to discover truth and teach without interference. Rank and tenure, however, is typically considered to be a 7-year probationary period. Academic administrators most often rise through the ranks of the professorate and usually are tenured professors as well as administrators. (There has been recent literature on what are called 360-degree evaluation trends outside of academia, but these are ephemeral and often either voluntary or not embodied in the traditions and policies of these other organizations). This tradition is well-established in academia and part of the governance structure. Even the judiciary have generally not ruled on or interfered with tenure decisions.

College and university management can be considered to be a strong and embedded form of participatory management, which in a host of other organizations has been the subject of a great deal of management research. Many advantages of participatory management have been documented in supervisory and management research studies and in the general management literature.

However beneficial the concept of participatory management may be, there is a potential caution in applying it to academia. In practice, the contemporary academic manager, and particularly the CEO, is constantly concerned with issues and organizational dilemmas where he or she must calculate the best objective management solution, while at the same time considering and being fully aware of the personality and often conflicting human relations aspects of decision making in general, and of specific decisions as well in the academic environment. For example, in evaluating a faculty member, or for any other major and far-reaching academic decision for that matter, deans especially, but also academic vice presidents and CEOs, must remember that these same faculty members will evaluate them.

In another example, when making a budgetary decision an academic manager must be aware that some departments and colleges are stronger, or at least more vocal than others, and may mount a campaign against the administrator, irrespective of the validity and objectivity of the decision (or in some cases because of it). A vote of confidence, the extreme measure of collegial dissatisfaction, often results in removing the administrator at some point. Because administrators are so often torn between their desire to support people and the fiscal or institutional realities that dictate their denial of many requests, the ability to communicate negative information without alienating the listeners has become an essential skill of an effective academic administrator, says Gary Olson (2007). Though there are exceptions, it is now rare for an academic manager to have an extended tenure as administrator. This is especially true of presidents and chancellors. Given the increasing political and other internal pressures, recent studies have shown that the average administrator survives the appointment for approximately 5 to 7 years. During the 1930s, 1940s, and even into the 1950s, it was not uncommon for a college president to be in office for 20 or more years or until retirement.

Typical University Organizational Structure

Although there are some differences among institutional categories, modern colleges and universities tend to have very similar organizational structures. This includes the office of the CEO, president (or chancellor), and other titles. CEO responsibilities tend to be similar among institutional categories. Some public colleges have their own independent governing boards; others operate under a state university system with a statewide governing board. A chancellor generally heads a state system and supervises individual campus presidents. The private giving—fundraising—function is preeminent in a president's office today, whether public or private, given the drastic cutbacks in public funds of recent years. Private fundraising has always been a preeminent concern for private institution presidents.

A president is assisted in the fundraising function by an office, called variously institutional advancement or university advancement, typically headed by a vice president, who handles day-to-day fundraising support for the president. A president's office, depending on the institution, may also include athletics, performing arts centers, and various community relations functions as well as state and federal legislative relations. A current lament is that the role and status of the university president has diminished greatly over the past 50 or so years from that of respected thinker and national leader of intellectual and social thought to, currently, that of chief institutional fundraiser. In addition to the recent decline in primarily state funds for higher education, which has elevated the fundraising function, many observers view the diminution of the role of the college/university president as a by-product of the country's increasing polarization.

The reasoning is that institutional leaders are beholden to the vagaries of the political and political funding processes (whether a public or private institution, as the 2007 Columbia University case of extending a speaking invitation to the president of Iran illustrates) (Wilson, 2007). Therefore, pronouncements and positions are likely to be vigorously, and sometimes vehemently, opposed by one interest group or another, often to the detriment of a president's position as leader.

Another major academic function and structure is that of academic administration, most often viewed as the number two position in any college or university. This office, often termed *academic affairs*, is considered to be the line or main function in academia, that of teaching and learning. The office of academic affairs supervises all academic functions such as academic departments, divisions, colleges, and programs. The standard manager classification in academic affairs is vice president for academic affairs and/or provost. In small to midsize institutions, this title is generally held by one person or office, called the provost/vice president for academic affairs. In large institutions these two positions may be separate, with the provost reporting to the academic vice president. Although the title of dean is widely recognized and popularized by the media, the title of provost, supervisor of the deans, is not well understood outside (and in many cases inside) academia.

The term *provost* stems from the 11th-century and Medieval times and is described by the Merriam-Webster Dictionary Online (2007) as "the chief dignitary of a collegiate or cathedral chapter, the chief magistrate of a Scottish burgh, the keeper of a prison," or simply as a "high-ranking university administrative officer." (Most provosts, when among other provosts, often find a bit of inside humor in these analogies.)

Typical functions under academic affairs and a provost may include institutional research, libraries, graduate school and graduate dean, off-campus academic programs and training or other extended learning, and, increasingly, the administration of student affairs through a dean of students. The functions and activities contained in student affairs vary by institution, but there are several typical functions and organizational structures under the student affairs umbrella. Typically, student affairs is administered by a dean of students, though some institutions may have a vice president for student affairs who supervises a dean of students. Student affairs generally includes student activities, judicial affairs, student development (learning support; testing, which typically includes counseling, testing, and emergency mental health functions at some universities; career services; writing laboratories; learning support laboratories and mentoring centers, etc.), and quite often university public safety/university police.

Most often federal TRIO programs as learning support programs are also located in student affairs. These include federal learning support programs such as Student Support Services, offering learning assistance aids to students from freshmen to seniors; Upward Bound, which grooms elementary through high school students for college; Talent Search, which also reaches into lower elementary grades to aid in college preparation; and the McNair Program of preparation of existing college students for graduate studies. Some universities also have a federally funded, non-TRIO program, GEAR-UP, which also grooms high school students for college entrance.

The student affairs function also often includes admissions or enrollment management, which may consist of the registrar and the financial aid office as well. Student health is also included in student affairs in most colleges and universities, with fully staffed student health centers, nurses, and contract or university-employed physicians in many cases. Student housing or residences are also most often located in student affairs.

Historically, there has been a disconnect between student affairs and academic affairs, and the literature of student affairs is replete with calls, recommendations, and programs to close this gap to elicit more effective student learning. There has recently been a small but significant trend to place student affairs under the provost/vice president for academic affairs as one structural method of addressing this disconnect.

In terms of other university organizational structures, there are, depending on the institution, other, more hierarchical structures. These include a vice president for administration and/or finance (by various names); a budget officer either under this vice president or directly under the president; and a business office. Additionally, there may be other offices with various names responsible for instructional and other technology, procurement, facilities, and human resources under this vice president.

Contemporary Management Issues in Universities and the Complexities and Challenges of Academic Management

Currently academia is facing a host of major and controversial public issues. Among these are accountability (often called the accountability crisis) and, concomitantly, evaluation has risen to the forefront as a major concern in recent years, as public institutions in particular are seen as more accountable for public funds, with overtones of cost containment similar to that of the nation's health care system. It often appears that public institutions are judged as valuable based on the low cost of their tuition, and private institutions on the basis of the high cost of theirs.

This accountability concern is heightened by a number of critical factors for which the public tends to view the university as being responsible, or at least for which it should provide solutions. These factors are such things as the pressing need for elementary and secondary teachers as well as nurses and other health professionals. Further pressure has come from the diminution of state funding for higher education (especially public higher education) and the resulting often-debated tuition and fee increases necessary to continue current levels of student learning.

Other contemporary issues include hate crimes, campus violence, and the university's role in public service. Public service—variously called engagement, the engaged university, or community or regional engagement—has become a major opportunity as well as a major source of internal tension between the purely academic and the more professional disciplines on a given regional public university campus, except for land-grant institutions, whose mission has always called for these activities. Other than land-grant institutions, regional public colleges and universities generally have viewed their role as primarily one of teaching, especially because many of them evolved from teacher education colleges. The new paradigm, however, appears to be a reliance on universities as economic development, state, regional, and community development engines as well as suppliers of workforce and job development services to meet societal needs. This has not been an easy role for many institutions to accept, nor is this role well-understood or developed in many regional state institutions. As a result of this need, all of the national higher education associations have created task forces or published issue papers on this function in the past decade or so.

Academic program development and expansion is another pressing issue, especially if the mission of a university is viewed as assisting with local or regional needs. In that case new academic programs to serve new businesses and industry are viewed as critical to these needs.

Enrollment management, including enrollment development and retention, is increasingly a major issue in many universities educating what are called first-generation college students (those whose parents were not college graduates and who may experience numerous barriers to graduation with much lower graduation rates).

As indicated previously, fundraising or the development of private funds and endowments, in the past decade of diminishing state funding of higher education, has become perhaps the preeminent issue in higher education today for presidents.

Conflicting and often colliding pressures for diversity, given the national retrenchment in affirmative action of recent years, have become a hot button issue, as has freedom of speech and/or academic freedom—generally where large segments of the public or political figures do not agree with what independent faculty are saying on campus. In the latter case a university and its CEO may be caught between the competing pressures of tenured faculty and academic freedom, a divided public, and often divisive politics, which for public universities most often include those legislators responsible for funding the institution. Other similar related issues are concerns about mascots in relation to cultural sensitivities.

In terms of administrative strategies, long-range and strategic planning has assumed a major role in university directions, as has the role of technology, especially that of instructional technology, online learning, and so forth. Community or public relations ability as a management strategy undergirds many of today's contemporary concerns, as do budgeting, budget management, and securing appropriations from state executive and legislative sources.

Universities are under increasing pressure to engage in expanding the reach of higher education to all areas of a given state. This includes linkages with local community colleges and the creation of matriculation agreements and joint higher education centers to reach underserved geographic areas of a state with academic programs. This has become increasingly important in recent years as well.

Is There a Social Work Manager Role in Higher Education?

Historically, there have been relatively few social workers in managerial roles in higher education other than social work department chairs or deans and directors of schools and colleges of social work, and even fewer serving as provosts or CEOs. Other than a relatively few, very prominent, deans of non-social-work academic functions such as a graduate school or undergraduate dean, there have been few deans or academic administrators of non-social-work colleges, even when social work is an academic program under a specific college.

The reasons for this are unclear, and the issue certainly begs for further research. Such questions arise as: Do social work managers not aspire to these positions? Are they not trained or oriented to assume these positions (to use social work terminology, is higher education not considered a field of practice other than to head social work academic programs)? Is professional social work education and/or are social work educators, through omission or commission, creating, abetting, or supporting such barriers (e.g., by a failure to focus on budgeting, human resources management, public relations, etc.)? Are there value barriers such as the attitude that the only proper role for a social work manager is to head a professional social work function (and management in social work itself has only been emphasized by a small group of social work manager advocates nationally)?

In addition, in academia the fast track to senior management and the CEO position does not generally favor academics and academic managers who head professional schools. This is one of the many biases that operate in academia and add to the various barriers facing social work managers in academia.

If the social work profession itself does not emphasize this academic management progression and these management roles, and the academy itself has barriers, then so-cial work managers with a career objective of academic administration operate under a dual handicap. However, factually speaking, an analytical observer can conclude that the education and training of social workers can be a good fit with many of the func-tions, issues, management, and leadership competencies in contemporary higher education management.

Social Worker "Fit" with Management in Academe

In 1997 the NNSWM established a credential, the Certified Social Work Manager (CSWM), which included Certification Competencies for social workers practicing as managers. These competencies are published in an NNSWM document titled *Leadership and Management Practice Standards* (NNSWM, 1997; revised 2004). The Network has shared these standards with many experts in the field and gathered and used their responses in formulating them.

> In the Network's ongoing efforts to address the needs of social work managers, and to inform the profession and other interested parties of the unique skills of social work managers, a set of practice standards has been developed. These are not minimum standards, but rather are descriptions of the level of practice that is expected of experienced and academically trained professionals. (NNSWM, 2004)

Like the bias against academic managers from the professions, other biases affect who is favored and hired to lead academic functions. These biases include but are not limited to what may be inferred as an unspoken "higher education caste system" hold-ing that only those coming from the specific Carnegie classification are qualified to manage other institutions in that category, that (though changing) only those who have risen through the ranks of academia can be the CEO. There are other such biases that operate as well in academe.

Nonetheless, a host of social work manager KSAVs inherent in the NNSWM's standards are a close, if not exact, fit with the actual skills requirements of academic administration. Many of the academic biases inherent in higher education, though generally accepted, have not been tested empirically. The Network standards are content-related to specific skills in relation to actual academic administration. The following NNSWM Standards appear to be very congruent with social work manager KSAVs.

The NNSWM standards (NNSWM, 2004) contain the 14 categories:
- Advocacy
- Communication and Interpersonal Relationships
- Ethics
- Evaluation (outcomes and data)
- Evaluation (of resource development opportunities)
- Financial Management
- Governance
- Human Resource Management and Development
- Information Technology

- Leadership
- Planning
- Program Development and Organizational Management
- Public/Community Relations and Marketing
- Public Policy

As a conceptual document, these NNSWM Standards not only list the specific skills (if diligently applied) required for success in academic management, but they also encompass, with almost no changes in definitions, most of the exact phraseology used in contemporary advertisements, requirements, and position descriptions for academic managers and CEOs. It appears that the simple addition of "academic" in front of "organization" in the Network Standards is all that is required to describe the skill set of a successful academic administrator. I use the qualifiers "if applied" and "successful," because even not all traditionally "trained" academic managers consistently apply these skill sets to their daily operations, and some have questioned whether there is enough formal training to assume the CEO role in academia, even for those rising through the ranks.

For example, higher education articles in *The Chronicle for Higher Education*; online resources such as *Academic Impressions* and *University Business*; and numerous local newspapers across the country are replete with articles about academic mismanagement. These have articles on fiscal overspending, mismanagement, and even outright fraud. Such mismanagement has resulted in some highly publicized criminal charges and convictions of college and university administrators.

Other reported higher education managerial abuses include lack of knowledge and understanding of effective systems and procedures for managing organizational resources, as one of the NNSWM Standards calls for; presidential indiscretion which is very similar to a lack of commitment to the social work values of social justice, as well as to principles of equity and fairness; management style issues (e.g., top-down authoritarianism, poor two-way communications, inappropriate, and culturally or gender insensitive remarks); miscalculations based on lack of fact or information, and so forth.

These are not blanket condemnations of academic administrators, but references to recent and well-documented cases of failure of some higher education managers and CEOs to live up to higher education manager standards. Faculty and staff in a given institution obviously know of a host of other deviations from standard practice and style discussed only internally in a given institution of higher education. These are issues of appropriate and applied standards; the point is that social work (management) standards already provide the basis for performance by those educated in social work schools to manage the majority of academic organizations.

The Path Ahead

If higher education management contains much of the same content as do the social work manager standards, then what must be done, and by whom, to create opportunities to bridge this practice gap? As stated at the beginning of this chapter, bridging this gap will not be easy. Realizing these opportunities requires a concerted effort by social work managers, educators, and professional associations, in concert with many other leaders and non-social-work national organizations.

A Change in Thinking

The first requirement to open doors to social work managers in academe, a conceptual shift, is for professional social work to recognize and prioritize academic administration formally as the major opportunity that it is, much as it first recognized social work in industry or corporate social work as a practice field some decades ago.

Second, this formal recognition should consist of analyzing the most appropriate fit of social work manager KSAVs and standards with the various functions and structures in academia: CEO, academic vice president, vice president and/or dean of students, academic dean, institutional advancement, community relations, human resources, department chair, and so forth. There are obvious skill sets that predominate in each academic organizational function.

Recognition of New Fields of Social Work Management Practice

NASW Role(s)

NASW, which has published practice standards in a number of fields (NASW, 2007), defines these standards as follows:

> Social work practice consists of the professional application of social work values, principles, and techniques to one or more of the following ends: helping people obtain tangible services; counseling and psychotherapy with individuals, families, and groups; helping communities or groups provide or improve social and health services; and participating in legislative processes. The practice of social work requires knowledge of human development and behavior; of social and economic, and cultural institutions; and of the interaction of all these factors. (NASW, 2007)

There are NASW Standards for a host of specific fields of practice, including the following.

- *NASW Standards for Social Work Practice with Clients with Substance Use Disorders*
- *NASW and ASWB Standards for Technology and Social Work Practice*
- *NASW Standards for Social Work Practice in Health Care Settings*
- *NASW Standards for Clinical Social Work in Social Work Practice*
- *NASW Standards for Social Work Practice in Child Welfare*
- *Standards for Social Work Practice in Palliative and End of Life Care*
- *Standards for Social Work Services in Long-Term Care Facilities*
- *Continuing Education and the Social Work Profession*
- *NASW Standards for the Practice of Social Work with Adolescents*
- *NASW Standards for Integrating Genetics into Social Work Practice*

- *For Cultural Competence in Social Work Practice*
- *For Continuing Professional Education*
- *For School Social Work Services*
- *Indicators for Cultural Competence in Social Work Practice*

It must be noted, as the NNSWM did as an occasion for its founding in 1985 (and, indeed, the original reason for the founding of the Network), that there are still no NASW standards regarding administration, management, or executive leadership practice. It would appear that drafting new academic administration or management standards or revisions of existing standards will fall to the Network, possibly working with NASW and other constituencies in some way, and probably through such strategies as joint task forces and committees.

CSWE Role(s)

Two areas of CSWE seem to have the most relevance to promoting social work managers in academic administration. First, the CSWE has the Office of Social Work Education and Research (OSWER),

> formed in 2004 to fulfill the organizational mission of advocating for social work education and research. The CSWE Board of Directors approved a research agenda for OSWER in February 2005, which outlines the need for research to inform policy and practice for CSWE staff, Board, the volunteer commissions and councils, and to serve the needs of CSWE member programs—their deans, directors, faculty, and students (CSWE, 2007a)

This office can work with the NNSWM to research the necessary content knowledge or refine the existing social work school curriculum content necessary for social workers to be better positioned for entry and/or advancement into higher education management.

Second, the CSWE has a Career Center that can also be of great utility in recognizing and soliciting job announcements (including publicizing social work managers to potential employers), and then listing the many academic management positions as a part of the center's services (CSWE, 2007b). This office can focus on and publicize appropriate higher education management positions and call them to the attention of potential social work management applicants.

In concert with other social work and non-social-work entities CSWE can also develop new or refined curricula to benefit social work managers in higher education administration. A logical starting point would be to forge links with other academic program associations and accrediting bodies. The following would probably be a starting point and a minimum list of organizations that must be formally accessed:

- The National Association of Student Personnel Administrators (NASPA) in higher education, which is

> the leading voice for student affairs administration, policy and practice and affirms the commitment of student affairs to educating the whole student and integrating student life and learning. With over 11,000 members at 1,400 campuses, and representing

462   Management and Leadership in Social Work Education

29 countries, NASPA is the largest professional association for student affairs administrators, faculty and graduate students. (NASPA, 2007)

Student affairs is probably a logical starting point for social work access as most of the functions of student affairs contain a majority of social work KSAVs.

* The National Association of State Universities and Land-Grant Colleges (NASULGC), which is "the nation's oldest higher education association. Dedicated to supporting excellence in teaching, research and public service, NASULGC has been in the forefront of educational leadership nationally for more than 120 years" (NASULGC, 2007). NASULGC is the national association of land-grant institutions and large major public research institutions.

* The American Association of State Colleges and Universities. AASCU is the national association of regional public institutions of higher education and "represents more than 400 public colleges, universities and systems of higher education throughout the United States and its territories. AASCU schools enroll more than three million students or 55 percent of the enrollment at all public four-year institutions" (AASCU, 2007).

There are no doubt other higher education bodies that must be accessed and coordinated with to move a social work management or executive in higher education agenda forward. This list comprises only a few key players in contemporary higher education. Accessing the various regional and specialized accrediting bodies will probably be necessary as well.

NNSWM Roles

As indicated previously, the future role of the NNSWM is as clear for this potential new field of management practice as it was for production of social work management standards in general. That role will consist of advocacy, including joint task forces, within the profession as well as with other pertinent constituencies. Given their missions, NNSWM and CSWE would probably be the leading organizations in this new endeavor.

It will probably fall to NNSWM and its members and committees to make overtures, create discussion forums, and initiate contacts and coordinate with various other associations and organizations to highlight and prioritize social work manager KSAVs relevant to higher education administration. It is clear from the history of new initiatives in social work management that the NNSWM must become the key player and advocate if this is to become a new national social work management initiative.

Social Work Manager Roles

Social work managers must become aware of these new opportunities, through the various functions and services of some of the resources listed previously. But more importantly, social work managers, once informed, must actually apply for relevant positions in higher education.

The Higher Education Community

There is a host of very pressing higher education issues facing America's colleges and universities and the national higher education community. Hence, the higher education community will be difficult to access and is likely to have little interest in pursuing this new initiative, which it may not interpret as being in line with existing higher education priorities and concerns. Advocacy for this initiative will fall to social work organizations to create interest and move it forward.

The Benefits

Establishing a new field of social work practice will be a formidable task, especially because it will require mobilizing one of the oldest and most entrenched professions in the world today—the academy. It will not be an easy task.

However, the benefits for both organized social work and student learners are many, including better service to students in their quest for knowledge and, at a minimum, improved retention and graduation rates with more personalized student services. Social work manager skills following appropriate standards can also be an important factor in addressing many of the higher education management ills chronicled so widely in today's higher education publications. The problem will lie in starting the initiative.

References

American Association of State Colleges and Universities. (AASCU). (2007). Welcome. Retrieved November 1, 2007, from http://www.aascu.org/leadership/about.htm

Carnegie Foundation for the Advancement of Teaching. (2007). Retrieved November 1, 2007, from http://www.carnegiefoundation.org/classifications/index.asp?key=785

Council on Social Work Education. (2007a). Office of Social Work Education and Research (OSWER). Retrieved October 15, 2007, from http://www.cswe.org/CSWE/research/

Council on Social Work Education. (2007b). Career and Professional Services. Retrieved October 15, 2007, from http://www.cswe.org/CSWE/career/

Dowdall, G., & Dowdall, J. (2005). Crossing over to the dark side: Considering a career in academic administration? Here's what you need to think about. *The Chronicle of Higher Education.* Retrieved November 1, 2007, from http://chronicle.com/weekly/v52/i05/05c00101.htm

Encyclopedia Britannica Online. College. (2007). Retrieved November 1, 2007, from http://www.britannica.com/eb/article-9024766/college

Maslyn, R. T. (2002). Why I founded the National Network for Social Work Managers. Retrieved November 1, 2007, from http://www.socialworkmanager.org/Articles/BobMaslynArticle.htm.

Merriam-Webster Online. (2007). Provost. Retrieved November 1, 2007, from http://www.m-w.com/dictionary/Provost

National Association of Social Workers (NASW). (2007). *Practice.* Retrieved October 15, 2007, from http://www.naswdc.org/practice/default.asp

National Association of State Universities and Land-Grant Colleges. (NASULGC). A public university association. Retrieved November 1, 2007, from http://www.nasulgc.org/NetCommunity/Page.aspx?pid=183&srcid=-2

National Association of Student Personnel Administrators (NASPA). (2007). About NASPA. Retrieved October 15, 2007, from http://www.naspa.org/about/index.cfm

National Network for Social Work Managers (NNSWM). (1997). Leadership and management practice standards, revised June 1, 2004. Retrieved October 30, 2007, from http://www.socialworkmanager.org/Standards.htm

Olson, G. A. (2007). The delicate art of rejection: Communicating negative information without alienating your audience is an essential administrative skill. *The Chronicle for Higher Education: Chronicle Careers.* Retrieved November 1, 2007, from http://chronicle.com/weekly/v54/i04/04c00301.htm

Onear, P. (2007). 5 reasons politicians hate us: Between the worlds of politics and higher education lies a lot of misunderstanding. *The Chronicle for Higher Education: Chronicle Careers.* Retrieved October 5, 2007, from http://chronicle.com/weekly/v54/i06/06c00301.htm

Wilson, R. (2007). Speech puts Bollinger back in the eye of a storm: Columbia's president wants to be seen as a defender of free speech, but past disputes left critics with another view. *The Chronicle of Higher Education: The Faculty.* Retrieved November 1, 2007, from http://chronicle.com/weekly/v54/i06/06a00801.htm

About the Contributors

Matt Aubry, MSW, oversees the Development Department at the YAI/National Institute for People with Disabilities Network, which is responsible for the organization's fundraising initiatives. Mr. Aubry received his MSW from the Hunter College School of Social Work. He teaches a course on not-for-profit fundraising at Baruch College of the City University of New York.

Lynn Uhlfelder Berman is senior manager of media relations for YAI/National Institute for People with Disabilities. A graduate of the University of Missouri School of Journalism, she worked for nearly 20 years in newspapers as a reporter, copy editor, assignment editor, and sports editor. Before joining YAI/NIPD, she worked at *The New York Times*.

Stanley Blostein, EdD, MSSW, is associate professor emeritus and retired associate dean, College of Social Work, The Ohio State University. He earned his EdD from the University of Kentucky, and his MSSW being from the University of Louisville. His practice experience includes director of planning for the Kentucky Department of Mental Health, chief of program and liaison for the Illinois Department of Mental Health, and director of the Salt River Mental Health Center, Louisville, KY. He has held faculty positions at West Virginia University, the University of Kentucky, and The Ohio State University.

Harold E. Briggs, PhD, is professor of social work at Portland State University. Between 1984 and 1990, Dr. Briggs was the associate executive director of Habilitative Systems Inc., and has provided consultation and technical assistance to nearly 50 family advocacy and support organizations representing diverse cultural communities. Dr. Briggs made a significant contribution to the knowledge base by establishing practice questions for use in planning delivery of evidence-based interventions emphasizing cultural values and preferences of communities of color.

Terri Moore Brown, EdD, is department chair, MSW program director, and associate professor of social work at Fayetteville State University. Dr. Brown has more than 11 years of university leadership and teaching experience and 7 years of practice experience. Dr. Brown received her BA in social work and sociology from Methodist College, her MA in social work from East Carolina University, and her EdD in higher education administration from North Carolina State University.

Michael Daley, PhD, is director of the social work program at the University of South Alabama in Mobile. He has 22 years of experience in academic administration including 15 years as a BSW program director. He has served in leadership positions in several professional organizations including president of the National Rural Social Work Caucus, president and treasurer of the Texas Chapter of NASW, and chair of the NASW National Ethics Committee.

Mark Ezell, PhD, is professor of social welfare at the University of Kansas in Lawrence. He has published widely in professional journals and presented numerous papers at conferences throughout the world. Dr. Ezell's book, *Advocacy in the Human Services* (Wadsworth), was published in October 2000. In 1997 he was selected by the U.S. Children's Bureau as a Child Welfare Research Fellow and received funding for research related to child welfare contracting.

Bruce D. Friedman, PhD, ACSW, CSWM, LCSW, is professor and director of the Social Work Program at California State University Bakersfield. He is president of the board of the National Network of Social Work Managers and serves on the editorial boards of *Social Thought* and *Administration in Social Work*. Professor Friedman has authored several books, including *How to Teach Effectively: A Brief Guide* (2008) and *The Research Tool Kit: Putting it All Together* (1996, 2006).

Fontaine H. Fulghum is an experienced human services administrator and policy planner. She has taught at the graduate schools of social work at Tulane University, Bryn Mawr College, and Rutgers University. She is coauthor (with R. S. Mayers) of *Cases, Readings, and Exercises in Financial Management for Nonprofit Human Service Organizations* (2008, CD-ROM, Charles C. Thomas Publisher). She has done doctoral work at Bryn Mawr College.

Colleen Galambos, PhD, is professor at the University of Missouri School of Social Work, teaching in the graduate and doctoral programs. She holds a BSW from Cornell University, an MSW from the University of Maryland, and a PhD from Catholic University National School of Social Service. Editor-in-chief of the *Journal of Social Work Education*, she also serves on the Publications Committee of the Council on Social Word Education and is the immediate past editor-in-chief of *Health and Social Work*.

Donna Hardina, MSW, PhD, is professor in the Department of Social Work Education at California State University, Fresno. She has graduate degrees in social work and public policy and has published extensively on community organization practice, nonprofit management, empowerment, and citizen participation. Her practice experience includes antihunger advocacy, coalition-building, nonprofit management, and community organization.

Eugene Herrington, PhD, MDiv, LCSW, is codirector of the Historically Black Colleges and Universities National Resource Center. A licensed clinician and educator with strong program development and administrative experience, Dr. Herrington was the recipient of the 2004 National Historically Black Colleges and Universities Substance Abuse Conferences Service Award. He is a member of the Addiction Technology Transfer Center National Advisory Group and the National Committee on Addiction Studies and Standards in Higher Education.

Paul R. Keys, MSW, PhD, CSWM, is professor at Governors State University in University Park, IL. He has written extensively on human services management with a focus on the chief executive officer. He is a cofounder of the National Network for Social Work Managers and has executive-level experience as a deputy state agency administrator in Wisconsin and as county department director in Broward County (Ft. Lauderdale), Florida.

Joel M. Levy, DSW, is chief executive officer of YAI/National Institute for People with Disabilities. He has held academic appointments at the University of Pennsylvania, Baruch College, Adelphi University, the John F. Kennedy Jr. Institute for New Worker Education at the City University of New York, New York University, Mount Sinai School of Medicine, and the University of Haifa in Israel. Dr. Levy has received numerous professional awards, including the 2008 Career Achievement Award from the Association for Community Organization and Social Administration, and has served on various national professional boards.

Philip H. Levy, PhD, is president of YAI/National Institute for People with Disabilities Network (YAI/NIPD), president and chief operating officer of YAI/NIPD, and chief executive officer of the National Institute for People with Disabilities of New Jersey. His private psychotherapy practice serves individuals and couples. Dr. Levy has received numerous awards and has been on the faculties of New York University, Columbia University, City University of New York, and Adelphi University. Dr. Levy received his PhD from New York University.

Rufus Sylvester Lynch, DSW, former dean of the Whitney M. Young, Jr. School of Social Work at Clark Atlanta University, is a forensic social worker who serves as president and principal investigator for the Institute for the Advancement of Working Families: A Forensic Education, Behavioral Change, and Employment Services Corp.; serves on the editorial board of the *Journal of Forensic Social Work*; is a National Judicial Fellow of the Institute for Court Management; and is national director of the Collaborative of Deans and Directors of Schools of Social Work Programs, housed within Historically Black Colleges and Universities. He received his DSW from the University of Pennsylvania, an MA from the University of Pittsburgh, and a BA in sociology from Morgan State College.

Lawrence L. Martin, MSW, MBA, PhD, is professor of public affairs and senior research associate with the Center for Community Partnerships at the University of Central Florida in Orlando. Dr. Martin also holds joint appointments with the Department of Public Administration and the School of Social Work.

Raymond Sanchez Mayers, PhD, is associate professor at the Rutgers University School of Social Work. He has taught financial management in the master's programs at Rutgers and the University of Texas. He is the author of *Financial Management for Nonprofit Human Service Organizations* (2004, Charles C. Thomas Publisher). He received his PhD from Brandeis University.

Bowen McBeath, PhD, is assistant professor in the School of Social Work and the Division of Public Administration at Portland State University. He has received awards and fellowships from the Academy of Management, the Association for Research on Nonprofit Organizations and Voluntary Action, the Council on Social Work Education, the James Madison Foundation, and the Society for Social Work and Research. He received his MSW and PhD from the University of Michigan.

Jacquelyn Mitchell, JD, LCISW, is director of the Title IV-E Program at the Whitney M. Young, Jr. School of Social Work at Clark Atlanta University. A forensic social worker, mediator, and attorney, she has taught in undergraduate and graduate social work programs, including three historically Black institutions. Her publications include "Is Social Work Y2K Compliant? Adapting to the Mandates of Future Practice" (in *Proceedings of the National Organization of Forensic Social Workers Conference 2000*, Haworth, 2002) and "Interdisciplinary Reaction: Critical Influences on Change" (with R. S. Lynch, in *The Seventh Learning College Principle: A Framework for Transformational Change*, NASPA, 2005).

Phoua Moua, BA, is marketing specialist in the Policy, Partnerships and Planning Unit with the Network for a Healthy California at the California Department of Public Health. She graduated from University of California, Davis with degrees in political science and communications.

Xong Moua, MSW-PPSC, is a graduate of the Department of Social Work Education at California State University, Fresno. She has more than 10 years of working experience in the Southeast Asian community in the Central Valley of California. She worked with Fresno County Department of Children and Family Services for 6 years as a social work practitioner. Currently, she is working with the Fresno Unified School District as a school social worker.

Ben Nivin is director of the Professional Information Department at YAI/National Institute for People with Disabilities. Mr. Nivin, who has been at YAI for more than 25 years, oversees the organization's publications, media relations, and public information. Mr. Nivin received his bachelor's degree from the City University of New York and holds graduate degrees from Columbia University's School of International Public Affairs and from the Graduate School of Arts and Sciences.

Peggy Pittman-Munke, MSW, PhD, is active in a variety of communities on boards, mostly focused on children's and family issues and substance abuse issues. Dr. Pittman-Munke has been a BSW educator for more than 30 years and is also a social welfare historian. She currently directs the social work program at Murray State University.

Cynthia Cannon Poindexter, MSW, PhD has been a social worker in the HIV field for more than 20 years, serving as an advocate, case manager, crisis counselor, supervisor, educator, program developer, grant writer, and program manager. She was the first social worker at the first AIDS Service Organization in South Carolina in the mid-1980s. She currently teaches HIV practice, HIV policy, management, supervision, and qualitative research at the Fordham University Graduate School of Social Service.

Joshua Rubin, MA, is a senior management fellow at YAI/National Institute for People with Disabilities Network. Prior to joining YAI/NIPD he served as the assistant commissioner for Mental Hygiene Policy in the Department of Health and Mental Hygiene of the City of New York. Mr. Rubin has an MA in public policy from the John F. Kennedy School of Government at Harvard University and a BA in religion and the humanities from the University of Chicago.

Jeanette C. Takamura, MSW, PhD, is dean of the Columbia University School of Social Work. She was assistant secretary for aging in the U.S. Department of Health and Human Services (1996–2001). For her efforts as assistant secretary, Dr. Takamura received the Secretary's Distinguished Service Award and the Lucy Stone Achievement Award. She is an elected fellow of the National Academy on Social Insurance and of the National Academy for Public Administration. She is also an invited principal of the Council for Excellence in Government.

Karen Wegmann, MBA, is chief financial officer with YAI/National Institute for People with Disabilities. She has been a lecturer on economics at the City University of New York (CUNY) and has lectured on financial management topics for nonprofit managers at Adelphi Graduate School of Social Work, CUNY Graduate School, and University of Pennsylvania Graduate School of Social Work. She holds an MBA from Pace University and a BA from Queens College.

Jane Yamaguchi, MSW, PhD, is associate professor in the Department of Social Work Education at California State University, Fresno. She has a PhD from the University of Chicago, School of Social Service Administration; an MSW from Smith College

School for Social Work; and her BA from Yale University. Her research and practice experiences include medical social work and services for people with severe and persistent mental illnesses and developmental disabilities.

Molly Yang, MSW-PPSC, obtained her MSW at California State University, Fresno. Currently, Ms. Yang is an academic high school counselor at Sunnyside High School in Fresno, California. Before becoming a counselor, she was a school social work for 4 years with Fresno Unified School District. Ms. Yang has facilitated workshops on Hmong teen suicide topics and Hmong mental health issues.

Joan Levy Zlotnik, PhD, ACSW, is executive director of the Institute for the advancement of Social Work Research. She has led the organization since 2000, working to build social work research resources and to translate research to practice, policy, and education. She is actively involved in the national policy arena, working on the promotion of social work research and behavioral and social science research opportunities, responding to the demographics of aging, promoting an understanding of the evidence-based practice paradigm, and in addressing the child welfare workforce crisis.

Index